PENGUIN REFERENCE

THE PENGUIN DICTIONARY OF ARCHITECTURE

John Fleming was born in 1919 and was educated at Rugby School and Trinity College, Cambridge. His main interests are eighteenth-century art and architecture, especially British and Italian. In 1961 he published *Robert Adam and His Circle in Edinburgh and Rome*, which was awarded the Bannister Fletcher Prize and the Alice Davis Hitchcock Medal. He is a FRSL.

Hugh Honour was born in 1927 and was educated at the King's School, Canterbury, and St Catherine's College, Cambridge. Since 1954 he has lived in Italy. He published *Chinoiserie: The Vision of Cathay* in 1961 and *The Companion Guide to Venice* in 1965. His *Neo-Classicism* (1968) and *Romanticism* (1979) have been published in the Penguin *Style and Civilization* series, of which he and John Fleming are the editors. For *The Image of the Black in Western Art, from the American Revolution to World War I* he received the Anisfield-Wolf Book Award in Race Relations 1990. He is a FBA and a FRSL.

John Fleming and Hugh Honour have collaborated on the *Penguin Dictionary of Decorative Arts* (1977) and *A World History of Art* (1982, 1991, published as *The Visual Arts: A History* in the USA, 1982, 1986, 1991), which was awarded the Mitchell Prize.

Sir Nikolaus Pevsner was born in 1902 and educated at Leipzig. From 1949 to 1955 he was Slade Professor of Fine Art and a Fellow of St John's College, Cambridge. In 1959 he became Professor of the History of Art at Birkbeck College, University of London, and he remained there until his retirement in 1969 when he became Emeritus Professor. He was a Royal Gold Medallist of the RIBA and honorary doctor of Leicester, York, Leeds, Oxford, Cambridge, East Anglia, Zagreb, Keele, Heriot-Watt, Edinburgh and Pennsylvania universities, an honorary fellow of St John's College, Cambridge, FBA and FBA. He was awarded the CBE in 1953 and received a knighthood in 1969. He was a member of the Historic Buildings Council and the Advisory Board on Redundant Churches.

From its inception he edited the *Pelican History of Art and Architecture* and wrote most of *The Buildings of England* by counties, as well as editing the whole series. He published many other books including *An Outline of European Architecture*, *Pioneers of Modern Design*, and *The Englishness of English Art* (Reith Lectures, 1955), which are also published by Penguin.

Sir Nikolaus died in 1983.

THE PENGUIN DICTIONARY OF

ARCHITECTURE

JOHN FLEMING

HUGH HONOUR

NIKOLAUS PEVSNER

DRAWINGS BY
DAVID ETHERTON

Fourth Edition

PENGUIN BOOKS

PENGUIN BOOKS

Published by the Penguin Group
Penguin Books Ltd, 27 Wrights Lane, London W8 5TZ, England
Penguin Books USA Inc., 375 Hudson Street, New York, New York 10014, USA
Penguin Books Australia Ltd, Ringwood, Victoria, Australia
Penguin Books Canada Ltd, 10 Alcorn Avenue, Toronto, Ontario, Canada M4V 3B2
Penguin Books (NZ) Ltd, 182–190 Wairau Road, Auckland 10, New Zealand

Penguin Books Ltd, Registered Offices: Harmondsworth, Middlesex, England

First published 1966
Second edition 1972
Third edition 1980
Fourth edition 1991
5 7 9 10 8 6 4

Printed in England by Clays Ltd, St Ives plc
Filmset in 8½ on 10 pt Imprint

Foreword to the Fourth Edition

This is the first edition to be published since the death of Nikolaus Pevsner, whose loss we acutely feel. From the book's inception, now more than twenty-five years ago, he was the guiding spirit and it was only at his repeated insistence that his name appears last on the title-page – 'alphabetical order, please! That is correct,' he would say. He wrote the entries for medieval and nineteenth- and twentieth-century architects, as well as the European and American national entries and most of the stylistic ones. He was assisted by Sabrina Longland in connection with definitions of medieval terms and by Enid Caldecott in connection with modern technical terms. We wrote the rest of the book. But for the third edition specialists contributed entries for Australian, Byzantine, Canadian, Russian and South African architecture and also for the entry on windows, all being signed by their authors, to whom we are most grateful. Sarah Pearson revised and in some instances re-wrote entries for the techniques of roof-construction.

For this fourth edition we have made additions to the national entries to take account of recent developments and have also re-written the Chinese, Indian, Japanese and other Far Eastern entries. Its increased size is, however, due mainly to the addition of entries for many contemporary architects, some of whom had not even begun their careers when the first edition went to press. We have also revised many entries in the light of the increased and more accurate knowledge of the history of architecture published in recent years. And we have appended very brief bibliographies to most of the biographical entries as well as some others (for those cited in abbreviated form full titles are given on pp. 493–8). Over the years we have received much help and advice and we should like to acknowledge that given us by Bruce Boucher, Adrian Edwards, Eileen and John Harris, Ruth Kamen, Alastair Laing, Renato Pedio, Rupert Scott, John Shearman and Sir John Summerson. We are also grateful to the Royal Commission on Historical Monuments (England) for permission to reproduce the cruck drawing (Fig. 34).

a

Aalto, Hugo Alvar Henrik (1898–1976). Among the most important modern architects, and certainly pre-eminent in his native Finland. Started neo-classically, in a typically Scandinavian idiom, c. 1923 5, and turned to the INTERNATIONAL MODERN with his excellent Library at Viipuri (1927, 1930–35), Convalescent Home at Paimio (1929–33), and factory with workers' housing at Sumila (1936–9, with large additions of 1951–7). He possessed a strong feeling for materials and their characters, which, Finland being a country of forests, inspired him to use timber widely. He also invented bent plywood furniture (1932). Timber figured prominently in his Finnish Pavilion at the Paris Exhibition of 1937 and in the Villa Mairea at Noormarkku (1938). Aalto's most original works date from after the Second World War. By then he had evolved a language entirely his own, quite unconcerned with current clichés, yet in its vigorous display of curved walls and single-pitched roofs, in its play with brick and timber, entirely in harmony with the international trend towards plastically more expressive *ensembles*. The principal works are a Hall of Residence at the Massachusetts Institute of Technology, Cambridge, Mass. (1947–9), with a curved front and staircases projecting out of the wall and climbing up diagonally; the Village Hall at Säynätsalo (1951); the Pensions Institute at Helsinki (1952–7), a more straightforward job; the church at Imatra (1952–8), on a completely free plan; and the Finlandia Concert Hall, Helsinki (1971), his last and perhaps his finest building.

K. Flieg, *A.A. (1922–62), (1963 –70), (1971–6)*, Zürich 1963, 1971, 1978; D. Porphyrios, *Sources of Modern Eclecticism: Studies on A.A.*, London 1982; G. Schildt, *A. A. The Early Years*, New York 1984, and *A.A. The Decisive Years*, New York 1986.

Abacus. The flat slab on the top of a CAPITAL: in Greek Doric a thick square slab; in Greek Ionic, Tuscan, Roman Doric and Ionic, square with the lower edge moulded; in Corinthian and Composite with concave sides and the corners cut off. *See* Fig. 66.

Abadie, Paul (1812–84), *see* VAUDREMER, Joseph-Auguste-Émile.

Abbey. A MONASTERY governed by an abbot or abbess.

Abramovitz, Max (b. 1908). American architect, a partner of Wallace K. HARRISON from the late 1930s until 1976. He designed the Philharmonic Hall for Harrison's Lincoln Center, New York (1962). His Assembly Hall (1963) and Krannert Center, Univer-

FIG. I. *Acanthus*

FIG. 2. *Acroterion, antefixa and general view*

KEY:
1. *Pediment* 2. *Acroterion* 3. *Antefixa*

sity of Illinois, Urbana (1969), are notable.

The Architecture of M.A., Champaign, Urbana 1963.

Abutment. Solid masonry placed to counteract the lateral thrust of a VAULT or ARCH. *See* Fig. 4.

Abyssinian architecture, *see* ETHIOPIAN ARCHITECTURE.

Acanthus. A plant with thick, fleshy, scalloped leaves used on carved ornament of Corinthian and Composite CAPITALS and on other mouldings. See Fig. 1.

Achaemenid architecture, *see* PERSIAN ARCHITECTURE.

Acropolis. The citadel of a Greek city, built at its highest point and containing the chief temples and public buildings, as at Athens.

Acroteria. Plinths for statues or ornaments placed at the apex and ends of a PEDIMENT; also, more loosely, both the plinths and what stands on them. *See* Fig. 2.

Adam, Robert (1728–92), the greatest British architect of the later C18, was equally if not more brilliant as a decorator, furniture designer, etc., for which his name is still a household word. He is comparable in his chaste and rather epicene elegance with his French contemporary SOUFFLOT, but without Soufflot's chilly solemnity. He was a typically hard-headed Scot, canny and remorselessly ambitious, yet with a tender, romantic side to his character as well. Both facets were reflected in his work, which oscillates between a picturesque version of neoclassicism and a classicizing version of neo-Gothic. His work has an air of unceremonious good manners, unpedantic erudition, and unostentatious opulence which perfectly reflects the civilized world of his patrons. Appreciating that it would be bad manners, and bad business, to make any violent break with established traditions, he devised a neo-classical style lighter and more gaily elegant than that of the Palladians who preceded or the Greek Revivalists who succeeded him. He avoided startling innovations such as the Greek Doric for classical buildings or the picturesquely asymmetrical for Gothic ones. He answered the current demand for a new classicism by enlarging the repertory of decorative motifs and by a more imaginative use of contrasting room plans derived largely from Imperial Roman Baths. In his cunning variation of room shapes and in his predilection for columned screens and apses to give a sense of spatial mystery, no less than in his neo-Gothic castles so massively romantic outside and so comfortably classical within – he answered the taste for the picturesque. He became the architect *par excellence* to the Age of Sensibility, as BURLINGTON had been to the English Augustan period. His influence spread rapidly all over England and beyond, as far as Russia and America. His output was enormous, and only the unlucky Adelphi speculation robbed him of the fortune he would otherwise have made.

His father William Adam (1689–1748) was the leading architect of his day in Scotland and developed a robust, personal style based on VANBRUGH, GIBBS, and the English Palladians, e.g. Hopetoun House, near Edinburgh (1723–42), and Duff House, Banff (1735–9). His brothers John (1721–92) and James (1732–94)

were also architects, and all three trained in their father's Edinburgh office: Robert and James attended Edinburgh University as well. Robert Adam's early work is no more than competent, e.g. Dumfries House (designed 1750–54). His genius emerged only after his Grand Tour (1754–8), most of which was spent in Rome studying Imperial Roman architecture under CLÉRISSEAU, with whom he also surveyed Diocletian's palace at Split in Dalmatia (later published by him as *Ruins of Spalatro*, 1764).

In 1758 he settled in London, where he was joined by his brother James after a similar Grand Tour with Clérisseau (1760–63). The columnar Admiralty Screen, London (1759–60), gave immediate proof of his ability and originality, but all his other early commissions were for the internal transformation of old houses or the completion of houses already begun by other architects. Nevertheless, his style rapidly matured, and the interiors of Harewood House (1758–71), Kedleston Hall (1760–61), Syon House (1760–69), Osterley Park (1761–80), Luton Hoo (1766–70), Newby Hall (1767–85), and Kenwood (1767–9) are perhaps his masterpieces of interior design. His meticulous attention to detail is revealed no less in the jewel-like finish of the painted decorations and very shallow stucco work than in the care he lavished on every part of each room from the carpets to the keyhole guards. No previous architect had attempted such comprehensive schemes of interior decoration. Although individual decorative motifs are often small in scale they are woven together with such skill that the general effect is rarely finicking, and although the same artistic personality is evident in each room the effect of a series is never monotonous. They perfectly illustrate those qualities for which he and James expressed their admiration in the introduction to their *Works in Architecture* (1773; 2nd vol. 1779; 3rd vol. 1822): movement or 'rise and fall, the advance and recess and other diversity of forms' and 'a variety of light mouldings'. His neo-classicism is most evident in the planning of Syon, with its varied geometric shapes (basilican hall, rotunda, projected central Pantheon, etc.), and on the south front of Kedleston, modelled on a Roman TRIUMPHAL ARCH.

His originality and ingenuity in planning culminated in his London houses of the 1770s – e.g. 20 St James's Square, 20 Portman Square – in which, however, the decoration became increasingly shallow and linear, tending towards the flippancy and frippery for which he was much criticized towards the end of his life.

Between 1768 and 1772 he and James embarked on their most ambitious enterprise, the Adelphi, a vast palatial group of houses on the banks of the Thames (now destroyed). Unfortunately the speculation failed and they were saved from bankruptcy only by the expedient of a lottery and by loans from their elder brother John in Edinburgh.

Partly as a result of the Adelphi fiasco the quality of Robert Adam's work declined sharply after 1775. But it recovered amazingly during the last decade of his life under the stimulus of large commissions in Edinburgh – the General Register House (begun 1774 and completed, with modifications, after his death), the University (begun 1789, completed by W. H. PLAYFAIR

to modified designs 1817–34, the dome added by Rowand Anderson (1834–1921) in 1887), and Charlotte Square (designed 1791). The entrance front to the University is his most monumental building and perhaps his masterpiece as an architect. To the same period belong most of his sham castles, e.g. Culzean Castle (1777–92) and Seton Castle (1789–91), which were much in advance of their date. His earlier neo-Gothic style, e.g. the interiors of Alnwick Castle (*c.* 1770, now destroyed), had been similar in its sophisticated elegance to his neo-classical style. Now he developed a much bolder manner. At Culzean he took full advantage of a dramatic site on the Ayrshire coast for a martial display of round towers and battlements embracing rooms of feminine delicacy inside. The charm of the place lies in this contrast, which would have been greatly relished by the C18 Man of Sensibility, who could here enjoy the chilling horror of storms at sea from an eminently safe and civilized interior.

Colvin 1978: Summerson 1983; J. Gifford, *W. A. (1689–1748)*, Edinburgh 1989.

Addorsed. Term applied to two figures, usually animals, placed symmetrically back to back; often found on CAPITALS.

Adler, Dankmar (1844–1900), *see* SULLIVAN, Louis Henry.

Adobe. Unbaked mud brick dried in the sun, commonly used for building in Spain and Latin America, also in New Mexico, e.g. Santa Fé.

Adyton or **Adytum.** The inner sanctuary of a Greek temple whence oracles were delivered; also, more loosely, any private chamber or sanctuary.

Aedicule. Properly a shrine framed by two columns supporting an ENTABLATURE and PEDIMENT, set in a temple and containing a statue; but also, more loosely, the framing of a door, window or other opening with two columns, piers or pilasters supporting a gable, lintel, plaque, or an entablature and pediment.

Aegricane, see BUCRANE.

Aeolic capital, see ORDER.

Aesthetic Movement. A late C19 English and American artistic movement in reaction against 'Philistine' taste. It derived from the 'art for art's sake' theories of Gautier, Baudelaire and, in England, Walter Pater, though it had no counterpart in France or elsewhere in continental Europe. The opening of the Grosvenor Gallery, London, in 1877 marked its apogee with Whistler and Oscar Wilde to the fore. Its chief influence was on painting and the decorative arts; in architecture its leading exponent was GODWIN. Other architects associated with it, notably ASHBEE and LETHABY, more properly belong to the ARTS AND CRAFTS. The two movements overlapped and had something in common. In the USA it had much less influence on architecture than on interior design and decoration.

J. D. Kornwolf in *In Pursuit of Beauty. Americans and the Aesthetic Movement*, New York 1986; E. Aslin, *The Aesthetic Movement*, London 1969.

Affronted. Term applied to two figures, usually animals, placed symmetrically facing each other; often found on CAPITALS.

Afghanistan architecture, see INDIAN AND PAKISTANI ARCHITECTURE.

African architecture, see EGYPTIAN ARCHITECTURE; ISLAMIC ARCHITECTURE; SOUTH AFRICAN ARCHITECTURE.

Agger. Latin term for the built-up foundations of Roman roads; also sometimes applied to the banks of hill-forts or other earthworks.

Agora. The open space in a Greek or Roman town used as a market-place or general meeting-place, usually surrounded by porticos as in a FORUM.

Agostino di Duccio (1418–81). Primarily a sculptor but worked with ALBERTI on the Tempio Malatestiano at Rimini, where his extremely individual and exquisitely refined relief sculpture is best seen. Equally sculptural and equally masterly is the façade he designed for the oratory of S. Bernardino at Perugia (1457–61). Very different in feeling is his monumental Porta S. Pietro or Porta delle Due Porte at Perugia (1473–81).

Heydenreich and Lotz 1974.

Ahmad Ustad or Ustad Ahmad Lahori (1580?–1649), known as Ahmad Mi'mar. He was chief architect to Shah Jahan at the vast Red Fort palace complex in Delhi and also at Agra (*see* INDIAN ARCHITECTURE).

Aichel, Jan Blazej Santini (1667–1723), see SANTINI-AICHEL, Jan Blazej.

Aida, Takefumi (b. 1927), see JAPANESE ARCHITECTURE.

Aillaud,.Émile (b. 1902). French architect notable for his (intentionally) eccentric housing estates outside Paris, e.g. Les Courtillières, formed of huge serpentine curves (1955–60), and La Grande-Borne, Grigny (1964–71).

J.-F. Dhuys, *L'Architecture selon É.A.*, Paris 1983.

Aisle. Part of a church, hall or other building, parallel to the main span and divided from it by an ARCADE of piers or columns or in rare cases by a screen wall. *See* Fig. 10.

Akkadian architecture, *see* SUMERIAN AND AKKADIAN ARCHITECTURE.

Alabaster. A fine-grained form of gypsum or limestone, white or reddish or yellowish white and translucent. It was used, cut into thin laminae, for church windows in the Middle Ages, notably in Italy, e.g. San Vitale, Ravenna.

Alan of Walsingham. Sacrist of Ely Cathedral at the time when the new Lady Chapel was begun (1321) and the tower over the Norman crossing collapsed (1322) and was replaced by the celebrated octagon. From the documents it is almost certain that the bold idea of replacing the square crossing tower by a larger octagon was his.

Harvey 1984.

Álava, Juan de (d. 1537), *see* JUAN DE ÁLAVA.

Alberti, Leone Battista (1404–72). Playwright, musician, painter, mathematician, scientist, and athlete as well as architect and architectural theorist, he came nearer than anyone to the Renaissance ideal of a 'complete man'. Aristocratic by temperament, he was the first great dilettante architect. He confined himself to designing, and had nothing to do with the actual building of his works. But his few buildings are masterpieces and his *De re aedificatoria* (1452, fully published 1485) is the first architectural treatise of the Renaissance. It crystallized current ideas on proportion, the orders, and ideal (symbolic) town planning. (English translation by J. Rykwent, *On the Art of Building in Ten Books*, Cambridge Mass., 1988.) But though he began with theory his buildings are surprisingly unpedantic and undogmatic. They progressed from the nostalgically archaeological to the boldly experimental. Perhaps his dilettante status allowed him greater freedom than his professional contemporaries. He designed only six buildings and saw only three of them completed. To some extent, he was indebted to BRUNELLESCHI, to whom (among others) he dedicated his treatise *Della pittura* (1436), but whereas Brunelleschi's buildings were elegantly linear his were massively plastic. Architectural beauty he defined as 'the harmony and concord of all the parts achieved in such a manner that nothing could be added, or taken away, or altered except for the worse' and ornament as 'a kind of additional brightness and improvement of Beauty'. By ornament he meant the classical vocabulary of orders, columns, pilasters, and architraves which he always used correctly and grammatically but frequently out of context, e.g. his columns always support architraves (not arches), but are frequently merely decorative and without real structural purpose. His most notable and influential achievement was the adaptation of classical elements to the wall architecture of the Renaissance.

The illegitimate son of a Florentine exile, he was probably born in Genoa. Educated in the humanist atmosphere of Padua, he later studied law at Bologna University and visited Florence for the first time in 1428. In 1431 he went to Rome, where he joined the Papal civil service which apparently allowed him ample time for both travel and the cultivation of his various talents. He became Papal adviser for the restoration of Rome (1447–55) and may have collaborated there with Bernardo ROSSELLINO. In 1450 he was commissioned to transform the Gothic church of S. Francesco, Rimini, into a memorial to the local tyrant, Sigismondo Malatesta, his wife, and courtiers. It was subsequently called the Tempio Malatestiano. He designed a marble shell to encase the old building, the front freely based on a Roman triumphal arch (symbolizing the triumph over death), the side walls pierced by deep arched niches each containing a sarcophagus. The front was never finished, and it is now difficult to visualize how he intended to mask the upper part of the old Gothic façade. As it stands it is a magnificent fragment, one of the noblest and most poignant evocations of the grandeur, *gravitas*, and decorum of Roman architecture. His next work was another addition to a Gothic church, the completion of the façade of S. Maria Novella, Florence (1456–70). Entirely coated with an inlay of different coloured marbles, it owes as much to the C11–12 church of S. Miniato, Florence, as to any Roman building, though the central doorway is derived from the Pantheon. But the whole design is based on a complex geometrical arrangement of squares, and is thus the first instance of the use of HARMONIC PROPORTIONS in the Renaissance. The upper part of the façade is in the form of a pedimented temple front linked to the sides by great scrolls which were to be much copied in later periods. It was commissioned by Giovanni Rucellai, whose name is inscribed across the top

with typical Renaissance confidence. For the same patron he designed the façade of Palazzo Rucellai, Florence (completed by 1460, under Rossellino's supervision), the exquisite, casket-like little marble-clad shrine of the Holy Sepulchre (1467) and perhaps also the Cappella Rucellai, Florence, in which it stands. The Palazzo Rucellai, with its rusticated walls articulated by three superimposed orders of pilasters (Ionic and Corinthian very freely interpreted), is indebted to Brunelleschi's Palazzo di Parte Guelfa. But it has certain novelties, e.g. square-headed door-cases, a vast cornice instead of eaves, and double windows with pilasters and a central column supporting an architrave beneath the rounded cap. The exquisite adjustment of the proportions distinguishes it from the palace designed in emulation of it at Pienza by Rossellino.

S. Sebastiano (1460 onwards) and S. Andrea (1470), both at Mantua, are the only buildings which Alberti designed entire, though neither was completed during his lifetime. For S. Sebastiano he chose a centralized Greek cross plan and designed a massively austere façade as a pilastered temple front, perhaps to be approached up a wide flight of steps. The entablature is broken with a rounded headed window (derived from the Roman arch of Tiberius at Orange), which increased its severity by reducing the pilasters from six to four. This alteration and his complete rejection of columns marks his increasing tendency to stray from correct classical usage in the creation of a more logical wall architecture. The church was completed, with further alterations, after his death. At S. Andrea his plans were carried out more faithfully, though the dome he designed to cover the crossing was never executed. The façade is a combination of a pedimented temple front and a triumphal arch, with shallow pilasters in place of columns and a deep central recess framing the main door. Inside he abandoned the traditional aisle structure for a barrel-vaulted nave flanked by side chapels. Interior and exterior are carefully integrated. The sides of the nave, with pilastered solids and arched recesses alternating, repeat the rhythmical pattern and the triumphal arch of the façade on exactly the same scale. These two buildings herald a new and less archaeological attitude to antiquity. They reach forward from the Early to the High Renaissance and beyond.

Wittkower 1988; Heydenreich and Lotz 1974; F. Borsi, *L.B.A.*, Oxford 1977.

Albini, Franco (1905–77). Studied and lived in Milan. His interior of the Palazzo Bianco Museum, Genoa, and of the treasury of Genoa Cathedral (1951 and 1954) established him as a display architect. His principal buildings were the municipal office, Genoa (1952–61), and the Rinascente department store, Rome (with Franca Helg, 1957–62). His stations for the Milan Metropolitana (1962 onwards) are also notable.

F. Moschini, *F.A.*, London 1979; S. Leet, *F.A.*, Princeton 1989.

Alcázar. A Spanish fortified palace, the most notable examples being those of Segovia, Seville and Toledo (*see* SPANISH ARCHITECTURE).

Alcove. 1. A recess or niche in a wall or an extension or recess (sometimes vaulted) to a room, e.g. for a bed. 2. A secluded bower or summerhouse in a garden.

Aldrich, Henry (1648–1710). Dean of Christ Church, Oxford, he was a virtuoso and architect of distinction. Only two buildings are certainly by him, or largely by him: All Saints', Oxford (1701–10, steeple revised 1717–20 by HAWKSMOOR, whom Aldrich knew), and Peckwater Quad, Christ Church (built by William Townesend 1707–14). Peckwater Quad is a remarkable early example of PALLADIANISM. Aldrich also designed Christ Church Library (built 1717–38) but his designs were completely recast by George Clarke (1661–1736) after Aldrich's death. The Fellows' Building, Corpus Christi College (1706–12), has been attributed to Aldrich; also, with less probability, Trinity College Chapel (1691–4) and Queen's College Library (1693–4). He wrote a Vitruvian–Palladian treatise which was posthumously published in 1789 as *Elementa architecturae civilis*.

Colvin 1978; Summerson 1983; Harris 1990.

Aleijadinho, António Francisco Lisboa (1730 or 1738–1814). The greatest Brazilian sculptor and architect. A mulatto (illegitimate son of a Portuguese architect), he worked in the rich gold-mining province of Minas Gerais, and combined barbarically rich and contorted sculptural decoration with the more dignified architectural forms of traditional Lusitanian church design. His masterpieces are São Francisco, Ouro Preto (1766–94), and the monumental scenic staircase in front of Bom Jesus de Matozinhos, Congonhas do Campo (1800–1805).

Kubler and Soria 1959.

Aleotti, Giovanni Battista (1546–1636), *see* SCAMOZZI, Vincenzo.

Alessi, Galeazzo (1512–72). The leading High Renaissance architect in Genoa. Born in Perugia and trained in Rome where he was much influenced by MICHELANGELO, he settled in Genoa by 1548. He was adept at turning difficult sloping sites to advantage, and made great play with monumental staircases, colonnades, and courtyards on different levels. His several palaces, notably Villa Cambiaso (1548), Palazzo Cambiaso (1565, now Banco d'Italia), and Palazzo Parodi (1567), set the pattern for Genoese domestic architecture. He also built the imposing S. Maria di Carignano, Genoa (1549–52), based on BRAMANTE's design for St Peter's. In Milan he designed Palazzo Marino (1557), now the Municipio, of which the courtyard is an outstanding example of MANNERIST architecture. The *salone maggiore* is also remarkable but was damaged in 1943 and is heavily restored. (The façade facing Piazza della Scala is by Luca Beltrami, 1889.) Other works by him in Milan include SS. Paolo e Barnaba (1561–7) and the façade of S. Maria presso S. Celso (completed by Martino BASSI after he left Milan in 1569).

Heydenreich and Lotz 1974; N. A. H. Brown, *The Milanese Architecture of G.A.*, New York 1980.

Alexander, Christopher (b. 1936). English architect and theorist, he founded the Center for Environmental Structures (CES), Berkeley, California, in 1967, where his experiments have been influential. In 1977 he published *A Pattern Language* consisting of 253 design precepts. A protagonist of low-tech self-built housing (*see* COMMUNITY ARCHITECTURE), his most notable projects have been for user-designed apartment buildings at St Quentin-en-Yvelines near Versailles,

France (1974), and for housing at Mexicali, Mexico (1976). His New Eishin Gakuen High School, Eishin University, Japan, dates from 1985–7.

Alfieri, Benedetto (1699–1767), Piedmontese nobleman (uncle of the poet), began as a lawyer, turned to architecture, and succeeded JUVARRA as royal architect in Turin (1739). He was largely employed in completing Juvarra's work in Palazzo Reale, Turin, and elsewhere. The Teatro Regio, Turin, was begun by Juvarra but is largely by Alfieri (1736–40). His main independent building is the vast parish church at Carignano (1757–64), with a severe façade and very rich interior on a peculiar kidney-shaped plan. He also designed the noble west portico of Geneva Cathedral in a surprisingly radical classicizing style (1752–6).

Pommer 1967; A. Bellini, *B.A.*, Milan 1978; C. Cancro, *B.A. (1699–1767) L'opera completa*, Milan 1980.

Algardi, Alessandro (1595–1654). Born in Bologna but settled in Rome, best known as a sculptor, representing the sobriety of Bolognese classicism in opposition to BERNINI. His reputation as an architect rests on the Villa Doria-Pamphili in Rome, of which he had the general direction. (The attribution of the design to his assistant Giovanni Francesco Grimaldi (1606–90) is now not accepted.)

J. Montagu, *A.A.*, London 1985.

Alicatado. Spanish term meaning 'cut work' applied to wall decorations composed of mosaics of variously coloured geometrically shaped pieces of glazed pottery in use from the C12 (e.g. Alhambra, Granada, and Alcázar, Seville) but soon superseded by uniformly shaped TILES. By the C15 it was used only to surround tilework.

Allio, Domenico dell' (d. 1563), *see* AUSTRIAN ARCHITECTURE.

Allio, Donato Felice (*c.* 1680–1770), *see* AUSTRIAN ARCHITECTURE.

Alliprandi, Giovanni Battista (1665–*c.* 1720), *see* CZECHOSLOVAK ARCHITECTURE.

Almonry. The room in a MONASTERY in which alms are distributed.

Almquist, Osvald (1884–1950). With Gunnar ASPLUND a pioneer of modern functionalist architecture in Sweden, e.g. his hydro-electric power plants near Hammersfors and Krangfors (1925–8).
 B. Linn, *O.A. Ein Arkitekt och Hans Arbete*, Stockholm 1967.

Almshouse. A house or, more usually, a group of houses built and endowed by private charity for the aged and poor – replacing, after the dissolution of the monasteries in England, monastic houses where alms and hospitality were dispensed. Many were built in Elizabethan and Stuart times, often as personal memorials to their founders. In type they range from those built round a courtyard with hall and chapel, to a simple row of cottages. The larger ones often have a gables over the street front. The Penrose Almshouses, Barnstaple (1627), have a gabled gatehouse. The more splendid and conspicuous foundations were often those of bishops and archbishops, e.g. Abbot's Hospital, Guildford (begun 1619). John NASH's Blaise Hamlet (1811) consists of ten almshouses.
 W. H. Godfrey, *The English Almshouse with Some Account of its Predecessor, the Medieval Almshouse*, London 1955; B. Bailey, *Almshouses*, London 1988.

Altana. A covered terrace or loggia raised above the roof, like a BELVEDERE. Venetian in origin and usually of wood, it was intended for drying clothes and is still so used in Venice. It later became a feature of C15–16 domestic architecture in Rome.

Altar. A structure on which to place or sacrifice offerings to a deity. In Greece and Rome altars took many different forms. The Christian altar is a table or slab on supports consecrated for celebration of the sacrament; usually of stone. In the Middle Ages portable altars could be of metal. After the Reformation communion tables of wood replaced altars in England.

Altar frontal, *see* ANTEPENDIUM.

Altar-tomb. A post-medieval term for a tomb resembling an altar with solid sides but not used as one. *See* TOMB-CHEST.

Alure. An alley or place to walk in, especially behind a parapet or round the roof of a church.

Álvares, Afonso (*fl.* 1551–75), *see* PORTUGUESE ARCHITECTURE.

Álvares, Baltasar (*fl.* 1570–1620), *see* PORTUGUESE ARCHITECTURE.

Amadeo or **Omodeo**, Giovanni Antonio (1447–1522). Born in Pavia, and primarily a sculptor, he was working at the Certosa there by 1466; then he worked in Milan (MICHELOZZO's Portinari Chapel in S. Eustorgio), where he encountered the Early Renaissance style. The immediate result was the Colleoni Chapel (1470–73) attached to S. Maria Maggiore, Bergamo – based on the Portinari Chapel but encrusted with Renaissance ornamentation in

Gothic profusion. He designed the elaborate façade of the Certosa outside Pavia (1491 onwards). The Gothic dome over the crossing of Milan Cathedral was built after designs by Amadeo and Dolcebuono, with advice from FRANCESCO DI GIORGIO.

Heydenreich and Lotz 1974.

Ambo. A stand raised on two or more steps, for the reading of the Epistle and the Gospel; a prominent feature in early medieval Italian churches. Sometimes two were built, one for the Epistle and one for the Gospel, on the south and north sides respectively. After the C13 the ambo was replaced by the PULPIT.

Ambry, see AUMBRY.

Ambulatory. A semicircular or polygonal aisle enclosing an APSE or a straight-ended sanctuary; originally used for processional purposes.

Ambulatory church. In Early Christian and Byzantine architecture a church in which a domed centre bay is enveloped on three sides by AISLES. See also CROSS-DOMED CHURCH.

American architecture, see BRAZILIAN, MESO-AMERICAN, MEXICAN, PERUVIAN and UNITED STATES ARCHITECTURE.

Ammanati, Bartolomeo (1511–92), was primarily a MANNERIST sculptor. His architectural masterpiece is the very graceful Ponte S. Trinità, Florence (1558–70, destroyed 1944 but rebuilt). With VIGNOLA and VASARI he played some part in designing Villa Giulia, Rome (1551–5). He enlarged and altered Palazzo Pitti, Florence (1558–70), building the almost grotesquely over-rusticated garden façade (begun 1560). He completed Palazzo

Grifoni, Florence (1557), and supervised the building of MICHELANGELO's vestibule stairway in the Laurenziana, Florence. Outside Florence, he designed the Tempietto della Vittoria, near Arezzo (1572). In Lucca he designed part of the Palazzo Provinciale (1578) with a handsome SERLIAN loggia.

Heydenreich and Lotz 1974.

Amphiprostyle. Term applied to a temple with porticos at each end, but without columns along the sides.

Amphitheatre. An elliptical or circular space surrounded by rising tiers of seats, as used by the Romans for gladiatorial contests, e.g. the Colosseum, Rome.

Amsterdam School, see DUTCH ARCHITECTURE; EXPRESSIONISM; KLERK, Michel de.

Anathyrosis. The smooth marginal dressing of the outer contact band of a masonry joint, the central portion being left roughened and sunk so as to avoid contact.

Ancones. 1. Brackets or CONSOLES on either side of a doorway, supporting a CORNICE. 2. The projections left on blocks of stone, such as the drums of a column, to hoist them into position.

Anderson, Sir Robert Rowand (1834–1921), see ADAM, Robert.

Ando, Tadao (b. 1941). Japanese 'new wave' architect, a leading exponent of 'Critical Regionalism' in reaction against METABOLISM. His revival of traditional materials and vernacular styles is combined with modern techniques. He has been influential both in his prolific writings and his buildings which are mainly domestic and small-scale, e.g. Matsumoto house, Waka-yama (1980), Koshino house, Osaka (1981), Rokko housing, Hyogo (1983), in which great refinement is achieved without any loss of vigour.

Y. Futagawa, *T.A.*, Tokyo 1981; Kunihiro and Eiserman, *T.A. The Yale Studio and Current Works*, New York 1989.

Andrea di Cione (*fl.* 1343–68), *see* ORCAGNA.

Andrea Pisano (d. 1348/9), *see* PISANO, Andrea.

Andrews, John (b. 1933). Australian architect, trained in Sydney and under J. L. SERT at Harvard. He made his name with Scarborough College, University of Toronto, Canada (1962–9), a pioneer MEGASTRUCTURE designed to accommodate 5,000 people in a self-suf-ficient institution. This was followed by students' housing at Guelph University, Canada (1965–8), Seaport Passenger Terminal, Miami, USA (1967), and the Gund Hall Graduate School of Design, Harvard University, USA (1968), which Philip JOHNSON called 'one of the six greatest buildings of the C20'. Of his recent buildings the American Express Tower, Sydney, Australia (1976), and the Canadian National Tower, Toronto, Canada (1977), should be mentioned.

P. Drew, *The Third Generation. The Changing Meaning of Architecture*, New York 1972.

Ang. In Chinese roof construction a long transverse bracket arm with the function of a lever. An *ang ton* is placed directly under a roof sloping down-wards to the eaves.

Anglo-Saxon architecture, *see* ENGLISH ARCHITECTURE.

Angular capital. An IONIC capital with all four sides alike, and the volutes turned outwards as in a Corinthian capital. A C16 innovation, probably due to SCAMOZZI and frequently employed until the late C18, when rejected as incorrect.

Annular. Ring-shaped, as in an annu-lar barrel vault or annular passage.

Annulet, *see* SHAFT-RING.

Anreith, Anton (1754–1822), *see* SOUTH AFRICAN ARCHITECTURE.

Anse de panier, *see* ARCH.

Anta. A PILASTER of which the base and CAPITAL do not conform with the ORDER used elsewhere on the building; it is usually placed at the ends of the projecting walls of a temple PORTICO or pronaos. If there are columns be-tween the *antae* they are called columns *in antis*; the portico and temple itself may also be called *in antis*, as distinct from being PROSTYLE.

Antechurch or **forechurch**. An ap-pendix to the west end of a church, resembling a porch or a NARTHEX, but several bays deep and usually consist-ing of nave and aisles.

Antefixae. Ornamental blocks on the edge of a roof to conceal the ends of the tiles. *See* Fig. 2.

Antelami, Benedetto (active 1177–1233), a sculptor and probably an ar-chitect also. Attributed to him are the Baptistery, Parma (1196–1216, com-pleted 1270), the cathedral of Borgo San Donnino, now Fidenza (1179–96 and 1214–18), and S. Andrea at Ver-celli (1219–25/6). This church already has features pointing in the direction of French Gothic. The transition from Romanesque to Gothic is obvious in his sculpture.

FIG. 3. *Anthemion*

K. W. Forster, *B.A.*, Munich 1961.

Antependium or **altar frontal**. A decorative, detachable covering for the front of an altar as distinct from the front itself. Antependiums are of various materials: painted wood, ivory, embroidered silk or other textiles, gold, silver or other metals, e.g. the gold antependium from Basel Cathedral of *c.* 1022/4 (Musée de Cluny, Paris) or that in the Palatine Chapel, Aachen, also of gold, of *c.* 1020. If the covering is continued round the sides and back it is called a PALIOTTO.

Anthemion. Ornament reminiscent of a honeysuckle flower alternating with palm leaves or PALMETTES, common in ancient Greek and Roman architecture. *See* Fig. 3.

Anthemios of Tralles. Geometrician and theorist rather than architect, he is known for sure to have designed only one building, but that among the greatest in the world: Hagia Sophia, Constantinople (AD 532–7). The dates of his birth and death are unknown. Born at Tralles in Lydia, he came of a Greek professional middle-class family; his father was a physician. In 532 Justinian chose him to design the new church of Holy Wisdom (Hagia Sophia) to replace a predecessor which had been burnt in riots. This vast undertaking was completed in the incredibly brief period of five years, to the gratification of Justinian, who claimed to have surpassed Solomon. Anthemios described architecture as 'the application of geometry to solid matter', and his great work with its dome 107 ft in diameter is remarkable as a feat of engineering (even though the dome collapsed in 558). But it is also much more, for by the cunning use of screened aisles and galleries around the central area of the church he concealed the supports of the dome which thus seems to float above the building, creating an atmosphere of mystery emphasized by the contrast between the light central space and the dark aisles. He was assisted by ISIDORUS OF MILETUS.

Krautheimer 1986; R. J. Mainstone, *Hagia Sophia*, London 1988.

Anticlastic. Of a surface, having curvatures in opposite senses (concave and convex) in different directions through any point, e.g. as in a HYPERBOLIC PARABOLOID ROOF.

Antis, in, *see* ANTA; PORTICO.

Antoine, Jacques-Denis (1733–1801). A leading architect in the reign of Louis XVI. His masterpiece is the Mint, Paris (1768–75) – huge, solemn, and very Roman, though he did not visit Italy until 1777. He built a number of Parisian *hôtels*, notably the Hôtel de Jaucourt (1782), and outside Paris, the Château de Herces near Houdan (1772) and the Chapelle de la Visitation at Nancy (1785).

Braham 1980.

Antonelli, Alessandro (1798–1888). Professor of Architecture at Turin from 1836 till 1857. His most famous works are the crazily high, externally classical and internally iron-supported towers of the so-called Mole Antonelliana at Turin (originally intended as

Antonio di Vincenzo

a synagogue and about 550 ft high) and of the cathedral of Novara (about 420 ft high). The former was designed in 1863, the latter in 1840.

Meeks 1966; F. Rosso, *A.A.*, Florence 1989.

Antonio di Vincenzo (*c.* 1350–1401/ 2), *see* ITALIAN ARCHITECTURE.

Antunes, João (1683–1734), *see* PORTUGUESE ARCHITECTURE.

Apadana or **apadhana.** In ancient Persia a free-standing columned hall apparently serving as a throne-room. Outstanding was the hundred-columned apadana built in Persepolis under Darius I (*see* PERSIAN ARCHITECTURE). The apadana often had a portico, and was itself mostly square in plan.

Apex stone. The top stone in a GABLE end, sometimes called the *saddle stone*.

Apollodorus of Damascus (active AD 97–130). Born in Syria, he went to Rome and became official architect to Trajan (AD 97–117), accompanying him on his military campaigns and designing or inspiring almost all the buildings erected under him. His first recorded work was the stone-and-wood bridge over the Danube at Dobreta (AD 104). But his masterpieces were naturally in Rome itself: an ODEON circular in plan (probably that built by Domitian in the Campus Martius), the Baths of Trajan, and Trajan's Forum. The latter, with its imposing axial planning and subtle play of symmetry, illustrates his style, a brilliant compromise between the Hellenistic and the pure Roman traditions. He also planned the markets at the extreme end of the Quirinal hill, and was probably involved in work at the port of Rome (Fiumicino)

and at Civitavecchia. The TRIUMPHAL ARCHES at Ancona and Benevento have been attributed to him. Though he was on less happy terms with Hadrian, he collaborated with him on at least one project, and dedicated to him his treatise on the construction of engines of assault, *Poliorketa*. But, according to Dio Cassius, Hadrian banished him from Rome in about AD 130, and later condemned him to death because of his harsh criticism of the Temple of Venus and Rome.

MacDonald 1965; Ward-Perkins 1981.

Apophyge. The slight curve at the top and bottom of a column where the SHAFT joins the CAPITAL or base.

Applied column, *see* ENGAGED COLUMN.

Apron. A raised panel below a window-sill, sometimes shaped and decorated.

Apse. A vaulted semicircular or polygonal termination, usually to a chancel or chapel. *See* Fig. 10.

Apsidiole or **absidiole.** A small, projecting apsidal chapel.

Apteral. An adjective describing a classical-style building with columns at the end, but not along the sides.

Aqueduct. An artifical channel for carrying water, usually an elevated masonry or brick structure supported on arches; invented by the ancient Romans, e.g. the CI BC Pont du Gard near Nîmes in France and the early CI to C2 AD aqueduct at Segovia, Spain, which still carries the town's water supply.

Ward-Perkins 1981.

Arabesque. Intricate and fanciful surface decoration generally based on geometrical patterns and using combinations of flowing lines, tendrils, etc., covering the surface with a network of zigzags, spirals, etc. Human figures were not used, as they were in GROTESQUE ornament. The origin of arabesque ornament is disputed, but the name derives from the belief that it was typically Saracenic, especially that on Venetian Saracenic metalwork. The development of arabesque ornament is contemporary with that of STRAPWORK at Fontainebleau in 1533–5, but the nature of the connection between them is unknown.

P. Ward-Jackson in *Victoria & Albert Museum Bulletin*, July 1967.

Araeostyle. With an arrangement of columns spaced four diameters apart. *See also* DIASTYLE; EUSTYLE; PYCNOSTYLE; SYSTYLE.

Arau, *see* BELGIAN ARCHITECTURE.

Arcade. 1. A range of arches carried on PIERS or columns, either free-standing or blind, i.e. attached to a wall. 2. A covered passage with shops on one or both sides.

J. F. Geist, *Arcades: The History of a Building Type,* Cambridge, Mass., 1983; M. Mackeith, *The History and Conservation of Shopping Arcades,* London 1986.

Arch. The spanning of an opening by means other than that of a LINTEL. The most primitive form was made by CORBELLING. True arches are curved and so constructed with wedge-shaped blocks over the opening that the downward thrust of the weight of their own material and of that above is converted into outward thrusts resisted by the flanking material. There are many different types.

Anse de panier is a French term for an arch whose curve resembles that of the handle of a basket; also called *basket arch*. It is formed by a segment of a large circle continued left and right by two segments of much smaller circles.

Basket arch or *three-centred arch, see above.*

A *catenary arch* is like an inverted CATENARY.

Corbel arch, see false arch.

Depressed arch, see four-centred arch.

Discharging arch, see relieving arch.

A *drop arch* is pointed with a span greater than its radii.

An *elliptical arch* is a half ellipse from a centre on the SPRINGING LINE.

Equilateral arch, see pointed arch.

A *false* or *corbel arch* is one constructed by progressive cantilevering or corbelling from the two sides with horizontal joints.

A *four-centred* or *depressed arch* is a late medieval form – an arch of four arcs, the two outer and lower ones springing from centres on the springing line, the two inner and upper arcs from centres below the springing line.

A *horseshoe arch* is often found in Islamic buildings; it can be either a pointed or a round horseshoe.

Keel arch, see ogee arch.

A *lancet arch* is pointed, with radii much larger than the span.

An *ogee arch* is pointed and usually of four arcs, the centres of two inside the arch, of the other two outside; this produces a compound curve of two parts, one convex and the other concave. Introduced *c.* 1300 it was popular throughout the late Middle Ages and in England especially in the early C14; also called a *keel arch.* In a *nodding ogee arch* the apex projects beyond the vertical plane of the wall or supporting member.

FIG. 4. *Arch*

KEY:
1. Keystone
2. Voussoirs
3. Impost
4. Abutment
5. Extrados
6. Intrados or soffit
7. Centre
8. Span
9. Springing line
10. Haunch
11. Crown

A *pointed arch* is produced by two curves, each with a radius equal to the span and meeting in a point at the top; also called an *equilateral arch*.

A *raking* or *rampant arch* has one impost higher than the other.

A *relieving arch* is usually of rough construction placed in a wall, above an arch or any opening, to relieve it of much of the superincumbent weight; also called a *discharging arch*.

A *rowlock arch* has bricks or small VOUSSOIRS in separate concentric rings.

A *segmental arch* is a segment of a circle drawn from a centre below the springing line.

A *segmental pointed arch* is drawn from two centres below the springing line.

A *shouldered arch* consists of a lintel connected with the jambs of a doorway by corbels. The corbels start with a concave quadrant and continue vertically to meet the lintel.

A *skew arch* has jambs not at right-angles to its faces.

Four-centred arch;
Tudor arch;
Ogee arch;
Stilted arch;
Horseshoe arch;
Basket arch;
Lancet arch

A *stilted arch* has its springing line raised by vertical PIERS above the IMPOST level.

A *strainer arch* is one inserted, in most cases, across a nave or an aisle to prevent the walls from leaning.

A *Tudor arch* is a late medieval pointed arch whose shanks start with a curve near to a quarter circle and continue to the apex in a straight line.

See Fig. 4.

Arch façade. A façade in the form of a large screen hollowed out into a series of deep, unornamented arches. In England it appears first in Norman churches and most dramatically in the west façade of Lincoln Cathedral and at the abbey church of Bury St Edmunds.

Archer, John Lee (1791–1852), *see* AUSTRALIAN ARCHITECTURE.

Archer, Thomas (*c.* 1668–1743). The only English Baroque architect to have studied continental Baroque at first hand. His buildings are unique in England in showing an intimate appreciation of BERNINI and BORROMINI. He came of good family and made a four-year Grand Tour after Oxford, returning home in 1695. A Whig, he was successful at Court and in 1703 obtained the lucrative post of Groom Porter. His buildings date between then and 1715, when he acquired the even more profitable post of Controller of Customs at Newcastle, whereupon he gave up architecture. The north front of Chatsworth (1704–5) and the garden pavilion at Wrest Park (1709–11) are his best surviving secular buildings but his reputation rests mainly on his three churches — Birmingham Cathedral (1710–15); St Paul, Deptford, London (1713–30); and St John, Smith Square, London (1713–30), with its spectacular and much-maligned towers. Heythrop House, Oxfordshire (1707–10), was his most grandiloquent effort but it was burnt and largely rebuilt in 1870.

Colvin 1978; Summerson 1983.

Archigram. English group formed in 1960 by Peter Cook (b. 1936). Their fantastic, utopian space-age visions of a flexible, disposable, plug-in Pop architecture in rapturous candy-colours were unrealized but influential. Cook's Montreal Tower project (1963) is a prototype HIGH TECH design. The 'machine-look' was anticipated by Michael Webb (b. 1937) in his Fur-niture Manufacturers project, 1957, which resembled an automobile engine. Archigram disbanded in 1975, their Capsule at Expo 70, Osaka, being almost their only realized project.

P. Cook, *Archigram*, London 1974; Klotz 1986.

Architects' Co-Partnership. A group of English architects founded in 1939 and refounded in 1945. An anonymous team approach and preference for industrialized building materials characterize their work, notably the Dunlop Semtex rubber factory, Brynmawr (1946–9), with Ove ARUP, and educational buildings such as the Biochemistry Building, Imperial College, London (1961–4), and the Wolfson Building, Trinity College, Cambridge (1972).

Architext, *see* AZUMA, Takamitsu.

Architrave. The lintel extending from one column or pier to another: also, the lowest of the three main parts of an ENTABLATURE; also, more loosely, the moulded frame surrounding a door or window (if this frame turns away at the top at right angles, rises vertically and returns horizontally, forming a shoulder, it is called a *shouldered architrave*). *See* Figs. 41, 44, 66.

Architrave-cornice. An ENTABLATURE from which the FRIEZE is elided.

Archivolt. The continuous architrave moulding of the face of an arch, following its contour; also the INTRADOS or under-side of an arch.

Archizoom. Italian 'new wave' group in Florence 1966–73 and Milan 1974. Mainly concerned with interior design, they heralded later developments with 'anti-design' and 'banal-design'.

A. Branzi, *The Hot House*, London 1985.

Arcosolia, see CATACOMB.

Arcuated. A term applied to a building dependent structurally on the use of arches or the arch principle, in contrast to a TRABEATED building.

Arena. The central open space of an AMPHITHEATRE; also, more loosely, any building for public contests or displays in the open air.

Ariss, John, the first professional architect in North America, emigrated from England in or shortly before 1751, when he advertised in the *Maryland Gazette* as being 'lately from Great Britain' and ready to undertake 'Buildings of all Sorts and Dimensions . . . either of the Ancient or Modern Order of Gibbs, Architect'. His work is unrecorded, but some of the finer Virginian houses were probably designed by him, e.g. Mount Airey, Richmond County (1755–8); they are English Palladian, with Gibbsian overtones.

Pierson and Jordy 1970; Whiffen and Koeper 1981.

Ark, see ECHAL.

Armenian architecture, see BYZANTINE ARCHITECTURE.

Arnolfo di Cambio (*c.* 1245–*c.* 1310). A Florentine sculptor and mason. Assistant of Nicola PISANO in 1266, he is already called a *subtilissimus magister* in 1277. He signed works of decorative architecture and sculpture combined in 1282, 1285, and 1293. The architectural forms used are truly Gothic, aware of French precedent, and contain trefoil-headed and trefoil-cusped arches. In 1296 the new cathedral of Florence was begun; Arnolfo was master mason. His design is recognizable in the nave and aisles, but the present centralizing east end with its

three polygonal apses is by Francesco TALENTI, though it only enlarged and pushed considerably farther east the east end as intended by Arnolfo, perhaps under the influence of Cologne. It is curious that Arnolfo, in the earliest source referring to him (though as late as *c.* 1520), is called a German. Several other buildings have been attributed to Arnolfo, among them, with convincing arguments, S. Croce (begun 1294/5), the Florentine Badia (begun 1284), and the tower of the Palazzo Vecchio (*c.* 1310).

A. M. Romanini, *A. di C. e lo 'stil novo' del gotico italiano* (1969), Florence 1980; White 1987.

Aronco, Raimondo d' (1857–1932), see SOMMARUGA, Giuseppe.

Arris. A sharp edge produced by the meeting of two surfaces.

Arruda, Diogo (active 1508–31). The leading practitioner of the MANUELINE STYLE in Portugal. His main work is the nave and chapterhouse of the Cristo church, Tomar (1510–14), with its almost surrealist sculptured decoration: sails and ropes around the circular windows, mouldings of cork floats threaded on cables, buttresses carved with patterns of coral and seaweed. His brother Francisco (active 1510–47) was mainly a military architect, but built the exotic, almost Hindu, tower at Belem (1515–20).

Kubler and Soria 1959.

Art Deco. The fashionable Jazz Age style concurrent with INTERNATIONAL MODERN in the 1920s and 1930s. The name derives from a Paris exhibition of decorative and industrial art in 1925. It is characterized by unfunctional 'modernism' – e.g. streamlining motifs in architecture. The French architect

Robert Mallet-Stevens (1886–1945) was its chief European exponent in architecture, e.g. his cubistic apartments and other buildings in rue Mallet-Stevens, Paris (1926–7). In the USA the style found its most notable expression in skyscrapers (e.g. the Chrysler building, New York, 1928–30, by William Van Alen, 1882–1954) and cinemas, etc. (e.g. Radio City Music Hall, Rockefeller Center, New York).

B. Hillier, *Art Deco*, Minneapolis 1971; R. H. Bletter and C. Robinson, *Skyscraper Style – Art Deco New York*, New York 1975.

Art Nouveau. The name of a shop opened in Paris in 1895 to sell objects of modern, i.e. non-period-imitation, style. The movement away from imitation of the past had started in book production and textiles in England in the 1880s (*see* MACKMURDO), and had begun to invade furniture and other furnishings about 1890. Stylistically, the origins lay in the designs of William MORRIS and the English ARTS AND CRAFTS. One of the principal centres from 1892 onwards was Brussels (*see* HANKAR, HORTA; van de VELDE). In France the two centres were Nancy, where in Émile Gallé's glass Art Nouveau forms occurred as early as the 1880s, and Paris, e.g. GUIMARD, JOURDAIN. Art Nouveau forms are characterized by the ubiquitous use of undulation like waves or flames or flower stalks or flowing hair. Some artists kept close to nature, others, especially van de Velde, preferred abstract forms as being a purer expression of the dynamics aimed at. The most important representatives of Art Nouveau are: in America, Louis C. Tiffany (1848–1933); in Germany (where it is called *Jugendstil*), Hermann Obrist (1863–

1927) and August Endell (1871–1925), whose Elvira Studio, Munich (1897–8), was notable; and in Italy (where it is called *Stile Liberty*), Raimondo d'Aronco (1857–1932), Ernesto Basile (1857–1932) and SOMMARUGA. In architecture by far the greatest is GAUDÍ. It has rightly been pointed out that Art Nouveau has a source and certainly a parallel in the paintings and graphic work of Gauguin, Munch, and some others. The climax in Britain, and at the same time the beginning of the end, is the work of Charles R. MACKINTOSH of Glasgow, in whose architecture and decoration the slender curves and the subtle opalescent colours of Art Nouveau blend with a new rectangular crispness and pure whiteness of framework. Vienna took this up at once, and found from it the way into the C20 emphasis on the square and the cube (*see* LOOS; HOFFMANN; LECHNER).

Nicoletti 1978; Loyer 1979.

Arts and Crafts. A late C19 English movement to revive handicrafts and reform architecture by using traditional building crafts and local materials (*see* VERNACULAR ARCHITECTURE). It was born in the wake of the 1851 Great Exhibition in London and in opposition to the machine-made furnishings etc. made possible by the Industrial Revolution. Inspired by RUSKIN and MORRIS it may be said to have started when Morris met Philip WEBB in 1856, though DEVEY had anticipated it at Penshurst in 1850. In 1859–60 Webb built for Morris his famous Red House, Bexley Heath, which exemplified the aims of the movement – informality, modesty, structural integrity, etc. Webb was followed by Norman SHAW and Eden NESFIELD and the movement culminated with ASHBEE, LETHABY, VOYSEY and the early LUTYENS, though others should be mentioned, notably Ernest Newton (1856–1922) and his Lethaby-influenced houses (Redcourt, Haslemere, 1895); Edward Schroeder Prior (1852–1932) and his butterfly-plan houses (The Barn, Exmouth, 1896–9); Halsey Ricardo (1854–1928) and his colourful, tile-covered houses (8 Addison Road, London, 1905–7); M. Hugh Baillie Scott (1865–1945) and his rough-cast and open-planned houses with inglenooks etc. inside (Blackwell School, Bowness-on-Windermere, 1900); and, in Scotland, Robert LORIMER. The movement played a notable part in early GARDEN CITIES AND GARDEN SUBURBS with Shaw's Bedford Park, London (1877), and the work of Voysey there and of Baillie Scott at Hampstead Garden Suburb and of UNWIN's partner Raymond Barry Parker (1867–1941) at Letchworth Garden City.

The movement contributed notably to church building with Lethaby's All Saints, Brockhampton (1900–1902). More typically Arts and Crafts are Holy Trinity, Sloane Street, London (1888), by John Dando Sedding (1838–91), and St Cyprian's, Clarence Gate, London (1902–3) by COMPER.

In England the movement declined after 1900 but it was influential in Europe, mainly in Germany through Hermann Muthesius (1861–1927), whose *Das englische Haus* (1904–5) is a classic and whose Haus Freudenberg, Berlin (1907–8), outdoes Baillie Scott; and through the DEUTSCHER WERKBUND, thus influencing BEHRENS, OLBRICH, and the early BAUHAUS. In the USA the movement's influence was felt as early as the 1870s with RICH-

ARDSON, but its outstanding exponent was Frank Lloyd WRIGHT, founder member of the Chicago Arts and Crafts Society in 1897. McKIM and WHITE and also George Washington Maher (1864–1926) should also be mentioned, as well as, on the west coast, GREENE & GREENE and even perhaps MAYBECK.

J. D. Kornwolf, *M.H. Baillie Scott and the Arts and Crafts Movement*, Baltimore and London 1972; T. Davey, *Arts and Crafts Architecture: The Search for an Earthly Paradise*, London 1980; M. Richardson, *Architects of the Arts and Crafts Movement*, London 1981; D. Hawkes, *Modern Country Homes in England: The Arts and Crafts Architecture of Barry Parker*, London 1986; W. Kaplan, 'The Art that is Life': *The Arts and Crafts Movement in America 1875–1920*, Boston 1987; P. Stansky, *Redesigning the World: William Morris, the 1880s and the Arts and Crafts*, Princeton 1988.

Arup, Ove (1895–1988). Studied philosophy before graduating in engineering in Copenhagen in 1922. Engaged first in civil engineering and then became involved in architecture, working with TECTON in London to produce Highpoint, the Penguin Pool and Finsbury Health Centre, where he applied new ideas of concrete construction and pioneered the use of load-bearing concrete walls. His own consulting practice became known for its fresh approach to the solution of difficult structural problems, and he collaborated closely with leading architects in England and overseas. A parallel partnership of architects and engineers, with Philip Dowson, Ronald Hobbs and others, was formed in 1963, called Arup Associates This multi-professional team aimed to practise close collaboration between professions. It has been responsible for Point Royal, Bracknell, buildings for Corpus Christi, Cambridge, and Somerville, Oxford, the Mining and Metallurgy Departments at Birmingham University and the buildings for CIBA at Duxford, and for Smith, Kline & French at Welwyn (1963). As a consultant Arup was involved in UTZON's Sydney Opera House (1956–74) and in PIANO and ROGERS' Centre Pompidou, Paris (1971–7). More recently Arup Associates have been responsible for some notable HIGH TECH buildings: Lloyds' offices, Chatham (1983), and especially 1 Finsbury Avenue, London (1984), and offices at Broadgate, Liverpool Street, London (1986).

M. Brawne, *A. Associates*, London 1983.

Asam, Cosmas Damian (1686–1739) and Egid Quirin (1692–1750), were brothers who always worked together as architects though sometimes separately as decorators (Cosmas Damian was a fresco-painter and Egid Quirin a sculptor). Sons of a Bavarian painter, they did not emerge from provincial obscurity until after visiting Rome (1711–14). As a result of this Roman training they remained essentially Baroque rather than Rococo architects. They seem to have admired the juicier C17 Italians rather than their elegant and frivolous contemporaries. They decorated many important churches (e.g. Michelfeld; Einsiedeln, 1727; St Jacobi, Innsbruck; Osterhofen; Freising Cathedral, 1723–4; St Maria Victoria, Ingolstadt; Aldersbach), but designed and built only four, in which, however, they carried to unprece-

dented lengths the melodramatic effects of concealed lighting, spatial illusionism, and other tricks which they had picked up in Rome. Their emotionalism is seen at its wildest in the fantastic *tableau vivant* altar-pieces at Rohr (1717–23) and Weltenburg (1716–35). They attempted something better in St John Nepomuk, Munich (1735–8), a church which is attached to their house and was entirely paid for by them. This is a tiny but sensational church, a masterpiece of German Baroque in which architecture and decoration are successfully combined to achieve an intense atmosphere of religious fervour. Their last work, the Ursulinenkirche, Straubing (1736–40), is almost equally good.

Hitchcock 1968; B. Rupprecht, *Die Brüder A. Sinn und Sinnlichkeit in bayerischen Barock*, Regensburg 1980.

Ashbee, Charles Robert (1863–1942). More a social reformer than an architect. His model was MORRIS and he became a leading member of the ARTS AND CRAFTS movement. In 1888 he founded his Guild and School of Handicraft in the East End of London. The guild moved into the country, to Chipping Campden, in 1902. The First World War killed it. His best architectural designs were for houses in Cheyne Walk, London – Nos. 72–3 (1897, destroyed in the Second World War) and Nos. 38 and 39 (1899–1901).

A. Crawford, *C.R.A.*, London 1985.

Ashlar. Hewn blocks of masonry wrought to even faces and square edges and laid in horizontal courses with vertical joints, as opposed to rubble or unhewn stone straight from the quarry.

Ashlar piece, *see* ROOF.

FIG. 5. *Astragal*

Aslin, Charles Herbert (1893–1959), *see* INDUSTRIALIZED BUILDING.

Asplund, Gunnar Erik (1885–1940), the most important Swedish architect of the C20, started in the Scandinavian classicism first developed by the Danes; his principal work in that style is the Stockholm City Library (1920–28) with its high circular reading room rising as a drum above the rest of the *ensemble*. With his work for the Stockholm Exhibition of 1930 he changed to the Central European Modern, but instead of treating it in the relatively massive manner then current, he lightened up his forms by means of thin metal members, much glass, and some freer forms of roof, etc., thereby endowing the style with a grace and translucency which had a great international impact. But Asplund was never demonstrative or aggressive. His buildings always observe a noble restraint. The finest of them are the extension of the Town Hall of Göteborg (1934–7), with its beautifully transparent courtyard, and the Stockholm Crematorium (1935–40), which may well be called the most perfect example of genuine C20 monumentality and religious architecture in existence.

C. Caldenby and O. Hultin, *A. 1885–1940*, New York 1985; D. Cruikshank (ed.), *G.A.*, London 1988; C. St John-Wilson, *G.A. Architect 1885–1940. The Dilemma of Classicism*, London 1988.

Asprucci, Antonio (1723–1808). A notable early neo-classical architect in Rome. His masterpiece is the interior of Villa Borghese, Rome (1782 onwards), and the elegant temples, sham ruins, and other follies in the park, where he was succeeded by Luigi Canina (1795–1856).

M. Chiarini in *DBI* 1962.

Assyrian architecture, *see* SUMERIAN AND AKKADIAN ARCHITECTURE.

Astragal. A small moulding circular in section, often decorated with a bead and reel enrichment. In Scotland a glazing bar. *See* Figs. 5, 44.

Asturian architecture, *see* SPANISH ARCHITECTURE.

Astylar. A term applied to a façade without columns or pilasters.

Atlantes. Supports in the form of carved male figures, used especially by German Baroque architects instead of columns to support an ENTABLATURE. The Roman term is *telamones*. *See also* CARYATID.

Atrium. 1. In Roman domestic architecture, an inner court open to the sky and surrounded by the roof. 2. In Early Christian and medieval architecture, an open court in front of a church; usually a colonnaded quadrangle.

Attached column, *see* ENGAGED COLUMN.

Attic base. The base of an IONIC column consisting of two large rings of convex mouldings (the lower of greater diameter) joined by a spreading concave moulding, used in Athens in the C5 and C4 BC.

Attic storey. 1. A storey above the main ENTABLATURE of a building and in strictly architectural relation to it, as, e.g., in Roman TRIUMPHAL ARCHES. 2. Also, more loosely, the space within the sloping roof of a house or the upper storey of a building if less high than the others.

Atwood, Charles B. (1849–95), *see* BURNHAM, Daniel Hudson.

Aumbry or **ambry**. A cupboard or recess used to keep sacred vessels in.

Austin, Henry (1804–91), *see* UNITED STATES ARCHITECTURE.

Australian architecture of the colonial period (1788–1850) is an extension of English Georgian architecture in its imperial phase. The first leading architects were Francis Howard GREENWAY in New South Wales and John Lee Archer (1791–1852), who had been trained by John RENNIE, in Tasmania. Archer's St John's Church in Hobart was completed in 1835. John Verge (1782–1861) built some of the best country and town houses, notably Camden Park, NSW (1831), and Elizabeth Bay House, Sydney (1832), with a fine elliptical staircase and hall.

Climate, the abundance of land, the availability of convict labour to work in stone, and the taste of military officers, many of whom had served in India and became settlers, favoured the rise of spacious single-storey residences and indeed mansions (Panshanger, Tasmania, of *c.* 1838, architect unknown, is a good example), often with wide verandas, thus making possible a characteristic integration of the roof with the Doric columnar support.

In public architecture the purposes and the needs of a penal colony determined the priority of types: barracks, churches, gaols, court houses, hospitals, customs houses, naval docks, and warehouses were built handsomely to the taste of the governing class with convict labour and skills. The ruins of Port Arthur, Tasmania, in an isolated coastal setting, provide a spectacle of penal architecture unrivalled elsewhere.

During this Indian summer of the Georgian Rule of Taste the first examples of neo-Gothic were comparatively severe. The popularity of verandas led to a demand for ornamental ironwork, imported at first mainly for town houses, and the development of local manufactures, culminating in the exceptionally rich ironwork of the Victorian period.

Apart from the siting of public buildings and some grid-planning in the central areas, urban development clung to the line of the main highways, still a characteristic of smaller Australian towns. A landmark in the history of town planning is Adelaide, laid out by Colonel Light from 1837. The idea of a green belt for new towns had been recently advocated by T. J. Mazlen (1832) and others in England, but Light was the first to carry it out on a spacious scale on all sides, averaging a mile in depth. By exploiting the course of the Torrens River and reserving the heights of North Adelaide and the opposing North Terrace of the city for the residences of the gentry, he achieved a plan which rivals Edinburgh New Town in its feeling for landscape.

The beginning of the Victorian period (1851–1900) coincided with the discovery of gold and the rapid expansion of pastoralism. The new optimism is expressed in government buildings, cathedrals, banks, and a spate of civic and municipal town halls with impressive porticoes and high towers. Government House in Melbourne (1872–6), by William Wardell (1823–

99), who also designed the large St Patrick's Cathedral (begun 1863), was based on the plan of Osborne House in the Isle of Wight. The high tower derives from the Capitol in Rome. The Anglican cathedral of St Paul's was designed after 1877 by William BUT-TERFIELD in England; some changes were made and the spires are later, but the interior with its use of coloured marble is highly original. The dome of the Law Courts in Melbourne (1877–82) is modelled on GANDON's Four Courts in Dublin. The Catholic cathedral of Adelaide, St Francis Xavier's (begun 1870 and still unfinished), reputedly goes back to a design by PUGIN. (It was built to a design by his son E. W. Pugin.)

In Sydney the dominant Victorian architect was Edmund Blacket (1817–83) whose Sydney University (1854–60) is Gothic in style but Palladian in plan. The opulence of the period is best studied in the town and country houses, built for the leading squatting families.

The collapse of the Land Boom in 1892–3, the two world wars, and the intervening Depression slowed down the building mania. ART NOUVEAU architecture and ornament derives mainly from England, but the growth of American influence culminated in the award by competition for the plan of Canberra to Walter Burley GRIFFIN, formerly with Frank Lloyd WRIGHT in Chicago, who arrived in 1913 and remained until 1935. By allowing no building on the surrounding hills and by spaciously separating the centres of civic growth, he achieved a grandiose landscape plan on which geometry is imposed but splendidly relieved by the irregular and dominant lake in the centre. Also notable are Griffin's

Capitol Theatre in Melbourne (1921–4) and Castlecrag housing, Sydney (1921–35).

A breakthrough for the modern school of architects, hitherto hampered by the conservatism of government and commercial patronage, was the Academy of Science, Canberra (1958–9), by Sir Roy Grounds (1905–81). Grounds was subsequently appointed the architect of the National Gallery of Victoria (1962–7) and the Arts Centre in Melbourne (in progress). In Sydney, Harry Seidler (b. 1923), who had studied under GROPIUS at Harvard and came to Australia in 1948, has had an extensive industrial and commercial practice; the Australia Square Tower (1967), financed by private enterprise, is a handsome and conspicuous civic landmark. His Australian Embassy in Paris (1977–9) is also notable. In Melbourne the 1970s Collins Place development has two tower blocks by I. M. PEI. More recently, the Australian architect John ANDREWS, after making a reputation in Canada and the USA, has worked extensively in Canberra (student residences for the National University, 1971–4, and for the College of Advanced Education, 1973–5), in Sydney (Hooker Tower, 1971–4, and American Express Tower, 1976) and in Brisbane (Chemical Engineering building, University of Queensland, 1973–5). Though small-scale the domestic work of Glen Morcutt (b. 1936) is notable for its combination of Miesian clarity and other qualities of Modernism with the revival of traditional Australian corrugated-iron construction – e.g. at Balmain, Sydney, in the 1970s. But the most famous modern building in Australia is the Sydney Opera House, designed by the Danish architect Jørn Utzon (b. 1918) after winning the competition in 1957. The circumstances leading to his resignation or dismissal occasioned a *cause célèbre* in which he was supported by almost the entire architectural profession in Austrialia. Although not finished to his design, it illustrates splendidly the triumph of an idea over practical, political, and bureaucratic difficulties, and has become one of the rare buildings to capture the popular imagination. [J. Burke]

Austrian architecture. Austria originated in the Ostmark (Eastern Marches) established in 803 by Charlemagne after he had subdued the Bavarians in 788. When the Hungarian invasion had been halted (955), the Ostmark was renewed and remained in the hands of the Babenberg dynasty from 976 to 1246. After that Austria passed to the Habsburgs. The archbishopric of Salzburg was created in 789; additional bishoprics came much later; Gurk in 1070, Seckau in 1218, and Vienna only in 1480.

Of pre-Romanesque architecture in Austria little is known. Salzburg Cathedral (767–74) was, according to excavations, nearly 200 ft long and had a straightforward Early Christian basilica plan with one apse. The Romanesque style is an interesting mixture of elements from Bavaria and Lombardy, although West Germany (especially Hirsau, the centre of Cluniac architecture for Germany) and even France also play a part. Bavarian influence means basilican churches with pillars (Hirsau stood for columns – see St Paul im Lavanttal in Austria), no transepts, and three parallel apses, while Lombardy was the source of much of the best decoration; it is to be found at Klosterneuburg (1114–33),

Gurk (1140s–*c.* 1200; crypt of a hundred marble columns), Millstatt, and even the portal of St Peter at Salzburg (*c.* 1240). Another source of ornament was Normandy (zigzag, etc.) via Worms, Bamberg, and Regensburg – see St Stephen, Vienna; St Pölten; and the Karner at Tulln. Karners are charnel houses with chapels, centrally planned, and they are an Austrian speciality. The largest church of the C12 was Salzburg Cathedral as rebuilt in 1181 onwards. It was as long as Old St Peter's in Rome, and had double aisles, round towers over apses in the end walls of the transepts, two (older) west towers, and an octagonal crossing tower.

Cistercian colonization was actively pursued in Austria, and Viktring (built 1142–1202) is indeed an early and faithful follower of Fontenay, the earliest preserved house in France; it has, for example, the pointed tunnel vaults of Fontenay. On the other hand Heiligenkreuz (begun *c.* 1150–60) has rib vaults with heavy square ribs, a Lombard characteristic. Heiligenkreuz received a choir in 1295, of the hall type. This is of course fully Gothic, and hall churches are characteristic of the German Late Gothic. The hall choir was suggested by an earlier Cistercian hall choir in Austria: Lilienfeld (1202–30), also nearly entirely Gothic. This is an extremely early case of the hall elevation and one which established Austria as one of the sources of German hall churches. Zwettl, also Cistercian, received its splendid hall choir with ambulatory and low radiating chapels much later (1343–83). From here influences again reached out to south and south-west Germany. The friars, the most active order of the later C13 and the C14, went in for halls too.

The principal achievement of the C14 and C15 is of course St Stephen in Vienna, not a cathedral originally. The hall chancel is of 1304–40, the glorious south tower of 1359–1433. Connections in the early C14 were principally with Bohemia (Vienna) and Bavaria (Franciscan church, Salzburg, begun 1408; by Hans STETHAIMER). Developments in architecture in the later C15 and early C16 were as great and important as they were in sculpture: intricate vaults, with star, net, and even rosette motifs, are characteristic, and culminate in the stucco ribs with vegetable details of Laas (*c.* 1515–20) and Kötschach (1518–27) in Carinthia. Supports may be twisted piers (Salzburg Castle, 1502) or even tree-trunk piers (Bechyně Castle, across the Bohemian border). The first secular buildings are also of these late years: the Bummerlhaus at Steyr (1497), the Goldenes Dachl at Innsbruck (completed 1500), and the Kornmesserhaus at Bruck on the Mur (1499–1505). The arcading here suggests Venetian influence.

But Italian influence was very soon to mean something quite different from the Gothic of the Kornmesserhaus. The portal of the Salvator Chapel in Vienna of just after 1515 is entirely Lombard Renaissance and must be the work of a sculptor from there. Similar works, especially funerary monuments, picked up the new forms at once. In architecture the next examples are the portal of the Arsenal at Wiener Neustadt (1524) and the elegant courtyard of the Portia Palace at Spittal (*c.* 1540); comparison with the much heavier courtyard of the Landhaus at Graz (1556–65; by Domenico dell'Allio, d. 1563) shows a characteristic development. The stage after this is represented by the courtyard of the Schalla-burg near Melk (1572–1600) with caryatids, etc. – what would in Britain be called Elizabethan. On the whole, Austria is less rich in first-rate Renaissance buildings than Bohemia. The Hofkirche at Innsbruck (1553–63) is a Gothic hall, though with slender columns instead of piers. The only fully Italian building in the ecclesiastical field is Salzburg Cathedral, by Santino SOLARI, with two west towers and a crossing dome, and this is of 1614–28. The cathedral, the Archiepiscopal Palace, and the Franciscan church show a very complete development of Italianate C17 stucco decoration.

In Vienna a remarkable number of churches were built and rebuilt, but they appear minor when one measures them by the achievements of the Austrian Baroque of *c.* 1690–1730. The great names are first the theatrical designer and engineer Lodovico Burnacini (1636–1707), who designed the wildly Baroque Trinity Monument on the Graben in 1687; then Domenico MARTINELLI of the two Liechtenstein palaces of *c.* 1700; and then FISCHER VON ERLACH and HILDEBRANDT. Little need be said about them here – of Fischer's brilliant centralizing church plans at Salzburg (Trinity, 1694–1702; Collegiate, 1694–1707), heralded by those of G. ZUCCALLI of 1685; of his Karlskirche in Vienna with its fantastic Trajan's Columns; of his restrained and courtly decoration; and of Hildebrandt's brilliant spatial interlocking and his fiery decoration (Upper Belvedere, Vienna, 1714–24). Meanwhile the great abbeys in the country were as busy rebuilding as the towns and the nobility: Melk (1702–14; by PRANDTAUER); St Florian (1686–1705; by CARLONE and then Prand tauer); Göttweig (begun 1719; by Hildebrandt); Klosterneuburg (begun 1730; by Donato Allio (*c.* 1680–1770)). Particularly splendid are the libraries in the abbeys (Altenburg, 1740; Admont, *c.* 1745).

The Louis XVI or Robert ADAM style of the later C18 is represented in Vienna by the Academy of the Sciences (1753; by JADOT DE VILLE ISSY) and the Josephinum (1783; by Isidore Canevale (1730–86)). The Gloriette, a large-scale eye-catcher in the park of Schönbrunn by Johann Ferdinand von Hohenburg (1732–1816), is, in spite of its early date (1775), in a neo-Cinquecento style. Neo-Grecian at its most severe are the Theseustempel (1820–23) and the Burgtor (1824), both by NOBILE (the latter originally designed by CAGNOLA).

C19 historicism is in full swing with the perfectly preserved Anif Castle near Salzburg (begun 1838), the church of Altlerchenfeld, Vienna (1848–61), by Eduard van der Null (1812–68), in neo-Romanesque, and the Arsenal (1849–56) by Christian Friedrich Ludwig von Förster (1797–1863) and others, also in a neo-Romanesque style. Shortly after, Vienna established herself as one of the centres of historicism on a grand scale with the abolition of the fortress walls of inner Vienna and the making of the Ringstrasse (begun 1859). Along this wide green belt a number of majestic public buildings were erected in various period styles: the Votivkirche (begun 1856) by Heinrich von Ferstel (1828–83), in Gothic; the Opera (begun 1861) by van der Null and August Siccard von Siccardsburg (1813–68), in free Renaissance; the Town Hall (1872–83) by Friedrich von Schmidt (1825–91) in symmetrical Gothic; the Museums (begun 1872) by SEMPER and Karl von Hasenauer (1833–94), in Renaissance to Baroque; the Academy (begun 1872–3; by Theophil von HANSEN), in Renaissance; the Parliament (begun 1873–, also by von Hansen), in pure Grecian; the Burgtheater (begun 1873; again by Semper and Hasenauer) in Renaissance; the University (by Ferstel) in a mixed Italian and French C16 style; and, finally, the Neue Hofburg (1872 and 1881 onwards; by Semper and Hasenauer), again in Renaissance. There are also large blocks of flats in the monumental, strung-out composition.

Vienna was one of the most important centres in the whole world when it came to abandoning historicism and creating a new idiom for the C20. The leaders were Otto WAGNER, whose Postal Savings Bank (1904) is remarkably fresh and enterprising, his pupil OLBRICH, whose Secession (1898) blazed the trail – though more towards ART NOUVEAU than towards the C20 – and the two even younger men, HOFFMANN and LOOS. When the C20 style began to settle down, and be accepted in the mid-twenties, a mild variety of it was applied to the many blocks of working-class flats, some of them vast, which the municipality of Vienna erected, e.g. the Karl-Marx-Hof (1927) by Karl Ehn (1884–1957).

After the Second World War, building recovered slowly but by the mid-1960s Austrian architects had regained their former leading position internationally with Hans HOLLEIN and Gustav Peichl (b. 1928), notable for his Austrian State Radio (ORF) studios (1968–81), and, more recently, with COOP HIMMELBLAU and the Viennese group Haus-Rucker-Co formed in 1967 and active since then also in Düsseldorf and New York.

Avant-corps

FIG. 6. *Axonometric projection*
Plan; Section aa; Elevation

Avant-corps. Part of a building projecting prominently from the main block or CORPS DE LOGIS.

Averlino, Antonio, *see* FILARETE.

Axial plan. Of a building planned longitudinally or along an axis, i.e. not CENTRALLY PLANNED, e.g. a basilica as opposed to an octagon.

Axis. An imaginary straight line about which the earth or any other body rotates; or, in architecture, an imaginary straight line passing centrally through a composition, ground-plan or façade so as to give an impression of balance.

Axonometric projection. A geometrical drawing showing a building in three dimensions. The plan is set up truly to a convenient angle, and the verticals projected to scale, with the result that all dimensions on a horizontal plane and all verticals are to scale, but diagonals and curves on a vertical plane are distorted. *See* Fig. 6.

Aymonino, Carlo (b. 1926). Italian architect best known for his city-centre planning (Turin and Bologna 1962, Reggio Emilia 1971, Florence 1978) and for his publications (*Piazze d'Italia. Progettare gli spazi aperti,* Milan 1988). His Gallaratese 2 complex, Milan (1967–73), includes a notable apartment block by Aldo ROSSI.

C.A., *Origine e sviluppo della città moderna,* Padua 1971; C.A., *Il significato delle città,* Bari 1975; C. Conforti, *C.A. L'architettura non è un mito,* Rome (1980) 1983.

Aztec architecture, *see* MESO-AMERICAN ARCHITECTURE.

Azulejos. Glazed pottery TILES usually painted in bright colours with floral and other patterns, much used on the outsides and insides of Spanish, Portuguese, and central and south American buildings.

Azuma, Takamitsu (b. 1933). Japanese architect, began as assistant to SAKAKURA but developed a self-consciously individual style of 'oppositional harmonies', e.g. Satsuki Kindergarten, Osaka (1969–73). He was a founder of the Architext group in 1971 which broke with the MET-ABOLISTS and argued for discontinuity and contradiction.

Bognar 1985.

b

Babylonian architecture, *see* SUM-
ERIAN AND AKKADIAN ARCHITEC-
TURE.

Bacini. Painted and glazed earthenware plates and bowls of *c.* 1200 im-
bedded as decoration on façades and
exteriors of Italian Romanesque
churches, campanili and occasionally
other buildings, e.g. S. Piero in Grado,
Pisa; SS. Giovanni e Paolo, Rome.

Backsteingotik, *see* GERMAN ARCHI-
TECTURE.

Bacon, Henry (1866–1924), *see*
UNITED STATES ARCHITECTURE.

Baguette or **bagnette.** A small mould-
ing of semicircular section, like an
ASTRAGAL; also a frame with a small
BEAD MOULDING.

Bähr, Georg (1666–1738). The leading
Baroque architect in Dresden. He
began as a carpenter and in 1705
became Ratszimmermeister (master
carpenter to the city) in Dresden. But
he had already begun to study mech-
anics (he invented a *camera obscura* and
a mechanical organ) and his first building was begun the same year, the parish
church of Loschwitz (1705–8) on an
elongated octagonal plan. Two Greek
cross plan churches followed, at
Schmiedeberg (1713–16) and Forch-
heim (1719–26) both in the Erzgebirge.

His masterpiece was the Frauenkirche
in Dresden (1722–38: destroyed 1944),
by far the grandest Protestant church
in Germany. Bähr's first design for it
dates from as early as 1722, a Greek
cross plan with octagonal galleries,
deriving from VISCARDI's Mariahilfkirche at Freystadt (1700–1708). But
in 1726 this design was revised in
favour of a square ground plan with a
circular arrangement of piers, with
angle turrets flanking the dome on all
four sides. The dome was also redesigned to increase its height and
pitch, thus producing a very bold
silhouette. The interior resembled a
centrally planned theatre with curving
galleries and a richly decorated organ
(by Gottfried Silbermann 1732–6) as
the main feature. The Dreikönigskirche in Dresden Neustadt (1732–9)
originally designed by PÖPPELMANN
was supervised by Bähr.

Hempel 1965.

Bailey. An open space or court of a
stone-built castle; also called a *ward*.
See also MOTTE-AND-BAILEY.

Baillairgé, Thomas (1791–1859), *see*
CANADIAN ARCHITECTURE.

Baillie Scott, Hugh Mackay (1865–
1945), *see* ARTS AND CRAFTS.

Baird, John (1798–1859), *see* METAL
STRUCTURES.

FIG. 7. *Ballflower*

Bakema, Jakob Berend (1914–81), *see* DUTCH ARCHITECTURE.

Baker, Sir Herbert (1862–1946), was born in Kent and remained an English countryman. Baker's most interesting work belongs to South Africa. He went out early, gained Cecil Rhodes's confidence, and built Groote Schuur for him in 1890 in the traditional Dutch Colonial idiom, and later private houses in Johannesburg, some very successful in an Arts and Crafts way (Stonehouse, 1902). His most prominent buildings were the Government House and Union Buildings in Pretoria (1905 onwards and 1910–13). Side by side with his friend LUTYENS he was called in at New Delhi, and was responsible there for the Secretariat Building (1912 onwards). His style is as imperially classical as Lutyens's but much weaker, less original, and less disciplined. This is especially evident in his later London buildings (Bank of England, 1921; India House, 1925; South Africa House, 1930). He was more at ease where he could use a less elevated style and a great variety of materials. This is why the War Memorial Cloister at Winchester College (1922–4) is one of his most successful buildings. He published *Architecture and Personalities* (1944). See also SOUTH AFRICAN ARCHITECTURE.

D. E. Greig, *H.B. in South Africa*, Cape Town and London 1970; R. G. Irving, *Indian Summer. Lutyens, B. and Imperial Delhi*, London 1981.

Balcony. A platform projecting from a wall, enclosed by a railing or balustrade, supported on brackets or columns or cantilevered out. A small, decorative balcony projecting from a window-sill, sometimes to hold flowerpots, is called a *balconette*.

Baldachin or **baldacchino**. A canopy over a throne, altar, doorway, etc. It may be portable, suspended from a ceiling, projecting from a wall or free-standing on columns or other supports. *See also* CIBORIUM.

Baldassari, Luciano (1896–1982), *see* ITALIAN ARCHITECTURE.

Balinese architecture, *see* INDONESIAN ARCHITECTURE.

Balistraria. In medieval military architecture, the cross-shaped opening in BATTLEMENTS and elsewhere for the use of the crossbow.

Ballflower. A globular three-petalled flower enclosing a small ball; a decoration in use in the first quarter of the C14. *See* Fig. 7.

Balloon framing. A method of timber-frame construction used in the USA and Scandinavia: the STUDS or uprights run from sill to eaves, and the horizontal members are nailed to them. It is said to have been invented in Chicago in 1832.

Ballu, Théodore (1817–85). French architect. His best-known building is Holy Trinity, Paris (1863–7), a design in the Early Renaissance of Italy and France. He completed GAU's Ste Clotilde, Paris.

M. Decouchy, *T.B.*, Paris 1875; Benevolo 1971.

Baltard, Louis-Pierre (1764–1846). French architect. He built the Law

FIG. 8. *Bargeboards*

Courts at Lyon (1836–41) which, with its long row of giant Corinthian columns, is a belated representative of the Empire style. Baltard taught first at the École Polytechnique, then at the École des Beaux Arts.

Baltard, Victor (1805–74), son of Louis-Pierre Baltard. His most famous work was Les Halles, Paris (1854–66, demolished), an important urban development, all glass and iron. His church St Augustine (1862–71) is externally a domed building of the Early French Renaissance but internally proclaims its iron construction.

Benevolo 1971.

Baluster. A short post or pillar in a series supporting a rail or COPING and thus forming a *balustrade*. *See* Fig. 81.

Balustrade, *see* BALUSTER.

Band or **plat band**. An unmoulded, projecting STRING COURSE.

Banded column, *see* RUSTICATED COLUMN.

Baptistery. A building for baptismal rites containing the font; often separate from the church.

Bar tracery, *see* TRACERY.

Barabino, Carlo Francesco (1768–1835), *see* ITALIAN ARCHITECTURE.

Barbican. An outwork defending the entrance to a castle.

Barelli, Agostino (1627–79). Born in Bologna, where he designed the Theatine church of S. Bartolomeo (1653), he later introduced the Italian Baroque style to Bavaria. He designed the Theatine church of St Cajetan, Munich (1663), completed by Enrico ZUCCALLI, on the model of S. Andrea della Valle, Rome. He also built the squarish central block of the electoral palace at Nymphenburg outside Munich (1663), completed by EFFNER in 1717–23.

N. Lieb, *München. Die Geschichte seiner Kunst*, Munich (1971) 1977.

Bargeboards or **vergeboards**. Projecting boards placed against the incline of the gable of a building, hiding the ends of the horizontal roof timbers; sometimes decorated. *See* Fig. 8.

Barlow, William Henry (1812–1902), *see* ENGLISH ARCHITECTURE.

Barn. A covered building for the storage of grain and other agricultural produce. Medieval barns were sometimes extremely large and their enormous roofs of CRUCK CONSTRUCTION gave them considerable architectural distinction. William Morris said the C13 Great Coxwell barn was 'as noble as a cathedral'. The Cholsey barn of *c.* 1200 (demolished 1815) was the largest in Europe, the second largest being that at Vaulerand in France. Tithe-barns for the storage of the priest's tithe were a feature of many ecclesiastical estates.

Baroque architecture. The architecture of the C17 and part of the C18. It is characterized by exuberant decoration, expansive curvaceous forms, a

Barragán

sense of mass, a delight in large-scale and sweeping vistas, and a preference for spatially complex compositions. The term applies fully to the C17 in Italy (notably BERNINI and BORROMINI) and to the C17 and part of the C18 in Austria, Germany and Spain, but with limitations to the C17 in France and the late C17 and early C18 in England. For all these latter cases the term Baroque Classicism has sometimes been adopted to denote that they are instances of the Baroque tempered by classical elements. This is especially evident in England, where the swelling forms of Baroque plans and elevations were never favoured. *See also* ENGLISH, FRENCH, GERMAN, ITALIAN, RUSSIAN and SPANISH ARCHITECTURE.

Barragán, Luis (1902–88). Mexican architect who, after travelling in Spain and France, where he attended lectures by Le Corbusier, settled in Mexico City in 1936. His early work combined the severe, geometrical forms he admired in Le Corbusier with Mexican vernacular elements and resulted in an individual style, e.g. his own house in Tacubaya (1947). His later work continued to recall the Mexican *pueblo*, especially in colour and in the settings he created for it, indeed he became almost as much a landscape architect as a designer of buildings. Most of his work was in or on the outskirts of Mexico City, e.g. the suburb of Pedregal. Notable examples are Satellite City Towers (1957), the Arboledas (1957–61) and Los Clunes (1961–4) residential quarters, the San Cristobal estate buildings and stables (1967–8) and the Gilardi House, Tacubaya (1976).

W. Arets and W. van der Bergh, *L.B. (1902–88) Architect*, Rotterdam 1990.

Barrel vault, *see* VAULT.

Barry, Sir Charles (1795–1860). The most versatile of the leading Early Victorian architects, an excellent planner and an energetic, tough, and hardworking man. With some inherited money he travelled in 1817–20 through France, Italy, Greece, Turkey, Egypt, and Palestine, studying buildings and doing brilliant sketches. In 1823 he won the competition for St Peter's, Brighton, and then for some years did 'pre-archaeological' Gothic churches, i.e. an inventive rather than a correct interpretation of the style. In 1824 he designed the Royal Institution of Fine Arts in Manchester – Grecian this time – and he followed this up with the Manchester Athenaeum (1836). But the Travellers' Club in London (1829–31) was Quattrocento, and this meant the start of the neo-Renaissance for England. With the Reform Club of 1837 his Renaissance turned Cinquecento, and with Bridgewater House (1847) a free, not to say debased, Cinquecento. This development from the reticent to the spectacular and from low to high relief permeates his work in general – see, now in the northern Renaissance field, the development from Highclere (1837), itself far busier than his early work, to the Halifax Town Hall (1859–62), which is asymmetrical and a jumble of motifs. It was completed by Barry's son Edward M. Barry (1830–80), who built the Charing Cross and Cannon Street Hotels, London.

But Sir Charles's *magnum opus* is, of course, the Houses of Parliament, won in competition in 1835–6 and begun in 1839; it was formally opened in 1852. Its ground plan is functionally excellent, its façade to the Thames still symmetrical in the Georgian way, but its

FIG. 9. *Bartizan*

skyline completely asymmetrical and exceedingly well balanced with its two contrasting towers and its flèche. Most of the close Perpendicular detail and nearly all the internal detail is by PUGIN, who was commissioned by Barry for the purpose.

A. Barry, *The Life and Works of Sir C.B.*, London 1867; J. M. Crook and H. M. Port, *The History of the King's Works*, vol. vi, London 1973; H. M. Port, *The Houses of Parliament*, London 1976; Hitchcock 1977; Colvin 1978

Barthélèmy, Jacques-Eugène (1799–1868), *see* FRENCH ARCHITECTURE.

Bartizan. A small turret projecting from the angle on the top of a tower or parapet. *See* Fig. 9.

Basement. The lowest storey of a building, usually below or partly below ground level or, if beginning at ground level, of less height than the storey above. It is a living-space, as distinct from a CELLAR.

Basevi, George (1794–1845), was articled to SOANE. In 1816–19 he was in Italy and Greece. His first buildings are Grecian, but his best-known build-

ing, the Fitzwilliam Museum at Cambridge (1836–45, completed with some alterations by C. R. COCKERELL in 1845–8), already shows the trend towards classical harmony becoming, with clustered giant columns and a heavy attic, more dramatic and indeed Baroque. It is the same trend which distinguishes the BEAUX ARTS style in France from the Empire style. Early in his career (c. 1825), Basevi also designed Belgrave Square (minus the corner mansions), London, and later Thurloe Square (1839–45) and Pelham Crescent and Pelham Place (now Egerton Place) (1833 onwards), London, and a number of country houses in various styles.

Colvin 1978.

Basile, Ernesto (1857–1932), *see* SOMMARUGA, Giuseppe.

Basilica. An ancient Roman colonnaded hall for public use (e.g. the basilicas of Trajan and Augustus, Rome; the basilica of Constantine, Trier, Germany, survives almost intact), later adopted as a building type for EARLY CHRISTIAN churches. The term indicated function and not form, but ancient Roman basilicas were often oblong buildings with aisles and galleries and with an apse opposite the entrance which might be through one of the longer or shorter sides. It was from public buildings of this type that Early Christian churches evolved (not from pagan religious architecture) and by the C4 they had acquired their essential characteristics: oblong plan; longitudinal axis; a timber roof, either open or concealed by a flat ceiling; a termination, either rectangular or in the form of an apse; and usually a nave with two or more aisles, the former higher and wider than the latter, lit by

Basket arch

FIG. 10. *Basilica*

KEY:
1. Narthex 3. Apse
2. Nave   4. Aisles

FIG. 11. *Battlements*

clerestory windows and with or without a gallery. *See* Fig. 10.

Ward-Perkins 1981; Krautheimer 1986.

Basket arch, *see* ARCH.

Bassi, Martino (1542–91). Milanese architect who succeeded ALESSI at S. Maria presso S. Celso, Milan, and from 1573 onwards rebuilt the Early Christian rotunda, S. Lorenzo, Milan. He became architect at the cathedral, Milan, in 1587. From 1578 he also worked at the Sacro Monte, Varallo.

R. Wittkower, *Gothic v. Classic*, New York 1974; Heydenreich and Lotz 1974.

Bastard, John (1688–1770) and William (*c.* 1689–1766). English provincial architects notable for rebuilding the centre of Blandford, Dorset, in a vernacular Baroque style after a fire in 1731.

Colvin 1978; Summerson 1983.

Bastion. A projection at the angle of a fortification, from which the garrison can see and defend the ground before the ramparts.

Bastle or **bastel-house.** A defensible farmhouse, accommodating animals on the ground floor, usually vaulted, and human beings above, found along the upland areas of the Scottish border, mostly dating from 1550–1650.

Bath stone. Building stone from the oolite formation near Bath but also quarried elsewhere in England and used throughout her architectural history.

Batter. The inclined face of a wall.

Battlement. A PARAPET with alternating indentations or EMBRASURES and raised portions or *merlons*; also called *crenellation. See* Fig. 11.

Baudot, Anatole de (1834–1915). A pupil of LABROUSTE and VIOLLET-LE-DUC. His St Jean de Montmartre in Paris (1894–1902) is the first building where all the structural members, including the vaulting ribs, are of exposed reinforced concrete. Yet the character remains Gothic. It can be called the most successful demonstration of the union of old and new advocated by Viollet-le-Duc in his *Entretiens.* Actually reinforced concrete is not strictly correct. The ribs were of bricks pierced with steel rods, the cells of reinforced cement.

Collins 1965; Hitchcock 1977.

Bauhaus. The Grand-Duke of Saxe-Weimar had founded a school of arts and crafts at Weimar in 1906. He appointed van de VELDE to the directorship – a very progressive move; for van de Velde believed in teaching in workshops rather than studios. When van de Velde left Germany, he suggested GROPIUS as his successor, and Gropius took over in 1919. He reorganized the school and called it the

Bauhaus. According to its first manifesto the school was to teach crafts, and all artists and architects were to work together towards the great goal of 'the building of the future'. The manifesto was enthusiastic in tone and had on its cover an Expressionist vision of a cathedral, a woodcut by Feininger. This first phase of the Bauhaus, inspired by MORRIS, MUTHESIUS and the ARTS AND CRAFTS movement, and sustained by the Expressionist mood of post-war Germany, did not last long. The aim now became industrial design, and stark cubic simplicity replaced the EXPRESSIONISM. This fundamental change of programme was accelerated by lectures which Theo van Doesburg (1883–1931) gave in 1922 introducing DE STIJL ideas and by the appointment of Moholy-Nagy (1895–1946) in 1923. The result was a memorandum by Gropius issued in 1924 and called *Art and Technology – A New Unity*. However, in the same year, political changes led to the dissolution of the Bauhaus in Weimar. At that moment the Burgomaster of Dessau offered the school a new field of activity. A new building was designed by Gropius and built in 1925–6, one of the paradigmatic masterpieces of the INTERNATIONAL MODERN style. In 1926 the Bauhaus received recognition as the State School of Art of Anhalt. This seemed to secure the future. A department of architecture was established, and Hannes Meyer (1889–1954) became its head. One year later, in 1928, Gropius resigned and suggested Hannes Meyer as his successor. Meyer was politically far more radical than Gropius. He organized the department of architecture, but was dismissed for political reasons in 1930. His successor was MIES VAN DER ROHE. However,

the growth of National Socialism in Anhalt led to his dismissal and, in 1932, to the closure of the school. Mies tried to carry on in Berlin, converting the school into a private enterprise. But in 1933 that also was closed by the Nazis.

The Bauhaus was the most important school of art of the C20. Its most significant achievement was that to the very end artists and craftsmen, and in the end architects, too, worked together. At the start of the Bauhaus the *Vorkurs*, as built up by Johannes Itten, comprised them all. The intention of the *Vorkurs* was to stimulate a theoretically and practically sound sense of form and colour. Later the Bauhaus became the only art school in which designs for industrial products were developed. Moreover, Gropius's own style of architecture became almost automatically a symbol of the programme of the school. But, when all is said, the most impressive fact about the Bauhaus is that Gropius succeeded in keeping together in happy co-operation such dissimilar artists as Kandinsky, Feininger, Klee, and Schlemmer.

After 1933 the staff dispersed, nearly all emigrating to the USA and carrying with them the Bauhaus ideals. In 1937 Moholy-Nagy became director of the New Bauhaus in Chicago, which failed. He then set up an independent school of design later renamed the Chicago Institute of Design. In 1951–6 Max BILL (b. 1908) revived the Bauhaus programme at the influential Design School at Ulm.

H. Wingler, *The Bauhaus: Weimar, Dessau, Berlin and Chicago*, Cambridge, Mass., 1969; G. Naylor, *The Bauhaus Reassessed. Sources and Design Theory*, London 1985.

FIG. 12. *Bay leaf garland*

Baulk-tie, see ROOF.

Bautista, Francisco (1594–1679). A Spanish Jesuit priest who built churches for his order in Madrid and Toledo. That in Madrid, S. Isidro el Real (1629), based on the plan of the Gesù in Rome, with a somewhat severe façade, is the most interesting. The church had considerable influence in Spain.

Kubler and Soria 1959.

Bawa, Geoffrey (b. 1919). Sri Lankan architect, trained in London but practising in Colombo. His sensitive adaptation of modern techniques to traditional Sri Lankan architecture characterizes his buildings, often set in lush gardens designed for them, e.g. the Bentota Beach Hotel (1969), the Triton Hotel, Ahungalla (1981), the New Parliament building Sri Jayawardenapura, Kotte (1982), and the University of Ruhuna, Matara (1984), all in Sri Lanka.

B. B. Taylor, *G.B.*, Singapore 1986.

Bay. A vertical division of the exterior or interior of a building marked not by walls but by fenestration, an order, buttresses, units of vaulting, roof compartments, etc.

Bay leaf garland. Classical decorative motif used to enrich TORUS mouldings, etc. *See* Fig. 12.

Bay window. An angular or curved projection of a house front filled by fenestration. If curved, also called a bow window. If on an upper floor only, called an *oriel* or *oriel window*.

Bazhenov, Vasily Ivanovich (1738–99). An early neo-classical architect, probably the most visionary Russian architect of any period. He was unlucky in his career, and his genius has to be judged on the basis of only half-a-dozen buildings and several projects. Of humble birth, he began under Ukhtomsky in Moscow and CHEVAKINSKY in Petersburg, later studying in Paris and Italy (early 1760s). In 1767 Catherine II commissioned him to design a great palace, embracing the existing monuments, in the Moscow Kremlin. It never rose above its massive foundations, but the plans and scale model already show him at his maturity – great Ionic colonnades binding the upper storeys above a severe rustication – and it established his reputation. His next commission was also frustrated – a remodelling of Catherine's palace and park at Tsaritsyno, near Moscow, in a most inventive mock-Gothic (with classical and Old Russian elements not far below the surface). His lesser structures survive, but the palace was dismantled on the verge of completion and the task given to KAZAKOV. Of his other possible essays in Gothic the church at Cherkizovo-Starki is especially interesting for its originality and early date (founded 1759).

Out of court favour, Bazhenov turned to private Moscow patrons: the Pashov House (1784), the circular bell-tower of the Skorbyashchenskaya church, and the Yushkov House with its dramatic rounded and colonnaded corner. With Paul's accession he produced his last and strangest public assignment: a moated neo-classical fortress, the 'St Michael Castle' in

FIG. 13. *Beakhead moulding*

Petersburg, an uningratiating yet fascinating building (the severity of its forms now somewhat masked with decorative additions by Vincenzo Brenna, 1745–1820). Its large detached pavilions are Bazhenov's final masterpiece. [R. R. Milner-Gulland]

Hamilton 1983.

BBPR, *see* ROGERS, Ernesto Nathan.

Bead and reel, *see* ASTRAGAL.

Bead moulding. A small cylindrical moulding enriched with ornament resembling a string of beads; used in the Romanesque period.

Beakhead. A Norman decorative motif consisting of a row of bird, animal, or human heads biting a ROLL MOULDING. *See* Fig. 13.

Beam. In roof construction a transverse, horizontal timber (*see* ROOF). In the body of a building a main horizontal timber supporting floor or ceiling JOISTS. A *dragon beam* is set diagonally and projecting at the corner of a building to support the joists of a JETTY on two adjacent sides.

Beaux Arts style. A very rich classical style favoured by the École des Beaux Arts in late C19 France, e.g. GARNIER's Opéra, Paris (1861–75), and much imitated elsewhere, e.g. Palais de Justice, Brussels, 1866–83, by Joseph Poelaert (1817–79). It was also very influential in the USA, where many of the leading late C19 architects had been trained at the École des Beaux Arts, e.g. HUNT, MCKIM, RICHARDSON.

A. Drexler (ed.), *The Architecture of the École des Beaux Arts*, New York 1972; D. D. Egbert, *The Beaux Arts Tradition in French Architecture*, Princeton 1980; Middleton 1982.

Becerra, Francisco (*c.* 1545–1605), *see* PERUVIAN ARCHITECTURE.

Bed moulding. A small moulding between the CORONA and the FRIEZE in any ENTABLATURE.

Beehive house. A primitive structure, circular in plan and built of rough stones set in projecting courses to form a dome. Prehistoric examples, called *nuraghi*, have been found in Sardinia, and others of later date in Ireland and Scotland (called *wheel-house* and *broch*). They are still inhabited in south-east Italy (Apulia), where they are called *trulli*. The finest example of beehive construction is the tomb called the 'Treasury of Atreus' at Mycenae (C13 BC).

Beer, Georg (d. 1600), *see* SCHICKHARDT, Heinrich.

Beer, Michael (d. 1666). He was born at Au in the Bregenzerwald and was the founder of the Vorarlberger school of architects which included, besides the Beer family, the MOSBRUGGER family and the THUMB family. The latter intermarried with the Beer family. The long series of buildings by this school, mostly for Benedictine monasteries in south-west Germany and Switzerland, was eventually to mark the triumph of German over Italian elements in south German Baroque architecture (i.e. over the domination of such Italians as

ZUCCALLI and VISCARDI from the Grisons). Michael Beer is known to have worked at the abbey church at Kempten (1652–4) and he was probably responsible for its design, which attempted a fusion of the longitudinal and centralized types of church. It has a curious, large-domed octagon between nave and chancel. His son Franz Beer (1660–1726) became one of the leading architects of the Vorarlberg school. He began at Obermarchtal abbey church, where he and Christian THUMB took over after the death of Michael THUMB in 1690. The influence of the Thumbs is still evident in his next building, Kloster Irsee (1699–1704). But he achieved an individual style and also great elegance and lightness at the abbey church at Rheinau in Switzerland (1704–11), where he emphasized verticality by setting the galleries well back from the pilaster ends of the internal buttresses which typify the Vorarlberg type of church. His style culminated in the Cistercian abbey church of St Urban in the Canton of Lucerne (1711–15) and at the Benedictine abbey church at Weingarten (1715–23), though his responsibility at the latter is uncertain. (He refused to direct the building operations, and the design was probably a collaboration with Johann Jakob Herkommer (1648–1717) and perhaps also Caspar MOSBRUGGER.) In 1717 he reconstructed the Premonstratensian abbey church at Weissenau near Ravensburg. Two plans (unexecuted) for the abbey church at Einsiedeln are attributed to him. His eldest daughter married Peter THUMB. Johann Michael Beer (1696–1780) designed the choir and east façade at the abbey church at St Gallen (1760–69) and Ferdinand Beer (1731–89) designed the administrative block of the monastery at St Gallen.

N. Lieb and F. Dieth, *Die Vorarlberger Barock-Baumeister*, Munich and Zürich (1960) 1983; W. Oechslin (ed.), *Die Vorarlberger Barockbaumeister*, exh. cat., Bregenz 1978.

Behnisch, Günter (b. 1922), *see* OTTO, Frei.

Behrens, Peter (1868–1940), started as a painter but after 1890 was attracted by design and crafts, under the direct or indirect influence of the teachings of MORRIS. He designed typefaces, was one of the founders of the Vereinigte Werkstätten at Munich, and for them designed table glass among other things. In 1899 Ernst Ludwig, Grand Duke of Hesse, called him to Darmstadt (*see* OLBRICH). The house he designed for himself there in 1900–1901 is original, vigorous, and even ruthless. In 1907 he was among the founders of the DEUTSCHER WERKBUND, became architect to the AEG in Berlin, and designed for them factories (notably the Berlin turbine factory of 1908–9), shops, products, and even stationery. The factories are among the earliest anywhere to be taken seriously architecturally and designed without any recourse to period allusions. For more representational jobs he used a more representational style which has been called a 'scraped classicism' (offices in Düsseldorf for Mannesmann, 1911–12; German Embassy, St Petersburg, 1911–12). Around 1910 GROPIUS, LE CORBUSIER and MIES VAN DER ROHE were all working in his office. After the First World War his style paid tribute first to the then current EXPRESSIONISM (offices for I. G. Farben, Höchst, 1920–24), then to the INTERNATIONAL MODERN (warehouse for the State Tobacco Administration, Linz, Austria, 1930). In 1925 he designed 'New Ways', 508 Wellingborough Road, Northampton – the earliest example of the c20 style in England. (The house incorporates a room designed by MACKINTOSH in 1907.)

A. Windsor, *P.B. Architect and Designer*, London 1981; T. Buddensieg, *Industriekultur, P.B. and the A.E.G. 1907–1914*, Cambridge, Mass., 1984.

Bélanger, François-Joseph (1744–1818). The most elegant Louis XVI architect and the leading French landscape gardener. Trained in Paris, he visited England in 1766. The following year he joined the Menus Plaisirs and in 1777 designed his masterpiece, the exquisite neo-classical Bagatelle in the Bois de Boulogne, Paris, which he built for the king's brother in sixty-four days to win a bet with Marie-Antoinette. The garden, laid out between 1778 and 1780, was the most famous *jardin anglais* of the period. It was followed in 1784 by the *jardin anglo-chinois* at another of his pavilions, the Folie Saint James at Neuilly, and in 1786 by the last of his great landscape gardens, Méréville. He also designed the exquisite pavilion in the garden of the Hôtel de Brancas, Paris (1771) and some interiors of great elegance, e.g. Hôtel de Mlle Desvieux, Paris (1788). In 1803 he designed a remarkable glass and iron dome for the Halle au Blé in Paris to replace the no less remarkable glass and wood dome of Legrand and Molinos of 1782.

Braham 1980; M. K. Deming, *La Halle au blé de Paris 1762–1813 . . .*, Brussels 1984.

Belcher, John (1841–1913), *see* ENGLISH ARCHITECTURE.

Belfast roof, see ROOF.

Belfry. Generally the upper room or storey in a tower in which bells are hung, and thus often the bell-tower itself, whether it is attached to or stands separate from the main building. Also the timber frame inside a church steeple to which bells are fastened. Derived from the Old French *berfrei* (= tower), the word has no connection with 'bell'.

Belgian architecture. In the Middle Ages the southern Netherlands belonged to the archdiocese of Cologne; hence Romanesque building drew its inspiration chiefly from Germany. The earliest building of major importance, St Gertrude at Nivelles (consecrated 1046), is, side by side with St Michael at Hildesheim, the best-preserved Ottonian church in the German orbit. The former St John at Liège was built to a central plan like Charlemagne's church at Aachen, the former Liège Cathedral had a west as well as an east chancel, St Bartholomew, also at Liège, has a typically German unrelieved façade block with recessed twin towers (cf. especially Maastricht), and the cathedral of Tournai has a trefoil east end (i.e. transepts with apsidal ends) on the pattern of St Mary in Capitol at Cologne; its group of five towers round the crossing may also be derived from Cologne.

Tournai had a great influence on the Early Gothic architecture of France (Noyon, Laon): the east end was rebuilt *c.* 1242, no longer on a German pattern but on that of such High Gothic cathedrals as Soissons and Amiens. The Gothic style in present-day Belgium was, in fact, imported from France; borrowings also occurred from Normandy and Burgundy, and as in other countries the Cistercians were among the pioneers. Orval of the late C12 is still Transitional, Villers (1210–72) is fully Gothic, as are the principal church of Brussels, Ste Gudule (begun before 1226, the façade C15), the beautiful chancel of St Martin at Ypres (begun 1221), and Notre Dame at Tongres (begun 1240). Later Gothic architecture in the southern Netherlands first drew mainly on French inspiration, dominant at Hertogenbosch (c. 1280–1330) and in the chancel of Hal in the C14. But in the C15 Belgium, admittedly influenced by French Flamboyant as well as German *Sondergotik* (*see* GERMAN ARCHITECTURE), developed a splendid style of her own. The principal buildings are Notre Dame at Antwerp (completed 1518), St Rombaut at Malines, St Peter at Louvain (begun 1425), and the Sablon Church at Brussels. Characteristic features are complicated lierne vaults of German derivation, proud towers – that of Antwerp 306 ft high, that of Malines about 320 ft and intended to be about 530 ft – and exceedingly elaborate Flamboyant fitments, such as rood screens.

The most spectacular castle is that of Ghent (inscribed 1180), with its oblong keep and its many towers along the curtain wall. But the sphere in which Belgium is in the forefront of European building is the town halls and guild halls of her prosperous towns. The Cloth Hall at Ypres (1202–1304, destroyed 1915, replaced by a replica), 440 ft long, was the grandest such building in all Europe, and there is the town hall of Bruges (tower c. 1376–1482, 350 ft high), then, ornately and lacily decorated, those of Brussels (begun 1402), Louvain (1448–63), Ghent (1517), and Oude-

narde (1525–30). Interiors were as rich as exteriors – see, for example, the magnificent chimney-piece in Courtrai Town Hall (1526). The names of the master masons are now mostly known: the Keldermans are the most familiar, notably Rombout (c. 1460–1531). There are also plenty of medieval town houses preserved; Romanesque buildings are mostly in stone (Tournai), Gothic most often in brick, frequently with crowstepped gables (as early as the C13).

The Renaissance appeared in occasional motifs in paintings as early as 1500 and was more widely represented after 1510. The most important date for the promotion of the Renaissance spirit is 1517, when Raphael's cartoons for tapestries in the Sistine Chapel reached Brussels, where the tapestries were to be made. In the same year the Stadtholderess Margaret of Austria had additions built to her palace at Malines in the Renaissance style. Their relative purity is exceptional; the usual thing in the twenties and thirties is a happy-go-lucky mixing of Renaissance with traditional motifs, sometimes quite restrained (The Salmon, Malines, 1530–34), but mostly exuberant (The Greffe, Bruges, with its fabulous chimney-piece, 1535–7; the courtyard of the former Bishop's Palace, Liège, 1526). In churches the Renaissance was confined to details; the proportions and the vaults remained Gothic (St Jacques, Liège, 1513–38). A very influential element in architectural decoration was introduced in Antwerp in the forties and spread all over northern Europe – the combination of STRAPWORK, inspired by Fontainebleau, and GROTESQUES, inspired by ancient Roman excavations. Cornelis FLORIS and later Hans Vredeman de VRIES were its most eminent practitioners.

But Floris also designed the Antwerp Town Hall (1561–6), and this, though provided with a big, dominating gable in the northern style, is in its motifs entirely developed from BRAMANTE and SERLIO, i.e. the Italian (and French) Cinquecento. The former Granvella Palace in Brussels (c. 1550) is also classical Cinquecento. However, the Jesuits, in their churches, clung to the Gothic well into the C17; an exception is St Charles Borromeo at Antwerp (1615–21), with a broad MANNERIST façade and a tunnel-vaulted interior with arcades on columns in two tiers. True C17 architecture came in under the influence of Italy and France (domes such as Notre Dame de Montaigu, begun 1609; St Pierre, Ghent, begun 1629; Notre Dame de Hanswyck, Malines, begun 1663), and after c. 1650 developed into a characteristic Belgian Baroque, inspired largely by Rubens. Church façades are without towers and covered with sumptuous and somewhat undisciplined decoration (St Michael, Louvain, 1650–66; St John Baptist, Brussels, 1657–77; St Peter, Malines, 1670–1709). Typical of the situation about 1700 are the houses round the Grand' Place in Brussels built after the bombardment of 1695 and with their gables basically still rooted in the Belgian past.

Of the C18 and early C19 little need be said; this period was dominated by French classicism (Royal Library, Brussels, c. 1750; Palais des Académies, Brussels, 1823–6). But in the later C19 Belgium found the way back to an exuberant Baroque. The cyclopean BEAUX ARTS STYLE Palais de Justice, Brussels (1866–83), by Joseph Poelaert (1817–79), is one of the most Baroque buildings of its time in Europe, though Poelaert could also work in a wild

Gothic (Laeken church, begun 1862). A generation later Belgium for the first time in her architectural history, and only for a few years, proved herself a pioneer; this was when attempts were being made to establish ART NOUVEAU as a viable architectural style. By far the most important architect in this movement was Victor HORTA of Brussels, and the key buildings are the Hôtel Tassel (designed 1892), the Hôtel Solvay (1895–1900), and the Maison du Peuple (1895–9), all of them with much of the undulating-line ornament of Art Nouveau, but also with a daring use of iron both externally and internally. Paul HANKAR developed a striking variant to Horta's style, while Henry van de VELDE, though Belgian, belongs to international rather than Belgian Art Nouveau.

Few Belgian architects were known internationally in the early C20, apart from van de Velde. But in the late 1960s and 1970s Belgium regained some of its former influence with Maurice Culot and Lucien Kroll (b. 1927). In Brussels in 1968 Culot formed ARAU (Atelier du Recherche et d'Action Urbaine) to plead for the renovation and restoration of the architectural substance when urban renewal is necessary, as then in Brussels, where the city centre was being destroyed to make room for anonymous European Community office blocks. Lucien Kroll's advocacy of 'creative participation' in building resulted most notably in his Student Centre at Wolluvé Saint-Lambert, Brussels (1970–77), the only major European example of *ad hoc* architecture.

Bell, Edward Ingress (1837–1914), *see* WEBB, Sir Aston.

Bell, Henry (1647–1711). English provincial architect, notable for his rebuilding of King's Lynn, Norfolk, after a fire in 1675, e.g. the Customs House (1683).

Colvin 1978; Summerson 1983.

Bell capital, see CAPITAL.

Bell gable, see BELLCOTE.

Bellcote. A framework on a roof to hang bells from; also called a *bell gable.*

Beltrami, Luca (1854–1933), see SOMMARUGA, Giuseppe.

Belvedere, see GAZEBO.

Bema. The Greek word means a speaker's tribune or a platform. 1. A raised stage for the clergy in the apse of Early Christian churches. 2. In Eastern usage, a space raised above the nave level of a church, which is shut off by the ICONOSTASIS and contains the altar. 3. In synagogues, the elevated pulpit from which are read the Pentateuch and Torah. Rabbinical authorities differ over its correct position: Maimonides (1204) maintains that the centre is correct, as does Moses Isserles of Cracow (C16), but Joseph Karo (1575) prescribed no fixed place. In modern times it has often been moved forward near the Ark for practical reasons. It is usually wooden and rectangular, and sometimes has a curved front and back, also open sides approached by steps.

Bench-ends, see PEW.

Benedetto da Maiano (1442–97). He was the younger brother of GIULIANO DA MAIANO and collaborated with him at the S. Fina chapel in the Collegiata in S. Gimignano (1466). Though primarily a sculptor, he was equally notable as an architect if the attribution to him of the portico of S. Maria delle Grazie, Arezzo (1490–91), is correct. It

is supremely elegant and airy, very different in feeling from Giuliano da SANGALLO's Palazzo Strozzi in Florence, with the construction of which he was certainly involved.

G. Pampaloni, *Palazzo Strozzi,* Rome 1963.

Benedictine architecture, see CLUNY.

Benjamin, Asher (1773–1845), see UNITED STATES ARCHITECTURE.

Bens, Adolf (b. 1894), see CZECHOSLOVAK ARCHITECTURE.

Bentley, John Francis (1839–1902). A pupil of Henry Clutton. Converted to Catholicism in 1861, he set up on his own in 1862. After a number of years spent mostly on designs for church furnishings and on additions and alterations, he built the Convent of the Sacred Heart at Hammersmith (1868 onwards) with a scrupulous simplicity and near-bareness; the serried chimneys are particularly impressive. Wider success came much later. Among the most memorable buildings are Holy Rood, Watford, a rich Gothic church, but also most intelligently thought out (1883–90), and St Francis at Bocking, Essex (1898). In 1894 he was commissioned to design Westminster Cathedral, London (1895–1903). The style here is Byzantine, the material brick with ample stone dressings and concrete for the domes. No iron is used: Bentley called it 'that curse of modern construction'. The campanile, asymmetrically placed, is the tallest church tower in London. The interior is superbly large in scale and extremely sparing in architectural detail, although according to Bentley's intention it should have been covered with mosaics and slabs of variegated marble (and this is gradually being done). However, Philip WEBB admired it bare as it was.

W. Scott-Moncrieff, *J.F.B.*, London 1924.

Berg, Max (1870–1947), *see* CONCRETE; GERMAN ARCHITECTURE.

Berlage, Hendrik Petrus (1856–1934), studied at the Zürich Polytechnic, then worked under CUYPERS. The building that made him famous, and is indeed a milestone in the development of Dutch architecture away from C19 HISTORICISM, is his Amsterdam Exchange (1897–1903). It does not mark a break with the past, but the treatment of period forms, derived from the Romanesque as well as the C16, is so free and the detail so original that it amounted to a profession of faith in an independent future. Specially characteristic are certain chunky, rather primeval details and others that are jagged and almost Expressionist. Berlage's style, indeed, prepared the way for the EXPRESSIONISM of the so-called School of Amsterdam (*see* KLERK; OUD). Berlage designed one building in England, the office building Holland House, Bury Street, City of London (1916–14). His last major works, the Nationale-Nederlander offices, The Hague, 1918–27 (enlarged by DUDOK 1953–4 following Berlage's plan), and the Gemeentemuseum, The Hague (1919–35), are less personal in style.

P. Singelenberg, *H.P.B.: Idea and Style. The Quest for Modern Architecture*, Utrecht 1972; S. Polano, *H.P.B. (1856–1934). Opera completa*, Milan 1987.

Berm. The level area separating ditch from bank on a hill-fort or barrow.

Bernard de Soissons, *see* JEAN D'ORBAIS.

Bernini, Gianlorenzo (1598–1680). The dominating figure in Roman Baroque art. Primarily a sculptor, like MICHELANGELO, he was almost as universal a genius, being painter and poet as well as architect. He was born in Naples of a Neapolitan mother and Florentine father, Pietro Bernini, a late Mannerist sculptor of the second rank. The family settled in Rome *c.* 1605. Bernini spent the whole of his working life there, and no other city bears so strong an imprint of one man's vision and personality. His buildings and sculpture perfectly express the grandeur, flamboyance, and emotionalism of the Counter-Reformation. He was already famous as a sculptor by the age of twenty, but his long and almost uniformly successful career as an architect began with the election of Urban VIII (Barberini) in 1623. He was appointed architect to St Peter's six years later. But most of his important buildings belong to his middle age, mainly during the pontificate of Alexander VII (Chigi, 1655–67). By then his fame was so great that Louis XIV begged him to come to Paris to enlarge the Louvre. Unlike his neurotic contemporary and rival BORROMINI, who accused him of stealing some of his designs, he was well-balanced and extrovert in temperament, polished and self-assured in manner. Yet he was devout and deeply religious: an ardent follower of Jesuit teaching. He combined to an exceptional degree a revolutionary artistic genius with the organizing ability of a man of affairs.

His first commissions (1624) were for the renovation of S. Bibiana and the baldacchino in St Peter's. Though interesting as an experiment, S. Bibiana suffers from a lack of assurance most uncharacteristic of its author and

Bernini

in striking contrast to the daringly original baldacchino (1624–33) he erected under Michelangelo's dome in the centre of St Peter's. With its gigantic bronze barley-sugar columns, buoyant scrolls and dynamic sculpture, this showy masterpiece is the very symbol of the age – of its grandeur, luxury, and lack of restraint. And by its glorification of the twisted columns used in Constantine's basilica and traditionally connected with the Temple of Jerusalem it celebrates the continuity of the Church and its triumph over the Reformation.

Various other commissions followed: the façade and staircase of Palazzo Barberini, the remodelling of Porta del Popolo, the Cornaro Chapel in S. Maria della Vittoria (1645–52). In the latter polychrome marbles, exaggerated perspective, and every trick of lighting and scenic illusion are exploited to heighten the dramatic effect of his marble group of the Ecstasy of St Teresa, placed as if behind a proscenium arch above the altar. But not until he was almost sixty did he get the chance to show his skill as a designer of churches, first at Castelgandolfo (1658–61), then at Ariccia (1662–4), and, finally and most brilliantly, at S. Andrea al Quirinale in Rome (1658–70), which perfectly realizes his conception of a church as a unified architectural setting for the religious mysteries illustrated by the sculptural decoration.

Of his two great secular buildings in Rome, Palazzo di Montecitorio (1650 onwards) and Palazzo Odescalchi (1664 onwards), the latter is by far the more important. It is composed of a richly articulated central part of seven bays with giant composite pilasters, between simple rusticated receding wings of three bays, and marks a decisive break with Roman tradition. It was very influential and became the model for aristocratic palaces all over Europe. Unfortunately, the composition was ruined by later alterations and enlargements. Bernini's last great secular enterprise, for the Louvre in Paris of 1664–6, was never carried out but was nevertheless influential, especially his third project for the east façade. His gift for the monumental and colossal found supreme expression in the Piazza of St Peter's (1656 onwards). The conception is extremely simple and extremely original – an enormous oval surrounded by colonnades of free-standing columns with a straight entablature above. This not only helped to correct the faults of MADERNO's façade by giving it the impression of greater height but expressed with overwhelming authority and conviction the dignity, grandeur, and majestic repose of Mother Church. Bernini himself compared his colonnades to the motherly arms of the Church 'which embrace Catholics to reinforce their belief'. The Piazza was to have been enclosed by a third arm, unfortunately never built, and the intended effect of surprise and elation on passing through the colonnades has now been idiotically destroyed by opening up the via della Conciliazione. The free-standing colonnades of the Piazza have been widely copied, from Greenwich to Leningrad. Bernini's last great work, the Scala Regia in the Vatican (1663–6), epitomizes his style – his sense of scale and movement, his ingenuity in turning an awkward site to advantage, his mastery of scenic effects (optical illusions, exaggerated perspectives, concealed lighting), and his brilliant use of sculpture to dramatize the climaxes of his com-

FIG. 14. *Billet*

position. He here achieved the perfect Baroque synthesis of the arts.

Wittkower 1982; F. Borsi, *B. architetto*, Milan 1980; Varriano 1986.

Bertotti-Scamozzi, Ottavio (1719–90), the leading Palladian-Revival architect in Italy, built numerous houses in and around Vicenza, notably Palazzo Pagello-Beltrame (1780) and Palazzo Franceschini (1770, now the Questura), distinctly neo-classical versions of PALLADIO. He is more important as the editor of Palladio's work: *Le fabbriche e i disegni di Andrea Palladio raccolti e illustrati* (1776–83) and *Le terme dei Romani, disegnate da A. Palladio* (1797).

L. Olivato, *O.B.-S. studioso di Andrea Palladio*, Vicenza 1976; C. Kamm-Kyburz, *Der Architekt O.B.-S. 1719–1790*, Bern 1983.

Béton brut. 'Concrete in the raw', that is, concrete left in its natural state when the FORMWORK has been removed. Sometimes special formwork is used to show clearly the timber graining on the concrete surface. Also called *board-marked concrete*.

Bianchi, Pietro (1787–1849), *see* ITALIAN ARCHITECTURE.

Bianco or **Bianchi**, Bartolommeo

(*c.* 1590–1657), a leading Baroque architect in Genoa, was born in Como, but was working in Genoa by 1619 when he began Palazzo Durazzo-Pallavicini. His best building is the University (1630–36), where he took full advantage of a steeply sloping site to produce a masterpiece of scenic planning with dramatic staircases and colonnaded courtyards on four levels.

Wittkower 1982.

Bibiena, *see* GALLI DA BIBIENA.

Bifora or **biforate window**, *see* WINDOW.

Bill, Max (b. 1908), *see* BAUHAUS; SWISS ARCHITECTURE.

Billet. A Romanesque moulding consisting of several bands of raised short cylinders or square pieces placed at regular intervals. *See* Fig. 14.

Bindesbøll, Michael Gottlieb Burkner (1800–1856), *see* DANISH ARCHITECTURE.

Bird's beak moulding. Moulding used in ancient Greek architecture and thought to resemble, in section, the beak of a bird.

Blacket, Edmund T. (1817–83), *see* AUSTRALIAN ARCHITECTURE.

Blade, *see* CRUCKS.

Blind arcade, *see* ARCADE.

Blind or **blank tracery.** Tracery applied to the surface of walls, wood panels, etc., in Gothic buildings.

Blind window. The elements of a window (the surround, mullion, etc.) applied to a wall without any aperture. It was used as a decorative device and is found from the Middle Ages onwards. It was often used in the later periods to give symmetry to the façade of an asymmetrically planned building.

Block capital, *see* CAPITAL.

Blocked. Term applied to columns, etc. with regular projecting blocks as in a GIBBS SURROUND or a RUSTICATED COLUMN.

Blocked column, *see* COLUMN.

Blocked rustication, *see* RUSTICA-TION.

Blocking course. In classical architecture, the plain course of stone surmounting the CORNICE at the top of a building; also a projecting cornice of stone or brick at the base of a building.

Blom, Piet (b. 1934), *see* DUTCH ARCHITECTURE.

Blondel, Jacques-François (1705–74). A minor architect (not related to Nicolas-François Blondel) but a very influential writer, theorist and teacher, becoming Professor at the Académie Royale de l'Architecture in 1762. Conservative in taste he exalted the French tradition as exemplified by MANSART and PERRAULT. His publications include *De la distribution des maisons* ... (1783); *L'Architecture française* (1752–6) known as the 'Grand Blondel' of which only four of the projected eight volumes appeared; *Discours sur la nécessité de l'étude de l'architecture* (1754) and *Cours d'architecture* (1771–7), which contains his public lectures and the substance of his teaching. The last two volumes were published posthumously by his pupil Patte. Of his buildings nothing survives except three sides of the Place d'Armes at Metz.

W. Herrmann, *Laugier and Eighteenth Century French Theory*, London 1962; Braham 1980; Rykwert 1980.

Blondel, Nicolas-François (1617–86), engineer and mathematician, was more interested in the theory than the practice of architecture. He expounded the rigidly classical and rationalist doctrines of the French Academy in his *Cours d'architecture* (1675, augmented ed. 1698). The Porte St Denis, Paris (1671), is his best surviving building.

Blunt 1982.

Blore, Edward (1787–1879), a topographical and antiquarian draughtsman before he became a practising architect. His great chance came in 1816 on meeting Walter Scott, then about to rebuild Abbotsford, to which Blore later contributed. After that he extended his practice considerably. Much was restoration. Among his original buildings are the domestic parts of Lambeth Palace, London (1829–48), the Pitt Press, Cambridge (1831–2), Worsley Hall, Lancashire (1840–45, demolished), Thicket Priory, Yorkshire (1844–7), and Great Moreton Hall, Cheshire (1841–6).

Colvin 1978.

Blum, Hans (*fl.* 1550). Blum published the most influential German treatise on the orders: *Quinque Columnarum Exacta descriptio atque delineatio* ... (Zürich 1550) and thus provided German architects with their first grammar in the classical language of architecture. It was based on SERLIO and often reprinted. Later editions (*Ein kunstrych Buoch von allerly Antiquiteten* ... Zürich *c.* 1560, *Warhafte Contrafacturen etlich alt u. schoner Gebauden* ... Zürich 1562) contain designs by Blum for churches, triumphal arches, etc. An English edition appeared in 1601.

Hitchcock 1981; Harris 1990.

Board-marked concrete, *see* BÉTON BRUT.

Boasted work. Stonework roughly blocked out preparatory to carving; also masonry finished with a boaster chisel.

Böblinger. A family of south German masons of which the two most important members were Hans Senior and Matthäus. Hans (1412–82) was a journeyman at Konstanz in 1435, then became foreman under Matthäus ENSINGEN at St Mary, Esslingen, and in 1440 master mason of this church. Matthäus (d. 1505) was one of Hans's sons and was probably trained in Cologne. He was later at Esslingen with his father, and then at Ulm where, after three years, he became master mason of the Minster (1480). He was successor there to Ulrich and Matthäus Ensingen, and replaced Ulrich's design for the west tower with one of his own. His steeple was completed in 1881–90 and became the highest church tower in Europe (530 ft). However, in 1492 Matthäus had to resign from the post and leave the town after cracks had appeared in the tower. He was called to a number of other places for consultation or to provide designs and supervise. Thieme and Becker's *Künstler-Lexikon* mentions eight more members of the family.

Baum 1956; Bucher 1979

Bodley, George Frederick (1827–1907), was of Scottish descent and George Gilbert SCOTT's first pupil (1845–c. 1850). Mostly but not exclusively a church architect, he always worked in the Gothic style; in his earlier works he was influenced by the French C13, later by English models. His style is as competent and knowledgeable as Scott's, but distinguished by a never-failing taste and by abundant and elaborate details, including the choice of those who were to do furnishings and fitments. An early patron of MORRIS, he also started C. E. Kempe on his career. Among his earliest works are St Michael, Brighton (1859–61); St Martin, Scarborough (1861–2); All Saints, Cambridge (1863–4). In 1869 he went into partnership with Thomas Garner (1839–1906), another pupil of Scott's; the partnership lasted till 1898, though after 1884 the partners designed and supervised jobs individually. Among their most lavish works is Holy Angels, Hoar Cross, Staffordshire (1871–7). St Augustine, Pendlebury (1870–74), on the other hand, is one of the most monumental by virtue of its simplicity; instead of aisles, it has passages through internal buttresses, a motif derived from Albi and Spain and often repeated by the younger generation. Perhaps the noblest of all Bodley's churches is that of Clumber (1886–9), now standing forlorn in the grounds of the demolished mansion. Bodley also designed the chapel of Queens' College, Cambridge (1890–91), and buildings for King's College, Cambridge (1893). His last commission was for Washington Cathedral, Washington, DC, for which he prepared designs (1906–7). The cathedral was begun in 1910 under Henry Vaughan (d. 1917) and completed in 1990. Among his pupils were C. R. ASHBEE and Sir Ninian COMPER (see ARTS AND CRAFTS).

Clarke 1969; Hitchcock 1977.

Bodt, Jean de (1670–1745). A Huguenot who left France after the revocation of the Edict of Nantes in 1685, was trained as an architect in Holland and after working for a time in England settled in 1698 in Berlin, where he soon became the most important architect after SCHLÜTER. In 1701 he built the

Fortuna Portal of the Potsdam Stadtschloss (retained by KNOBELS-DORFF in his rebuilding of 1744) and completed NERING's Arsenal in Berlin (*c.* 1706) and Parochialkirche, modifying both designs. In about 1710 the east front of Wentworth Castle, Yorkshire, was built to his designs for the Earl of Strafford. (The Earl of Strafford was ambassador to the King of Prussia 1706–11.) In 1728 he settled in Dresden, where he was appointed Superintendent of the Royal Works and thus was in charge of PÖPPEL-MANN's work at the Japanisches Palais. But all his own ambitious projects for buildings in Dresden and elsewhere in Saxony remained on paper.

Colombier 1956; Hempel 1965.

Boffrand, Gabriel Germain (1667–1754), the greatest French Rococo architect, began as a sculptor, studying under Girardon in Paris (1681), but soon turned to architecture. He became the pupil and later the collaborator of J. HARDOUIN-MANSART. In 1711 he became Premier Architecte to the Duc de Lorraine, for whom he built the château of Lunéville (1702–6) and its chapel (1720–23). Nearly all his work in Nancy has been demolished. He made a large fortune, mainly by the speculative building of Parisian *hôtels* (e.g. Hôtels de Montmorency, 1712; de Seignelay, 1713; de Torcy, 1714), but he lost the bulk of it in the Mississippi Bubble of 1720. Like his contemporary de COTTE he had great influence outside France, especially in Germany (e.g. on the Residenz, Würzburg). His virtuosity is well seen in the Hôtel de Montmorency, Paris, built round an oval court with rooms of various shapes and sizes, including a pentagon. The elevations, as always

with Boffrand, are of the utmost simplicity and reticence, while the interior is of course very luxurious. His finest interior is probably that of the pavilion he added (*c.* 1733–40) to the Hôtel de Soubise (now the Archives Nationales), Paris. His Rococo ideal of elegant informality and sophisticated simplicity was realized in his Château de Saint Ouen, a brilliant and original conception consisting of a tiny Trianon-like pavilion of three rooms, set in a spacious courtyard formed by the guests' apartment, offices, stables, etc. He published *Livre d'architecture contenant les principes généraux de cet art* in 1745.

Kalnein and Levey 1972; M. Gallett and J. Garms, *G.B. 1667–1754*, Paris 1986.

Bofill, Ricardo (Levi) (b. 1939). Spanish architect who founded the interdisciplinary workshop Taller de Arquitectura in Barcelona in 1962 and quickly made his name with low-cost housing complexes in a provocative mixture of brick and other regional Spanish vernacular materials and styles, e.g. the Xanadu apartments, Calpe (1967), and the Walden 7 Residential complex, Sant Just Desvern, near Barcelona (1970–75). These were followed by enormous POST-MODERN Classical housing developments on a Piranesian scale in France: Les Arcades du Lac, St Quentin-en-Yvelines, near Paris (1978–83), Les Espaces d'Abraxas, Marne-la-Vallée, near Paris (1978–82), La Place Nombre d'Or, Montpellier (1978–84), and Les Échelles du Baroque, Montparnasse, Paris (1983–86). Rhetorical, even megalomaniac, these *tours de force* introduce a sense of grandeur and monumentality into the public spaces they very powerfully generate. He has published *L'Architecture d'un homme* (Paris 1978).

W. A. James, *R.B. Taller de Arquitectura*, New York 1989.

Bogardus, James (1800–1874). An inventor of many things in many fields, Bogardus concerns us here for his cast-iron façades of commercial buildings. The earliest was his own factory in New York, built in 1848 (*see* METAL STRUCTURES). He published *Cast-Iron Buildings. Their Construction and Advantages* (New York 1856). His iron façades played an important role in the development of prefabricated building parts. Even more interesting was his proposed design for the New York exhibition of 1853 which has a central tower from which the roofs were suspended on the principle of suspension bridges.

Condit 1968; Benevolo 1971.

Bohigas, José Oriol (Guardiola) (b. 1925), *see* SPANISH ARCHITECTURE.

Böhm, Dominikus (1880–1955). German EXPRESSIONIST church architect, e.g. St Engelbert, Cologne-Riehl (1930–32). His later work is more conventional, e.g. S. Maria Königin, Cologne-Marienburg (1954).

A. Hoff, H. Muck and R. Thoma, *D.D. Leben und Work*, Munich and Zürich 1962, G. Stalling, *Studien zu D.B.*, Berne and Frankfurt 1974.

Böhm, Gottfried (b. 1920). Son of Dominikus Böhm, whose practice he inherited. He developed an extremely dramatic, sculptural style, e.g. the Town Hall, Bensberg (1963–9), and the Pilgrimage Church, Neviges (1963–8), but later abandoned the rather ponderous plasticity of this for lighter, airier, glass and steel buildings, e.g. the

Landesamt für Datenverarbeitung und Statistik, Düsseldorf (1969–76), and the Gemeindezentrum, Rheinberg (1977–80).

S. Raev, *G.B. Bauten und Projeckte 1950–1980*, Cologne 1982; S. Raev, *G.B., Lectures, Buildings and Projects*, Stuttgart 1987.

Boileau, Louis-Auguste (1812 96). French architect. One of the first to use iron construction in church architecture. His only familiar work is St Eugène in Paris (1854–5), earlier than BALTARD's St Augustine and VIOLLET-LE-DUC's defence of iron in the *Entretiens*. However, earlier still than St Eugène is the Ste Geneviève Library by LABROUSTE. St Eugène was the model for the church of Vésinet (1863). Boileau also wrote a book on the use of iron in architecture, *Nouvelle Forme architecturale* (Paris 1853).

Hitchcock 1977; C. Behnisch and G. Hartung, *Eisenkonstruktionen des 19 Jahrhunderts*, 1982.

Boiserie. French term for wood panelling or other fitted woodwork for an interior scheme of decoration (*see* PANEL). The term is usually applied to French C17 and especially C18 panelling elaborately decorated with shallow relief carvings of foliage etc., notably by such Rococo ornamental sculptors as François-Antoine Vassé (1681–1736), Jules Degoullons (1671–1738), François Roumier (d. 1748) and Jacques Verberckt (1704 71). They also carried out ecclesiastical schemes, notably choir stalls with panelling – e.g. in Notre Dame, Paris, and Orléans Cathedral. In C18 Germany boiseries were often combined with STUCCO decorations on the ceiling to form unified schemes of decoration, e.g. at the Residenz, Munich, and the Amalienburg

FIG. 15. *Bolection moulding*

KEY:
1. Bolection moulding 2. Panel
3. Frame

at Nymphenburg, where the stucco work is by J. B. ZIMMERMANN and the boiseries by the Paris-trained Wenzelaus Miroffsky (d. 1759) and Joachim Dietrich (d. 1753) – probably to designs by the architect François CUVILLIÉS. It is seldom known to what extent the ornamental sculptors were responsible for the design of their boiseries and how much the supervising architects, such as GABRIEL, HARDOUIN-MANSART and de COTTE, were involved.

A. Laing in A. Blunt (ed.), *Baroque and Rococo Architecture and Decoration*, London 1978; B. Pons, *Les Sculpteurs ornemantistes parisiens et l'art décoratif des Bâtiments du roi*, Strasbourg 1985.

Boito, Camillo (1836–1914), *see* SOMMARUGA, Giuseppe.

Bolection moulding. A moulding used to cover the joint between two members with different surface levels. It projects beyond both surfaces. *See* Fig. 15.

Bollard. A thick post of wood, metal or stone for securing ropes and hawsers, usually on a ship or wharf but also elsewhere; also, by analogy, similarly shaped posts used in series to limit vehicular access to an area, sometimes with intervening chains.

Bon or **Buon,** Bartolomeo (*c.* 1405–*c.* 1467). Venetian sculptor-architect, son of Giovanni Bon (*c.* 1362–1443), with whom he worked at the Ca' d'Oro (1424–31) and then on the Porta della Carta, Doges' Palace (1438–43) where late Venetian Gothic reached its apogee. His portals at S. Giovanni e Paolo (1458–63) and Madonna dell'Orto (1460–66) are more classicizing, as is his upper storey of the Arco Foscari in the Doges' Palace (1460–64). His unfinished Ca' del Duca (Palazzo Corner), Grand Canal, would have been precociously Renaissance (only the basement is by him). The Arsenal Gate (1460–62) has been attributed to him.

McAndrew 1980; Lieberman 1982; Howard 1987.

Bon or **Bono,** Bartolomeo (d. 1529). Lombard architect working in Venice (unrelated to his namesake), where the ground floor of the Scuola di San Rocco (1516–24) is his best-known work. It was completed by Antonio Abbondi, called Scarpagnino (d. 1549).

McAndrew 1980; Lieberman 1982; Howard 1987.

Bonatz, Paul (1877–1956). German architect notable for his Stuttgart railway station (1911–27), inspired by Eliel SAARINEN's Helsinki station, and for his work with Fritz Todt (1891–1942) on the Autobahn system (1935–40), especially the bridges, which he designed. He published *Leben und Bauen* (Stuttgart 1950).

N. Bongartz *et al.*, *P.B. 1877–1956*, Stuttgart 1977.

Bonavia, Santiago (d. 1759), *see* SPA-
NISH ARCHITECTURE.

Bond, *see* BRICKWORK.

Bond stone, *see* PARPEN.

Bonnet tile. A curved tile used for
joining plain tiles along the hip of a roof.

Bonneuil, Étienne de (*fl.* 1287–8), *see*
SCANDINAVIAN ARCHITECTURE.

Bonomi, Joseph (1739–1808). Born
and trained in Italy, he came to England in 1767 at the invitation of the
ADAM brothers for whom he worked.
But by the 1780s he was practising
independently. His masterpiece is the
small but very imposing church of St
James, Great Packington, Warwickshire (1789–90). It is extremely severe:
plain brick outside, Greek Doric inside
with smooth, painted ashlar. It is the
only building in England which can be
compared with the contemporary work
in France by Ledoux and in Prussia by
Gilly. Bonomi's other work is less original. His large country house Rose-
neath (1803–6) outside Glasgow was
demolished in 1961. His son Ignatius
(*c.* 1787–1870) was an architect in
Durham, designing both country
houses (e.g. Burn Hall, 1821–34) and a
number of churches including the neo-
Norman Duddo (1832) and Oxenhope
(1849) in Northumberland and Yorkshire. He retired in 1855. His second
son, also Joseph (1796–1878), designed
the flax mill of Marshall & Co., Leeds,
the most grandiose Egyptian-style
building in Europe (1842).

Colvin 1978; Summerson 1983; P.
Meadows, *J.B. Architect (1739–1808)*,
exh. cat., London 1988.

Borromini, Francesco (1599–1667).
The most original genius of Roman
High Baroque architecture and the
jealous rival of his almost exact contemporary BERNINI. A late starter,
lonely, frustrated, and neurotic, he
eventually committed suicide. Born at
Bissone on Lake Lugano, the son of a
mason, he worked in Milan before
going to Rome in late 1619. He
remained there for the rest of his life.
Befriended by his distant relation
MADERNO, he found employment as a
stone-carver at St Peter's, mainly on
decorative *putti*, festoons, etc., e.g. the
wrought-iron gates to the Cappella del
SS. Sacramento (1627), which are after
his designs. After Maderno's death
(1629) he continued under Bernini,
later becoming his chief assistant and
occasionally contributing to the designs
both at St Peter's and at Palazzo
Barberini. But their relationship was
uneasy. Himself a first-rate craftsman,
Borromini despised Bernini's technical shortcomings; Bernini's success
rankled. The two men parted for good
in 1634 when Borromini's great opportunity came with the commission
for S. Carlo alle Quattro Fontane.
Despite its miniature size, S. Carlo
(1637–41) is one of the most ingenious
spatial compositions ever invented and
displays Borromini's mastery of his
art and revolutionary disregard for
convention. The oval plan, emphasized
by the honeycomb dome, is based on
geometric units (equilateral triangles),
but the swaying rhythm and sculptural effect of the undulating walls and
restless, intertwined plastic elements
produce an almost voluptuous effect.
The concave-convex-concave façade
was begun in 1665. S. Carlo was
quickly followed by S. Ivo della Sapienza (1643–60). Borromini's triangular
planning system here produced a star-
hexagon, which he worked out vertically with dynamic effect. The fantastic

FIG. 16. *Boss*

dome culminates in an extraordinary ZIGGURAT-like spiral feature.

His style reached its zenith at S. Ivo. Later buildings were either left unfinished or inhibited by complexities of site or by his having to take over plans by previous architects. Unfinished works include S. Maria dei Sette Dolori (1642–8); the interior remodelling of S. Giovanni in Laterano (1646–9), which still lacks the intended nave vaulting; and S. Andrea delle Fratte (1653–65), where the dome is still without its lantern though the drum-like casing and three-storey tower outdo even S. Ivo in fantasy. At S. Agnese in Piazza Navona (1653–7) he took over from Carlo RAINALDI, changing the character of his interior designs by seemingly minor alterations and completely redesigning the façade on a concave plan. The dramatic grouping of high drum and dome framed by elegant towers is one of his best and most typical compositions, though he was dismissed as architect before its completion and further changes were made (notably in the pediment). An awkward site cramped his style at the Oratory of St Philip Neri (1638–50), remarkable for its ingenious dual-purpose façade uniting chapel and monastic buildings. His domestic architecture is fragmentary but no less startling – *trompe l'œil* arcade at Palazzo Spada, river front and loggia at Palazzo Falconieri, grand *salone* at Palazzo Pamphili (after 1647) and the library at the Sapienza. The latter was the prototype of many great C18 libraries. His Villa Falconieri at Frascati (*c.* 1644) was altered by FUGA.

He became increasingly unorthodox, and his last work, the Collegio di Propaganda Fide (1647–64), shows a remarkable change of style towards monumentality and austerity, the capitals, for example, being reduced to a few parallel grooves. Its façade in via di Propaganda – heavy, oppressive, nightmarish – is unlike anything before or since. Reproached in his own day for having destroyed the conventions of good architecture, Borromini had little immediate influence in Italy except superficially in ornamentation. (His revolutionary spatial concepts were to bear abundant fruit later on in central Europe.) His style was too personal and eccentric, especially in its combination of Gothic and post-Renaissance elements. His Gothic affinities were noted by his contemporaries (e.g. Baldinucci), and indeed they went beyond a partiality for medieval features such as the SQUINCH, for his geometrical system of planning and emphasis on a dynamic skeleton brought him close to the structural principles of Gothic. Yet his blending of architecture and sculpture and his voluptuous moulding of space and mass tie him to the Italian anthropomorphic tradition.

A. Blunt, *B.*, London 1979; Wittkower 1982; J. Connors, *B.'s Roman Oratory*, Cambridge, Mass., 1980; P. Portoghesi, *B. nella cultura europea*, Rome (1964) 1982; Varriano 1986.

Boss. An ornamental knob or projection covering the intersection of ribs in a vault or ceiling; often carved with foliage. See Figs. 16, 87.

Botta, Mario (b. 1943). Swiss architect, the leading member of the Italo-Swiss 'Ticino School'. His usually small-scale buildings are notable for their elemental forms, sensitive use of the regional vernacular and sympathetic relationship to the landscape, e.g. Casa Bianchi, Riva San Vitale (1971–2), the Casa Rotondo, Stabio (1981). His recent office building at Lugano (1981–5) is exceptional both in scale and in its provocatively free use of modern construction techniques.

S. Wrede, *M.B.*, New York 1987; F. Dal Co, *M.B. Architettura 1960–85*, Milan 1988.

Boulevard. A wide street, usually with trees either down the middle or along the sides.

Boullée, Étienne-Louis (1728–99). A leading neo-classical architect, he probably had more influence than LEDOUX, though he built little (the Hôtel Alexandre, Paris, 1763–6, is the most interesting survivor), and his treatise on architecture remained unpublished until as recently as 1953, for he had many and important pupils, such as J.-N.-L. DURAND who wrote the most influential treatise of the Empire period. His best designs date from the 1780s and 1790s and are, if anything, even more megalomaniac than Ledoux's e.g. a 500 ft high spherical monument to Newton and they are also, like Ledoux's, expressive or *parlantes* in intention despite their apparently abstract, geometrical simplicity. In his treatise he pleads for a felt, as much as reasoned, architecture, and for character, grandeur, and magic.

J. M. Pérouse de Monclos, *E.-L. B. 1728–1799: de l'architecture classique à l'architecture révolutionnaire*, Paris 1969; H. Rosenau, *B. and Visionary Architecture*, London 1976; Braham 1980.

Bourgeau, Victor (1809–88), *see* CANADIAN ARCHITECTURE.

Bow window, *see* BAY WINDOW.

Bowstring roof, *see* ROOF.

Bowtell. A term in use by the C15 (e.g. William of Worcester's notes; masons' contracts) for a convex moulding. A form of ROLL MOULDING usually three-quarters of a circle in section; also called *edge roll*. See Fig. 17.

Box. A small country house, e.g. a shooting box. A convenient term to describe a compact minor dwelling, e.g. a rectory.

Box-frame. A box-like form of concrete construction, where the loads are taken on cross-walls. This is suitable only for buildings consisting of repetitive small cells, such as flats or hostels. Sometimes called *cross-wall* construction. *See* Fig. 18.

Box-pew, *see* PEW.

Boytac, Diogo (fl. 1490–1525), *see* PORTUGUESE ARCHITECTURE.

Brace. A subsidiary timber, curved or straight, set diagonally to strengthen a timber frame. *See also* ROOF.

Bracket. A small supporting piece of stone or other material, often formed of scrolls or VOLUTES, to carry a projecting weight. *See also* ANCONES; CORBEL.

Bracket moulding. A Late Gothic moulding composed of two ogee mouldings with convex facings adjoining, sometimes called a *double ogee* or *brace*.

FIG. 17. *Bowtell*

FIG. 18. *Box-frame*

Bramante, Donato (Donato di Pascuccio d'Antonio, 1444–1514). The first of the great High Renaissance architects. He began under the shadow of ALBERTI and MICHELOZZO, and was profoundly influenced by LEONARDO DA VINCI, from whom he derived his interest in centrally planned churches. In Rome he evolved a classic style of imposing monumentality which was to have a deep and lasting effect on the development of Italian architecture. PALLADIO declared that he 'was the first who brought good architecture to light'. He was born near Urbino, where he probably met the leading artists at the humanist court of Federigo da Montefeltro, Piero della Francesca, and FRANCESCO DI GIORGIO, to whom he presumably owed his interest in the problems of perspective. He is first recorded in 1477 painting perspective decorations on the façade of Palazzo del Podestà, Bergamo, and he later (1481) made a drawing which was engraved as a perspective model for painters. He entered the service of Duke Ludovico Sforza *c.* 1479, for whom he worked at Vigevano as both decorative painter and architect. His first building of importance is S. Maria presso S. Satiro, Milan (begun 1482). Here he encased the tiny c9 Cappella della Pietà in a drum decorated with niches flanked by slender pilasters, and crowned it with a rather chunky octagonal lantern. He entirely rebuilt the rest of the church on a Latin cross plan. Alberti's influence is apparent in the design for the façade (never completed), the use of shallow pilasters on the side wall and the barrel-vaulted nave. There was no room for a chancel so he feigned one in *trompe l'œil* painting and relief (still deceptive if seen from the right spot). Above the crossing he built a dome with coffered interior, the first since Roman times. He also built an octagonal sacristy, very richy decorated with carvings. In 1488 he was appointed consultant to Pavia Cathedral but only the crypt was carried out according to his proposals. He designed a centrally planned east end for the Gothic church of S. Maria delle Grazie, Milan, in which Leonardo was involved with him, spacious and airy internally, but with a lavish use of elegant but rather finicking carving on the exterior of the apses and the sixteen-sided drum which encases the dome (though much of this ornament may have been added without the warrant of his designs). For S. Ambrogio, Milan, he designed the Canons' Cloister (1492, only one wing built) and a further group of four cloisters (1497, two completed after 1576 to his plans). In the Canons' Cloister he used slender Corinthian columns with high friezes and boldly projecting impost blocks, and four columns in the form of tree trunks with the stumps of sawn-off branches protruding from the cylinders.

In 1499 the French invasion of Lombardy and the fall of the Sforzas forced him to flee to Rome, then the artistic centre of Italy. Apart from some frescoes, his first work in Rome was a cloister at S. Maria della Pace (1500), astonishingly different from anything he had previously designed. It has sturdy Doric piers and attached Ionic columns derived from the Colosseum on the ground floor, and an open gallery on the first with alternate Corinthian columns and Composite piers supporting not arches but an architrave. The effect is wholly Roman in its quiet gravity. He became still graver and more Roman in his next building, the circular Tempietto of S. Pietro in Montorio, Rome (commissioned 1502 but perhaps not built until *c.* 1510), the first great monument of the High Renaissance, which has a majestic solemnity belying its small size. Surrounded at the base by a Tuscan Doric colonnade with a correct classical entablature, it has no surface decorations apart from the metopes and the shells in the niches. It was intended to have been set in the centre of a circular peristyle which would have provided the perfect spatial foil to its solidity, for it is conceived in terms of volume rather than space, like a Greek temple. Here the Renaissance came closer to the spirit of antiquity than in any other building.

The election of Pope Julius II in 1503 provided Bramante with a new and wholly congenial patron who commissioned him to draw up a vast building plan for the Vatican and St Peter's. A range of buildings later incor-porated in the Cortile di S. Damaso was promptly begun, with three tiers of superimposed arcades. Though massive, this was relatively modest in comparison with the scheme for the Cortile del Belvedere, a huge courtyard on three levels measuring about 950 ft by 225 ft, flanked by arcaded buildings, with a theatre at the lower end and a museum for classical antiquities with a central exedra closing the upper court. Work began at the museum end, but only the first storey was completed to his designs (much altered later). The only one of his works in the Vatican which survives intact is the handsome spiral ramp enclosed in a tower of the Belvedere (*c.* 1505). For St Peter's he proposed a church that would have been the *ne plus ultra* in centralized planning – a Greek cross with four smaller Greek crosses in the arms, roofed by a vast central dome as large as the Pantheon's with four smaller domes and four corner towers, all standing isolated in an immense *piazza*. The foundation stone was laid in 1506 and building was begun but little was completed before the Pope's death in 1513 brought all work to a halt. (There are analogies between his designs for St Peter's and the 'Ninfeo' at Genazzano now attributed to him.) The choir for S. Maria del Popolo, Rome (1505–9), is small in scale but grand in conception, with a massively coffered vault and shell-capped apse. The Santa Casa at Loreto (begun 1509) is almost as Roman as the Cortile del Belvedere, though heavily and richly decorated with sculptures by Andrea Sansovino, Tribolo, Baccio Bandinelli, G. B. della Porta, and others. He also designed and began Palazzo Caprini, Rome (*c.* 1510, later altered out of recognition), with a heavily rusticated basement and five pedimented windows between coupled half-columns on the upper floor, a design which was to be widely imitated. The house was later acquired by RAPHAEL, who inherited his position as leading architect in Rome.

A. Bruschi, *B.*, London 1977; L. Patetta, *L'architettura del quattrocento a Milano*, Milan 1987.

Bramantino (*fl.* 1503–36), *see* SUAR-DI, Bartolomeo.

Branch tracery, *see* TRACERY.

Brattishing. An ornamental cresting on the top of a screen or cornice usually formed of leaves, Tudor flowers, or miniature battlements.

Brazilian architecture. Brazil was settled by the Portuguese early in the C16 and remained a Portuguese colony till 1807. The country became an independent empire in 1822, and a republic in 1889. Architecture during the colonial centuries remained dependent on Portugal; one of the earliest Baroque churches is S. Bento at Rio of 1652. The centres of the Baroque, however, are S. Salvador de Bahia and the towns of Minas Gerais, where gold was discovered in the late C17. At Bahia the Terceiros church of 1703 is exuberantly CHURRIGUERESQUE; so is the decoration of the church of S. Francisco (1708 onwards). The architectural climax of Brazilian Baroque, however, is Ouro Preto near Belo Horizonte, with its many churches of the second half of the C18, mostly with two façade towers and elongated central plans. To the same group belongs the church of Bom Jesus at Congonhas do Campo (1777): sculpture here and in several of the Ouro Preto churches is by ALEIJA-DINHO.

A revulsion from the Baroque came only after 1815. French artists immigrated, including A. H. V. Grand-jean de Montigny (1776–1850), who finished the Customs House at Rio in 1820. A little later, but still French Classical, is the theatre at Recife by Louis Vauthier (*c.* 1810–77), and the rather more American-Colonial-looking theatre at Belém do Pará (1868–78) with its attenuated giant portico. The neo-Baroque is best illustrated by the opera house at Manáus of 1890–96.

While all this had been first colonial and then peripheral, Brazil became one of the leading countries of the world in architecture after the Second World War. The Modern Movement had been introduced by the white cubic houses built from 1928 onwards by Gregori Warchavchik (1896–1972), who had published his *Manifesto on Modern Architecture* in 1925. LE COR-BUSIER visited Brazil briefly in 1929, and again in 1936, in connection with the proposed new Ministry of Education at Rio. The building was begun to an amended plan by a group of young Brazilian architects in 1937. Among them were both Lucio COSTA and Oscar NIEMEYER, now the most famous Brazilian architects. Niemeyer was especially important for his early buildings at Pampulha, a club, a dance hall, and a casino of 1942, and a church of 1943. They were the earliest buildings in any country resolutely and adventurously to turn away from the international rationalism then just being accepted by progressive authorities and clients in most countries. Instead, Niemeyer introduced parabolic curves in elevation, a tower with tapering sides, passages under canopies snaking their way from one building to another, a pair of monopitch roofs slanting downward to where they meet. Other architects whose names have become familiar are Marcelo and Milton Roberto (1908–64 and 1914–53), Rino Levi (1901–65) and Affonso Eduardo Reidy (1909–64) whose Pedregulho Housing development (1947–55) and Museum of Modern Art, Rio (1954–7), are outstanding.

Lucio COSTA's name became a household word overnight when in 1956 he won the competition for the plan of Brasilia, the new capital of Brazil. The principal buildings there are by Niemeyer: the hotel, the brilliant president's palace, the palaces of the three powers, and the ministry buildings. Niemeyer's centrally planned cathedral was dedicated in 1970. The landscape architect Roberto Burle Marx (b. 1909) contributed notably to the setting.

Brenna, Vincenzo (1745–1820), *see* CAMERON, Charles.

Bressumer or **breastsummer**. A horizontal timber which carries a wall above, such as the beam supporting a projecting gable or the lintel of a wide opening like a fireplace.

Brettingham, Matthew (1699–1769), was undistinguished, but had a large practice and built Holkham Hall to KENT's designs. He later claimed to have designed it himself. Few of his own works survive; Langley Hall (c. 1745) is probably the best. In London he designed several important town houses: Norfolk House (1748–52, demolished 1938), York House, Pall Mall (1761–3, demolished), and No. 5, St James's Square (1749). His son Matthew (1725–1803) was also an architect, equally successful and equally undistinguished.

Colvin 1978; Summerson 1983.

Breuer, Marcel (Laiko) (1902–81). Born in Hungary, he studied at the BAUHAUS from 1920. In 1925 he was put in charge of the joinery and cabinet workshop, and in that year designed his first tubular steel chair. He went to London in 1935, to Harvard in 1937, and was in a partnership with GROPIUS (1937–40). His independent practice in America started effectively only after the Second World War. He was first commissioned to design private houses in New England. A sympathy with natural materials (rubble, timber), derived perhaps from his Bauhaus days, had already been apparent in some of his work in England. Later his practice spread to other countries (Bijenkorf, Rotterdam, with Elzas, 1953; Unesco, Paris, with Zehrfuss and NERVI, 1953–8), and his style then followed the rather less rational, more arbitrary trend of architecture in general (Abbey of St John, Collegeville, Minnesota, 1953–61, and the Lecture Hall for New York University on University Heights, Bronx, New York, 1956–61). The Whitney Museum of American Art, New York (1963–6), and the IBM complex at Boca Raton, Florida (1967–77), were his last important works. He published *Sun and Shadow. The Philosophy of an Architect* (ed. P. Blake) in 1956.

C. Jones (ed.), *M.B. 1921–1961 Buildings and Projects*, London 1962; T. Papachristou, *M.B. Neue Bauten und Projekte*, Stuttgart 1970.

Brickwork. A *header* is a brick laid so that the end only appears on the face of the wall, while a *stretcher* is a brick laid so that the side only appears on the face of the wall. A *closer* is half a header and is sometimes used to finish the

Bridge

English bond

Header   Stretcher

Flemish Bond

FIG. 19. *Brickwork*

brickwork of every other course at the end of a wall or against an opening.

English bond is a method of laying bricks so that alternate courses or layers on the face of the wall are composed of headers or stretchers only. *English garden wall bond* is a method of laying bricks so that three courses of stretchers alternate with one course of headers on the face of the wall. *Flemish bond* is a method of laying bricks so that alternate headers and stretchers appear in each course on the face of the wall. *Heading bond* is composed of headers only. *Nogging* is the name given to brickwork used to fill the spaces between the timbers in a timber-framed building. *See* Fig. 19.

Bridge. A built construction spanning a river, canal, ravine, etc. or connecting two points at a height above the intervening ground and allowing free passage beneath. The main types are: *girder bridges*, resting on supports at either end; *arch bridges*, borne on arches or arched vaults (*see also* AQUE-DUCT; VIADUCT); *suspension bridges*, with the framework hung from high

masts (e.g. TELFORD's Menai Straits Bridge of 1819–26), and *cantilever bridges*. There are three main types of movable bridges: the simple *drawbridge*, the *swing bridge*, which moves horizontally, and the *bascule bridge*, which moves vertically on the see-saw principle (e.g. Tower Bridge, London). The earliest surviving bridge of any length is that of Martorell in Spain, *c.* 219 BC, with a centre arch 130 ft across. Cast iron was used for bridges from 1779 (first at Coalbrookdale, England) and the C19 introduction of railways led to swift developments in bridge-building, notably by George Stephenson (1781–1848), Robert Stephenson (1803–59), and BRUNEL in England, EIFFEL in France, and John A. Roebling (1806–69) in the USA. Roebling's most famous bridge is the Brooklyn Bridge, New York, begun in 1867 and completed by his son Washington in 1883. The outstanding bridges of the early C20 reflect developments in concrete construction, notably those by FREYSSINET, HEN-NEBIQUE, MAILLART and, more recently, MORANDI. *See also* CLAPPER BRIDGE.

R. Mainstone, *Developments in Structural Form*, London 1975; C. Jurecka, *Brücken. Historische Entwicklungen – Faszination der Technik*, Vienna and Munich 1979; F. Leonhardt, *Brücken – Ästhetik und Gestaltung*, Stuttgart 1982.

Brinkman, Johannes Andreas (1902–49), *see* DUTCH ARCHITECTURE.

Brise-soleil. A sun-break or check; now frequently an arrangement of horizontal or vertical fins, used in hot climates to shade the window openings.

Broach spire, *see* SPIRE.

Broach-stop, *see* STOP-CHAMFER.

Broch, *see* BEEHIVE HOUSE.

Brodrick, Cuthbert (1822–1905). A Yorkshire architect whose capital work is the Leeds Town Hall (1853–8), a grand edifice with a many-columned dome, influenced by COCKERELL and WREN. More original is his Leeds Corn Exchange (1861–3), elliptical in plan, Italian Renaissance in style, and with little in the way of enrichment. He also did the wondrously big and heavy Grand Hotel at Scarborough in a style paying tribute to the then fashionable French Renaissance (1863–7), and the Town Hall of Hull (1862–6).

T. B. Wilson, *Two Leeds Architects: C.B. and George Corson*, Leeds 1937; Hitchcock 1977.

Broek, Johannes Hendrik van der (1898–1978), *see* DUTCH ARCHITECTURE.

Broken pediment, *see* PEDIMENT.

Brongniart, Alexandre-Théodore (1739–1813), a prominent neo-classical architect, was born in Paris and trained under J. F. BLONDEL. In 1765 he began his very successful independent practice, designing the theatre at Caen (destroyed) and the Hôtel de Montesson, Paris. For his private houses he adopted a graceful and unpedantic neo-classical style, the nearest equivalent in architecture to the sculpture of Clodion, who was several times employed to decorate them (e.g. Hôtel de Condé, Paris, designed 1780). For the Capuchin convent in the Chaussée d'Antin, now Lycée Condorcet (1780–82, façade rebuilt 1864), he developed a much more severe manner, designing a colon-

nade of Paestum Doric columns for the cloister. In 1804 he was entrusted with the new cemetery of Père-Lachaise in Paris and its *jardin anglais* layout was very influential. His last important work was the Paris Bourse, an appropriately grandiose Corinthian building in the Imperial Roman style (begun 1807, altered and enlarged 1895).

Braham 1980; *A.-T.B. 1739–1813*, exh. cat., Musée Carnavalet, Paris 1985.

Brooks, James (1825–1901). A Gothic-Revival church architect whose directness of approach is comparable to BUTTERFIELD's; but where Butterfield is obstinate and perverse, Brooks excels by a simplicity which LETHABY called big-boned. His favourite material was stock brick, his favourite style that of the early C13 with lancet windows and apse. His principal churches are all in London: first a group in the poor north-eastern suburbs (St Michael, Shoreditch, 1863; Holy Saviour, Hoxton, 1864; St Chad, Haggerston, 1867; St Columba, Haggerston, 1867); and then, a little more refined, three individual masterpieces, among the best of their date in the country: the Ascension, Lavender Hill, 1874; the Transfiguration, Lewisham, 1880 (recently mutilated by the insertion of a *mezzanine* floor above the arcades); and All Hallows, Gospel Oak, 1889. The latter was intended to be vaulted throughout.

Clarke 1969; Hitchcock 1977; Dixon and Muthesius 1978.

Brosse, Salomon de (*c.* 1571–1626), was born at Verneuil, where his maternal grandfather Jacques Androuet DU CERCEAU was building the *château*. His father was also an architect. He settled in Paris *c.* 1598, and was appointed architect to the Crown in 1608. Unlike his relations in the Du Cerceau family and his predecessor BULLANT he conceived architecture in terms of mass and not merely of surface decoration. This plastic sense is evident in his three great *châteaux* of Coulommiers (1613), Luxembourg (begun 1615, enlarged and altered C19), and Blérancourt (1612–19, one pavilion survives). The latter is the finest, and was revolutionary in its day, being a free-standing symmetrical block designed to be seen from all sides. In 1618 he began the Palais du Parlement at Rennes, to which his feeling for sharply defined masses and delicacy of classical detail gives great distinction. (There are some C19 alterations.) In 1623 he built the Protestant Temple at Charenton. His frenchified classicism is epitomized in the façade of St Gervais, Paris (1623), which combines VIGNOLA's Gesù scheme with L'ORME's frontispiece at Anet with three superimposed orders. He was the most notable precursor of François MANSART, whom he anticipated in some ways.

R. Coope, *S. de B. and the Development of the Classical Style in French Architecture from 1565 to 1630*, London 1972.

Brown, Lancelot (nicknamed Capability, 1716–83). The architect of several Palladian country houses, e.g. Croome Court (1751–2) and Claremont House (1771–4). But he is much more important as a landscape gardener. In 1740 he became gardener at Stowe, where he worked on KENT's great layout, and in 1749 he became a consulting landscape gardener. Very soon he developed an artfully informal manner and devised numerous parks with wide expanses of lawn, clumps of trees, serpentine lakes, which provided a perfect setting for the neo-Palladian country seat. Nature was not fettered, as in the formal schemes of LE NÔTRE, but tamed, and a thick planting of trees served both to conceal the bounds of the idyllic park and to protect it from the unimproved landscape beyond. His probably apocryphal remark on his lake at Blenheim, 'Thames, Thames, you will never forgive me,' sums up his attitude. His parks were less an alternative to the formal garden than an alternative to nature which proved irresistibly appealing not only in England but also on the Continent. His best surviving parks are: Warwick Castle (*c.* 1750), Croome Court (1751), Bowood (1761), Blenheim (1765, much altered), Ashburnham (1767), Dodington Park (1764), and Nuneham Courtenay (1778).

D. Stroud, *C.B.*, London (1950) 1975.

Brownstone. A dark or reddish brown sandstone much used for building in the eastern USA from the mid C19. It gave its name to the typical New York terrace house of the late C19.

Bruant or **Bruand**, Libéral (*c.* 1635–97), built the Hôtel des Invalides in Paris (1670–77), notable for the Roman gravity of its arcaded courts, and the highly original Salpêtrière Chapel in Paris (*c.* 1670). He designed a house for the Duke of York, later James II, in Richmond, *c.* 1662. He was a greatly gifted architect who never achieved the success he merited. His brother Jacques (d. 1664) designed the Hall of the Marchands Drapiers (*c.* 1655–60), the façade of which is in the Musée Carnavalet, Paris.

Blunt 1982.

Bruce, Sir William (*c.* 1630–1710), introduced the classical style into Scotland. He came into prominence after the Restoration, for which he had vigorously intrigued, and was rewarded with the lucrative Clerkship to the Bills (1660). He was created baronet 1668, and in 1671 appointed King's Surveyor and Master of Works in Scotland. His work at Holyrood House, Edinburgh (1671 onwards), is frenchified but still rather gauche. Kinross House (1686–93) and Hopetoun House (1699–1703) are more accomplished in the PRATT tradition.

J. G. Dunbar, *Sir W.B.*, exh. cat., Edinburgh 1971; J. Macaulay, *The Classical Country House in Scotland 1660–1800*, London 1987.

Brückwald, Otto (1841–1904), *see* SEMPER, Gottfried.

Brunel, Isambard Kingdom (1806–59). The son of Sir Marc Isambard Brunel (1769–1849), who had been born in Normandy, had worked in the French Navy, then as city engineer in New York, and had settled in England in 1799; his most famous English work is the Thames Tunnel from Wapping to Rotherhithe (1824–43). The son was educated in Paris and trained in his father's office. In 1829 he designed the Clifton Bridge at Bristol, one of the noblest of English suspension bridges. He was also responsible for the Great Western line from London to Bristol, including the Box Tunnel and Paddington Station, London (1850–55, with Sir Matthew Digby WYATT and Owen Jones). His best-known bridge is the Saltash Bridge, opened in 1859. He also built ships (the *Great Western*, which took only fifteen days to America, and the even larger *Great Eastern*) and in addition, docks (Bristol, Monkwearmouth).

L. T. C. Rolt, *I.K.B.*, London 1957; A. Pugsley (ed.), *The Works of I.K.B.*, Cambridge 1980.

Brunelleschi, Filippo (1377–1446), the first Renaissance architect and one of the greatest, as elegant and refined as Botticelli and as springlike. Far less dogmatic and antiquarian than his immediate successors, e.g. ALBERTI and MICHELOZZO, he was less concerned with the revival of antiquity than with practical problems of construction and the management of space. He, more than anyone else, was responsible for formulating the laws of linear perspective, and a preoccupation with the linear conquest of space characterizes his architecture. In his buildings the horizontals are marked by thin lines which seem to follow the guides of a perspective framework, while the verticals, columns, and fluted pilasters have a spidery, linear attenuation.

Born in Florence, he began as a goldsmith and sculptor, joining the Arte della Seta in 1398, then working for a goldsmith in Pistoia (silver altar, Pistoia Cathedral, *c.* 1399), and competing in 1401–2 for the second bronze door of the Florence Baptistery (he tied with Ghiberti but refused to collaborate with him). In 1404 he was admitted as a master to the Goldsmiths' Guild, and in the same year his advice was sought about a buttress for the cathedral in Florence. (A visit to Rome he is said to have made with Donatello after 1402 is now discounted.) He continued as a sculptor for a while, but gradually turned his attention exclusively to architecture. In 1415 he repaired the Ponte a Mare at Pisa; in 1417 he advised on the projected dome of Florence Cathedral. His first major works, all in Florence, date from 1418 onwards – a domed chapel in S. Jacopo sopr'Arno (destroyed), the Barbadori Chapel in S. Felicità (partly destroyed), the Palazzo di Parte Guelfa (much altered, but the prototype Early Renaissance palace), and S. Lorenzo. While these were in progress he began, in 1420, to build his masterpiece, the dome of Florence Cathedral, and in 1419 the Ospedale degli Innocenti in Florence.

At S. Lorenzo he began with the sacristy (finished 1428), a cube roofed by a very elegant dome with narrow ribs radiating from the central lantern, a type of construction he called *a creste e vele* (with crests and sails), which neatly expresses its appearance of canvas stretched over the quadrant ribs. The whole interior is painted white, while taut bands of grey *pietra serena* outline the main architectural members; this is the first instance of this strikingly effective decorative scheme. The church itself he designed as a basilica, adding shallow transepts and also chapels attached to the side aisles. But he drew his inspiration not from Imperial Rome so much as the Tuscan Romanesque or proto-Renaissance of the C11–12.

He was commissioned to build the cathedral dome in partnership with Ghiberti, who gradually slipped out of the picture. The dome is Gothic in outline with elegantly curved white ribs springing up to the centre, but it is essentially Renaissance in its engineering technique – herringbone brickwork in the Roman manner. The skeleton was completed in 1436, and a further competition held for the lantern – won this time by Brunelleschi alone. In 1438 he designed the semicircular tribunes with shell-capped niches and coupled Corinthian columns which stand beneath the drum.

The Ospedale degli Innocenti, Florence (designed 1419, built 1421–44), is often claimed as the first Renaissance building. It consists of an arcade of slender, even spindly, Corinthian columns with blue-and-white glazed terracotta plaques between the arches, and a first floor with widely spaced pedimented windows above the centre of each arch. The wide spacing of the arches harks back to C11 and C12 Tuscan work, but the detail is distinctly Roman.

In 1429 he began the Pazzi Chapel in the cloister of S. Croce, Florence. The plan is more complex than that of the S. Lorenzo Sacristy: an atrium in the ratio of 1:3, the main building 2:3, and a square chancel. (It was built on the foundations of an earlier chapterhouse.) The interior decoration is more forceful than S. Lorenzo, with virile semicircular arcs of *pietra serena*, Corinthian pilasters, and, in the spandrels, glazed terracotta reliefs. The façade is odd, closer to the tribune of a basilica than a temple portico – slender Corinthian columns supporting a blank attic storey with shallow carved rectangular panels and coupled pilasters. It was not completed until long after Brunelleschi's death and may not have been designed by him. (A second visit to Rome he is said to have made in 1433 is now also discounted.) S. Maria degli Angeli, Florence, was his most archaeological design, though unfortunately building stopped after three years and only the lower parts of the walls remain. It was the first centrally planned church of the Renaissance (an octagon with eight chapels surrounding the central space, sixteen-sided outside with flat walls and deep niches alternating). At S. Spirito, Florence (begun 1436), he reverted to the basilican Latin

FIG. 20. *Bucranium*

cross plan, but gave it an entirely new centralized emphasis by running an aisle round the whole church (the west section never built). Once again the proportions are straightforward – an arrangement of cubes, half-cubes, and double cubes – creating that balance and feeling of tranquil repose which was among the chief aims of Renaissance architects. The classical ornamentation is correct and vigorous though sometimes employed in a slightly unorthodox fashion. Several other works have been attributed to him, notably the centre of Palazzo Pitti, Florence, which he may have designed shortly before his death. Though astylar it is clearly an Early Renaissance building, with its massive rusticated stonework inspired by Roman work and with proportions governed by a simple series of ratios.

Brunelleschi became the first Renaissance architect almost by accident. He seems to have been drawn towards ancient Rome less for aesthetic than for practical, engineering reasons. An eclectic empiricist, he hit by instinct on those ideas which were to be developed by his successors. Perhaps his greatest merit was to have preserved Early Renaissance architecture from the dry pedantry of archaeology and revivalism.

E. Battisti, *F.B.*, (Milan 1976) London 1981.

Brutalism or the **New Brutalism**. A term coined in England in 1954 to characterize the style of LE CORBUSIER at the moment of Marseille and Chandigarh, and the style of those inspired by such buildings: in England the SMITHSONS and STIRLING and GOWAN; in Italy Vittoriano Viganò (Istituto Marchiondi, Milan, 1953–9); in America Paul RUDOLPH; in Japan MAYEKAWA, TANGE, and many others. Brutalism nearly always uses concrete exposed at its roughest (BÉTON BRUT) and handled with overemphasis on big chunky members which collide ruthlessly.

R. Banham, *The New Brutalism*, London 1966.

Bryce, David (1803–76), *see* SCOTTISH ARCHITECTURE.

Bryggman, Erik (1891–1955), *see* FINNISH ARCHITECTURE.

Bucrane or **bucranium**. In classical architecture, a sculptured ox-skull, usually garlanded, often found in the METOPES of a Doric frieze. A similar relief of a ram's or goat's head or skull is called an *aegricane*. *See* Fig. 20.

Buddhist railing. A barrier of stone carved to resemble a wooden fence, with horizontal slats woven through the verticals, made to surround a STUPA (as at Sanchi in India), but also carved in relief as a symbol.

Bulfinch, Charles (1763–1844), came of a wealthy, cultivated Boston family. He graduated at Harvard and was, on his European journey in 1785–7, advised by JEFFERSON. His principal works are the Beacon Monument (1791) in Boston, a Doric column 60 ft high; the State House in Boston (1795–8); and the Court House, also in Boston (1810). They are perhaps the most dignified American public buildings of their time. In Boston extensive street planning and the building of terraces of houses with unified façades was also done under Bulfinch's chairmanship, notably Tontine Crescent (1793, demolished 1858). In his church plans (Holy Cross, Boston, 1805; New South Church, Boston, 1814; Church of Christ, Lancaster, Massachusetts, 1816) he was influenced by WREN, in his secular work by CHAMBERS and ADAM. From 1817 to 1830 Bulfinch was in charge of work on the Capitol in Washington.

H. Kirker, *The Architecture of C.B.*, Cambridge, Mass., 1969; Whiffen and Koeper 1981.

Bulgarian architecture, *see* BYZANTINE ARCHITECTURE.

Bullant, Jean (*c.* 1520/25–78). His early, rather pedantic classical style is based on L'ORME and the study of antiquity (he visited Rome *c.* 1540–45), but it rapidly acquired MANNERIST complexities and, finally, in his late works for Catherine de' Medici, showed a fantasy similar to that of his rival DU CERCEAU. Much of his work has been destroyed. His additions to the Château of Écouen illustrate his characteristically pedantic accuracy in classical details and no less characteristic misunderstanding of the spirit that stood behind them, as witness his most unclassical use of the colossal order. Mannerist features are striking in his bridge and gallery at Fère-en-Tardenois (1552–62) and in the Petit Château at Chantilly (*c.* 1560). Of his work for Catherine de' Medici only his additions to Chenonceau survive – the western arm of the forecourt and gallery over the bridge (*c.* 1576). He published *Reigle générale d'architecture* (1563) and *Petit traicté de géométrie* (1564).

Blunt 1982.

Bullet, Pierre (1639–1716), a pupil of N.-F. BLONDEL, began in the classical academic tradition and did not display much originality until towards the end of his career at the Hôtels Crozat and d'Évreux in the Place Vendôme, Paris (1702–7). Built on irregular corner sites, they foreshadow the freedom and fantasy of Rococo architects in the shape and disposition of rooms. He wrote a theoretical treatise, *L'architecture pratique* (1691).

Blunt 1982.

Bull's eye window. A small circular window like an ŒIL-DE-BŒUF.

Bungalow. A detached, single-storey house in its own plot of land. The term first occurs in 1784 as an anglicization of the Indian word '*bangla*' and was given to lightly constructed dwellings with verandas erected for English officials in mid-C19 Indian cantonments and hill stations. Later the term was used for similarly light, simple dwellings built as second homes in England and America. In England the pioneer examples were at Westgate-on-Sea and Birchington (1869–82). So many of these were later built by unqualified designers that certain areas became known as 'bungaloid growths'.

A. D. King, *The Bungalow: The Production of a Global Culture*, London 1984; C. Lancaster, *The American Bungalow 1880–1920s*, New York 1985.

Bunning, James Bunstone (1802–63), *see* LABROUSTE, Pierre-François-Henri.

Bunshaft, Gordon (b. 1909), *see* SKIDMORE, OWINGS & MERRILL.

Buon, Bartolomeo (*c.* 1405–*c.* 1467), *see* BON, Bartolomeo.

Buontalenti, Bernardo (1531–1608). Florentine Mannerist architect, painter and sculptor, and also a prolific designer of masques, fireworks (hence his nickname 'delle Girandole') and other entertainments for the Tuscan Grand Ducal court. He was even more sophisticated and stylish than his contemporaries AMMANATI and VASARI, e.g. the fantastic *trompe l'œil* altar steps in S. Stefano (1574–6), the perverse Porta delle Suppliche at the Uffizi (*c.* 1580), and the grottoes in the Boboli Gardens (1583–8), all in Florence. But this preciosity and sense of fantasy was necessarily restrained in his major works, of which the most notable are the Villa di Artimino at Signa (1594), the *galleria* and *tribuna* of the Uffizi (1584), the façade of S. Trinità (1592–4), the Fortezza del Belvedere (1590–95) and the Palazzo Nonfinito (1593–1600), all in Florence, and the Loggia dei Banchi in Pisa (the design of 1605 was executed by Puglioni). He also produced a fantastic design for the façade of the cathedral at Florence (1587) and carried out much engineering work for the Grand Duke, notably at the harbour of Leghorn and a canal between Leghorn and Pisa (1571–3). His grand-ducal villa at Pratolino (1569–75) was destroyed in the C19.

I M Botto in *DBI* 1972; A. Fara, *B.B. Baumeister aus Florenz*, Basel 1990.

Burges, William (1827–81), trained in engineering, then in the offices of Blore and Matthew Digby WYATT. He travelled in France, Germany, and Italy, and was always as interested in French as in English Gothic forms. In 1856, he won, with Henry Clutton (1819–93), the competition for Lille Cathedral, but in the event the building was not allotted to them. In 1859 he added the east end to Waltham Abbey, where for the first time the peculiar massiveness and heavy-handedness of his detail come out. He was a great believer in plenty of carved decoration, and specialized much less in ecclesiastical work than the other leading Gothic Revivalists. His principal works are Cork Cathedral (1862–76), still in a pure French High Gothic; the substantial addition to Cardiff Castle (1868–85); the remodelling of Castell Coch near Cardiff (1875–91); the Harrow School Speech Room (1872); and his own house in Melbury Road, Kensington (1875–80). Hartford College, Connecticut, was also built to his designs (1873–80).

J. M. Crook, *W.B. and the High Victorian Dream*, London 1981.

Burghausen, Hans von (d. 1432), *see* STETHAIMER.

Burle Marx, Roberto (b. 1909), *see* BRAZILIAN ARCHITECTURE.

Burlington, Richard Boyle, 3rd Earl of (1694–1753), was the patron and high priest of English PALLADIANISM and a gifted architect in his own right. He first visited Italy in 1714 15, but his conversion to Palladianism came after his return to London, which coincided with the publication of CAMPBELL's *Vitruvius Britannicus* and LEONI's edition of Palladio's *Four Books of Architecture*. He immediately replaced GIBBS with Campbell as architect of Burlington House and set out once more for Italy to study the master's buildings at first hand. He returned (1719) with his protégé William KENT, and for the next thirty years dominated the architectural scene in England. The widespread fashion for Palladio was largely due to his influence. He financed Kent's *Designs of Inigo Jones* (1727) and in 1730 published Palladio's drawings of Roman *thermae*. But there was a marked difference between his own and his followers' interpretation of the master. For him Palladianism meant a return to the architecture of antiquity as explained and illustrated by Palladio, and he avoided, whereas his followers blindly accepted, all the non-classical and Mannerist features in the master's style. Cold, intellectual, and aristocratic, he was described by Pope as a 'positive' man, and both the strength and weakness of Palladianism derive from his obsessive, puritanical urge to preach absolute classical standards – those just and noble rules which were in due course to 'Fill half the land with imitating fools' (Pope). His fastidious but dogmatic character is equally evident in his buildings, which became increasingly dry and pedantic. They have a staccato quality – an over-articulation or overemphasis of individual features – suggesting a formula-loving mind. His *œuvre* appears to have consisted of about a dozen buildings designed mostly for himself or friends, beginning in 1717 with a garden pavilion – the Bagno (demolished) – at Chiswick, where he built his best-known work, the ornamental villa based on Palladio's Rotonda (*c.* 1723–9). His only other important works to survive are the Dormitory, Westminster School, London (1722–30, rebuilt 1947), Northwick Park, Worcestershire (1730), and the Assembly Rooms, York (1732, refronted 1828). This latter is an exact model of Palladio's Egyptian Hall, based on VITRUVIUS. In addition to his independent work, he may be credited as part author of several buildings by his protégé Kent, notably Holkham Hall.

Wittkower 1974; Summerson 1983; C. Carré, *Lord B. (1694–1753) le connaisseur, le mécène, l'architecte*, Clermont-Ferrand 1985.

Burmese architecture. In Burma as elsewhere in South-East Asia durable materials were reserved for religious buildings, which are the only ones surviving from before the C19. As Buddhism has been, since an early period, the main national religion, STUPAS (confusingly known in Burma as pagodas) abound. The most sacred and famous, the Shwedagon in Rangoon, is traditionally said to have been founded in C5 BC but has been enlarged several times (finally in 1768) to its present height of 342 ft from its tiered platform. Covered in gold and encrusted with precious stones, its present characteristically Burmese form, with a spreading base from which a hemisphere merges into a spire, was probably a magnification of that given it in the C14. There are remains of C5–8 stupas and temples at the site of the city of Sri Ksetra, near Prome. But the largest group of ancient Burmese buildings is at Pagan, in a bend of the Irrawaddy, a city founded probably in C2 AD, much developed after 1044 and covering an area of 35 sq. miles by 1287, when it was sacked by Mongols under Kublai Khan. Of its numerous surviving buildings the most notable are the Ananda temple (begun 1090), with a spiky, many-spired exterior constructed of stone on a Greek-cross plan with four porticos leading to two narrow vaulted concentric corridors for passage round a solid central block against which 30-ft-high statues of the Buddha stand; the elegant stucco-decorated Schwegugyi temple, smaller but with more interior space (1131); the Kubyaukgy temple (1215, restored 1468), a brick-built imitation of the Mahabodi shrine at Bodh Gaya, India; and the massive brick Mingalazedi stupa, begun in 1274. After the fall of Pagan the building of stupas continued at Pegu, Mingun and Rangoon. In 1857 a new capital was founded at Mandalay in northern Burma with an extensive, very intricately decorated wood-built royal palace, of which only a single pavilion survived destruction in the Second World War, in a square enclosure surrounded by walls and a moat. Buildings dating from the British occupation (beginning in south Burma in 1824) are numerous in Rangoon but undistinguished.

Burn, William (1789–1870), *see* SCOTTISH ARCHITECTURE; SHAW, Richard Norman.

Burnacini, Lodovico Ottavio (1636–1707), *see* AUSTRIAN ARCHITECTURE.

Burnet, John (1814–1901), *see* SCOTTISH ARCHITECTURE.

Burnham, Daniel Hudson (1846–1912), came of an old Massachusetts family. His father moved to Chicago, and there, after several false starts, the son went into an architect's office, where he met J. W. ROOT. The two went into partnership, an ideal pair: Root was poetic and versatile, Burnham practical and a skilled administrator. Burnham and Root have an important share in the evolution of the so-called CHICAGO SCHOOL. Their best-known buildings are the Montauk building (1881–2, demolished), which heralded the advent of the skyscraper; the Monadnock building (1889–91), still a load-bearing masonry structure,

though severely direct and unornamented; the Masonic Temple (1890–92, demolished), with its twenty-two storeys the tallest building in the world at the time it was built and with a complete steel skeleton (as introduced slightly before by HOLABIRD & ROCHE); the Reliance building, Chicago (1890 extended 1894); and the Flat-iron building in New York (1902). Burnham was made Chief of Construction for the World's Columbian Exposition in Chicago, which took place in 1893. Buildings were designed by HUNT, McKIM, Mead and WHITE, Charles B. Atwood (1849–95), POST, SULLIVAN, and others. The most monumental of them were classical and columnar, and this demonstration of BEAUX ARTS ideals cut short the life of the Chicago School. Later Burnham concentrated more and more on town and area planning: his plans for the District of Columbia (1901–2) are the start of comprehensive town planning in America. They were followed by the plan for Chicago (1906–9) and many others.

T. S. Hines, *B. of Chicago: Architect and Planner*, New York 1979.

Burton, Decimus (1800–1881). The son of James Burton (1761–1837), a successful London builder. As early as 1823 he designed the Colosseum in Regent's Park with a dome larger than that of St Paul's and a Greek Doric portico. It housed a panorama of London. In 1825 he began the Hyde Park Improvements which included the Hyde Park Corner screen. He designed several housing estates (e.g. at Tunbridge Wells, 1828 onwards), the centre of Fleetwood (1836–43), the great Palm Houses at Chatsworth (with PAXTON) and Kew (1844–8, with R.

Turner), many villas (e.g. some in Regent's Park), the Athenaeum, London (1829–30), and country houses.

Colvin 1978; Summerson 1983; G. R. Williams, *D.B.*, London 1984.

Buscheto or **Busketus** (*fl.* 1063–1110), *see* ITALIAN ARCHITECTURE.

Bush-hammering. A method of obtaining an even, rough, 'rusticated' texture on concrete after it has set, by using a bush-hammer (a mechanically operated percussion tool) with a specially grooved head which chips the surface.

Buszko, Henryk (b. 1924), *see* POLISH ARCHITECTURE.

Butterfield, William (1814–1900), a High-Church Gothic-Revivalist, was aloof in his life (a bachelor with a butler) and studious in his work. The peculiar aggressiveness of his forms – one jarring with the other – and of his colours – stone and multicoloured brick in stripes or geometrical patterns – was tolerated by the purists of the Cambridge Camden movement and their journal *The Ecclesiologist*, partly because he was their personal friend (he drew much for the *Instrumenta ecclesiastica* of 1847), partly because he must have had a great power of conviction. His earliest church (and parsonage) of importance was Coalpit Heath (1844). This was followed by St Augustine's College, Canterbury, quieter than most of his work. The eruption of his fully developed personal style came with All Saints, Margaret Street, London (1849–59), a ruthless composition in red brick of church and accessory buildings on three sides of a small courtyard. The steeple is slender, noble, north German Gothic, and asym-

metrically placed. St Matthias, Stoke Newington, London, followed in 1850–52 – yellow brick, with a nave crossed by two transverse arches; then St Alban's, Holborn, London, in 1863; Keble College, Oxford, in 1867–75; the Rugby School buildings in 1870–86; and many others. Nearly all his work, apart from that for colleges and schools, was ecclesiastical. An exception is the robustly utilitarian County Hospital at Winchester (1863). His early cottages (*c.* 1848–50) are also remarkably free from HISTORICISM. They are the pattern for WEBB's Red House.

P. Thompson, *W.B.*, London 1971; Hitchcock 1977.

Buttress. A mass of masonry or brickwork projecting from or built against a wall to give additional strength, usually to counteract the lateral thrust of an arch, roof, or vault.

Angle buttresses. Two meeting at an angle of 90° at the angle of a building.

Clasping buttress. One which encases the angle.

Diagonal buttress. One placed against the right angle formed by two walls, and more or less equiangular with both.

Flying buttress. An arch or half-arch transmitting the thrust of a vault or roof from the upper part of a wall to an outer support or buttress.

Lateral buttress. A buttress standing at the corner of a building on axis with one wall.

Pier buttress. An exterior pier which counteracts the thrust of a vault or arch.

Setback buttress. A buttress set slightly back from the angle. *See* Fig. 21.

Byzantine architecture. The culmination of Early Christian architecture. This style developed after AD 330 when

Angle buttress   Diagonal buttress   Setback buttress   Clasping buttress

Flying buttress

FIG. 21. *Buttress*

Constantine established the Imperial capital at Byzantium (renamed Constantinople) on the Bosphorus. The arts in Rome were then at a low ebb, but no efforts were spared to make the new capital as traditionally Roman as possible. Such a building as the aqueduct of Valens differs little from those built in the West during the previous 300 years. But gradually a new and original style emerged. Classical concepts, such as the ORDERS, were no longer observed; classical detail of all kinds was coarsened and the lush relief decorations popular in Rome were abandoned in favour of flat, rather lacy ornaments. Early c5 churches in Cilicia (e.g. Kandirli and Cambazli), built in a mixture of Syrian and Roman styles, suggest that some of the new influences came from the East. The later c5 church of St John in Studion, Constantinople, also shows a tendency to depart from classical precepts. Yet classicism, or at least a desire to recapture the splendours of the classical past, was to remain a force of recurrent importance throughout Byzantine art, especially in the secular arts where the taint of paganism probably mattered less to early Christians. Very little is known of Byzantine domestic architecture, but recent excavations have revealed that the Imperial Palace in Constantinople was among the greatest buildings of its time.

In the c5 two forms of church were evolved: the BASILICA and the centrally planned church reserved for the shrines of martyrs. The latter, called *martyria*, were usually built on a Greek cross plan and were domed – the combination of a dome with a square base being a Byzantine introduction from the Near East. It was the achievement of c6 architects to combine these two forms of church and to create interiors in which a wholly unclassical play of void and solid, dark and light, produced an effect of mystery which is perhaps the most striking feature of the Byzantine church. The outstanding masterpiece of Byzantine church architecture, Hagia Sophia, Constantinople (built AD 532–7 by ANTHEMIOS of TRALLES and ISIDORUS OF MILETUS), shows this quality to perfection. But it was the mathematical and intellectual rather than the emotive qualities of Hagia Sophia that impressed contemporaries. 'Through the harmony of its measurements it is distinguished by indescribable beauty,' wrote Procopius. The same author commented that 'a spherical-shaped Tholos standing upon a circle makes it exceedingly beautiful'. At this time mathematics was considered the highest of the sciences, and Anthemios was a notable mathematician who believed that architecture was 'the application of geometry to solid matter'.

By the c9 symbolism began to play a greater part in Byzantine church architecture. The church was now regarded as a microcosm of all earth and sky, as the setting of Christ's life on earth, and at the same time as the image of the liturgical year. This complex triple symbolism was expressed in painted or mosaic decorations where the very colours used had an emblematic significance. The mystique of numbers also found reflection in church design. To the Byzantine these intellectual concepts were as important as the air of mystery created by screens and galleries dividing the well-lit central area from those surrounding it. The typical Byzantine CROSS-IN-SQUARE church plan (a Greek cross inscribed in a square and capped by a central dome and subsidiary domes) provided a perfect background for the display of this elaborate painted or mosaic decoration.

As early as the C5 the Byzantine style began to influence architecture in Italy, especially Ravenna (S. Giovanni Battista, S. Croce, and the so-called Mausoleum of Galla Placidia). The basilican S. Apollinare in Classe, Ravenna (c. 536–50), and the octagonal S. Vitale, Ravenna (c. 526–47), are among the greatest and least altered of all Byzantine buildings. Though erected by Byzantine architects, and probably by Byzantine masons as well, both reveal slight Western peculiarities, notably in the decoration of the exterior. Later, Western buildings began to show more radical departures from Byzantine precedents – e.g. S. Marco, Venice, with its very rich marble-clad exterior.

The C7–9 marked a prolonged crisis for Byzantine civilization, under threat not only from external enemies (Persians, Arabs, Bulgars, etc.) but from the protracted and enigmatic internal schisms of the Iconoclast controversy – whose resolution in favour of the holy images (843) had not only theological but important aesthetic consequences for East Christian art and architecture, henceforth to be comprehensively and organically linked. The Middle Byzantine (i.e. C9–12) decorative system – representations of sacred persons and events, disposed with the more 'heavenly' scenes in the higher and eastern parts of the building, utilizing glass mosaic or true fresco and tempera panel-paintings (icons) – predicated appropriate architectural forms, of which the cross-in-square church, whose elements were picturesquely massed so as to culminate in a central dome on a tall drum resting (via pendentives or squin-

ches) on four columns or piers, developed in this age as the characteristic type. To the basic quincunx of the ground-plan various additions or modifications could be made: these normally included three apses to the east and one or more narthexes (porches) to the west; subsidiary domes were often placed over the corner-bays.

The cross-in-square church-type – particularly suitable for smaller buildings – proliferated and refined itself throughout the middle and late (i.e. post-1261) Byzantine periods; in Russia it outlived the Fall of Constantinople (1453) by at least two centuries. Its spread coincided with greater attention not only to the interior but to the exterior surfaces of the masonry: polychrome brick, stone and plaster-work, ceramic inlays, chiselled mouldings, low-relief sculpture, pseudo-Kufic 'lettering' become common decorative features. Though this can lead in late examples to fussiness, it generally gives Byzantine architecture a renewed liveness and joyful picturesqueness of total effect (cf. C14 examples such as Holy Apostles, Salonica or Pammakaristos, Constantinople). A small but important group of C11–12 churches (Hosios Loukas, Dafni, etc.) are built on a grander scale, their comparatively wide domes supported on an octagon of piers. Basilican plans do not entirely die out; most such churches are small, but an example impressive in its C11 remodelling is St Sofia at Ohrid, Yugoslavia. The later Byzantine period has also left us some scanty remains of domestic architecture: the palace known as Tekfur Saray in Constantinople, several monastic *ensembles* (notably on Mount Athos).

At no stage is it easy to define the

geographical scope of Byzantine architecture, and the problem becomes particularly acute from the middle Byzantine period onwards: while the actual frontiers of the Empire tended to contract, its missionary activity and cultural prestige grew throughout Eastern and (more sporadically) Western Europe. 'Provincial' architecture from Aachen to Armenia, from Sicily to the White Sea, exhibits a wide variety of forms that are in obvious respects related to the Byzantine heritage, while they can with equal justice be placed in the context of the early development of national traditions. The religious division of Europe into Roman Catholic and Orthodox did not make itself deeply evident until the Western sack of Constantinople (1204), after which the cultural community of the East Christian world tends to be more closely felt. While, however, Constantinople continued to the end to be the chief focus for cultural endeavour in Eastern Europe and the chief repository (in particular) of classicizing tendencies in art and architecture, the history of so-called Byzantine architecture is by the late Middle Ages more and more to be read in the variety of surviving monuments originating beyond the direct sphere of Constantinopolitan influence – though this was capable of reasserting itself at any time up to the Fall. We shall therefore briefly examine each of the main national schools of East Christian architecture in turn.

The Transcaucasian states (Armenia and Georgia), Christian since the c4, preserve an exceptional wealth of building in fine local stone from all periods. Both basilican and (very inventive) centralizing plans are met with throughout, but particularly outstanding are some well-preserved dome churches from the beginning of c6 (St Hripsime at Etchmiadzin, Armenia, and Dzhvari at Mtskheta, Georgia); they seem more closely related to the Near-Eastern church architecture of Syria than to anything in Constantinople, and the extent to which Armenian builders actually originated (rather than followed) certain developments in Byzantine and even Western European architecture has been the subject of much inconclusive debate. By the beginning of the c11 great domed basilicas such as the cathedral of Ani, Armenia, and Sveti-Tskoveli, Mtskheta, have developed vaulting systems and decorative features that startlingly foreshadow the vocabulary of Romanesque and even Gothic church architecture. The massing of forms in smaller churches (e.g. Metekhi at Tbilisi, Georgia, 1278) has a more Byzantine feel. But certain features remain characteristic of the architecture of the region: low-relief patterned carving (sometimes figurative – notably at Aghthamar, Armenia, c10) and prominent mouldings; faceted domes on high polygonal drums; a tendency for the external ground-plan to conceal rather than reveal the inner articulation. Independent Armenian architecture was extinguished with Armenia itself in the late Middle Ages, but in Georgia impressive (though no longer innovative) churches were still being produced in the c17 (Ananuri). Both countries preserve a certain amount of early secular building (e.g. the c13 monastic refectory of Hagartsin, Armenia; many fortresses in Georgia).

In Bulgaria, an independent and powerful state from the c7 to the early c11, excavations have revealed remarkable and extensive remains of the early palace complex at Pliska and the so-called Round Church at Preslav. The Byzantine coastal outpost of Mesembria (Nesebur) preserves, despite earthquake damage, a wealth of middle to late Byzantine churches; from the second period of Bulgarian independence (c13–14) many small cross-in-square and basilican churches survive in the capital, Turnovo, and elsewhere. After the Turkish conquest Bulgaria is notable for the quality of its vernacular wooden houses (at Arbanasi, Plovdiv, Ohrid – now in Yugoslavia – etc.).

Serbia became a unified state in the late c12, and a large number of interesting buildings survive from that time until Turkish domination became complete in 1459. Characteristic of the great c13 monastic churches such as Studenica, Mileševo, and Sopoćani (the Raška School) is the combination of Romanesque exterior features, derived through the Dalmatian coast, with the full and magnificent interior decorative scheme of an Orthodox domed basilica. The last and most ambitious of this series is Dečani (1327), said to contain the largest surviving area of medieval fresco-painting in the world. In the c14 Serbia expanded southwards, and the cross-in-square plan, often multi-domed, becomes usual. A magnificently ingenious variant of this is the pyramidally tiered church of Gračanica (1326). In the reduced Serbian state of c15 architectural activity and innovation continue with a series of buildings (the Morava School) of tall, narrow proportions, an abundance of external decoration and a trefoil ground plan at the east end derived from churches on Mount Athos. The most remarkable and monumental work of the Morava School is probably the fortress-monastery of Manasija (1407). At Smederevo, the last capital, an extensive citadel with walls recalling those of Constantinople was built (1444 onwards).

Romanian architecture in the old heartlands of Wallachia and Moldavia carried on where Serbian architecture left off. No masonry churches survive from before the c14; though there are early examples at Cozia and Curtea-de-Argeş (St Nicholas) in Wallachia and at Radauţi in Moldavia, the 'golden age' of Romanian architecture starts in the post-Byzantine period at the turn of the c15–16 and lasts into the c17. In comparison with Serbian Morava architecture, Romanian churches are even more ornate, casket-like, elongated, tall, narrow, and fancifully adorned, with the occasional admixture of imported decorative features (e.g. Gothic window tracery). Most notable and original is a group of Moldavian churches decorated between c. 1520 and 1600 with complete cycles of frescoes on the exterior (protected by overhanging eaves) as well as inside. The most bizarrely impressive building is the monastic cathedral at Curtea de Argeş (1517), representing a post-Byzantine mannerism whose extreme forms are equalled only in the near-contemporary St Basil's in Moscow (no direct connection is to be postulated).

RUSSIAN ARCHITECTURE is dealt with separately; Byzantine masons and mosaicists worked in c11 Kiev, and cross-in-square forms established themselves firmly from an early stage: the Byzantine heritage was not fully worked out until the post-Petrine modern age.

Finally, it must be noted that certain Greek areas (Trebizond, the 'monastic republic' of Mount Athos) remained independent of Constantinople in the late Byzantine period, and developed their own architectural traditions – notably the Athonite monastic cathedral-type, with cross-arms ending in semicircular apses, that was to provide the basic ground-plan for late Serbian and Romanian churches.

The Fall of Constantinople (1453) and Turkish conquest of the Balkans brought Byzantine architecture in the former Empire to an effective end; church architecture became extremely modest, externally visible domes a rarity. Turned in on itself, Orthodox architecture in the next four centuries developed aesthetic originality in only one direction: the vernacular art of elaborately carved wooden icon-screens, whose charm could only partially compensate for the rapid decline not only in architectural form, but in the decorative schemes of wall-paintings and icons. [R. R. Milner-Gulland]

Krautheimer 1986; C. Mango, *Byzantine Architecture*, London 1986.

C

FIG. 22. *Cable moulding*

Cable moulding. A Romanesque moulding imitating a twisted cord. *See* Fig. 22.

Cable structures, *see* OTTO, Frei.

Cabled fluting, *see* FLUTING.

Caen stone. Stone from Caen, Normandy, used in English medieval buildings.

Cagnola, Marchese Luigi (1762–1833). A neo-classical architect who played a leading role in the Napoleonic transformation of Milan, designing the severe Ionic Porta Ticinese (1801–14) and the much richer Arco della Pace (1806–38). He also designed a Pantheon-like parish church at Ghisalba (c. 1830), a fantastic campanile crowned with CANEPHORAE supporting a dome at Urgnano (c. 1820), and his own many-columned Grecian villa Inverigo (begun 1813).

Meeks 1966; G. Mezzanotte, *Architettura neoclassica in Lombardia*, Naples 1966; P. Favole in *DBI* 1973.

Caisson. 1. An air chamber, resembling a well, driven down to a firm foundation stratum in the soil and filled with concrete. It is used for construction below water (e.g. for the piers of a bridge) or on water-logged ground. 2. A sunken panel in a flat or vaulted ceiling (*see* COFFERING).

Caldarium. The hot-room in a Roman bath.

Calderini, Guglielmo (1837–1916), *see* ITALIAN ARCHITECTURE.

Callicrates was the leading architect in Periclean Athens, and with ICTINUS designed the Parthenon (447–438 BC). He probably designed and built the exquisite little Ionic temple of Athena Nike on the Acropolis, Athens (448–after 421 BC). He also built the south and central portion of the Long Walls from Athens to Piraeus, and perhaps restored part of the city walls.

R. Carpenter, *The Architects of the Parthenon*, Harmondsworth 1970.

Calotte, *see* DOME.

Camarín. A small chapel behind and above the high altar in Spanish churches. It is usually visible from the nave. The earliest example is in the church of the Desamparados in Valencia (1647–67).

Camber. Of a horizontal timber, usually a tie-beam or a collar-beam (*see* ROOF), in which the centre is higher than the ends.

Cambio, Arnolfo di (*c.* 1245–*c.* 1310), *see* ARNOLFO DI CAMBIO.

Cambodian architecture, *see* KHMER ARCHITECTURE.

Came. A metal strip used for LEADED LIGHTS.

Cameron, Charles (*c.* 1743–1812), son of a London mason, visited Rome 1766–9, and published *The Baths of the Romans* in 1772. Nothing more is known of him until he was summoned to Russia in 1779 by Catherine the Great. He lived there for the rest of his life. For Catherine he decorated several apartments in RASTRELLI'S palace at Tsarskoe Selo (now Pushkin) near Leningrad (1780–85), and also designed the Agate Pavilion and Cameron Gallery there. For the Grand Duke Paul he built the great palace at Pavlovsk (1782–5) and the circular Doric peripteral Temple of Friendship in the English Park – the first of its kind in Russia. In about 1787 he was superseded as architect-in-chief by his pupil Vincenzo Brenna (1745–1820), and when Catherine died in 1796 he was dismissed from royal service. But he stayed on in Russia, building for private patrons, e.g. the Razumovsky Palace at Baturin in the Ukraine (1799–1802, unfinished). He returned to favour after the death of Paul I, and in 1805 designed the naval hospital and barracks at Kronstadt. He was an admirer and close follower of CLÉRISSEAU and Robert ADAM, especially in interior decoration, though lacking Adam's finesse.

T. Talbot-Rice and A. A. Tait (eds.), *Charles Cameron*, exh. cat., Edinburgh and London 1967–8; A. Kuchamov, *Pavlosk, Palace and Park*, Leningrad 1975.

Campanile. The Italian word for a bell-tower, usually separate from the main building. The earliest surviving Italian campanili are at Ravenna – circular and probably of the C9. The earliest recorded campanile was square and was attached to St Peter's in Rome. It went back to the mid C8.

Campbell, Colen (1676–1729). Little is known about him until 1715, when the first volume of *Vitruvius Britannicus* appeared and he built Wanstead House (now demolished), which became the model for large English Palladian country houses. With Baldersby Park, Yorkshire (1720–28), he initiated the neo-Palladian villa. He was probably responsible for Lord BURLINGTON'S conversion to PALLADIANISM and was comissioned to remodel Burlington House, London (1718–19). Mereworth Castle (1722–5) is perhaps the best of the English versions of Palladio's Rotonda design. Houghton Hall (1721, executed with modifications by Ripley) is enormous and imposing, but Ebberston Lodge, near Scarborough (1718), and Compton Place, Eastbourne (1726–7), are more elegant and refined.

H. E. Stutchbury, *The Architecture of C.C.*, Manchester 1967; Summerson 1983; Harris 1990.

Campen, Jacob van **Kampen** or (1595–1657). A wealthy and erudite painter-architect and the leading exponent of Dutch PALLADIANISM, an unpretentious, placid and economic form of classicism characterized by its use of brick mixed with stone and its straightforward, almost diagrammatic use of pilasters. He studied in Italy and probably knew SCAMOZZI, who certainly influenced him greatly, rather more indeed than Palladio. Van

Campen's style is epitomized in his masterpiece the Mauritshuis, The Hague (1633–5), entirely Palladian in plan, with giant Ionic pilasters, raised on a low ground floor and supporting a pediment, crowned with a typically Dutch hipped roof rising in a slightly concave line from the eaves. His great Town Hall in Amsterdam (now the Royal Palace: 1648–55), built entirely of stone, is heavier but very imposing – the grandest of all town halls. More original is the Nieuwe Kerk in Haarlem (1645–9), of the Greek CROSS-IN-SQUARE type. He also designed the Coymans house on the Keizersgracht, Amsterdam (1624), the earliest example of Palladianism in Holland, the Noordeinde Palace, The Hague (1640), and the Accijnhuis and theatre in Amsterdam (1637). With Christian Huygens he was responsible for the general conception of decoration by Jordaens and others in Pieter POST's Huis-ten-Bosch. His domestic style had great influence through his followers Post, Arend van 's GRAVESANDE and Philip VINGBOONS. And it was later introduced into England by Hugh MAY and others.

K. Freemantle, *The Baroque Town Hall of Amsterdam,* Utrecht 1959; Kuyper 1980.

Campus. A self-contained architectural composition of separate buildings arranged round a park-like expanse of lawn, often sited in open country, housing a community of students and scholars. It superseded the medieval quadrangle arrangement for universities. The first was Downing College, Cambridge, by WILKINS, begun 1806, though it seems to have been unknown to JEFFERSON when he conceived the University of Virginia at Charlot-

tesville (1817–26). This was very influential and began a long tradition of university building in the USA – right up to the present day, e.g. Eero SAARINEN's Morse and Stiles Colleges at Yale.

R. P. Dober, *Campus Planning*, New York 1964; P. V. Turner, *Campuses: An American Planning Tradition*, Cambridge, Mass., 1984.

Canadian architecture. History and geography combined to make Canada a colony first of France, then of Britain and finally, a nation entirely dependent for its continuing existence – unacknowledged as the fact may be – on the armed forces of a benevolent neighbouring power. Its architecture manifests these circumstances.

Not that it is necessarily impoverishing to follow rather than lead. Excesses and exaggerations can thereby be successfully avoided. The best of the past is oftenest preserved where pressure for innovation is least. In architecture, as in speech, colonies preserve forms longer than mother countries. Occasionally too, striking combinations of new and old can result from colonial conditions. All of which principles are demonstrable in Canadian architectural history.

For example, the parish church architecture evolved in mid-C17 French Canada constituted for all intents and purposes a genuinely creative response to colonial conditions. Its fusion of a Romanesque tradition, common from Carolingian times on, with certain up-to-date C17 Baroque details has a few parallels in France in locales where conditions roughly approximated those in Quebec, but is not a copy of anything in France. A good many examples of this architecture are known from old photographs and drawings – e.g. the parish church at St Laurent, Île d'Orléans, begun 1695, façade reconstructed 1708 by Jean Maillou (1668–1753, Royal Architect of New France), demolished 1864; Ste-Anne-de-Beaupré (built 1689 by master-mason Claude Baillif, demolished 1878); the old parish church of Les Trois-Rivières with Louis Quinze interior (1710, burnt out 1908). The best extant example is the chapel of the Ursuline Convent in Quebec, with its *récollette* retable executed 1734–9 by Noël Levasseur (1680–1740) and his cousin Pierre-Noël (1690–1770).

So distinctive was this church-type that after the Cession of 1763 it was successfully revived as a symbol of French resistance to assimilation in the form of a standard plan devised by Abbé Pierre Conefroy (1752–1816) which was applied in over thirty parish churches around Montreal, the region most threatened with assimilation. Good surviving examples are the churches of Lacadie (1801) and St Mathias, Rouville (1813). Conefroy's own church at Boucherville still stands, built in 1813, but considerably altered by later additions. This body of architecture is one of the earliest examples anywhere of typically C19 architectural eclecticism for associative reasons.

In the C19 parish organization remained the chief institution ensuring survival of a distinctive French culture in North America: accordingly, the C19 parish churches of Quebec constituted its most notable architecture. In the Quebec region, Thomas Baillairgé (1791–1859) created a body of architecture worthy in many respects of a place in any history of world architecture, even though his climactic effort, the

façade of the Basilica of Quebec, was abortive (1844–6). St Joseph Lauzon (1830–32, enlarged by insertion of an extra section in the nave, 1954) is a good representative example of Baillairgé's single-spired church-type; of his twin-towered façades Deschambault (1834–8) is characteristic (this design also includes deliberate reminiscences of the 1803 Anglican cathedral of Quebec and the 1666–1807 Jesuit church in Quebec). Best-known and indeed a unique *pièce d'occasion* is the triple-towered façade of Ste-Famille, Île d'Orléans, resulting from Baillairgé's addition of a central spire in 1843 to mark the centenary of the original 1743 twin-towered structure.

Montreal's two major C19 churches are also important examples of eclectic architectural symbolism. Notre Dame, the 1722 parish church built by the Sulpicians, was replaced in 1824–9 by one of the continent's earliest and largest Gothic Revival churches, designed by an Irishman from Brooklyn, James O'Donnel (1774–1830). It was commissioned, apparently, with a view to asserting French Catholic presence in the English Protestant part of Montreal by a design supposed to resemble the medieval cathedral of Notre Dame in Paris – the whole concept being related to the Bourbon restoration and the Gothic Revival of 1815–35 in France. The Cathedral of St Jacques was one of the last examples of the medieval practice of architects being sent to copy other buildings for associative reasons. Its genesis was in a visit to Rome by the diocesan architect, Victor Bourgeau (1809–88), commissioned by the Bishop of Montreal, Ignace Bourget, in 1870 for the purpose of reproducing St Peter's on a reduced scale as a new Montreal cathedral to symbolize Canadian support for the Holy See in its contest with Italian liberalism. Built in 1875–85 by Joseph Michaud (1822–1902) with Bourgeau's collaboration, this replica of St Peter's may still be seen in the heart of Montreal.

The bulk of English Canada's architectural history consists of later styles. Already in 1750 a typical variant of Gibbs's parish church-type with Palladian detail had appeared in Halifax – St Paul's, whose frame was prefabricated in Boston (almost totally altered by remodellings in 1812 and 1867). But the bulk of these churches date from the Loyalist time after the American Revolution when they had ceased to appear, for obvious reasons, in the old colonies. Typical were churches like St Mary's, Auburn, Nova Scotia (1790); St Stephen's, Chester, Nova Scotia (1795), in the diocese of the violently anti-American bishop Charles Inglis; Holy Trinity, Quebec (designed in 1803 by Major William Rose, one of a typical family of soldiers and Empire administrators) and St George, Kingston, Ontario (designed in 1859 by George Browne of Belfast). c18 Baroque was likewise perpetuated in public buildings in early Upper Canada as a symbol of devotion to the Old Empire, e.g. Kingston's City Hall (1843 by George Browne); Victoria Hall, Cobourg (1856–60 by Kivus Tully of Belfast); Osgoode Law Courts, Toronto (1829 and later, original design by John Ewart); and St Lawrence Hall, Toronto (1850 by William Thomas).

A late Gothic Revival superseded Georgian in English Canada from c. 1840, shading into Italianate predominance by c. 1860, thence into miscellaneous picturesqueness. Ecclesiologist architects designed cathedrals for St John's, Newfoundland (1846–85, substantially by the two Gilbert SCOTTS and Fredericton (1843, substantially completed to designs by BUTTERFIELD), but these are more transplanted English than Canadian architecture. The most striking Canadian examples of picturesque mid-c19 styles come in a body of polychromatic brick farmhouses in southern Ontario from the 1870s to 1890s, their distinctive decorative detail deriving from a revealing complex of British origins – High Gothic Revival of medieval polychromy by Pugin, Butterfield and Ruskin plus characteristic Nonconformist middle-class industrial and commercial architecture as well as housing and small shop-fronts, throughout the Midlands, Ulster and Lowland Scotland. The Late Victorian similarly persisted in Canada a good generation after losing its dominance in Britain. Edward Lennox's Casa Loma, Toronto (1911), for example, is essentially the kind of adapted Scottish Baronial employed in Sir James Gowans's houses in Edinburgh in the 1870s and '80s (not to mention Balmoral Castle).

This *retardataire* pattern changed somewhat in modern times with the versatile Ernest Cormier (1885–1980), whose Art Deco building for the University of Montreal (1928–55), classicizing Supreme Court, Ottawa (1938–50), and curtain-wall National Printing Bureau, Hull (1950–58), should be mentioned. Works like the Malton International Airport, Toronto (1963–6), the Union Railway Station, Ottawa (1969), and the New National Gallery of Canada, Ottawa (1976), all by John C. Parkin (b. 1922); the City Hall, Toronto (1958–64), by Viljo Revell (1910–64); and, more recently, Simon Fraser University, Burnaby, British

Canadian architecture

Columbia (1963–5), and Lethbridge University, Alberta (1971), by Arthur ERICKSON, or Scarborough College, Ontario (1962–9 with additions 1972), and Student Housing Complex, Guelph University, Ontario (1965–8), by John ANDREWS, must certainly count as major examples of current *avant-garde* modes. All major Canadian cities have examples of modern urban layouts and total environments: Place Ville-Marie, Montreal (1960 by I. M. PEI for William Zeckendorf) and Dominion Centre, Toronto (1963–9 by MIES VAN DER ROHE), being the best-known perhaps. Also famous internationally, as a result of Expo '67, was Moshe SAFDIE's Habitat, a seminal example of mass housing. St Mary's Church, Red Deer, Alberta (1968), and the Kehewen (1975) and later schools in Alberta, all by Douglas Cardinal (b. 1934) are notable. More recently the City Hall, Mississauga, Toronto (1986–8), by Edward Jones (b. 1939) in a classicizing POST-MODERN style *à la* LEDOUX is outstanding.

Special conditions in Canada have resulted in a number of outstanding works of historic architecture. University College, the main and for long the only building of Toronto University, designed in 1856 by William Frederick Cumberland (1821–81), a classmate and friend of John Ruskin at Oxford, has been compared to the Oxford Museum, designed on Ruskin's principles by Deane and Woodward; but University College is a better example of those principles, and an earlier one – a major monument of High Victorian picturesque eclectic style, as well as the typical High Victorian formal block with centre and corner towers. The design for the Dominion Parliament Buildings in Ottawa (1859, completed 1866, destroyed by fire in 1916 except for the Library, and rebuilt in a chastened vein), by Thomas Fuller (1822–98), clearly followed the mode of University College but Gothicized the detail to conform with Westminster Palace and express continuity of tradition between Old Britain and New Canada. Thus came into being a Canadian national style, carried through in many other government buildings all over the country, and most dramatically in the '*château*-style' hotels erected by the Canadian Pacific Railroad and its competitors from the 1880s into the 1930s. Its most representative examples are Château Frontenac, Quebec, and the Empress, Victoria, both dating from the 1890s and early c20, both deliberately composed as symbols of Canadian nationality marking the eastern and western entrances to the country by sea – and with Scottish castle details making both, as more than one critic has suggested, climactic monuments to Canada's status as a 'Scotch colony' in those first five decades when Canadian politics, business, railroading, journalism and homesteading were decisively dominated by Scottish immigrants.

Finally, any history of Canadian architecture should refer to the remarkable body of domestic architecture by Samuel Maclure of Victoria (1867–1929) in response to a curious social situation existing in the capital of British Columbia between 1890 and 1930 whereby an entire governing class effectively withdrew from concern with practical affairs to create an ideal world of retirement and refined leisure, the very image of *rentier* capitalism at its height. For this clientele, Maclure created a series of remarkable houses, mostly Tudor in detail, perfectly manifesting the values and lifestyles of an expatriate British aristocracy. Most still survive, typical examples being the Biggarstaff Wilson and John J. Shallcross houses in Victoria (1905–6 and 1907) and the Hon. Walter C. Nicol house in Sidney (1925). With his partner Cecil Croker Fox, Maclure also designed a number of mansions and public buildings for magnates in booming Vancouver, e.g. Boys Residential School, now RCMP headquarters (1914).

The impressive restorations undertaken by successive Canadian governments after the Second World War should be mentioned, notably Fort Louisbourg on Cape Breton Island, Nova Scotia, and the Hudson's Bay Post at Lower Fort Garry, Manitoba. [A. Gowans]

Cancelli. In early Christian architecture, a latticed screen or grille separating the choir from the main body of a church.

Candela, Felix (b. 1910), was born in Spain but has lived in Mexico since 1939. He is one of the most resourceful concrete engineers of the age, notably for SHELL vaulting, and is also important architecturally. He was inspired initially by TORROJA. Among his most significant works, both in Mexico City, are the Church of Our Lady of Miracles (1953–5), an extreme example of mid-century EXPRESSIONISM, and the Cosmic Ray Pavilion, University City (1952), which is a tiny four-legged shed with a HYPERBOLIC PARABOLOID roof only about 1 in. thick at the ridge. Later buildings by Candela are the Chapel of the Missionaries of the Holy Spirit at Coyoacán (1956, with Enrique de la Mora) with a simple saddle-shaped canopy on rough stone walls;

the restaurant at Xochimilco (1958, with Joaquín Alvarez Ordóñez) placed in the water gardens like an eight-petalled flower of paraboloids; the Market Hall at Coyoacán (1956, with Pedro Ramírez Vásquez and Rafael Mijares) with the mushroom-shaped umbrellas which Candela has since used at the John Lewis warehouse, Stevenage, England (1963, with Yorke, Rosenberg and Mardall); and the Olympic Stadium (Mexico City 1968). From 1971 to 1978 he taught at the University of Illinois, Chicago.

C. Faber, *C. The Shell Builder*, New York and London 1963; C. B. Smith, *Builders in the Sun: Five Mexican Architects*, New York 1967.

Candi. Javanese term for an ancient temple or shrine (*see* JAVANESE ARCHITECTURE).

Candid, Peter, or Peter de Wit or de Witte (1548–1628). MANNERIST painter and architect, born in Bruges. He was the son of a Flemish sculptor, Elias de Witte, with whom he went to Florence c. 1573. He studied painting in Italy, perhaps under VASARI, and worked as a painter both in Florence and Rome. In 1586 he settled in Munich under the patronage of Duke Wilhelm V and Maximilian I, who had already attracted thither Friedrich SUSTRIS and the Mannerist sculptor Hubert Gerhard. Candid was involved as an architect in the later stages of the building of the Munich Residenz.

Hitchcock 1981.

Candilis, Georges (b. 1903). Russian-born French architect and town-planner. With LE CORBUSIER 1945–50 and from 1955 with Alexis Josic (b. 1921) and Shadrach Woods (1923–73). They planned the new towns of

FIG. 23. *Cantilever beam*

Bagnols-sur-Cèze (1956) and Toulouse le Mirail (1964–77) and designed a complex of buildings for the Free University, Berlin-Dahlem (1967–79). In 1977 he published *Bâtir la vie: Un architecte témoin de son temps*.

Canephora. A sculptured female figure carrying a basket on her head.

Canes, *see* QUARRY.

Canevale, Isidore (1730–86), *see* HUNGARIAN ARCHITECTURE.

Canina, Luigi (1795–1856), *see* AS-PRUCCI, Antonio.

Canopy. A hood suspended or projected over a door, window, tomb, altar, pulpit, niche, etc.

Canterbury, *see* MICHAEL OF CANTERBURY.

Cantilever. A horizontal projection (e.g. a step, balcony, beam or canopy) supported by a downward force behind a fulcrum. It is without external bracing and thus appears to be self-supporting. *See* Fig. 23.

Cantoria. Italian term for a singers' gallery, sometimes a prominent feature in Italian Renaissance churches, e.g. those of marble with reliefs by Andrea della Robbia and Donatello (Museo dell'Opera del Duomo, Florence).

Cap. The crowning feature of a windmill, usually a domical roof; also an abbreviation for CAPITAL.

Cap house. A small roofed super-structure to a stair leading to a parapet walk.

Cape Dutch architecture, *see* SOUTH AFRICAN ARCHITECTURE.

Capital. The head or crowning feature of a column.

Aeolic capital. See ORDER.

Basket capital. A Byzantine form, hemispherical or approximately so, decorated with a wicker design like a basket.

Bell capital. A form of capital of which the chief characteristic is a reversed bell between the SHAFT or NECKING and the upper moulding. The bell is often enriched with carving.

Block capital, see cushion capital.

Crocket capital. An Early Gothic form, consisting of stylized leaves with endings rolled over similar to small VOLUTES.

Cube capital, see cushion capital.

Cushion capital. A Romanesque and Byzantine capital cut from a cube, with its lower parts rounded off to adapt it to a circular shaft; the remaining flat face of each side is generally a LUNETTE. Also called a *block* or *cube capital.*

Lotus capital. An ancient Egyptian type in the form of a lotus bud.

Palm capital. An ancient Egyptian type, like the crown of a palm tree.

Protomai capital. A capital with half-figures, usually animals, projecting from its four corners.

Scalloped capital. A development of the *block* or *cushion capital* in which the single lunette on each face is elaborated into one or more truncated cones.

See also STIFF-LEAF; WATER-LEAF; and, for capitals in classical architecture, ORDER. *See* Figs. 24, 66.

KEY:
1. Cushion
2. Scalloped
3. Water-leaf
4. Crocket
5. Stiff-leaf

FIG. 24. *Capital*

Caracol or **caracole**. A spiral staircase (*see* STAIR).

Caratti, Francesco (d. 1677), was born at Bissone near Como, and went in 1652 to Prague, where he became the leading architect. His masterpiece is the Černin Palace (begun 1668), with a row of thirty giant attached Corinthian columns and a rusticated basement which breaks forward to provide bases for the columns and bulges out into a central porch. The strong chiaroscuro created by the projections makes this façade one of the most exciting of its

time. He also built the Mary Magdalen Church, Prague (begun 1656), and the east wing of the palace at Roudnice (1665).

Hempel 1965.

Cardinal, Douglas J. (b. 1934), *see* CANADIAN ARCHITECTURE.

Carlone, Carl Martin (1616–67), *see* HUNGARIAN ARCHITECTURE.

Carlone, Carlo Antonio (d. 1708), is the most important member of a large family of Italian artists working in Austria and south Germany. His masterpiece is the richly stuccoed interior of the Italianate Priory Church of St Florian (1686–1705). Other works include the Jesuitenkirche zu den Neun Chören der Engel, Vienna (1662), with a rather secular street façade, and the charming little pilgrimage church of Christkindl (begun 1706), which was finished by PRANDTAUER, who was much indebted to Carlone.

Brucker 1983.

Carolingian architecture takes its name from Charlemagne (King from 768, Emperor 800–814) and his descendants and the style extends in time from the late c8 into the c10, and in space through those countries which formed part of Charlemagne's Empire, especially France, Germany, and the Netherlands. Anglo-Saxon architecture in England and Asturian architecture in Spain stand outside this style, which is composite and the result of conflicting trends in these formative centuries of Western civilization. Charlemagne himself promoted a renaissance of Roman – i.e. Constantinian – Christianity. This is evident in poetry, in script, in illumination, and also in the plans and elevations of cer-

tain churches which follow Early Christian examples (St Denis, Fulda, etc.). But indigenous characteristics also make themselves felt and point forward to the ROMANESQUE. In this category are prominent towers, strongly stressed west ends and east ends (Centula, plan for St Gall), and also heavier, more massive members. The most spectacular building preserved from Charlemagne's time is the Palatine chapel at Aachen, designed by Odo of Metz, begun in 792 and dedicated 805. *See also* GERMAN ARCHITECTURE; FRENCH ARCHITECTURE.
Conant 1979.

Carpenter's Gothic. Contemporary term for the early GOTHIC REVIVAL in England, e.g. designs by Batty LANGLEY; later used in the USA for C19 building with much exterior woodwork incorporating Gothic motifs.
A. de C. and D. B. McArdle, *C.G.*, New York (1978) 1983.

Carr, John (1723–1807). A late and provincial exponent of PALLADIANISM, working mainly in Yorkshire. He began life as a mason in his father's quarry near Wakefield, and in his twenties built Kirby Hall to the design of Lord BURLINGTON and Roger MORRIS. He was later associated with Robert ADAM in the building of Harewood House (begun 1759). From then onwards he designed and built many large country houses. He was unoriginal, but could be refined and dignified in a quiet way, e.g., Denton Park (*c.* 1778) and Farnley Hall (*c.* 1786). His largest and perhaps his best work is the Crescent at Buxton (1780–90), where he very successfully combined the younger WOOD's invention of the monumental residential crescent with the arcaded ground floor surmounted by giant pilaster order used by Inigo JONES at Covent Garden.

J. Carr, *The Works in Architecture of J. C.*, York 1973; I. Hale (ed.), *J. C.*, Hull 1973; Colvin 1978; Summerson 1983.

Carrel or **carol**. A niche in a cloister where a monk might sit and work or read; sometimes applied to BAY WINDOWS.

Cartouche. An ornamental panel in the form of a scroll or sheet of paper with curling edges, usually bearing an inscription and sometimes ornately framed.

Carvalho, Eugenio dos Santos de (1711–60), *see* PORTUGUESE ARCHITECTURE.

Caryatid. A sculptured female figure used as a column to support an entablature or other similar member, as on the Erechtheum. The term is also applied loosely to various other columns and pilasters carved wholly or partly in the form of human figures; ATLANTES (male caryatids), CANEPHORAE (females, carrying baskets on their heads), HERMS (three-quarter-length figures on pedestals), Telamones (another name for Atlantes), and TERMS (tapering pedestals merging at the top into human, animal, or mythical figures). *See* Fig. 25.

Casemate. A vaulted room, with EMBRASURES, built in the thickness of the ramparts or other fortifications, and used as a barracks or battery, or both.

Casement. 1. The hinged part of a window, attached to the upright side of the window-frame. 2. The wide concave moulding in door and window JAMBS and between COMPOUND columns or piers, found in Late Gothic architecture. The term was in use by the middle of the C15 (William of Worcester's notes).

Casement window. A metal or timber window with the sash hung vertically and opening outwards or inwards.

Casino. 1. An ornamental pavilion or small house, usually in the grounds of a larger house. 2. In the C18 a dancing saloon, today a building for gambling.

Cassels, Richard, *see* CASTLE, Richard.

Cast iron. Iron shaped by pouring into moulds. It was used in building from the late C18 (e.g. the Iron Bridge, Coalbrookdale, 1775–9) until superseded by steel in the mid C19 (see INDUSTRIALIZED BUILDING; METAL STRUCTURES).

Castellamonte, Carlo Conte di (1560–1641), was trained in Rome. He became architect to the Duke of Savoy in 1615 and played a large part in developing the city plan of Turin, where he designed Piazza S. Carlo (1637) and several churches. He began Castello di Valentino, Turin (1633), completed in the French style with a high hipped roof (1663) by his son Amadeo (1610–83), who succeeded him as court architect.

G. Brino *et al.*, *L'opera di C. e A. di C.* Turin 1966; Wittkower 1982.

Castellated. Decorated with BATTLE-MENTS.

Castle. A fortified habitation. The planning and building of castles is primarily directed by the necessities of defence; it rarely extends as a whole into architecture proper, though certain features may. In the earlier Middle

FIG. 25. *Caryatid*

Ages the principal elements of castles were the donjon or KEEP and the hall in France and England, the Bergfrid and the Palas in Germany. The keep is a tower spacious enough to act as living quarters in time of war for the lord or governor and the garrison; the Bergfrid is a tower of normal proportions; the Palas is the hall-range. The earliest dated donjon is at Langeais (*c*. 990), the earliest surviving major hall at Goslar (mid C11).

England built some hall-keeps, i.e. keeps wider than they are high (Tower of London). In France and Italy in the early C13 Roman precedent led to symmetrical compositions with angle towers and a gatehouse in the middle of one side. Some castles of Edward I in Britain took this over, and where in the late Middle Ages castles were still needed (south coast, Scottish border), they were often symmetrically composed. The rule in Britain at this time, however, was that castles could be replaced by unfortified manor houses. Towards the end of the Middle Ages the spread of firearms changed the castle into the fortress, with low BASTIONS for mounting cannon and no towers.

Fortress Elements

Casemate. Vaulted chamber in a bastion for men and guns.

Cavalier. Raised earth-platform of a fortress used for look-out purposes or gun placements.

Counterscarp. The face of the ditch of a fortress sloping towards the defender.

Demi-Lune, see *Half-Moon*.

Glacis. The ground sloping from the top of the rampart of a fortress to the level of the country around.

Half-Moon. Outwork of a fortress, crescent-shaped or forming an angle.

Hornwork. Outwork of a fortress with two demi-bastions.

Ravelin. Similar to a *Half-Moon*.

Redoubt. Small detached fortification.

Scarp. The side of the ditch of a fortress sloping towards the enemy.

Sconce. Detached fort with bastions.

Castle, Richard (*c*. 1690–1751). A German, formerly Cassels, who settled in Ireland in 1727–8, worked for PEARCE on the Parliament House, Dublin, and became the leading architect of his day in Ireland. His surviving works conform to English PALLADIANISM without any trace of his foreign origin: e.g. Tyrone House (1740–45) and Leinster House (1745–51) in Dublin, and his two great country houses, Carton, Kildare (1739–45), and Russborough, Wicklow (1742–55).

Summerson 1983.

Castrum (Latin). Roman military camp, built on a common rectangular layout throughout the Empire. A castrum was surrounded by a rampart and a wall with towers, and crossed by two main streets, the *cardo* and *decumanus*, running between four gates – the *porta praetoria*, *porta dextra*, *porta sinistra*, and *porta decumana*. The headquarters (*praetorium*) lay at their intersection, and the barracks, armoury and other essential military buildings in the four quarters made by the streets. Camps were strategically placed along the *limes* to secure the border.

Catacomb. An underground cemetery, sometimes on several levels, consisting of linked galleries with shelf-tombs (*loculi*) and chambers (*cubicula*) with tomb niches (*arcosolia*). The word *catacumbas* (of uncertain

FIG. 26. *Cavetto moulding*

derivation) was first applied in the c5 to the Christian cemetery initiated some two hundred years earlier beneath the church of S. Sebastiano on the Appian Way outside Rome. It was later extended to cover the many similar Early Christian cemeteries in and around Rome and in Naples, Sicily, and North Africa, which vary in plan (e.g. originally gridiron in Rome and radial in Syracuse). Paintings on the walls of the Roman catacombs are among the earliest (c3–4) examples of Christian art. Christians had, however, preferred open-air cemeteries from the c3, and catacombs were rarely used for burials after the c6. The term catacomb is also applied to other and later subterranean cemeteries (e.g. the c18 catacombs of Paris), including those of non-Christian cults.

Krautheimer 1986.

Catenary. The curve formed by a chain or rope uniformly loaded along its length and freely suspended from two points horizontally separated. For catenary arch, *see* ARCH.

Cathedra. The bishop's chair or throne in his cathedral church, originally placed behind the high altar in the centre of the curved wall of the APSE.

Cathedral. Bishop's church, from CATHEDRA.

Caul and **caulcole.** The main stalk of a leaf on a Corinthian capital (*see* ORDER) from which grow the lesser stalks or

caulcoles (Latin *cauliculi*) supporting the VOLUTES.

Caus or **Caux**, Isaac de (*fl.* 1612–55) and Salomon de (d. 1626), *see* JONES, Inigo.

Cavalier. In military architecture, a raised earth-platform of a fortress, for look-out purposes or gun placements.

Cavetto moulding. A hollow moulding, about a quarter of a circle in section. *See* Fig. 26.

Cell. One of the compartments of a groin or rib VAULT, in the Romanesque period usually of plastered rubble, in the Gothic period of neatly coursed stones; the earliest known example is St Denis of 1140–44. Also called a *web*.

Cella. The main body of a classical temple (containing the cult image), as distinct from the portico, etc.

Cellar. A room below or partly below ground for storage, etc. as distinct from a basement, which is a living-space.

Celure. The panelled and adorned part of a wagon roof (*see* ROOF) above the ROOD or the altar.

Cenotaph. A monument to a person or persons buried elsewhere.

Centoring. Wooden framework used in arch and vault construction; it is removed (or 'struck') when the mortar has set.

Centrally planned. Of a building which radiates from a central point, as distinct from one on an AXIAL PLAN, e.g. an octagonal building as opposed to a BASILICA.

Ceylon (Sri Lanka), *see* SRI LANKAN ARCHITECTURE.

Chaînes. Vertical strips of rusticated

masonry rising between horizontal string mouldings and cornice, dividing a façade into bays or panels; much used in C17 French domestic architecture.

Chair-rail or **dado-rail**. A moulding round a room to prevent chairs, when pushed back against the walls, from damaging their surface.

Chaitya. A Sanskrit word for a sacred mound, especially a Buddhist STUPA.

Chaitya arch. An English term for a recurrent motif in Indian Buddhist and Hindu architecture, resembling in miniature the arches (derived from the cross-section of a vaulted wooden building) which crown the entrance to CHAITYA HALLS.

Chaitya hall. An early Indian Buddhist or Hindu temple or shrine, in form not unlike a Christian BASILICA, having a long hall divided into a central nave with side aisles by two rows of columns, terminating in a part-circular or apsidal end to allow a passage way round the votive CHAITYA or STUPA. The earliest were free-standing timber structures, none of which survives. Rock-cut chaitya halls imitate them. In plan they remained constant, but the entrance façade evolved from the simple C2 BC screens to later and increasingly elaborate porticos with horse-shoe windows and flanked by niches for Buddha images. *See also* INDIAN AND PAKISTANI ARCHITECTURE.

Chalet. A Swiss herdsman's hut or mountain cottage. The term is now loosely applied to any house built in the Swiss style.

Chalgrin, Jean-François-Thérèse (1739–1811). A pupil of SERVANDONI and BOULLÉE and Rome scholar (1758–63). He began in the rather epi-

cene neo-classical manner then current (e.g. in the work of SOUFFLOT), and reintroduced the basilican plan in his St Philippe-du-Roule, Paris (designed 1768 and built by 1774), with an imposing Doric portico. But much of the elegance of Chalgrin's design has not survived later alterations. In 1776 he completed Servandoni's St Sulpice, Paris, designing the north tower and the exquisite baptistery at its base. His masterpiece, the Arc de Triomphe, Paris (1806–35), is more Romantic-Classical in the style of Boullée, with its imperial symbolism and megalomaniac scale. He did not live to see it finished, and the sculptural decoration by Rude and others gives it a distinctly C19 appearance. He rebuilt the Odéon, Paris, in 1807, following the original designs by Joseph Peyre and Charles de WAILLY.

Braham 1980; T. W. Gaehtgens, *Napoleon's Arc de Triomphe*, Göttingen 1974.

Chamberlin, Powell & Bon. A London partnership (Peter Hugh Girard Chamberlin, b. 1919, Geoffry C. Hamilton Powell, b. 1920, and Christopher Bon, b. 1921). The partners won the competition in 1952 for a City of London housing estate round Golden Lane, including the Barbican Arts Centre (1978). The whole redevelopment was finished in 1982. Their building for New Hall, Cambridge (begun 1960), is decidedly *outré* in its forms, as much of their work tends to be, e.g. at the University of Leeds (1972–5).

Chambers, Sir William (1723–96), the greatest official architect of his day in England, was born in Göteborg, Sweden, the son of a Scottish merchant. At sixteen he joined the Swedish

East India Company and for nine years made voyages to India and China. His architectural training began in 1749 in Paris under J.-F. BLONDEL, and was continued in Italy from 1750 until 1755, when he settled in London. He was an immediate success. His appointment (1756) as architectural tutor to the Prince of Wales established him in royal favour, and he became successively Architect to the King, jointly with Robert ADAM (1760), Comptroller (1769), and Surveyor General (1782). In 1770 the king allowed him to assume a knighthood on receiving the Order of the Polar Star from the King of Sweden.

His career was that of a supremely successful official and his buildings are extremely competent; fastidious in ornament, impeccable in the use of orders, but rather academic, despite his famous Pagoda in Kew Gardens, and much less spectacular than those of his rival Robert Adam. His style is scholarly but eclectic, based on English PALLADIANISM smoothed out and refined by the neo-classicism of SOUFFLOT and his contemporaries, whom he had known in Paris and with whom he afterwards kept in touch. Usually best on a small scale, his scholarly finesse is well illustrated by two of his earlier works, the Casino at Marino, Dublin (1757–69), an exemplary combination of strictly classical elements to fit a Greek cross plan, and the Pagoda at Kew (1757–62), in which he aspired to similar archaeological accuracy in another manner. He was notable for his staircases, e.g. Gower House, London (c. 1769, destroyed), Melbourne House, London (c. 1772, destroyed), and Somerset House, London. His country houses are neo-Palladian in plan and composition – e.g. Lord

Bessborough's villa, now a school, at Roehampton (c. 1760) and Duddingston House, Edinburgh (1762–4) – while the Strand façade of his largest and best-known work, Somerset House, London (1776–86), is a conscious imitation of a Palladian composition by Inigo JONES on the site. The courtyards and river façade display more vivacity and originality, and some of the interior decoration equals anything by Adam for refinement, particularly in the Strand block in which some rooms represent the earliest examples of a mature Louis XVI style in England. Though never as fashionable as Adam, he exerted great influence both as official head of his profession and through his numerous pupils. His *Treatise on Civil Architecture* (1759) became a standard work.

J. Harris, *Sir W. C.*, London 1970.

Chambiges, Martin (d. 1532), *see* FRENCH ARCHITECTURE.

Chamfer. The surface made when the sharp edge or ARRIS of a stone block or piece of wood, etc., is cut away, usually at an angle of 45° to the other two surfaces. It is called a *hollow chamfer* when the surface made is concave.

Champneys, Basil (1842–1935), *see* ENGLISH ARCHITECTURE.

Chancel. That part of the east end of a church in which the main altar is placed; reserved for clergy and choir. From the Latin word *cancellus*, which strictly means the screen that often separated it from the body of the church. The term more usually describes the space enclosed and is applied to the whole continuation of the nave east of the CROSSING.

Chancel arch. The arch at the west end of a CHANCEL.

FIG. 27. *Chatri*

Chantry chapel. A chapel attached to, or inside, a church, endowed for the celebration of Masses for the soul of the founder or for the souls of such others as he may order.

Chapel. A place for worship in honour of a particular saint, usually forming part of a church but sometimes a separate, detached building.

Chapterhouse. The place of assembly for abbot or prior and members of a monastery for the discussion of business or for reading the chapters of the monastic rule. It is reached from the CLOISTERS, to whose eastern range it usually belongs, and in England is often polygonal in plan. *See* Fig. 63. In cathedrals it usually belongs to the secular canons.

Chareau, Pierre (1883–1950). French architect and furniture designer notable for his Maison de Verre, Paris (1928–32, with Bernard Bijvoet), in which mass-produced components were assembled on a flexible plan. He emigrated to the USA in 1940.

M. Vellay and K. Frampton, *P.C. Architect and Craftsman 1883–1950*, London 1985.

Chatri. Pillared pavilions surmounted by a dome, a feature of Indo-Islamic architecture which first appeared in the early C16, often round the drum of a domed building. *See* Fig. 27.

Chattra. In early Buddhist sculpture and architecture, a stone parasol, often crowning a STUPA; if more than one, superimposed one on another, called a *chattravalli*.

Chedi. In THAI ARCHITECTURE, a STUPA.

Chelles, Jean de and Pierre de, *see* JEAN DE CHELLES.

Chequer-work. A method of decorating walls or pavements with alternating squares of contrasting materials (e.g. stone, brick, flint) to produce a chessboard effect.

Chermayeff, Serge (b. 1900). Russian architect in partnership with MENDELSOHN 1933–6 in England. In 1940 he emigrated to the USA, where he experimented with wood-frame structures and became an influential teacher and theorist.

Chersiphron (*fl.c.* 560 BC), *see* GREEK ARCHITECTURE.

Chevakinsky, Savva (1713–1770s). Appointed architect to Tsarskoe Selo in 1745, he was responsible (with A. Kvasov) for most of the work there apart from RASTRELLI's, e.g. the Rococo Hermitage. His greatest surviving work is the St Nicholas Marine Cathedral (1752) in Leningrad, the finest Late Baroque church in Russia. Though overshadowed by Rastrelli, he had his own lively artistic personality. [R. R. Milner-Gulland]

Chevet. The French term for the east end of a church, consisting of APSE and

FIG. 28. *Chevron*

AMBULATORY with or without radiating chapels.

Chevron. A Romanesque moulding forming a zigzag; so called from the French word for a pair of rafters giving this form. *See* Fig. 28.

Chiattone, Mario (1891–1957), *see* SANT'ELIA, Antonio.

Chiaveri, Gaetano (1689–1770). Late Baroque architect, born in Rome but worked mainly in northern Europe – St Petersburg (1717 27), Warsaw and Dresden (*c.* 1737–48). His masterpiece was the Hofkirche in Dresden (begun 1738, badly damaged 1944), a Roman Catholic church intended to rival the grandeur of BÄHR's Lutheran Frauenkirche. It has a very elegant campanile with an open-work top section which provided the perfect foil to the solidity of Bähr's dome, as did also the exterior of the church itself with its rhythmically advancing and receding walls crowned by numerous statues. Chiaveri provided plans for the river front of the royal palace in Warsaw (1740, only partly adopted) and somewhat theatrical designs for a royal palace in Dresden (*c.* 1748, not executed). He published a volume of engraved designs: *Ornamenti diversi di porte e finestre* (1743–4).

Hempel 1965.

Chicago School. A term of disputed definition, perhaps best understood as referring to a group of architects working in Chicago between *c.* 1880 and *c.* 1910 and their development of utilitarian multi-storey buildings characterized by their external expression of the skeleton frame and the repetitious use of identical fenestration for storeys of similar plan and also by an emphasis on verticality – e.g. JENNEY, RICHARDSON, BURNHAM & ROOT, HOLABIRD & ROCHE, SULLIVAN, WRIGHT, and others.

Condit 1964.

Chicago window. A window occupying the full width of a bay and divided into a large fixed sash flanked by a narrow movable sash on each side, as in the Marquette building by HOLABIRD & ROCHE (1894) and SULLIVAN's Carson Pirie & Scott store (1899–1904) in Chicago.

Chigi. Japanese term for the scissorslike finials on the roof of a Shinto temple.

Chimney bar. The bar above the fireplace opening which carries the front of the CHIMNEY-BREAST.

Chimney-breast. The stone or brick structure projecting into or out of a room and containing the flue.

Chimney-piece, *see* MANTELPIECE.

Chimney shaft. A high chimney with only one flue.

Chimney-stack. Masonry or brickwork containing several flues, projecting above the roof and terminating in chimney-pots.

Chinese architecture. Features that characterize the architecture of China, and the rest of East Asia, are already evident in the remains of two Shang dynasty (*c.* 1750–1045 BC) cities excavated beneath modern Zhengzhou and Anyang (He nan province) – the former a rectangle covering some two sq. miles surrounded by a vast earthwork estimated at having been some 33 ft high and 65 ft wide. The more important buildings were set on raised platforms and were of wooden trabeated construction, with walls of light material serving simply as protective screens. Paintings, relief carvings and little pottery models dating from the Han dynasty (c. 202 BC to AD 220) record such buildings and also indicate the importance given to tiled roofs. Underground tombs of the Han period reveal that the technique of tunnel vaulting with brick and stone had been mastered, but most of their stone elements imitate trabeated wooden construction, notably columns crowned by spreading consoles or brackets to carry beams. Stone was used for fortifications and for bridges, the earliest surviving being that built 605–617 at Zhao xian (He bei province) with a flattened arch spanning 123 ft. Otherwise the earliest stone buildings are PAGODAS erected after the introduction of Buddhism from India. The twelve-sided pagoda built c. 520 in the Song shan monastery (near Luo yang, He nan province) is derived from an Indian SIKHARA. The much larger seven-storey square-plan Great Wild Goose pagoda at Xi an (He nan province) owes more to Han dynasty watchtowers (known from pottery models) and the corbels supporting its roofs simulate woodwork. By the time of the Song dynasty (960–1279) pagodas had been given a wholly Chinese form – tall towers of uniform width or very slightly tapering with roofs marking each storey – followed until the late C19, sometimes of stone or brick but usually of wood with ceramic tiles (the earliest surviving wooden example,

of 1058, is at Ying xian, Shan xi province).

Few wooden buildings survive from before the C16 in China. But Chinese styles and structural techniques were adopted for Buddhist monasteries in C7–8 Japan, where very fine examples have been preserved (see JAPANESE ARCHITECTURE). By this time a complex system of wooden construction had been devised to carry heavy ceramic-tiled ROOFS (pitched, gambrel or hipped), with the ridge-pole resting on a framework of columns joined horizontally by tie-beams and purlins, with elaborate corbels to spread the load, especially under wide-spreading eaves. A single storey was normal (libraries were the main exception, e.g. that of the C11 in the Long xing monastery at Zheng ding in He bei province), but the appearance of an upper floor was sometimes given by a lean-to roof immediately above the level of the entrance, either extending the interior space or covering an open colonnade. In 1103 Li Jie, an architect of the imperial Board of Works, published *Methods and Designs of Architecture* which formulated a system of proportions, derived from the vertical breadth of a bracket arm, to govern the size and spacing of columns and beams, and also described the various types of carved ornament. The treatise was officially prescribed for use throughout the empire.

The earliest surviving wooden building in China is the great hall of 847 in the Fo guang monastery on mount Wu tai in Shan xi province. Song dynasty buildings include the large temple of the Holy mother (1023–32) at Jin ci near Tai yuan in Shan xi province. The Daoist Yongle temple (Shan xi province) built under the Yuan dynasty

(1260–1368) is architecturally simple but provides a clear example of the normal system of axial planning, with a gate-house, large hall and two smaller halls on axis. (It was dismantled and faithfully re-erected 1959–63.) Architectural principles over-ruled religious differences even in the exteriors of mosques (e.g. in Beijing and Xi an), though pagodas were reserved for Buddhist establishments. The only exceptions were lamaist monasteries, which followed TIBETAN precedents (e.g. in Beijing and at Cheng de in He bei province). And although the vast majority of early Chinese temples were extensively restored or entirely rebuilt under the Ming (1368–1644) and Qing (1644–1912) dynasties their essential original forms were maintained. The temple of Confucius at his birth-place Qu fu in Shan dong province was built to replace its predecessor destroyed by fire in 1724 and is unusual only in that it has ten marble columns wreathed round with dragons supporting the eaves on its lower roof on the south front. The residence of the descendants of Confucius next to it, dating partly from the Ming period, is virtually the only surviving large non-imperial palace – an axial succession of halls similar to temples approached through courtyards flanked by smaller buildings, with a garden at the north end.

Apart from the Great Wall, which was given its present appearance 1368–1500, the imperial palace or 'Forbidden City' in Beijing (literally 'northern capital') is the major architectural achievement of the Ming and Qing dynasties, indeed one of the most impressive in the world. With three huge courtyards dominated by buildings on high platforms, the plan follows a very ancient tradition. It was begun in 1407, but the

Grand Ancestral Shrine erected in 1464 to replace a predecessor destroyed by fire is the only survivor among its many buildings dating entirely from the Ming period: the others are C18 reconstructions and much of their decoration is still later. But respect for tradition gives to the whole complex a stylistic unity extending from the great ceremonial halls in the southern half to the imperial living quarters and the numerous small houses for widows and concubines, each composed of detached buildings set round a courtyard (similar to private houses elsewhere in the city, though very few now survive). Imperial building work continued with a marked decline in the quality of decorative detail until shortly before the end of the régime: the Summer Palace, Yi he yuan, outside Beijing, begun 1888 as a replacement for its predecessor sacked by European troops in 1860; in the city itself the great circular Hall of Annual Prayers (popularly called the Temple of Heaven), with its blue tiled roofs, was begun after 1889 as the replica of an early C15 building that had been destroyed by fire.

In the mid C18 an addition to the imperial summer palace Yuan ming yuan (of which only ruins survive) was built under the supervision of Jesuits in an Italianate Baroque style. This was a unique instance of Western influence in the imperial period, though Europeans erected buildings in their own styles for their own use, e.g. the Baroque Catholic church of Xuan wu Men, Beijing (1657), the red-brick Gothic Holy Trinity church, Shanghai, by George Gilbert SCOTT and William Kidner (1866–9), the French Gothic Catholic cathedral, Shanghai (1896–1910), as well as consulates, banks, etc. in the treaty ports. Many more such buildings went up after the Republican Revolution of 1911, most prominently in Shanghai. The Chinese-based British firm Palmer & Turner provided designs in an enterprising range of styles – in Shanghai the over-blown BEAUX ARTS STYLE Hong Kong and Shanghai Bank (1921–3) the simplified ART DECO style Peace Hotel (1926–8) and the half-timbered Tudor style Sassoon Villa (1930). European styles were also taken up by a few Chinese architects, e.g. the pidgin-neo-Georgian lecture hall of Nanjing University. But there was also a politically inspired Chinese revival, e.g. the Sun Yat Sen mausoleum begun 1926 by Lu Yan-zhi (1894–1929) and the Central Museum of 1937, both in Nanjing. Attempts were also made to apply Chinese decorative features to Western-style buildings: the Municipal Government Building, Shanghai (1930), is among the worst examples, the Zhong shan hospital, Shanghai (1937), among the best. The INTERNATIONAL MODERN style was introduced for a few private houses in the 1930s and for hotels since 1949. But this term can hardly be applied to the recent proliferation of high-rise blocks throughout the country, built economically to accommodate the urban populations: they are purely utilitarian. The most prominent post-Second World War public buildings date from the time of close Sino-Russian alliance and Soviet influence is evident – the daunting Great Hall of the People and Museum of Chinese History (both 1959) which have massive colonnaded façades and a few discreet Chinese decorative details on either side of Tian an men square, Beijing. The Memorial Hall of Chairman Mao (1977) in the same square is smaller and more recognizably Chinese even though it is flat roofed. The most interesting recent buildings are hotels for foreign tourists, ranging in styles from Chinese to nondescript Western but including the Xiang shan Hotel outside Beijing of 1979–83 by M. I. PEI.

Chinoiserie. European imitations or evocations of Chinese art which first appeared in the C17, became very popular in the C18 – especially in England, Germany, France and Italy – and lingered on into the C19. Numerous PAGODAS were built in Europe. Of the larger buildings in the style, the teahouse at Potsdam (1754–7), the pavilion at Drottningholm, Sweden (1763–9), the Palazzina La Favorita, Palermo (1799), and the interior of the Royal Pavilion, Brighton (1802–21), are the most important.

Chochol, Josef (1880–1956), *see* CZECHOSLOVAK ARCHITECTURE.

Choir. The part of a church where divine service is sung, usually part of the chancel.

Choir screen. A partition of wood or stone, elaborately carved, separating the choir and chancel from the nave and transepts of a church. It corresponds approximately to the ICONOSTASIS in a Byzantine church.

Churriguera, José Benito de (1665–1725). The eldest of three architect brothers, the others being Joaquín (1674–1724) and Alberto (1676–1750). They came of a family of Barcelona sculptors specializing in elaborately carved retables and began in this way themselves; hence their peculiar architectural style with its lavish piling up of surface ornamentation, now known as the Churrigueresque style. Some of its more fantastic and barbaric features may have been inspired by native art in Central and South America. José Benito settled early in Madrid as a carver of retables (e.g. Sagrario in Segovia Cathedral) and did not turn architect until 1709, when he laid out the town of Nuevo Baztán, the most ambitious and original urban scheme of its period in Spain. His brother Joaquín's best works date from the next decade, e.g. the patio of the Colegio de Anaya and Colegio de Calatrava at Salamanca. The youngest brother, Alberto, was the most talented, but did not emerge as an architect in his own right until after the death of his two elder brothers. The Plaza Mayor at Salamanca (begun 1729) is his first great work. San Sebastian, Salamanca, followed in 1731, but seven years later he left Salamanca and resigned as architect in charge. His last works are small but among his best: e.g. the parish church at Orgaz (1738) and the portal and façade of the church of the Assumption at Rueda (1738–47).

Kubler and Soria 1959.

Churrigueresque style. The lavish over-decorated style named after the CHURRIGUERA family, though the term is often extended to include all the more florid, Late Baroque architecture in Spain and Spanish America, especially Mexico. Pedro de RIBERA and Narciso TOMÉ were its best practitioners in Spain, where it was popular mainly in Castille.

J. M. Pla Dalman, *La arquitectura barroca española y el Churriguerismo*, Madrid 1951.

CIAM or **Congrès International d'Architecture Moderne**. Founded in 1928, it became the chief instrument for disseminating Modernist ideas on architecture and town planning. Dominated in the 1930s by LE CORBUSIER, it emphasized functionalism and rational planning. CIAM had two periods of great influence: 1930–34 and 1950–56. The so-called 'Athens Charter' issued by CIAM in 1933 set out principles for urban planning in which the primary functions were identified as 'residential, work, recreation and traffic' – COSTA's Brasilia was to be its great exemplar. In the late 1950s the younger generation (represented by 'Team X' and including BAKEMA and van EYCK, the SMITHSONS and CANDILIS) rejected the ideals of the older generation. The last meeting of CIAM took place in 1959.

A. Smithson, *Team 10 Primer*, Cambridge, Mass., 1963; M. Steinman, *CIAM: Dokumente 1928–1939*, Basel and Stuttgart 1979.

Ciborium. A canopy raised over the high altar. It is normally a dome supported on columns. *See also* BALDACHIN.

Cill, *see* SILL.

Cima recta, cima reversa, *see* CYMA RECTA, CYMA REVERSA.

Cimborio. The Spanish term for a LANTERN admitting light over a crossing tower (*see* CROSSING) or other raised structure above a roof.

Cincture. A small convex moulding round the SHAFT of a column.

Cinquefoil, *see* FOIL.

Circus. 1. In Roman architecture a long oblong building with rounded ends and with tiered seating on both sides and at one end; if used for horse-racing, a hippodrome. 2. In the C18 a circular or nearly circular range of houses. 3. In modern town planning a circular road or street junction.

Ciriani, Henri (b. 1936), *see* FRENCH ARCHITECTURE.

Cistercian architecture. The Cistercian Order was founded in 1098. It was named after Cîteaux in Burgundy. The third abbot, and the one to establish the rules of the Order, was the Englishman Stephen Harding. The most famous Cistercian is St Bernard of Clairvaux (1090–1153), named after Clairvaux, the second mother abbey of the Order. The other two were Pontigny and Morimond, all in Burgundy. The Order pleaded for reform, and an exacting life. One of the rules was to settle in wild country and to colonize and cultivate it. The Cistercians became extremely successful landowners. They settled in near and far countries. At the time of the death of St Bernard there were 339 houses, in 1200 about 525 (including nunneries). Whereas the Cluniacs (*see* CLUNY) did not impose rules of architectural planning, a Cistercian house is at once recognizable by plan and elevation in whatever country it may be. Both plans and elevations, at least up to about 1150, were kept demonstratively simple. Choirs had straight ends, chapels extending east of the transepts ended straight too. The standard plan had two to each transept, but there could be up to four. Apses are rare (except in Spain). Details were simple too, but great efforts were made to achieve fine workmanship. The earliest completely preserved church is Fontenay in Burgundy (1139–47), the grandest preserved Burgundian church Pontigny (*c.* 1140–1200). England possesses the finest ruins: Fountains,

Rievaulx, Kirkstall, Roche, Tintern, etc. The best-known Italian houses are Casamari, Fossanova, and Chiaravalle; the best-known Spanish ones Moreruela, La Oliva, Poblet and Santas Creus; the best-known in Germany Eberbach, Ebrach, Maulbronn, Bronnbach, Walkenried and Riddagshausen; in Austria Heiligenkreuz, Lilienfeld and Zwettl.

W. Braunfels, *Abendländische Klosterbaukunst*, Cologne (1969) 1978; P. Fergusson, *Architecture of Solitude. Cistercian Abbeys in Twelfth Century England*, Princeton 1984; C. Norton and D. Parks (eds.), *Cistercian Art and Architecture in the British Isles*, London 1986; R. Stalley, *The Cistercian Monasteries of Ireland*, New Haven and London 1987.

Citadel. In military architecture, a fort with from four to six bastions. It was usually sited at a corner of a fortified town but connected with it, e.g. Lille or Arras.

Cladding. An external covering or skin applied to a structure for aesthetic or protective purposes. *See also* CURTAIN WALL.

Clapboard. In the USA and Canada the term for WEATHERBOARD.

Clapper bridge. A bridge made of large slabs of stone, some built up to make rough PIERS and other longer ones laid on top to make the roadway.

Clarke, George (1661–1736), *see* ALDRICH, Henry.

Clason, Isak Gustaf (1856–1930), *see* SWEDISH ARCHITECTURE.

Clasp, *see* INDUSTRIALIZED BUILDING.

Classicism. A revival of or return to the principles of Greek or (more often)

Roman art and architecture. The word 'classic' originally signified a member of the superior tax-paying class of Roman citizens. It was later applied, by analogy, to writers of established reputation; and in the Middle Ages it was extended to all Greek and Roman writers and also to the arts of the same period, though always with an implication of 'accepted authority'. The various classical revivals were thus attempts to return to the rule of artistic law and order as well as evocations of the glories of ancient Rome. Although most phases of medieval and later European art have to some extent been influenced by antiquity, the term 'classicism' is generally reserved for the styles more consciously indebted to Greece and Rome.

The first of these revivals was the CAROLINGIAN *renovatio* of the c8–9 – a politically, no less than aesthetically, inspired return to late Imperial Roman art and architecture. The Tuscan c11 Proto-Renaissance represents a somewhat similar attempt to revive Roman architectural forms. The few monuments produced under it exerted considerable influence on the earliest works of BRUNELLESCHI and thus the initial phase of the RENAISSANCE proper. But from the c16 onwards the Renaissance reinterpretation of antiquity was to exert almost as much influence on classicizing architects as antiquity itself. For it was during the Renaissance that writers began to evolve a classical theory of architecture based largely on the confused and confusing treatise of VITRUVIUS, which had been rediscovered in 1414. Throughout the c17 architectural theory remained essentially classical, though practising architects often paid no more than lip-service to it. But there

was a practical as well as a theoretical return to classical standards in late c17 France (notably in the work of PERRAULT and MANSART). And in early c18 England such architects as Colen CAMPBELL, Lord BURLINGTON, and William KENT led a return to classicism by way of Inigo JONES and PALLADIO. This PALLADIANISM has sometimes been interpreted as the first phase of the late c18 neo-classical movement.

This movement, generally referred to as neo-classicism, began in the 1750s as a reaction against the excesses of the Late BAROQUE and ROCOCO and as a reflection of a general desire for established principles based on laws of nature and reason. In art and architecture these also embodied the 'noble simplicity and calm grandeur' which Winckelmann regarded as the prime qualities of Greek art. Fresh attention was given to surviving antique buildings in Europe and Asia Minor. PIRANESI's etchings inspired a new vision of Roman architecture, emphasizing its formal and spatial qualities. Classically 'incorrect' motifs were rejected in favour of those more archaeologically correct. But the mere copying of Greek and Roman buildings was rarely practised and never recommended. Theorists like LAUGIER and LODOLI demanded rational architecture based on first principles, not one which imitated Roman grandeur.

These new ideas were bound up with a nascent primitivism – a belief that architecture, like society, had been at its purest and best in its simplest and most primitive form. This led to an appreciation of the severity of Greek DORIC, made possible by the publications of James STUART and others and by the discovery of the early Doric temples in Sicily and at Paestum – though for the more fundamentalist architects (e.g. C. A. Ehrensvärd in Sweden) even the latter were insufficiently plain, sturdy and masculine. It also led to the creation of an architecture of pure geometrical forms – the cube, pyramid, cylinder and sphere – which found its most extreme expression in the designs of BOULLÉE, LEDOUX, and GILLY, and in buildings by SOANE in England, LATROBE in the USA and ZAKHAROV in Russia. But if few late C18 architects took neo-classical principles to their logical conclusion equally few remained entirely immune to them.

Neo-classical buildings are solid and rather severe. Decoration, including classical enrichments, is restrained and sometimes eliminated altogether. The orders are used structurally rather than ornamentally, with columns supporting entablatures and not merely applied to the walls. Volumetric clarity is emphasized both internally and externally by unbroken contours. The Baroque organic principle by which a façade is unified by interlocking its various parts (so that the wings flow out of the central block and the main storey into those above and below) is rejected in favour of an inorganic one by which the masses are rigidly defined and, sometimes brutally, juxtaposed.

In the early C19 these severe neo-classical ideas were abandoned in favour of styles richer in decoration, more picturesque in composition and more literary in their allusions to the past. In France, under the Empire, the richly luxurious and dramatically expressive Roman Imperial style was revived as propaganda for the régime. Architects once more played for effect rather than sought to express visually a high intellectual ideal. Thus the classical tradition survived, in Europe and the USA and in various European colonies in Asia and Africa, throughout the C19, but simply as a form of HISTORICISM – whether Greek, Roman or Renaissance (see GREEK REVIVAL). And although many individual buildings in these styles are of high quality (notably those by BARRY, ELMES, SMIRKE, PLAYFAIR, STRICKLAND, SCHINKEL, KLENZE, HITTORF, etc.) they show little further development. Ironically enough, the leading tenets of the neo-classicists (logical construction, truth to materials, etc.) were taken up and developed in an anti-classical way by the architects of the GOTHIC REVIVAL.

By the late C19 these historicizing styles had come full circle from neo-classical austerity, logical simplicity and purity to the lavish and heavily ornamented BEAUX ARTS STYLE which persisted well into the C20, especially in the USA with Paul CRET and others. In the 1920s and 1930s classicism was once again purged of superfluous ornament in a so-called 'stripped' style superficially similar to late C18 neo-classicism and much promoted for official buildings by the Fascist and Nazi regimes, from which it got a bad name (see ITALIAN ARCHITECTURE; GERMAN ARCHITECTURE). At the same time, however, there were many architects who were indifferent or averse to modernism without any political or ideological motives and were able to draw inspiration freely from ancient Roman, Renaissance and also C17–18 versions of classicism, e.g. Philip Trammell Shutze (1890–1982) whose Citizens and Southern National Bank, Atlanta, USA (1929), has an interior of Imperial Roman grandeur. More recently POST-MODERNISM and other trends opposed to modernism have led to the revival of classical elements in the work of several notable architects, from STIRLING and OUTRAM in England to STERN and others in the USA, and, in Europe, BOFILL, BOTTA, KRIER, ROSSI and several others.

Clerestory or **clearstory**. The upper stage of the main walls of a church above the aisle roofs, pierced by windows; the same term is applicable in domestic building. In Romanesque architecture it often has a narrow wall-passage on the inside.

Clérisseau, Charles-Louis (1721–1820). A French neo-classical draughtsman and architect who exerted a wide influence through his pupils and patrons, William CHAMBERS, Robert and James ADAM, and Thomas JEFFERSON. He also provided designs (not executed) for Catherine the Great. His own buildings are uninspired, e.g. the Palais de Justice, Metz (1776–89).

Kalnein and Levey 1973; Braham 1980.

Clerk, Simon (d. c. 1489). Master mason of Bury St Edmunds Abbey from 1445 at the latest, and also of Eton College, c. 1455–60 (in succession to his brother John), and King's College Chapel, Cambridge, from 1477 to 1485. Of his work at Bury nothing survives; at Eton and Cambridge he continued work, that is, he did not initiate, and so his style remains unknown to us. He is named here as an example of the way distinguished masons were given responsibility in several places.

Harvey 1984.

Clocher. The French term for a bell-tower.

Cloister. An enclosed space, usually a quadrangle or open court, surrounded by roofed or vaulted passages or ambulatories with an open arcade or colonnade on the interior side and a plain wall on the other; it connects the monastic church with the domestic parts of the MONASTERY; usually south of the NAVE and west of the TRANSEPT. *See* Fig. 63.

Cloister vault. The American term for a domical VAULT.

Cluny. A Burgundian monastery founded in 910. It generated the reform of the Benedictine Order, and the militancy of the Church in the C11. Urban II, who summoned Europe to the First Crusade, was once a monk there, as were later Popes such as Gregory VII and Paschal II. In the early C12 the abbey church of Cluny, of which little survives, was the largest in all Europe (*see* FRENCH ARCHITECTURE). It was built in the characteristic Burgundian style; but this style was not, as with the CISTERCIANS, mandatory upon its daughter-houses; these took their character from the locality. La Charité-sur-Loire, Vézelay, St Martial in Limoges, Moissac and St Martin-des-Champs in Paris are among the best-known of them. The mother-house in England was Lewes, the chief houses in Switzerland were Romainmôtier and Payerne, and in Germany, Hirsau. Around AD 1200 the Order had about 1,500 establishments.

J. Evans, *Romanesque Architecture of the Order of Cluny*, Farnborough, (1938) 1972; M. Eschapasse, *L'Architecture bénédictine en Europe*, Paris 1963; Conant 1979.

Clustered pier, *see* COMPOUND PIER.

Clutton, Henry (1819–93), *see* BENT-LEY, John Francis; BURGES, William.

Coade stone. An 'artificial stone' marketed by Mrs Eleanor Coade (1709–96) of Lambeth from 1769 and, after her death, by William Croggan until 1833. Finer than STUCCO and other available compositions, it was probably a type of pottery (stoneware) and was widely used for all kinds of architectural ornament from capitals and key-stones to whole doorways (as still *in situ* in Bedford Square, London). The fan-vaulted screen in St George's Chapel, Windsor, by Henry Emlyn (1787), is of Coade stone.

A. Kelly, *Mrs C.'s Stone*, London 1990.

Coates, Wells (Windemut) (1895–1958). English architect notable chiefly for his Lawn Road Flats in Hampstead (1932–4) and Palace Gate flats (1937–9), London, pioneer work in England in INTERNATIONAL MODERN style.

S. Cantacuzino, *W.C.*, London 1978.

Cob. Walling material made of clay mixed with straw, gravel and sand. It can be used with or without formwork (*see* PISÉ).

Cockerell, Charles Robert (1788–1863), son of S. P. COCKERELL, studied under his father and assisted Sir Robert SMIRKE. From 1810 to 1817 he was abroad, first in Greece, Asia Minor, and Sicily, then in Italy. Keenly interested in archaeology, he was excellent at classical and modern languages; in Greece he worked on the discoveries of Aegina and Phigaleia. However, Cockerell combined his passion for Greek antiquities with a great admiration for WREN, and the result is a style which is the English parallel of

the Paris BEAUX ARTS STYLE of about 1840: grander than before, fond of giant orders and sudden solecisms, yet still firmly disciplined. Cockerell is an architects' architect, and PUGIN hated him passionately. Among his buildings the following only can be referred to: the Cambridge University (now Law) Library (1837–42) with its splendid coffered tunnel vault; the Taylorian (Ashmolean) building in Oxford (1841–5); various branch buildings for the Bank of England, whose architect he became in 1833 (e.g. those in Manchester and Liverpool, both begun in 1845); and a number of insurance office buildings (e.g. the Liverpool & London and Globe Insurance, Dale Street, Liverpool, of 1855–7). He was Professor of Architecture at the Royal Academy, the recipient of the first Gold Medal of the Royal Institute of British Architects, and a member of the academies of Paris, Rome, Munich, Copenhagen, etc. He also wrote on the iconography of the west front of Wells Cathedral.

D. Watkin, *The Life and Work of C.R.C.*, London 1974.

Cockerell, Samuel Pepys (1753–1827), began in TAYLOR's office along with NASH. He acquired numerous surveyorships – Admiralty, East India Company, St Paul's, Foundling Hospital, etc. – but is remembered for his fantastic country house, Sezincote (1805), the first Indian-style building in England. Elsewhere he showed French influence of an advanced kind, e.g. the west tower of St Anne's, Soho, London. In 1792 he restored Ticken-cote church in the Norman style, thus anticipating C19 restorations.

Colvin 1978.

Coderch y Sentmenat, José Antonio

(1913–84), *see* SPANISH ARCHITEC-
TURE.

Codussi or **Coducci**, Mauro (*c.* 1440–
1504). Born near Bergamo, he had
settled in Venice by 1469 and was
largely responsible, with LOMBARDO,
for replacing Venetian Gothic with a
classicizing style achieving a remarkable synthesis of the Veneto-Byzantine
and Renaissance. His earliest-known
work is S. Michele in Isola (1469–77),
the first Renaissance church in Venice,
with a façade derived from ALBERTI's
Tempio Malatestiano but capped by
a semicircular pediment of Veneto-
Byzantine inspiration. Between 1480
and 1500 he completed S. Zaccaria,
begun in 1458 by Antonio Gambello
(d. 1481), with its very tall façade on
which columns and niches are piled up
on one another, and with classical ornament in most unclassical profusion. He
was more restrained in S. Giovanni
Crisostomo (1497–1504). Palazzo Zorzi
a San Severo (*c.* 1480), Palazzo Cor-
ner-Spinelli (*c.* 1485–90) and Palazzo
Vendramin-Calergi (begun *c.* 1502)
have been attributed to him. In 1492–
1504 he rebuilt S. Maria Formosa on
the plan of its C12 predecessor (exterior
and dome are C16 and C17). His surviving masterpiece is the great double
staircase at the Scuola di S. Giovanni
Evangelista (1498). His staircase at
the Scuola di S. Marco (1490–95) was
destroyed in the C19. He also designed
the campanile of S. Pietro di Castello
(1482–8). The clock tower in Piazza S.
Marco has been attributed to him.

L. O. Puppi and L. Puppi, *M.C. e
l'architettura veneziana del primo
rinascimento*, Milan 1977; McAndrew
1980; Lieberman 1982; Howard 1987.

Coffering. Decoration of a ceiling, a
vault, or an arch SOFFIT, consisting of

sunken square or polygonal ornamental
panels. *See also* CAISSON; LACUNAR.

Coia, Jack (1898–1981), *see* SCOTTISH
ARCHITECTURE.

Coignet, François (1814–88), *see* CON-
CRETE.

Cola da Caprarola (Cola di Matteucci) (*fl.* 1499–1519), *see* LEONARDO
DA VINCI.

Collar-beam, *see* ROOF.

Collcutt, Thomas, *see* ENGLISH AR-
CHITECTURE.

Colonia, Juan, Simón, Francisco, *see*
SIMÓN DE COLONIA.

Colonial style, *see* UNITED STATES
ARCHITECTURE.

Colonnade. A row of columns carrying an entablature or arches.

Colossal order. Any ORDER whose
columns rise from the ground through
several storeys, sometimes called a
giant order.

Column. A free-standing upright
member of circular section and usually
slightly tapering, normally intended as
a support but sometimes erected independently as a monument. In classical architecture it consists of a shaft,
capital and, except in Greek Doric, a
base (*see* ORDER). A *blocked column* has
alternate rectangular blocks and circular drums. For the twisted column
which appears in Baroque architecture,
see SOLOMONIC COLUMN.

Columna rostrata or **rostral column.**
In Roman architecture, an ornamental
column decorated with ships' prows to
celebrate a naval victory. *See* Fig. 29.

Common rafter, *see* ROOF.

Communion table, *see* ALTAR.

FIG. 29. *Columna rostrata*

FIG. 30. *Compound pier*

Community architecture. An English movement for low-tech labour-intensive user-designed and user-built housing. Foreshadowed by Ralph ERSKINE's 'participatory design process' at Byker in 1969–80, it was pioneered in the 1970s by Walter Segal (1907–85) with timber-frame construction self-built housing. Schemes for both new housing and the rehabilitation of old housing followed in the 1980s. The precepts of Christopher ALEXANDER may be associated theoretically with the movement.

N. Waites and C. Knevitt, *Community Architecture: How People are Creating their Own Environment*, London 1987; J. McKean, *Learning from Segal*, Basel, Boston, Berlin 1989.

Comper, John Ninian (1864–1960). A pupil of BODLEY, he continued the ARTS AND CRAFTS tradition in a series of crisp and noble Late Gothic Revival churches – from St Cyprian's, Clarence Gate, London (1902–3), St Mary's, Wellingborough (1904–31), All Saints Convent, London Colney (1923–7), to St Philip's, Cosham, Portsmouth (1937). He was knighted in 1950.

A. Symondson, *Sir N.C. The Last Gothic Revivalist*, London 1988.

Compluvium. Rectangular opening in the atrium of an ancient Roman house towards which the roof sloped, throwing off rainwater into a shallow cistern or impluvium in the floor.

Composite order, *see* ORDER.

Compound pier. A pier with several SHAFTS, attached or detached, or demi-shafts against the faces of it; also called a *clustered* pier. *See* Fig. 30.

Conch. A semicircular niche surmounted by a half-dome.

Concrete. Concrete is 'mortar mixed with small stones to produce a hard monolithic mass' (P. Collins, *Concrete*, 1959). It was used in ancient ROMAN ARCHITECTURE and became a determining factor in its development. Unlike modern concrete, which can be mixed and poured, ancient Roman concrete had to be laid in courses as it dried out quickly. But about the time of Augustus (early CI AD) a slow-drying mortar was discovered and this revolutionized architecture. Combined with the arch and vault it enabled ancient Roman architects to cover, without any internal support, spaces far larger and of far greater flexibility of form than had been possible before. It brought about an architecture of space rather than of mass. The earliest example is Nero's Golden House by SEVERUS. Trajan's Market and the Pantheon, Rome, are other notable examples.

After the fall of the Roman Empire it was almost forgotten and only revived in the late C18. The revival started in France, where the word for concrete is *béton*. Among the pioneers in the late C18 and early C19 are F. Cointereau and F. M. Lebrun. The story became more consistent only after 1850. The leaders were François Coignet (1814–88), who in 1864 built the shell of the church of Le Vésinet of concrete. Meanwhile experiments had gone on with iron reinforcement of the concrete. LOUDON in 1832 mentioned concrete floors with embedded iron lattice work. Joseph Monnier made flower-pots with reinforcement in the 1860s and columns and beams in 1877. Scholarly calculations began in the 1870s in the USA (W. E. Ward, T. Hyatt) and Germany (Wayss, Koenen). But the breakthrough was due to François HENNEBIQUE who started factories with a framework of reinforced concrete in 1895 and was soon kept busy. Hennebique's American counterparts were Ernest L. Ransome (1884–1911) and, after 1905, Albert KAHN (1869–1942) of Detroit, who pioneered industrial methods of standardization and team design in his factories for the Ford Motor Company, General Motors, and others. The first exposed concrete (or rather reinforced cement and steel rods piercing bricks) appeared in the church of St Jean de Montmartre in Paris, 1894–1902, by BAUDOT, a pupil of VIOLLET-LE-DUC. The next step in the history of concrete was taken by MAILLART in 1905. Maillart recognized that concrete could be handled for bridges, not trabeated but arcuated, arch and roadway being a structural unity. A few years later, in 1910–13, Max Berg (1870–1947) built the grandiose dome of the Hala Ludowe at Wroclaw (formerly Jahrhunderthalle, Breslau) of reinforced concrete. In 1919 PERRET, who only very rarely departed from trabeated concrete construction, built the vast Esders clothing workshop in Paris with elegantly slender transverse arches. A unity of pier and vault could also be achieved by what is called mushroom slabs. These were developed by Maillart in Switzerland from 1910 onwards, and concurrently in America. Reinforced concrete also made it possible to build very far-projecting canopies, for instance in GARNIER'S designs for an industrial city, published in 1917. In 1916 FREYSINNET began his airship hangars at Orly. They were of parabolic section with a transversely pleated surface. The greatest master of concrete in our day was – needless to say – NERVI.

Collins 1959; Davey 1961; Mainstone 1975; J. Faber and D. Alsop, *Rein-*

forced Concrete Simply Explained, London 1979; A. Allen, *Reinforced Concrete Design to BS 8110*, London 1988.

Condominium. A building or building complex, usually residential and of low density, in which each unit is individually owned but subject to group control and restrictions.

Conefroy, Abbé Pierre (1752–1816), *see* CANADIAN ARCHITECTURE.

Confessio. In early medieval churches a subterranean chamber or recess located below or near the altar and sheltering a relic.

Conoid. In form like a cone, a term commonly used in connection with the lower part of a medieval vault where the ribs converge, forming approximately an inverted half-cone.

Conservatory, greenhouse or **winter garden.** A glazed building either detached from or attached to a house and opening out of it. The earliest were C17 glass and stone structures, e.g. at Versailles (1684–6), Kew (1761, by CHAMBERS) and the Jardin des Plantes, Paris, by MOLINOS (1795). The great development of conservatories came with the introduction of the wrought-iron glazing bar and metal structures. The first iron and glass conservatory was of 1789 at Stuttgart-Hohenheim. LOUDON built iron and glass greenhouses from 1817 onwards and they culminated in PAXTON's enormous and famous curvilinear iron and glass conservatory at Chatsworth (1836–40), that at Kew by BURTON (1844–8) and that at Lyon in 1847 by Hector Horeau (1801–71). The oldest surviving example is the Camellia House at Wollerton Hall by T. Clarke of 1823.

J. Hix, *The Glasshouse*, London (1974) 1981; S. Koppelman, *Glasshouses and Wintergardens of the Nineteenth Century*, London 1981; Kohlmaier and Von Sartory, *Houses of Glass. A Nineteenth-Century Building Type*, Cambridge, Mass., 1986; M. Wood and A. S. Warren, *Glasshouses. A History of Greenhouses, Orangeries and Conservatories*, London 1988.

Console. An ornamental bracket with a compound curved outline and usually of greater height than projection. *See* ANCONES; BRACKET; CORBEL; MODILLION.

Constructivism. Less a movement – still less a style – than a whole aesthetic (in some respects anti-aesthetic) ideology, crystallized in Soviet Russia *c.* 1920 from ideas already adumbrated by early practitioners of modernism (*see* MALEVICH; TATLIN; INTERNATIONAL MODERN). Though potentially embracing all the arts, its most important achievements were in architecture and design: in the 1920s and early 1930s the VESNIN brothers, LISSITZKY, K. MELNIKOV, N. Ladovski, I. Leonodov and many others produced an outstandingly advanced and functionally effective series of (mostly) public buildings, as well as *avant-garde* exhibition designs and theatrical sets, in the Constructivist spirit of utilitarian simplicity and respect for the logic of materials. Russian Constructivism spawned many competing factions and theoretical '-isms', some extremely iconoclastic (e.g. A. Gan's slogan 'Art is dead!', 1922); the suppression of artistic groupings in the USSR in 1932 signalled a change of Soviet artistic policy that would lead to the return of heavy pseudo-Renaissance pastiche styles for a couple of

decades (cf. RUSSIAN ARCHITEC-
TURE). But the Constructivist heritage
has lived on to the present, to some
extent in Russia, more obviously in the
West, whither it was largely dissemin-
ated through the BAUHAUS. [R. R.
Milner-Gulland]

K. Lodder, *Russian Constructivism*,
London and New Haven 1983; S. O.
Khan-Magomedov, *Pioneers of Soviet
Architecture: The Search for New
Solutions in the 1920s and 1930s*, Lon-
don 1987.

Contant d'Ivry, Pierre (1698–1777),
see VIGNON, Pierre-Alexandre.

Continuous imposts, *see* IMPOST.

Conurbation. A term used in town
planning to denote a group of towns
linked together geographically, and
possibly by their function, e.g. the
towns of the Black Country or the
Potteries. The word was first used by
Patrick GEDDES about 1910.

Cook, Peter (b. 1936), *see* ARCHI-
GRAM.

Coop Himmelbau. An Austrian
group formed in 1968 by Wolf D.
Prix (b. 1942), Helmut Swiczonsky
(b. 1944) and Rainer Michael Holzer,
who left in 1971. Influenced by HOL-
LEIN and by HAUS-RUCKER Co they
developed an aggressive approach with
the Reiss bar (1977), Flammenflügel
bar (1980) and Roter Engel bar (1981),
all in Vienna. Their Merz-Schule project (1981) and Media Skyline complex
for Hamburg (1985) realize better their
radical aims. They published *Architektur Muss Brennen* (Graz) in 1980.

Klotz 1986; K. Offerman, *Coop
Himmelbau*, Stuttgart 1989.

Coping. A capping or covering to a wall,
either flat or sloping to throw off water.

Coptic architecture, *see* EGYPTIAN
ARCHITECTURE.

Corazzi, Antonio (1792–1877), *see*
POLISH ARCHITECTURE.

Corbel. A projecting block, usually of
stone, supporting a beam or other
horizontal member. A series, each one
projecting beyond the one below, can
be used in constructing a vault or arch.

Corbel arch, *see* ARCH.

Corbel course. A continuous projecting course of stones supporting beams
or other horizontal members.

Corbel-ring, *see* SHAFT-RING.

Corbel table. A projecting course of
masonry supported by a range of
CORBELS, forming a parapet; often
found in Norman buildings.

Corbelling. Brick or masonry courses,
each built out beyond the one below
like a series of corbels, to support a
BARTIZAN, chimney-stack, projecting
window, etc., or to form a rough arch,
vault or dome.

Corbie steps or **crow steps.** Steps on
the COPING of a gable, used in Flanders, Holland, north Germany and
East Anglia, and also in C16 and C17
Scotland.

Cordemoy, Jean-Louis de. An early
neo-classical theorist about whom
very little is known except that he was
a priest (prior of St Nicholas at La
Ferté-sous-Jouars) and was not, as is
sometimes said, identical with L. G.
de Cordemoy (1651–1722). His *Nouveau traité de toute l'architecture* (1706)
was the first to preach truth and simplicity in architecture and to insist
that the purpose of a building should
be expressed in its form. His ideas

anticipated and probably influenced those of LAUGIER and LODOLI.

Herrmann 1962; R. Middleton in *Journal of the Warburg and Courtauld Institutes*, 1962; Rykwert 1980.

Cordon. In military architecture, the rounded stone moulding or band below the parapet of the revetment of the rampart, going all round the fort.

Coretti. Small galleries like the boxes of a theatre, often inserted into the choir wall of Baroque churches.

Corinthian order, *see* ORDER.

Cormier, Ernest (1885–1980), *see* CANADIAN ARCHITECTURE.

Cornice. In classical architecture, the top, projecting section of an ENTABLATURE; also any projecting ornamental moulding along the top of a building, wall, arch, etc., finishing or crowning it. That along the sloping sides of a pediment is called a raking cornice. *See* Figs. 44, 66.

Corona. The vertical-faced projection in the upper part of a CORNICE, above the BED MOULDING and below the CYMATIUM, with its SOFFIT or undersurface recessed to form a drip.

Corps de logis. The French term for the main building forming a self-contained dwelling, as distinct from the wings, pavilions, service quarters, stables, etc.

Correa, Charles Mark (b. 1930). Indian architect trained in the USA under Buckminster FULLER and, briefly, Yimoru YAMASAKI. In 1956 he returned to India and has moved steadily away from Modernism towards a more flexible, low-cost style derived from Indian vernacular architecture and building practice, using local materials with great sensitivity, e.g. Bharat Bhavan (1972) and the Parliament building (1984), Bhopal. He has also been active in town planning on a large scale, notably his project for a new Bombay housing estate for two million people.

H. U. Khan (ed.), *C.C.*, Singapore and London (1984) 1987.

Cortile. The Italian term for a courtyard, usually internal and surrounded by ARCADES.

Cortona, Pietro Berrettini da (1596–1669), painter and architect, second only to BERNINI in the history of Roman Baroque art, was born at Cortona, the son of a stone mason. Apprenticed to the undistinguished Florentine painter Commodi, he went with him to Rome *c.* 1612 and settled there. He can have received only superficial training in architecture, if any at all. First patronized by the Sacchetti family, for whom he designed the Villa del Pigneto (1626–36, now destroyed, but a landmark in villa design), he was soon taken up by Cardinal Francesco Barberini and his cultivated circle. Thereafter he had architectural and pictorial commissions in hand simultaneously. His first important building, SS Martina e Luca, Rome (1634–69), is also the first great, highly personal, and entirely homogeneous Baroque church, conceived as a single plastic organism with a single dynamic theme applied throughout. It is notable especially for the pliable effect given to the massive walls by breaking them up with giant columns: these are not used to define bays or space, as they would have been by a Renaissance architect, but to stimulate the plastic sense. The decoration is extremely rich, even eccentric (e.g. the wildly undulating forms of the dome coffering), with here and there Florentine MANNERIST traits. In contrast to Bernini he excluded figure sculpture entirely; he also excluded colour and had the interior painted white throughout.

His use of concave and convex forms in the façade of S. Maria della Pace, Rome (1656–9), is typically Baroque. More original is his application of theatre design to the *piazza*: he treated it as an auditorium, the side entrances being arranged as if they were stage doors and the flanking houses as if they were boxes. The gradual elimination of Mannerist elements from his style and his tendency towards Roman simplicity, gravity, and monumentality are apparent in the façade of S. Maria in Via Lata, Rome (1658–62). Comparison between his early and late works, notably the dome of S. Carlo al Corso, Rome (begun 1668), illustrates his remarkable progress from eccentricity and complexity, with effervescent decoration, to serene classical magnificence. Most of his grander and more ambitious schemes remained on paper (Chiesa Nuova di S. Filippo, Florence; Palazzo Chigi, Rome; Louvre, Paris). Though equally great as painter and architect he said that he regarded architecture only as a pastime.

Wittkower 1982; Varriano 1986.

Cosmati work. Decorative work in marble with inlays of coloured stones, mosaic, glass, gilding, etc., much employed in Italian Romanesque architecture, especially in and around Rome and Naples, C12–13. Roman marble workers of this period were known collectively as the Cosmati from the name Cosma, which recurs in several families of marble workers.

E. Hutton, *The Cosmati. The Roman Marble Workers of the XIIth and XIIIth Centuries*, London 1950.

Costa, Lucio (b. 1902). Born at Toulon in France. Brazilian architect, planner, and architectural historian. He was the leading member of the team which, with LE CORBUSIER as consultant, produced the Ministry of Education, Rio de Janeiro (1937–43). The block of flats in Eduardo Guinle Park (1948–54) is his. As a planner he suddenly rose to fame by winning the competition for Brasilia, the new capital (Nova Cap) of Brazil, in 1957. The plan is a formal one, yet not at all formal in the BEAUX ARTS sense. It has the shape of a bow and arrow or a bird, the head being the square with the two houses of parliament and the parliamentary offices, the tail being the railway station. Close to this are sites for light industry; nearer the head, but on the way along the straight monumental axis towards the station, follows the quarter of hotels, banks, theatres, etc., which lies at the junction of body and wings. The long curved wings (or the bow proper) are for housing; this area is divided into large square blocks, called *superquadre*, each with its freely arranged high slabs of flats, schools, church, etc.

It exemplifies the urban planning principles promoted by CIAM in the 'Athens Charter' and provides an impressive setting for NIEMEYER's buildings.

J. O. Gazenco and M. M. Scarone, *L.C.*, Buenos Aires 1959; F. Bullrich, *New Directions in Latin American Architecture*, New York 1969.

Cottage orné. An artfully rustic building, usually of asymmetrical plan, often with a thatched roof, much use of fancy WEATHERBOARDING, and very rough-hewn wooden columns. It was a product of the picturesque cult of the late c18 and early c19 in England: a group of such cottages was built by NASH at Blaise Hamlet (1811). It might serve merely as an ornament to a park or as a lodge or farm labourer's house, but several, intended for the gentry, were built on a fairly large scale. J. Malton's *Essay on British Cottage Architecture* (1798) focused attention on old English cottages and numerous designs were published during the following decades, e.g. PAPWORTH's *Designs for Rural Residences* (1818). By this date it had become as popular as the small *villa* for middle-class clients. The term 'cottage ornée' was not, of course, used by ARTS AND CRAFTS architects.

C. Hussey, *The Picturesque*, London 1924; Summerson 1983; S. Lyall, *Dream Cottages*, London 1988.

Cotte, Robert de (1656–1735), an early Rococo architect, was instrumental in the diffusion abroad, especially in Germany, of French architectural and decorative fashions. He began under his brother-in-law J. HARDOUIN-MANSART, who established him professionally and whom he later succeeded as Premier Architecte (1709). His main work for the Crown was remodelling the choir of Notre Dame, Paris (completed 1714), with decoration by Pierre LE PAUTRE. His Parisian *hôtels* date from 1700 onwards, the most notable among those that survive being the Hôtel de Bouvallais (*c.* 1717) and the redecoration of François MANSART's Hôtel de Toulouse, now the Banque de France, in which the gallery (1718–19) is a Rococo masterpiece (the decoration is by François-Antoine Vassé). He also worked extensively outside Paris (e.g. Palais Rohan, Stras-

bourg, 1727–8, built 1731–62), and was frequently consulted by German patrons, e.g. for extensions to the *château* at Bonn and for Schloss Clemensruhe at Poppelsdorf (1715); his designs or advice were not always accepted (e.g. at Schloss Brühl, Schloss Schleissheim and the Residenz at Würzburg).

Kalnein and Levey 1972; R. M. Neumann, *R. de C. Architect of the Late Baroque*, Ann Arbor and London 1980.

Coupled roof, *see* ROOF.

Cour d'honneur. The front court of a palace or *château* where honoured guests might alight from their carriages and be formally received.

Course. A continuous layer of stones, bricks, etc., in a wall. A *lacing course* binds the facing to the core of the wall.

Court style, *see* RAYONNANT.

Courtonne, Jean (1671–1739), *see* FRENCH ARCHITECTURE.

Covarrubias, Alonso de (1488–1570), was a mason and decorative sculptor in a limpid, playful Early Renaissance style, though for structural members he still adhered to the Gothic tradition. He appears first as one of the nine consultants for Salamanca Cathedral in 1512, a sign of remarkably early recognition. From 1515 he did decorative work at Sigüenza. The church of the Piedad at Guadalajara (1526) is now in ruins, but the Chapel of the New Kings at Toledo Cathedral (1531–4) survives complete and is a delightful work. The fine staircase of the Archbishop's Palace at Alcalá is of *c.* 1530, the richly tunnel-vaulted Sacristy at Sigüenza of 1532–4. Covarrubias was master mason of Toledo Cathedral and architect to the royal castles (1537 onwards); see the courtyard of the Alcázar at Toledo.

Kubler and Soria 1959.

Cove or **coving.** A large concave moulding, especially that produced by the arched junction of wall and ceiling in a 'cove ceiling'. In a ROOD SCREEN the concave curve supporting the projecting ROOD LOFT is called the coving.

Cover fillet. A moulded strip used to cover a joint in panelling, etc.

Cowl. A metal covering, like a monk's hood, fixed over a chimney or other vent, and revolving with the wind to improve ventilation.

Cradle roof, *see* ROOF.

Craig, James (1744–95), *see* SCOTTISH ARCHITECTURE.

Cram, Ralph Adams (1863–1942). American neo-Gothic architect, he admired BODLEY and took up his Perpendicular Gothic at All Saints, Ashmont (1891), St Thomas's, New York (1905–13, with GOODHUE), and the Chapel and Graduate College, Princeton University (1911 onwards, with Ferguson). His Cathedral of St John the Divine, New York (begun 1911), essays French Gothic. He published *The Gothic Quest* (1907) and *The Substance of Gothic* (1917).

D. S. Tucci, *R.A.C. American Medievalist*, Boston 1975; A. M. Daniel, *The Early Architecture of R.A.C. 1889–1902*, 1980; R. Muccigrosso, *American Gothic. The Mind of R.A.C.*, 1980.

Cramp. A metal pin or other device to bind together stones of the same course. *See* DOWELL.

Credence. A small table or shelf near the altar, on which the Sacraments are placed.

Crenellation, *see* BATTLEMENT.

Crepidoma. The stepped base of a Greek temple.

Crescent. A semi-elliptical row of houses. Invented by John WOOD the younger at the Royal Crescent, Bath (1767–75), which was followed by John CARR's Crescent at Buxton (1780–90), where Wood's invention of a monumental residential crescent was combined with an arcaded ground floor. John Palmer (*c.* 1738–1817) went further with his concave–convex Lansdown Crescent, Bath (1789–93). Crescents became a feature of C19 town planning.

Crest or **cresting.** An ornamental finish along the top of a screen, wall, or roof; usually decorated and sometimes perforated.

Cret, Paul (1876–1945). French architect who settled in the USA in 1903. He built the Pan-American Union (1912–13), the Folger Shakespeare Library (1932) and the Federal Reserve Board Building (1935), all in Washington, DC.

Cretan and Mycenaean architecture. Excavations have revealed the earliest examples of European architecture at Knossos and Phaestos in Crete. Although many of the discoveries are of controversial significance, and most of the proposed reconstructions are unconvincing, enough survives to reveal certain general characteristics. At both Knossos and Phaestos there were elaborate palaces, richly coloured and decorated with selinite revetments, destroyed in the (probably seismic) catastrophe of *c.* 1700 BC which marks the first break in Cretan history. The palaces built to replace them were more carefully integrated with the surrounding landscapes; they had hanging

FIG. 31. *Crocket*
KEY:
1. Finial 2. Crocket

gardens, cool courtyards, and colon-naded walks. Planning seems to have been wilfully asymmetrical, and long corridors linked a bewildering series of tiny rooms with the courtyards and pillared halls. Decorations proliferated, and both interiors and exteriors were boldly and brightly painted in a manner which must have been almost jazzy. Another dramatic destruction occurred *c.* 1400 BC; shortly afterwards Crete seems to have come under Myce-naean control.

The Mycenaeans of the Greek main-land developed the MEGARON and also the *tholos* or BEEHIVE tomb, of which the best surviving example is the so-called 'Treasury of Atreus at Mycenae (C15 BC). Between 1400 and

1200 BC, when the Mycenaeans held the upper hand in the Greek world, they produced an architecture of great monumentality and sophistication. The great cyclopean walls surviving at Mycenae and Tiryns reveal their engineering abilities. They developed the fortified acropolis as the civic and religious centre of the city. They began to use stone sculpture (e.g. the Lion Gate at Mycenae) as well as painting for decoration and, for especially fine rooms, incrustations of alabaster. But their most important achievement was in monumental planning. Ab-andoning the haphazard systems of the palaces at Knossos and Phaestos, they enhanced the majestic impact of the acropolis at Mycenae by arranging a succession of courtyards, staircases, and rooms on a single axis. The My-cenaeans were overthrown and their buildings destroyed by incursions from the north in the C12 BC but two My-cenaean architectural elements – the *megaron* and the acropolis – were destined to survive in GREEK ARCHI-TECTURE.

Crinkle-crankle wall. A serpentine or continuously snake-like curving or undulating wall.

Crocket. A decorative hook-like spur of stone carved in various leaf shapes and projecting at regular intervals from the angles of spires, pinnacles, canopies, gables etc., in Gothic archi-tecture. Also used in Gothic capitals in place of leaves and volutes (*see* CAPI-TAL; Fig. 31).

Crocket capital, *see* CAPITAL.

Cromlech, *see* MEGALITH.

Cronaca, Simone del Pollaiuolo (1457–1508), was a Florentine but, like Giuliano da SANGALLO with

FIG. 32. *Cross*

KEY:

1. Greek cross
2. Latin cross
3. St Anthony's cross
4. St Andrew's cross
5. Double cross
6. Forked cross
7. Maltese cross
8. Clover-leaf cross
9. Cross of Lorraine
10. Papal cross

whom he was to be closely associated, he spent several years in Rome when young (1475–85). He collaborated with Giuliano da Sangallo at the sacristy of S. Spirito, Florence, and with BENEDETTO DA MAIANO at Palazzo Strozzi, Florence, for which he designed the magnificent and famous cornice (1490–1504). His masterpiece is S. Francesco (S. Salvatore) al Monte, Florence (1487–1504) – extremely elegant yet robust and dignified. The Palazzo Guadagni in Florence (1503–6) has been attributed to him.

Heydenreich and Lotz 1974; Goldthwaite 1980.

Cross. One of the most ancient symbolical ornamental devices, found in many cultures from prehistoric times. In ancient Egypt a form of cross called an *ankh*, composed of a T surmounted by a loop, was the symbol of life. The *swastica*, a cross in which the arms are bent at right angles in the same relative direction, is of similarly ancient origin (supposedly a solar symbol), notably in ancient India. A cross became the main Christian symbol when it was adopted by the Emperor Constantine in the early C4, signifying specifically 'Triumph over Death'. It has been used in ornament and has also determined the plans of churches. There were two main types: (1) The Latin cross, with a long arm and a shorter one placed more than halfway up; (2) the Greek cross, with equal arms fixed on a short handle, as represented in Byzantine art from the C5, which signified the thaumaturgical power of Christ. The Greek cross plan was used mainly for Byzantine and Italian Renaissance churches, the Latin cross plan for churches in northern Europe from the Middle Ages onwards. For ornamental use the Christian Church developed various types of cross, sometimes in association with saints (e.g. St Andrew's cross, St Anthony's cross), sometimes by a process of decorative elaboration (e.g. clover-leaf cross). For the main types of cross, *see* Fig. 32.

Cross-domed church. In early Christian and Byzantine architecture, a church plan whose core, enveloped on three sides by aisles and galleries, forms a cross. The core is surmounted by a dome in the centre and four barrel vaults resting on four corner piers. Sometimes called an *ambulatory church*.

Cross-in-square, cross-inscribed, *croix inscrite* or quincunx. The most widely spread Byzantine church plan, of obscure origin. The Nea, completed in 880, is said to have been the first example in Constantinople. It is composed of nine bays. The centre bay is a large square, the corner bays are small squares and the remaining four bays are rectangular. The tall central bay is domed (resting on four piers or

FIG. 33. *Cross-window*

columns), the corner bays are either domed or groin- or barrel-vaulted and the rectangular bays are usually barrel-vaulted.

Cross-rail. A main horizontal member of a timber-framed wall placed between the WALL-PLATE at the top and the SILL at the bottom (*see* TIMBER-FRAMING).

Cross-vault, *see* VAULT.

Cross-window. A window with one MULLION and one TRANSOM. *See* Fig. 33.

Crossing. The space at the intersection of the nave, chancel, and transepts of a church; often surmounted by a crossing tower or dome.

Crow steps, *see* CORBIE STEPS.

Crown. The top part of an ARCH including the keystone. *See* Fig. 4.

Crown-post, *see* ROOF.

Cruciform. Shaped like a cross, as in the plan of a Christian church.

Cruck construction. A category of medieval architecture, of obscure origin, which culminated in such great roofs as those of the C13 Great Coxwell BARN and of Westminster Hall, London (1395–6), where the roof has a span of slightly over 67 ft. It is a multi-tiered construction, combining the hammerbeam and the arch-brace-and-

collar type of ROOF. In cruck construction the CRUCKS or blades extend from the ground or low side-walls to the ridge of the roof. They are the chief load-bearing members that support the roof.

N. W. Alcock, *Cruck Construction: An Introduction and Catalogue,* London 1981.

Crucks. Pairs of inclined timbers known as blades, usually curved, in CRUCK CONSTRUCTION. There are several types. *Base* blades rise from ground level to a tie- or collar-beam (*see* ROOF) upon which the roof truss is carried; in timber buildings they support the walls. *Full* blades rise from ground level to the apex of a building; they serve as the main members of a roof truss and in timber buildings they support the walls. *Jointed* blades are formed from more than one timber; the lower member normally rises from ground level and acts as a wall-post; it is usually elbowed at wall-plate level and jointed just above. *Middle* blades rise from half-way up the walls to a tie- or collar-beam upon which the roof truss is supported. *Raised* blades rise from half-way up the walls to the apex. *Upper* blades are supported on a tie-beam and rise to the apex. *See* Fig. 34.

Crusader castles. The mainly C12 military architecture of the Crusaders in the Holy Land was notable for pilgrim forts, coastal fortifications and, especially, strategic inland castles of which the most notable is the Krak des Chevaliers in Syria, built to secure the Homs Gap by the Knights Hospitaller 1150–1200. It survives almost intact.

T. S. R. Boase, *Castles and Churches of the Crusader Knights,* London 1967.

Crypt. In a church, a chamber or vault

Full cruck

Base cruck

Raised cruck

Middle cruck

Upper cruck

Jointed cruck

FIG. 34. *Crucks*

beneath the main floor, not necessarily underground, and usually containing graves or relics. *See also* CONFESSIO. The term *ring crypt* is used for semi-circular corridor crypts below the apse of a church. They are early medieval and the first seem to belong to the late c6 (St Peter's in Rome).

FIG. 35. *Curtain wall*

Cryptoporticus. In Roman architecture, an enclosed gallery having walls with openings instead of columns; also a covered or subterranean passage.

Cubitt, Thomas (1788–1855), began as a carpenter and became the greatest London speculative builder and developer. He took the crucial step towards INDUSTRIALIZED BUILDING by setting up in 1815 a firm employing all building trades on a permanent wage basis. He accumulated a fortune. Bloomsbury, Tyburn, Belgravia and Pimlico were largely built by him from the 1820s onwards. He or his firm, which included until 1832 his architecturally more gifted brother Lewis (1799–1883), designed most of the buildings, e.g. the west side of Tavistock Square, Gordon Square, Eaton Square, Albert Gate, etc. Belgrave Square itself (by BASEVI) is an exception. Thomas Cubitt also designed and built Osborne House, Isle of Wight (1845–8), under the direction of the Prince Consort. Lewis Cubitt designed and built independently the south side of Lowndes Square, London (1837–9), but is famous for King's Cross station (1851–

2), a masterpiece of railway architecture.

P. Hobhouse, *T.C. Masterbuilder*, London 1971.

Cuijpers, Petrus Josephus Hubertus (1827–1921), *see* CUYPERS, Petrus Josephus Hubertus.

Cul-de-lampe. An ornamental support or pendant of inverted conical form.

Culot, Maurice, *see* BELGIAN ARCHITECTURE.

Cumberland, William Frederick (1821–81), *see* CANADIAN ARCHITECTURE.

Cupola. A DOME, especially a small dome on a circular or polygonal base crowning a roof or turret.

Curtail step. The lowest step in a flight, with a curved end which projects beyond the newel.

Curtain wall. 1. In medieval architecture, the outer wall of a castle, surrounding it and usually punctured by towers or BASTIONS. 2. A non-load-bearing wall which can be applied in front of a framed structure to keep out the weather. In 1918 Willis Polk (1870–1924) gave the Hallidie Building in San Francisco a continuous curtain wall of steel and glass which hung in front of the main frame, thus separating 'structure' from 'cladding'. There are now many types manufactured from a variety of materials; sections may include windows and the spaces between. *See* Fig. 35.

Hart, Henn and Sontag 1985.

Curvilinear tracery, *see* TRACERY.

Cushioned frieze. A frieze with a convex profile, also called a pulvinated frieze.

Cusp. Projecting points formed at the meeting of the FOILS in Gothic TRACERY, etc. *See* Fig. 48.

Cutwater. The wedge-shaped end of a pier of a bridge, so constructed to break the current of water.

Cuvilliés, François (1695–1768). One of the most accomplished Rococo architects. Though he derived inspiration from the French Rococo, his decoration is much more exuberant than anything in France. His masterpiece, the Amalienburg in the park of Nymphenburg near Munich, has an easy elegance and gossamer delicacy which makes it the supreme secular monument of the Rococo. Born at Soignies-en-Hainaut, he entered the service of the exiled Elector Max Emanuel of Bavaria in 1708. As court dwarf, he travelled in the Elector's train through France, and in 1714 accompanied him on his return to Munich. Too small for the army, he began by working as a military architect and showed such promise that he was sent to Paris (1720–24) to study under J.-F. BLONDEL. In 1725 he was appointed Court Architect in Munich with EFFNER. For the Elector's brother he replaced SCHLAUN as architect at Schloss Brühl near Cologne (1728) and designed the beautiful little house of Falkenlust in the park. His first work in Bavaria was the decoration of the Reiche Zimmer in the Residenz, Munich (1729–37, partly destroyed). In 1733 he provided designs for the abbey church of Schäftlarn and for Palais Königsfeld (now the Archbishop's Palace), Munich. His next work was the Amalienburg (1734–9). It is a single-storey building with a large circular room in the centre which makes the garden façade curve outwards gracefully. The carved wood and silvered decorations in the main rooms are of exquisite refinement and the colour schemes are remarkably subtle – a cool watery blue background in the centre, citron yellow in one of the side rooms, and straw yellow in the other. In 1747 he provided plans for Wilhelmstal, near Kassel (erected by C.-L. Du RY). His last major work was the Residenztheater, Munich (1751–3; partly destroyed 1944, restored 1958), one of the last insouciant extravaganzas of the Rococo, liberally decorated with exquisitely carved *putti*, caryatids, swags, trophies of musical instruments, and those frothy cartouches which characterize the style. In 1767 he completed the façade of the Theatine church of St Cajetan in Munich. He published a *Livre de cartouches* in 1738.

H. R. Hitchcock, *Rococo Architecture in Southern Germany*, London 1968; W. Braunfels, *F.C. (1695–1768). Der Baumeister der galanter Architektur des Rokoko*, Munich 1986.

Cuypers, Petrus Josephus Hubertus (1827–1921), the most important Dutch architect of the C19, studied at the Antwerp Academy and in 1850 became City Architect at Roermond. In 1852 he set up a workshop there for Christian art. In 1865 he went to Amsterdam, where he built his two most famous buildings, both in the Dutch brick Renaissance style, and both restrained and without the exuberance of others working in the northern Renaissance styles. The two buildings are the Rijksmuseum (1877–85) and the Central Station (1881–9). But the majority of Cuypers's works

FIG. 36. *Cyma recta; cyma reversa*

are neo-Gothic churches. It is hard to single out a few from the large total: they might be St Catharina, Eindhoven (1859); St Wilibrordus and Sacred Heart, both in Amsterdam (1864–6 and 1873–80); St Bonifatius, Leeuwarden (1881); St Vitus, Hilversum (1890–92); and Steenbergen (1903). Cuypers also restored and enlarged the castle of Haarzuylen (1894–6).

Hitchcock 1977.

Cyclopean masonry. In pre-classical Greek architecture, masonry composed of very large irregular blocks of stone; also any polygonal masonry of a large size. *See* Fig. 75.

Cyma recta. A double-curved moulding, concave above and convex below; also called an *ogee moulding. See* Figs. 36, 44.

Cyma reversa. A double-curved moulding, convex above and concave below; also called a *reverse ogee moulding. See* Figs. 36, 44.

Cymatium. The top member of a CORNICE in a classical ENTABLATURE.

Czechoslovak architecture. In the Middle Ages architecture in Bohemia and Moravia formed part of German architecture. The oldest Christian buildings date from the C10 (Rotunda, Hradshin, Prague, excavated). The principal Romanesque buildings of the C12 and early C13 are St George at Prague, the crypt of Doksany and Strahov Abbey in Prague. At Třebič in the mid C13 French Gothic influence begins to make itself felt. Its climax is Prague Cathedral, begun in 1344 by Matthias of Arras and inspired by Narbonne. It was continued after Matthias's death (d. 1353) by Peter PARLER (choir completed 1385 and much of the south transept before he died in 1399), and his work is the architectural parallel to Charles IV's great epoch in Bohemian history. Charles made Prague the capital of the Empire, added large, boldly planned areas to the city, and built not far from Prague his castle Karlstejn (1348–67). Peter Parler represents a stylistic link with south Germany which was never to snap. With the flowing tracery in its windows, the complicated rib vaults, the flying ribs and the superb portrait heads on the triforium, Prague Cathedral blazed the trail for the architecture of the C15 and early C16 in Germany and Austria. Peter Parler was also the architect of the chancel of Kolin, added to a hall nave of c. 1280 – the first in Bohemia, and of course derived from Germany. Parler also began the cathedral-like church of S. Barbara, Kutná Hora, in 1388. Yet another important church of Charles's time is the octagonal Karlov church in Prague.

Of the other Late Gothic churches the most notable are those of Třeboň, Český Krumlov, Olomouc, Košice, Plzeň, Brno, Most (Brüx) of 1517, and finally Louny (Laun) of 1529 etc. by Benedikt Rieth.

For by then Benedikt RIETH had reached his full maturity. His (though begun by M. Rajsek) are also the fabulously intertwined vaults of Kutná Hora, but his centre was of course Prague. On the Hradshin a predecessor, in the 1480s, had done the amazing oratory in the cathedral with its intricate decorative ribs in the form of branches and twigs. This may or may not be by Rajsek. Rieth's *magnum opus* is the Vladislav Hall on the Hradshin (1493–1502). This combines another intertwined vault with windows of pure Italian Renaissance forms and other details in an insouciant mixture of Latest Gothic and Renaissance.

The last years of the C15 are an early date for Renaissance features in the East, later, it is true, than the years of King Matthias in Hungary, but earlier than the earliest pieces in Poland – and indeed in Austria and Germany. Only one generation later Paolo della Stella (d. 1552) and Bonifaz Wohlmut (d. 1579) built the Belvedere (1534–63) in the Hradshin gardens in the purest and most elegant Cinquecento style. It is of a precociousness as astonishing as Rieth's work. However, with the one exception of Hrezda castle near Prague, a star-shaped hunting-lodge of 1555 with exquisite wholly Italian stucco decoration, it remained alone, and the common development is more similar to the German and the Polish socalled Renaissance. The number of buildings and such features as portals is great. The Schwarzenberg Palace on the castle hill has shaped gables and diamond-cut ashlar blocks (1545 onwards), the Ball Court on the Hradshin (1567–9 by Wohlmut) rich sgraffito decoration. The same technique of decoration appears in a house of 1555 at Telč, whose crazy gable is reminiscent of Poland. Among the most characteristic features are colonnaded courtyards, in two or even three tiers (Bučovice, Velké Losiny).

Count Waldstein, the ambitious general, led architecture back to the Italian grandeur and simplicity with his vast palace in Prague and especially its Loggia corresponding in height to three storeys of the palace (1623–34, by Andrea Spezza (d. 1628) and others). Vienna has nothing to compare with it or the Franco-Italian Schloss Troya, Prague (1679–96) by Jean-Baptiste MATHEY; but the two largest palaces of the second half of the C17 are in the same vein as contemporary work in Vienna (and Hungary). They are the Lobkowicz Palace at Roudnice (1655) and the Černin Palace in Prague (begun 1668), both by Francesco CARATTI. The Černin Palace is twenty-nine windows wide and four storeys high, with no pavilions or other projections, but with the heaviest diamond rustication on the ground floor and serried attached giant columns above. The change from this massed display to the splendidly curvaceous Bohemian C18 style was due to two members of the Bavarian DIENTZENHOFER family: Christoph and Kilian Ignaz. Christoph's principal work is the church of St Niklas on the Kleinseite (Malá Strana) at Prague (1703–11). The source of the style is GUARINI, who designed a church near Prague, and there are also close relations to HILDEBRANDT's work. The most characteristic features of Christoph Dientzenhofer's churches are façades curving forward and backward, interlocked oval spaces inside, and skew or three-dimensional arches. A particularly bold motif is the diagonally set façade towers of Kilian Ignaz Dientzenhofer's St John Nepomuk on the Rock (1730). Among domestic buildings there is much influence from FISCHER VON ERLACH in the early c18 (Liblice Castle by Alliprandi, 1699). A layout of exceptional boldness was that of Kuks, built from 1707 onwards for Count Sporck. A palace, no longer extant, faced a vast block of almshouses across a valley in which was a race-course, and extremely Baroque sculpture adorns the terrace of the almshouses and extends into the dense woods near by. The most interesting architect of these years was Jan Blazej SANTINI-AICHEL with his remodellings of Gothic churches in a queer Baroque-Gothic all his own, though inspired by Rieth and BORROMINI.

The best examples of the turn to neo-classicism are the neo-Palladian mansion of Kačina (1802) by Christian Friedrich Schuricht (1753–1832) and the beautiful saloon in the Rohan Palace, Prague, of 1807 by Louis Joseph Montoyer (c. 1749–1811). The style carries on to the colonnade, baths, etc. of the Chotek gardens at Kroměříž (Kremsier) of the 1830s and 1840s. Little needs singling out between 1850 and 1900, foremost the National Theatre (1868–84) and the Rudolfinum (1884) in Prague by Josef Zítek (1832–1909). Both are Italianate, the theatre richer, the Rudolfinum more restrained and refined.

For the c20 Jan Koteřa (1871–1923),

a pupil of Otto WAGNER in Vienna, was very influential, notably through Josef Gočár (1880–1945) and Josef Chochol (1880–1956), who promoted c. 1910–14 a weird Expressionist, so-called Cubist architecture, of which Chochol's apartment block in Neklan Street, Prague, of 1913 is a remarkable surviving example. In 1920 the commission to reconstruct Prague Castle and its gardens as a presidential palace for the new republic went to another Wagner pupil, Josef PLEČNIK. The INTERNATIONAL MODERN style was going strong before 1930 when MIES VAN DER ROHE built his most important European period house – the Tugendhat house – at Brno, where an exhibition of Modern Culture had been held in 1928. A very notable group of small houses was designed and built for this 1928 exhibition by Jan Visek, Jaroslav Grunt and Bohuslav Fuchs (1895–1972), whose Vesna girls' school and boarding school at Brno of 1929–30 is an outstanding early example of the International style, as are also the Machnac Sanatorium at Trenčianske Teplice (1929–32) by Joromír Krejcar (1895–1949), the Ministry of Pensions, Prague, designed in 1928 by Josef Havlíček (1899–1961) and Karel Honzík (1900–1966), and the Electricity Company building, Prague, by Josef Kriz (b. 1895) and Adolf Bens (b. 1894) of 1926 with its large, glazed inner courtyard. Only a few years later came the plans for the industrial centres of Hradec Králové (which were directed by Gočár) and for Zlin, now Gottwaldov, the town of the Bata shoe factory.

d

FIG. 37. *Dagger*

Dado. 1. In classical architecture, the portion of a PLINTH or PEDESTAL between the base and CORNICE; also called a *die*. See Fig. 68. 2. In modern architecture, the finishing of the lower part of an interior wall from floor to waist height.

Dado-rail, *see* CHAIR-RAIL.

Dagger. A TRACERY motif of the Decorated style: a lancet shape, rounded or pointed at the head, pointed at the foot, and cusped inside. See Fig. 37.

Dagoba, *see* STUPA; SRI LANKAN ARCHITECTURE

Dahlerup, Jens Vilhelm (1836–1907), *see* DANISH ARCHITECTURE.

Dais. A raised platform at one end of a medieval hall, where the head of the house dined with his family circle.

Dance, George (1741–1825), son of George Dance senior (1695–1768, architect of the Mansion House, London, 1739–42), went at seventeen to Italy for seven years with his brother Nathaniel, the painter, winning a gold medal at Parma in 1763 with some surpris-

ingly advanced neo-classical designs. His early buildings are equally original and advanced, and might almost suggest an acquaintance with his more *avant-garde* French contemporaries, LEDOUX and BOULLÉE, because of his use of the elements of architecture as a means of expression rather than of abstract geometrical design. His first building after his return from Italy was the exquisitely pure and restrained All Hallows, London Wall (1765 7). This was followed by his daring and highly imaginative Newgate Prison, London (1770–80, demolished), the most original and dramatic building of its period in England. His ability appears to have been quickly recognized, despite his unorthodoxy, for he was elected a founder member of the Royal Academy in 1768. His later buildings show no decline in originality or imagination: indeed, some of them anticipate SOANE – e.g. the Council Chamber of London Guildhall (1777, destroyed), in which the dome was treated like a parachute with fine lines radiating from the glazed opening in the centre, and the library of Lansdowne House, London (1788–91, completed by SMIRKE), which was lit by concealed windows in the semi-domed *exedrae* at either end of the long flat-vaulted room. After the turn of the century his style became increasingly austere and at Stratton Park (1803–6, only the portico survives) and the College of Surgeons, London (1806–13), he foreshadowed the Greek Revival of Smirke and WILKINS. But his principal artistic legatee was his pupil Soane. His unorthodoxy was exhibited in such works as the neo-Gothic south front of the Guildhall, London (1788–9), and the Tudor Gothic exterior of Ashburnham Place, Sussex (1813–17, demolished).

D. Stroud, *G.D. Architect 1751–1825*, London, 1971; Summerson 1983.

Dancing steps. Shaped steps on a turn, the tapered end being widened to give a better foothold; also called *danced stairs* or *balanced winders*.

Danish architecture. (For medieval and earlier architecture in Denmark, *see* SCANDINAVIAN ARCHITECTURE.) The Renaissance made itself felt late and slowly in Denmark. A house like Hesselagergård of *c.* 1550 has semicircular gables on the Venetian pattern, but otherwise shows little of a true understanding of the Renaissance. The two great castles or country palaces of the Danish kings, Frederick II's Kronborg and Christian IV's Frederiksborg, date from 1574–85 and *c.* 1602–20 respectively. In style they derive from the Netherlands, and Antonius van Opbergen (1543–1611) and Hans Steenwinckel the elder (*c.*1545–1601), working at Kronborg, and Hans and Lourens van Steenwinckel (1587–1639 and *c.* 1585–1619), the architects of Frederiksborg, were in fact Dutchmen. Rosenborg in Copenhagen, a summer palace, dates from 1606–17, the delightful Exchange in Copenhagen by the Steenwinckels, from 1619–25. Its spire, in the form of three entwined dragons' tails, is a landmark. The style of all

these buildings is close to that of the Netherlanders who built at Danzig or Emden, and not too distant from that of Jacobean England. The same style in ecclesiastical architecture appears in Holy Trinity, Kristianstad in Sweden of 1618 etc., probably by the Steenwinckels. The church is a hall church with very slim piers and still has the shaped gables of the Netherlandish style. The burial chapel of Christian IV attached to Roskilde Cathedral was begun even a few years earlier (1614) and has Netherlandish gables of a slightly more advanced type and in addition Gothic windows, a case of Revival rather than Survival.

In 1662 the area of Copenhagen east of Kongens Nytorv and towards the new Citadel was laid out with a grid of straight streets, and in the course of the late C17 and the C18 this area filled up with private palaces and houses as stately as those of the best quarters of Paris during the same period. Their style throughout is the classical style which by then had begun to dominate Denmark and Scandinavia, usually Dutch in inspiration, e.g. the Charlottenborg Palace, Copenhagen (1672–83), in the new area mentioned above, and the Church of Our Saviour, Copenhagen (1682–96), by Lambert van Haven (1630–95), of which the interior recalls de KEYSER's churches in Amsterdam. The former Sophie-Amalienborg in Copenhagen of 1667–73, on the other hand, is an attempt at the Italian villa in Denmark.

Openness to influences from several countries remained characteristic throughout the C18. Frederiksborg (1707–9) and Fredensborg (*c.* 1720) were Italian in inspiration (both were much altered later), Christiansborg, the former royal palace in Copenhagen, was south German, as was the charming Hermitage, Dyrehaven, north of Copenhagen, of 1734 by Laurids de Thura (1706–59). The finest mid-c18 building in Denmark is the Amalienborg in Copenhagen by EIGTVED, laid out in 1750–54 as an octagonal 'place' with four palaces at the diagonals and four streets branching off in the main directions. The style is French, the quality of the highest. Eigtved also designed the Frederiks church, magnificent, with a dominating dome on a high drum, but this was not carried out; Laurids de Thura made another, more classical design, and Nicholas-Henri Jardin (1720–99), called in from France, a third, in its detail even more classical, with a giant portico of detached columns and columns round the drum.

The neo-classical phase of the classical revival began remarkably early in Denmark, where the Moltke Chapel at Karise of 1761–6 and the Chapel of Frederik V in Roskilde Cathedral (final design 1774) by Caspar Frederik Harsdorff (1735–99) are among the purest works of their date anywhere. The leader of the Greek Revival in Denmark was Christian Frederick HANSEN (1756–1845), his principal works being the Law Courts on the Nytorv of 1803–16 and the Church of Our Lady of 1810–26, both in Copenhagen. All on his own is Gottlieb Bindesbøll (1800–1856), whose Thorvaldsen Museum in Copenhagen of 1839–47 is as original within the Greek Revival as the work of Greek THOMSON in Glasgow. For later historicist revival architecture the best examples are the Copenhagen University Library of 1855–61 in the RUNDBOGENSTIL by Johan Daniel Herholdt (1818–1902), with elegant exposed iron

members inside; the Italian Renaissance style Royal Theatre of 1872–4 by Jens Vilhelm Dahlerup (1836–1907), the Magasins du Nord of 1893 onwards by Albert Christian Jensen (1847–1913) with French pavilion roofs, and the French Baroque-style Frederik church, Copenhagen, of 1876–94 by Ferdinand Meldahl (1827–1908), following the style of Jardin's design.

From the 1890s onwards, however, some Danish architects joined the vanguard of those who endeavoured to get away from Victorian obtrusiveness and from historicism. The Copenhagen Town Hall by Martin Nyrop (1849–1921) was begun in 1893 and is as important as BERLAGE's Exchange in Amsterdam as an example of the imaginative treatment of elements from various styles of the past to achieve an original whole. KLINT's famous Grundtvig church, Copenhagen, which was begun finally only in 1919, straddles the gap between traditionalism and post-First World War EXPRESSIONISM. But the Grundtvig church is an exception in Denmark. The way to the c20 was as a rule not via a free Gothic but via Classicism. The paramount examples are the Faborg Museum, Copenhagen, of 1912–15 by Carl Petersen (1874–1923) and the Copenhagen Police Headquarters of 1919–24 by Hack Kampmann (1856–1920) and Aage Rafn (1890–1953). Then Denmark entered its moderate, sensitive c20 style, illustrated at its most Danish in Aarhus University of 1931 onwards by Kay Fisker (1893–1965) with C. F. Møller and P. Stegmann, at its most international by the impeccable work of Arne JACOBSEN and a few others. Only Jørn Utzon (b.1918) has broken with Danish restraint in his rhapsodic design for the Sydney Opera House (begun 1956). His Bagsvaerd church, Copenhagen, of 1974–6 is no less remarkable, as are also his influential courtyard housing schemes – two- or three-storey mass housing with closed alleys to create privacy and segregation of traffic.

D'Aronco, Raimondo (1857–1932), *see* ITALIAN ARCHITECTURE; SOMMARUGA, Giuseppe.

Davis, Alexander Jackson (1803–92) was born in New York, joined Ithiel Town (1784–1844) as a draughtsman and became his partner in 1829. Town had already designed the Connecticut State Capitol with a Greek Doric portico in 1827. The partners now designed more capitols of the same type, but with domes a little incongruously rising over the middle of the longitudinal blocks (Indiana, 1831; N. Carolina, 1831; Illinois, 1837; Ohio, 1839). They are among the grandest of the Greek-Revival buildings in America. Their United States Custom House, New York (1833–42, now the Federal Hall Memorial Museum), should also be mentioned. But Davis could also do collegiate Gothic (New York University, Washington Square, 1832 onwards) and other versions of Gothic, e.g. Lyndhurst, Tarrytown, NY (1838–42), and was versed in the cottage style too, e.g. Gatehouse, Blithewood, Barrytown, NY (1836–51). At the same time he was interested in modern materials – he did an iron shop-front as early as 1835 – and was in fact an exceptionally versatile designer. He was one of the founders of the American Institute of Architects and of the villa estate of Llewellyn Park, NJ (1857).

R.H. Newton, *Town and Davis Architects. Pioneers in American Revivalist Architecture 1812–1870*, New York 1942; W. Andrews, *Architecture, Ambition and Americans. A Social History of American Architecture*, New York (1947) 1978.

De Bodt, Jean (1670–1745), *see* BODT, Jean de.

De Brosse, Salomon (*c.* 1571–1626), *see* BROSSE, Salomon de.

De Carlo, Giancarlo (b.1919), *see* ITALIAN ARCHITECTURE.

De Caux or **De Caus,** Isaac (*fl.* 1612–55) and Salomon (d. 1626), *see* JONES, Inigo.

De Cotte, Robert (1656–1735), *see* COTTE, Robert de.

De Key, Lieven (*c.* 1560–1627), *see* KEY, Lieven de.

De Keyser, Hendrick (1565–1621), *see* KEYSER, Hendrick de.

De Klerk, Michel (1884–1923), *see* KLERK, Michel de.

De Rossi, Giovanni Antonio (1616–95), *see* ROSSI, Giovanni Antonio de.

De Sanctis, Francesco (1693–1740), designed the Spanish Steps in Rome (1723–5), the vast and fabulous external Baroque stairway of elegant, curvilinear design, mounting from Piazza di Spagna to S. Trinità dei Monti; a masterpiece of scenic town planning.

N. A. Mallory, *Roman Rococo Architecture from Clement XI to Benedict XIV (1700–1758)*, New York 1978.

De Stijl. Dutch art and architecture movement founded in 1917 by the theorist Theo van Doesburg (1883–1931). The architects OUD, RIETVELD and Robert van't Hoff (1887–1979) were prominent members, but the painter Mondrian dominated the movement and the group's early buildings were influenced by his theories, e.g. van't Hoff's concrete cubistic houses of 1914–16 near Utrecht. They were also influenced by Frank Lloyd WRIGHT. Rietveld's Schröder house, Utrecht (1924), epitomizes De Stijl architecture. Van Doesburg lectured at the Bauhaus in 1921 and at about this date Oud left the group, which was joined by others, notably LISSITSKY, through whom Constructivism became a strong influence. After van Doesburg's death (1931) the group disbanded. It was very influential, more so than its achievements in architecture would warrant.

M. Friedman (ed.), *De Stijl 1917–1931. Visions of Utopia*, New York 1982; N. J. Troy, *The De Stijl Environment*, Cambridge, Mass., 1983.

De Wailly, Charles (1730–98), *see* WAILLY, Charles de.

Deane, Thomas (1792–1871), *see* RUSKIN, John.

Decastyle. Of a PORTICO with ten fronted columns.

Decker, Paul (1677–1713). German Baroque architect famous for his book of engraved designs: *Fürstlicher Baumeister, oder: Architectus civilis* (1711, 2nd edition with supplementary plates 1716). He worked under SCHLÜTER in Berlin from 1699, later settled in Nuremberg and finally, in 1712, in Bayreuth. Little is known of his work and he appears to have built nothing of importance. But his magnificent and fantastic designs, illustrating the most extravagent type of Baroque architecture and decoration (the latter derived from Bérain through Schlüter) had considerable influence on later German and Austrian architecture, e.g. FISCHER VON ERLACH. Decker's post-

humous *Architectura Theoretica-Practica* (1720) is a handbook to ornament.

E. Schneider, *P.D. der Altere (1677–1713), Beiträge zu seinem Werk*, Düren 1937.

Decorated style or 'Dec'. Historical division of English Gothic architecture 1250–1360 (*see* ENGLISH ARCHITECTURE).

Deinocrates, a Hellenistic architect, contemporary with Alexander the Great, appears to have been the architect, with Paeonius, of the temple of Artemis at Ephesus (*c.* 356 BC). He is credited with the town plan of Alexandria and various other important undertakings, some of them rather fanciful, e.g. the project to transform Mount Athos into a colossal statue of the king, holding in one hand a city and in the other a huge cup into which the mountain streams would be gathered and then cascade into the sea.

R. Martin, *L'Urbanisme dans la Grèce antique*, Paris 1956.

Delafosse, Jean-Charles (1734–91). French architect known mainly for his ornamental designs in a rather ponderous version of the Louis XIV style, with much use of heavy swags and chunky Greek frets. Two of the houses he built in Paris survive – Hôtel Titon and Hôtel Gioux (nos. 58 and 60 rue du Faubourg-Poissonnière) of 1776–80, both discreetly decorated with his favourite type of ornament.

Kaufmann 1955; Braham 1980.

Della Porta, Giacomo (1533–1602), *see* PORTA, Giacomo della.

Delorme, Philibert (1500/15–1570), *see* L'ORME, Philibert de.

Demi-column or **half-column.** A column half sunk into a wall; a type of

Demilune

FIG. 38. *Diaper work*

ENGAGED COLUMN, to be distinguished from a PILASTER.

Demilune. In military architecture, a detached crescent-shaped or triangular outwork, built in the moat.

Dentil. A small square block used in series in Ionic, Corinthian, Composite, and more rarely Doric CORNICES. *See* Figs. 44, 66.

Depressed arch, *see* ARCH.

Desornamentado. The severe, unornamented style of Juan de HERRERA which became the official style of Philip II's reign in Spain.

Desprez, Jean-Louis (1743–1804), *see* SWEDISH ARCHITECTURE.

Deutscher Werkbund. A German association of *avant-garde* manufacturers, architects, artists and writers founded in Munich in 1907 inspired by BEHRENS and others and guided by similar ideas to those of the Deutsche Werkstätten, founded in Dresden in 1898, i.e. to create a national art without any stylistic imitation, based on sound construction and the cooperation of artisan, artist and architect. It was very influential in early industrial design. Their 1914 exhibition in Cologne included notable buildings by GROPIUS, TAUT and van de VELDE. Their influential 1927 experimental housing at Stuttgart (Weissenhofseidlung) was supervised by MIES and

included buildings by LE CORBUSIER, OUD and STAM. By that date, however, its ideas had been taken over by Gropius for the BAUHAUS. Closed in 1934, it reopened in 1945 in East Germany and later in West Germany, but its pioneering days were over.

L. Burckhardt (ed.), *The Werkbund: History and Ideology 1907–33*, New York 1980; R. Pommer and C. F. Otto, *Weissenhof and the Modern Movement in Architecture*, Chicago 1990.

Devey, George (1820–86). Trained as a watercolourist under J. S. Cotman, he anticipated the ARTS AND CRAFTS movement in his love and knowledge of vernacular building – e.g. his cottages and other estate buildings at Penshurst (1850). His later buildings – Betteshanger (1856–61), St Alban's Court, Nonington (1864), and Hall Place, Leigh (begun 1871), all in Kent – are larger and lack the informality and spontaneity of his cottages. Though a pioneer he had little influence (except through VOYSEY) and was overshadowed by MORRIS and WEBB despite their Red House (1860) being much less pure in its use of the vernacular.

M. Girouard, *The Victorian Country House*, London 1979.

Diaconicon. In Byzantine architecture, a room attached to or enclosed in a church; in Early Christian times, utilized for the reception of the congregation's offerings and serving as archive, vestry and library; later used only for the latter functions (also, a sacristy).

Diaper work. All-over surface decoration of a small repeated pattern such as lozenges or squares. *See* Fig 38.

Diaphragm arch. A transverse arch

124

(*see* VAULT) across the nave of a church, carrying a masonry gable. Diaphragm arches divide wooden roofs into sections and were probably used to prevent fire spreading.

Diastyle. With an arrangement of columns three diameters apart. *See also* ARAEOSTYLE; EUSTYLE; PYCNO-STYLE; SYSTYLE.

Die. The part of a PEDESTAL between the plinth and the cornice, also called the DADO. *See* Fig. 68.

Dientzenhofer, Christian or Christoph, *see* DIENTZENHOFER, Kilian Ignaz.

Dientzenhofer, Georg (1643–89). The eldest member of an important Bavarian family of Baroque architects. His main works are the Cistercian abbey church at Waldsassen (1685–1704, with A. Leuthner); the nearby pilgrimage church at Kappel (1685 9), built on an unusual trefoil plan with three minaret-like towers to symbolize the Trinity; and the façade of St Martin, Bamberg (1686–91).

Dientzenhofer, Johann (1663–1726), the son of Georg, studied first in Prague then in Italy (1699–1700). His Italianate cathedral of Fulda (1704–12) reflects BORROMINI's remodelling of S. Giovanni in Laterano. His most impressive church is that of the Benedictine abbey of Banz (1710–18), where his brother Leonhard (d. 1707) had built the conventual buildings; it has a complex ground plan based on a series of ovals and derived perhaps from GUARINI. His masterpiece is Schloss Pommersfelden, one of the largest and finest of German Baroque palaces, built in the remarkably short period of seven years (1711–18), with

vastly imposing staircase (for which the patron, Lothar Franz von Schönborn, sought advice of HILDEBRANDT and also contributed ideas of his own), marble hall, gallery, hall of mirrors, and numerous richly stuccoed apartments.

Dientzenhofer, Kilian Ignaz (1689–1751), the most distinguished member of the Dientzenhofer family, was the son of Christian or Christoph (1655–1722, a brother of Johann who settled in Prague, where he built several churches, notably St Niklas on the Kleinseite, 1703–11, and St Margeretha, Břevnov, 1708–15). Trained first under his father, then under HILDEBRANDT, Kilian Ignaz soon became the leading Baroque architect in Prague. His style is sometimes a little theatrical, and he makes much play with contrasting concave and convex surfaces. His first independent building is the pretty little Villa Amerika, Prague (1717–20), with an almost Chinese roof in two tiers and very elaborate window surrounds. He also built the Palais Sylva-Tarouca, Prague (1749), on a much larger scale. His originality is best seen in his churches, the Thomaskirche, Prague (1723), with its intentionally jarring details; St Johann Nepomuk am Felsen, Prague (1730), with diagonally set towers on either side of the façade, a device he used again at St Florian, Kladno (*c.* 1750), and St Niklas in the Old City in Prague (1732–7). His many other churches are notable for the variety of their Baroque plans – a circle at Nitzau, pure oval at Deutsch-Wernersdorf, a succession of ovals at St Mary Magdalen, Karlovy Vary (1733–6), an elongated octagon with straight sides at Ruppersdorf, and with convex inner and concave outer sides at Hermsdorf

FIG. 39. *Dogtooth*

(near Hallstadt) and star shaped for the Chapel of St Mary of the Morning Star above Wockersdorf. He added a bold dome and towers to his father's St Niklas (1737–51). At the abbey church of Unter-Rotschow (1746–7) he showed for the first time a tendency towards classical restraint.

C. Norberg-Schultz, *K.I.D. e il barocco boemo*, Rome 1968; M. Vilimkova and J. Brucker, *D.*, Rosenheim 1989.

Dietterlin, Wendel (1551–99). German architect and engraver important mainly for his publication *Architectura und Ausstheilung der V. Seuln* (1593–4), with plates which represent the northern MANNERIST conception of architectural decoration at its most bizarre – with frantically interlaced STRAPWORK etc. The complete edition of 1598 has additional plates which are sober by comparison.

Diglyph, *see* TRIGLYPH.

Dinkeloo, John (1918–81), *see* ROCHE, Eamonn Kevin.

Diocletian window, *see* THERMAL WINDOW.

Diotisalvi (*fl.* C12), *see* ITALIAN ARCHITECTURE.

Dipteral. A term applied to a building with a double row of columns on each side.

Discharging arch, *see* ARCH.

Distyle in antis. In classical architecture, a PORTICO with two columns between pilasters or ANTAE.

Dixon, Jeremy (b.1939), *see* ENGLISH ARCHITECTURE.

Dobson, John (1787–1865). The architectural character of the centre of Newcastle, as laid out from *c.* 1835 onwards by the enterprising builder and developer Richard Grainger (1797–1861), is due to Dobson. He studied in London under the watercolourist John Varley and afterwards returned to Newcastle. He could work in the Gothic style, but was at his best in a very restrained Grecian or classical, e.g. Eldon Square, Newcastle (1835, now demolished). His most important buildings are along the triangle of Grey Street–Market Street–Grainger Street (built *c.* 1835–7) and the well-known Central Railway Station (1849–50). His Royal Arcade (1831–2) has been demolished, but his entrance to Newcastle General Cemetery (1836) survives. Of his country houses Nunnykirk (1825) and Meldon Park (1832) are Grecian; Beaufront Castle (1837–41) Gothic; and Lilburn Tower (1829–37) Tudor – all in Northumberland.

T. Faulkner and A. Greg, *J.D.*, Newcastle 1987.

Dodecastyle. Of a PORTICO with twelve frontal columns.

Doesburg, Theo van (1883–1931), *see* DE STIJL.

Dog-leg staircase, *see* STAIR.

Dogtooth. Early English ornament consisting of a series of four-cornered stars placed diagonally and raised pyramidally. *See* Fig. 39.

Dolmen, *see* MEGALITH.

Dome. Vault of even curvature on a circular base. The section can be segmental, semicircular, pointed, or bulbous.

Squinch arches

KEY:
1. Pendentive
2. Drum
3. Dome
4. Lantern

Sail vault; Domical vault; Umbrella vault

FIG. 40. *Dome*

If a dome is to be erected on a square base, members must be interpolated at the corners to mediate between the square and the circle. They can be pendentives or squinches. A *pendentive* is a spherical triangle; its curvature is that of a dome whose diameter is the diagonal of the initial square. The triangle is carried to the height which allows the erection on its top horizontal of the dome proper. A *squinch* is either an arch or arches of increasing radius projecting one in front of the other, or horizontal arches projecting in the same manner. If squinches are placed in the corners of the square and enough arches are erected on them they will result in a suitable base-line for the

dome. In all these cases the dome will have the diameter of the length of one side of the square. It can be placed direct on the circular base-line, when this is achieved, or a drum, usually with windows, can be interpolated. If the dome has no drum and is segmental, it is called a *saucer* dome. If it has no drum and is semicircular, it is called a *calotte*.

Another method of developing a dome out of a square is to take the diagonal of the square as the diameter of the dome. In this case the dome starts as if by pendentives, but their curvature is then continued without any break. Such domes are called *sail vaults*, because they resemble a sail with the four corners fixed and the wind blowing into it.

A *domical vault* is not a dome proper. If on a square base, four webs (CELLS) rise to a point separated by GROINS (*see* VAULT). The same can be done on a polygonal base.

An *umbrella, parachute, pumpkin* or *melon dome* is a dome on a circular base, but also divided into individual webs, each of which, however, has a base-line curved segmentally in plan and curved in elevation. *See* Fig. 40

Doménech I Montaner, Lluis (1850–1923), *see* SPANISH ARCHITEC-TURE.

Domical vault, *see* VAULT.

Domus. In Roman architecture, a house for a single well-to-do family, as distinct from the huts or tenements of the poor and the apartment houses (IN-SULAE) of the middle class. *See* ROMAN ARCHITECTURE.

Donjon, *see* KEEP.

Door, *see* Fig. 41.

FIG. 41. *Door*

KEY:
1. Architrave
2. Top rail
3. Shutting stile
4. Hanging stile
5. Top panel
6. Frieze rail
7. Muntin
8. Middle panel
9. Lock rail
10. Bottom panel
11. Bottom rail

FIG. 42. *Dosseret*

KEY: 1. Dosseret 2. Capital

D'Orbay, François (1631–97), *see* ORBAY, François d'.

Doric order, *see* ORDER.

Doric style, *see* GREEK ARCHITECTURE.

Dormer window. A window placed vertically in a sloping roof and with a roof of its own. It usually serves sleeping quarters, hence the name. Also called a LUCARNE. The gable above a dormer window is often formed as a pediment and called a *dormer head.*

Dorter, *see* MONASTERY.

Dortsman, Adriaan (d. 1682), *see* DUTCH ARCHITECTURE.

Doshi, Balkrishna (b. 1927), *see* INDIAN ARCHITECTURE.

Dosseret. The French term for an additional high block or slab set on top of an ABACUS and placed between it and the SPANDREL of the arch above; also called a *super-abacus.* Common in Byzantine work, and found in some Romanesque buildings. *See* IMPOST BLOCK; Fig. 42.

Dotti, Carlo Francesco (*c.* 1670–1759). A leading Late Baroque architect in Bologna. His sanctuary of the Madonna di S. Luca, Bologna (1723–57), is a masterpiece of dramatic grouping, with a domed church built on an elliptical plan and a boldly undulating colonnade sweeping out from the main façade.

A. M. Matteucci, *C.F.D. e l'architettura bolognese del settecento,* Bologna 1969.

Double-framed roof, *see* ROOF.

Double-pile house. An English C17 type: a rectangular block two rooms deep, the two rows of rooms usually being separated by a corridor running the length of the house. The type was adumbrated in JONES's Queen's House, Greenwich.

Double-return stairs, *see* STAIR.

Dowell. A metal pin between stones

of different courses to prevent shifting; *see also* CRAMP.

Downing, Andrew Jackson (1815–52), the son of a nurseryman and from the beginning an enthusiast for landscape and plants, became America's leading writer on landscape gardening, cottages, and country houses, America's REPTON or LOUDON. His chief writings are *A Treatise on the Theory and Practice of Landscape Gardening,* 1841; *Cottage Residences,* 1842; *Notes about Buildings in the Country,* 1849; and *The Architecture of Country Houses,* 1850. For architectural commissions he was in partnership with Calvert Vaux (1824–95).
Hitchcock 1977.

Dragon beam, *see* BEAM.

Dravidian architecture. A term for south INDIAN ARCHITECTURE.

Dressings. Stones worked to a finished face, whether smooth or moulded, and used around an angle, window, or any feature.

Drip. A projecting member of a cornice, etc., from which rainwater drips and is thus prevented from running down the face of the wall below.

Drip-joint. A joint between two pieces of metal on a roof, acting as a water conductor and preventing water from penetrating between the metal.

Dripstone, *see* HOOD-MOULD.

Drop. The lower projecting end of a newel (*see* STAIR).

Drop arch, *see* ARCH.

Drop ornament. A carved ornament in the form of a pendant.

Drop tracery. A border of pendant tracery on the SOFFIT of a Gothic arch.

Drops. English term for GUTTAE.

Drum. A vertical wall supporting a DOME or CUPOLA; it may be circular, square, or polygonal in plan. Also the cylindrical blocks of stone that make up a column.

Dry masonry. Masonry laid without mortar.

Du Cerceau. A family of French architects and decorators. Jacques Androuet the elder (*c.* 1520–*c.* 1585) was the founder of the dynasty; he is, and always was, more famous for his engravings than for his buildings, none of which survives. The *châteaux* of Verneuil (1568) and Charleval (1570, abandoned unfinished 1574) were probably the best. But he was essentially an inventor of ornament, not an architect, and indulged in the most wanton and grotesque designs, generally in a Late MANNERIST style. His first *Livre d'architecture* (Paris, 1559) reveals his personal vein of fantasy and lack of refinement. It had considerable influence, and some of the more practical designs may even have been built. But he was best known for his *Les plus excellents bastiments de France* (1576–79). His son Baptiste (*c.* 1545–90) succeeded LESCOT as architect at the Louvre in 1578. In 1584 he became Architecte Ordinaire du Roi but had to leave Paris the following year as a Protestant refugee. He provided designs for the Pont Neuf, Paris (1578) and may have designed the Hôtel d'Angoulême, now Lamoignon, Paris (1584). His younger brother Jacques II (1550–1614) was, with LOUIS MÉTEZEAU, the favourite architect of Henry IV. He became Architecte du Roi in 1594 and probably designed the pavilions of the Place des Vosges, Paris. Baptiste's son Jean (*c.* 1590–after 1649) became Architecte Ordinaire du Roi in 1617. He built the *escalier en fer de cheval* at Fontainebleau (1634) and designed two of the most typical Louis XIII Parisian *hôtels* – the Hôtel Sully (1625–9) and the Hôtel de Bretonville (1637–43). They are both remarkable for the richness of their elaborately carved decoration – sculptural friezes, pediments with scrolls and masks, and allegorical figures in niches.

Blunt 1982; R Coope, *Salomon de Brosse and the Development of the Classical Style in French Architecture from 1565 to 1630*, London 1972; D. A. Chevalley, *Der grosse Tuilerientwurf in der Überlieferung Ducerceaus*, Bern and Frankfurt 1973.

Du Ry, Paul (1640–1714). He came of a family of French architects and was the grandson of Charles (*fl.* 1611–36), the son of Mathurin (*fl.* 1639) and nephew of de BROSSE. A Huguenot, he left France after the revocation of the Edict of Nantes in 1685 and settled in Kassel, where he built the Oberneustadt to house other Huguenot refugees. This trim piece of urban layout included the simple, centrally planned Karlskirche (1698–1710, badly damaged but restored). In his post of Oberbaumeister in Kassel he was succeeded by his son, Charles-Louis (1692–1757), who built the Mint and the Militarkasino (both destroyed). Simon-Louis (1726–99), the son of Charles-Louis, was an architect of greater importance. He began under his father, then studied under the Swedish court architect Carl Hårleman in Stockholm (1746–8) and Jacques-François BLONDEL in Paris before beginning a tour of Italy from which he returned in 1756. His first work was

at Schloss Wilhelmstal near Kassel, where he was involved in completing the building begun according to designs of CUVILLIÉS and added the two severely simple little lodges (1756–8). In Kassel he was responsible for laying out the spacious rectangular Friedrichsplatz with the austerely Palladian Fredericianum (1768–79), which is important as the first ever museum-library building designed as such. At Wilhelmshöhe, outside Kassel, he built the south and north wings of the vast and imposingly classical Schloss (1786–90), completed later by H. C. JUSSOW, and probably some of the follies in the Park (e.g. Der Mulang, a Chinese village and the 'Felseneck'). He was also responsible for numerous buildings in Kassel, most of which were destroyed in 1945.

Kaufmann 1955; Hempel 1965; H. K. Boehlke, *S.-L.D.R. Ein Wegbereiter klassizistischer Architekte in Deutschland*, Kassel 1980.

Duban, Félix-Jacques (1797–1870), *see* VIOLLET-LE-DUC, Eugène-Emanuel.

Dudok, Willem Marinus (1884–1974), was architect to the small town of Hilversum near Amsterdam from 1916. He designed many schools and other public buildings, and his style appears to be complete as early as 1921 (Dr Bavinck School, Public Baths): exposed brick; asymmetrical compositions of rectangular blocks, usually with a tower; long bands of low windows. The style reached its climax with the Hilversum Town Hall of 1924–31, internationally one of the most influential buildings of its date. Of Dudok's later buildings, the Utrecht Theatre (1938–41) and the Royal Dutch Steel Works at Velsen (Ijmuiden, 1948) are the most notable.

Hitchcock 1977; M Cramer *et al.*, *W.M.D. 1884–1974*, Amsterdam 1981.

Durand, Jean-Nicolas-Louis (1760–1834), was probably the most widely influential architectural theorist of the early C19, not only in France but also in Germany. He was trained partly under BOULLÉE and partly under the civil engineer Rodolphe Perronet (1708–94), designer of the Pont de la Concorde, Paris). He built little (Maison La Thuile, Paris, 1788, destroyed in C19) but he was employed on festival decorations during the Revolution and submitted numerous projects for public buildings to the Convention. In 1795 he was appointed professor of architecture at the new École Polytechnique, which replaced and was modelled on the royal school of military engineering, retaining this post until 1830. He published in 1800 *Recueil et parallèle des édifices en tout genre* in which public buildings of various periods and countries (including non-European) were illustrated according to his theory of modular proportions. But his major work is the two-volume *Précis et leçons d'architecture* (1802–5, frequently reprinted and translated into German) in which he stated a rationalist ideal of utilitarian functionalism. 'One should not strive to make a building pleasing, since if one concerns oneself solely with the fulfilment of practical requirements, it is impossible that it should not be pleasing,' he wrote. 'Architects should concern themselves with planning and with nothing else.' Yet he abandoned neither the use of historical ornament nor the principle of strictly symmetrical planning.

Hitchcock 1977; W. Szambien, *J.-N.-L. D. 1760–1834*, Paris 1984; J.

Villari, *J.-N.-L. D. (1760–1834): Arte e scienza dell'architettura*, Rome 1987.

Dutch architecture. The oldest preserved buildings in the northern Netherlands belong to the CARO-LINGIAN fringe. They are the WEST-WORK of St Mary at Maastricht and the Valkhof Chapel at Nijmegen, which was built in strict imitation of Charlemagne's palace chapel at Aachen. The ROMANESQUE style proper appears first at Deventer, St Peter at Utrecht and the more impressive abbey church of Susteren (*c.* 1060 onwards), the latter clearly dependent on Werden and Essen. A little later is the grand westwork of St Servatius at Maastricht, again German in type. Even more patent is the German origin of the trefoil-shaped early C12 chancel of Rolduc (Cologne). The mature and late Romanesque of the Rhineland is represented by St Mary at Maastricht and the splendid Roermond Abbey, begun as late as 1219–20. It was Cistercian but shows nothing of Cistercian architectural customs. Its nearest parallel is at Neuss, and, just as in such churches of the Rhineland, a general Romanesque mood is combined with French Early Gothic motifs.

The GOTHIC style was accepted late. The cathedral of Utrecht was begun in 1254. Its style is derived from that of Soissons via the chancel of Tournai only completed in 1255. The vaulting pattern of ambulatory and radiating chapels shows the dependence. The smaller Buur church at Utrecht has the French High Gothic type of piers and was started shortly after 1253. Halls were occasionally built on Westphalian pattern (Zutphen), but the type of the major later medieval churches, the large number and size of which testifies to the prosperity of Holland, is basilican and remarkably simple, with an inner elevation of arcade and clerestory divided by no more than a triforium, a blind triforium or a narrow wall passage. To this type belong the major churches of Breda, Delft (New Church), Dordrecht, Haarlem, The Hague (Great Church), Leiden, all begun in the late C14. The New Church in Amsterdam followed later. All these churches have an ambulatory, but the majority leave out the radiating chapels. Some have very large transepts. The Great Church in The Hague has a specially airy hall nave, which continued inspiring architects into the C17. The only church of richly decorated interior and exterior is St John at Hertogenbosch, started again in the late C14. Of other typical features of the Dutch Gothic the widespread use of brick must be remembered, also with patterns on the façade (as in north Germany) and the great prominence of Late Gothic west steeples with pretty and daring openwork details (Utrecht Cathedral, C14; Zierikzee, 1453 onwards, mostly destroyed; Amersfoort St Mary, later C15; Rhenen, begun 1492).

Concerning secular architecture the earliest noteworthy structures are the circular castles or enclosures of Leiden, Egmond, Teilingen, etc. They are of the late C11 and C12, and some have had as their centre a keep. The most spectacular secular building is the Great Hall of the Binnenhof at The Hague, built in the second half of the C13 and more akin to Westminster Hall than to continental great halls. For the late Middle Ages the lively façades of some town halls (Middelburg, 1412–1599, rebuilt after 1945)

and houses with stepped gables are characteristic.

Holland has some fine Early Renaissance monuments of the 1530s built by Italians, notably the tower of Ijsselstein church (1532–5) by Alessandro Pasqualini (d. before 1559) of Bologna and the courtyard of Breda castle (begun 1536) by Tommaso Vincidor (*c.* 1495–1560) also of Bologna. Buildings such as the town halls of Nijmegen (*c.* 1555) and The Hague (1564–5) show how the new Renaissance motifs are absorbed into the native traditions. Soon, however, out of tradition and the enjoyment of the multifariousness of available Renaissance motifs and the modifications and distortions they were capable of, a gay, boisterous national style with ornate gables and extensive play with brick and stone mixtures was developed. It culminates in the work of Lieven de KEY at Haarlem (Meat Hall, 1602–3, tower New Church, 1613) and in Leiden (Town Hall, 1593–7) and the churches by Hendrick de KEYSER in Amsterdam, which are extremely interesting for their centralizing Protestant plans. This style, as exemplified by buildings like the Kloveniersdoelen at Middelburg (*c.* 1607–10), had immense influence along the German seaboard as far as Gdansk (Danzig) and in Denmark. Architects from the Netherlands are found in most of these places.

At the same time as in England and France classical restraint replaced these 'Jacobean' displays. The first signs of a change were Honselersdijk of 1621–*c.* 1630 and Rijswijk of 1630, both inspired from France and both by unknown architects. But at a time between these two country houses of the Stadholder, Jacob van CAMPEN began his activity; his are the most important classical buildings in Holland. His earliest is the Coymans house in Amsterdam (1624), and in the thirties and forties plenty more outstanding classical buildings appeared, especially van Campen's Mauritshuis in The Hague (1633–5), his magnificent Amsterdam Town Hall, now Royal Palace (begun 1648), and his Nieuwe Kerk at Haarlem (1645–9). Other architects also contributed to this noble and restrained style: Pieter POST with Huis-ten-Bos, The Hague (begun 1645), the Weighhouse at Leiden (1657) and the Town Hall of Maastricht (begun 1659) with its splendid entrance hall, Arend van's GRAVESANDE with the octagonal Mare church at Leiden (1638–48), Adriaan Dortsman (d. 1682) with the circular Lutheran church in Amsterdam (1668–71) and Justus VINGBOONS with the ambitious Trippenhuis in Amsterdam (1662), built as a private house for two brothers. Altogether no other town in Europe is as rich as Amsterdam in prosperous private houses. They allow us to see the whole development from the time of de Keyser into the late c18.

With the late c17 French influence became paramount not only in painting but also in architecture. The finest examples are William of Orange's Het Loo of c. 1685–7 by J. Roman and the French refugee Daniel MAROT, the beautiful town hall of Enkhuisen of 1686–8 by Steven Vennecool (1657–1719), and then such remarkably ambitious private (or formerly private) houses as the Middelburg Library of 1733 (by J. P. van Baurscheidt Jun. of Antwerp), the Royal Library at The Hague of 1734–6 (by Marot) and Felix Meritis in Amsterdam. The latter, by J. Otten Husley (1738–94), is of 1778, hence on the way to neo-classicism.

The Pavilion at Haarlem for Henry Hope, the banker, followed in 1785–8. The best early neo-classical church is St Rosalia in Rotterdam of 1777–9 (by Jan Giudice). This is on the pattern of the palace chapel of Versailles, while the ballroom in the Knuiterdijk Palace in The Hague of the 1820s (by Jan de Greef) is on the pattern of the Vitruvian Egyptian Hall and of its English imitators.

The first third of the c19 was unquestioningly classical and more or less Grecian (Scheveningen, Pavilion, 1826; Leeuwarden, Law Courts, 1846). Then about 1840 neo-Gothic made a late start (Catholic Church, Harmelen, 1838; Gothic Hall behind the Kneuterdijk Palace, The Hague 1840; Riding School, The Hague, 1845; former station, Rotterdam, 1847). Concurrently neo-Romanesque appears, though more rarely (Coolsingel Hospital, Rotterdam, 1842 onwards). As in other countries the Gothic soon turns from the romantic to the archaeologically accurate, and the best examples of this serious-minded Gothicism are the churches by CUYPERS. But Cuypers is famous for his large neo-1600 buildings, clearly disposed and resourcefully detailed (Rijksmuseum and Central Station Amsterdam, 1877–85 and 1881–9).

From there a way into the c20 was found by the brilliant and typically Dutch BERLAGE. His Exchange in Amsterdam of 1897–1903 is in style transitional between historicism and the c20. From Berlage, whose detail tends to be arty-crafty and often very curious, one line went to Johann Melchior van der Mey (1878–1949) and his crazy Scheepvarthuis in Amsterdam (1913–17) and to the EXPRESSIONISM of the Amsterdam School; another line went into the rationalism of DE STIJL and the INTERNATIONAL MODERN, notably the Van Nelle Tobacco Factory, Rotterdam (1926–30), by Johannes Andreas Brinkman (1902–49) and Johannes Hendrik van den Broek (1898–1978), who was later in partnership with Bakema (see below). Cubistic but fantastic is Gerrit RIETVELD's Schroeder house at Utrecht of 1925, cubic and rational and extremely well grouped the buildings of DUDOK. OUD's work during and after the Second World War represents a turn away from rationalism which took place in other countries as well. A noteworthy Dutch achievement after the Second World War was the rebuilding of the centre of Rotterdam, with the Lijnbaan shopping centre (1953–5) by van der Broek and Jakob Berend Bakema (1914–81). More influential has been the work of Aldo Van Eyck (b. 1918), especially his Children's Home, Amsterdam (1958–60), Arnhem Pavilion (1966) and his recent urban renovation work, notably

at Zwolle (1975–7) with Théo Bosch. Among prominent contemporary architects Herman Hertzberger (b. 1932) and Piet Blom (b. 1934) were widely acclaimed for, respectively, the Old Age Home, Amsterdam (1975), and 't Speelhuis, Helmund (1975–8). More recently Rem Koolhaas (b. 1944) has become influential internationally with his OMA (Office for Metropolitan Architecture), formed in 1975, and their subsequent promotion of a cool contextualism, for example the Parliament extension in The Hague (1978) and projects for the Berlin 1984 Bauaustellung. In 1978 he published *Delirious New York* (New York and London).

Dutert, Charles-Louis-Ferdinand (1845–1906), *see* GLASS.

Dwarf gallery. A wall-passage with small arcading on the outside of a building; usual in Romanesque architecture, especially in Italy and Germany.

e

Eames, Charles (1907–78). A universal artist. He designed furniture (the famous Eames Chair of 1940–41, developed in collaboration with Eero SAARINEN), made films (*Black Top*, 1950), and built his own house at Santa Monica in California (1949), No. 8 in John Entenza's Case Study programme and a much admired masterpiece of INDUSTRIALZED BUILDING. Windows and doors were prefabricated standard items from a manufacturer's catalogue. Yet, with these elements Eames succeeded in achieving a light, grid-like effect of Japanese finesse. The metal frames are filled in with transparent and translucent glass and stucco.

A. Drexler, *C.E.*, New York 1973.

Early Christian architecture. The first Christian structures date from after AD 200 and were of three types: meeting-houses, CATACOMBS and MARTYRIA. The meeting-house comprised an assembly room for celebrating the Eucharist, a baptistery and various other rooms, as at Dura Europos in Syria of 200–230, the earliest known. After the recogniton of Christianity by Constantine in 313 the modest meeting-houses were gradually replaced by churches for which the model was found in Roman administrative meeting-halls, not in pagan temples. Thus evolved the Christian BASILICA, e.g. the C4 Lateran Basilica and Old St Peter's in Rome. At first, however, Constantinian church architecture varied from aisleless halls to centralized buildings (e.g. S. Costanza, Rome, *c.* 350; S. Lorenzo, Milan, *c.* 370; S. Gereon, Cologne, *c.* 380) though the latter were usually martyria. With the banning of all heathen cults in 391 Christianity became the official religion of the Roman Empire and the basilica attained its canonical form, e.g. S. Maria Maggiore, Rome, 432–40. Outside Italy early Christian architecture developed similarly (e.g. S. Demetrios, Salonika, C5; S. Leonidas, Corinth-Lechaion, late C5–C6), sometimes with regional variations as at the very imposing ruined church of four basilical cross-arms meeting in an octagon at Qal'at Si'man, Syria, *c.* 480–90. For subsequent developments, *see* BYZANTINE ARCHITECTURE.

Krautheimer 1986.

Early English or 'E.E.'. Historical division of English medieval architecture *c.* 1190–*c.*1250. *See* ENGLISH ARCHITECTURE.

Easter sepulchre. A recess with TOMB-CHEST, usually in the north wall of a CHANCEL; the tomb-chest was designed to receive an effigy of Christ for Easter celebrations.

Eaves. The underpart of a sloping roof overhanging a wall.

Echal. In a synagogue, the fitting enclosing the Ark or cupboard in which are kept the rolls of the Law; often of wood. An ornate example of the C18 exists in London at Bevis Marks, in the form of a large tripartite REREDOS.

Echinus. A convex moulding below the ABACUS of a Doric CAPITAL. *See* Fig. 66. Also the moulding, covered with EGG AND DART, under the cushion of an IONIC capital.

Eclectic. A term applied to works of art and especially C19 and C20 architecture combining elements from two or more historical styles.

École des Beaux Arts, *see* BEAUX ARTS STYLE.

Edge roll, *see* BOWTELL.

Edicula, *see* AEDICULE.

Edwardian architecture, *see* ENGLISH ARCHITECTURE.

Effner, Joseph (1687–1745), born in Munich, was the son of the chief gardener to Max Emanuel, Elector of Bavaria, who sent him to be trained as an architect in Paris under BOFFRAND (1706–15). In 1715 he was appointed Court Architect. He was in Italy in 1718. Between 1719 and 1725 he completed ZUCCALLI's Schloss Schleissheim and designed the magnificent monumental staircase. He also completed Agostino BARELLI's Schloss Nymphenburg outside Munich (1717–23), converting Barelli's Italianate villa into a German Baroque palace and adding several exquisite little pavilions in the park; the Pagodenburg (1717–19, classical exterior with chinoiserie in-

terior), the Roman Badenburg (1719–21), and the precociously picturesque Magdalenklause (1725–8). At the Munich Residenz he was in charge of the new Grottenhof from 1715 where the sparkling Ahnengalerie or Gallery of Ancestors (1726–31) was designed by him, though the ceiling is by CUVILLIÉS. His only later building of note is the Preysing palace in the Residenzstrasse, Munich (1727–34).

Hempel 1965: P. Stadler, *J.E. (1687–1745): Hofbaumeister Max Emanuels*, exh. cat., Dachau 1987.

Egas, Enrique de (d. probably 1534), was the son either of Hanequin of Brussels, who built the upper parts of the towers of Toledo Cathedral and the Portal of the Lions (1452), or of Egas Cueman, his brother, a sculptor who died in 1495. In 1497 Enrique became master mason of Plasencia Cathedral – where work, however, soon stopped and was later continued by JUAN DE ÁLAVA and Francisco de COLONIA – and in 1498 of Toledo Cathedral. Enrique's masterpieces are the hospitals of Santiago de Compostela (1501–11) and Toledo (1504–14), where the north Italian Early Renaissance appears early and at its most delightful. He was consulted at the Seo of Saragossa in 1505, and at Seville Cathedral in 1512 and 1525, and also on cathedral projects at Malaga (1528) and Segovia (1529). He was also connected with the designs for the Royal Chapel at Granada (begun *c.* 1504), and designed Granada Cathedral (begun 1523, but soon turned Renaissance from Enrique's Gothic by SILOE).

Kubler and Soria 1959.

Egg and dart or **egg and tongue.** An OVOLO MOULDING decorated with a pattern based on alternate eggs and arrow-heads. *See* Fig. 43.

FIG. 43. *Egg and dart*

Egyptian architecture. As Herodotus pointed out, the ancient Egyptians regarded the dwelling-house as a temporary lodging and the tomb as a permanent abode. Houses were built of clay, sometimes but not always in the form of baked bricks; tombs and temples reproduced the elements of this domestic architecture on the grandest possible scale and in the most durable materials. Thus the bundles of papyrus stalks used as supports in mud huts were transformed into the majestic carved stone papyrus columns of the temples. No efforts were spared to secure the permanence of the tombs and their attendant temples by such devices as the use of the living rock and the steep BATTER of walls to resist earthquake shocks. The result is an architecture of inhuman, impersonal, and to this day daunting monumentality. Features peculiar to ancient Egyptian architecture include the PYRAMID, the OBELISK, the steeply battered PYLON, the symbolical lotus column, and incised relief decoration without any structural relevance.

The earliest large-scale work in stone is the funeral complex at Saqqara, built by the architect IMHOTEP for King Zoser, founder of the third dynasty (*c.* 2650–2600 BC) – a vast stepped pyramid almost 200 ft high, surrounded by a columned processional hall and other buildings to provide a habitation for the dead king and a realistic stage-setting for ritual, all enclosed by a niched limestone wall. The stepped pyramid was superseded by the regular pyramid, of which the most famous examples are at Giza, built for kings of the fourth dynasty (*c.* 2600–2480 BC). The collapse of the Old Kingdom (*c.* 2000 BC) created the first break in the history of ancient Egyptian architecture. There was a temporary revival in the period of the Middle Kingdom (1991–1650 BC): earlier styles were slightly simplified and less durable materials were used (as in the pyramid of Sesostris I at Lisht). But not until the New Kingdom period (1570–1085 BC) were great buildings once again erected. The most notable monuments are the mortuary temple of Queen Hatshepsut at Deir el Bahari (*c.* 1480 BC) by Senmut, with its pillared halls, colonnades, and gigantic ramps connecting the different levels; the magnificent temple of Amon at Karnak (*c.* 1570–1085 BC); and the many-columned temple of Amon-Mut-Khonsu at Luxor (*c.* 1570–1200 BC). The final revival took place under the rule of the Ptolemies, whom Alexander the Great had established on the Egyptian throne. Numerous temples survive from this period (323–30 BC), still built in the traditional manner, e.g. the temples of Horus at Edfu and the temples on the island of Philae. For later architecture in Egypt *see* HELLENISTIC ARCHITECTURE; ISLAMIC ARCHITECTURE; Hassan FATHY.

Egyptian hall. A hall with an internal PERISTYLE as derived by PALLADIO from VITRUVIUS. It was especially popular with neo-Palladian architects e.g. Lord BURLINGTON's Assembly Rooms in York. It has no direct connection with Egyptian architecture.

Egyptian revival. The art of ancient Egypt interested Europeans from the Renaissance onwards, but the first large-scale imitations (apart from pyramids and obelisks) date from the late c18 and were purely decorative, beginning with the interior of the English coffee-house in Rome by PIRANESI, who published engravings of it in 1769. In France, Napoleon's Egyptian campaign of 1798 stimulated a taste for Égyptiennerie manifested in the decorative arts and a few built structures, notably a fountain of 1809 in rue de Sèvres, Paris. The publication by one of the *savants* who took part in the campaign, Vivant Denon's *Voyage dans la basse et haute Égypte* (Paris 1802, reprinted London 1802), with the first extensive corpus of accurate illustrations of Egyptian monuments, inspired several free imitations in England, beginning with the Egyptian Hall for exhibitions, Piccadilly, London, 1811–12 (demolished), by Peter Frederick Robinson (1776–1858). As the debt of Greece to Egypt was generally acknowledged, windows of trapezoid shape like Egyptian doors were sometimes inserted in GREEK REVIVAL buildings (e.g. by BINDESBØLL and THOMSON). But explicitly Egyptian palm-, lotusbud- and Hathor-columns were used for their associations on a limited range of buildings (the flax mill of Marshall & Co., Leeds, by J. BONOMI II in 1842, the elephant house of 1858 in the Antwerp zoo) and also for cemetery entrances (Sharrow Vale, Sheffield, 1836; Highgate, London, 1839–42) and many later both in England and the USA. Egyptian motifs were taken up in the 1920s by ART DECO architects and designers, e.g. Carreras cigarette factory, Hampstead Road, London, 1928, by A. G. Porri.

R. Carrott, *The Egyptian Revival*, Berkeley 1978; J. S. Curl, *The Egyptian Revival*, London 1982.

Ehn, Karl (1884–1957), *see* AUSTRIAN ARCHITECTURE.

Ehrenkrantz, Ezra (b. 1933), *see* INDUSTRIALIZED BUILDING.

Ehrensvard, Carl August (1745–1800), *see* SWEDISH ARCHITECTURE.

Eiermann, Egon (1904–70), was a pupil of POELZIG. By concentrating on industrial buildings, Eiermann managed to carry the INTERNATIONAL MODERN of the thirties through the Nazi years in Germany. Of his many post-war factories one of the finest is at Blumberg (1951). His international fame was established by the German Pavilion at the Brussels Exhibition of 1958, a perfect blend of crisp, clear, cubic, transparent blocks and their grouping in a landscape setting. The solution to the problem of grouping the new Kaiser-Wilhelm Gedächtniskirche at Berlin (1959–62) with the dramatic neo-Romanesque ruin of the old is more questionable. Other buildings of special importance are the offices of the Essener Steinkohlen-Bergwerke, Essen (1958–60); the wholesale warehouses, etc., for Messrs Neckermann at Frankfurt (1958–61); and the German Embassy, Washington (1961–3). In 1968 he designed an office block for an Italian firm in Frankfurt with towers like inverted chalices.

W. Schirmer (ed.), *E.E. Bauten und Projekte*, Stuttgart 1984.

Eiffel, Gustave (1832–1923), the French engineer, is famous chiefly for the Eiffel Tower, built for the Paris Exhibition of 1889. At 1,010 ft, the tower was the highest building in the world until the Chrysler and then the Empire State buildings were erected in New York. The Eiffel Tower in its immensely prominent position in the centre of Paris marks the final acceptance of metal, in this case iron, as an architectural medium. Eiffel's iron bridges are technically and visually as important as the Eiffel Tower (Douro, 1876–7; Garabit Viaduct, 1880–84). He was also engineer to the Bon Marché store in Paris (1876), and to the Statue of Liberty in New York, both of which have remarkable iron interiors.

M. Besset, *G.E. 1832–1923*, Paris 1957; J. Harriss, *The Tallest Tower. E. and the Belle Époque*, Boston, Mass., 1975; B. Lemoine, *G.E. 1832–1923*, Paris 1984.

Eigtved, Nils (1701–54). Danish Rococo architect famous for the Amalienborg in Copenhagen, the finest c18 urban group outside France. Trained in Dresden and Warsaw under Carl Friedrich PÖPPELMANN (1725–33), he also visited Paris and Rome before settling in Copenhagen in 1735. As court architect he laid out an entire new section of the city with the octagonal Amalienborg (1750–54) and its four palaces set diagonally at its centre. He designed the Frederiks church on axis with it but his designs were greatly altered in execution. His Rococo interiors (1734 onwards) in the royal palace of Christiansborg were destroyed in 1794.

K. Voss, *Arkitekten N.E. 1701–1754*, Copenhagen 1971.

Eisenman, Peter (b. 1932). American architect associated with the NEW YORK FIVE since 1972. He took their concern with 'form' and disdain for function to its furthest limits, his designs for single-family houses being conceived almost as abstract sculptures, e.g. House VI (Frank House), West Cornwall, Conn., 1972. He published *House of Cards* in 1978 and in the 1980s began moving towards a more flexible, almost a 'narrative', conception of architecture, e.g. his 1987 project for a Biocentre at the University of Frankfurt.

Klotz 1988; Jencks 1988.

El Wakil, Abdel-Wahed (b. 1943), *see* FATHY, Hassan.

Eldem, Sedad Hakki (b. 1908), *see* TURKISH ARCHITECTURE.

Elevation. The external faces of a building; also a drawing made in projection on a vertical plane to show any one face (or elevation) of a building. *See* Fig. 6.

Elias of Dereham or **Durham** (d. 1245) was Canon of Salisbury and Wells and a confidant of Archbishops Hubert Walter and Stephen Langton, Bishop Jocelyn of Wells, Bishop Hugh of Lincoln, Bishop Poore of Salisbury, and Bishop des Roches of Winchester. He was present at the sealing of Magna Carta and at the translation of the relics of Thomas à Becket in 1220. He was, in addition, in charge of the King's Works at Winchester Castle and Clarendon Palace, and '*a prima fundatione rector*' of Salisbury Cathedral. *Rector* sounds like administrator rather than designer, but he was also paid for making a vessel for Salisbury Cathedral and is called *artifex* in connection with the new shrine of Thomas à Becket; so he was certainly something of an artist, and it is likely that he was, like ALAN OF WALSINGHAM a hundred years later, a man capable also of designing buildings and of discussing details constructively with the master masons.

Harvey 1984.

Elizabethan and Jacobean architecture, *see* ENGLISH ARCHITECTURE.

Ell. In the USA a single-storey lean-to wing containing a kitchen. Ells were added in the C17 to WEATHER-BOARDED, timber-framed buildings in New England.

Elliot, Archibald (1760–1823), *see* SCOTTISH ARCHITECTURE.

Elliot, James (1770– 1810), *see* SCOTTISH ARCHITECTURE.

Elliptical arch, *see* ARCH.

Ellis, Peter (1804–84). A Liverpool architect now famous as a pioneer of the modern office building. His Oriel Chambers in Water Street, Liverpool, of 1864, with its façade glazed throughout in the form of angular oriels separated by very slender mullions, foreshadows the Chicago skyscraper of twenty years later. The back is almost entirely of glass, cantilevered out in front of the frame, itself of cast iron with brick arches. The back of his office block, No. 16 Cook Street, Liverpool (1866), is even more advanced, consisting of a wall and spiral staircase entirely of glass except for the thinnest of iron mullions.

Hitchcock 1977.

Elmes, Harvey Lonsdale (1814–47). The son of James Elmes (1782–1862), architect and writer, a champion of the Elgin Marbles, of Keats, and of Wordsworth. James wrote on prison reform, and in 1823 edited the life and works of Wren. Harvey was a pupil of his father and in 1836 won the competition for St George's Hall, Liverpool (designed 1840). Even though, in its grouping and its massing of columns, it is no longer of Grecian purity, the building is convincedly classical. The interior was completed brilliantly by C. R. COCKERELL in 1851–4.

Colvin 1978.

Ely, *see* REGINALD OF ELY.

Emberton, Joseph (1890–1956), *see* ENGLISH ARCHITECTURE.

Embrasure. A recess for a window, door, etc., or a small opening in the wall or PARAPET of a fortified building, usually splayed on the inside.

Empire style, *see* CLASSICISM.

Encaustic tiles. Earthenware tiles glazed and decorated, much used in the Middle Ages and in Victorian churches for flooring.

Enceinte. In military architecture, the main enclosure of a fortress, surrounded by the wall or ditch.

Endell, August (1871–1925), *see* ART NOUVEAU.

Enfilade. The French system of aligning internal doors in a sequence so that a vista is obtained through a series of rooms when all the doors are open. They are usually placed close to the windows. The arrangement was introduced *c.* 1650 and became a feature of Baroque palace planning.

Engaged column. A column attached to, or partly sunk into, a wall or PIER; also called an *applied column* or *attached column. See also* DEMI-COLUMN.

Engel, Carl Ludwig (1778–1840). German but active from 1815 in Finland. He knew SCHINKEL's work and had lived several years in St Petersburg. These are the two sources of his neo-classical style. His main buildings are the Senate (1818–22), the Old Church (1826), the University (1818–32), the Cathedral (1830–40) and the University Library (1836–44), all at Helsinki. The cathedral is strictly centrally planned, a Greek cross with four porticos outside, a quatrefoil inside. Above the centre is a tall dome. The university library has two splendid oblong reading-rooms with detached giant columns all round.

J. M. Richards, *A Guide to Finnish Architecture*, London 1966; N. E. Wickberg, *E.*, exh. cat., Berlin 1970.

English architecture. The Romans left England in 410. No datable document of architecture exists of before the c7, but excavations have proved in places as distant from one another as Tintagel and Llantwit Major in Cornwall and Whitby in Yorkshire that early monastic establishments were of the Egyptian coenobitic type with separate detached huts clustered round a centre with the church and probably a refectory. At Abingdon it must have been the same, and Nendrum is an Irish example. The type reached England via Ireland. Of the same c7 are also the earliest surviving churches. They fall into two groups, one in the south-east, characterized by apses and a triple arcade dividing the choir from the nave, the other in the north, with long, tall, narrow nave and straight-ended chancel: the first group includes St Pancras and St Martin at Canterbury, Reculver, and Bradwell-on-Sea; the latter, Monkwearmouth, Jarrow, and Escomb. None of these has aisles, but instead they had side chambers, called *porticus*. Towers did not exist, but there were west porches. Between the two groups stand Brixworth in Northamptonshire, larger than the others and with aisles, and Bradford-on-Avon in Wiltshire. But the typically Anglo-Saxon decoration of Bradford, with its pilaster-strips, flat blank arches, triangles instead of arches – the whole

applied like the timbering of timber-framed work – is as late as the c10 and is indeed the most prominent decorative feature of later Anglo-Saxon architecture. Towers seem to have made their appearance in the c10 too; they are either at the west end or placed centrally between nave and chancel. Highly decorated examples are to be found at Earls Barton and Barton-on-Humber. Transepts also appear, and aisles become a little more frequent. That churches of timber, which must have been the rule in the earliest centuries, still went on as late as the c11 is proved by Greensted in Essex, which can be dated *c.* 1013. Many churches of the later c11 have Anglo-Saxon side by side with Norman motifs; the mixture is called the *Saxo-Norman overlap*.

What is called Norman architecture in England is not the art of Normandy but that brought by William the Conqueror to England, i.e. really what on the Continent is called Romanesque. The Norman style in fact begins just before the Conquest, with Westminster Abbey as rebuilt by Edward the Confessor. This is a close parallel to such buildings in Normandy as Jumièges, Mont St Michel, and the churches of Caen: internally with arcade, gallery (ample or small, with large or subdivided openings towards the nave), CLERESTORY, and open timber roof; externally with two façade towers and a square crossing tower (Canterbury, Southwell). The volume of building was enormous. Nearly every cathedral and abbey church was rebuilt, and most of the bishops and abbots came from Normandy. But apart from the system of Normandy, there are also interesting variations of divers origin: the mighty single west tower of Ely on the pattern of Germany; the giant niches of the façades of Tewkesbury and Lincoln, also on German patterns; the gallery tucked in below the arch of the arcade (Jedburgh); and the giant round piers of Tewkesbury and Gloucester, perhaps on a Burgundian pattern (as at Tournus). Ornament is prevalently geometrical (zigzag, CRENELLATION, chain, reel, and similar motifs). Figure sculpture is rarely concentrated on the portals as in the French royal domain (York, chapterhouse of St Mary); its connections are rather with the west of France and with Lombardy.

In only one respect does England appear to lead in the European Romanesque style; in the VAULTING of Durham Cathedral. For while England has no parallel to the mighty tunnel vaults of so many French naves and the groin vaults of so many German naves, Durham was rib-vaulted from the beginning (1093), and hers seem to be the earliest rib vaults not only of northern Europe but possibly of Europe altogether. While it may be that some of the elementary rib vaults of Lombardy are in fact of earlier date, those of Durham are without question infinitely more accomplished, and they and their descendants in France (Caen, St Étienne, Beauvais) led to the triumphant adoption of rib vaulting at St Denis and in the whole Gothic style, first in France and then everywhere.

The Gothic style reached England first by means of the CISTERCIAN Order. Its first English buildings of c. 1130–60, however, though provided with pointed arches, have Burgundian Cistercian sources of a Romanesque kind, and where rib vaults first appear, they are derived from Durham rather than France. Cistercian churches go Gothic very gradually about 1160–80 (Roche), and a few non-Cistercian churches take part in this development (Ripon). But the real, the only fully convinced, beginning of Gothic architecture in England is the east end of Canterbury Cathedral, begun by WILLIAM OF SENS in 1174 and brought to completion in 1185 by William the Englishman. Sens and Paris Cathedrals are the precursors, the retrochoir at Chichester and the nave of the Temple Church the immediate successors. Also immediately follows the retrochoir at Winchester, a hall choir, a form liked in England (on the pattern of Anjou churches), as it reappears at Salisbury, the Temple and Barking Abbey.

But real, thoroughly English Gothic, i.e. the so-called Early English style, begins with Wells c. 1175–1239 and Lincoln c. 1190–1280. Here there is more stress on horizontals than in France, there are straight east walls (not radiating chapels), and the details also keep right away from the central French development. The chancel of Lincoln in particular with its crazy vault has no French parallel and begins a distinguished series of figured vaults which precedes those of any other country. The first star vaults are in the Lincoln nave, and the acme of this system is Exeter of the late C13. Less original but equally impressive are Salisbury of 1220– c. 1266 and the east transept of Durham.

Durham Cathedral lies on the castle hill and late C11 as well as C12 domestic parts survive. Altogether, although English castles are primarily castles with keeps, like the French donjons (the Tower in London, Colchester, Rochester, etc.), these keeps were not normally used domestically, but great halls, chapels, etc. were also built. A reform of the defensive system was brought about by the Crusades, in England as (a little earlier) in France. Emphasis was now laid on the defence not of one tower but of the whole wall with its many smaller towers, and often even on more than one concentric wall, on the pattern ultimately of the walls of Constantinople. Such castles are Dover, the Tower of London and the splendid late C13 castles of Wales (Conway, Caernarvon, Harlech, Beaumaris).

In church architecture the late C13 marks the change from the Early English to the Decorated style. This lasted into the second half of the C14, and is characterized first and foremost by the OGEE, a double or S-curve, which occurs chiefly in arches and in the TRACERY of windows. The other main characteristic is a maximum of decoration covering surfaces (e.g. in foliage DIAPERS) and encrusting arches, gables, etc.; the leaves are not naturalistic but stylized, with nobbly forms reminiscent of certain seaweeds. Spatially the Decorated style favours the unexpected vista, especially in diagonal directions. Principal works are the east parts of Bristol Cathedral (begun in 1298) and Wells Cathedral (c. 1290 c. 1340), the Lady Chapel and the famous Octagon at Ely (1321-53), and screens (Lincoln), funerary monuments (Edward II, Gloucester Cathedral; Percy Tomb, Beverley), stalls (Exeter), etc. No other country has anything as novel, as resourceful and as lavish as the English Decorated style, though when a similar direction was taken by Peter PARLER at Prague, it is likely that English influence played a determining part. The start at Prague was in 1353.

At that time, however, England was already turning her back on the Decorated. The Perpendicular style, beginning in London c. 1335 and reaching a full climax in the Gloucester chancel in 1337-57, is the very reverse of the Decorated. Perpendicular is characterized by the stress on straight verticals and horizontals, by slender, vertically subdivided supports and large windows, by window tracery with little fantasy and inventiveness. The signature tune is the panel motif, which is simply arched but with the arch cusped. This occurs in rows and tiers everywhere in the tracery, and almost as frequently in blank-wall decoration. In vaulting the Perpendicular first favours lierne VAULTS, therein following the inventions of the Decorated, and later fan VAULTS, introduced about 1350-60 either in the cloisters at Gloucester or in the chapterhouse at Hereford. For the Early Perpendicular the chancel of Gloucester Cathedral is the most important work; for the time about 1400 the naves of Canterbury (1379-1405 by Henry YEVELE) and Winchester (c. 1360 but mostly c. 1394-1410); for the Late Perpendicular St George's Chapel at Windsor (begun 1474), King's College Chapel at Cambridge (1446-61, 1477-85 and 1508-15) and the chapel of Henry VII at Westminster Abbey (1503-19) and its predecessor, the chancel vault of Oxford Cathedral (c. 1478 onwards). But for the Perpendicular style parish churches are as significant as the major buildings so far noted. The grandest of these are in Suffolk and Norfolk, in Somerset (especially towers), and in the Cotswolds, demonstrating the riches which the wool and cloth trade made for the middle class. The Perpendicular style, once it had been established, went on without major changes for 250 years, and it can be argued that the Elizabethan style in England is more Perpendicular than it is Renaissance.

It was in Henry VII's Chapel that the first works in England in the Italian Renaissance style were put up, the tombs of the Lady Margaret and Henry VII by Pietro Torrigiani of Florence (1512–18). Henry VIII and his court favoured the new style which was impressively promoted in the crafts by Holbein's designs. But the Renaissance in England remained till about 1550 a matter of decoration, and it was coarsened as soon as it fell into native hands. The Protector Somerset in Somerset House was the first to understand Italian or rather by then French Renaissance principles more fully, and from Somerset House the Elizabethan style proceeded. It combines the symmetry of façades, as the Renaissance had taught it, and Renaissance details, with Netherlandish decorative motifs (STRAPWORK) and the Perpendicular belief in very large windows with MULLIONS and TRANSOMS. Longleat (mainly 1568 onwards, by SMYTHSON) is the first complete example: others are Burghley House (1552–87), Montacute (1580–99), Wollaton (1580–85) and Hardwick (1591–7). The first fifteen years of the reign of James I brought no change. Among the principal buildings are Hatfield (1607–12), Audley End (1603–16), Bramshill (1605–12). Plans of houses are often of E or H shape, if they do not have internal courtyards as the largest have. Windows are usually very large and may dominate the walls. Gables, straight or curved in the manner of the Netherlands, are frequent. Wood and plaster decoration is rich and often over-extravagant. Ecclesiastical architecture was almost at a standstill, and even the ample Jacobean-looking church furnishings are usually Jacobean only in style but as late as the 1630s.

By then the greatest revolution in English architecture had, however, already taken place, the revolution achieved by Inigo JONES. His Queen's House at Greenwich was begun in 1616, his Banqueting House in Whitehall in 1619. Jones's strictly Palladian classicism was continued by John WEBB, Sir Roger PRATT, and Hugh MAY. Another contributing factor was the domestic architecture of Holland, which influenced England first in a semi-classical form with Dutch gables. The Jones style was too pure and exacting to find favour immediately outside the most cultured circles. The universal acceptance of classical architecture came only with the time of WREN, but in domestic building the so-called Wren type of house – quite plain, with a middle pediment, a pedimented doorway, and a hipped roof – is not a creation of Wren. Stuart churches are a rarity. They also become more frequent only at the time of Wren and are largely the result of the Fire of London. They are of a wide variety of plans, longitudinal or central or a synthesis of the two, and also of a wide variety of elevational features, especially in the steeples. The range of forms used by Wren is immense. It goes from the noble classical simplicity of the dome of St Paul's to the dramatic Baroque of the west towers of St Paul's and of Greenwich and the Hampton Court plans, to the brick domesticity of Kensington Palace and even to the Gothic Revival of a few of the city churches.

HAWKSMOOR, Wren's favourite

pupil, and the ingenious VANBRUGH followed Wren's lead in working towards a synthesis of Baroque and Gothicism or a general medievalism. The creation of picturesque landscaping in England about 1715–20 is closely allied to this medievalism, which was much stronger than in any other country. The fact that the architects of the generation after Vanbrugh and Hawksmoor returned to the Palladianism of Jones is only at first sight a contradiction. Palladian houses and picturesque grounds must be seen as the two sides of the same coin. The architects in question are men such as Colen CAMPBELL, Lord BURLINGTON, and KENT (the latter, however, much inspired by the Vanbrugh style as well). GIBBS continued rather in the Wren vein: he is chiefly remembered for his churches, which had much influence in America as well as in England. Palladianism ruled until modified by the more elegant and varied style of Robert ADAM, but essentially the Palladian tradition maintained its hold until the 1820s (NASH's Regent's Park terraces).

Georgian architecture is classical in its major exteriors; but on the smaller domestic scale it still has the sensible plainness of the Queen Anne style. Interiors are more elaborate than exteriors; here also Palladianism was the rule at first, but it was handled with greater freedom and verve. A brief phase of ROCOCO followed about the middle of the century: then the enchantment of Robert Adam's delicate decoration captured nearly everybody. Grecian interiors were rare until about 1820, but Victorian licence and exuberance are already heralded in certain Regency interiors (Brighton Pavilion).

But Victorian architecture is not all licence and exuberance. At the other end of the scale is the respect for the past, a historicism taken very seriously as a matter of religious or social responsibility. The licence is usually paramount in domestic, the seriousness in ecclesiastical architecture. Not that historicism did not dominate domestic architecture too, but there it was taken in a less demanding way. Victorian church architecture is almost entirely Gothic, though in the 1840s there was a passing fashion for neo-Norman and neo-Early-Christian or neo-Italian-Romanesque (T. H. WYATT, Wilton). The revived Gothic was treated as a rule correctly (SCOTT); but some of the very best (PEARSON) were able to allow themselves freedom within the Gothic *ensemble*. The Gothic phase most readily imitated was first Perpendicular (Houses of Parliament), then from c. 1840 onwards, thanks chiefly to PUGIN, the so-called Second Pointed or Middle Pointed, i.e. the style of c. 1250–1300, and then from the seventies onwards, again Perpendicular (BODLEY). At the end of the century historicism began to break down, and Norman SHAW could use domestic C17 elements in a church (St Michael, Bedford Park) and John Dando Sedding (1838–91) yet freer, but always sensitively handled, elements, e.g. Holy Redeemer, Clerkenwell, London (1887–8).

In secular architecture the possibility of using Gothic side by side with classical had already been handed down from Wren and Hawksmoor via the Rococo Gothic of Horace Walpole's Strawberry Hill and the romantic Gothic of James WYATT's Fonthill. Other styles had also occasionally been tried, though not seriously (CHINOISERIE, also the Indian of the Brighton Pavilion). But Gothic was given publicly the same weight as classical only with BARRY's Houses of Parliament (1836–68). At the same time Barry introduced a neo-Quattrocento (Travellers' Club) and neo-Cinquecento (Reform Club) and a neo-Elizabethan (Highclere, 1837). So by *c.* 1840 a wide range of historical possibilities were accepted. To them in the late fifties the French Renaissance with its prominent pavilion roofs was added.

Quite separate from all this was the great engineering development. England had been first in the Industrial Revolution (and the size of the new mansions and size and frequency of the new churches bear witness to England's unprecedented industrial and consequently commercial prosperity). The first iron bridges belong to England (TELFORD, BRUNEL), and the largest iron and glass conservatories (PAXTON, BURTON). In BUNNING's Coal Exchange (1846–9) iron and glass first appeared with architectural ambitions, and only two years after its completion Paxton's Crystal Palace was entirely of iron and glass, the whole 1,800 ft length of it. But iron and glass in architecture remained after that confined to exhibition buildings, train sheds (notably St Pancras station, London, of 1864–8 by the engineer William Henry Barlow (1812–1902), with a single span of 74 m rising to 30 m high), and, on the fringe of architecture, to warehouses and office buildings. The functional self-sufficiency of these new materials and the shunning of over-decoration which followed from their convinced use, however, made them unpopular with the High Victorian architects. But from 1877 onwards William MORRIS fought publicly for simplicity, for truth to materials and against over-decoration, though he did so in a militant anti-industrial spirit. Hence those who were convinced by Morris's teachings were less attracted by an alliance with industry and commerce than by an application of Morris's principles to the human scale of domestic architecture. The leaders were Morris's friend Philip WEBB and the more richly endowed Norman SHAW. They, from the sixties onwards, built houses for a small section of the middle class which were fresher and aesthetically more adventurous than anything done at the same time abroad (*see* ARTS AND CRAFTS). Working-class architecture, on the other hand, i.e. housing provided by manufacturers and then by trusts (Peabody Trust), remained grim and was only humanized when HOWARD's garden city principle had begun to be applied to factory housing (Port Sunlight, Bournville). About 1900 England was still leading both in the planning conception of the garden suburb and in the architecture of the so-called Domestic Revival. This, in the work of VOYSEY, and the early work of LUTYENS, was beginning to move out of historicism towards a greater independence of period motifs and towards that simplicity and directness which in the commercial field had already been achieved by the CHICAGO SCHOOL.

The pre-First World War years were notable for the work of MACKINTOSH, BENTLEY, COMPER, HOLDEN and the eccentric Harrison TOWNSEND, though the eclectic Aston WEBB was perhaps more representative of the Edwardian period as typified by such stylistically heterogeneous buildings as the Imperial Institute, London (1887–93, demolished 1957), by Thomas Collcutt (1840–1924), the Rylands Memorial Library, Manchester (1890–99), by Basil Champneys (1842–1935), or the Ashton Memorial, Lancaster (1904–9), by John Belcher (1841–1913). However, when radical innovation became the demand of the more go-ahead architects England lagged behind France, Germany and Austria and contributed only occasionally in the later 1920s and a little more frequently in the 1930s with the work of a few adherents of the INTERNATIONAL MODERN movement, in particular the ARCHITECTS' CO-PARTNERSHIP, COATES, FRY, Francis Yorke (1906 62), Owen Williams (1890–1969) and Joseph Emberton (1890–1956). The Boots factory, Beeston (1931), Peckham Health Centre, London (1935), by Williams, and the Royal Corinthian Yacht Club, Burnham-on-Crouch (1936), by Emberton, are notable *incunabula* of Modernism.

In the immediate aftermath of the Second World War the contributions of the London County Council under MATTHEW and MARTIN to mass-housing and schools were notable as were, slightly later, the public buildings of LASDUN, Sir Basil Spence (1907–76) and others. But already by the late 1950s the first of several reactions against Modernism made itself felt with BRUTALISM in the early work of STIRLING and the SMITH-SONS, followed by the more radical, unproductive but influential ARCHIGRAM. A few years later POST-MODERNISM found its most talented exponents in England in Jeremy Dixon (b. 1939), whose London housing schemes at St Mark's Road, North Kensington (1975–80), Lanark Road,

Maida Vale (1982), and Dudgeon's Wharf, Isle of Dogs (1986–8), are distinctive; Terry Farrell (b. 1938), whose Alban Gate, London Wall (1987), and Charing Cross redevelopment are notable; and the highly original and colourful John Outram (b. 1934), whose Harp Central Heating building at Swanley, Kent (1984), and Blackwall Pumping Station, Isle of Dogs, London (1988), are outstanding. However, recent English architecture is notable mainly for HIGH TECH as developed by FOSTER, PIANO and ROGERS and in recent work by ARUP Associates, Michael HOPKINS, Nicholas Grimshaw (b. 1939) and others. High Tech is unusual for being exclusively English – the only English architectural movement of international significance this century – though some of its major achievements have been for foreign clients. It can be seen as the culmination of several Modernist trends and as sparking off such reactionary, traditionalist responses as the 'fake Georgian' development at Richmond Riverside by Quinlan Terry (b. 1937), comparable to François Spoerry's Port Grimaud in France and Port Liberté, New York.

Ensingen, Ulrich von (d. 1419), and his son Matthäus (d. 1463), the two most important members of a south German family of masons. Ulrich was sufficiently distinguished by 1391 for him to put his name forward as master mason to the cathedral authorities at Milan. In 1392 he became master mason for Ulm Minster (begun 1377). He changed plan and elevation boldly and designed the west tower with its splendid porch. The upper parts of the tower were built to a changed design by Matthäus BÖBLINGER. In 1394

FIG. 44. *Entablature: Corinthian*

KEY:

1. Cyma recta   5. Dentils
2. Fascia   6. Cyma reversa
3. Modillions   7. Astragal
4. Ovolo

Ulrich went after all to Milan, but was not satisfied or able to convince the authorities, and so left in 1395. In 1397 he was appointed master mason at Ulm for life. In 1399, in addition to his job at Ulm, he was put in charge of the continuation of the west tower at Strassburg. Here it was he who started the single tower instead of the two originally projected and built the enchanting octagon stage. The spire, however, is by his successor Johann HÜLTZ. He also worked at the Frauenkirche, Esslingen, from 1398 onwards, and probably designed the west tower, which was carried out (and probably altered) by Hans BÖBLINGER.

Ulrich had three sons who became masons. One of them is Matthäus, who first worked under his father at Strassburg, then became master mason at Berne, where he designed the new minster in 1420–21. From Berne he also undertook the job of master mason at Esslingen, but was replaced there in

1440 by Hans Böblinger. From 1446 he was master mason at Ulm. Of his sons three were masons.

Frankl 1972; L. Mojon, *Der Münsterbaumeister M.E.*, Bern 1967; R Wortmann, *600 Jahre Ulmer Münster*, Ulm 1977; B. Schock-Werner in Recht 1989.

Entablature. The upper part of an ORDER, consisting of ARCHITRAVE, FRIEZE and CORNICE. *See* Figs. 44, 66.

Entasis. The very slight convex curve used on Greek and later columns to correct the optical illusion of concavity which would result if the sides were straight. Also used on spires and other structures for the same reason.

Entresol, *see* MEZZANINE.

Eosander (von Göthe), Johann Friedrich (1670–1729). A pupil of TESSIN, he succeeded SCHLÜTER in Berlin, where he was employed at Charlottenburg from 1702 onwards. The domed tower is his as well as much of the interior. In 1722 he went to Dresden, where he built the Ubigau palace (1724–6).

R. Biederstedt, *J.F.E. Grundzüge einer Bibliographie*, Stockholm 1961; Hempel 1965.

Equilateral arch, *see* ARCH.

Erdmannsdorf, Friedrich Wilhelm Freiherr von (1736–1800). Neo-classical architect inspired by the English neo-Palladians, then fashionable at Frederick the Great's Potsdam, rather than by Palladio himself. He decided to become an architect when travelling in England in 1763. His work is elegant and polite, very different from the radical and severe neo-classicism of his exact contemporary LEDOUX. In 1765–6 he travelled in Italy with his patron the Duke of Anhalt and met both Winckelmann and CLÉRISSEAU. He also visited England again. On his return to Germany he built the neo-Palladian palace at Wörlitz (1768–73). His later buildings in Dessau have all been destroyed: the Schlosstheater (1777), Schloss Georgium (c. 1780) and the Stables and Riding School (1790 91).

F.W. von E., 1736–1800, exh. cat., Wörlitz 1986; H.-J. Kadetz, F.W. von E. 1736–1800. Wegbereiten des deutschen Frühklassizismus in Anhalt-Dessau, East Berlin 1986.

Erickson, Arthur Charles (b. 1924). Canadian architect notable for his pragmatic and eclectic large-scale public projects, the Simon Fraser University, Burnaby, British Columbia (1963–5), Lethbridge University, Alberta (1971), and the Government Offices and Courthouse complex, Vancouver (1973–80), a huge and remarkable urban layout.

E. Iglauer, Seven Stones. A Portrait of A.E. Architect, Seattle 1981; The Architecture of A.E., London 1988.

Erskine, Ralph (b. 1914). Born in England, he settled in Sweden in 1939 and opened an architectural practice in 1946 at Drottningholm. He excelled in low-cost housing, e.g. at Fors in Dalecarlia (1950–53), at Tibro (1959–64) and Kiruna (1959–65), all in Sweden. He became known internationally for his Byker housing at Newcastle-upon-Tyne (1969–80), where the residents were closely consulted throughout the 'participatory design process'. At Byker two-storey terrace houses with irregular small windows and other openings are ranged behind an immense outer wall eight storeys high and one kilometre long. This defensive

conception was later developed by Erskine for a new town at Resolute Bay, Canada (1973 onwards).

S. Ray, R.E., Bari 1978; P Collymore, The Architecture of R.E., London 1982; D. Lasdun, Architecture in the Age of Scepticism, London 1984.

Ervi, Aarne (1910–77), see FINNISH ARCHITECTURE.

Erwin von Steinbach (d. 1318) is one of the most famous medieval architects, because Goethe wrote his prose poem Von deutscher Baukunst (1772) on Strasbourg Cathedral, and especially its façade and steeple, round Erwin's name. The Chapel of the Virgin (1275–1319, destroyed 1682; fragment in the Musée de l'Œuvre de Notre Dame, Strasbourg) bore an inscription saying that 'Master Erwin built this work'. He is mentioned in documents as master of works at Strasbourg from 1284 onwards and on his tomb he is called the 'Gubernator' of the fabric. However, the steeple was not built during his lifetime. But it is likely that the west façade and the famous drawing for it of c. 1275, known as 'dessin B', are by Erwin (Musée de l'Œuvre de Notre Dame, Strasbourg)

Recht 1989.

Escarp or **scarp.** In military architecture, the bank or wall immediately in front of and below the rampart. It is often the inner side of the fosse or ditch.

Eseler, Nicolaus (c. 1400–1492), see GERMAN ARCHITECTURE.

Esonarthex, see NARTHEX.

Espagnolette. An elongated and hinged fastening used on double French doors and windows. Despite the name, it appears to have been of

French, not Spanish, origin and to have come into use in the early C17.

Estípite. A type of PILASTER tapering towards the base, extensively used in Spanish post-Renaissance architecture.

Etruscan architecture. The main building materials were wood, rubble, clay (sometimes baked); stone was used only for the foundations of temples and secular buildings, for fortifications, and for tombs. As the Romans were anxious to erase all memory of the Etruscans very few of their buildings survive above ground level. Their most notable surviving constructions are city walls dating from the C6 to the C4 BC (Tarquinia, Chiusi, Cortona, etc.) – sometimes with handsome if rather heavy arched gateways – though most of these are later (e.g. Falerii Novi, *c.* 250 BC; Perugia, *c.* 300 BC). After the C5 BC temples were built on a plan derived from Greece, but with rather widely spaced, stocky, wooden, unfluted columns, wooden beams, and richly modelled terracotta facings and ACROTERIA applied to them. Underground tombs were usually hewn out of the living rock; their interiors were very elaborately painted and occasionally decorated with stucco reliefs (e.g. Tomb of the Stucchi, Cerveteri, C3 BC).

Boethius 1978.

Eulalius designed the Church of the Holy Apostles, Constantinople (536–45, destroyed), the prototype Greek cross-plan church with five domes. It inspired S. Marco, Venice, and S. Front, Périgueux.

Eustyle. With an arrangement of columns two and a quarter diameters apart. *See also* AEROSTYLE; DIASTYLE; PYCNOSTYLE; SYSTYLE.

Exedra. In classical architecture, a semicircular or rectangular recess with raised seats; also, more loosely, any APSE or niche or the apsidal end of a room or a room opening full width into a larger, covered or uncovered space.

Exonarthex, *see* NARTHEX.

Expressionism. The style dominant in northern Europe about 1905–25. In architecture it is partly a continuation of ART NOUVEAU and was itself continued after the Second World War, e.g. by BRUTALISM. Buildings should not be confined to functioning well but create sensations of freely shaped abstract sculpture. GAUDÍ in his late work was the greatest architect of Expressionism. In Holland Expressionism is represented by the Amsterdam School, notably by the housing estates of Michel de KLERK and most wildly by van der Mey's Scheepvarthuis of 1913–17, both in Amsterdam. In Denmark the Grundtvig church in Copenhagen (1913–26), by KLINT is gothicizing Expressionism. In Germany the most radical architectural Expressionism was never built, notably the fantastic sketches by Hermann Finsterlin (1887–1973), which often do not look like buildings at all, and POELZIG's House of Friendship for Istanbul (1916) and sketches for the Salzburg Festival Theatre (1920). The style of the latter was only once allowed to appear in reality: in the remodelling of a circus in Berlin as the Grosses Schauspielhaus (1918–19). The Einstein Tower at Potsdam by MENDELSOHN (1919–21), the Chile-Haus in Hamburg (1922–3) by Fritz Höger (1877–1949) and St Engelbert, Cologne-Riehl (1930–32), by Dominikus Böhm, are notable Expressionist buildings. Even GROPIUS and MIES VAN

DER ROHE for a short time sacrificed on the altars of Expressionism: Gropius in his monument to the revolutionaries who were killed in the March Riots (1912), Mies in his glass skyscrapers of 1919–21 and the monument to Liebknecht and Rosa Luxemburg (1926).

W. Pehnt, *Expressionist Architecture*, London 1973.

Extrados. The outer curved face of an arch or vault. *See* Fig. 4.

Eyck, Aldo Van (b. 1918), *see* DUTCH ARCHITECTURE.

Eye-catcher or **gloriette.** A decorative building, such as a sham ruin, usually built on an eminence in a landscape park to terminate a view or otherwise punctuate the layout. *See also* FOLLY.

f

Façade. The front or face of a building, emphasized architecturally.

Facing. The finishing applied to the outer surface of a building.

Falconetto, Giovanni Maria (1468–1535), anticipated SANSOVINO's and PALLADIO's classicism in his remarkable loggia and Odeon in Padua (1524, now part of Palazzo Giustiniani). His town-gates, Porta S. Giovanni (1528) and Porta Savonarola, Padua (1530), and the Monte di Pietà, Padua (1531–5), are also fine.

Heydenreich and Lotz 1974.

False arch, *see* ARCH.

False gallery, *see* GALLERY.

Fan vault, *see* VAULT.

Fanlight. 1. A window, often semi-circular, over a door, in Georgian and Regency buildings, with radiating glazing bars suggesting a fan. 2. Also, less commonly, the upper part of a window hinged to open separately.

Fanzago, Cosimo (1591–1678), was born at Clusone near Bergamo, but settled in 1608 in Naples, where he became the leading Baroque architect. Trained as a sculptor, he also worked as a decorator and painter, and was interested less in planning than in decoration. His exuberant style is epitom-

ized in the fantastic Guglia di S. Gennaro (1631–60), and in such effervescent façades as those of S. Maria della Sapienza (1638–41), S. Giuseppe degli Scalzi (*c.* 1660), and his vast unfinished Palazzo Donn'Anna (1642–4). His earlier buildings are more restrained and elegant, e.g. the arcades of the Certosa di S. Martino above Naples (1623–31).

Wittkower 1982; Blunt 1975.

Farrell, Terry (b. 1938), *see* ENGLISH ARCHITECTURE.

Fascia. A plain horizontal band, usually in an ARCHITRAVE, which may consist of two or three fasciae oversailing each other and sometimes separated by narrow mouldings. *See* Figs. 44, 66.

Fathy, Hassan (1900–1989). Egyptian architect notable as a pioneer in the use of traditional materials and methods and for his sensitive adaptation of local vernacular styles. He became known internationally for his village of New Gournia near Luxor (1945–8), largely built of sun-dried brick. His later housing complexes of Bariz in the Kharga oasis (1964) and of Sidi Crier on the Mediterranean coast (1971) were not fully realized. He published *Architecture for the Poor* (1973) and *Natural Energy and Vernacular Architecture* (Chicago 1986). His pupil Abdel-

FIG. 45. *Festoon*

Wahed el Wakil (b. 1943) is outstanding, e.g. the house for Esmat Halawa at Agamy, Egypt (1975), and Al Qiblatain mosque (1987).

D. Rastofer, *H.F.*, London 1985; J. Steele, *H.F.*, London 1988.

Faubourg. A suburb or quarter of a medieval city outside the walls.

Federal style. A chronological rather than stylistic term for North American arts from the establishment of the Federal Government in 1789 to c. 1830.

I. Craig, *The Federal Presence*, Cambridge 1984.

Fehling, Hermann (b. 1909), *see* GERMAN ARCHITECTURE.

Fellner, Jacob (1722–80), *see* HUNGARIAN ARCHITECTURE.

Fenestration. The arrangement of windows in a building.

Feretory. A shrine for relics designed to be carried in processions; kept behind the high altar.

Ferro-concrete, *see* REINFORCED CONCRETE.

Ferstel, Heinrich von (1828–83), *see* AUSTRIAN ARCHITECTURE.

Festoon. A carved ornament in the form of a garland of fruit and flowers, tied with ribbons and suspended at both ends in a loop; commonly used on a FRIEZE or panel and also called a *swag. See* Fig. 45.

Figueroa

Fielded panel, *see* PANEL.

Fieldstone. The American word for RUBBLE.

Figini, Luigi (1903–84), and POLLINI, Gino (b. 1903). Figini and Pollini in 1926 established with TERRAGNI and a few others RATIONALISM or 'Gruppo 7', the first Italian group with an ostensibly modern programme. Their best-known works were done for Olivetti's at Ivrea (headquarters building 1948–50). The church of the Madonna dei Poveri at Milan (1952–6) shows the development from the rational International Style of the thirties to the freer forms of the second half of the century. Of their later buildings the church of SS. Giovanni e Paolo, Milan (begun 1966), may be mentioned.

C. Blasi, *F. e P.*, Milan 1963; V. Savi, *L.F. and G.P. Architects*, 1980.

Figueroa, Leonardo de (1650–1730), the creator of the Sevillian Baroque style, was the first to make use of the cut-brick construction in white or yellow walls surrounded with red trim so intimately associated with the city. His style is rich in an abundance of glazed tiles, patterned columns, SALOMÓNICAS, ESTÍPITES, tassels, foliated brackets, undulating cornices, statues of saints and caryatids and mermen. All his works are in Seville: e.g. Hospital de Venerables Sacerdotes (1687–97); Magdalena church (1691–1709); Salvador church (1696–1711); and the very ornate west entrance to S. Telmo (1724–34). S. Luis, the richest and finest Baroque church in Seville (1699–1731), is usually attributed to him. His son Ambrosio (1700–1775) maintained his style in Seville (S. Catalina, 1732; chapel of the Cartuja,

153

FIG. 46. *Fillet*

1752–8; and Sacrament chapel in El Arahal 1763–6), and the family tradition was carried on over the threshold of the neo-classical period by his grandson Antonio Matías (*c.* 1734–96?), who built the elegant campanile at La Palma del Condado (1780).

Kubler and Soria 1959.

Filarete, Antonio Averlino (*c.* 1400–69), built little but played an important part in the diffusion of the Early Renaissance style. Born in Florence, he adopted the Greek name Filarete (lover of virtue) fairly late in life. He began as a sculptor and executed a bronze door for St Peter's (1443) in Rome. In 1451 he was commissioned by Francesco Sforza to build the Ospedale Maggiore in Milan, which he designed on a very elaborate symmetrical plan. He built only the first storey of the central block, a sturdy basement carrying an elegant Brunelleschian arcade, begun in 1456. While in Milan he completed his *Trattato d'architettura*, which VASARI called the most ridiculous book ever produced; it circulated widely in manuscript but was not printed until the C19. Owing little to VITRUVIUS or ALBERTI, it is a highly original work written as a dialogue and inspired partly by Platonic philosophy, about which he seems to have learned from the Greek scholar at the Sforza court, Francesco da Tolentino called Filelfo. One of its novelties was the association of the Greek orders (he admitted neither the Tuscan nor the Composite) with the classes of society for whom buildings were intended. It also includes numerous designs for hopelessly impractical buildings and plans for two ideal cities, Sforzinda inland and Plousiapolis on the coast, which were to be blessed with every amenity, including a ten-storey tower of Vice and Virtue, with a brothel on the ground floor and an astronomical observatory on the top.

Heydenreich and Lotz 1974; L. Patetta, *L'architettura del quattrocento a Milano*, Milan 1987; Onians 1988.

Fillet. A narrow, flat, raised band running down a shaft between the flutes in a column or along an arch or a ROLL MOULDING; also the uppermost member of a CORNICE, sometimes called a *listel. See* Fig. 46.

Finial. A formal ornament at the top of a canopy, gable, pinnacle, etc.; usually a detached foliated FLEUR-DE-LIS form. *See* Fig. 31.

Finnish architecture. Although Finland lies between Sweden and Russia, Eastern inspiration remained very sporadic right down to the beginning of the C19. The principal influence came throughout the centuries from Sweden and north Germany. Nothing exists that is older than the C13; the earliest buildings are village churches. Brick soon became the favourite material – apart of course from wood. In the village churches detail is elementary. The only large church is the cathedral of Turku (Åbo), which dates from the C14. Star vaults and ornamented brick gables came from Germany, detached wooden campanili (such as also exist in England) from Sweden. The extremely copious wall-paintings have their parallel in Sweden too.

Gothic plan types survived very long, and there is no Early Renaissance decoration. The turn to a classical style came only with the C17, and then again on Swedish patterns. The best early example is the manor house of Sarvlax of 1619, with giant pilasters already of a classical kind. Then in the late C17 the churches – being all Protestant – adopted cruciform and other central plans, again in connection with Swedish patterns (St Katharine, Stockholm). Wood, however, remained the favourite material.

The first climax of Finnish architecture came immediately after the country had become Russian. Helsinki was made the capital in 1812, and a plan for a new centre was made in 1817 (by J. A. Ehrenstrom). Thus C19 Helsinki is a planned town with streets as wide as in the Russian provinces and a large central square. The main buildings around this square are all the work of C. L. ENGEL. They are in a neoclassical idiom of mixed SCHINKEL and Petersburg elements. They culminate in the cathedral of 1830–40. But even as late as 1848 a large church in the country was still built of wood (Kerimaki).

The second climax falls into the years between c. 1850 and c. 1910. They are the years of a national romanticism. Like Sweden, like Russia, like Hungary, Finland looked to a romanticized and very colourful past for inspiration. Alex Gallén, the painter (and of course Sibelius), are the best-known representatives of this trend. In architecture it is exemplified by the National Museum at Helsinki (1904–10) by Eliel SAARINEN, Armas Lindgren (1874–1929) and Hermann Gesellius (1874–1916), and Tampere Cathedral, 1899–1907, by Lars Sonck

(1870–1956). They are quite irregular in outline, use assorted motifs of the past freely and emphasize boldly local materials. Saarinen won the competition for the Helsinki station, and this (1905–14) is a blend of a rational plan with motifs partly curvaceous and fantastical and partly (already) rectangular. The latter motifs come close to those used in the same years by OLBRICH and BEHRENS.

Finland achieved independence at last in 1917. AALTO was nineteen then and the much less known Erik Bryggman (1891–1955) twenty-six. A mere twelve years later Aalto had, with the Paimio Sanatorium and the Viipuri Library (Viipuri was taken away from Finland by Russia in 1940), achieved international fame within the current central European modern style. But Aalto was not just one of many. His strong personality had come through already by 1937, and in his work from 1947 onwards he is one of the leaders of a style of free curves, unexpected skylines, bold rhythms of glass and windowless walls. He liked to use timber and hard red brick. Side by side with him are others, first Bryggman, whose Cemetery Chapel at Turku of 1939 is as bold and novel as anything by Aalto himself, and then a younger generation led by Viljo Revell (1910–64; Toronto City Hall). The place to see the high standard of recent Finnish architecture at its most concentrated is Tapiola outside Helsinki, a 'new town' of c. 17,000 inhabitants, planned as a 'garden city' by Aarne Ervi (1910–77) and carried out from 1952 onwards with many buildings also by him (1962–74) and by Reima Pietilä (b. 1923), whose central buildings in Hervanta New Town, near Tampere (1979), were followed by the lavish palace and administrative complex for the Emir of Kuwait (1970–81).

Fioravanti, Aristotele (c. 1415–86), *see* RUSSIAN ARCHITECTURE.

Fischer, Johann Michael (1692–1766), the most prolific of south German Rococo architects, built no less than twenty-two abbeys and thirty-two churches. Though less gifted than his contemporaries NEUMANN and ZIMMERMANN, he had great sensitivity to spatial relationships and could obtain monumental effects. His masterpiece is the Benedictine abbey church at Ottobeuren (1748–67), with a fine soaring façade and magnificently rich interior frothing with effervescent decoration. The smaller church at Rott-am-Inn (1759–63) shows a tendency towards greater restraint and provides a perfect setting for the statues by Ignaz Günther. Other works include St Anne, Munich (1727–39), on an oval plan; the abbey church at Diessen (1732–9); the church at Berg-am-Laim (1735–43); the Benedictine abbey at Zwiefalten (1741–65), even larger than Ottobeuren and still richer inside; and finally, the Brigittine abbey church at Altomünster (1763–6).

Hitchcock 1968; N. Lieb, *J.M.F. Baumeister und Raumschöpfer im späten Barock Suddeutschlands*, Regensburg 1982.

Fischer von Erlach, Johann Bernhard (1656–1723), a leading Baroque architect in Austria, was more restrained and intellectual than his rival HILDEBRANDT, but also more courtly and traditional. Born near Graz, he began as a sculptor and stucco worker, then went to Italy probably in 1674 and perhaps received some training in architecture under Carlo FONTANA in

Rome. In 1685 he settled in Vienna. There he was eventually appointed Court Architect in 1704. His first building of note is Schloss Frain in Moravia (1690–94), with an imposing oval hall. Italian influence, especially that of BORROMINI, is very evident in his three churches in Salzburg, the Dreifaltigkeitskirche (1694–1702), Kollegienkirche (1694–1707), and Ursulinenkirche (1699–1705). His masterpiece, the Karlskirche in Vienna (begun 1716), is a unique design with no antecedents and no successors, but his Roman memories are again quite explicit, notably in the opening theme of a Pantheon portico framed by a couple of Trajan's columns, expressive of his conscious striving after imperial grandeur. His secular buildings include the façade and monumental staircase, with its monumental ATLANTES, of the Stadtpalais of Prinz Eugen, Vienna (1695–8); the Palais Batthyány-Schönborn, Vienna (*c.* 1700); the Palais Clam Gallas, Prague (1707–12); the Palais Trautson, Vienna (1710–16); and finally, the Hofbibliothek in the Hofburg, Vienna, which he began the year of his death (1723) and which was finished by his son Joseph Emanuel (1693–1742). This library is one of the most imposing interiors in Europe and illustrates his imperial manner at its grandiloquent best. He assumed the title 'von Erlach' on being knighted by the Emperor. His wide scholarship found expression in his *Entwurf einer historischen Architektur* (published Vienna 1721), which was the first architectural treatise to include and illustrate Egyptian and Chinese buildings, and which thus exerted a great influence on various later architectural exoticisms.

H. Aurenhammer, *J.B.F. von E.*,

London 1973; H. Keller (ed.), *F. von E., Entwurf einer historischen Architektur* (1721) 1978; Brucker 1983.

Fisker, Kay (1893–1965), *see* DANISH ARCHITECTURE.

Flamboyant. The late Gothic style in France. In Flamboyant TRACERY the bars of stonework form long wavy divisions (*see* FRENCH ARCHITECTURE).

Flank. In military architecture, the side of a BASTION returning to the courtine from the face.

Flèche. A slender spire, usually of wood, rising from the ridge of a ROOF; also called a *spirelet*.

Flemish bond, *see* BRICKWORK.

Fleur-de-lis. French for lily-flower; originally the royal arms of France.

Fleuron. A decorative carved flower or leaf.

Flight. A series of stairs unbroken by a landing.

Flitcroft, Henry (1697–1769), was a protégé of Lord BURLINGTON, who procured him various posts in the Office of Works, where he eventually succeeded KENT as Master Mason and Deputy Surveyor. He was known as 'Burlington Harry'. Competent but uninspired, he was little superior to the 'imitating fools' who, according to Pope's prophecy, followed Lord Burlington's just and noble rules. His colossal east front at Wentworth Woodhouse (*c.* 1735–70), the longest façade in England, illustrates the empty pomposity into which PALLADIANISM declined: Woburn Abbey is equally derivative (1747–61). His town houses are more successful, notably 10 St James's Square, London (1735). St Giles-in-

the-Fields, London (1731–3), is an unflattering imitation of St Martin-in-the-Fields.

Colvin 1978; Summerson 1983.

Floris, Cornelis (1514/20–75). Primarily a sculptor and ornamentalist (*see* GROTESQUE) but also the leading MANNERIST architect in the southern Netherlands. He visited Rome *c.* 1538. The tall, grave and classicizing Antwerp Town Hall (1561–6) is his masterpiece. Other notable works include the House of the German Hansa, Antwerp (*c.* 1566) and the rood screen in Tournai Cathedral (1572). His style was widely diffused (and debased) by the engravings of Hans Vredeman de VRIES.

Tafuri 1966.

Flötner or **Flettner**, Peter (*c.* 1485–1546). German Renaissance architect, sculptor, goldsmith, and an influential ornamental designer. He published at Nuremberg innumerable engraved designs for furniture, arabesques, etc. In 1518 he was working at the Fugger chapel in St Anna, Augsburg, and later travelled in Italy before settling in Nuremberg in 1522. His rather fanciful version of the Renaissance style can be seen in the fountain in the market-place at Mainz (1526), but his masterpiece as an architect was the Hirschvogelsaal in Nuremberg (1534, destroyed), the earliest and perhaps most accomplished example of Renaissance domestic architecture in Germany.

Hitchcock 1981; M. Angerer, *P.F. Entwürfe*, Kiel 1984.

Flowing tracery, *see* TRACERY.

Flush bead moulding. An inset bead or convex moulding, its outer surface being flush with adjacent surfaces. *See* Fig. 47.

Flushwork

FIG. 47. *Flush bead moulding*

FIG. 48. *i: Detail of flowing tracery showing elaborate use of cusping*

ii: Foil (aa: cusp in section)

Flushwork. The decorative use of KNAPPED FLINT in conjunction with dressed stone to form patterns, such as TRACERY, initials, etc.

Fluting. Shallow, concave grooves running vertically on the SHAFT of a column, PILASTER, or other surface; they may meet in an ARRIS or be separated by a FILLET. If the lower part is filled with a solid cylindrical piece it is called *cabled fluting*. See Fig. 66.

Flying buttress, *see* BUTTRESS.

Flying façade. The continuation of the façade wall of a building above the roof-line, especially in Mayan architecture.

Foil. A lobe or leaf-shaped curve formed by the CUSPING of a circle or an arch. The number of foils involved is indicated by a prefix, e.g. trefoil, multifoil. *See* Fig. 48.

Foliated. Carved with leaf ornament.

Folly. A costly but useless structure built to satisfy the whim of some eccentric and thought to show his folly; usually a tower or a sham Gothic or classical ruin in a landscaped park intended to enhance the view or picturesque effect.

Fontaine, Pierre-François-Léonard (1762–1853), the son and grandson of architects, became Napoleon's favourite architect and was largely responsible, with his partner PERCIER, for the creation of the Empire style. He studied in Paris under Antoine-François Peyre (1739–1823), then in Rome 1786–90. Percier joined him in Paris the following year, and they remained together until 1814. Their decorative style is well illustrated at Malmaison, where they worked for Napoleon from 1802 onwards, Joséphine's tented bedroom being completed in 1812. They extended the north wing of the Louvre to the Tuileries, and built the beautifully detailed Arc du Carrousel (1806–7) between the Tuileries and the Grande Galerie. Their joint works also include the rue de Rivoli, Paris (1801); the fountain in the Place Dauphine, Paris (1802); and much restoration and decoration at the royal *châteaux* (Fontainebleau, Saint-Cloud, Compiègne,

Versailles) and at the Louvre, notably the Salle des Cariatides. Their influence spread rapidly throughout Europe mainly by means of their publications: *Palais, maisons, etc., à Rome* (1798) and especially their *Recueil de décorations intérieures* (1801). The most notable of Fontaine's independent works are the restoration of the Palais Royal, Paris (1814–31, including the Galerie d'Orléans), and the Hôtel-Dieu, Pontoise (1823–7).

M. L. Biver, *P.F., premier architecte de l'empereur*, Paris 1964; Braham 1980.

Fontana, Carlo (1638–1714), was born near Como but settled in Rome *c.* 1655. He began as assistant to CORTONA, RAINALDI, and BERNINI, working under the latter for ten years. His accomplished but derivative style is best seen in the façade of S. Marcello al Corso, Rome (1682–3), and in the many chapels he built in Roman churches: Cappella Cibo in S. Maria del Popolo (1683–7); baptismal chapel in St Peter's (1692–8). Less successful is the Jesuit church and college at Loyola in Spain. He restored and largely rebuilt SS. Apostoli, Rome (1702), and completed Bernini's Palazzo di Montecitorio, Rome, including the main entrance (1694–7). His secular buildings are undistinguished, e.g. Palazzo Spreti, Ravenna (1700), and Ospizio di S. Michele, Rome (1700–1703). By industry and perseverance he became undisputed leader of his profession in Rome and was largely responsible for the classicizing, bookish academicism into which the Baroque style declined. He had an enormous influence all over Europe through his numerous pupils, who included FISCHER VON ERLACH and

HILDEBRANDT in Austria, GIBBS in England, and PÖPPELMANN in Germany.

A. Braham and H. Hager, *C.F. The Drawings at Windsor Castle*, London 1978; Wittkower 1982.

Fontana, Domenico (1543–1607), was born near Lugano, settled in Rome *c.* 1563, and became architect to Sixtus V (1585–90), under whom he laid the foundations of Baroque Rome (Vatican obelisk 1586, four streets radiating from S. Maria Maggiore). His *magnum opus* is the Lateran Palace in Rome (1586), followed by the Vatican Library (1587–9). He assisted Giacomo della PORTA in building the dome of St Peter's. In 1592 he settled in Naples, where he was appointed 'Royal Engineer' and obtained many large commissions including the Royal Palace (1600–1602).

Wittkower 1982.

Fontana, Giacomo (1710–73), *see* POLISH ARCHITECTURE.

Forderer, Walter-Maria (b. 1928), *see* SWISS ARCHITECTURE.

Forechurch, *see* ANTECHURCH.

Formeret. In a medieval VAULT, the rib against the wall, known also as a *wall rib*.

Formwork. Commonly called *shuttering*, this is the temporary form that 'wet' concrete is poured into; it is constructed of braced timber or metal. When the formwork is removed, the concrete is found to have the texture of the material imprinted upon its surface. The formwork may be re-used if the type of construction is suitable, as in walls or repeating floor BAYS.

Förster, Christian Friedrich Ludwig

von (1797–1863), *see* AUSTRIAN AR-
CHITECTURE.

Fortress, *see* CASTLE.

Forum. In Roman architecture, a central open space usually surrounded by
public buildings and colonnades: it
corresponds to the Greek AGORA.

Fosse. A ditch or moat, whether dry
or wet, used in defence.

Foster, Norman (b. 1935). Leading
English HIGH TECH architect. He was
in partnership with Richard ROGERS
as 'Team 4' until 1967. Foster's work
is notable for the elegance and precision
of its sophisticated engineering approach. His chief works to date are the
Willis Faber & Dumas insurance company offices, Ipswich (1975), the Sainsbury Centre for the Visual Arts, Norwich (1977), the Renault warehouse,
Swindon (1983), the Hong Kong Bank
headquarters, Hong Kong (1986),
and, in course of construction, the
Médiathèque, Nîmes.

D. Sudjic, *N.F., Richard Rogers,
James Stirling*, London 1986; I. Lam-
bot, *N.F. Buildings and Projects of
Foster Associates*, London 1990; A.
Benedetti (ed.), *N.F.*, Bologna 1988.

Four-centred arch, *see* ARCH.

Foyer. The vestibule or entrance hall
of a theatre.

Frame construction, *see* FRAMED
BUILDING.

Frame house. In the USA a sawn-
timber house of FRAMED construction,
usually covered with SHINGLES or
WEATHERBOARDING.

Framed building. A structure whose
weight is carried by the framework
instead of by load-bearing walls. The
term includes modern METAL and
REINFORCED CONCRETE structures,
as well as TIMBER-FRAMED (half-
timbered) buildings. In the former
the frame is usually encased within a
FACING (or CLADDING) of light material; in the latter the infilling may be
of WATTLE AND DAUB, brick, etc.

Francesco di Giorgio Martini
(1439–1501/2), a leading Early Renaissance theorist, wrote a treatise
which, though not printed until the
C19, exerted considerable influence,
especially on LEONARDO DA VINCI,
who owned a copy of it. He was born in
Siena, the son of a poultry dealer, and
trained as a sculptor and painter.
Before 1477 he moved to Urbino and
entered the service of Federigo da Montefeltro, who employed him as a medallist and military engineer. He wrote
c. 1482 his *Trattato di architettura civile
e militare*, based partly on VITRUVIUS
(whom he translated or had translated)
and ALBERTI, but showing a more
practical attitude to the problems of
architectural symbolism. Much of it
is devoted to church planning: he
produces a symbolic rationalization of
the church with a long nave and centralized east end, and he also deals with
the placing of the altar in a centralized
church or tribune, stating the case for
a central position to symbolize God's
place in the universe, and for a peripheral position to symbolize his infinite
distance from mankind.

His work as an architect is poorly
documented. He probably contributed
to the design of Palazzo Ducale, Urbino (perhaps the exquisitely beautiful
loggia looking out over the surrounding hills). In 1485 he provided a model
for the Latin cross church of S. Maria
del Calcinaio, Cortona (completed

1516), a masterpiece of Early Renaissance clarity, harmony, and repose. He also provided a design for the austerely simple Palazzo del Comune, Jesi (1486; but much altered). Many other works have been attributed to him: S. Maria degli Angeli, Siena; S. Bernardino, Urbino; and Palazzo Ducale, Gubbio. He was also renowned as a designer of fortifications and war machinery.

A. S. Weller, *F. di G.*, Chicago 1943; R. Papini, *F. di G.M. architetto*, Florence 1946; P. Rotondi, *Il Palazzo Ducale di Urbino*, Urbino 1950; Heydenreich and Lotz 1974.

Francke, Paul (1538–1615), *see* GERMAN ARCHITECTURE.

Frater, *see* MONASTERY.

Fréart de Chambray (1606–76), Roland, *see* LEMERCIER, Jacques.

Freestone. Any stone that cuts well in all directions, especially fine-grained limestone or sandstone.

French architecture. The earliest Christian buildings in France, such as the baptisteries of Fréjus, Mélas, Aix and Marseille Cathedral, all dating from the C5, are of the same Early Christian type as baptisteries of that century in Italy and other Mediterranean countries. The origin of the plan types is Imperial Roman. Of the Merovingian period the two most interesting buildings are the so-called crypt of Jouarre near Meaux and the baptistery of St Jean at Poitiers. The former was not a crypt at all, but an attachment to a church. It was much changed in the C11 and C12, but the columns and the coarsely sub-Roman capitals are probably of the late C7. St Jean is also essentially of the C7, and still has a pediment of Roman descent, but a group of oddly triangular and semicircular windows. Chronicles tell us of more civilized and more Italo-Early Christian buildings (Tours, Clermont Ferrand, both C5) with aisles, columns, transepts and apses. Such buildings must have continued or been revived in the CAROLINGIAN age. However, nothing of any ambition has survived. Germigny-des-Prés is tiny, though with its central plan of Byzantine origin (via Spain?) interesting. The excavations of St Denis have revealed a building of Early Christian type there, with aisles, transepts and apse. It was consecrated in 775. In 790–99 Centula (St Riquier) was built. All we know of it is deduced from texts and parallels with other buildings. It was of revolutionary novelty in plan and elevation, with a WESTWORK, nave and aisles, transepts, a chancel and an apse, and with towers of identical details, perhaps of timber, over the west as well as the east crossings. They were flanked by round stair turrets. The result must have been as proud and as lively as any of the later German Romanesque cathedrals on the Rhine.

The Romanesque style can be said to have started in the C10, when two new types of plans were evolved, both to become Romanesque standard and both devised to allow for the placing of more altars. One is connected with the second building of Cluny Abbey, the centre of a much-needed monastic reform. This was consecrated in 981 and had chancel aisles flanking the east apse, and moreover apsidal chapels on the east sides of the transept. In contrast to this so-called staggered plan is the plan with ambulatory and radiating chapels which seems to have been derived from such a crypt as that of

St Pierre-le-Vif at Sens and to have been adopted in the late C10 or anyway about 1000. Early examples are Tournus and Notre Dame de la Couture at Le Mans. The building to popularize it all over present-day France was, it seems, St Martin at Tours (begun after 997, now largely demolished). From here it became one of the distinguishing features of a small but important group of late C11 to early C12 churches in the country. They are or were St Martial at Limoges, St Sernin at Toulouse and to a lesser degree St Foy at Conques. Their other characteristics are transepts with aisles and, in elevation, galleries and tunnel VAULTS.

The vaulting of the main spaces of churches was a practical as well as an aesthetic need. A stone vault increases security against fire when a church is struck by lightning, and at the same time creates a spatial unity which a timber ceiling on stone walls can never achieve. Yet most French churches before the later C11 had timber ceilings (St Remi at Reims 1005–49, Jumièges in Normandy c. 1040–67, St Étienne, c. 1060–81, and Ste Trinité, 1062–c. 1130, at Caen). The great exception to the rule is St Philibert at Tournus in Burgundy, which has early C11 vaults of such a variety and used in such a variety of ways that it appears to us a laboratory of vaulting. There are tunnel vaults longitudinal and transverse, groin vaults and half-tunnels.

Tournus has a separate forechurch or antechurch, two-storeyed, aisled and of three bays in depth. Such an antechurch, though single-storeyed, had already been done at Cluny and was repeated when in 1088 a new church was begun at Cluny. This was, with its antechurch and its two pairs of

east transepts, to be the largest church of Europe, c. 600 ft long. In elevation it differed from the Tours–Toulouse type. It had a blind triforium, clerestory windows and a pointed tunnel vault. Pointed arches are by no means an invention of Gothic builders. The details at Cluny and otherwise in Burgundy show signs of an appreciation of the ancient Roman remains in the area. Autun Cathedral, consecrated in 1132, has much in common with Cluny. Vézelay (c. 1104–32 and later) on the other hand is inspired by the Rhineland. It has no gallery or triforium and groin instead of tunnel vaults.

Tunnel vaults are the most usual system of vaulting in Romanesque France. The regions to which we must now turn have them as their standard. They are Auvergne (Clermont-Ferrand, Issoire), similar to the Tours–Toulouse type, but more robust in detail and built with the local volcanic materials, Poitou with HALL CHURCHES of steep and narrow proportions (the finest by far is St Savin), and Provence (Arles, St Paul-trois-Châteaux), also tall and narrow but with clerestory lighting. Provençal churches are often aisleless. Where they have aisles, groin vaults or half-tunnels are used.

Exceptions to this standard are two regions, Normandy and the Angoumois and Périgord. The former was slow in taking to major vaulting. After the Conquest anyway the weight of Norman activity and ambition shifted to England, and here at the end of the C11 rib vaulting was introduced, a technically superior form of groin vaulting (Durham). The churches of Caen took it over about 1115–20 in sexpartite forms. The Angoumois and Périgord on the other hand placed their faith in vaults of a different type, inspired, it seems, by Byzantium – either direct or via Venice. They kept away from aisles, and put on their solid outer walls domes on PENDENTIVES. Cahors, Angoulême and Périgueux are the foremost examples. Angers Cathedral, begun *c.* 1145, is of this type too, but in its details it is unmistakably Gothic, though a Gothic deliberately different from that of the Royal France which was the Angevins' enemy.

The Gothic of Royal France, i.e. the Gothic sooner or later for most of Europe, begins at St Denis and Sens about 1140. It is characterized by the combining of pointed arch and rib vault into a system of great logic and structural ingenuity. St Denis moreover has an ambulatory and chapels of a suppleness which makes all Romanesque east ends appear elementary additions of separate parts. Both St Denis and Sens have two-tower façades. This motif which became Gothic standard is derived from such Norman buildings as St Étienne at Caen, just as the rib vault with the sophisticated profiles of St Denis had its origin in Norman architecture. St Denis also possessed the first of the Gothic figure portals, with column-like figures standing erect in the jambs. At St Denis they are not preserved, but they are at Chartres in the west front, where they date from *c.* 1145–50.

The great Early Gothic cathedrals are Sens, *c.* 1140; Noyon, 1145–1228; Laon, *c.* 1160–*c.* 1230; Paris, 1163–1250. They have the sexpartite rib vaults of Caen and show a development to higher proportions, thinner members, larger openings, and less inert wall. At Noyon and Laon CROCKET capitals begin to appear, a symbol of the resilience and freshness of the

Early Gothic style. Noyon and Laon have four-tier elevations inside, i.e. galleries as well as triforia. This represents a quickening of rhythm and a further opening of the wall.

Chartres, as rebuilt from 1194, turned Early Gothic into High Gothic. Its quadripartite rib vaults, tall arcades, tall clerestory windows, flying buttresses and its replacement of the gallery by a low triforium band all convey a sense of greater coherence, a yet quicker rhythm and yet more open walling. The system created at Chartres was taken over for the rebuilding of the cathedrals of Reims (1211 onwards) and Amiens (1220–70), and the abbey church of St Denis (1231 onwards), with the scale and the daring of slender supports and large openings ever increasing, until Beauvais reached a height of *c.* 155 ft. Bar TRACERY started at Reims; so did naturalistic foliage, the convincing concomitant of the High Gothic mood. Of the major cathedrals of these years, only Bourges stands apart, a very individual synthesis of conservative Early Gothic with the most boldly High Gothic elements. The greatest subtlety and refinement but also a first step away from High Gothic clarity appear in St Urbain at Troyes of 1262 and St Nazaire at Carcassonne of *c.* 1270. The later C13 cathedrals built as a sign of the spreading of royal power to the south and the west followed the lead of Reims and Amiens. Only in a few provinces did regional features manage to hold their own. Thus Poitou and also Anjou persisted with hall churches, even if their proportions and their spatial feeling changed in the Gothic direction. In the south a type established itself, probably on a Catalan pattern, with high proportions and chapels between internal buttresses instead of aisles (Albi, 1282–1390).

The greatest part of the C14 in France was a period of less architectural progress and this changed only gradually after about 1375, when Flamboyant tracery began to establish itself – more than two generations after flowing tracery had become the standard in England. The Flamboyant style, as the French call it, i.e. French Late Gothic, got a firm foothold only in the C15, although even then it remained more a matter of decoration than of plan and elevation. The richest province is Normandy (St Ouen, Rouen, and the west porch of S. Maclou, Rouen, of c. 1500–1514). Other notable examples are the church of Brou, Bourg-en-Bresse (1516–32) and the west front of Troyes Cathedral (c. 1507) by Martin Chambiges (d. 1532), who was master mason at Beauvais and Sens Cathedrals from 1490.

Castle building is first characterized by the KEEP or donjon, turning very early from square or oblong to round or rounded. In consequence of the experience of eastern fortification during the Crusades the keep was given up about 1200 and systems were designed instead where defence is spread along the whole CURTAIN WALL, which is sometimes doubled and has many towers. Shortly after 1200 (Louvre, Dourdan) this new system was occasionally regularized and made into a symmetrical composition of four ranges with angle towers round a square or oblong courtyard. In the course of the C15 the manor house or country house (Plessis-lès-Tours, 1463–72) began to replace the castle. The Flamboyant style created many splendid and ornate public and private buildings in the towns, such as the

Law Courts of Rouen (1499–1509) and, the finest of all private houses, the House of Jacques Cœur at Bourges (1442–53).

The Renaissance arrived early in France, but in a desultory way. Italians were working in Marseille in 1475–81. Odd Quattrocento details in painting occur even earlier. They also appear in architectural decoration (Easter Sepulchre, Solesmes, 1496). The earliest examples of a systematic use of Quattrocento pilasters in several orders is Gaillon (1502–10). With François I full acceptance of such motifs as this is seen at Blois (1515–24) and in other *châteaux* along the Loire. The most monumental of them is Chambord (1519–47), a symmetrical composition with a square main building having an ingenious double-spiral staircase in the centre and tunnel-vaulted corridors to north, south, west and east with standard lodgings in the corners. The largest of the *châteaux* of François I is Fontainebleau (1528 onwards) by Gilles le Breton (d. 1553), and here, in the interior (Gallery of François I, 1532–40), Mannerism in its most up-to-date Italian form entered France (*see* Francesco PRIMATICCIO). By the middle of the C16 France had developed a Renaissance style of her own, with French characteristics and architects. The most important of them were LESCOT, who began the rebuilding of the Louvre in 1546, and L'ORME. L'Orme introduced the dome and proved himself an ingenious technician as well as a creator of grand compositions (Anet, 1541–63). BULLANT at Écouen (1538–55) appears as L'Orme's equal. His use of giant columns, internationally very early, had a great influence on France.

The wars of religion shook France

so violently that little on a large scale could be built. The palace of Verneuil (begun *c.* 1568) was built slowly, while the palace of Charleval (begun 1570) was abandoned very soon. Both are by the elder Du Cerceau, and both show an overcrowding of the façades with restless and fantastical detail. The typically French pavilion roofs make their appearance here. Another example of the restlessness of these years is the Town Hall at Arras (1510 onwards).

With Henri IV things settled down. His principal contributions are *places* in Paris, i.e. town planning rather than palace architecture. The Place des Vosges (1605 onwards) survives entirely, the Place Dauphine fragmentarily, and the Place de France, the first with radiating streets (an idea conceived under Sixtus V in Rome), was never built. The elevations are of brick with busy stone DRESSINGS, a style which remained typical up to about 1630 (earliest part of Versailles, 1624). Henri IV's ideas on *places* as focal points of monumental town planning were taken up enthusiastically under Louis XIV and Louis XV, and reached their climax in the Paris of Napoleon III (Louis XIV: Place des Victoires, Place Vendôme, layout of Versailles).

The leading architects under Louis XIV were at the start François Mansart and Le Vau, then Perrault and Jules Hardouin-Mansart. François Mansart (like Corneille in literature and Poussin in painting) guided France into that classical style to which she remained faithful till beyond 1800, though it looks as if Salomon de Brosse, the important architect under Louis XIII, had in his last work, the Law Courts at Rennes (begun 1618), preceded Mansart. Mansart is of the

same fundamental importance in *châteaux* (Blois, 1635–8), town *hôtels* (Vrillière, begun 1635; Carnavalet, 1660), and churches. In church architecture de Brosse had started on tall façades crowded with Italian columns (St Gervais, 1623). Mansart toned them down to something closer to the Roman Gesù pattern, and he established the dome as a feature of ambitious Parisian churches (Visitation, 1632; Minims, 1636). His grandest church is the Val-de-Grâce, begun in 1645 and continued by Lemercier. But Lemercier had preceded Mansart in the field of major domed churches: his Sorbonne church with its remarkably early giant portico of detached columns was begun in 1635. Le Vau was a more Baroque designer than Mansart, as is shown by his liking for curves, and particularly for ovals, externally and internally. His first Paris house is the Hôtel Lambert (1642–4), his first country house Vaux-le-Vicomte (1657–61), with its domed oval central saloon, where Louis XIV's team of Le Vau, Lebrun (the painter) and Le Nôtre appeared together for the first time.

In 1665 Louis XIV called Bernini to Paris to advise him on the completion of the Louvre. But Bernini's grand Baroque plans were discarded in favour of Perrault's elegant, eminently French façade with its pairs of slender columns and straight entablature in front of a long loggia (1667–70). The king's architect during Louis XIV's later years was Hardouin-Mansart. He was not a man of the calibre of the others, but he was a brilliant organizer, and it fell to him vastly to enlarge and to complete Versailles (1678 onwards). The magniloquent grandeur of the interiors is his but also the noble simplicity of the Orangery and the informal layout of the Grand Trianon (1690s). He also designed the truly monumental Dôme-des-Invalides (1680–91). In Mansart's office the Rococo was created by younger designers (e.g. Pierre LEPAUTRE) about 1710–15. It became essentially a style of interior decoration. Otherwise the difference between the C17 and C18 *hôtel* or country house is greater finesse and delicacy of detail, and a more cunning planning of cabinets and minor rooms, and a decrease in scale, e.g. Hôtel de Matignon, Paris, by Jean Courtonne (1671–1739). BOFFRAND and de COTTE were both very influential in Germany. The most impressive major work of the mid-century is perhaps the planning and building of the new centre of Nancy by HÉRÉ (1752).

From the middle of the C18 onwards France turned to classicism, first with some theoretical writings (Cochin, 1750, LAUGIER, 1753), then in actual architecture too. A moderate, still very elegant classicism prevails in the work of GABRIEL (Place de la Concorde, 1753–75, Petit Trianon, designed 1761). More radical is SOUFFLOT's Panthéon (1757–90) with its exquisite dome (inspired by Wren's St Paul's) resting on piers of Gothic structural daring, its Greek-cross shape and its arms accompanied by narrow aisles or ambulatories, the separation from the arms being by columns carrying straight lintels. The last quarter of the C18 saw even more radical endeavours towards architectural reform. They were made mostly by young architects back from the French Academy in Rome. There they found inspiration not only in classical antiquity but even more in its bewitching interpretation by PIRANESI. One such was M.-J.

PEYRE, whose influential *Œuvres d'architecture* came out in 1765. But the most influential of all – BOULLÉE – had not been in Rome. His Hôtel de Brunoy of 1772 belongs to the earliest examples of the new simplicity and rectangularity. Others are the Mint (1768–77) by J.-D. ANTOINE (1733–1801), the Hôtel de Salm (1782) by Pierre Rousseau (1751–1810), and CHALGRIN's brilliant St Philippe-du-Roule of 1768–77. But Boullée's influence was exerted less by what he built than by drawings he made for a future book. They and LEDOUX's buildings at Arc-et-Senans and in Paris together with his published drawings represent a new radicalism of form and at the same time a megalomania of scale. Boullée's most influential follower was J.-N.-L. DURAND, not because of his buildings but because of the publications which came out of his lecture courses at the École Polytechnique. They were used abroad as much as in France (*see* e.g. SCHINKEL). Durand's two books were issued in 1800 and 1802–9. But the most successful architects of the years of Napoleon's rule were PERCIER and FONTAINE. In their works and in e.g. the Bourse (1807) by A.-T. BRONGNIART, the façade of the Palais Bourbon (1803–7) by Bernard Poyet (1742–1824) and the Madeleine (1804–45) by P.-A. VIGNON the style of Boullée and Ledoux became less terse and demanding and more rhetorical and accommodating. Side by side with this classical development from Revolution to Empire runs the development of Romanticism in the form of the *jardin anglais* and its furnishings. Examples are the Bagatelle by BÉLANGER of 1778 and the part of Versailles where Marie-Antoinette's Dairy was built in 1782–6 by Richard MIQUE.

The interaction between classical and Gothic went on in the C19. The grand chapel of Louis XVIII at Dreux was built classical in 1816–22, but enlarged Gothic in 1839. Ste Clotilde (1846–7) by F. C. GAU is serious neo-Gothic; so is Notre Dame de Bon Secours outside Rouen (1840–47) by J.-E. Barthélèmy (1799–1868), and in the 1840s also VIOLLET-LE-DUC began his highly knowledgeable if drastic restorations. Medieval scholarship reached its acme with his publications. Meanwhile HITTORF began St Vincent de Paul (1824) in a classical turning Early Christian. His later work is in a free Italianate, and in his two circuses of 1839 and 1851 he used glass and iron domes. The understanding among architects of what role iron could play was wider in France than in Britain. LABROUSTE's Ste Geneviève Library of 1838–50 is of a very pure, refined Italian Renaissance outside but has its iron framework exposed inside. Viollet-le-Duc in his *Entretiens* pleaded for iron, and already before their publication, in 1854–5, L.-A. BOILEAU had built St Eugène essentially of iron.

Concerning façades rather than structure, the French Renaissance was now added to the *répertoire*, first in the enlargements of the Louvre by Louis Visconti and H.-M. LEFUEL (1853 onwards), then in the façade of St Augustin by Victor BALTARD. The church (1862–71) again has iron inside. Shortly after, the full Baroque triumphed in GARNIER's Opéra of 1861–75, a masterpiece of BEAUX ARTS architecture. Those less ready for lush displays now rediscovered the Romanesque (VAUDREMER, 1864 etc.; Abadie, Sacré Cœur, 1874 etc.) and with this sparked off the style of RICHARDSON in America and with it the great rise of American architecture.

But while Paris remained leading in the development of iron and steel (Halles des Machines and Eiffel Tower, both for the exhibition of 1889), in architecture proper she produced nothing to emulate the English ARTS AND CRAFTS or the American CHICAGO SCHOOL. France came into her own again only about 1900 with the ART NOUVEAU structures of GUIMARD and its ART DECO and other derivatives by Henri-Frédéric Sauvage (1873–1932), and the pioneer designs of PERRET and Tony GARNIER. From them the way was open to the INTERNATIONAL MODERN of the 1920s in the hands of LE CORBUSIER, Robert Mallet Stevens (1886–1945) and André Lurçat (1894–1970). The latter designed the villa Hefferlin, Ville-d'Avray, 1932. His 1945 town plan for Maubeuge was remarkable, his residential complexes at St Denis (1952–8) less so. Jean PROUVÉ was the most interesting French experimenter in structure, together with Bernard Zehrfuss (b. 1911), who collaborated on the CNIT building (1958) and Unesco building (1958) in Paris with BREUER and NERVI.

The housing developments of Georges CANDILIS near Nîmes and on the south-east littoral should be mentioned, as well as those by AILLAUD outside Paris and, more recently, those by BOFILL at Montpellier and near Paris. The large-scale neo-Mediterranean vernacular resort town of Port Grimaud near St Tropez (1967–75) by François Spoerry (b. 1912) is startling and was derided by Modernists as a fake fishing village. But in 1984 Spoerry was commissioned to design the New England vernacular Port Liberté in New York harbour. Outstanding among recent buildings in

FIG. 49. *Fret*

Paris – apart from the Centre Pompidou by PIANO and ROGERS – are the apartments 'Le Cour d'Angle' at St Denis (1982–3) by Henri Ciriani (b. 1936), the Conservatoire de Musique (1984) by Christian de Portzamparc (b. 1944), the enormous Institut du Monde Arabe (1987) by Jean NOUVEL and the layout and buildings of the Parc de la Villette (1985 onwards) by Bernard Tschumi (b. 1944).

French window, *see* WINDOW.

Fret. A geometrical ornament of horizontal and vertical straight lines repeated to form a band, e.g. a *key pattern* or *meander*. *See* Fig. 49.

Freyssinet, Eugène (1879–1962). One of the leading CONCRETE designers of his generation. His fame rests principally on the two airstrip hangars at Orly (1916). They were of parabolic section, with a transversely folded surface and over 200 ft high. They were destroyed in 1944. Freyssinet also designed important concrete bridges, e.g. those at Plougastel (1925–30), Esbly (1946–50) and the St Michel bridge at Toulouse (1959). He published *Une Révolution dans les techniques du béton* (Paris 1926).

G. Günschel, *Grosse Konstrukteure. F. – Maillart – Dischinger – Finsterwalder*, Berlin, Frankfurt, Vienna 1966; J. Fernandez Ordoñez, *E.F.*, Barcelona 1978.

Frieze. 1. The middle division of an ENTABLATURE, between the ARCHITRAVE and CORNICE; usually decorated but may be plain. *See* Figs. 44, 66. 2. The decorated band along the upper part of an internal wall, immediately below the cornice.

Frisoni, Donato Giuseppe (1683–1735). He was born at Laino, between Como and Lugano, and began as a stucco-worker. In this capacity he was employed in 1709 on the vast palace at Ludwigsburg. In 1714 he succeeded the previous architect there (Johann Friedrich Nette, 1672–1714) and became responsible for the final form of the palace with its imposing second CORPS DE LOGIS (1725–33) and the trefoil-shaped Court church. He also designed the elegant small banqueting house, Favorite, on the hill opposite (begun 1718). But perhaps his major achievement is the town plan of Ludwigsburg, very unusual for its integration of the palace and its garden with a regular system of streets.

Hempel 1965.

Frontal. The covering for the front of an altar (*see* ANTEPENDIUM).

Frontispiece. The main façade of a building or its principal entrance BAY.

Fry, Edwin Maxwell (1899–1987). One of the pioneers in England of the INTERNATIONAL MODERN of the 1930s. His early buildings were private houses, dating from 1934 onwards. From 1934 to 1936 he was in partnership with GROPIUS. The most important outcome of this is the Impington Village College (1936). Of his later, post-war work done in partnership with his wife Jane Beverley Drew (b. 1911) and specializing in tropical architecture and design, the university and other buildings at Ibadan, Nigeria, and housing at Chandigarh, Pakistan (1951–4), where he was senior architect with LE CORBUSIER, should be mentioned. He published with his wife *Tropical Architecture in the Dry and Humid Zones* (London 1966).

H. A. N. Brockman, *F., Drew, Knight, Cramer. Architecture*, London 1978.

Fuchs, Bohuslav (1895–1972), *see* CZECHOSLOVAK ARCHITECTURE.

Fuga, Ferdinando (1699–1781), was born in Florence and died in Naples. But his principal works are all in Rome, e.g. Palazzo della Consulta (1732–7), the façade of S. Maria Maggiore (1741–3), and Palazzo Corsini (1736 onwards), in which his sophisticated Late Baroque style is seen at its elegant best. In 1751 he settled in Naples, where he received several important commissions (Albergo de' Poveri, Chiesa dei Gerolamini), but his early virtuosity had by then faded to a tame classicism and his late works are notable mainly for their size.

Blunt 1971; E. Kieren (ed.), *F.F. e l'architettura romana del settecento*, exh cat., Rome 1988.

Fulcrum. A support about which free rotation is possible or about which rotation occurs.

Fuller, Richard Buckminster (1895–1983). After working in a variety of commercial jobs, he started work in 1922 on structural systems for cheap and effective shelter, light in weight as well as quick to erect. The first was his Dymaxion House project of 1927, intended for low-cost mass-production and derived from the techniques of aircraft and vehicle construction. He later developed a bathroom unit (1937) and the Autonomous Living Package

(1949). They were all notable contributions to INDUSTRIALIZED BUILDING. His main concern, however, was with covering large spans. The result was his *geodesic domes* developed after the Second World War. They were made by him on the SPACE-FRAME principle in many different materials: timber, plywood, aluminium, paper board, PRESTRESSED CONCRETE, and even bamboo. The best-known are the Union Tank Car repair shop, Baton Rouge, Louisiana, 1958 (with a diameter of 384 ft), the Climatron, St Louis, 1960, the US pavilion at the Montreal Exhibition, 1967, and the weather radome, Mount Fuji, Tokyo, 1973. He also developed a system known as Tensegrity Structures, spatial skeletal structures utilizing distinct elements in compression and tension rods, the latter being joined together only via elements in compression.

He was an inspiring teacher and had wide and considerable influence especially in the USA but also elsewhere. He published *Intuition* (New York 1972), and his writings were collected and edited by J. Meller as *The Buckminster Fuller Reader* (London 1970).

R. W. Marks and R. B. Fuller, *The Dymaxion World of B.F.*, Garden City, N.Y., (1960) 1973; J. Ward (ed.), *The Artifacts of R.B.F.*, New York 1985.

Fuller, Thomas (1822–98), *see* CANADIAN ARCHITECTURE.

Functionalism. The creed of the architect or designer who holds that it is his primary duty to see that a building or an object designed by him functions well. Whatever he wishes to convey aesthetically and emotionally must not interfere with the fitness of the building or the object to fulfil its purpose. Though best known through SUL-LIVAN's slogan 'Form follows Function' and the writings of Otto WAGNER and Adolf LOOS, Functionalism has a long history in aesthetic theory.

E. R. de Zurko, *Origins of Functionalist Theory*, New York 1957; J. M. Richards, *The Functional Tradition*, London 1958.

Furness, Frank (1839–1912). A Philadelphia architect who for a short time employed SULLIVAN. Furness's style is very idiosyncratic, comparable in mood to that of TEULON and Bassett Keeling (1836–86) in England. It must be called Gothic, but all features are gross and some are original. The Provident Life and Trust Company, Philadelphia (1876–9; 1888–90, demolished), and the National Bank, Philadelphia (1883–4, demolished), were remarkable. The earlier Pennsylvania Academy of Fine Arts, Philadelphia (1872–6) survives.

Hitchcock 1977; J. F. O'Gorman, *The Architecture of F.F.*, Philadelphia (1973) 1987.

Furttenbach, Josef (1591–1667), *see* GERMAN ARCHITECTURE.

Futurism, *see* SANT'ELIA, Antonio.

g

Shaped gable   *Dutch gable*

FIG. 50. *Gable*

Gabetti, Roberto (b.1925), *see* ITALIAN ARCHITECTURE.

Gable. The triangular upper portion of a wall at the end of a pitched roof corresponding to a pediment in classical architecture. It can be used non-functionally, e.g. on the portal of a Gothic cathedral. It normally has straight sides, but there are variants. A crow-stepped or corbie stepped gable has stepped sides. A Dutch gable (characteristic of c. 1630–50) has curved sides crowned by a pediment (*see* Fig. 50). A hipped gable has the uppermost part sloped back. A shaped gable (characteristic of c. 1600–1650) has multi-curved sides (*see* Fig. 50).

Gable roof, *see* ROOF.

Gablet. A decorative motif in the form of a small gable, as on a buttress, above a niche, etc. For gablet roof, *see* ROOF.

Gabriel, Ange-Jacques (1698–1782). The greatest C18 architect in France and perhaps in Europe. His genius was conservative rather than revolutionary: he carried on and brought to its ultimate perfection the French classical tradition of François MANSART, by-passing, as it were, the Rococo. He resembled his great contemporary CHARDIN in his solid unostentatious good taste, which reached its highest pitch of refinement in small intimate buildings such as his Hermitage or Pavillon de Pompadour at Fontainebleau (begun 1749) and in his great masterpiece, the Petit Trianon in the park at Versailles (designed 1761). His father was a successful architect, Jacques Gabriel (1667–1742), who built several good Parisian *hôtels*, notably the Hôtel Peyrenne de Moras (now the Musée Rodin), and the Place Royale at Bordeaux (begun 1728), a masterpiece of Rococo urbanism. In 1735 he succeeded de COTTE as Premier Architecte and Director of the Academy. Ange-Jacques Gabriel was trained in Paris under his father and never went to Italy. He worked under and with his father for the Crown, and in due course succeeded him as Premier Architecte. In this position he built exclusively for the king, Louis XV, and Mme de Pompadour. Additions and alterations to the various royal palaces – Fontainebleau, Compiègne, Versailles – took up most of his time. They were sometimes Rococo to match existing work. His theatre and the projected reconstruction of the Marble Court at Versailles are extremely elegant. His largest commissions outside Versailles were for the École Militaire, Paris (1751–88), and the layout of the Place de la Concorde, Paris (1753–75); while the two great palaces (Hôtel de Crillon and Ministère de la Marine, 1757–75) flanking his rue Royale – their façades with screens in the style of PERRAULT's great east front of the Louvre – are his most successful buildings on the monumental scale. The Pavillon Français, Versailles (1750), the small hunting-boxes or Pavillons de Butard (1750) and de la Muette (1753–4) and the Petit Château at Choisy (1754–6) foreshadow the civilized intimacy of his masterpiece. The Petit Trianon may owe something to the sober dignity of English PALLADIANISM, but the extreme elegance and refinement of this perfectly proportioned cubical composition is wholly French and achieves a serenity and distinction different in kind and quality from any other contemporary building.

C. Tadgell, *A.-J.G.*, London 1978; Braham 1980; M. Gallet and Y. Bottineau, *Les G.*, Paris 1982.

Gadrooned. Decorated with convex curves; the opposite of fluted (*see* FLUTING).

Galilee. A vestibule or occasionally a chapel, originally for penitents and usually at the west end of a church. Sometimes called a NARTHEX or PARADISE.

Galilei, Alessandro Maria Gaetano (1691–1737), born in Florence and

trained there, went to England in 1714–19 (designed Castletown, Co. Kildare, Eire, built by PEARCE 1722, and the portico for Kimbolton Castle, 1718–19). In 1731 he won the competition for the façade of S. Giovanni in Laterano, Rome, with a somewhat tight and severely classical design (executed 1733–6). He also designed the Corsini Chapel there (1732–5) and the façade of S. Giovanni dei Fiorentini, Rome (1734).

Wittkower 1982.

Gallery. In church architecture, an upper storey over an aisle, opening on to the nave. Also called a *tribune* and often, wrongly, a TRIFORIUM. A *false gallery* is a middle storey comparable in height to a gallery but opening into the roof space over the aisles without external windows. Found as an exterior feature with continuous small open ARCADING in medieval Italian and German churches, and sometimes called a DWARF GALLERY.

In secular architecture: 1. A platform or mezzanine supported on columns or brackets and overlooking the main interior space of a building, e.g. a theatre. 2. A long room, often on an upper floor, for recreation or entertainment and sometimes used for the display of paintings, etc. (hence the modern term 'art gallery'). In England such rooms were often called 'long galleries'. The most famous is the Galerie des Glaces, Versailles (begun 1678), widely copied in palace architecture. 3. In Italy a shopping ARCADE is called a *galleria*.

Galleting. Inserting into mortar courses, while still soft, small pieces of stone, chips of flint, etc., sometimes for structural but usually for decorative reasons.

Galli da Bibiena. The leading family of QUADRATURA painters and theatrical designers in early C18 Italy. They came from Bibiena near Bologna. Several members of the family were spirited draughtsmen and accomplished painters of *trompe l'œil* architecture; a few were architects as well. Ferdinando (1657–1743) designed the church of S. Antonio Abbate, Parma (1712–16), with a very effective double dome. In 1711 he published his important *L'architettura civile preparata sulla geometria e ridotta alle prospettive*. His brother Francesco (1659–1731) became the greatest designer of theatres and established a long-surviving tradition. His main theatres (only partly surviving) are the Opera House, Vienna, and theatres of Nancy, Verona (Teatro Filarmonico) and Rome (Teatro Aliberti, 1720). One of Ferdinand's sons, Giuseppe (1696–1757), worked as a theatrical designer in Vienna and in Dresden (1747–53) and in 1746–8 designed the wonderfully rich interior of the theatre at Bayreuth; while another son, Antonio (1700–1774), designed several theatres in Italy, of which only four survive: Teatro Rinnovati, Siena (1753), Teatro Comunale, Bologna (1756–63), Teatro Scientifico, Palazzo dell'Accademia Virgiliana, Mantua (begun 1767), and Teatro Lauro Rossi, Macerata (executed by C. Morelli). Antonio also built the chapel in the Immacolata, Sabbioneta (*c.* 1770), with a remarkable dome decorated internally with an open, detached network of stucco ornamentation. A third son, Alessandro (1687–1769), became Architect-General to the Elector Palatine in Mannheim, where he built the opera house (1737, destroyed) and began the fine Jesuit church (1738–56). The very

elaborate stage designs by members of the family may have exerted some influence on JUVARRA and PIRANESI.

H. A. Mayor, *The B. Family*, New York 1945; Wittkower 1982.

Gambrel roof, *see* ROOF.

Gameren, Tylman van (d.1706), *see* TYLMAN VAN GAMEREN.

Gandon, James (1743–1823). A pupil of CHAMBERS, he became the leading neo-classical architect in Dublin. He was of French Huguenot descent and his work is sometimes surprisingly advanced and close to his *avant-garde* French contemporaries, e.g. Nottingham County Hall (1770–72), of which the façade survives. In 1781 he went to Dublin to supervise the construction of the Custom House on the Liffey (completed 1791, interior destroyed 1921). But his masterpiece is the Four Courts, also on the Liffey, where he took over from T. Cooley (1786–1802, interior destroyed 1922). Also in Dublin are his portico of the Bank of Ireland (1785) and the King's Inns (begun 1795 but later enlarged). He published, with J. Woolfe, two supplementary volumes to *Vitruvius Britannicus* in 1769 and 1771.

Colvin 1978; Summerson 1983; E. McParland, *J.G. Vitruvius Hibernicus*, London 1985.

Ganghofer, Jorg (d.1488), *see* GERMAN ARCHITECTURE.

Garden city and garden suburb. The garden city scheme, conceived by Ebenezer HOWARD, was first translated into reality at Letchworth (begun 1903) by Raymond UNWIN. The first garden suburbs in England were Bedford Park, London (begun 1877, by

Norman SHAW), Port Sunlight (1888 onwards) and Bournville, Birmingham (mainly 1893 onwards), but the finest English specimen is the Hampstead Garden Suburb in London, started in 1906. In Germany the most interesting garden city is that planned by Richard RIEMERSCHMID in 1907 at Hellerau near Dresden, begun in 1909. *See also* NEW TOWNS; RADBURN PLANNING.

G. Benoit-Lévy, *La Cité-jardin*, Paris 1904; W. L. Creese, *The Search for Environment. The Garden City: Before and After*, London and New Haven (1960) 1966; R.Fishman, *Urban Utopias in the Twentieth Century*, New York 1977.

Garderobe. Wardrobe. Also the medieval name for a lavatory.

Gargoyle. A water spout projecting from a roof, or the PARAPET of a wall or tower, and carved into a grotesque figure, human or animal.

Garner, Thomas (1839–1906), *see* BODLEY.

Garnier, Jean-Louis-Charles (1825–98), won the Grand Prix of the Academy in 1848, and went to Rome in the same year and to Athens in 1852. Back in Paris in 1854, he worked under BALLU. In 1861 he won the competition for the Opéra, and the building was completed in 1875. Prominently placed in one of HAUSSMANN's many grand *points de vue*, it is the most splendid incarnation of the Second Empire and a masterpiece of the BEAUX ARTS STYLE. The exterior, the ample staircase, the glittering foyer are frankly Baroque, and openly endeavour to beat the Baroque at its own game. At the same time Meyerbeer, Wagner, Verdi could not be heard in more sympathetic surroundings, since the building is most intelligently planned for its particular purpose of combining a setting for opera with a setting for social display. The same is true, in its own intentionally more meretricious way, of the Casino at Monte Carlo (1879–85), which had great influence in Europe on light-hearted resort architecture. Garnier's own villa at Bordighera (1874), with its asymmetrically placed tower, is Italianate and not Baroque.

M. Steinhauser, *Die Architektur der Pariser Oper*, Munich 1970; A. Drexler (ed.), *The Architecture of the École des Beaux-Arts*, New York 1972.

Garnier, Tony (1869–1948). When he gained the Prix de Rome in 1899 and duly went to Rome, he spent much of his time not measuring and studying ancient buildings, but working on the designs for a Cité Industrielle. These designs were submitted in 1904, exhibited, and finally published in 1917. They represent a completely new approach to town planning, in radical opposition to the academic principles of town planning as taught by the École des Beaux Arts, principles of symmetry and imposed monumentality. Garnier instead gave himself a site that was imaginary and yet realistic, since it resembled the country near his native Lyon: he decided that his town should have 35,000 inhabitants, located industry, railway lines, station, town centre, and housing, and related them rationally to each other. Moreover, he proposed that all the buildings should be made essentially of CONCRETE. He designed small houses of quite novel cubic simplicity placed among trees, and some major buildings with the large CANTILEVERS which REINFORCED CONCRETE had just begun to make possible, with glass and concrete roofs, etc. In 1905 Garnier was called by the newly elected mayor, Édouard Herriot, to Lyon to be municipal architect. He built the slaughterhouse in 1909–13, the stadium in 1913–16.

D. Wiebenson, *T.G. The Cité Industrielle*, London 1969; Hitchcock 1977; R. Jullian, *T.G. (1869–1948). Utopiste et constructeur*, Paris 1987.

Garth. An enclosed area, usually a garden enclosed by cloisters.

Gärtner, Friedrich von (1792–1847), the son of an architect, studied at the Munich Academy, then for a short time with WEINBRENNER, and after that in Paris with PERCIER and FONTAINE. In 1815–17 he was in Italy, and in 1818–20 in Holland and England. After that he held a chair at the Munich Academy. On a second journey to Italy in 1828 he was introduced to King Ludwig I of Bavaria, and from then was, side by side and in competition with KLENZE, the king's favourite architect. Gärtner's speciality was what the Germans call the RUNDBOGENSTIL, the style of round arches, be they Italian Romanesque or Italian Quattrocento: it is said that it was King Ludwig rather than Gärtner who favoured this post-classical style. In Munich Gärtner built the Ludwigskirche (1829–40), the State Library (1831–40), and the University (1835–40), all three in the Ludwigstrasse, and at its south end the Feldherrnhalle, a copy of the Loggia dei Lanzi in Florence (1840–44) and an essay in the Tuscan Gothic. In 1835–6 Gärtner was in Athens, where he designed the palace of the new king, a son of Ludwig.

O. Hederer, *F. von G. (1792–1847). Leben-Werk-Schüler*, Munich 1976; Hitchcock 1977.

Gau, Franz Christian (1790–1853), was born in Cologne, went to Paris in 1810, and in 1815 with a Prussian grant to Rome, where he became a friend of the Nazarenes (Overbeck, Cornelius, etc.). In 1818–20 he was in Egypt and Palestine, but returned to Paris in 1821. Gau was more widely known during his lifetime as an Egyptian scholar than as an architect. Yet his Ste Clotilde (1846–57; completed by BALLU) is the one outstanding neo-Gothic church in Paris. The style is a rich High Gothic, the façade has two towers with spires like St Nicaise at Reims, and the roof construction is of iron.

Hitchcock 1977.

Gaudi y Cornet, Antonio (1852–1926), was born at Reus (Tarragona), where his father was a coppersmith and pot- and kettle-maker. So he grew up acquainted with metals, and it is not surprising that the savagery of his ornamental invention appeared first in metal railings and gates. Nor was the architecture of the building for which these were designed – the Casa Vicens at Barcelona – tame or imitative in the sense of C19 historicism. The house, built in 1878–80, is in fact a nightmarish farrago of Moorish and Gothic elements; indeed, Moorish and Gothic – and in addition, it seems, Moroccan – are the sources of Gaudi's style. The Casa Vicens was followed in 1883–5 by El Capricho, a house at Comillas in northern Spain – equally crazy and less dependent on any past style.

In 1883 Gaudi was put in charge of the continuation of a large church in Barcelona, the Sagrada Familia, begun as a conventional neo-Gothic building. He did the crypt in 1884–91 and began the transept façade in 1891. By then he had been taken up by Count Güell, an industrialist who remained his faithful patron. His town house, the Palacio Güell (now a theatre museum), dates from 1885–9, and here there first appeared the parabolic arches and the wild roof excrescences which were to become part of Gaudí's repertoire. But far more fiercely extravagant than anything he or any architect had done before were the designs for the chapel of Sta Coloma de Cervelló which Gaudí began to build in 1889 for one of Count Güell's estates: it was never completed. It has an entirely free, asymmetrical, jagged plan, with pillars set at a slant, warped vaults, an indescribable interplay of exterior and interior, and ostentatiously crude benches. For the Parque Güell, a park at Barcelona, begun in 1900, similar motifs were used, and in addition the snakily undulating back of a long seat running along the sides of a large open space was faced with bits of broken tile and crockery in arbitrary patterns as effective as any invented by Picasso (who lived at Barcelona during these very years, 1901–4).

In 1903 Gaudí began the upper part of the transept of the Sagrada Familia. The lower part had gradually reached an ever freer interpretation of Gothic motifs, but the turrets at the top defeated comparison with anything architectural from the past or the present. Instead, comparisons with termite hills or with crustaceous creatures come at once to mind. The ceramic facing is similar to that in the Parque Güell. Aesthetically as surprising and socially more so than any earlier building are Gaudí's two blocks of luxury flats, the Casa Batlló and the Casa Milá (both begun 1905); for here was acceptance by wealthy Barcelonians of Gaudí's unprecedented architecture. The façades

undulate, rise and fall, and are garnished with fantastical top excrescences and sharp, piercing, aggressive wrought-iron balconies. Moreover, the rooms have no straight walls, no right angles. The principles behind ART NOUVEAU (*see* HORTA; MACKINTOSH; MACKMURDO; van de VELDE), usually confined to decoration and mostly two-dimensional decoration, could not well be pushed to a further architectural extreme. But *see* SPANISH ARCHITECTURE.

G. R. Collins, *A.G.*, London 1960; E. Casanelles, *A.G.A Reappraisal*, New York 1967; R. Descharnes and C. Prévost, *G. the Visionary*, New York (1969) 1971; O. Bohigas, *Arquitectura Modernista, Barcelona*, Barcelona (1968) 1973; G. R. Collins and J. Bassegoda-Nouelle, *The Designs and Drawings of A.G.*, Princeton 1983.

Gazebo. A small look-out tower or summerhouse with a view, usually in a garden or park but sometimes on the roof of a house; in the latter case it is also called a *belvedere*.

Geddes, Sir Patrick (1854–1932). If Raymond UNWIN was the greatest British town-planner of his day in practice, Geddes was the greatest in town-planning theory, a theory which he established in the present much-widened sense of the word, with emphasis laid on the necessity of preliminary surveys, on 'diagnosis before treatment', and on the dependence of acceptable town planning on sociological research bordering on biological work. Geddes was, in fact, a trained biologist and zoologist though he never took a degree. He was Professor of Botany at Dundee from 1889 to 1918, and of sociology at Bombay from 1920 to 1923. He was knighted shortly before his death. His principal work on town planning is *City Development* (1904).

P. Boardman, *The Worlds of P. G. (1854–1932)*, London 1978.

Gehry, Frank O. (b.1929), *see* UNITED STATES ARCHITECTURE.

Genelli, Hans Christian (1763–1823), *see* GILLY, Friedrich.

Genga, Girolamo (*c.* 1476–1551). Late Renaissance painter and architect from Urbino. His buildings are heavier and more scenographic than RAPHAEL's, e.g. additions to Villa Imperiale, Pesaro (1535), which recall the Villa Madama, Rome. It has elaborate and very fine illusionistic architectural painted decorations, also by Genga with a team of assistants. His only other building of importance is S. Giovanni Battista, Pesaro (1543 onwards), similarly solemn and monumental. The Villa Imperiale was built for the Duke of Urbino and was influential, e.g. on the Villa Giulia, Rome, through AMMANATI.

Tafuri 1966; A. Pinelli and O. Rossi, *G. architetto. Aspetti della cultura urbinata del primo '500*, Rome 1971; M. Groblewski, *Die Kirche San Giovanni Battista in Pesaro von G.G.*, Regensburg 1976.

Geodesic dome. A hemispherical SPACE FRAME construction of lightweight rods joined to form hexagons, developed by Buckminster FULLER.

Geoffrey de Noiers (active *c.* 1200), was called *constructor* of the choir of St Hugh at Lincoln Cathedral (begun 1192). The term may mean only supervisor, but more probably he is the designer of this epoch-making building. The design is, in spite of Geoffrey's name, entirely English, not merely in its proportions and the curious layout of the east chapels, but especially in its vault, the earliest vault whose ribs make a decorative (and a very wilful) pattern rather than simply express their function.

N. Pevsner, *The Choir of Lincoln Cathedral*, Oxford 1963.

Geometric staircase, *see* STAIR.

Geometrical tracery, *see* TRACERY.

Georgian architecture, *see* ENGLISH ARCHITECTURE; BYZANTINE ARCHITECTURE.

Gerbier, Sir Balthazar (1592–1663), a Dutch-born Huguenot who settled in England in 1616, was courtier, diplomat, miniaturist, and pamphleteer as well as architect. He almost certainly designed the York Water Gate, Victoria Embankment Gardens, London (1626–7), a direct imitation of the Fontaine de Médicis at the Luxembourg in Paris. Nothing else by him survives. He designed Hampstead Marshall (*c.* 1660), completed by William WINDE.

H. R. Williamson, *Four Stuart Portraits*, London 1949; Colvin 1978; Summerson 1983.

German architecture. We know more about early German churches now than we did fifty years ago. Until then there was the rotunda of St Mary on the Würzburg fortress and the traces of the grand basilica of St Boniface at Fulda, both c8 and both of Early Christian inspiration. Excavations have now told us of small aisleless churches with straight-ended chancels, much as in northern England.

But all this is small fry in comparison with Charlemagne's buildings, especially the happily preserved palace chapel of Aachen and the large abbey church of Centula (St Riquier) only known from descriptions and derivations. Aachen was a palace of the Emperor, Ingelheim was another. Both were spacious, axially planned, and apparently aware of Imperial Roman plans. The large Aachen chapel dedicated in 805 is externally a polygon of sixteen sides, and internally has an ambulatory round an octagonal centre; above the ambulatory is a gallery and on top of the octagon a domical VAULT. Details are amazingly pure in the Roman tradition, as indeed is so much – script, poetry, illumination – that issued from the Emperor's circle. This applies also, e.g., to the curious gatehouse of Lorsch Abbey. At Aachen the most original feature is the WESTWORK, and as for Centula, consecrated in 799, all is original – a westwork with a tower repeating the shape of the crossing tower, transepts emanating from the crossing, and transept-like wings off the westwork, a chancel and an apse. As original is the vellum plan for St Gall Abbey, datable to about 820. This has a west as well as an east apse and a pair of round campanili, the earliest church towers of which we have a record.

Centula can be called the pattern from which the German Romanesque style derived. The years of development are the late C10 – with the westwork of St Pantaleon in Cologne, consecrated in 980, and the nunnery church of Gernrode (begun 959–63). At St Michael in Hildesheim of c. 1010–33 the Romanesque style is complete. Its climax is the great cathedrals and abbeys of the Rhineland dating from the mid C11 to the early C13: Speier 1030–61 and later, Mainz 1009, 1181 and later, Maria Laach 1093–1156

and Worms late C11 and C12. Internationally speaking the mid C11 was the time of the great superiority of the work in the Empire over work in England, Italy, and most parts of France, as it was the time of the Salians, the most powerful of the emperors. The principal buildings are the following: the hall-range of the palace of Goslar of c. 1050 not matched anywhere, Speier Cathedral already mentioned, with its ruthlessly grand inner elevation and the groin vaults which the nave received about 1080–90, the first major vault in Germany. The decoration is inspired by northern Italy, the elevational system probably inspired by the Roman basilica of Trier. Trier Cathedral is another of the masterpieces of these years – a lengthening of a centrally planned Roman building. The west front has the first so-called dwarf gallery, i.e. an arcaded wall-passage, earlier than any in Italy. But the most coherent major building of these years is St Mary-in-Capitol (c. 1040–65) at Cologne, built on a trefoil plan for the east end and with tunnel vaults. The details are very severe – e.g. BLOCK CAPITALS, as had been introduced at St Pantaleon and at Hildesheim. Beneath is a crypt of many short columns; Speier has another. The trefoil east end became the hallmark of the Romanesque school of Cologne. Cologne before the Second World War had more Romanesque churches than any other city in Europe. They go on into the early C13, when motifs tend to get fanciful and decoration exuberant–baroque, as it has been called. The west end of Worms, completed c. 1230, shows this at its most outré, but also shows that now the French Gothic began to make its mark.

But we cannot leave the Romanesque without referring to a developing liking for HALL CHURCHES in Westphalia (Kirchlinde *c.* 1175) and also in Bavaria (Waldersbach *c.* 1175) and to the style promoted by the Congregation of Hirsau, i.e. the German Cluniacs. Their churches are not much like French Cluniac churches. The main church at Hirsau was begun in 1082; specially good other Hirsau-type churches are Alpirsbach and Paulinzella, the latter of 1112–32. The Hirsau type had an antechurch (like Cluny) with two west towers, nave arcades with columns, mostly with plain block capitals, and two slim towers over the east bays of the aisles.

Now for the relation to the Gothic in France which had been created there about 1135–40. Germany did not take any notice of it until about 1200 with Gelnhausen (*c.* 1200–1230), the 'PARADISE' of the abbey church of Maulbronn (*c.* 1210–20), St Gereon at Cologne (1219 onwards) and Limburg on the Lahn (consecrated 1235). The result here is a mixture, resourceful and entertaining, but impure and not guided by any understanding of what Gothic architecture really is about. That changed suddenly and very dramatically with St Elizabeth at Marburg, started in 1235, the church of the Virgin at Trier, started a few years later (a centrally planned building making ingenious use of French elements) and Cologne Cathedral, started in 1284. St Elizabeth with its rib vaults and bar-tracery presupposes Reims, started in 1211, but with its trefoil east end derived from Cologne. The church after a change of plan was built as a hall church, and that is a motif of Westphalian derivation. It became the hallmark of the Late Gothic in Germany. Cologne Cathedral is French in general

and in particular. Amiens and Beauvais are closest to it. It was to be the largest and the highest of all High Gothic cathedrals, but only the east end was built, and that was consecrated only in 1322. The rest is mostly C19.

To proceed with German Gothic development one must watch for the spread of the hall church. One group is hall chancels of Austrian abbeys – Lilienfeld (consecrated 1230), Heiligenkreuz (consecrated 1295) and Zwettl (begun 1343). Meanwhile Westphalia turned from Romanesque to Gothic halls (Osnabrück, 1256–92, nave at Münster, *c.* 1267 onwards). Halls also established themselves in north-east and east Germany and especially in the architecture of the Friars. An early example (*c.* 1240) is the Frankfurt Blackfriars.

The full maturity of the German hall church is reached in south Germany from 1351, the date when the chancel of Schwäbisch-Gmünd was begun, probably by Heinrich PARLER, and through the C15 into the C16. The architects spreading this Late Gothic style (called *Sondergotik*) were the PARLER family, with Peter, the greatest, who in 1353 became the Emperor Charles IV's architect of Prague Cathedral and introduced here complicated rib vaults and incidentally amazing portrait sculpture (in the triforium). A Michael Parler worked at Ulm, a Johann was called to Milan, another Johann appears at Freiburg, but the fantastic spire with its filigree tracery all over is earlier than that Parler. Altogether we hear of more architects' names now (*see* ENSINGEN; BÖBLINGER; HEINZELMANN) and also of the statutes of masons' lodges. There are many outstanding Late Gothic parish churches in south Germany and Austria, such as St Martin at Landshut (and the Salzburg Greyfriars) by Hans STETHAIMER, Nördlingen (1427 onwards) and Dinkelsbühl (1448 onwards) by Nicolaus Eseler (c. 1400–1492), Amberg (1420 onwards), the Frauenkirche in Munich (1468 onwards) by Jörg von Ganghofer (d. 1488) and the chancel of St Lorenz in Nuremberg (begun 1439) by Heinzelmann and RORICZER. Nor is north Germany poor in Late Gothic churches.

But the pride of north Germany is its brick churches, in an impressive and very simplified Gothic (called *Backsteingotik*), and its brick town halls such of those of Lübeck and Stralsund and the overwhelming one, mainly of the late C14, at Torun (Thorn) in the territory of the Prussian Knights. Their castles are as overwhelming, especially the C14 Malbork (Marienburg).

Altogether Germany is rich in Late Gothic secular work. At the castle at Meissen the rebuilding of 1471–c. 1485 demonstrates the transition from castle to palace. So does, on an even grander scale, the work of Benedict RIETH VON PIESTING on the Hradchin at Prague. The Vladislav Hall belongs to the years 1493–1502. Its curvaceous rib vaults are the acme of German Late Gothic fantasy.

But the Vladislav Hall also has motifs of the Italian Renaissance. The infiltration started in fact earlier in Bohemia, Hungary and Poland than in Germany. In Germany Dürer and Burkmayr used Renaissance detail elegantly in 1508, and in 1509 the Fuggers of Augsburg founded a chapel in S. Anna, Augsburg, which was intended to look north Italian as an ensemble. In the second quarter of the C16 much decoration *à la* Como or Pavia can be found (Georgentor, Dresden 1534). Ensembles however remained rare – e.g. the Johann-Friedrichs-Bau (1533–6), Schloss Hartenfels, Torgau, by Konrad Krebs (1491–1540). The purest is part of the Stadtresidenz at Landshut (1537–43) inspired by GIULIO ROMANO, to whom it has been attributed. But soon, in any case, purity was no longer the ideal. As the wholly national Elizabethan style emerges in England, so does the so-called German Renaissance in Germany, with gables, stubby columns and coarse, more Flemish than Italian, decoration. Examples are the Town Halls of Leipzig (1556) and Rothenburg (1573–8), the Lusthaus, Stuttgart (1584–93, demolished), by George Beer (d. 1600) and SCHICKHARDT, the Plassenburg, Kulmbach (1559 onwards), and the Pellerhaus in Nuremberg (1602–7, gutted but rebuilt), by Jacob WOLFF. There are, however, also some more international-looking buildings, i.e. buildings of French (Schloss Aschaffenburg 1605–14, gutted 1944 but rebuilt, by RIDINGER) or Flemish (Ottheinrichsbau, Heidelberg, 1556–9; Town Hall portico, Cologne, 1567–70) or Italian inspiration (St Michael, Munich, 1583–92 by SUSTRIS, Hans Krumpper (c. 1570–1635) and others). The most original churches about 1600 are Protestant and north German: those of Wolfenbüttel by Paul Francke (1538–1615) and Bückeburg (1613–23). But all this has little to do with the Renaissance.

Just as in England with Inigo Jones, a true understanding of the High Renaissance came only after 1600 and even then very rarely, e.g. Josef Furttenbach (1591–1667), important mainly for his publications. The key building is Elias HOLL's Augsburg Town Hall of 1615–20. But then – and this singles out Germany – the Thirty Years' War interrupted this organic development.

It left the country devastated and impoverished, and when building again became possible, the situation in the country – and indeed taste – had changed. The most important architectural events took place in the Catholic south, and the source of inspiration was Italy, and at first even the architects were Italian, as, e.g., BARELLI and ZUCCALLI, who built the Theatinerkirche in Munich (1663–88). About 1700, Germans replaced the Italians. Of the first generation are SCHLÜTER, who built the Palace and the Arsenal in Berlin, the great FISCHER VON ERLACH in Vienna and PÖPPELMANN of the Zwinger in Dresden (1709 onwards). All three were born about 1660. HILDEBRANDT in Vienna was a little younger. While Fischer von Erlach, despite his ingenious plans with their centralizing tendencies and their ovals, is a classicist at bottom, Hildebrandt represents the BORROMINI and GUARINI party in Europe, as do the DIENTZENHOFERS in Franconia and Bohemia (Johann: Banz 1710–18; Christoph: Břevnov near Prague 1708–15; Kilian and Christoph Ignaz: the two St Nicholases, Prague, 1730s). The Fischer Hildebrandt antinomy is equally patent in Dresden, but here it is a Catholic–Protestant antinomy: BÄHR's Protestant Frauenkirche begun 1722, the town church v. CHIAVERI's Catholic church of 1738 onwards, the Court church.

As for other northern centres Frederick the Great's early Sanssouci at Potsdam (1745–7) with KNOBELS-DORFF looked to Rococo France (even if not with such abandon as CUVILLIÉS's Amalienburg at Nymphenburg near Munich of 1734–9), his later buildings, including the Gothic Nauener Gate at Potsdam of 1755, to England. The Rhineland naturally looked to France, but even there – Brühl, Bruchsal – in the end the greatest German architect of the century won.

He is, needless to say, Balthasar NEUMANN, and his masterworks are the Episcopal Palace of Würzburg (1720–44), still in some elements guided by Hildebrandt, and the splendid churches of Vierzehnheiligen (1742 onwards) and Neresheim (1747 onwards). Neumann lived at Würzburg, i.e. in Franconia. The three greatest Bavarian church builders were ASAM, ZIMMERMANN and J.M. FISCHER, all born between 1685 and 1695. The Asam brothers, also painters and sculptors, are the most Italian – influenced by Borromini, and rich in their brown and gold decoration (Weltenburg; St John Nepomuk, Munich). Fischer (Ottobeuren, Zwiefalten, Rott) is all large and light in colours and ingenious in planning as well. Zimmermann is primarily remembered – rightly so – for the Wies church (1745–54). There were two Zimmermann brothers as well, the other being a painter, and the *unisono* of all the arts is of course one of the most characteristic features of the Baroque. The great abbeys of south Germany and even more Austria show that in all their sumptuous parts (see e.g. Melk, St Florian, Klosterneuburg).

No wonder then that the total reaction against the Rococo was a Protestant and a north German initiative. Friedrich GILLY in Berlin came from Huguenot stock. He never visited Italy, but he visited Paris and London.

German architecture

What London meant to him we do not know, but Paris meant the most radical innovators of Europe – the Odéon, the Théâtre Feydeau, the rue des Colonnes. Gilly died too young to build more than negligibly, but his designs for a National Monument to Frederick the Great and for a National Theatre prove him to be one of the few architects of genius of the period.

SCHINKEL was his pupil, again one of the greatest of the period in all Europe, less brilliantly endowed perhaps, but of rare competence and as resourceful as Gilly. He started as a painter, especially as a theatrical painter, in the romantic vein. His design of 1810 for a mausoleum for Queen Luise is Gothic. When after Napoleon's defeat building started again, he built in a pure but highly original Grecian. The New Guard House, the Theatre, the Old Museum (all in Berlin and all designed in 1816–22) are among the noblest of the Greek Revival anywhere. He became Superintendent of Building in Prussia and his influence stretched far, even into Scandinavia and Finland. Later in life he experimented with more original forms – centrally planned churches, façades of public buildings of exposed brick and functional bareness (Academy of Architecture of 1831–6, designs for a library and a bazaar). When he visited England in 1826, his principal interests were industrial products and the new huge mills.

KLENZE, Schinkel's opposite number in Bavaria, was more accommodating but equally resourceful. His œuvre already comprises the full HISTORICISM of the C19: the Greek (Glyptothek, Munich and Walhalla, Regensburg), the Quattrocento and Cinquecento parts of the Royal Palace,

Munich, the Early Christian of the church of All Saints, Munich, the originality of the Hall of Liberation above Kelheim. As for C19 historicism Germany made the RUNDBOGENSTIL one of her specialities. In the Italian Renaissance vein SEMPER did such beautiful buildings as the Dresden Gallery (1847 onwards) and the Dresden Opera. The difference between the first and second Opera (1838 onwards and, after a fire, 1871 onwards) is that between C19 neo-Renaissance and neo-Baroque. The neo-Baroque appeared at its best in the Houses of Parliament, Berlin, by Paul Wallot (1841–1912) (1884 onwards). Compare then the Parliament with Ludwig von Hoffmann's Supreme Court at Leipzig (1887 onwards), and you will get a first idea of the development from ornateness to simplicity.

Germany was indeed one of the leading countries in overcoming Historicism and establishing the new functional style of the C20, in which the DEUTSCHER WERKBUND played a notable role. The key works are by Peter BEHRENS of c. 1904–14, buildings including the famous factories for the AEG. Behrens's pupils were GROPIUS and MIES VAN DER ROHE. Gropius's *magnum opus* remains the BAUHAUS building at Dessau. Mies's greatest work was done after his emigration to Chicago. Other leaders in the so-called INTERNATIONAL MODERN were Max Berg (1870–1947) of the Centennial Hall at Wroclaw (Breslau) of 1913 – the first (apart from bridges) to take into account the possibilities of arcuated concrete – and MENDELSOHN of the Einstein Tower of 1919–20.

But the Einstein Tower is pre-the-International-Modern of Mendelsohn. It belongs to that EXPRESSIONISM which for a brief moment even Gropius and Mies fell victim to. Most convincedly Expressionist in the years about 1920 were Dominikus BÖHM, POELZIG, SCHAROUN, and to some extent Hugo Häring (1882–1958), e.g. the Garkau farm buildings of 1923, and Heinrich Tessenow (1876–1950), e.g. the Sächsische Landeschule, Dresden, of 1925–7. After 1933 the most prominent buildings were Nazi, e.g. the Haus der Deutsches Kunst, Munich (1933–7) by Paul Ludwig Troost (1878–1934), the Autobahn (1935–40) by Fritz Todt (1891–1942) and BONATZ, who designed the bridges etc. for it, and the new Berlin Chancellery and Nuremberg party rally buildings etc. by SPEER. In the immediate post-war period came the Expressionist revival with Scharoun's Berlin Philharmonie concert hall (1956–63) and Gottfried BÖHM's Bensberg Town Hall (1963–9), carried on into the 1980s by Hermann Fehling (b. 1909) and Daniel Gogel (b.1927) with their observatory at Gaveling, Munich (1976–80). Neo-Expressionism also informs the brilliant structural conceptions of Frei OTTO, while the International Modern tradition was carried on by EIERMANN and HENTRICH. More recently Oswald Mathias Ungers (b. 1926) and Josef Paul Kleihues (b. 1933) have taken up a new 'rationalistic' approach (*see* NEO-RATIONALISM) and as planning director of the International Bauausstellung in Berlin (IBA 1987) Kleihues has promoted the work of Rob KRIER.

Gesellius, Herman (1874–1916), *see* FINNISH ARCHITECTURE.

Gesso. A composition of gypsum or chalk and size, sometimes with other materials. It provides a smooth absorbent white surface. The term is some-times used for *plaster of Paris*, a white gypsum powder that forms a paste when mixed with water and hardens into a solid: used by sculptors for moulds and casts.

Giant order, *see* COLOSSAL ORDER.

Gibberd, Sir Frederick (1908–84). One of the first in England to accept the INTERNATIONAL MODERN style of the 1930s (Pulman Court, Streatham, London, 1934–5). His best-known works after the Second World War are the plan and some of the chief buildings for the New Town of Harlow (1947), the terminal buildings for London Airport (1950–69), the Roman Catholic Cathedral, Liverpool (1960), and the Central London Mosque, Regent's Park (1969).

Gibbs, James (1662–1754). The most influential London church architect of the early C18. In contrast to his predominantly Whig and neo-Palladian contemporaries, he was a Scot, a Catholic, and a Tory with Jacobite sympathies, and had the unique advantage of training under a leading Italian architect, Carlo FONTANA. Born in Aberdeen he went to Rome c. 1703 to study for the priesthood, but left the Scots College after a year. He stayed on in Rome until 1709, and appears to have studied painting before turning to architecture. His first building, St Maryle-Strand, London (1714–17), is a mixture of WREN and Italian Mannerist and Baroque elements. Rather surprisingly, he was then taken up by Lord BURLINGTON, though only to be dropped in favour of Colen CAMPBELL, who replaced him as architect of Burlington House. He had no further contact with the neo-Palladians and remained faithful to Wren and his

FIG. 51. *Gibbs surround*

Gibbs surround. The surround of a doorway or window consisting of alternating large and small blocks of stone, quoinwise, or of intermittent large blocks; sometimes with a narrow raised band connecting up the verticals and along the face of the arch. Named after the architect James GIBBS though used by other architects, e.g. PALLADIO, CAMPBELL. *See* Fig. 51.

Gigliardi, Domenico, *see* ZHILYARDI, Domenico.

Gil de Hontañón, Juan (d. 1526) and Rodrigo (d. 1577), father and son. Juan is the designer of the last two Gothic cathedrals of Spain, Salamanca and Segovia: at Salamanca he was consulted in 1512 (with eight others) and made master mason; at Segovia he started the new building in 1525. An earlier work of his is the cloister of Palencia Cathedral (begun 1505). He was consulted in 1513 for Seville Cathedral and designed the new lantern, etc., also still Gothic (1517–19).

Rodrigo appears first in 1521 at Santiago, probably as an assistant of JUAN DE ÁLAVA; then, in 1526, as one of the five architects consulted on the projected vast collegiate church of Valladolid (the others are his father, his master, Francisco de COLONIA, and Riaño). He was master mason at Astorga Cathedral (from 1530), where he built the nave; at Salamanca Cathedral (from 1537), where the transepts must be his; at the cloister of Santiago (from 1538), where he followed Álava; at Plasencia Cathedral (1537 or 1544), where the contributions of various masons are obscure; and at Segovia Cathedral (from 1563), where the east end is his. His finest secular work is the PLATERESQUE façade of the University at Alcalá de Henares (1537–53). He also wrote a

Italian masters, although he absorbed into his eclectic style a few Palladian features. St Martin-in-the-Fields, London (1722–6), is his masterpiece, and was widely imitated, especially in its combination of temple-front portico and steeple rising from the ridge of the roof. The monumental side elevations of recessed giant columns and giant pilasters have windows with his characteristic GIBBS SURROUND.

His best surviving secular buildings are outside London: the Octagon, Twickenham (1720); Sudbrooke Park, Petersham (*c.* 1720); Ditchley House (1720–25); and the Senate House (1722–30) and King's College Fellows' Building at Cambridge (1724–49). Several of these display his ebulliently Italian Baroque style of interior decoration at its sumptuous best. His last and most original building, the Radcliffe Library, Oxford (1737–49), is unique in England in showing the influence of Italian Mannerism. He exerted great influence both in Britain and in America through his *Book of Architecture* (1728), one of the plates from which probably inspired the White House in Washington.

T. Friedman, *J.G.*, New Haven and London 1984; Harris 1990.

book on architecture which is known only at second-hand.

Kubler and Soria 1959.

Gilbert, Cass (1859–1934). He designed the Woolworth Building in New York (1913) which until 1930 was the highest building in America (*c*. 260 m.). With its Gothic details it still belongs to HISTORICISM.

Gill, Irving John (1870–1936). American architect, working in California after training in Chicago under SULLIVAN 1890–93 alongside WRIGHT. He started his own practice in San Diego in 1893. His early buildings experimented with various styles, notably SHINGLE but also PRAIRIE, English cottage vernacular, Spanish Mission and others, though always adhering to ARTS AND CRAFTS principles even when he evolved his own style *c*. 1907 with the Laughlin House, Los Angeles. The Dodge House, Los Angeles (1916, now demolished), and the Horatio West apartments, Santa Monica (1919), illustrate his developed style, emphatically cubic and with large concrete blocks. It is curiously similar to advanced work in Europe of the same years.

E. McCoy, *Five California Architects*, New York 1960; D. Gebhard, *Architecture in Southern California*, Los Angeles 1965; W. Kaplan, *The Art that is Life; The Arts and Crafts Movement in America 1875–1920*, Boston 1987–8.

Gilles le Breton (d. 1553), *see* LE BRETON, Giles.

Gilly, Friedrich (1772–1800), came of a French Huguenot family which had moved to Berlin in 1689, and was the son of the architect David Gilly (1748–

1808). In spite of his neo-classical convictions he started as a Gothic enthusiast, drawing the Marienburg in West Prussia (1794). The king bought one of the drawings and gave young Gilly a four-year travel grant which, because of the war, he could not take up. In 1796 the idea of a national monument for Frederick the Great was revived. The king had died in 1786, and in the following year the monument had first been suggested: Hans Christian Genelli (1763–1823) at once submitted a Greek Doric temple, a very early case of faith in Grecian ideals (*but see* LEDOUX and SOANE). Gilly now designed a great funerary precinct and in its centre, raised on a high platform, a much larger Greek Doric temple – a Parthenon for the Prussian king. The precinct is strikingly original and strikingly severe in its forms. It is true that Gilly leant on the most recent work of young Parisian architects and their model PIRANESI (e.g. in the tunnel-vaulted triumphal arch), but the absolutely unmoulded cubic shapes are all his.

The year after, he took up his grant, but went to France and England instead of Italy: what he drew in Paris shows the sympathies already indicated by the monument. On his return in 1798 Gilly was made Professor of Optics and Perspective at the newly founded Academy of Architecture. In the same year he did his design for a national theatre for Berlin; in spite of certain motifs derived from Paris it is perhaps the most unimitative design of the age. It seems easier to reach the C20 from this unrelieved geometrical shape than from anything between Gilly and 1890. The functions of the various parts of the building are made perfectly clear, and the semicircular front in particular, taken from Legrand and Molinos's Théâtre Feydeau (which Gilly drew in Paris), was handed by him to Moller (Theatre, Mainz, 1829), and from there reached SEMPER.

H. Reelfs and K. Frössli, *F.G. 1772–1800* . . ., exh. cat., Berlin 1984; Watkin and Mellinghoff 1987.

Giocondo, Fra Giovanni (1433–1515). A Dominican friar, born in Verona. The Palazzo del Consiglio, Verona (1476–93), used to be attributed to him. He was in Naples 1489–93, where he succeeded GIULIANO DA MAIANO at Poggioreale, then in Paris 1495–1505, where he was responsible for the construction of a bridge over the Seine *c.* 1500. In 1511 he published the first illustrated edition of VITRUVIUS. He produced a plan for St Peter's (1505–12) and was appointed architect to St Peter's with RAPHAEL in 1514.

Heydenreich and Lotz 1974; V. Fontana, *Fra G.G. Architetto 1433–1515,* Vicenza 1988.

Giotto di Bondone (*c.* 1266–1337) was appointed master mason to the cathedral and city of Florence in 1334 on account of his fame as a painter. His architectural work was limited to the campanile of the cathedral, which he began in that year. It seems certain that only the first storey of the socle was finished when he died. It was completed, with alterations, by Andrea PISANO and Francesco TALENTI in the 1340s and 1350s.

Trachtenberg 1971; White 1987.

Giuliano da Maiano (1432–90). He was the elder brother of BENEDETTO DA MAIANO. He began as a wood-carver (choirstalls in Pisa Cathedral, cupboards in New Sacristy, Florence Cathedral, 1463–5) but later worked mainly as an architect and was appointed architect to Florence Cathedral from 1477 until his death. He helped to diffuse the Early Renaissance style of BRUNELLESCHI and MICHELOZZO throughout Tuscany and beyond to the Marches and Naples. He designed the chapel of S. Fina in the Collegiata at S. Gimignano (1466), Palazzo Spannochi, Siena (begun 1473), and Palazzo Venier, Recanati (1477, much altered later). His masterpiece is the cathedral of Faenza (1474–86). At Naples he designed the Palazzo di Poggio Reale (*c.* 1488, destroyed) and the quadrangular Porta Capuana (*c.* 1485) and, probably, the Piccolomini, Terranova and Tolosa chapels in S. Anna di Monteoliveto, Naples.

Heydenreich and Lotz 1974.

Giulio Romano (Giulio Pippi or Giuliano Giannuzzi, 1499–1546), was born in Rome and began, as both painter and architect, in the classical shadow of RAPHAEL, under whom he was trained. He worked on the painted and stucco decorations at the Villa Madama and may have contributed to its design. But he rapidly developed a strongly personal and dramatically forceful MANNERIST style. His first building, the Palazzo Adimari Salviati, Rome (begun *c.* 1520 but much altered later), the Villa Lante on the Gianicolo, Rome (begun 1520/21, now the Finnish Academy), and the Palazzo Stati Maccarani in Piazza S. Eustachio, Rome (begun 1522/3, now Palazzo di Brazza), already display his originality, especially the Palazzo Maccarani, which is extremely wilful and eccentric in its use of the classical repertory of form. (Palazzo Cicciaporci, Rome, was for long attributed to him, erroneously.) In 1524 he went to work for Federigo Gonzaga at Mantua, where all his most notable buildings were constructed. Palazzo Te (1524–34) was designed for Federigo's honeymoon and as a summer villa. One storey high, it is built around an enormous courtyard and looks on to a garden terminated by a semicircular pilastered colonnade. Much in the plan derives from ancient Rome by way of Raphael's Villa Madama, but the careful interrelation of house and garden is new. Still more revolutionary were the façades: one of them smooth, with the SERLIAN MOTIF repeated as a blind arcade towards the garden; the others excessively rough with irregular rustication, Tuscan columns, massive keystones and wilfully misused classical details (the centre triglyph of each intercolumniation looks as if it had slipped out of place). He decorated the interior with frescoes, mainly of an erotic nature. One room gives a key to his strange personality: it has only one door and no windows and the walls and ceiling are painted to represent the Fall of the Titans, so that the shape of the room is entirely effaced and the visitor finds himself engulfed in a cascade of boulders and gigantic nude figures some 14 ft high.

On the façade of his own house in Mantua (c. 1544) he again indulged in a truculently licentious misuse of classical detail, but this time with a different intention. It is elegantly aloof and sophisticated instead of oppressive and neurotic. For the Palazzo Ducale, Mantua, he designed the 'appartamento di Troia' (1536–9), with its elaborate stucco decorations, and the adjacent Cortile della Cavallerizza (1539 onwards), with coupled twisted columns on the first floor and much heavy rustication, one wing being pierced by arches and square windows

to afford a view across the nearby lake. He also designed the abbey church of San Benedetto Po or in Polirone (1540 onwards) and remodelled Mantua Cathedral (1545 onwards) with double aisles supported by sturdy Corinthian columns whose repeated drum-beat monotony draws the visitor towards the high altar – another instance of his preoccupation with the effect a building would make rather than with the perfection of its form. The Palazzo Italiano at Landshut, Bavaria (1537 onwards), has been attributed to him.

Heydenreich and Lotz 1974; E. Verheyen, *The Palazzo del Te in Mantua*, Baltimore 1977; C. L. Frommel *et al.*, *G.R.*, Milan 1989.

Giurgola, Romualdo (b. 1920), *see* KAHN, Louis.

Glacis. In military architecture, the ground sloping from the top of the parapet of the covered way till it reaches the level of the open country, so that every part of it can be swept by the fire of the ramparts.

Glass. Although used for windows since ancient Roman times, glass was not used as a building material until the late C18, first in greenhouses etc. (*see* CONSERVATORIES), then in vaults and domes (*see* FONTAINE; BÉLANGER) and then for complete structures (PAXTON's Crystal Palace, London, 1851, and August Voit's Glaspalast, Munich, 1853–4, both burnt down in the 1930s), supported by metal framework (*see* METAL STRUCTURES). The large-span glazed roof was developed in the mid C19 for railway stations (Paddington station, London, 1854), covered markets (Les Halles, Paris, 1853) and stores (Bon Marché, Paris, 1876), culminating in the Galerie des

Glazed bricks

Machines at the Paris 1889 exhibition by Charles-Louis-Ferdinand Dutert (1845–1906) and the engineer Victor Contamin (1840–93). The introduction of the glazed CURTAIN WALL (*see also* ELLIS; CHICAGO SCHOOL) led to the continuous glass façades of BEHRENS, GROPIUS, TAUT, etc. and the glass-clad skyscrapers of MIES VAN DER ROHE. Tinted solar glass is nowadays used for large expanses, e.g. Willis Faber office, Ipswich (1975 by Norman FOSTER). Special glass products – glass slabs, glass bricks, glass tubing for walls, etc. – have also been exploited structurally by such architects as LE CORBUSIER and Frank Lloyd WRIGHT.

W. Blaser, *Filigrane Architektur . . .* 1980; G. Kohlmann and B. Sartory, *House of Glass*, Cambridge, Mass., 1986.

Glazed bricks. Polychrome glazed bricks were developed in the ancient Near East (Assyria) in the late second millennium BC and were used for wall decoration on a large scale at Khorsabad (C8 BC) and Babylon (*c.* 575 BC) and Susa (C5 BC). Those from Khorsabad and Susa are now in East Berlin (Staatliche Museum) and Paris (Louvre).

W. Andrae, *Coloured Ceramics from Assur*, London 1925.

Gloriette, *see* EYE-CATCHER.

Gočár, Josef (1880–1945), *see* CZECHOSLOVAK ARCHITECTURE.

Godefroy, Maximilien (1765–1840?). French *émigré* architect who introduced Parisian NEO-CLASSICAL ideals to the USA. He was trained in Paris where he probably knew LEDOUX. He arrived in America in 1805. His chief works are the advanced neo-classical

Unitarian Church in Baltimore (1817–18) and the Commercial and Farmer's Bank in Baltimore (1812–13) of which only the doorway survives. His masterpiece is the Battle Monument in Baltimore (designed 1810, built 1814–27), the first great civic monument in the USA and a precursor of MILLS's Washington Monuments in Baltimore and Washington. But Godefroy's neo-classical ideals did not prevent him from indulging in neo-Gothic, e.g. the chapel of St Mary's Seminary, Baltimore (1807). He left America in 1819, settling first in London, unsuccessfully, and in 1827 returned to France.

Hitchcock 1977; R. L. Alexander, *The Architecture of M.G.*, Baltimore 1974.

Godwin, Edward William (1833–86). Godwin was born in Bristol, where in 1862 he designed a warehouse in a massive style with rows of round-arched openings, rather similar to the warehouses of Boston, Massachusetts. In the same year he moved to London, having won the competition for Northampton Town Hall. This, built 1861–4, is Gothic. So are Congleton Town Hall (1864–6) and Dromore Castle, Limerick (1866–73). But Godwin was not content to be a revivalist. His 'art furniture' of 1871 and later is inspired by Japan, but at the same time decidedly original. In architecture this originality could be even bolder, e.g. White House, Tite Street, Chelsea, built for Whistler in 1877–9 (demolished) and the even more original designs for 44 Tite Street (1878, modified in construction). Later on Godwin was engaged in theatrical decoration.

D. Harbron, *The Conscious Stone. The Life of E.W.G.*, London 1949; Hitchcock 1977.

Goff, Bruce Alonzo (1904–82). An extreme individualist and typically American loner, Goff always practised in the mid-West, usually for clients of moderate means, and only towards the end of his life became more widely known. His work is mainly residential but is otherwise unclassifiable in its maverick originality. He delighted in combining opposites – flowing, free-form curves with complicated geometrical configurations, organic materials with standard prefabricated parts. Notable are his Ford House, Aurora, Illinois (1948), a radially divided circle in plan, constructed of curved steel ribs and standard Quonset-hut members; Bavinger House, Norman, Oklahoma (1949–55), a continuous snail-like spiral of open spaces suspended from a steel mast and cables; Glen Harder House, near Mountain Lake, Minnesota (1970), like an Indian encampment; the Price House, Bartlesville, Oklahoma (1956–76), formed of interlocking polygons; and the Barby II Residence, Tucson, Arizona (1974–6).

D. DeLong, *The Architecture of B.G. Buildings and Projects 1916–1977*, New York 1977; J. Cook, *The Architecture of B.G.*, London 1978; D. G. DeLong, *B.G. Toward Absolute Architecture*, Cambridge, Mass., 1988.

Gogel, Daniel (b. 1927), see GERMAN ARCHITECTURE.

Golden section. An irrational proportion, probably known to the ancient Greeks (perhaps Euclid) and thought to be divine by Renaissance theorists, notably Luca Pacioli (*De divina proportione*, 1479, published 1509). It may be defined as a line cut in such a way that the smaller section is to the greater as the greater is to the whole. This cannot be worked out mathematically, hence its fascination. Approximately it would be 5:8.

M. Boissavlievitch, *Le Nombre d'or et l'esthétique scientifique de l'architecture*, Paris 1952; O. Hageneier, *Der goldene Schnitt*, 1977.

Golosov, Ilyal A. (1883–1945), *see* RUSSIAN ARCHITECTURE.

Gondouin or **Gondoin,** Jacques (1737–1818). French neo-classical architect trained under J.-F. BLONDEL and at the French Academy in Rome (1761–4), then travelled in Holland and England. His masterpiece is the École de Chirurgie in Paris (1769–75), designed as a temple of Aesculapius. The street façade is in the form of an Ionic colonnade (correctly Greek in detail) with a TRIUMPHAL ARCH motif in the centre giving access to a square court on the far side of which a Corinthian portico leads into the semi-circular anatomy theatre covered by a half Pantheon-dome. The building also included a small hospital, library, laboratories, etc. Monumental in design and practical in plan it is one of the finest and most advanced public buildings of its period anywhere. The anatomy theatre became the prototype for the Chamber of Deputies in the Palais Bourbon (1795–7 but rebuilt 1828–33) and for many later legislative buildings including LATROBE's House of Representatives in the Capitol at Washington. Gondouin established a successful private practice but was ruined by the Revolution and went into hiding. Under the Empire he re-emerged and designed the column in the Place Vendôme, Paris (completed 1810), first of the giant columns to be erected in the early C19 from Baltimore to Leningrad.

Braham 1980.

FIG. 52. *Gopura*

Goodhue, Bertram Grosvenor (1869–1924). American church architect, rather more versatile than his partner CRAM at St Thomas's, New York (1905–13). His St Vincent Ferrer church, New York (1914–18), the Rockefeller Chapel, University of Chicago (1918–28), and St Bartholomew's, New York (1914–19), inspired by BENTLEY's Westminster Cathedral, are notable. His masterpiece is the Nebraska State Capitol, Lincoln (1920–32). The National Academy of Science, Washington, DC (1919–24), is also by him.

R. Oliver, *B.G.G.*, New York and London 1983.

Gopura. The elaborate high gateway to a Hindu temple, usually very richly decorated with sculpture. Notable examples survive in southern India. *See* Fig. 52.

Gothic architecture. The architecture of the pointed arch, the RIB VAULT, the FLYING BUTTRESS, the walls reduced to a minimum by spacious arcades, by GALLERY or TRIFORIUM, and by spacious CLERESTORY windows. These are not isolated motifs; they act together and represent a system of skeletal structure with active, slender, resilient members and membrane-thin infilling or no infilling at all. The motifs are not in themselves Gothic inventions. Pointed arches had existed in ROMANESQUE Burgundy, southern France, and also Durham. Rib vaults had existed in Durham too; and the principle of flying buttresses as half-arches or half-tunnel vaults under the roofs of aisles or galleries above aisles is also found in French and English Romanesque. Even the verticalism of Gothic churches is only rarely more pronounced than that of, say, St Sernin at Toulouse or Ely (both Romanesque churches). The earliest completely Gothic building is the lower part of the east end of St Denis Abbey, dating from 1140–44 (see Abbot SUGER). For the development of the style in France and then in all other countries, *see* FRENCH, ENGLISH, GERMAN, SPANISH ARCHITECTURE etc.

Gothic Revival. The movement to revive the Gothic style belongs chiefly to the late C18 and the C19. Before the late C18 it must be distinguished from the Gothic Survival, an unquestioning continuation of Gothic forms, which is of course largely a matter of out-of-the-way buildings. Of major buildings mostly churches are concerned, and St Eustache in Paris and the chapel of Lincoln's Inn in London were completed well within the C17. By then, however, the new attitude of Revival had also appeared – the conscious choice of the Gothic style in contrast to the accepted current style. The first cases are those of the finishing of Gothic buildings, cases of Gothic for the sake of conformity (flèche, Milan Cathedral; façade, S. Petronio, Bologna), but soon the choice was also made for new buildings, though rarely before *c.* 1720. Then cases multiply, at least in England (HAWKSMOOR). Sanderson Miller (1717–80) began building sham castles in the 1740s, and with Arbury Hall, Warwickshire (*c.* 1760–70) by Henry Keene (1726–76) and especially Horace Walpole's Strawberry Hill (*c.* 1750–70) the Gothic Revival became a fashion. It affected France and Germany in the later C18, and a little later also Italy, Russia, America, etc. With the growth of archaeological knowledge, the Gothic Revival became more competent but also more ponderous (*see* HISTORICISM). For churches Gothic remained the accepted style well into the C20 (Episcopalian Cathedral, Washington, DC, begun to a design by BODLEY in 1907). Of public buildings, the epoch-making one was the Houses of Parliament in London (BARRY and PUGIN, 1836–65): other major examples are the Town Hall, Vienna (1872–83), by Friedrich von Schmidt (1825–91); the Houses of Parliament, Budapest (1883–1902), by Imre Steindl (1839–1902); the Law Courts, London (1866–82), by STREET; the University, Glasgow (1866–71), by Sir Giles Gilbert SCOTT, and the Rijksmuseum, Amsterdam (1877–85), by CUYPERS. *See also* CARPENTER'S GOTHIC.

K. Clark, *The Gothic Revival*, London (1928) 1962; Clarke 1969; P.

Frankl, *The Gothic*, Princeton (1960) 1966; G. German, *Gothic Revival in Europe and Britain*, London 1973; W. Andrews, *American Gothic*, New York 1975; C. Baur, *Neugotik*, Munich 1981; M. McCarthy, *Origins of the Gothic Revival*, London 1987.

Gowan, James (b. 1923), *see* STIRLING, James.

Grassi, Giorgio (b. 1935), *see* NEO-RATIONALISM.

Graves, Michael (b. 1934). Leading POST-MODERN architect in the USA of the generation after VENTURI. He emerged in 1969 as one of the NEW YORK FIVE and developed towards a colourful and sophisticated neo-historicism which his Public Services Building, Portland, Oregon (1980–82), made famous internationally though his Humana Tower, Louisville, Kentucky (1986), surpasses it. His extremely personal use of 'classical' and 'vernacular' elements achieves great distinction and elegance, e.g. the Environmental Education Center, Liberty State Park, Jersey City, 1983.

K. Nichols and P. Burke, *M.G. Buildings and Projects*, Princeton 1988.

Gravesande, Arent van's (d. 1662). A follower of van CAMPEN and a leading exponent of Dutch classicism. His style was already well developed in his earliest known building, the Sebastiaansdoelen in The Hague (1636). His mature work is all in Leiden, where he was municipal architect – the Cloth Hall (1639), the Bibliotheca Thysiana and his masterpiece the Marekerk (1638–48), an octagonal domed church with Ionic columns supporting the drum of the dome. He later began a variant of this design in the Oostkerk at Middelburg (1646).

Kuyper 1980.

Great Britain *see* ENGLISH ARCHI-TECTURE; IRISH ARCHITECTURE; SCOTTISH ARCHITECTURE.

Greek architecture. Commenting on the buildings on the Acropolis at Athens, Plutarch remarked: 'They were created in a short time for all time. Each in its fineness was even then at once age-old; but in the freshness of its vigour it is, even to the present day, recent and newly wrought.' No better description of the aims and achievements of Greek architects has ever been written. Their ambition was to discover eternally valid rules of form and proportion; to erect buildings human in scale yet suited to the divinity of their gods; to create, in other words, a classically ideal architecture. Their success may be measured by the fact that their works have been copied on and off for some 2,500 years and have never been superseded. Though severely damaged, the Parthenon remains the most nearly perfect building ever erected. Its influence stretches from the immediate followers of its architects to LE CORBUSIER. Greek architecture was, however, predominantly religious and official. Whereas temples and public buildings were of the greatest magnificence, private houses seem to have been fairly simple single-storey affairs, built of cheap materials.

Although the technique of constructing arches was known to the Greeks and the materials used for building temples, after the C6 BC, were normally stone or marble, their architecture was TRABEATED and preserved many of the techniques of wooden construction. A deep respect for tradition led them to preserve as decorative elements in their stone buildings many of the constructional elements of wooden ones: TRIGLYPHS representing the end of cross-beams, GUTTAE the pegs used for fastening them, and METOPES the space between them. They derived much from other Mediterranean civilizations – the plan of the temple from Asia Minor or Mycenae (*see* MEGARON), the columnar form from Egypt.

But the Doric temple form evolved in the late C7 BC was as original as it was typically Greek in its bold simplicity, unity of design, and use of decoration to emphasize (never to mask) structure. The earliest Doric temple to survive is that of Hera at Olympia (before 600 BC); it originally had wooden columns, which were gradually replaced in stone. Fragments from the temple at Korkyra, Corfu (*c.* 600 BC), reveal that sculpture was already used for the pediments. Other notable early Doric temples include the Temple C at Selinunte in Sicily (mid C6 BC), the so-called Basilica at Paestum (*c.* 530 BC), and the temple of Zeus Olympios at Agrigento in Sicily (*c.* 500–470 BC). In all these the columns are rather stocky and primitive-looking, partly because their smooth stucco coverings have flaked off. Much greater refinement marks the temple of Hephaistos, Athens (*c.* 449–444 BC). The summit was reached at the Parthenon (447–438 BC), with its perfect proportions and nicely balanced relation of sculpture to architecture. Here, as in other Doric temples, great pains were taken to correct optical illusions by the subtle use of ENTASIS. The temple to Athena Nike (448–421 BC) and the Erechtheum (421–406 BC), also on the Acropolis, reveal a tendency towards the exquisite; and the latter, with its graceful Ionic capitals and wonderful CARY-

ATIDS, also points towards a new appreciation of architectural movement.

The so-called Dorian people who dominated most of mainland Greece and the western colonies regarded Doric as their national architectural style. Ionians of the Aegean islands and the coast of Asia Minor developed the more delicate Ionic ORDER, as in the temple of Artemis at Ephesus (c. 560–550 BC) by the Cretan architect Chersiphron of Knossos, whose son Metagenes completed the building. It first appeared on the mainland in the buildings they contributed to the sanctuary at Delphi. And probably for political as much as aesthetic reasons, in the C5 BC the Athenians, then allied with the eastern Greeks against the Persians, admitted the Ionic order for the Erechtheum on the Acropolis in Athens (dedicated to the ancestor Dorians shared with the Ionians). The Ionic order was otherwise used on the mainland for interiors, notably in the temple of Apollo Epikourios at Bassae (late C5), which also included one column with a Corinthian capital, at the end of the CELLA. Until the HELLENISTIC period, the Corinthian order was used exclusively for interiors, e.g. Great Tholos at Delphi (c. 400 BC), temple of Athena Alea at Tegea (c. 360 BC), Tholos of Epidaurus (c. 350 BC). The only exception was the Choragic Monument of Lysicrates in Athens (334 BC), a kind of enlargement of a bronze offering table. This little building, with an almost over-bred elegance (which had great appeal in the C18), illustrates the final stage of Greek architectural development on the eve of the Macedonian conquest by Philip and his son Alexander the Great. A tendency towards superhuman monumentality as well as lavish ornamenta-

tion culminated in the Mausoleum at Halicarnassus (modern Bodrum) in 355–330 BC, where the role of the sculptors was greater than that of the architect.

Although the main Greek achievement was in the evolution of the Doric temple, many other types of religious buildings were of great beauty. The grandest were the theatres, notably that of Dionysus under the Acropolis in Athens (C5 BC, but much altered) and that at Epidaurus (c. 350 BC), which reveal as perfect a command of acoustics as of visual effects. Theatres of this type were much imitated, especially in Asia Minor, during the HELLENISTIC period. See also CRETAN AND MYCENAEAN ARCHITECTURE; BYZANTINE ARCHITECTURE.

Greek cross. A cross with four equal arms.

Greek key, see FRET.

Greek Revival. Greek as against Roman architecture became known to the West only about 1750–60 (see CLASSICISM). It was at first regarded as primitive and imitated by only a few architects. The earliest example is a garden temple at Hagley by 'Athenian' STUART (1758). A Grecian fashion began only in the 1780s. Among the earliest believers in the positive value of the simplicity and gravity of the Greek C5 were LEDOUX and SOANE. The Greek Revival culminated in all countries in the 1820s and 1830s, even, with the HANSENS, in Athens itself. (See also GILLY, SCHINKEL, SMIRKE, WILKINS, STRICKLAND, HAMILTON, PLAYFAIR, etc.)

Crook 1972; Honour 1977 and 1979; Middleton and Watkin 1977; R. G.

Kennedy, *Greek Revival. America*, New York 1989.

Greene & Greene. South Californian architects: Charles Sumner Greene (1868–1957) and Henry Greene (1870–1954). They specialized in massive timber construction and followed the ARTS AND CRAFTS movement in exposing joints. Their *œuvre* was almost exclusively domestic. Their very low-pitched roofs are reminiscent of Frank Lloyd WRIGHT and the Prairie style. They particularly liked the juxtaposition of timber with boulders. Examples of their work are the J. H. Cuthbertson House of 1902, Blacker House of 1907 and Gamble House of 1908–9, all in Pasadena, California, and the Pratt House of 1909 in Ojai, California.

R. L. Makinson, *C. and H.G. and Their Work*, 1978; and *G. & G. Architecture as a Fine Art*, Santa Barbara (1977) 1985.

Greenhouse, *see* CONSERVATORY.

Greenway, Francis Howard (1777–1837). A pupil of NASH, he was active first in Bristol and Clifton, where he designed the Assembly Rooms (1806, completed by Joseph Kay). Declared insolvent in 1811, he was accused of forgery in 1812 and condemned to death but transported to Australia instead. The verdict was for fourteen years, but he was at once recommended by a retired admiral to Governor Macquarie and very soon found himself busy designing buildings in and around Sydney. He became Acting Civilian Architect in 1816. His principal buildings belonged to only five or six years: the lighthouse and Macquarie Tower; the churches of St Matthew, Windsor, St Luke, Liverpool, and St James, Sydney; the Government House at Sydney, the Hight Park Barracks and the Liverpool Hospital. Greenway's style appeared at first to be Late Georgian, but individual motifs occur, especially in St Matthew. But his success did not, alas, last long. After quarrelling with Macquarie he was less busy.

M.H. Ellis, *F.G. His Life and Times*, Sydney and San Francisco (1949) 1966; M. Herman, *Early Australian Architects (1788–1850) and their Work*, Sydney and London 1954.

Gregotti, Vittorio (b. 1927). Italian architect associated with NEO-RATIONALISM notable for his large-scale topographically determined urban projects, of which the University of Calabria complex near Cosenza (1972 onwards) is the most spectacular.

M. Tafuri, *V.G. Buildings and Projects*, Milan (1982) 1988.

Griffin, Walter Burley (1876–1937). An American PRAIRIE SCHOOL architect, he worked for Frank Lloyd WRIGHT in Chicago 1901–5 and then on his own, contributing notably to the Rock Crest Rock Glen development, Mason City, Iowa (1908–17). In 1912 he won the competition for a new capital city at Canberra, settled in Australia and created at Canberra a gigantic GARDEN CITY (only the centre still bears the imprint of his conception). He also planned the community suburb of Castlecrag, Sydney (1921–35), and designed some notable buildings, e.g. Capitol Theatre, Melbourne (1921–4), before settling in 1935 in Lucknow, India, where he provided plans for the university campus, the Pioneer Press and a number of houses for Indian clients.

M. L. Peisch, *The Chicago School of Architecture: Early Followers of Sul-*

livan and Wright, New York 1964; J. Birrell, *W.B.G.*, Brisbane 1964; D. L. Johnson, *The Architecture of W.B.G.*, Melbourne 1977.

Grimshaw, Nicholas (b. 1939), *see* HIGH TECH.

Groin. The sharp edge formed by the intersection of vaulting surfaces.

Groin vault, *see* VAULT.

Gropius, Walter (1883–1969). Studied at the Colleges of Technology of Berlin and Munich. He received his introduction to the C20 problems of architecture and the responsibilities of the architect in the office of Peter BEHRENS, who believed in the architect's duty to provide well-designed buildings for working in, and also well-designed everyday products. He spent the years 1907–10 with Behrens. The outcome of this was that Gropius, as soon as he had established a practice of his own (1910), submitted a memorandum to a powerful potential client on the mass-producing of housing and equipment. One year later he built, with Adolph Meyer (1881–1929), the Fagus factory at Alfeld, which was one of the earliest buildings in any country to be in full command of the elements of architecture which were to constitute the INTERNATIONAL MODERN style: glass CURTAIN WALLING, unrelieved cubic blocks, corners left free of visible supports. For the Werkbund Exhibition at Cologne in 1914, Gropius produced, also with Adolph Meyer, a Model Factory and Office Building, equally radical in its statement of new principles. Apart from Behrens, Frank Lloyd WRIGHT was now a source of inspiration; for two publications about him had appeared in Berlin in 1910 and 1911. On the strength of the Werkbund

Exhibition building, Henry van de VELDE, then head of the School of Arts and Crafts at Weimar, advised the Grand Duke to make Gropius his successor. Gropius accepted and, when the First World War was over, settled down at Weimar to convert the school into a completely new establishment, for which he coined the name BAUHAUS (House of Building). This name alludes to Gropius's conviction that, as with the medieval cathedral, the building ought to be the meeting-place of all arts and crafts teaching; all should work towards this ultimate unity. He also believed that all artists should be familiar with crafts, and that the initial training of artists and craftsmen should be one and the same – an introduction to form, colour, and the nature of materials. This part of the teaching programme, first worked out by Johannes Itten, was known as the Basic Course (*Vorkurs*).

Gropius, in the first years of the Bauhaus, was propelled by the ideas of William MORRIS on the one hand, by the enthusiasm of the EXPRESSIONISTS on the other. There are, indeed, a few works by him belonging to these first years which are entirely Expressionist in style, notably the jagged concrete monument to those killed in the March Rising (1921) and the large log-house for the timber manufacturer Adolf Sommerfeld (1921–2), the latter equipped by Bauhaus staff and students. But then in 1923, stimulated by contacts with the Dutch group of DE STIJL (led by Theo van Doesburg), Gropius returned to the ideals of his early years. The Bauhaus turned from emphasis on craft to emphasis on industrial design, and Gropius's own style followed once again the line laid down by the Fagus factory. The principal monument of this change is the Bauhaus's own new premises at Dessau (1925–6), functionally planned and detailed. Other important designs of these flourishing years in Germany are those for a Total Theatre (1926) and the long slabs of 'rational' housing for Siemensstadt (1929).

The rising tide of National Socialism killed the Bauhaus, but Gropius had already left it in 1928. After Hitler assumed power, Gropius left Germany and, following a short spell of partnership with Maxwell FRY in London (1934–7) – the most influential outcome of which was the Impington Village College near Cambridge – he went to Harvard, where his principal job was once again teaching. His and Konrad WACHSMANN's General Panel system was a notable experiment in prefabricated housing and in 1945, in accordance with his faith in cooperative work, he started his own firm as TAC (The Architects' Collaborative) – a group of younger men working with him in full freedom. Of the achievements of this cooperative the Harvard Graduate Centre (1949), a block of flats for the Berlin Hansa quarter (Interbau Exhibition 1957) and the Pan Am Building, New York (1958–63), may be mentioned, together with Gropius's own US Embassy, Athens, of 1957–61.

M. Franciscono, *W.G. and the Creation of the Bauhaus in Weimar*, Chicago and London 1971; R. R. Isaacs, *W.G. Der Mensch und sein Werk*, Berlin 1983–4; H. Probst and C. Schadlich, *W.G.*, Berlin 1986.

Grosch, Christian Henrik (1801–65), *see* NORWEGIAN ARCHITECTURE.

Grotesque. Fanciful ornamental decoration composed of small, loosely connected motifs, not unlike ARABESQUES but including human figures, monkeys, sphinxes, etc. It derived from ancient Roman decorations, either painted or in low relief, which came to light in the Renaissance after being buried for centuries in subterranean ruins known as *grotte*, hence the name *grotesques*. At first details only were used, but in 1516 complete schemes were revived by RAPHAEL in the Vatican and these became famous when Raphael used them *c.* 1519 to decorate the Vatican Logge, largely executed by Giovanni da Udine, who decorated the Villa Madama, Rome, in a similar manner (1520–21). Within a few years engravings of grotesques were in circulation. By the mid C16, grotesques had spread from Italy to the rest of Europe and during the next 300 years were widely used, often in combination with STRAPWORK.

P. Ward-Jackson in *Victoria & Albert Museum Bulletin*, April and July 1967; N. Dacos, *La Découverte de la Domus Aurea et la formation des grotesques à la Renaissance*, London and Leiden 1971; A. Chastel, *La grotesque*, 1988.

Grotto. An artificial cavern, usually with fountains and other water-works and decorated with rock- and shell-work, also sculpture, ceramic reliefs and panels etc. Known to have been a feature of ancient Roman gardens, the grotto was revived in the Renaissance, notably by MANNERIST architects such as BUONTALENTI, e.g. grottoes in the Boboli Gardens, Florence (1583–8). In a more rustic form they became a feature of the PICTURESQUE garden and park in the C18.

B. Jones, *Follies and Grottoes*, London (1955) 1974; Heydenreich and Lotz 1974.

Ground-plan, *see* PLAN.

Grounds, Sir Roy (1905–81), *see* AUSTRALIAN ARCHITECTURE.

Gruen, Victor (1903–80). German architect who emigrated to the USA in 1938, where he invented the 'shopping centre' sited out of town for car-owners, e.g. his Northland Shopping Center, Detroit, 1952. His plan for Fort Worth, Texas (1955), was notable and in 1964 he published *Heart of our Cities*.

C. Tunnard, *Man-Made America*, New Haven 1963.

Gruppo 7, *see* RATIONALISM.

Guarini, Guarino (1624–83), was born in Modena and was a Theatine father, well known as a philosopher and mathematician, before he won fame as an architect. (He expanded Euclid and even foreshadowed Monge in his learned *Placita philosophica* of 1665.) Since he was first a mathematician and second an architect, his complex spatial compositions are sometimes difficult to understand. All his important surviving buildings are in Turin, where he spent the last seventeen years of his life. His admiration of BORROMINI is very obvious in Collegio dei Nobili (1678) and Palazzo Carignano (1679), especially the latter with its oval saloon and undulating façade in the style of S. Carlo alle Quattro Fontane. To inflate Borromini's miniature church to palatial grandiloquence was daring enough, yet his originality had already carried him even farther in the Cappella della SS. Sindone (1667–90) and in S. Lorenzo (1668–87). Both churches are crowned with fantastic and unprecedented cone-shaped domes. That of SS. Sindone is built of superimposed segmental arches that diminish in span as they ascend, the abstract geometric poetry of this free construction being emphasized by the diaphanous light which filters through the grids. The S. Lorenzo dome is equally unusual: it is composed of interlocking semicircular arches forming an octagon on a circular drum. The inspiration for this odd conception may have come from Hispano-Moresque architecture, perhaps from the similar dome in the mosque of al Hakim at Cordova (AD 965) or from French Gothic, which he certainly studied when in France. Guarini's structural ingenuity was not confined to domes, and his other experiments, notably those with banded vaults and diagonal, forward-tilted, or three-dimensional arches, were to be very influential in Germany and Austria. None of his important buildings outside Turin has survived: e.g. SS. Annunziata and Theatine Palace in Messina (1660); Ste Anne-la-Royale, Paris (1662 onwards); St Mary of Altötting, Prague (1679); and S. Maria Divina Providencia, Lisbon. His influence was greatly increased by his *Architettura civile*, published posthumously in 1737: engravings from it were known from 1668 onwards.

Wittkower 1982; H. A. Meek, *G.G. and his Architecture*, New Haven and London 1988.

Guas, Juan (d. 1496). A Spanish mason of French descent, probably the designer of S. Juan de los Reyes at Toledo (1477 onwards). Towards the end of his life Guas was master mason of Segovia and Toledo Cathedrals. It is likely that the wildly Late Gothic façade of S. Gregorio at Valladolid is his (1487–96).

Kubler and Soria 1959.

Gucewicz, Wawrzyniec (1753–98), *see* POLISH ARCHITECTURE.

FIG. 53. *Guilloche*

Guedes, Amancio d'Alpoim Miranda (b. 1925), *see* SOUTH AFRICAN ARCHITECTURE.

Guêpière, Pierre-Louis-Philippe de la (*c.* 1715–73). French architect who, alongside PIGAGE, introduced Louis XVI taste and standards into Germany. In 1750 he published *Recueil de projets d'architecture* and in the same year was summoned to Stuttgart, where he succeeded Leopoldo Retti as Directeur des Bâtiments in 1752 and designed the interiors of Retti's Neues Palais (destroyed). His masterpieces are the small and exquisite La Solitude (1763–7) outside Stuttgart and Mon Repos (1764–7) near Ludwigsburg. The interior of the latter was partially modified *c.* 1804 in an Empire style. He returned to France in 1768 but built nothing of note there. His designs for the Hôtel de Ville at Montbéliard were executed after his death with considerable alterations. He published *Recueil d'esquisses d'architecture* in 1762.

Colombier 1956; H. A. Klaiber, *Der Württemberg Oberbaudirektor P. de la G.*, Stuttgart 1959; H. J. Wörner, *Architektur der Frühklassizismus in Suddeutschland*, Munich 1979.

Guilloche. A pattern of interlacing bands forming a plait and used as an enrichment on a moulding. *See* Fig. 53.

Guimard, Hector (1867–1942), was professor at the École des Arts Décoratifs from 1894 to 1898. He is the best of the French ART NOUVEAU architects. At the beginning of his career (in 1893) he was influenced, it seems, by HORTA. His most remarkable building is the block of flats called Castel Bérenger in Paris (1894–8). The use of metal, faïence, and glass-bricks is bold and inventive, though the exterior is of less interest. On the other hand his Métro stations (1899–1904) are nothing but exterior – open metal arches in extreme Art Nouveau shapes – a daring thing for an architect to design, and perhaps an even more daring thing for a client to accept.

F. L. Graham, *H.G.*, New York 1970; Y. Brunhammer and G. Naylor, *H.G.*, London 1970; M. Rheims and G. Vigne, *H.G. 1867–1942*, New York 1988.

Gumpp, Johann Martin (1643–1729). The most important member of a family of architects working in Innsbruck, where he was Hofkammerbaumeister and a pioneer exponent of the Baroque. His main works are the Fugger-Taxis palace (1679–80), the remodelling of the old Government House (1690–92) and the Spitalkirche (1700–1701). His son Georg Anton (1682–1754) followed him as master mason to the Innsbruck court and was responsible for the boldly unconventional Landhaus (1725–8).

M. Krapf, *Die Baumeister G.*, Vienna and Munich 1979–80.

Guttae. Small drop-like projections carved below the TENIA under each TRIGLYPH on a Doric ARCHITRAVE. *See* Fig. 66.

Gwathmey, Charles (b. 1938), *see* NEW YORK FIVE.

Gymnasium. In ancient Greece a place for games and exercise, also for teaching. English has taken over the athletic, German and Italian the educational connotations of the word.

J. Delorme, *Gymnases. Étude sur les monuments consacrés à l'éducation dans la Grèce ancienne*, Paris 1960.

h

Hadfield, George (1763–1826), was born in Leghorn and trained at the Royal Academy Schools, London, winning the Gold Medal (1784) and studying in Italy 1790–91. In 1795 he went to America to supervise the construction of the new Capitol in Washington, replacing Étienne Sulpice (called Stephen) Hallet (c. 1760–1825). He disapproved of the design (by Thornton) and Hallet's revisions, but the radical alterations he suggested, such as the introduction of a colossal order, were not approved and he was dismissed in 1798. He continued to practise in Washington and impressed his neo-classical taste on the new city, e.g. the City Hall (1820, now the District of Columbia Courthouse), United States Bank (1824), Fuller's Hotel, Gadsby's Hotel, Van Ness's mausoleum (1826) and the imposing Paestum portico of Arlington House (1818), one of the most splendid examples of the Greek Revival in America.

Colvin 1978; Whiffen and Koeper 1981.

Hagioscope, see SQUINT.

Halfpenny, William (Michael Hoare, d. 1755). Holy Trinity, Leeds (1722–7), and the Redland Chapel, Bristol (1740–43), have been erroneously attributed to him, but he published some twenty architectural manuals for country gentlemen and builders which were enormously successful and influential. His designs are mostly Palladian but also include some rather ham-fisted attempts at Rococo sophistication, CHINOISERIE, GOTHIC REVIVAL, etc. *Practical Architecture* (1724), *A New and Compleat System of Architecture* (1749) and *Rural Architecture in the Chinese Taste* (c. 1750) are among the best of his books.

Colvin 1978; Summerson 1983; Harris 1990.

Half-timbering, see FRAMED BUILDING; TIMBER-FRAMING.

Hall church. A German type of church in which nave and aisles are of approximately equal height. Thus the nave is not lit from above but from the large windows of the aisles. Transepts and a distinct chancel are omitted. The earliest example is the C11 Chapel of St Bartholomew in Paderborn: the finest by STETHAIMER.

Hallet, Étienne Sulpice (called Stephen) (c. 1760–1825), see HADFIELD, George; THORNTON, William.

Hamilton, Thomas (1784–1858), was the leading GREEK REVIVAL architect in Edinburgh alongside W. H. PLAYFAIR. His masterpiece is the Royal High School, Edinburgh (1825–9). It is as forceful and dramatic – and as accomplished – as any Greek Revival building anywhere. But he was never able to repeat this success and his later work lacks impetus, e.g. the Assembly Rooms, Ayr (1827–30), the Dean Orphanage, Edinburgh (1833–6), the Burns Monument on Calton Hill, Edinburgh (1830), and the ingenious, refined but unconvincing Royal College of Physicians, Edinburgh (1843–6).

Colvin 1978; Summerson 1983; J. Rock, *T.H. Architect 1784–1858*, exh. cat., Edinburgh 1984.

Hammerbeam, *see* ROOF.

Hankar, Paul (1859–1901). Contemporary of HORTA, to whose ART NOUVEAU style he developed a striking variant, e.g. Maison Ciamberlani (now Bulgarian embassy), Brussels, 1897.

F. Loyer, *P.H. La naissance de l'Art Nouveau*, Brussels 1986.

Hans von Burghausen (d. 1432), *see* STETHAIMER or SETTHEIMER, Hans.

Hansen, Theophil von (1813–91). His father Christian Frederick (1756–1845) was the leading GREEK REVIVAL architect in Denmark (*see* DANISH ARCHITECTURE). Theophil became a leading exponent of C19 HISTORICISM, specializing in Italian Renaissance but equally at home with Greek Revival and Venetian Byzantine. He was trained in Copenhagen and travelled to Berlin, Munich, Italy and Greece and settled there, in Athens, for eight years (1838–46). His elder brother Hans Christian Hansen (1803–83) had been in Athens since 1833, became the Royal Architect and built Athens University (1839–50) in an appropriate Greek Revival style. Theophil Hansen's buildings in Athens, also Greek Revival, date from some years later – the Acad-

emy (1859–87) and Library (1885–92). In 1846 he had settled in Vienna, where he spent the rest of his life. In 1851 he married the daughter of Ludwig Förster, with whom he had collaborated on the Army Museum in the Arsenal in Vienna (1850) and who was mainly responsible for the Ring and the consequent urban development in Vienna. Hansen designed several of the more prominent public buildings on or near the Ring: Heinrichshof (1861–3, destroyed 1945); Musikverein (1867–9); Stock Exchange (1874–7); Academy of Art (1872–6); Parliament (1873–83).

Paulsson 1958; J. Travlos, *Neo-Classical Architecture in Greece*, Athens 1967; R. Wagner-Rieger, *Der Architekt T. von H.*, Vienna 1977; idem and M. Reissberger, *T. von H. Die Wiener Ringstrasse*, Wiesbaden 1980.

Hardouin-Mansart, Jules (1646–1708), the grand-nephew of François MANSART, by whom he may have been trained, owed more to LE VAU, whose grand manner he and Lebrun brought to perfection in the Galerie des Glaces at Versailles. He understood perfectly the artistic needs of Louis XIV's court and excelled as an official architect, being competent, quick, and adaptable. (He was appointed Royal Architect in 1675, Premier Architecte in 1685, and Surintendant des Bâtiments in 1699.) His meteoric career aroused jealousy, and Saint-Simon accused him of keeping tame architects in a backroom to do all his work for him. He was certainly lucky in having such gifted assistants as Pierre Lassurance (1650–1724) and Pierre LE PAUTRE, but he had real ability himself and a vivid sense of the splendour and visual drama required for a royal setting. From 1678 onwards he was in charge of the vast extensions to Versailles. These were disastrous externally, for he filled in the central terrace of Le Vau's garden façade and trebled its length. The stables, orangery, Trianon, and chapel are more successful (the latter being finished by Robert de COTTE). His Baroque tendencies reached their height in the Invalides Chapel in Paris (1680–91), while the Place Vendôme (1698 onwards) illustrates his genius for the spectacular in town planning. Towards the end of his life, notably in a number of rooms at Versailles, Trianon, and Marly, redecorated under his direction in the 1690s, he veered away from Baroque splendours towards a lighter and more elegant style which marks the first step towards the Rococo.

G. Cattani and P. Bourget, *J.H.-M.*, Paris 1956; Blunt 1982.

Hardwick, Philip (1792–1870). He stopped practising in the course of the 1840s. His son and grandson were also architects. In 1815 he was in Paris, and he spent 1818–19 in Italy. His *œuvre* does not seem to have been large, but it is of high quality and varied interest. His most famous building was Euston station, with its majestic Greek Doric propylaea (1836–9) which became famous when it was infamously destroyed by the British Transport Commission in 1962. The station building was quite independent of the propylaea, whose spiritual function was that of a worthy introduction to that miracle of human ingenuity, the London-to-Birmingham railway. The range of stylistic possibilities open to Hardwick was great, and he was remarkably good at all of them: a monumentally plain, strictly utilitarian classicism of brick and short Tuscan columns for the St

Katherine's Dock warehouses (1827–8); an at the time most unusual restrained English Baroque for the Goldsmiths' Hall (1829–35); Jacobean for Babraham Hall, Cambridgeshire (1831); and a convincing and unaffected Tudor for Lincoln's Inn Hall and Library (1842–5). On the latter, PEARSON was assistant, and it is possible that the refined detailing is his; at all events, the building is effortlessly convincing and has no longer the character of romantic make-believe of early C19 Tudor imitations.

A. and P. Smithson, *The Euston Arch*, London 1968; Colvin 1978.

Häring, Hugo (1882–1958), *see* GERMAN ARCHITECTURE.

Hårleman, Carl (1700–1753), *see* SWEDISH ARCHITECTURE.

Harling. The Scots term for ROUGHCAST.

Harmonic proportions. A system of proportions relating architecture to music. The Ancients discovered that if two cords are twanged the difference in pitch will be one octave if the shorter is half the length of the longer, a fifth if one is two thirds of the other, and a fourth if the ratio is 3:4. It was therefore assumed that rooms or whole buildings whose measurements followed the ratios 1:2, 2:3, or 3:4 would be harmonious. Early Renaissance architects, notably ALBERTI, seized on this discovery as the key to the beauty of Roman architecture and also to the harmony of the universe. The idea was further developed by PALLADIO who, with the aid of Venetian musical theorists, evolved a far more complex scale of proportions based on the major and minor third – 5:6 and 4:5 – and so on.

Wittkower 1988.

Harrison, Peter (1716–76). The only architect of distinction in pre-Revolutionary America. Born in England, he married an American heiress, emigrated in 1740, and settled in Newport, Rhode Island, as a trader in wines, rum, molasses, and mahogany. He presumably taught himself architecture but quickly acquired competence in the Palladian style, as his first work shows – Redwood Library, Newport (1748–50), a timber building imitating rusticated stone. Other buildings show Gibbsian influence: King's Chapel, Boston (1749–54); Synagogue, Newport (1759–63). But he returned to Inigo JONES and the English Palladians for inspiration in his later works: Brick Market, Newport (1761–72), and Christ Church, Cambridge, Massachusetts (1760). He settled in New Haven, Connecticut, in 1761, and became Collector of Customs there in 1768, suffering some persecution in his later years as a loyalist and government official.

C. Bridenbaugh, *P.H. First American Architect*, Chapel Hill 1949; Whiffen and Koeper 1981.

Harrison, Thomas (1744–1829). A Yorkshire architect, he designed some of the best and most gravely imposing neo-classical buildings in England. He was trained in Rome (1769–76) but never went to Greece. His masterpiece is Chester Castle, a complex of public buildings on which he worked for most of his life, though they were largely designed between 1786 and 1790. He won the commission in competition in 1785. The Prison, Exchequer Court, and Grand Jury Rooms were built 1788–91, the Shire Hall 1791–1801, the barracks and armoury wings 1804 onwards and the great Doric Propy-

laeum 1810–22. His other buildings include the Lyceum Club, Liverpool (1800–1802), the former Portico Library (now Lloyds Bank), Manchester (1802–6).

Crook 1972; Colvin 1978; Summerson 1983.

Harrison, Wallace Kirkman (1895–1981). With Raymond HOOD and others he was responsible for the Rockefeller Center, New York (1931–40), and with his partner Max ABRAMOVITZ headed the team, which included LE CORBUSIER, for the United Nations Headquarters, New York (1947–53). The mammoth New York State Center at Albany (1962–78) and the Lincoln Center, New York (1962–8), were also theirs, Harrison designing the new Metropolitan Opera House for the latter.

V. Newhouse, *W.K.H. Architect*, New York 1989.

Harsdorff, Caspar Frederik (1735–99), *see* DANISH ARCHITECTURE.

Hasenauer, Karl von (1833–94), *see* SEMPER, Gottfried.

Haunch. Part of an ARCH, roughly midway between the springing line and crown, where the lateral thrust is strongest. *See* Fig. 4.

Haus-Rucker-Co, *see* AUSTRIAN ARCHITECTURE.

Haussmann, Baron Georges-Eugène (1809–91). A Protestant from Alsace who became a lawyer and civil servant. He was ruthless, canny, and obstinate. Napoleon III made him Prefect of the Seine Department in 1853 and entrusted to him his sweeping plans for city improvement. Haussmann kept the post till 1870, and did as much as, or perhaps more than, the emperor expected. Haussmann's improvements follow the traditional principles of French town planning as established by Henri IV and developed by Louis XIV, and finally – Haussmann's direct model – by the so-called Artists' Plan of 1797: long straight boulevards meeting at *rond-points* are the principal motifs. It is often said that Haussmann made these boulevards to obtain good firing-lines in case of a revolution, but he was at least as much guided by traffic considerations (e.g. the connecting of railway stations) and was without doubt also passionately devoted to vistas towards monuments or monumental buildings such as the Arc de Triomphe or the Opéra. In 1890–93 he published his *Mémoires* (3 vols.).

D. H. Pinkney, *Napoleon III and the rebuilding of Paris*, Princeton 1958; Loyer 1987.

Haviland, John (1792–1852). American architect. He was a pupil of James ELMES and went to live in Philadelphia in 1816. In 1818–19 he brought out *The Builder's Assistant*, the first American book to illustrate the ORDERS of columns. His *magnum opus* is the Eastern Penitentiary at Cherry Hill, Philadelphia (1821–9), much imitated in Europe. It has battlements, whereas Haviland's Institute for the Deaf and Dumb (1824) has classical features and The Tombs in New York (1836–8), Law Courts and Prison, in one, is neo-Egyptian.

Whiffen and Koeper 1981.

Havlíček, Josef (1899–1961), *see* CZECHOSLOVAK ARCHITECTURE.

Hawksmoor, Nicholas (1661–1736), the most original of English Baroque architects except VANBRUGH, came from a family of Nottinghamshire farmers. At eighteen he became WREN's amanuensis and was closely associated with him at Greenwich Hospital and other buildings until his death. Vanbrugh also found him an able assistant and employed him from 1690 onwards, notably at Castle Howard and Blenheim Palace. Indeed, he became more than just an assistant to both Wren and Vanbrugh, though it is impossible now to assess how much they owed to him. It was presumably his expertise that enabled the untrained Vanbrugh's designs to be realized. His independent works have great originality, and only his dour, capricious character and lack of push denied him greater opportunities and worldly success. Vigorous, odd, bookish, yet massively plastic in feeling, his style is a highly personal Baroque amalgam of Wren, classical Rome, and Gothic. Like Vanbrugh, but unlike Wren, his passion was for dramatic effects of mass, and he has been criticized for heaviness as a result. He began working on his own c. 1702 at Easton Neston, a compact rectangular building with a giant order all round; it combines Wren's grandeur and urbanity, and in some details foreshadows Vanbrugh. In 1711 he was appointed Surveyor under the Act for Building Fifty New Churches, and the six he designed himself form the bulk of his *œuvre*. All of them are minor masterpieces: St Anne's, Limehouse (1714–30), with its medieval steeple in classical dress; St Mary Woolnoth (1716–24), with its square within a square plan; St George's, Bloomsbury (1716–30), the most grandiose and least odd of all his buildings; and Christchurch, Spitalfields (1714–29), as perverse and megalomaniac as anything by Vanbrugh. His other buildings are only slightly less notable – the quadrangle and hall at All Souls', Oxford (1729), and the west tower of Westminster Abbey (1718), all in his neo-Gothic manner; and finally, the grim and austere circular Doric mausoleum at Castle Howard (1729), where he returned to Rome and BRAMANTE for inspiration.

Colvin 1978; Summerson 1983; K. Downes, H. (1661–1736), London (1970) 1987.

Hayberger, Gotthard (1699–1764), see HUEBER, Joseph.

Header, see BRICKWORK.

Heinzelmann, Konrad (d. 1454), was at Ulm in the 1420s. He was called to Nördlingen in 1429 as master mason to design and build the church of St George, then to Rothenburg in 1428 to work on the church of St Jakob. In 1439 he went to Nuremberg, and there designed and began the beautiful chancel of St Lorenz.

Frankl 1972.

Hejduk, John (b. 1929), see NEW YORK FIVE.

Helix. A spiral motif, especially the inner spiral of the volute of a Corinthian capital.

Hellenistic architecture. The style developed in the Hellenistic kingdoms created out of the empire conquered by Alexander the Great (356–323 BC). Several of the finest surviving buildings are on the west coast of modern Turkey. The tendency towards greater elegance and elaboration in small buildings (e.g. the Choragic Monument of Lysicrates, Athens) and a more richly sculptural and monumental style for large ones (e.g. the Mausoleum of Halicarnassus and the Ionic temple of Artemis at Ephesus), already evident in early C4 GREEK ARCHITECTURE, was accelerated. The greatest Hellenistic city was Alexandria, laid out on a regular grid plan with numerous vast and very splendid buildings, none of which survives. The Ionic temple of Athena Polias, Priene (c. 335 BC), and of Artemis Leukophryene at Magnesia by HERMOGENES (c. 150 BC) are representative of the style. Doric temples were still built, but the columns became much more slender and motifs from the Ionic order were introduced, as in the Temple of Hera Basileia at Pergamum (c. 150 BC). The richer Corinthian order was more to the taste of the new civilization: at Athens the great Olympeion (begun 174 BC, though not completed until AD 131) is the first Corinthian building on the grand scale, and provides a piquant contrast to the sober solemnity of the Parthenon on the Acropolis above it.

Many of the finest Hellenistic buildings are civic rather than religious: the Bouleuterion at Miletus (174–65 BC) and various colonnaded walks like the recently restored Stoa in the Athenian AGORA (c. 150 BC). A new interest was also manifested in urban planning. At Pergamum (c. 190–133 BC) a library, large theatre, palace, barracks and several temples (including the remarkable Altar of Zeus, now Staatliche Museen, Berlin) were visually related to one another and placed scenographically to take full advantage of a terraced hill-top site. Grid planning was more usual, as at Priene, but with greater attention than before to monumental effects and the creation of vistas. Inventiveness was shown also in the planning of sanctuaries, notably that of Asclepios on Kos and the

Temple of Apollo at Didyma (begun 313 BC). Military engineering was brought to a new height of efficiency and many forts and walls, with handsome crisply cut masonry and sometimes with arched gateways, survive both in Greece and in Asia Minor (e.g. Priene). Excavations have revealed that private houses were built on a much grander scale than before. Techniques of construction developed in the Hellenistic kingdoms included the KEYSTONE arch and the TUNNEL VAULT (used mainly for tombs but occasionally for substructures and passages) both of which were later exploited by the Romans.

The Hellenistic style survived the conquest of Asia Minor by the Romans; indeed, Imperial Roman architecture may be regarded as its logical development. The main buildings of the two great Syrian sites, Baalbek (the very rich Temple of Bacchus, courts, and portico, c. AD 120–200) and Palmyra (Temple of the Sun, c. ADI; Temple of Baal, AD 131), are predominantly Hellenistic in feeling, though their vaults, arches, and domes are typically Roman.

Helm roof, see ROOF.

Hennebique, François (1842–1921). One of the pioneers of concrete architecture. He first used REINFORCED CONCRETE in 1879. His most important patents are of 1892. In 1894 he built at Viggen in Switzerland the first bridge of reinforced concrete, in 1895 at Roubaix the first grain elevator. His concrete and glass factories begin in 1894. For an exhibition at Geneva in 1896 he built a cantilevered concrete staircase, and for a small theatre at Morges in 1899 cantilevered galleries. In a small theatre at Munich in 1903

he was allowed to leave the concrete frame exposed. His own crazy concrete villa at Bourg-la-Reine dates from 1904.

Collins 1959; Pevsner 1968.

Henri Deux style, see FRENCH ARCHITECTURE; HISTORICISM.

Henry of Reyns, Master of the King's Masons to Windsor Castle in 1243, and later to Westminster Abbey. He was dead, it seems, by 1253. This means he was King's Master Mason when Westminster Abbey was begun and so was probably its designer. Reyns sounds temptingly like Reims, and Reims Cathedral is, in fact, the stylistic source of much at Westminster (tracery, the wall-passages in the east chapels), together with work at Amiens, Royaumont and the Sainte Chapelle in Paris, only just completed when the abbey was begun. However, there are other features, such as the large gallery and the ridge-rib of the vault, which are entirely English and may make it more likely that Henry was an Englishman who had worked at Reims. Judging by style, Henry may also have designed the King's Chapel at Windsor Castle (built c. 1240).

Webb 1965; Harvey 1984.

Hentrich, Helmut (b. 1905). Studied at Freiburg, Vienna, and Berlin, and in New York under Norman Bel Geddes 1930–31. He was with Hubert Petschnigg from 1954 in a partnership known as HPP. Among their most prominent buildings are the Thyssen building at Düsseldorf (Dreischeibenhaus) of 1957–60, the Aweta building at Ludwigshafen of 1960–63, the Klöckner-Humboldt Haus at Deutz of 1961–4, the Bonhoeffer church at Düsseldorf of 1964–5 and the University buildings at Bochum begun in 1961. Their Finland

House at Hamburg is the first high block in suspension construction in Europe (1966), followed by their Standard Bank, Johannesburg, with Ove ARUP (1967–9). Recent buildings: Concert Hall, Düsseldorf (1978), and Town Hall at Rheydt (1981–4).

H. B. Adams, *H.P.P.*, Düsseldorf 1989.

Héré de Corny, Emmanuel (1705–63). The architect of the Place Royale (Place Stanislas) in Nancy, the finest example of Rococo urbanism anywhere. He was trained under BOFFRAND in Paris but returned *c.* 1740 to Nancy to become architect to Stanislas Leszczynski, ex-king of Poland, for whom all his work was carried out – Hôtel des Missions Royales (1741–3), Château de Malgrange (1743), Place Royale (1752 onwards, with the Place de la Carrière leading into the Hemicycle) and the Place d'Alliance, all in Nancy. The Place Royale owes much to the superb ironwork by Lamour. Héré published his works in *Recueil des plans*, etc. (1750) and *Plans et élévations de la Place Royale de Nancy* (1753).

Kalnein and Levey 1972; J. Rau, *E.H. Premier architecte von Stanislas Lescynski in Lothringen (1705–1763)*, Berlin 1972; A. France-Lanord, *E.H. Architecte du Roi Stanislas*, Nancy 1984.

Herholdt, Johan Daniel (1818–1902), *see* DANISH ARCHITECTURE.

Herland, Hugh (d. *c.* 1405). Carpenter in the king's service probably from *c.* 1350, and in charge of the king's works in carpentry from 1375, when William Herland, presumably his father, died. His *magnum opus* is the hammerbeam roof of Westminster Hall, done in the

1390s; it has a span of about 67 ft. He also worked for William of Wykeham (with WILLIAM OF WYNFORD) at New College, Oxford, and probably at Winchester College.

Harvey 1984.

Herm. Originally, a rectangular pillar terminating in a head or bust (usually of Hermes), used to mark boundaries, etc. in ancient Greece. The form was adopted by Renaissance and post-Renaissance architects.

Hermogenes (*c.* 150 BC). Architect and apparently the most influential architectural theorist of the Hellenistic period. He was probably born at Priene, where he designed an altar. Critical of the Doric ORDER, because 'the distribution of the triglyphs and metopes is troublesome and unharmonious', he designed two important Ionic temples – that of Dionysos at Teos and the large pseudodipteral temple of Artemis Leukophryene at Magnesia on the Meander. He commented on these works in writings which are lost but were known to and quoted by VITRUVIUS.

Lawrence 1983; J. Onians, *Art and Thought in the Hellenistic Age*, London 1979.

Herrera, Juan de (1530–97), travelled abroad, mainly in Italy, from 1547 to 1559. He was appointed to succeed Juan Bautista de TOLEDO at the Escorial in 1563, though he did not design any additions until after 1572: the infirmary and chapel (1574–82) were his main contributions. But his majestic if sometimes rather solemn and Italianate style is best seen at the Palace of Aranjuez (1569), at the Exchange at Seville (1582), and in his designs for Valladolid Cathedral (*c.* 1585), which were only partly executed but had enormous influence, e.g. on Salamanca, Mexico, Puebla, and Lima Cathedrals. The severity and lack of ornament of Herrera's style became the official style during Philip II's reign – known as *estilo desornamentado*.

Kubler and Soria 1959; G. Kubler, *Building the Escorial*, Princeton 1982.

Herringbone work. Stone, brick, or tile work in which the component units are laid diagonally instead of horizontally. Alternate courses lie in opposite directions, forming a zigzag pattern along the wall-face.

Hertzberger, Herman (b. 1932), *see* DUTCH ARCHITECTURE.

Hewn stone. The American term for ASHLAR.

Hexastyle. Of a portico with six frontal columns.

High Gothic architecture, *see* GOTHIC ARCHITECTURE.

High Renaissance architecture, *see* MANNERISM; RENAISSANCE.

High-rise building, *see* SKYSCRAPER.

High Tech. A concept of or approach to architecture, rather than a style. Based on engineering and on construction and other (e.g. space) technologies and their visual expression, it was developed by English architects in the 1970s, notably by FOSTER and ROGERS. High Tech buildings are characterized by exposed structure (of steel and other metals), exposed services (pipes and air ducts etc.), by a smooth, impervious skin (often of glass) and by flexibility to create, internally, service zones and not rooms or sequences of rooms. The origins of High Tech may be sought in PAXTON's Crystal Palace and other C19 engineering structures, more recently in the work and theories of Buckminster FULLER, the plug-in fantasies of ARCHIGRAM and the tensile structures of Frei OTTO. The Centre Pompidou, Paris (1977), by PIANO and Rogers and the Sainsbury Centre for the Visual Arts, Norwich (1977), by Foster were High Tech's first notable buildings. Lloyd's of London (1986) and the Hong Kong Bank Headquarters, Hong Kong (1986), by Rogers and Foster respectively are among the latest. Also notable are several recent works by M. HOPKINS (especially the Schlumberger Research Laboratories, Cambridge, 1985), by ARUP Associates (1 Finsbury Avenue, London, 1984, and offices at Broadgate, Liverpool Street, London, 1986) and by Nicholas Grimshaw (b. 1939), whose Oxford ice-rink (1985) and Financial Times printing works, London (1988), are outstanding.

C. Davies, *High Tech Architecture*, London 1989.

Hilbersheimer, Ludwig (1885–1967). German theoretician of city planning. In 1924 he published *Hochhausstadt*, which promoted the high-rise city, layered on two levels. After 1932 he abandoned this vertical centralized city plan for horizontally planned decentralization. An associate of MIES, he was at the Bauhaus from 1928 and at Chicago from 1938.

R. Pommer *et al.*, *In the Shadow of Mies. L.H. Architect, Educator and Urban Planner*, New York 1988.

Hild, Joszef (1789–1867), *see* HUNGARIAN ARCHITECTURE.

Hildebrandt, Johann Lukas von (1668–1745). The leading Baroque architect in Austria alongside FISCHER

VON ERLACH, he was born in Genoa, the son of a captain in the Genoese army and an Italian mother. Italian always remained his first language. He studied with Carlo FONTANA in Rome before settling in Vienna. He was appointed Court Architect in 1700 and knighted by the emperor in 1720. He succeeded Fischer von Erlach as First Court Architect in 1723. His style is lighter than SCHLÜTER's and more Italianate than Fischer von Erlach's, livelier too and homelier, with typically Viennese charm. He much admired GUARINI, as his early (1699) Dominican church at Gabel in north Bohemia shows. It has Guarini's characteristic three-dimensional arches and a complicated and imaginative Guarinesque plan (concave corners hidden by convex balconies etc.). The influence of BORROMINI is evident in much of the carved decoration of his masterpiece, the Lower and Upper Belvedere in Vienna, built for Prince Eugene (the former completed 1714–15, the latter built 1720–24). His secular buildings are notable for their oval and octagonal rooms (Palais Schwarzenberg in Vienna, begun 1697; Summer Palace Ráckeve in Hungary, 1701–2; Palais Starhemberg-Schönborn in Vienna, 1706–17) and for their ingeniously planned and spatially dramatic ceremonial staircases (Palais Daun-Kinsky of 1713–16 and the Upper Belvedere in Vienna, Schloss Mirabell in Salzburg of 1721–7 and his addition to the Palais Harrach in Vienna of 1727–35). In 1711 he was consulted about the great staircase at Johann DIENTZENHOFER's Pommersfelden Palace and added the three-storey gallery there. From 1720 to 1723 and again from 1729 to 1744 he collaborated with NEUMANN on the rebuilding of the Residenz at Würzburg, contributing the designs for the lavishly decorated upper part of the central pavilion facing the gardens and the interiors of the Imperial hall and chapel. Though primarily a secular architect Hildebrandt built several churches including the Church of the Seminary at Linz (1717–25) with its boldly *mouvementé* façade, the parish church of Gollersdorf (1740–41) and probably the Piaristenkirche in Vienna (plan dated 1698, begun 1716 but later modified by K. I. DIENTZENHOFER), octagonal in plan and bright, rhythmical and Borrominesque inside. In 1719 he began the palatial enlargement of Göttweig abbey, magnificently sited above the Danube.

B. Grimschitz, *J.L. von H.*, Vienna 1959; Hempel 1965; H. and G. Auremhammer, *Das Belvedere in Wien*, Vienna and Munich 1971; Brucker 1983.

Hindu architecture, *see* INDIAN ARCHITECTURE.

Hip. The external angle formed by the meeting of two sloping roof surfaces. *See* ROOF; Fig. 72.

Hipped roof, *see* ROOF.

Hippodamos of Miletus (*fl. c.* 500–440 BC). Town-planner, political theorist and philosopher interested in the problem of urbanism. According to Aristotle (*Politics*), he originated the art of town planning and devised an ideal city to be inhabited by ten thousand citizens, divided into three classes (soldiers, artisans, and husbandmen), with the land also divided into three (sacred, public and private). The gridiron plan associated with his name had been in use since the C7 BC in Ionia though not in Attica. And his social ideas were hardly forward looking. But he seems to have been the first to appreciate that a town plan might formally embody and clarify a rational social order. He taught the Athenians the value of having a clear, regular, and strictly functional town plan instead of the haphazard layouts of archaic Greek towns. He lived in Athens and became a friend of Pericles, whose social ideas he appears to have shared. Though not an architect and never in charge of the actual construction of any town, he was probably responsible for the town plan of Miletus *c*. 475 BC and the layout of Piraeus (founded by Themistocles *c*. 470 BC) on a gridiron system with a formal, enclosed AGORA as its central feature. He possibly inspired the plan of Thourioi (founded 443 BC) as a Pan-Hellenic centre. The town plan of Rhodes has been less plausibly attributed to him. The gridiron plan was much used in later classical and Hellenistic periods. Thanks to Aristotle he has influenced writers on urbanism since the Renaissance (e.g. Sir Thomas More in *Utopia*).

F. Castagnoli, *Ippodamo di Mileto e l'urbanistica a pianta ottagonale*, Rome 1956; R. Martin, *L'Urbanisme dans la Grèce antique*, Paris 1956; J. B. Ward-Perkins, *Cities of Ancient Greece and Italy. Planning in Classical Antiquity*, New York 1974.

Hippodrome. In ancient Greece and Rome a course for horse and horse-and-chariot races, corresponding to the STADIUM for men. Early examples were usually without masonry; for later developments *see* CIRCUS.

Hirsau style, *see* AUSTRIAN ARCHITECTURE; GERMAN ARCHITECTURE.

Historicism. From the German *Historismus*, a pejorative term coined in the 1880s for the emphasis then given to history and later, by analogy, for the C19 philosophy of history (mainly Hegelian). Later, with reference to architecture, it was used for the C19 respect for the past and revival of historical styles as a matter of religious or social responsibility, or, more loosely, simply for C19 as opposed to earlier revivals – from the GREEK and GOTHIC REVIVALS to Byzantine, Early Christian, Romanesque, Italian Renaissance, French Renaissance, (*'Henri Deux'*), English Elizabethan, and Jacobean, etc. Architects aimed to work in the spirit of a style, taking care to observe its rules and imitating ornamental details with an accuracy previously reserved for classical styles. In this they were aided by a growing number of books on architecture, with detailed and often measured illustrations, also by museum collections of architectural details or plaster casts of them. Throughout the century demands for 'an architectural style of the C19' were reiterated (first by Heinrich Hübsch, 1795–1863, in his book *In welchem Style sollen wir bauen?*, 1828), but buildings unembellished with ornament (usually historical) were rarely regarded as 'architecture' by contemporaries (e.g. PAXTON's Crystal Palace). In England from the 1860s the use of historical ornament began to diminish (e.g. Philip WEBB and Norman SHAW whose so-called 'Queen Anne style' is usually dissociated from Historicism). ART NOUVEAU was the first international reaction against historical revivals.

K. Dohmer, *In welchem Style sollen wir bauen? Architekturtheorie zwischen Klassizismus und Jugendstil*, Munich 1976; W. J. Streich (ed.), *Der Historismus in der Architektur des 19 und 20 Jahrhunderts*, Berlin 1984; J. M.

Crook, *The Dilemma of Style*, London 1988.

Hittite architecture, *see* TURKISH ARCHITECTURE.

Hittorf, Jakob Ignaz (1792–1867), was born at Cologne, went to Paris in 1810 with GAU and placed himself under PERCIER. He then worked under BÉ-LANGER just at the time when the latter was busy with the glass and iron dome of the Corn Market. In 1819–23 Hittorf travelled in Germany, England, and Italy. After that, till 1848, he was Royal Architect. His first major building, executed with his father-in-law Lepère, is St Vincent de Paul, Paris (1824), still with an Ionic portico, but Early Christian rather than classical inside, with its two superimposed orders and its open roof. The exterior already shows the change from the pure classical to the new, grander, more rhetorical classical of the École des Beaux Arts as it culminated in Hittorf's Gare du Nord (1859–66). He also did extensive decorative work; laid out the Place de la Concorde in its present form (1832–40) and the Champs Élysées (1834–40); built two Circuses (des Champs Élysées, 1839; Napoléon, 1851) with iron and glass domes; and, with Charles Rohault de Fleury (1801–75) and Pellechet, designed the Grand Hôtel du Louvre – all of which proves his interest in new functions and new materials. Hittorf also made a name as an archaeologist, chiefly by his discovery of the polychromy of Greek architecture (1830), a 'Victorian' discovery shocking to the older generation of Grecian purists.

D. D. Schneider, *The Works and Doctrine of J.I.H. (1792–1867)*, New York 1977; Hitchcock 1977; *J.I.H. (1792–1867). Ein Architekt aus Köln*

im Paris des 19 Jahrhunderts, exh. cat., Cologne 1987.

Hoban, James (*c.* 1762–1831), was born in Ireland, emigrated to America after the Revolution, and was advertising in Philadelphia in 1785. But he settled in South Carolina until 1792, designing the State Capitol at Columbia (completed 1791, burnt down 1865), based on L'ENFANT's designs for the Federal Hall in New York. But he is remembered chiefly for the White House, Washington, which he designed in 1792, basing the front on a plate in GIBBS's *Book of Architecture*. He may also have had Leinster House, Dublin, in mind, though the White House is not, as has been suggested, a mere copy. It was built 1793–1801, and Hoban also supervised its rebuilding after 1814 (completed 1829). He also designed and built the Grand Hotel (1793–5) and the State and War Offices (begun in 1818), Washington. He ended his life as a solid and much respected councillor of that city.

Summerson 1983; W. Ryan and D. Guinness, *The White House. An Architectural History*, New York 1980.

Hoff, Robert van't (1887–1979), *see* DE STIJL.

Hoffmann, Josef (1870–1956), was a pupil of Otto WAGNER in Vienna and one of the founders of the Wiener Werkstätte (1903), based on the William MORRIS conviction of the importance of a unity between architecture and the crafts. His style developed from ART NOUVEAU towards a new appreciation of unrelieved square or rectangular forms ('Quadratl-Hoffmann') – a change not uninfluenced by MACKINTOSH, whose furniture and other work had been exhibited by the

Secession (*see* OLBRICH) in 1900. The Convalescent Home at Purkersdorf outside Vienna (1903–11) is one of the most courageously squared buildings of its date anywhere in the world, and yet it possesses that elegance and refinement of detail which is the Viennese heritage. With his Palais Stoclet in Brussels (1904–15) Hoffmann proved that this new totally anti-period style of unrelieved shapes could be made to look monumental and lavish by means of the materials used – in this case white marble in bronze framing outside, mosaics by Gustav Klimt inside. Hoffmann later built many wealthy villas, notably the neo-classical Haus Primavesi, Vienna (1913–15), some Austrian Pavilions for exhibitions (e.g. Paris 1925) and also some blocks of flats, but his chief importance lies in his early works.

E. F. Sekler, *J.H. The Architecture,* (Vienna 1982) Princeton 1985.

Höger, Fritz (Johann Friedrich) (1877–1949), *see* EXPRESSIONISM.

Hohenburg, Johann Ferdinand von (1732–1816), *see* AUSTRIAN ARCHITECTURE.

Holabird & Roche. William Holabird (1854–1923) went to West Point in 1873–5 and to Chicago in 1875, where he took an engineering job in the office of W. Le B. JENNEY. In 1880 he formed a partnership with Martin Roche (1855–1927). Their Tacoma building (1887–8), following Jenney's Home Insurance and going decisively beyond it, established steel-skeleton construction for SKYSCRAPERS and with it the CHICAGO SCHOOL style. Their Marquette building (1894) has the same importance stylistically as the Tacoma building has structurally. Its

horizontal windows and its crisp, un-enriched mouldings pointed the way into the c20.

Zukowsky 1988; R. Bruegmann, *H & R.,* New York 1990.

Holden, Charles (1876–1960). Holden was born to poverty in Lancashire. When he was at last able to devote himself to architecture he joined C. R. ASHBEE in 1897 and later Percy Adams, becoming a partner in 1907. The practice specialized in hospitals. Holden's most ambitious hospital is the King Edward VII Sanatorium at Midhurst (1903–6) and his most original work belongs to these years, i.e. Law Society annexe, London (1903–4), Bristol Public Library (1906), and British Medical Association (now Zimbabwe House), London (1906–8). In style they are not like pioneer Continental buildings of the time; nor are there direct British precedents, although MACKINTOSH and John James Joass (1868–1952) of Mappin House (1906–8) and the Royal Insurance Building, London (1907–8), might have to be named.

In 1923 Holden began working for Frank Pick of London Transport and a new phase of his development began. He designed station buildings and soon far more: stop signs for buses, shelters, platforms, etc. At first the underground stations were block-like, as were his earlier buildings (e.g. Mansion House station 1926), but from 1930 onwards they accepted the Continental Modern of e.g. Fritz Schumacher (e.g. Sudbury Town, Sudbury Hill, Southgate and Arnos Grove underground stations 1931–3). The headquarters of London Transport (55 Broadway, London), built in 1926–9, is again stocky. A noteworthy feature of this building is the external sculpture of Eric Gill, Epstein and Henry Moore. In 1932 Holden was commissioned to design the new buildings for London University in Bloomsbury. Here, alas, all his courage seems to have abandoned him. Neo-Georgian features are paired with tame modern details. In the last fifteen or twenty years of his life he was principally engaged with problems of London planning with Sir William HOLFORD.

E. Karol and F. Allibone, *C.H. Architect 1875–1960*, London (Heinz Gallery) 1988.

Holford, Sir William (1907–75). Leading town-planner in England, responsible with Charles HOLDEN for the post-war plan for the City of London (1946–7) and for the precinct of St Paul's Cathedral (1955–6), executed with some unfortunate modifications.

G. E. Cherry, *H.: A Study in Architecture, Planning and Civic Design*, London 1985.

Holl, Elias (1573–1646). The leading Renaissance architect in Germany where he holds a position parallel historically to that of his exact contemporaries Inigo JONES in England and de BROSSE in France and to the slightly younger van CAMPEN in Holland. He came of a family of Augsburg masons who had risen to prominence under the Fuggers. He travelled in Italy, visiting Venice 1600–1601 and presumably studying PALLADIO and other Italian architects. In 1602 he was appointed city architect of Augsburg, where he was responsible for a large building programme including houses, warehouses, guildhalls, market halls for the various trades, schools, gates and

towers for the city walls, the arsenal and the Town Hall. As a Protestant he suffered from the religious wars and was out of office 1630–32 and finally dismissed in 1635. His first building after his nomination as city architect was the arsenal, begun 1602. He believed in symmetry and classical proportions – e.g. St Anne's School (1613) with its high arcades encircling the court, regular fenestration, horizontal emphasis and remarkably well-designed classrooms lit from both sides; and the Hospital of the Holy Ghost (1626–30), which had high arcades encircling a court. But his masterpiece is the Town Hall (1615–20, damaged in the Second World War but rebuilt), a handsome, simple, rather severe building, much in advance of anything previously built in Germany. His aim was, he said, 'to obtain a bolder, more heroic appearance' and he claimed it was well proportioned. His first, unexecuted, design for it was more advanced stylistically than that built and made much play with Palladian windows almost in the manner of Palladio's Basilica in Vicenza. As built it is distinctly German in its verticality, especially in the central section of the façade, which contrasts strikingly with the more classically pure bays on either side. His work outside Augsburg was less important but includes additions to the Willibaldsburg at Eichstätt (1608) and, probably, the designs for the Schloss at Bratislava (Pozsony: Pressburg, 1632–49).

Hempel 1965; Hitchcock 1981; B. Roeck, *E.H. Stadtbaumeister und Architekt vom Europäischen Rang*, Regensburg 1984.

Holland, Henry (1745–1806), began

under his father, a Fulham builder, then became assistant to 'Capability' BROWN, whose daughter he married. His first independent work, Brooks's Club, London (1776–8), was quickly followed by his greatest, Carlton House, London, which he enlarged and altered for the Prince of Wales (1783–5, demolished 1827–8). Also for the Prince of Wales he built the Marine Pavilion at Brighton (1786–7), later transformed into the Royal Pavilion by NASH. His style owed something to both CHAMBERS and ADAM, with various Louis XVI elements added. Though lacking originality, the refined taste and 'august simplicity' of his interior decoration approached French neo-classicism in elegance. His best country houses are Southill (1796) and Berrington Hall (1778). He laid out and built Hans Town, Chelsea (1771 onwards), but this has been largely rebuilt.

D. Stroud, *H.H.*, London 1966; Colvin 1978; Summerson 1983.

Hollein, Hans (b. 1934). Austrian architect, typically Viennese in his extreme and often ironic sophistication, as shown in the small *de luxe* commercial buildings which made his name, e.g. the Schullin jewellery shop (1974) and the Austrian State Travel Agency (1976–8), both in Vienna. His recent large-scale Abteilberg Museum, Mönchengladbach (1972–82), is remarkable, especially the interior.

G. Pettena, *H.H. Opere 1960–88*, Florence and Milan 1988; Klotz 1988.

Holmgren, Herman Theodor (b. 1842), *see* SWEDISH ARCHITECTURE.

Holy sepulchre. A structure imitating (sometimes only in general form) the tomb of Christ as rediscovered by Constantine. This had been encased by Constantine in a miniature temple placed in a round (or polygonal?) church, both razed and rebuilt many times. Imitations of both shrine and church followed, at first by association, as cemetery chapels (earliest at Fulda, 820–21). The shrine was most commonly imitated in Germany (e.g. Constance C13, Görlitz 1481–1504) and Italy (e.g. ALBERTI's Rucellai *tempietto*, 1467), while England produced the variant of EASTER SEPULCHRES and a number of round churches (e.g. Cambridge and Northampton).

N. C. Brooks, *The Sepulchre of Christ in Art and Liturgy*, London 1921.

Hood, Raymond Mathewson (1881–1934). He won the competition for the Chicago Tribune Building in 1922 together with John Mead Howells (1868–1959). It was built 1923–5. His McGraw-Hill building in New York (1931) is one of the first skyscrapers designed in the INTERNATIONAL MODERN style. In his Daily News building (1930) he stressed the closely set verticals, and this must have inspired the Rockefeller Center (begun 1931).

W. H. Kilham, *R.H. Architect of Ideas*, New York 1973; R. A. M. Stern, *R.H.*, New York 1981.

Hood-mould. A projecting moulding to throw off the rain, on the face of a wall, above an arch, doorway, or window; can be called *dripstone* or, if rectangular, a *label. See also* LABEL-STOP; Fig. 54.

Hooke, Robert (1635–1703). English

FIG. 54. *Hood-mould*

scientist and WREN's closest architectural associate. His independent works were imposing but undistinguished – Royal College of Physicians (1672–7), Bethlehem Hospital (1674–6), Montagu House (1675–9), all in London and all demolished.

Colvin 1978; Summerson 1983.

Hopkins, Michael (b. 1935). Less severe and more relaxed than FOSTER, with whom he worked 1969–75, he has skilfully exploited the more 'acceptable face' of HIGH TECH. His own house in Hampstead, London (1976), and the Greene King brewery, Bury St Edmunds (1979), were followed in 1985 by the Schlumberger Research Laboratories, Cambridge (1985), and the widely acclaimed Mound Stand at Lord's Cricket Ground, London (1987).

Hopper, Thomas (1776–1856). English eclectic architect whose neo-Norman castles were bold and original – Gosford in Ireland (*c.* 1820) and Penrhyn in Wales (1825–37). In 1807 he designed a cast-iron neo-Gothic conservatory and other additions to Carlton House, London (demolished 1827–8).

Colvin 1978; N. Burton in Brown 1985.

Horeau, Hector (1801–72), *see* CONSERVATORY.

Hornwork. In military architecture, an outwork of two demi-bastions connected by a curtain and joined to the main work by two parallel wings.

Horseshoe arch, *see* ARCH.

Horta, Baron Victor (1861–1947), a Belgian architect, studied in Paris in 1878–80, then at the Brussels Academy under Balat. He appeared in the forefront of European architecture with his Hôtel Tassel, Brussels, now the Mexican Embassy (designed 1892). This is the same year as that of van de VELDE's first exploration of ART NOUVEAU typography and design. The Hôtel Tassel is less startling externally, but its staircase with exposed iron supports, floral iron ornament, and much linear decoration on the wall is Art Nouveau architecture of the boldest. The Hôtel Tassel was followed by the particularly complete and lavish Hôtel Solvay (1895–1900); the Maison du Peuple (1895–9), with a curved glass and iron façade and much structural and decorative iron inside the great hall; the store L'Innovation (1901; destroyed); and several more private houses; his own house (1898–1901) is now the Musée Horta. Later Horta turned to a conventional classicism (Palais des Beaux Arts, Brussels, 1922–9).

R. L. Delevoy, *V.H.*, Brussels 1958; F. Borsi and P. Portoghesi, *V.H.*, Rome 1969; A. Hoppenbrouwers *et al.*, *V.H. architectonographie*, Brussels 1975.

Hôtel. In France a town house of which the standard design was established by SERLIO's 'Grand Ferrare' in Fontainebleau (1544–6), i.e. a CORPS DE LOGIS with narrower wings forming a courtyard which is enclosed towards the street by a wall or by a stable and kitchen block, broken in the middle by the entrance door. The best surviving early example is the Hôtel Carnavalet in Paris by LESCOT of *c.* 1545. It was usual to have a garden or small park behind the *corps de logis*. The latter often contained a gallery on the first floor. MANSART's Hôtel de la Vrillière, Paris (1635–45), became the model for the classical type of Parisian hôtel.

Gallet 1964; Loyer 1987.

Howard, Sir Ebenezer (1850–1928), started as a clerk in the City of London, rose to be a valued shorthand writer, and remained that nearly to the end. During a stay of five years in America (1872–7), he learned to know and admire Whitman and Emerson, and began to think of the better life and how it could be made to come true. In 1898 he read Edward Bellamy's utopian work *Looking Backward*, and this gave him the idea of his lifetime: that of the GARDEN CITY, which is an independent city and not a suburb – this is important – and is placed in the green countryside and provided with countrified housing as well as industry and all cultural amenities. His book *Tomorrow* came out in 1898, in 1899 the Garden City Association was founded, in 1902 the book was republished as *Garden Cities of Tomorrow*, and in 1903 Letchworth was started, to the design of Parker and UNWIN. This was the earliest of the garden cities and greatly influenced the post-war SATELLITE TOWNS of Britain. Howard was knighted in 1927.

D. MacFadyen, *Sir E.H. and the Town Planning Movement*, London 1933; R. Beevers, *The Garden City Utopia. A Critical Biography of E.H.*, London 1988.

Howe, George (1886–1955). Designed in collaboration with William Lescaze (1896–1964) the Philadelphia Savings Fund Building (1929–32), one of the first skyscrapers in the INTERNATIONAL MODERN style.

R. Stern, *G.H. Towards a Modern Architecture*, New Haven and London 1975.

Howells, John Mead (1868–1959), *see* HOOD, Raymond Mathewson.

Hua. In Chinese roof construction a bracket, usually one of several comprising a TOU KUNG.

Hübsch, Heinrich (1795–1863), *see* HISTORICISM.

Hueber, Joseph (d. 1787). Late Rococo architect working in Styria. Son of a Viennese mason, he began as a journeyman mason in Bohemia, Saxony and central and southern Germany. In 1740 he took over the architectural practice of Giuseppe Carlone in Graz on marrying his widow. He built the handsome twin towers of the Mariahilfkirche in Graz (1742–4) and two pilgrimage churches – St Veit am Vorgau (1748–51) and the Weizbergkirche (1756–8), with an elaborate interior like a stage set – and the great library at Admont Abbey (*c.* 1770–74), though this has been attributed to Gotthard Hayberger (1699–1764), who designed the library at St Florian (1744–51).

Hempel 1965; Laing 1978.

Hültz, Johann (d. 1449), was master mason of Strassburg Cathedral and as such designed the openwork spire with its fabulous spiral staircase. The work was completed in 1439. Hültz was the successor to Ulrich von ENSINGEN, who built the octagon (the stage below the spire).

Frankl 1972.

Hungarian architecture. Medieval architecture in Hungary reflects the events in various centres of the West. Sometimes inspiration came from one centre, sometimes from more than one. As in other countries the beginnings are tantalizing. A building like Feldebrö of the C10 is mysterious in its stylistic pedigree. It is a square in plan with three apses in the middle of three sides. Should one link it with Germigny-des-Prés? Zalavár of the C9 has three parallel east apses like the contemporary buildings in Switzerland. The Romanesque style is, as one would expect, most closely linked with south Germany and Austria and with Lombardy. The latter appears most clearly in the grand though over-restored cathedral of Pécs with its four towers flanking the west and east end of the nave. The splendid west portal of Ják has German but also north Italian and even Norman elements. The abbey churches of Ják, Lébény and Zsámbék are the most conspicuous Romanesque churches of German descent in Hungary. They have in common a relatively late date (first half C13), three east apses, two west towers and a west gallery.

As in other countries the CISTER-CIANS and the Premonstratensians brought into Hungary a new plan and new details, all first developed in France. The finest buildings are of the C13. They are Bélapátfalva (founded in 1232), Pannonhalma, the latter (1217–24) not Cistercian, though Cistercian in style with sexpartite rib vaults, and Osca with polygonal instead of straight-edged east chapels. Sexpartite rib vaults are a French Early Gothic feature, and the Gothic of, e.g., Noyon

is also mixed with Romanesque, especially Norman detail in the elegant chapel in the castle of Esztergom.

Of the High Gothic style Hungary possesses no major monument.

As for the Late Gothic, it is clearly dependent on south Germany and Austria. The churches are of the HALL type. They are high, with slender piers, sometimes without capitals, and they have complicated figured rib vaults. Examples are Sopron, Koloszvár, and Brassó (chancel). The friars built much in Hungary during these centuries.

Among the castles of Hungary three at least must be mentioned: Buda, where much restoration and reconstruction of the great halls and the chapel is taking place, Visegrád with its mighty keep of *c.* 1260, square with triangular projections on two opposite sides, and Diósgyőr of the second half of the C14, which is oblong with an inner courtyard and four prominent angle towers.

Internationally speaking the most important phase in Hungarian architecture is that of King Matthias Corvinus (1458–90) and the decades after his death. The king was a patron of Mantegna, Verrocchio, Ercole Roberti, BENEDETTO DA MAIANO and other Italians. His library of illuminated manuscripts in the Renaissance style is unparalleled north of the Alps, and he also favoured the new style in architecture. Earlier than in any country outside Italy – including even France – are the friezes from Buda castle now in the Castle Museum and the well in Visegrád castle whose stepped terraces, still largely Gothic, are of great magnificence. In ecclesiastic art the Bakócz Chapel in Esztergom Cathedral, begun as early as 1506, is purely Italian. The architect is unknown; the altar (1519) is by Andrea Ferrucci of Fiesole.

After these years of enthusiasm Hungary settled down to a less adventurous later C16 and early C17. The fancy battlements and arcaded courtyards of houses are generally Eastern. The monuments of Turkish domination (mosques, minarets, baths, and funerary chapels at Pécs, Eger, Budapest) look odd side by side with them. As a sign of the war against the Turks some fortresses were erected (Győr, etc.) by Italian engineers on the new Italian models. The Turkish occupation ended only in the late C17, and in the C18 Austrian and Bohemian Baroque held the stage. The most interesting buildings are the Eszterházy palace at Eisenstadt across the Austrian border (1663–72) by Carl Martin Carlone (1616–67), Prince Eugene's delightful Ráckeve (1701–2) by HILDEBRANDT and then St Anne, Budapest (1740 onwards), the huge Eszterházy palace at Fertőd (1764–6) and the Lyceum at Eger (1765–85) by Jacob Fellner (1722–80).

The turn away from the Baroque in the direction of neo-classicism was taken early in Hungary. Vác Cathedral (1763–77) by Isidore Canevale (1730–86), with its giant portico of detached columns carrying a heavy attic, not a pediment, and with its central dome and coffered vaults, would be highly remarkable even if it stood in Paris. Classicism of a Romantic cast culminates in the immensely impressive cathedral of Esztergom (1822–c. 1850) by Janos Páckh (1796–1839) and Jozsef Hild (1789–1867), with its central plan, its many-columned dome and its eight-column giant portico, and in the competent but more conventional neo-Greek work of Mihály POLLAK, e.g. the National Museum, Budapest (1836–45).

The climax of C19 eclecticism is the richly Italianate Opera in Budapest (1875–84) by Miklos Ybl (1814–91), and the surprisingly late Gothic-Revival Houses of Parliament (1883–1902) by Imre Steindl (1839–1902). The ART NOUVEAU reaction against eclecticism had an unusually brilliant exponent in Ödön LECHNER. The Modern Movement set in as a branch of LOOS and HOFFMANN's Vienna with Béle Lajta (1875–1920), e.g. his Martinelli Place Emporium, Budapest (1912–14). The International Style reached Hungary in the 1930s, most notably through Farkas Molnár (1897–1945), who had studied at the Bauhaus. His own villa at Budapest (1932) and the Sanatorium at Pestujhely (1936) are exemplary. More recently the buildings of Imre Makovecz (b. 1935) has attracted international attention, e.g. his Richter House, Budapest (1985).

Hungry joint, *see* POINTING.

Hunt, Richard Morris (1827–95), came of a wealthy early Colonial family. They moved to Paris in 1843, and there Hunt joined LEFUEL's *atelier* and the École des Beaux Arts. He also worked on painting with Couture and on sculpture with Barye. He travelled widely before he was made an *inspecteur* under Lefuel of the Louvre in 1854. This first-hand knowledge of the French-Renaissance Revival he took back to America in 1855. He settled in New York and, side by side with his practice, ran an *atelier* on the Parisian pattern. But he returned to Europe again in the 1860s and only in 1868 finally came to rest. He designed the Tribune building in New York (1873, one of the first with lifts), and then rich men's residences at Newport, Rhode Island, in New York (W. K.

FIG. 55. *Hyperbolic paraboloid*

Vanderbilt, 1878 onwards; J. J. Astor, 1893), and elsewhere (Biltmore, Ashville, North Carolina, 1895, and Ochre Court, Newport, 1892). The French Renaissance remained his favourite style. Hunt was also the designer of the Administration building at the Chicago Exposition of 1893 and the façade of the Metropolitan Museum, New York (built in 1900–1902). He was one of the founders of the American Institute of Architects.

Hitchcock 1977; P. R. Baker, *R.M.H.*, Cambridge, Mass., 1980; S. R. Stein, *The Architecture of R.M.H. (1828–1895)*, Chicago 1986.

Hurtado Izquierdo, Francisco (1669–1725), one of the greatest Spanish Baroque architects, was quite the most exuberantly rich. His work is confined to interiors, which are of a fantasy unparalleled in Europe. Born and educated in Cordova, he became a captain in the army and possibly visited Sicily. He may have designed the Victoria *camarín* above the Mausoleum of the Counts of Buenavista, Málaga (1691–3). Most of his work is in Granada, where he designed the relatively simple *sagrario* (Sacrament Chapel) for the cathedral (1704–5). The Sacrament Chapel of the Cartuja (1702–20), walled with marble, jasper, and porphyry and containing a marble tabernacle sup-

ported by red and black SALOMÓNICAS, is a masterpiece of polychromatic opulence. He called it 'a precious jewel', and claimed that there was nothing like it in all Europe. In 1718 he designed the very complex *camarín*, liberally decorated with grey-and-coral-coloured marble and lapis lazuli, for the Cartuja of El Paular, Segovia. He has also been credited with the design of the still more bizarrely rich sacristy of the Granada Cartuja (executed 1730–47), where the tendency to muffle the structure in a riotous welter of ornament is taken to its final extreme.

Kubler and Soria 1959.

Husk garland. A FESTOON of nutshells diminishing towards the ends.

Husley, Jacob Otten (1738–94), *see* DUTCH ARCHITECTURE.

Hypaethral. Without a roof, open to the sky.

Hyperbolic paraboloid roof. A special form of double-curved shell, the geometry of which is generated by straight lines. This property makes it fairly easy to construct. The shape consists of a continuous plane developing from a parabolic arch in one direction to a similar inverted parabola in the other. It was pioneered by Matthew Nowicki (1910–51) at the Dorton Arena, Raleigh, N. Carolina (1948–53). *See* Fig. 55.

Mainstone 1975.

Hypocaust. The underground chamber or duct of the Roman system of central heating, the floor being heated by the hot air circulating below. The gases escaped up flues in the walls, thus heating these also.

Hypogeum. An underground room or vault.

Hypostyle. A hall or other large space over which the roof is supported by rows of columns like a forest.

Hypotrachelium. The groove round a Doric column between the SHAFT and the NECKING.

i

Iconostasis. A screen in Byzantine churches separating the sanctuary from the nave and pierced by three doors; originally a lattice of columns joined by a decorated PARAPET and COPING. Since the C14–15 it has become a wooden or stone wall covered with icons, hence the name.

Ictinus. The leading architect in Periclean Athens and one of the greatest of all time. With CALLICRATES he designed and built the Parthenon (447/6–438 BC), about which he later wrote a book, now lost, with Carpion. He was commissioned by Pericles to design the new Telesterion (Hall of Mysteries) at Eleusis, but his designs were altered by the three new architects who took over on the fall of Pericles. According to Pausanias he was also the architect of the Doric temple of Apollo at Bassae, begun after the Great Plague of 304 BC.

R. Carpenter, *The Architects of the Parthenon*, Harmondsworth 1970.

Imbrex. In Greek and Roman architecture, a convex tile to cover the join between two flat or concave roofing tiles.

Imhotep. Ancient Egyptian high priest and chief minister to King Zoser (third dynasty, *c.* 2650–2600 BC), Imhotep later acquired a mythological character as a healing deity and also as an architect. According to the C3 BC Egyptian historian Manetho, the Greeks attached some importance to Imhotep as an architect but only recently has his name been recovered in this connection (on a statue base of Zoser at Saqqara). He was architect of the Step Pyramid at Saqqara, a daring structure rising like a gigantic staircase to the heavens, and this led to the exploration of building with stone. Thus Imhotep laid the basis for the development of stone masonry on a large scale.

Smith and Simpson 1981.

Imperial staircase, *see* STAIRCASE.

Impluvium. The basin or water cistern, usually rectangular, in the centre of an ATRIUM of a Roman house to receive the rain-water from the surrounding roofs. The term is also used, loosely, for the uncovered space in the atrium as well as the water cistern.

Impost. A member in the wall, usually formed of a projecting bracket-like moulding, on which the end of an arch appears to rest. In Gothic architecture, mouldings on an arch sometimes continue without break to the floor and are called *continuous imposts*. *See* Fig. 4.

Impost block. A block with splayed sides placed between ABACUS and CAPITAL.

In antis, *see* ANTA

Inca architecture, *see* PERUVIAN ARCHITECTURE.

Indent. A shape chiselled out in a stone slab to receive a brass effigy.

Indian and Pakistani architecture.

The history of architecture in the Indian sub-continent – present-day India, Pakistan and Bangladesh – is complicated by major differences in climate and availability of building materials in an area as large as Western Europe, constantly shifting internal frontiers, invasion from outside, and a diversity of religious beliefs that inspired most of the structures that survive from before the C17. It begins with the remains of cities of the Indus valley or Harappan civilization which, during its most highly developed period *c.* 2100–1750 BC, extended from present-day Pakistan and Afghanistan as far south as the Gulf of Cambay and east to the Ganges valley. Mohenjo-Daro (Pakistan) is the most fully excavated site, a city about one mile across laid out on a grid plan with wide streets, sophisticated water-supply and drainage systems, numerous blocks of houses with internal courtyards built of bonded fire-burned brick of a standard size, a vast granary, a hypostyle hall and an asphalt-lined bath – none decorated. After the decline of this civilization nothing is known of Indian architecture for more than a millennium. Literary sources reveal that by the time of the birth of the Buddha *c.* 563 BC there were cities in the north-east and the consecutive history of Indian architecture begins at Pataliputra (beneath modern Patna), capital of the Mauryan dynasty that came to power *c.* 323 BC and, under Asoka (*c.*

272–231 BC), spread its rule over the north and centre of the sub-continent. Little remains of Pataliputra (said to have covered some 14 sq. miles) apart from the foundations of a HYPOSTYLE hall with 80 stone-based pillars. Buildings were of impermanent materials but their forms were simulated in carved stone entrances to C3 BC caves in the Barabar Hills (nr Gaya) which served as retreats for ascetics during the rainy season – notably the gable end of a wooden structure with a rounded thatched roof supported on rafters and rising to a central peak, the earliest form of the horseshoe arch that was to recur in Indian architecture, notably in the entrances to CHAITYA halls. Asoka, a convert to Buddhism, promoted the erection of STUPAS which probably established their essential form – a solid brick hemisphere flattened at the top to carry a stone parasol (*chattra*) surrounded by a square railing of stone simulating woodwork. The finest early example is at Sanchi, begun under Asoka, enlarged to 120 ft in diameter in the C2 when it was faced with stone and surrounded by a 10 ft high stone railing to which four elaborate gateways were added in C1 BC. Small stupas, placed in apses to permit ritual circumambulation, are features of Buddhist chaitya halls, distinguishing these caves from those of Jains and Hindus of the same period. Though excavated rather than built, these halls cut into the face of cliffs, beginning at the top with simulated rafters and descending around pillars, their entrances richly carved with figures, mark the beginning of Indian temple architecture in stone and range in date from C2 BC at Bhaja to the outstanding C5 AD examples at Ajanta and the last notable examples, at Ellora, of the C9. Caves with cells surrounding a rectangular central space were also excavated to serve as VIHARAS or monasteries. By a similar process freestanding Hindu temples were carved from the living rock – the five 'pancha rathas' each fashioned from a single boulder at Mamallapuram (C7) and the very much larger Kailasa temple with rich sculptural decoration at Ellora (mid C8). The earliest stone constructions are small cubical shrines on platforms dating from the end of the Gupta period (C3–5) in central India, at Nachna, Sanchi and Tigawa. The C6 Vishnu temple at Deogarh is more imposing, with superb carvings round the entrance and in false doors on the other three sides. Temples were also built of brick in the C5, sometimes with a more complex plan but similarly enclosing a cubical sanctuary (that at Bhitargaon is the largest and least ruined). From the C8 greater importance was given to the SIKHARA above the sanctuary and to the porch in front of it and sometimes extended to a long hall (e.g. at Aihole). Roofs were made of large stone slabs and early *sikharas* often have the appearance of one laid on top of another, diminishing in width to make a curved profile. But fully developed temples give an impression of sculptured mass rather than tectonic form. As their size increased the figurative carvings on their exteriors became ever more exuberant: the most notable examples include the Rajarana and Lingaraja temples at Bhubaneshwar; the Sasbahu temple at Gwalior; the Kandariya and Mahadeva temples at Khajuraho, all of the C11; and the Temple of the Sun at Konarak of the mid C13. These are all in northern styles (with some regional differences), brought to their highest expression at the time of the first Muslim invasions which put an end to temple building for some centuries. By this time Buddhism had lost its following in India. But the Jain religion continued to flourish (as it still does) if only in a few areas, notably Rajasthan and Gujarat; its temples differ from those dedicated to Hindu gods in that they are externally simpler but internally far richer, with more varied spaces and much intricate, mainly non-figurative, carving in the preferred medium of white marble, e.g. Adinatha temple on Mount Abu (C11), Adinatha temple at Ranakpur (mid C15).

In the south of India distinct Hindu styles emerged in the C7 (Meguti temple at Aihole and Malegitti Shivalaya temple at Badami) and continued to evolve without a break until the C18. Its distinguishing features are boldly moulded plinths, walls divided into projecting and recessed bays by pairs of pilasters, and overhanging eaves surmounted by parapets. The most notable C8 examples include the Shore temple at Mamallapuram and the richly sculptured Kailasantha temple at Kanchipuram. Under the Chola dynasty of kings who ruled in Tamil-Nadu C9–13 a vast number of temples were built, mostly small in scale but also the huge and imposing Brihadeshvara temples at Thanjavur and Gangaikondacholapuram, and the Nataraja temple at Chidambaram. To the north-west in Karnatika a distinctive style was created under the kings of the Hoysala dynasty C12–13. At Belur, Halebid and (the best preserved) Somnathpur, temples were built on very complicated plans with many angled projections, in a hard local stone which permits a sharpness of carving in their elaborate decorations which have the appearance of metal-

work. From the late C13 India was
under attack from Muslims, but in the
C15 most of the south was united in the
realm of the staunchly Hindu kings of
Vijayanagara whose defiance was expressed in the massive size of buildings,
many of which were added to earlier
temples – towering GOPURAS which
dwarf the sanctuaries in the enclosures
to which they give access, long processional corridors and halls with flat roofs
supported on numerous elaborately
carved pillars (sometimes with horses
rearing up out of them), e.g. at Kanchipuram, Srirangam and Vellore as
well as the capital city of Vijayanagara
(modern Hampi), which was sacked by
Muslims 1565, though much survives.
Temple building continued throughout the C17, most notably at Madurai,
and the practice of colouring the stucco
figures of deities on *gopuras* has never
ceased. At Madurai the C17 royal
palace, like the remains of the larger
and earlier one at Vijayanagara, is in
the Indo-Islamic style.

The invasion of the Indian sub-
continent by Muslims from western
Asia began in the C8 when present-day
Pakistan was occupied, but apart
from the remains of a C8 mosque near
Karachi and the undistinguished mid-
C12 Solah Khambi mosque at
Bhadreshwar in Kutch, the earliest
Islamic buildings date from the
establishment of the Delhi sultan-
ate in 1193. The Quwwat-ul-Islam
(Might of Islam) mosque, Delhi,
was built 1193-7 on the site of a
Hindu temple and with materials
from other demolished temples as
well. Surviving parts include the
entrance with a 20-ft-high gently
pointed arch carved in low relief
with a distinctly Indian foliage ornament, and the Qutb minar, or

tower of victory, which served also as
a MINARET, originally 238 ft high
(later enlarged) of four storeys diminishing in section and separated by
balconies resting on brackets with
stalactite mouldings. The large arch
and the minaret were new to India;
so too were domes and the tombs
or mausolea they often crowned, one
of the earliest surviving being that
of Ghiyas-ud-din Tughluq, Delhi,
of 1540-45, five storeys high with a
central dome surrounded by little
domed pavilions (the CHATRIS that
became a distinguishing feature of the
Indo-Islamic style), which set a new
standard for the magnificence of such
structures, followed by the tombs of
Humayun, Delhi (1565), and Akbar,
Sikander, nr Agra (1604-12), both
set in formal gardens, the latter of
red stone encrusted with geometrical
patterns in marble. Akbar's main architectural achievement was the palace-
city of Fatehpur Sikri (1571-85), an
extraordinary complex of buildings –
mosques, audience halls, the superb
tomb of Shaikh Salim Chishti, living
quarters for the emperor and his court
etc., all in a successful amalgam of
Persian–Islamic and Indian styles. The
tomb of Itmad-Ud-Daula at Agra
(1622-8) is exquisite rather than imposing, built of white marble with grilles
of lace-like carved tracery (simulating
MUSHRABEYEH work) and incrustations of semi-precious stones. The
much larger Taj Mahal, Agra, of
1630-53 presents an almost uniquely
successful combination of delicacy and
monumentality – refined in every detail
of carved and inlaid work, grandiose in
scale but of an opalescent colour which
gives it an appearance almost of weight-
lessness, perfectly balanced in its proportions and the relationship of the

mausoleum with its great bulbous dome to the four minarets standing out from its corners, to the red sandstone mosques on either side and to the great gateway which is separated from it by a Persian-style 'paradise garden' crossed by ornamental canals. It was designed by a Persian master-builder Ustad Isa Khan Effendi with his pupil AHMAD USTAD and, for the dome, Ismail Khan, on commission from Shah Jahan as the tomb for his favourite wife. Of the Moghul rulers, Shah Jahan, who reigned 1628–57, was the most fastidious patron of architecture: the works he commissioned include the several halls and pavilions in the Red Fort at Delhi (begun 1639), the Jami Masjid in Delhi (1644–58) – the largest mosque in India – and most of the buildings in the Red Fort at Agra, notably the Moti Masjid or Pearl Mosque. The style perfected under Shah Jahan was imitated by the architects of later Moghul emperors and minor rulers in north and central India with a marked decline in form as well as detail (already evident in the Bibi-Ka-Maqbara of 1678 at Aurangabad, which was intended, but signally failed, to rival the Taj Mahal). Of c18 building the Sikh Golden Temple at Amritsar is the most interesting. By this date, however, most of India had come under European dominance.

The earliest European buildings are churches at Goa – St Francis of Assisi (begun 1527), Immaculate Conception (1541), Cathedral (1562–1619) and Bom Jesus (1594–1605), all in Portuguese styles with prominent use of the classical ORDERS. There are architectural relics of the French presence at Pondicherry laid out on a grid pattern within a circular road 1756–77 but including earlier buildings, notably

the governor's palace (1752). The fantastic La Martinière boys' school at Lucknow (c. 1780–1800), designed and built by Major-General Claude Martin, Lyonnais soldier, banker and political agent, is more French than anything else. British buildings appeared first in the three main stations of the East India Company – Bombay (Cathedral begun 1672, St Andrews Kirk 1819, Town Hall 1820–23); Madras (St Mary's church 1678–80, Banqueting Hall 1802); and Calcutta (St John's church 1787; Government House, based on ADAM's Kedleston, of 1799–1802). They are all classical in style, mainly neo-PALLADIAN and GREEK REVIVAL and, like much that followed the spread of British rule, the work of army officers who were amateur architects, as is often only too obvious. In the later c19 Gothic was adopted for churches and public buildings, most exuberantly in Bombay – High Court (1871–9) by General James Augustus Fuller and the Victoria Terminus (1878–87) by F. W. Stevens. Indo-Islamic elements were employed with equal abandon on the High Court, Madras (1888–92), by J. W. Brassington and others. The most prominent of later British buildings are those by LUTYENS and BAKER at New Delhi, mainly Imperial Roman with a few, not always very happy, references to Indian Buddhist, Hindu and Islamic traditions.

The independence and partition of India and Pakistan in 1948 brought no liberation from Western architecture. LE CORBUSIER and Maxwell FRY were commissioned to design the city of Chandigarh as a new capital of the Punjab. In Pakistan, the new capital Islamabad was laid out in 1960 by Doxiadis Associates according to contemporary Western ideals of town planning. Though a fine mosque is by a Pakistani architect, Khwaja Zaheer-ud-Din, the huge secretariat and main hotel are by Gio PONTI. The main official buildings at Dacca, the new capital of East Pakistan (from 1971 Bangladesh), are by Louis KAHN (begun 1965). In India the Centre for Environmental Planning and Technology, Ahmadabad (1967–81), by Balkrishna Doshi (b. 1927) is one of the most successful public buildings. High-rise blocks have converted the waterfront of Bombay into an Asian Manhattan, but the popular housing designed by Charles CORREA is of greater architectural interest. *See also* BURMESE, NEPALESE, SRI LANKAN and TIBETAN ARCHITECTURE.

Indonesian architecture. Stone building was introduced with Hinduism and Buddhism from India, the earliest surviving structures being small late c7 temples in central Java (Dieng plateau). Borobudor in the same region was begun *c.* 780 (probably as a Hindu monument) but completed *c.* 833 as the greatest Mahayana Buddhist monument anywhere – a sacred mountain of stone approximately 360 ft across at the base and 115 ft high, on a mandala plan with nine terraces linked by stairways ascending from the cardinal points and passing under corbelled arches. Figurative reliefs of high quality line the galleries which, together with statues of the Buddha, were the monument's *raison d'être*. A few other Buddhist temples of the same date survive, e.g. Candi Mendut near Borobudor. In 832 central Java came under Hindu rulers who had temples built, notably at Prambanam (835–56), dedicated to Siva, Visnu and Brahma,

encrusted with much fine relief sculpture and with numerous tiers of spirelets which give a strong vertical accent in contrast to the spreading horizontality of Borobudor. Sculpture is less prominent on later temples, Kidal (*c.* 1260), Singosari (*c.* 1300) and Penataran (1347–75), all in eastern Java, with prominent horizontal mouldings richly carved. At Trowulan in central Java the tall temple form, divided vertically into halves and set apart, was adopted *c.* 1350 to make an entrance way or 'split gate'. The latest temple in Java is Candi Sukhu, built *c.* 1430 on a hill above Surakata, incorporating a truncated pyramid uncannily similar to Meso-American structures. Hinduism declined in Java after the introduction of Islam in the late c15 but survived together with local spirit cults on Bali. Bali temple architecture derived initially from Java, e.g. 'split gate' entrances to precincts, but soon acquired individuality, notably with the 'Merus', PAGODA-like towers with up to eleven roofs (Pura Taman Ayun at Mengwi, begun 1634). Mainly of wood, the temples have been frequently restored and embellished by worshippers.

On Java, Islamic architecture was mainly of wood, the earliest surviving mosques being at Demak (founded in 1478) and Kudus (begun 1549), the latter on the site of a Hindu temple of which the brick tower was converted into a minaret. Dutch-style buildings, from the period of colonial rule (1667–1949), were numerous but undistinguished. Indigenous Javanese styles survived in the kratons or palaces of the Sultans, notably at Yogyakarta and Surakarta (both mainly c18–19). The basic element was the *pendopo*, an open post-and-lintel pavilion with a pitched or hipped roof. The Batak villages of

Sumatra are notable for their vernacular buildings, on piles with very high pitched roofs curving forward at either end and often richly painted. Of recent architecture, the vast Istiqial mosque in Jakarta was completed in 1987 and the Sukarno-Hatta airport (completed 1985) is a remarkably successful evocation of traditional Javanese architecture using modern materials and technology.

Industrialized building. The mass-production of building parts may be traced from the late c18 onwards in England with Abraham Darby's Iron Bridge at Coalbrookdale (1775–9) and Benyon, Bage & Marshall's iron-framed flax mill at Shrewsbury (1796). It was greatly developed in the c19 in both England and the USA, e.g. Boulton & Watt's seven-storey cotton mill at Salford (1801), BOGARDUS's cast-iron façades in New York, PAXTON's wholly prefabricated cast-iron and glass Crystal Palace, London (1851). Even BARRY's Houses of Parliament, London (1839–52), had its bronze window frames mass-produced. The metal window typifies industrialized building, together with the CURTAIN WALL and other forms of prefabricated cladding. They were, later, used with SPACE FRAME construction as it was developed by FULLER, PROUVÉ and others, while PRECAST CONCRETE systems were pioneered by PERRET and NERVI. Fuller's Dymaxion House project (1927), derived from aircraft and vehicle construction, was notable, as were, in Germany, the contemporary experiments by Konrad WACHSMANN which culminated, after he emigrated to the USA, in the 'Mobilar Structure' wide-span system (1946) and, with GROPIUS, the General Panel System

for prefabricated housing. The EAMES house (1949) was another landmark. Of later systems those developed for school building in England by Charles Herbert Aslin (1893–1959) and by the CLASP (Consortium of Local Authorities Special Programme) from 1955 onwards and, in the USA, the steel-framed SCBSD system developed in California in 1965 by Ezra Ehrenkrantz (b. 1933) must be mentioned. SAFIE's 'Habitat' raised industrialized building to a new level architecturally.

G. Herbert, *The Dream of the Factory-Made House*, Cambridge, Mass., 1984; Klotz 1986.

Inglenook. A recess for bench or seat built beside a fireplace, sometimes covered by the CHIMNEY-BREAST.

Ingo or **ingoing.** The return face of a wall to provide a recess, usually for a door or window.

Insula, *see* ROMAN ARCHITECTURE.

Intercolumniation. The space between columns measured in diameters. Vitruvius established five main ratios, $1\frac{1}{2}$D Pycnostyle, 2D Systyle, $2\frac{1}{2}$D Eustyle, 3D Diastyle, 4D Araeostyle.

International Modern or **International Style.** A term coined in America in 1932 (*see* Philip JOHNSON) for the new architectural style of the c20, as created before the First World War by such architects as WRIGHT, GARNIER, LOOS, HOFFMANN and GROPIUS, and as accepted first in central Europe in the twenties and then in other countries of Europe and in America from the late twenties onwards, where it reached its height with MIES VAN DER ROHE. The style is characterized by asymmetrical compositions, unrelievedly cubic general shapes, metal and glass framework often resulting in large windows in horizontal bands, an absence of mouldings, a predilection for white rendering and open ground-plans, loosely arranged. Typical of the style were Gropius's 1925–6 Bauhaus Building, Dessau, the Weissenhof Siedlung or Deutscher Werkbund housing exhibition of 1926–7 at Stuttgart and LE CORBUSIER's Salvation Army Hostel, Paris, of 1929–33.

The reaction was slow in coming, first with the sculptural anti-rational late style of Le Corbusier, followed by similarly 'expressive' works by such architects as Eero SAARINEN, Kenzo TANGE and others (*see* BRUTALISM); secondly by the more articulate POST-MODERNISM.

Intrados. The inner curve or underside of an arch; also called a *soffit*. *See* Fig. 4.

Inwood, Henry William (1794–1843). The son of an architect (William Inwood, *c.* 1771–1843), with whom he designed his only building of note, St Pancras Church, London (1819–22), one of the great monuments of the GREEK REVIVAL in England. Every detail is faithfully copied from the Erechtheum, Tower of the Winds, Choragic Monument, and other well-known Athenian buildings. Sometimes his archaeological material is rather recondite, but he always uses it with sensibility.

Crook 1972; Colvin 1978; Summerson 1983.

Ionic order, *see* ORDER.

Iranian architecture, *see* PERSIAN ARCHITECTURE.

Irish architecture. The most rewarding and original phase is that before the Normans, the phase of monastic communities where coenobites lived in round or square huts, stone-vaulted by pseudo-vaults of horizontally laid stones corbelled forward gradually. There were several oratories in such communities, tapering round towers and the glorious High Crosses. The most famous sites are Skellig Michael, Nendrum, Glendalough, Clonmacnois, and Monasterboyce. The buildings are mostly C10–11.

The Hiberno-Romanesque style has its most dramatic monument in Cormac's Chapel at Cashel (dated 1134); it has a tunnel-vaulted nave and a rib-vaulted chancel. There are plenty of monuments in the Norman style with only minor national characteristics. The CISTERCIANS came in the 1140s, and the east end of Christ Church Cathedral, Dublin, shows their influence. The fully Gothic style in a wholly Early English version appears in the nave of Christ Church (connected with Wells and St David's) and the largely rebuilt St Patrick's Cathedral, also in Dublin. The most conspicuous Irish contribution to Gothic architecture is her friaries, mostly rurally sited; they have the tower between nave and chancel, which is also typical of English friaries.

Medieval architecture lasted into the C17. The English promoted such new towns as Londonderry, with its Gothic cathedral of 1628–33, and such houses as Carrick-on-Suir and Strafford's Jigginstown, both of the 1630s. Gothic gradually gave place to hipped roofs or parapets, and such buildings as Beaulieu and the Kilmainham Hospital of 1679 are entirely English in style. PALLADIANISM also bore an ample harvest in Ireland, the chief architects

Islamic architecture

being Sir Edward Lovett PEARCE, Richard CASTLE, James GANDON, and Francis Johnston (1761–1829). Examples are Castletown; Parliament House, Dublin, by Pearce; Powerscourt by Castle; the Customs House and the Four Courts, Dublin, by Gandon; the house of the Provost of Trinity College, Dublin; Caledon, by NASH; Townley Hall, and many others. Ireland is indeed exceedingly rich in Georgian houses, though for lack of a function they are rapidly decreasing. In Dublin very much is still preserved, and the city may well claim to be the finest major Georgian city in the British Isles. If any Victorian buildings are to be singled out, they would again have to be essentially English ones: Cork Cathedral by BURGES; Queen's University, Belfast, by Lanyon; and the Trinity College Museum by Deane & Woodward – all Gothic in style. Among contemporary architects the best known are Michael Scott (b. 1905), who built the new Abbey Theatre, Dublin (1959), and Bank of Ireland, Dublin (1973), and Kevin ROCHE, who has worked in the USA since 1948. One of the best recent buildings in Ireland is the new Library of Trinity College, Dublin, by Ahrends, Burton & Koralek (1963–7).

Iron structures, see METAL STRUCTURES.

Isabellino style. In Spanish architecture the style associated with Ferdinand and Isabella (1474–1516), equivalent to the MANUELINE STYLE in Portuguese architecture.

Isidorus of Miletus assisted ANTHEMIOS OF TRALLES in the building of Hagia Sophia, Constantinople (AD 532–7), and was, like him, a geo-

metrician who turned his attention to architecture. He is not to be confused with a younger Isidore, who rebuilt the dome of Hagia Sophia in 558.

Krautheimer 1986.

Islamic architecture. The origins are very obscure. The Bedouin Arabs, who were the original followers of Mohammed and responsible for the first Islamic conquests in Syria, Palestine, and Persia, were a nomadic people who lived in tents. In the cities they conquered they began by converting old buildings, and Christian churches became MOSQUES; in Damascus a pagan temple transformed into a Christian church was incorporated in the Great Mosque (706–15). The earliest and one of the most beautiful of Islamic buildings is the Dome of the Rock, Jerusalem, built as a sanctuary (not as a mosque) on a circular plan (685–705, but much altered later, especially in 1561, when the exterior was cased in Persian tiles and the interior lined with marble). The first MINARETS were converted church towers in Syria, and that built at Kairouan, Tunisia (724–7), is modelled on such a tower. True to their nomadic origins the Umayyad rulers preferred country residences to town palaces. Several survive as ruins – Kas al-Khayr al Sharki (c. 728–9), Khirbat al-Mafjar (c. 739–44) and Mshatta near Amman, Jordan (c. 744 50). In plan these groups of buildings were derived from Roman frontier stations. But both religious and secular buildings of the period incorporate elements which were to become distinguishing features of Islamic architecture: the horse-shoe arch, tunnel vaults of stone and brick, rich surface decoration in carved stone, mosaic, and painting. During the Um-

229

ayyad period the mosque took on its permanent architectural form, dictated by liturgical needs – minarets from which the faithful could be called to prayer; a wide courtyard with a central fountain for ablutions, with surrounding colonnades to give protection from the sun; a large praying chamber, marked externally by a dome (as a sign of importance) and internally by the mihrab or niche indicating the direction of Mecca, towards which the faithful must turn in prayer. The last survivor of the Umayyad dynasty became the founder of the Emirates at Cordova in Spain, where the early style of Islamic architecture was brought to perfection in the Great Mosque (786–990).

Under the Abbasids, who supplanted the Umayyads in 750, Persian influence began to dominate the Islamic world. The main achievements in architecture were the foundation of the new capital at Baghdad, built on a circular plan (762–7, now largely destroyed), and slightly later, the smaller city of Raqqa, Syria, of which little survives except richly decorated gateways. It was at this period that Islamic architecture began to depart radically from HELLENISTIC and BYZANTINE conventions. An elaborate court etiquette, derived from Persia and contrary to Bedouin ideas of informality, was introduced, and palaces were designed for the new caliphs on more formal and grandiose lines, e.g. the palaces at Ukhaidir (*c.* 764–78) and Samarra (*c.* 849–59) in Iraq. These large buildings were run up very quickly: stone was abandoned in favour of brick; there was much use of decorative stucco. The main C9 achievements were the Great Mosque of Kairouan, Tunisia (836); the mosque of Bu Fatata, Susa, Tunisia (850–51); the Great Mosque of Samarra, Iraq, with its strange ZIGGURAT-like minaret (*c.* 850); and the very well preserved mosque of Ibn Tulun, Cairo (876–7). Building materials were usually rough but dressed with intricate geometrical or floral surface decorations in painted stucco, mosaic, glazed tiles, or shallow relief carving. Local traditions influenced the decorative style in various regions (*see* CHINESE, INDIAN AND PAKISTANI, PERSIAN, and TURKISH ARCHITECTURE).

In the original nucleus of the Islamic world the most notable later mosques are those at Tabriz, Persia (1204), Cairo (Mosque of Sultan Barquq, 1384), and Isfahan, Persia (1585). Most of the earlier religious buildings, including the Masjid-el-Aksa and the Dome of the Rock in Jerusalem, were also altered and more richly decorated in these centuries. In southern Spain a local style of great opulence was developed: its principal monuments are the Giralda tower, Seville (1159), and the Alhambra, Granada (1309–54).

Isometric projection. A geometrical drawing to show a building in three dimensions. The plan is set up with lines at an equal angle (usually 30°) to the horizontal, while verticals remain vertical and to scale. It gives a more realistic effect than an AXONOMETRIC PROJECTION, but diagonals and curves are distorted. *See* Fig. 56.

Isozaki, Arata (b. 1931). Japanese POST-MODERN architect. He worked under TANGE until 1963 and made his name with the Fukuoka Mutual Bank, Kyushu (1966), which led to a series of important public commissions in which he developed his austere, refined

FIG. 56. *Isometric projection* plan;
section aa; elevation

cubistic style inspired partly by Western architecture, notably that of LEDOUX, partly by traditional Japanese art which combines and reconciles 'popular' content with surface elegance and sophistication. He has described the result as schizoid; but his best buildings achieve a unique and impressive East–West synthesis – e.g. the Fujimi Country Clubhouse, Oita (1972–4); the Gunna Prefectural Museum, Takasaki (1974); the Civic Centre, Tsukuba (1979–83); the Museum of Contemporary Art, Los Angeles (begun 1984), and the extension to the Brooklyn Museum, New York (begun 1986).

P. Drew, *The Architecture of A.I.*, New York 1982; B. Baratucci and B. di Russo, *A.I. architetture 1959–1982*, Rome 1983; H. Yatsuka and H. Suzuki, *A.I. 1976–1984*, Tokyo 1986.

Italian architecture. (For pre-Christian architecture in Italy *see* ETRUSCAN ARCHITECTURE; ROMAN ARCHITECTURE.) EARLY CHRISTIAN churches in Italy are mostly of the BASILICA type: nave and aisles separated by columns carrying arches or straight entablatures, and an apse, sometimes flanked by two subsidiary chambers. The best preserved of the type in Rome is S. Sabina (*c.* 422–32). Transepts are rare but occur in the more monumental churches: Constantine's S. Giovanni in Laterano (*c.* 313–20, later remodelled), Old St Peter's (*c.* 320–30 with double aisles, not preserved), S. Paolo fuori le Mura (late C5 also with double aisles, rebuilt after a fire in 1823) and S. Maria Maggiore (*c.* 432–40). Some centrally planned buildings also exist, but they are not numerous. The most notable in Rome is S. Stefano Rotondo (468–83), on a circular plan. The baptistery of S. Giovanni in Laterano (*c.* 315 and *c.* 432–40) is octagonal, a central plan being functionally advantageous for baptisteries. S. Costanza (*c.* 350), one of the most beautiful Early Christian buildings, is circular, with an ambulatory. Here the explanation is that it was a mausoleum and for mausolea the ancient Roman tradition was a circular plan.

Next to Rome, Ravenna was the most important centre (*see* BYZANTINE ARCHITECTURE). It became the capital of the Roman West in 404, of Odoacer in 476 and of Theodoric in 493, and of the Byzantine bridgehead in Italy in 540. Here also the majority of the churches are basilican: e.g. S. Apollinare Nuovo of *c.* 510–20 and S. Apollinare in Classe of *c.* 550. More original and varied are the centrally planned buildings: S. Vitale, completed in 547 and entirely Byzantine with its complex and ingenious octagonal plan, the Mausoleum of Galla Placidia of *c.* 450 which is a Greek cross, and the two octagonal baptisteries. The Mausoleum of Theodoric, as befitted this Gothic king, is much more massive. Moreover, it is of stone, whereas the other buildings are of brick. Characteristic features of these latter are external blank arcading or LESENES connected by a small frieze of blank arches, a motif which became typical of the north Italian Romanesque style. The earliest Italian CAMPANILI are also at Ravenna. They are circular and were probably a C9 addition. The earliest campanile of which we know is the square one once attached to St Peter's in Rome, and this went back to the mid c8.

At least two Early Christian buildings not in Rome or in Ravenna must be mentioned. One is S. Salvatore at Spoleto, of the late C4–6, several times restored, with a complete façade, its details and those of the interior still strikingly Late Roman, but with an oval dome over the chancel which is a motif of Syria or Asia Minor. The other is S. Lorenzo in Milan (c. 352–75, later partly remodelled), already exhibiting spatial subtleties as thrilling as those of S. Vitale. Milan possesses more early churches, at least in substantial parts, than had been known until recently, e.g. S. Simpliciano (late C4).

The transition from Early Christian to Early Medieval is imperceptible in Italy. S. Agnese in Rome of 625–38 is still entirely Early Christian, but S. Maria in Domnica and S. Maria in Cosmedin of the early C9 are in plan and elevation not essentially different. Nor is S. Prassede, although the latter has a transept, like that at Fulda probably a self-conscious reversion to Constantinian greatness. S. Maria in Cosmedin has a hall crypt, one of the earliest ever. Both Cosmedin and Domnica end in three parallel apses, and this is so in the most important early

C9 churches in north Italy too: S. Pietro, Agliate (early C11), and S. Vincenzo in Prato, Milan (C11). But on the whole these and other north Italian churches continue the Early Christian type as well (S. Salvatore, Brescia, Pomposa abbey). Innovations are the square piers of e.g. S. Pietro in Silvis, Bagnacavallo, of c8–9 and the small tunnel vaults of S. Maria in Valle at Cividale of c. 762–76 (the latter has also the finest early medieval sculpture in Italy). Cividale is extraordinary in plan as well, as was the interesting S. Maria delle Cinque Torre, Cassino (778–87, destroyed), which introduced the Byzantine plan of the inscribed cross and had moreover groin and tunnel vaults and three parallel apses.

It is not easy to decide where to start using the term Romanesque in Italy. The basilican plan, the columns of the arcades, the apse continuing the nave without a transept remain the Italian norm in the C11 and into the C12. The essential innovations in plan which France and Germany introduced in the late C10 and early C11 did not at once touch Italy and remained the exception even later. Ambulatories with radiating chapels for instance are rare (S. Antimo, near Siena, begun c. 1118; and Aversa Cathedral, near Naples, begun before c. 1150), although vestigial ambulatories had occurred remarkably early (S. Stefano, Verona, rebuilt c. 990; and Ivrea Cathedral, before 1002). The new elements which came in in the C11 seem to have been derived from the Empire. Montecassino of 1066 onwards had a transept, though one not projecting. It also still had the typically Italian three parallel apses. At Salerno Cathedral, consecrated in 1084, the transept stretches out beyond the aisle lines, and S. Nicola at Bari, the most important southern building (begun immediately after 1087), has transepts, alternating supports in the nave, a gallery, two west towers placed Norman fashion outside the aisle lines and the stumps of two east towers as well. Such east towers also occur, and here clearly under German influence, at S. Abbondio at Como, consecrated in 1095. S. Fedele at Como is later but still on a trefoil plan inspired by Cologne. S. Abbondio has no transept, but Aquileia of c. 1020 onwards already has, although for the rest it follows Early Christian tradition.

The C12 and the early C13 in Italy are hard to summarize. There is little of regional standards, at least in plans and elevations, though decorative motifs differ considerably from area to area. The great C12 cathedrals of the north Italian plain are truly Romanesque, though they also differ in many respects. But they have mostly alternating supports and galleries inside and the so-called dwarf galleries, small arcaded wall-passages, outside. Their towers are campanili, not integrated with the buildings themselves. Modena, begun in 1099, is the first, with a transept not projecting, and with the traditional three parallel apses. This is the same at S. Ambrogio in Milan with its solemn façade and its beautiful atrium. But the most important aspect of S. Ambrogio is the rib vaults with heavy ribs of plain rectangular section. This type occurs also in the south of France, and the several examples in Lombardy are probably all of the C12, i.e. later than the much more sophisticated ribs of Durham. The other principal north Italian cathedrals are Parma of after 1117, with a more German plan (far projecting transepts with apses and only one east apse), Piacenza

of c. 1120, Cremona and Ferrara. A spectacular appendix to these north Italian cathedrals is their large, detached, octagonal baptisteries. The most famous of the Italian baptisteries, however, is in central Italy, that of Pisa begun in 1153. Pisa Cathedral, exceptionally large, is exceptional in other ways as well. It was started as early as 1063 by Buscheto (fl. 1063–1110) and has long-aisled transepts with end-apses, a double-aisled nave and no vaults. The campanile, i.e. the leaning tower, arcaded in many tiers all round, was started in 1173. The Baptistery (1153–1265) bears an inscription to its architect, Diotisalvi. The same predilection for outer arcading in tiers is to be found at Lucca. Florence is different. Here already in the late C11 a movement arose which deserves the name Proto-Renaissance. It favoured ancient Roman motifs and has a graceful elegance unique in Romanesque Europe. The principal examples are the Baptistery, S. Miniato and SS. Apostoli, all in Florence, and the Badia at Fiesole, none of them exactly datable. A comparable interest in ancient Rome is found in and around Rome in the early C13 (façade, Città Castellana Cathedral, 1210; and façade, S. Lorenzo fuori le Mura, Rome, 1220 now altered). An exception in central Italy is the church of S. Claudio al Chienti, Macerata, which is on the Byzantine inscribed-cross plan.

The relations of the Italian Romanesque to Byzantium are manifold and interesting. The major monument, totally Byzantine, is of course St Mark's in Venice (1063 onwards), with a central plan and five domes. Domes were also placed over naves in a few major south Italian churches (Canosa Cathedral, 1071 onwards; Molfetta

Italian architecture

Cathedral, *c.* 1160 onwards). The inscribed-cross plan appears here and there in different parts of southern Italy, at Stilo, at Otranto (S. Pietro), at Trani (S. Andrea). The Byzantine elements in Sicilian architecture are fascinatingly overlaid with Saracen and Norman elements. The island had been under Byzantium from the c6, under Islam from 827, under the Normans from 1061. But during the years of the greatest Sicilian architecture, the country was one of the centres of the Hohenstaufen emperors. The Norman motifs of Cefalù and Monreale Cathedrals (1131 onwards and 1166 onwards) are patent to English visitors. On the other hand the Martorana at Palermo (1143 onwards) is on the Byzantine inscribed-cross plan, and S. Cataldo in Palermo looks wholly Arabic. This applies even more to the royal palaces and pavilions such as the Ziza and the Cuba at Palermo.

Romanesque Italy has much of secular architecture to offer. Here only a few buildings can be referred to – some byzantinizing palaces of Venice (especially the Fondaco dei Turchi) and the equally byzantinizing c11 Palazzo della Ragione at Pomposa, the slender towers of the nobility, especially famous those of San Gimignano and the two in the centre of Bologna, and the Town Halls of Como (1216), Orvieto and Massa Marittima. All these are of the c13.

But at that time the Gothic style had started on its Italian course. It had come, as in all countries, from France and, as in most countries, by means of the CISTERCIANS (Fossanova, 1187–1208, Casamari, 1203 onwards with rib vaults, both in Lazio, S. Galgano in Tuscany, 1227 onwards). The collegiate church of S. Andrea at Vercelli of *c.* 1220 onwards is transitional between Italian Romanesque and French Gothic. The most original of the early Gothic buildings in Italy is S. Francesco at Assisi, begun in 1228 and, oddly enough, inspired by the French West and most probably Angers Cathedral. Another early French (Burgundian) inspiration explains the splendid castles of Frederick II in the south of Italy and in Sicily (Augusta; Maniace, Syracuse; Ursino, Catania) and especially Castel del Monte of *c.* 1240 onwards, where French Gothic structure is fascinatingly mixed with ancient Roman detail used in a spirit of Renaissance. The plans of these castles are regular, mostly with angle towers, a plan introduced at the same time in France and thus continued in both countries (e.g. Ferrara, 1389 onwards).

Altogether the Italy of the c13 and c14 is rich in remarkable secular buildings, the public halls of Genoa, Orvieto and Piacenza, all c13 and all continuing the Romanesque type, the slightly later and less peacefully open Town Halls of Perugia (1283 onwards), Siena (1288 onwards) and Florence (Palazzo Vecchio, 1298 onwards), the Loggia dei Lanzi in Florence of 1376 with its strangely un-Gothic round arches, the Doge's Palace in Venice of 1309–1424, unique in size and composition, and some c14 palaces in Florence and Siena, and early c15 palaces in Venice (Ca' d'Oro 1424–36). North Italian Late Gothic detail is more ornate, more northern than that further south (Porta della Carta, Doge's Palace, 1438–43).

This northern, trans-alpine character applies with much greater force to Milan Cathedral, begun in 1386 and the work of a mixture of masters from Lombardy, Germany, and France, all fighting each other. The scale of

Milan Cathedral incited the starting on a similar scale of the Certosa of Pavia (1396 onwards, built slowly) and S. Petronio, the largest parish church of Bologna (1390 onwards, unfinished) by Antonio di Vincenzo (c. 1350–1401/2). But meanwhile, i.e. in the C13 and earlier C14, the Gothic style had made progress everywhere in Italy. In Bologna itself the friars' church of S. Francesco in 1236 started with a French ambulatory with radiating chapels. The friars otherwise built large but without an accepted system of plan or elevation. S. Francesco at Siena of 1326 onwards has no aisles and no vault, S. Croce in Florence, the Franciscan church there, of 1294/5 (attributed to ARNOLFO DI CAMBIO) has aisles and no vault. The east ends of both are in the Cistercian tradition. The Frari (Franciscan) and SS. Giovanni e Paolo, Venice (Dominican; both C14), have aisles, high round piers and rib vaults. The airiness of these churches is fundamentally different from the spatial feeling of the French Gothic. This Italian-ness of Italian Gothic expresses itself most strongly in S. Maria Novella in Florence (Dominican; 1278 onwards) and Florence Cathedral (begun by ARNOLFO in 1296). The arcades are much more generously opened than in France so that nave and aisles appear part of one space and not three parallel vessels. The measure of each bay opening of the arcades is c. 64 ft; at Amiens it was c. 25 ft. The campanile of Florence Cathedral (by GIOTTO) is the finest of all Italian Gothic campanili. The finest Gothic façades are Siena (1284 onwards, by Giovanni PISANO) and Orvieto (c. 1310 onwards, by MAITANI). As against Florence, Rome had little to contribute. The only important Gothic church is S. Maria sopra Minerva of c. 1280 onwards.

For the introduction of the Renaissance also Florence took precedence over Rome, however much the Renaissance masters owed to ancient Rome. However, even that debt is less great than C19 scholars assumed. It is certain that BRUNELLESCHI in his churches looked more to the Tuscan Proto-Renaissance (see above) than to Imperial Rome. For Florence the date of the conversion to the Renaissance is c. 1420; for Venice, Milan, and also Rome it is a generation later. For Rome ALBERTI, who was more in sympathy with the ancient Roman character in architecture than anyone else, was instrumental in establishing the Renaissance, though he had probably nothing to do with the courtyard of the Palazzo Venezia of c. 1470 which was the first to take up the ponderous motif of orders of attached columns to separate arched openings such as the Romans had used for the Theatre of Marcellus and the Colosseum. But on the whole the Quattrocento prefers arcades of slender columns carrying arches, i.e. rather delicate members, and a graceful lively decoration. Examples of the former are Brunelleschi's earliest façade, that of the Foundling Hospital in Florence (1419 onwards), and such palace courtyards as that of MICHELOZZO's Palazzo Medici in Florence (1444 onwards) or the Ducal Palace at Urbino (1460s), which also has some of the most exquisite Quattrocento decoration. Palace façades, especially in Tuscany, are still forbidding, in direct continuation of the Trecento. Heavy rustication was favoured (Palazzo Medici, Palazzo Strozzi), though Alberti in his Palazzo Rucellai, Florence, used a more elegant articulation by tiers of pilasters, and this was taken up at the Cancelleria in Rome (*c.* 1485). Church plans are usually longitudinal: Brunelleschi's with nave and aisles and slim arcades, Alberti's S. Andrea at Mantua aisleless, but with side-chapels, a system with a great future. But both Brunelleschi and Alberti and others as well (Giuliano da SANGALLO) favoured central plans and developed them in a variety of ways (Brunelleschi, S. Maria degli Angeli, Florence, 1434 onwards; Alberti, S. Sebastiano, Mantua, 1460 onwards; Sangallo, S. Maria delle Carceri, Prato, 1486 onwards).

Central Italians (MICHELOZZO, FILARETE) had introduced the Renaissance to Milan in the 1450s, and at the same time it appeared in Venice (Arsenal portal, 1457). In contrast to central Italy, however, the north of Italy went in for extremely busy decoration of façades as well as interiors (Verona and Brescia Town Halls, Certosa of Pavia, Como Cathedral, 1470s to 1490s and after 1500). These façades had considerable influence on the Early Renaissance in trans-alpine countries. Even BRAMANTE, in his early years in Milan, used this rich and playful decoration, though at S. Maria presso S. Satiro it is rather Alberti (in Mantua) who inspired him. Bramante lived in Milan in the same years as LEONARDO DA VINCI, but it is impossible to say what their relationship was. Leonardo sketched architectural ideas, but did not build. Nearly all his church plans are of central types, and he reached unprecedented complexities. Bramante clearly was attracted by the same problem, even if none of the central churches of Lombardy can with certainty be ascribed to him (Lodi, Crema).

With Bramante's move from Milan to Rome in 1499 the High Renaissance was established, with more substantial and also more Roman forms and character (St Peter's, Belvedere Court Vatican, Palazzo Caprini). RAPHAEL (Villa Madama), PERUZZI (Villa Farnesina), and GIULIO ROMANO were Bramante's successors, but the latter two soon turned away from his style to Mannerism. The solecisms of Giulio's Palazzo Te (1525 onwards) and his own house (1544), both at Mantua, are both eloquent and painful. At the same time MICHELANGELO designed in the Mannerist way (Medici Chapel and Laurentian Library, Florence, 1520s; exterior of St Peter's, 1546 onwards; and Porta Pia, Rome, 1561). Mannerism produced exquisite works (Farnese Palace, Caprarola, by VIGNOLA, 1547 onwards; Villa Giulia by Vignola, 1551 onwards, Casino of Pius IV by LIGORIO, 1559 onwards, both Rome; Uffizi, Florence, by VASARI, begun 1560), as well as perverse ones (Casa Zuccari, Rome, 1590), but it never ruled unchallenged. In the north of Italy the Renaissance spirit was alive throughout the C16, as is demonstrated by buildings such as SANSOVINO's Library of S. Marco, Venice (1537) and Palazzo Corner, Venice (before 1561), SANMICHELI's palaces and city gates of Verona (1520s to 1550s), and PALLADIO's palaces inside and villas outside Vicenza. Though in the work of Palladio, especially his churches in Venice, Mannerist traits are easily discovered, most of his secular work must be classed as Renaissance. The problem of Vignola in Rome is similar, but whereas Palladio, where he is not Mannerist, belongs to the past, Vignola, where he is not Mannerist, points forward to the Baroque.

There can be no doubt that Vignola's Gesù, Rome (begun 1568), established a canon of church plan and elevation for the Baroque: chapels instead of aisles, transepts and a dome (S. Andrea della Valle, S. Carlo al Corso, and others in Rome). The completion of St Peter's by MADERNO was also longitudinal. But the most interesting Baroque churches are those on central or elongated central plans. Vignola had used the oval as early as 1573, but it became a standard element only in the C17, varied inexhaustibly, especially by the greatest Roman Baroque architects BERNINI and BORROMINI. Bernini uses the oval transversely at S. Andrea al Quirinale, and RAINALDI uses a grouping of elements which gives the impression of a transverse oval at S. Agnese. The façade of this church, with its two towers and its concave centre, is by Borromini, whose façade of S. Carlino is even more complex in its use of concave and convex parts. There the interior carries the interaction of curves to the highest point it achieved in Rome, but the acme of spatial complications was reached by GUARINI at Turin. Bernini's work at St Peter's was concerned with decoration on the grandest scale (Baldacchino, Cathedra Petri) and with the forecourt in front of Maderno's façade. The elliptical colonnades and their splaying-out connection with the façade are aesthetically and from the planning point of view equally satisfying.

In the field of major urban planning Rome had already taken the lead in the late C16, when the long streets radiating from the Piazza del Popolo had been laid out. In secular architecture Rome contributed less, though the open façade of the Palazzo Barberini and the giant pilasters of Bernini's Palazzo Odescalchi had much influence. For Baroque palaces Genoa is the most interesting city, e.g. those on ALESSI's Strada Nuova.

As early as about 1700 Italy began to tone down the Baroque (FONTANA, then JUVARRA in Turin: Superga 1715–31; Palazzo Madama, 1718 onwards) and in the Veneto a Palladian revival took place (Scalfarotti's S. Simeone, Venice, 1718 onwards; Preti's Villa Pisani, Strà, 1735 onwards).

The C19 is more interesting in Italian architecture than most tourists realize. The neo-classical, especially neo-Greek style has produced much outstanding work. French influence is occasionally patent (S. Carlo Theatre, Naples (1820–44) by Antonio Niccolini (1772–1850)). The most monumental church is S. Francesco di Paola, Naples (1817–28), by Pietro Bianchi (1787–1849). Neo-Greek are JAPELLI's Caffè Pedrocchi, Padua (1816–31), and the Temple at Possagno (1819–30) by Antonio Canova; more wayward are the Cemetery at Staglieno (1835) and the Carlo Felice Theatre, Genoa (begun in 1827), which are both by Carlo Francesco Barabino (1768–1835), and the grandiose Cisternone, Livorno (1829), by Pasquale Poccianti (1774–1858). A curious anachronism is the use of classical forms and ornament by ANTONELLI in his two monster towers at Novara and Turin. In the sixties other styles had taken the place of the classical, a Super-Renaissance in MENGONI's Galleria in Milan, a Lombardo-Gothic in the Milan Cemetery by Carlo Maciachini (1818–99) and others, notably Camillo Boito (1836–1914), the brother of Verdi's librettist. As in other continental countries the neo-Renaissance – e.g. the Banco d'Italia (1885–92) and Palazzo Margherita, now the American Embassy (1886–90), both in Rome, by Gaetano Koch (1849–1910) – was followed by the neo-Baroque in such prominent buildings as the Palazzo di Giustizia, Rome (1888–1910), by Guglielmo Calderini (1837–1916). And the neo-Baroque was followed by Art Nouveau, e.g. Villa Igea, Palermo (1898), by Ernesto Basile (1857–1932). Italian Art Nouveau, called *stile floreale* or *stile Liberty*, was inspired at first by Vienna in the work of Raimondo d'Aronco (1857–1932) but became more original in that of SOMMARUGA and was continued with undiminished exuberance by Gino Coppedé (1866–1927) whose extraordinary apartment building in via Po, Rome, is as late as 1921.

The C20 started with SANT'ELIA's Futurist dreams of skyscrapers. The new international style did not make itself felt until the mid C20 and did not get a chance of showing itself in buildings until after 1930, e.g. Casa del Fascio, Como (1932), by TERRAGNI. This was the masterpiece of Italian RATIONALISM, a movement led by Terragni, FIGINI, POLLINI and a few others which produced a number of remarkable buildings – Press Pavilion for Milan Triennale 1933 by Luciano Baldessari (1896–1982), Palestra per la Scherma, Rome (1934–6), by Luigi Moretti (1907–73), Florence railway station (1933–6) by MICHELUCCI and others – before it foundered in its alliance with Fascism with such pomposities as the Foro Mussolini, Rome (1927–32), Città

Universitaria, Rome (1932–5), and the 1942 Universal Exhibition buildings, now EUR, Rome (1935–41), all of which are by Marcello Piacentini (1881–1960).

The immediate post-Second World War period was notable for PONTI's Pirelli skyscraper and BBPR's Torre Velasca, both in Milan, and especially for the structurally inventive and aesthetically sensitive work of NERVI. They were followed by several notable architects of disparate gifts – e.g. Gabetti and Isola (b. 1925 and 1928), Giorgio Grassi (b. 1935), Paolo Portoghesi (b. 1931), Gino Valle (b. 1923) – as well as by the urban planners Carlo AYMONINO snd Giancarlo De Carlo (b. 1919). The experimental groups ARCHIZOOM and Superstudio were formed in Florence in 1966 and had some influence internationally, though less than the NEO-RATIONALISM promoted by Vittorio GREGOTTI and Aldo ROSSI. Among younger Italian architects Renzo PIANO is outstanding, but has as yet had little opportunity to build in Italy apart from the Olympic Stadium, Bari (1989).

Iwan or **Liwan**. In Near-Eastern architecture, a large porch or shallow hall with a pointed barrel vault, as in the Sassanian palace at Ctesiphon, Iraq (mid C6 AD), and many later Islamic buildings where it may serve as an entrance, as at the Great Mosque, Yazd, Iran (*c.* 1330), or face a courtyard as at the Lutfullah Mosque, Isfahan, Iran (1602–16).

Ixnard, Michel d' (1723–95), a French early neo-classical architect, worked mainly in the Rhineland. Born at Nîmes and trained in Paris, he became architect to the Elector of Trier. His main work is the very large, severe, and rather heavy abbey church of St Blasien in the Black Forest (1764–84), with a Doric exterior and solemn Corinthian rotunda.

E. Franz, *P.M. d'I.* *1723–1795*, Weissenhorn 1985.

Izenour, Steven (b. 1930), *see* VEN-TURI, Robert.

j

Jacobean architecture, *see* ENG-
LISH ARCHITECTURE.

Jacobsen, Arne (1902–71). His style is
the most refined, meticulous INTER-
NATIONAL MODERN; he was initially
influenced by ASPLUND's Stockholm
Exhibition of 1930 and appeared as an
International Modern architect with
work of 1931, at a time when Copenhagen was reaching the climax of a
classicism as refined and meticulous in
its own way as Jacobsen's architecture
was to be. He built chiefly private
houses and housing until shortly before
the Second World War, when he was
also commissioned for work on a larger
scale. The Town Hall of Aarhus (with
Erik Møller, 1938–42) had a concrete
skeleton tower. Søllerød, an outer
suburb of Copenhagen, got a town hall
by Jacobsen in 1939–42. The Munk-
egård School at Gentofte, another
outer suburb of Copenhagen, is characterized by the many small play-yards
between classrooms (1952–6). The
Town Hall of Rødovre, yet another
outer suburb of Copenhagen, is Jacobsen's most exquisite public building
(1955–6), quite unmannered, without
any cliché or gimmick, nothing really
but the formal apparatus of the International thirties, yet handled with an unparalleled precision and elegance. The
same is true of his cylinder-boring factory at Aalborg (1957) and the SAS
Hotel at Copenhagen (1960; a tower
block on a podium of the Lever House
type – *see* SKIDMORE, OWINGS &
MERRILL). In 1964 St Catherine's College at Oxford was completed to Jacobsen's designs. During the fifties he
also designed some fine and original
furniture and cutlery.

T. Faber, *A. J.*, Stuttgart 1964; P.E.
Shriver, *A.J.*, Copenhagen 1972.

Jadot de Ville Issy, Jean-Nicolas
(1710–61). He was trained in France
and became at an early age architect to
the Archduke Franz I of Lorraine
whom he accompanied to Vienna on
his marriage to Maria Theresia. He
built the Academy of Sciences and
Letters in Vienna (1753) and the
menagerie at Schönbrunn, both in
an accomplished Louis XV style: and
he probably provided the plan for the
royal palace in Budapest (1749, greatly
altered in the C19). He also designed
the Arco di S. Gallo in Florence,
erected to mark the Archduke's accession to the Grand Duchy of Tuscany
in 1739.

Kalnein and Levey 1972.

Jahn, Helmut (b. 1940). German architect who emigrated to the USA
in 1966, joining a long-established
Chicago practice (C. F. Murphy Associates, now called Murphy/Jahn) as

director of design in 1973. Their recent notable buildings include the One South Wacker building (1979–82) and the State of Illinois Center (1980–83), both in Chicago.

N. Miller, *H.J.*, New York 1986; Klotz 1986.

Jalousie. A blind or shutter with slats which slope upwards from without to exclude rain and sun but admit air and some light; also an open-work grille covering a gallery in a church or a box in a theatre.

Jamb. The vertical face of an archway, doorway, or window; the part of the jamb which lies between the glass or door and the outer wall-surface is called a *reveal*.

Jamb shaft. A small shaft with capital and base placed against the jamb of a door or window, mainly in medieval architecture.

James, John (*c.* 1672–1746), built St George's, Hanover Square, London (1720–25), with its hexastyle portico of free-standing giant Corinthian columns and pediment. This idea was quickly taken up by GIBBS (St Martin-in-the-Fields). Wricklemarsh, Blackheath (1727–33), was his masterpiece, but it was demolished. He rebuilt St Mary's church, Twickenham, except for the west tower (1713–15). Appuldurcombe House, Isle of Wight, may be his. He published an English edition of Claude PERRAULT's book on the Orders in 1708

Downes 1966; Colvin 1978; Summerson 1983; Harris 1990.

Japanese architecture. Temples of the indigenous Shinto religion have been periodically demolished and built anew following a design developed by

the C3 AD from primitive huts, that at Ise being the best-known example. They are of stained (persimmon-orange colour) wood but unpainted, with pitched roofs of thatch supported on frames of intersecting spars which project above the ridge-pole. In the c6 an entirely different style was introduced 'ready-made' from China, with a complex system of roof construction, for the buildings in the first Japanese Buddhist monasteries – pagodas and halls for the display of images and for teaching. The earliest that survive are in the Horyuji, near Nara, founded in 607 but destroyed by fire in 670 and reconstructed with the gateway, pagoda and *kondo* (image hall) still entirely Chinese but disposed in a manner that broke away from the axial symmetry invariable in China, creating a distinctly Japanese composition of balanced solids and voids. Although most plans were bilaterally symmetrical, more emphasis was given to width than was usual in China and the size of the monasteries seems sometimes to have been greater: the Daibutsuden of the Todaiji, Nara, begun 743 though rebuilt in 1709 to the original design with a diminution in plan, is still the largest wooden building in the world. Nara, the first permanent capital of Japan, was laid out in 710 on a grid with wide avenues in emulation of Changan in China, the Tang dynasty capital. But deviations from Chinese forms began to appear in the c8 (e.g. the pagoda of the Yakushiji, Nara, with the ground storey wider than the tower, which has roofs of alternating size supported on brackets of unprecedented form) and became more pronounced after the Imperial Court moved to Kyoto in 794, especially during the Fujiwara period (898–1185), when there were few direct contacts with the Asian mainland. China proved the model for Japanese imperial administration and in the palace at Kyoto the great hall of state was placed at the end of a courtyard on axis with the main gateway to the enclosure. But living quarters and administrative buildings were disposed with more regard for convenience than symmetry and already had features that were to distinguish Japanese domestic architecture: shingles or thatch rather than ceramic tiles for roofs, veranda corridors as passages from one room or building to another, floors of wood (not of tile and stone with raised platforms as in China), and the division of interior spaces by sliding screens painted with landscapes etc. Externally, the buildings of the imperial and other palaces were similar to temples of the same period, of which the finest surviving example is the Hoodo (Phoenix Hall) dedicated to the Bodhisattva Amida, of the Byodoin at Uji, near Kyoto, founded by a Fujiwara prince in 1052. It has almost dandified elegance, with roofs so dashingly uplifted at their corners that they seem to float above the horizontal lines of the structure. Elegance is also the mark of a type of religious building peculiar to Japan, the *tahoto* or single-storey pagoda, with two wide-spreading roofs sheltering a STUPA and crowned by a tall mast (e.g. that of 1194 in the Ishiyamadera temple overlooking Lake Biwa). In these buildings the woodwork of the elaborate bracketing (more decorative than strictly functional) and of the carved ceilings is often of the greatest refinement. By the beginning of the Kamakura period (1185–1333) the main elements of Japanese religious architecture had been established

(with minor variants for several different Buddhist sects) and were to be respected in numerous reconstructions, though new buildings show a tendency towards richer and heavier decoration, taken to its extreme at Nikko, in the mausoleum (1634–6) of Tokugawa Ieyasu, founder of the Shogunate that ruled Japan during the Edo period (1615–1867). The most interesting developments were, however, in domestic architecture, with an entirely different tendency.

The three-storey Kinkakuji (or Golden Pavilion), Kyoto, built in 1397 (burned down 1950 but rebuilt as an exact replica) had decorations in gold leaf on its exterior but was otherwise ostensibly simple, with a structure of squared undecorated timbers, asymmetrical grouping of supports, no elaborate bracketing and a shingle roof. The smaller two-storey Ginkakuji (called the Silver Pavilion), built in 1483, is similar but with a ground floor of more pronounced asymmetry. Both these pavilions were set in artificially 'natural' gardens and intended as places of retirement for study and meditation, commissioned by devotees of Zen Buddhism and bequeathed to Zen monasteries. A different impression is given by the fortified castles built by war-lords in the late C16, e.g. at Himeji, where the asymmetry of its several storeys may have been determined to assist defence. Within the fortifications of the Nijo Castle of the Shoguns in Kyoto, begun 1602, the single-storey buildings for reception halls are on a staggered plan, squares arranged angle to angle so that passage from one to another along the flanking corridors necessitates repeated right-angle turns – partly to foil intruders. But the more complex rambling plan of the Katsura villa outside Kyoto, begun c. 1620, was determined aesthetically, to provide each room with a different view of the surrounding garden. Here the building materials are ostentatiously simple – sometimes rough un-worked tree-trunks for posts and beams – but employed with the greatest refinement. It is a large-scale expression of the quintessentially Japanese cult of rusticity and artificial naturalness which was taken to its extreme in the small houses and rooms for the tea ceremony (which had originated in Zen monasteries). Here as elsewhere, however, freedom in planning, the articulation of walls etc. was held in check by an inviolable rule of proportions based on the double square of the *tatami* straw and rush mat – approximately 6 by 3 ft (for imperial buildings 7 by 3 ft 6 ins), with halves but no other fractions permitted. The rule was obeyed for housing at all levels of society. And this combined with asymmetry and open planning – interior spaces that can be enlarged or reduced by sliding screens – was to appeal strongly to European architects in the early C20 (e.g Bruno TAUT).

The Westernization of Japan after 1868 had a less depressing influence on architecture than on the other arts, domestic traditions being rigorously maintained. A new period began after the arrival of Frank Lloyd WRIGHT and his Czech assistant Antonin Raymond (1889 1976) to build the Imperial Hotel, Tokyo (1916–20, demolished). Raymond settled in Japan. His Sogo store, Osaka (completed by Togo Murann, 1932), introduced the INTERNATIONAL MODERN style, and his own house at Karinizawa (1932) and Reader's Digest Offices, Tokyo (1949), were influential. But the 1930s

were also marked by a nationalist–traditionalist revival, e.g. the Imperial Museum, Tokyo (1938), by Hitoshi Watanabe (b. 1905). It was only after the Second World War that modern Japanese architecture – like that of Brazil slightly earlier – won international fame, and the decisive influence in Japan, as in Brazil, was LE CORBUSIER. Kunio MAYEKAWA, Junzo Sakakura (1904–69) and Takamasa Yoshisaka (1917–80) all worked in his office and later went in for extremely massive concrete and bold, heavily fanciful forms, e.g. Mayekawa's Festival Halls, Tokyo and Kyoto (both 1961); Sakakura's Town Hall, Hajima (1959); and Yoshisaka's Gotsu Town Hall (1962). The leading contemporary architect is Kenzo TANGE, whose mature works are all in concrete left as rough as possible and used for the most dramatic effects, e.g. Olympia Sports Stadium, Tokyo (1963–4), with suspended roof, and Yamanashi broadcasting centre, Kofu (1966–7). His disciples include the METABOLISM group – Kyonori KIKUTAKE, Kisho KUROKAWA, Fumihiko Maki (b. 1928) and Masato Otaka (b. 1923). His former colleagues Sachio Otani (b. 1924) and Arata ISOZAKI are also outstanding, e.g. Otani's International Conference Building, Kyoto (1963–6). The Architext group, founded by Takamitsu AZUMA, Takefumi Aida (b. 1927) and others in 1971, broke with the Metabolists. Also notable during the 1970s were Kazuo Shinohara (b. 1925) and Minoru Takeyama (b. 1934), whose Ni-Ban-Khan stores in Tokyo (1970, redesigned 1977) and Beverley Tom Hotel, Hokkaido (1973), epitomize the decade. More recently Tadao ANDO has made his name internationally with such small-scale works as the Matsumoto residence, Wakayama (1980), and the Rokko housing, Hyogo (1983).

Japelli or **Jappelli,** Giuseppe (1783–1852), a leading Italian romantic architect and landscape gardener, was a true eclectic of a type rare in Italy, able to work happily in a wide range of styles. Beginning at the Caffè Pedrocchi, Padua (1816–31), in a very elegant version of neo-classicism, he then turned to a severe manner derived from the astylar backs of Palladian villas – e.g. Villa Vigodarzere, Saonara (1817) – then to a bold Grecian style for the Doric slaughterhouse in Padua (1821, now the Istituto d'Arte). After a visit to France and England he added a neo-Gothic wing to the Pedrocchi (1837), and finally built the neo-Rococo Teatro Verdi, Padua (1847). His landscape parks are consistently in the English manner; most of them are in the Veneto (e.g. Saonara, Ca' Minotto, Rosà), but one of the finest was at Villa Torlonia, Rome (1840).

Meeks 1966; G. Mazza (ed.), *G.J. e il suo tempo*, Padua 1977; L. Puppi, *Il Caffè Pedrocchi di Padova*, Vicenza 1980.

Jardin, Nicolas-Henri (1720–99), *see* DANISH ARCHITECTURE.

Jean de Chelles. Master mason to Notre Dame in Paris and responsible for the façade bays of the transepts – that to the north came first in the 1240s, that to the south was begun in 1258 to a design by PIERRE DE MONTEREAU, who succeeded him at Notre Dame in 1265. A kinsman, Pierre de Chelles, was master mason of the cathedral in the early C14 and was still active in 1316, when he was called to Chartres as a consultant.

Frankl 1972; R. Branner, *St Louis and the Court Style in Gothic Architecture*, London 1965.

Jean d'Orbais. The names of the first four master masons of Reims Cathedral were recorded in a maze on the floor (known from C18 transcriptions). The order was in all probability Jean d'Orbais, Jean Le Loup, Gaucher de Reims and Bernard de Soissons. Bernard's headship lasted, it seems, to *c.* 1290; Gaucher's from *c.* 1245 to 1253; Le Loup's from *c.* 1229 to 1245 and Jean d'Orbais's from *c.* 1211 to 1229. So the first total plan was by Jean d'Orbais. The cathedral was begun in 1211 and the choir was consecrated in 1241.

Frankl 1972; Bony 1983.

Jefferson, Thomas (1743–1826), legislator, economist, educationalist, and third President of the United States of America (1801–9), was also an able and immensely influential architect. The son of a surveyor, he inherited a considerable estate in Albemarle County, where in 1768 he chose a high romantic site for his own house, Monticello (1770–79, remodelled 1796–1808). He derived the plan from Robert MORRIS's *Select Architecture*, but modified it with reference to GIBBS and Leoni's edition of PALLADIO. It had porticos front and back and a great forecourt with octagonal pavilions at the corners and square pavilions terminating the wings. It is very carefully thought out, both in its planning, on which he had strong personal views, and in its adaptation of Palladian elements. He was interested in Palladio mainly as the interpreter of Roman villa architecture, and looked back to antiquity for the 'natural' principles of his architectural theory. In 1785, while he was in Europe, he was asked to design the Virginia State Capitol for Rich-mond. With the help of CLÉRISSEAU, he produced a temple design based on the Maison Carreé (16 BC) at Nîmes, but Ionic instead of Corinthian and with pilasters in place of half-columns on the flanks and rear. The Virginia State Capi-tol (completed 1796 with the assistance of LATROBE) set a pattern for official architecture in the USA. As Secretary of State to George Washington he played a leading part in planning the new federal capital in Washington from 1792 onwards. After he became Presi-dent he entrusted Latrobe with the task of completing the new Capitol (1803, burnt 1814). Latrobe also assisted him with the University of Virginia, Charlot-tesville – a group of porticoed houses (each containing a professor's lodging and a classroom) linked by colonnades in a formal plan, with a great Pantheon at one end of the oblong composition (1817–26) – the first great CAMPUS plan.

W. H. Adams (ed.), *The Eye of T.J.*, Washington, DC, 1976, and *J.'s Mon-ticello*, New York 1983.

Jenney, William Le Baron (1832–1907), was born in Massachusetts, studied at the École Centrale des Arts et Manufactures in Paris, was an engineer in the Civil War, and opened a practice in architecture and engineering in Chi-cago in 1868. In 1869 he published a book called *Principles and Practices of Architecture*. By far his most import-ant building was the Home Insurance building (1883–5, demolished), as its iron columns, iron lintels and girders, and indeed steel beams, prepared the way for the skeleton construction of the CHICAGO SCHOOL. The Second Leit-er Building, Chicago (1889–90), is an eight-storey metal-framed building.

T. Turak, *W.L.B.J. A Pioneer of Modern Architecture*, Ann Arbor 1986; Zukovsky 1988.

Jensen, Albert Christian (1847–1913), *see* DANISH ARCHITECTURE.

Jensen-Klint, Peter Vilhelm (1853–1930), *see* KLINT, Peter Vilhelm Jensen.

Jesse window. A window in which the tracery represents the branches of the tree of Jesse – a genealogical tree showing the ancestors of Christ ascend-ing from the root of Jesse.

Jetty. In a TIMBER-FRAMED building the projection of an upper storey beyond the storey below made by the BEAMS and JOISTS of the lower storey oversailing the external wall. On their outer ends is placed the sill of the wall-ing for the storey above. Buildings can be jettied on several sides, in which case a *dragon beam* is set diagonally at the corner to carry the joists to either side.

Jib door or **gib door.** A concealed door flush with the wall-surface painted or papered to correspond with the walls. The DADO and other mouldings are similarly carried across the door.

Joass, John James (1868–1952), *see* HOLDEN, Charles.

Joggle, Joggling. Masons' terms for joining two stones in such a way as to prevent them from slipping or sliding, by means of a notch in one and a corres-ponding projection in the other. It is often seen exposed on the face of a flat arch. If the joggle is concealed it is called a 'secret joggle'. *See* Fig. 57.

John of Ramsey, *see* WILLIAM OF RAMSEY.

FIG. 57. *Joggled joint*

Johnson, Philip Cortelyou (b. 1906), invented the term INTERNATIONAL STYLE (1932, with Henry-Russell Hitchcock), but his fame was first spread by the house he built for himself in New Canaan, Connecticut (1949) – very much in the style of MIES VAN DER ROHE – a cube with completely glazed walls all round. The siting is romantic, and perhaps in the years about 1950 one should already have been able to guess that Johnson would not remain faithful to Mies's principles. In the guest-house (1952) close to his own house vaults began to appear, inspired by SOANE, and the synagogue at Port Chester, New York (1956), made it clear that he would prefer variety, the unexpected effect, and elegance to the single-mindedness of Mies. Buildings of more recent years are the Amon Carter Museum at Fort Worth, Texas (1961), the Art Gallery for the University of Nebraska at Lincoln (1962), the New York State Theater for the Lincoln Center in New York (1962–4), the indianizing shrine at New Harmony, Indiana (1960), additions to the Boston Public Library (1964–73), Corpus Christi, Art Museum of South Texas (1970–72), Minnesota IDS Center, Minneapolis (1970–73), and Penzoil Place, Houston, Texas (1970–76). His AT&T Building, New York (1978–83), has been called the first 'major monument' of POST-MODERNISM. His *Writings*, edited by R. A. M. Stern, were published in 1979 (New York and Oxford).

N. Miller, *The Buildings and Projects of P.J.*, New York 1979.

Jointing. Finishing the surface of mortar joints in brickwork or masonry while the mortar is fresh, instead of raking it out and POINTING.

Joists. Horizontal parallel timbers laid between the walls or the beams of a building to carry the floorboards. The undersides are either exposed to the room below and then often moulded, or have ceiling laths nailed to them for a plaster ceiling.

Jonas, Walter (1910–79), *see* ENGLISH ARCHITECTURE.

Jones, Edward (b. 1939), *see* CANADIAN ARCHITECTURE.

Jones, Inigo (1573–1652), a genius far in advance of his time in England, imported the classical style from Italy to a still half-Gothic north and brought English Renaissance architecture to sudden maturity. He was the same age as Donne and Ben Jonson, and only nine years younger than Shakespeare. Born in London, the son of a Smithfield clothworker, he appears to have visited Italy before 1603, being then a 'picture-maker'. Not until 1608 is he heard of as an architect (design for the New Exchange, London); his earliest known buildings date from later still. Meantime he had become a prominent figure at Court as a stage-designer for masques in the most lavish and up-to-date Italian manner. Many of his designs survive, of fantastic Baroque costumes and hardly less fantastic architectural sets, executed in a free, spontaneous style of draughtsmanship he had presumably picked up in Italy. In 1613 he went to Italy again, this time for a year and seven months, with the great collector Lord Arundel. He returned with an unbounded admiration for PALLADIO and a first-hand knowledge of Roman monuments unique in England at that date. (He met SCAMOZZI in Venice.) At this period he is sometimes said to have worked at Heidelberg with Salomon de Caus (d. 1626), with whose nephew Isaac (*fl.* 1612–55) he was later connected in England (see below).

From 1615, when he became Surveyor of the King's Works, until the Civil War in 1642 he was continuously employed at the various royal palaces. Immediately he built three startlingly novel buildings which broke uncompromisingly with the Jacobean past: the Queen's House, Greenwich (1616–18 and 1629–35); the Prince's Lodging, Newmarket (1619–22, now destroyed); and the Banqueting House, Whitehall, London (1619–22). The Queen's House is the first strictly classical building in England, though there was a long break in its construction (the foundations were laid in 1616, but the elevations and interior date from 1632–5). The Prince's Lodging, modest in size, set the pattern for the red-brick, stone-quoined, hipped-roof house with dormers, so popular later in the century. The Banqueting House is Jones's masterpiece; it perfectly expresses his conception of architecture – 'sollid, proporsionable according to the rules, masculine and unaffected' – as also his adoration of Palladio. But though every detail is Palladian it is not a mere imitation. Everything has been subtly transmuted and the result is unmistakably English: solid, sturdy, and rather phlegmatic. The Queen's Chapel, St James's Palace, London (1623–5), was also something new for England – a classical church, consisting

of an aisleless parallelogram with a coffered segmental vault, a pedimented front, and a large Venetian window. Equally striking but more elaborate was the Bramantesque temple design he used for King James's hearse in 1625.

His principal buildings for Charles I have been destroyed, except for the Queen's House at Greenwich. This is an Italian villa sympathetically reinterpreted, whose chastity and bareness must have appeared daringly original. The upper-floor loggia is very Palladian, as is also the two-armed, curved open staircase to the terrace; but, as always with Jones, nothing is a direct copy. The proportions have been slightly altered and the general effect is long and low and very un-Italian. Inside, the hall is a perfect cube and symmetry prevails throughout. Also to the 1630s belong his great Corinthian portico at Old St Paul's, transforming the medieval cathedral into the most Roman structure in the country, and Covent Garden, the first London square, of which the church and a fragment of the square survive, the latter rebuilt. The square was conceived as one composition, the houses having uniform façades with arcaded ground floors and giant pilasters above (perhaps influenced by the Place des Vosges, Paris). In about 1638 he also produced elaborate designs for an enormous Royal Palace in Whitehall. These reveal his limitations and it is perhaps fortunate for his reputation that they were never executed.

The year 1642 brought his brilliant career at Court to an end. He was with the King at Beverley, but nothing more is heard of him until 1645. Although his property was sequestrated he was pardoned in 1646 and his estate restored. From then onwards he seems to have swum quite happily with the political tide, working for the Parliamentarian Lord Pembroke. The great garden front at Wilton House was for long thought to have been built by him at about this date, but is now known to have been designed c. 1636 by Isaac de Caus or Caux (fl. 1612–55), whom Jones is said to have recommended and also advised. It was badly damaged by fire c. 1647 and the famous state rooms therefore date from about 1649, by which time Jones was too old to give much personal attention; he put it in the hands of his pupil and nephew by marriage, John WEBB. He was responsible for the celebrated double-cube room, until recently thought to have been by Jones himself. Innumerable buildings have been attributed to Jones, of which a few may have had some connection with him, notably the pavilions at Stoke Bruerne Park (1629–35). Though profound, his immediate influence was confined to Court circles. In the early C18 he largely inspired the Palladian revival of BURLINGTON and KENT. In 1727 Kent published *The Designs of Inigo Jones*, but the designs are largely by Webb.

Colvin 1978; Summerson 1983; J. Summerson, *I.J.*, Harmondsworth (1966) 1983; J. Harris and G. Higgot, *I.J. Complete Architectural Drawings*, London 1989; Harris 1990.

Jourdain, Frantz (1847–1935). Architect of the famous department store La Samaritaine, Paris (1901–10), a masterpiece of ART NOUVEAU though unfortunately renovated in 1926–30 in the ART DECO style.

M. L. Clausen, *F.J. and the Samaritaine*, Paris 1987.

Juan de Álava (d. 1537), a Spanish master mason on the verge of Late Gothic and Early Renaissance, appears first as consultant at Salamanca Cathedral in 1512 (with eight others) and Seville Cathedral in 1513 (with three others), in the latter years as master to the newly restarted work at Plasencia Cathedral (first with Francisco de Colonia – see SIMÓN DE COLONIA – who soon quarrelled with him). Then we come across him as the designer of the cloister of Santiago Cathedral (1521 onwards) and finally as master mason to Salamanca Cathedral after the death of Juan GIL DE HONTAÑÓN in 1526. S. Esteban at Salamanca (1524 onwards) is also by him; this and the work at Plasencia round the crossing are perhaps his finest.

Kubler and Soria 1959.

Juan de Colonia (d. c. 1511), see SIMÓN DE COLONIA.

Jubé. The French name for ROOD SCREEN.

Jugendstil, see ART NOUVEAU.

Jumsai, Sumet (b. 1939), see THAI ARCHITECTURE.

Jussow, Heinrich Christoph (1754–1825). He was born in Kassel, was given a classical education and then studied law at Marburg and Göttingen before joining the Landgräflichen Baudepartment under Simon Louis DU RY in 1778. He later studied architecture in Paris under de WAILLY and visited Italy and England (1784–8). He completed du Ry's Schloss Wilhelmshöhe outside Kassel and built numerous ornamental buildings in the Roman, Chinese and Gothic tastes in the park. Among these is his masterpiece, the picturesque castle Löwenburg (1793–8), much influenced by the English

Gothic Revival and the most elaborate c18 essay in the genre anywhere on the Continent. Built on a dramatic hillside site and approached by drawbridge across a moat, it is amply provided with ramparts, towers and (originally) guards in medieval costumes.

H. Vogel, *H.C.J.*, exh. cat., Kassel 1958–9; H. Bien, *Die Löwenburg im Schlosspark Wilhelmshöhe*, Berlin 1965; Honour 1979.

Juvarra, Filippo (1678–1736), born in Messina of a family of silversmiths, is the greatest Italian c18 architect and a brilliant draughtsman. His elegant and sophisticated Late Baroque buildings are as typical of their period as Tiepolo's paintings and equally accomplished; they have a Mozartian gaiety and fecundity of decorative invention. Trained in Rome under FONTANA (1703/4–14), he first won fame as a stage-designer, and this theatrical experience was to leave a mark on nearly all his subsequent work.

In 1714 he was invited to Turin by Victor Amadeus II of Savoy, who appointed him 'First Architect to the King'. Apart from a trip to Portugal, London, and Paris, in 1719–20, he remained in Turin for the next twenty years. His output was enormous, ranging from churches, palaces, country villas, and hunting-lodges to the layout of entire new city quarters in Turin – not to mention work as an interior decorator and designer of furniture and the applied arts. Of his churches the Superga (1715–31) and the chapel of the Venaria Reale (1716–21), both near Turin, are spectacular, the former

being by far the grandest of all Italian Baroque sanctuaries, comparable with Melk in Austria and Einsiedeln in Switzerland. S. Filippo Neri (1715), S. Croce (1718 onwards), and the Carmine (1732–5, gutted during the war) in Turin are all very fine. His city palaces in Turin include Palazzo Birago della Valle (1716), Palazzo Richa di Covasolo (1730), and Palazzo d'Ormea (1730), while his work for the king is remarkable for the four great palaces and villas in or near Turin – Venaria Reale (1714–26), Palazzo Madama (1718–21), Castello di Rivoli (1718–21, but only partly executed), and his masterpiece Stupinigi (1729–33). In all these works he had the assistance of numerous highly skilled painters, sculptors, and craftsmen, who were summoned from all parts of Italy to execute his designs.

Though little development is discernible in his style, which is a brilliant epitome of current ideas rather than an original invention, it reached its fine flower in Stupinigi, especially in the great central hall, whose scenic quality and skeletal structure suggest an influence from north of the Alps. In 1735 Juvarra was summoned to Spain by Philip V, for whom he designed the garden façade of S. Ildefonso near Segovia and the new Royal Palace in Madrid, executed with alterations after his death by G. B. SACCHETTI. He died suddenly in Madrid in January 1736.

Pommer 1967; S. Boscarino, *J. architetto*, Rome 1973; Wittkower 1982; H. Millon, *F.J. Drawings from the Roman Period 1704–1714*, Rome 1984.

k

Kahn, Albert (1869–1942). German architect who emigrated to the USA 1880. From 1905 he worked in Detroit, where he pioneered methods of standardization and team design in his factories for the Ford Motor Company, General Motors and others. By the 1920s he was the leading industrial architect in the USA, e.g. the Rouge River Plant, Dearborn, Michigan (1917–39). He worked in Russia 1929–32.

G. Hildebrand, *Designing for Industry. The Architecture of A.K.*, Cambridge, Mass., 1974; W. H. Ferry, *The Legacy of A.K.*, Detriot 1987.

Kahn, Louis Isadore (1901–74). Born on the island of Osel, Estonia, he went to the USA in 1905. He studied at the University of Pennsylvania, and much later taught at Yale (1947–57) and at the University of Pennsylvania (from 1957 onwards). He was internationally noticed only fairly late in life, first with the Yale University Art Gallery (with D. Orr, 1951–3), then with the Richards Medical Research Building, Philadelphia (1958–60). The Art Gallery has for its main exhibition space a SPACE-FRAME ceiling. The Medical Research Building has all ducts gathered in a number of sheer, square towers projecting from and rising above the outer walls; the reason is

said to be functional, but the effect is curiously dramatic and indeed aggressive – an original version of BRUTALISM. However, Kahn's works have, with their elementary geometrical shapes and large unbroken surfaces, a majesty and severity all their own. His most significant later buildings include the first Unitarian Church at Rochester, NY (1962); the Eleanor Donnelly Erdman dormitory at Bryn Mawr College, Pennsylvania (1965); the Salk Institute Laboratories, La Jolla, California (1959–65); the Indian Institute of Management, Ahmedabad (1963); the Kimbell Art Museum, Fort Worth (1967–72); and the Paul Mellon Center for British Studies at Yale (1969–77). At Dacca (Bangladesh) he planned the National Assembly complex, of which the major buildings are impressive (1965–76). Among his pupils Romualdo Giurgola (b. 1920) is outstanding.

A. Tyng, *Beginnings: L.K.'s Philosophy of Architecture*, London 1984; H. Ronner *et al.*, *L.I.K. The Complete Works 1935–74*, Basel, Stuttgart and Boulder (1977) 1987; R. S. Wurman, *What Will Be Has Always Been. The Words of L.K.*, New York 1986; Klotz 1988.

Kampen, Jacon van, *see* CAMPEN, Jacob van.

FIG. 58. *Keel moulding*

Kampmann, Hack (1856–1920), *see* DANISH ARCHITECTURE.

Kamsetzer, Jan Baptist (1753–95), *see* POLISH ARCHITECTURE.

Kazakov, Matyey Fyodorovich (1738–1813). Russian neo-classical architect, he worked almost entirely in the Moscow area and (unusually) neither travelled abroad nor studied at the Petersburg Academy. From a poor family, he trained under Ukhtomsky. His opportunity came as one of the team replanning and rebuilding Tver (now Kalinin) after the fire of 1763; already Baroque elements were yielding to neo-classicism in his first independent work there. Cooperation with BAZHENOV in the Kremlin palace project (1767–74) contributed to his mature style, first fully manifest in the rich yet restrained Senate building in the Kremlin (1776, today housing the Council of Ministers of the USSR). His *œuvre* includes private houses (e.g. for the Demidov, Gubin, Razumovksy families), typically with the main porticoed façade set back between symmetrical projecting wings, public commissions (Golitsyn Hospital, 1796; Moscow 'Old' University, 1786, remodelled by Zhilyardi, 1817) and the rotunda church of St Philip (1777). His excursions into Gothic antiquarianism are less convincing than Bazhenov's (Petrovsky Palace, 1775; Palace at Tsarityno, 1786). His style tended to become plainer and more Palladian, though never puristically so; domes and their fenestration fascinated him from first to last and he created fine interiors (e.g. 'Hall of Columns' in the Nobleman's Club, 1784). He was the chief initiator of the notable tradition of Moscow neo-classical architecture culminating in D. I. Zhilyardi or Gigliardi (1788–1845). [R. Milner-Gulland]

Hamilton 1983.

Keel moulding. A curved moulding with a nib or arris so that in profile it resembles the keel of a ship – a pointed arch in section. *See* Fig. 58.

Keene, Henry (1726–76), *see* GOTHIC REVIVAL.

Keep. The principal tower of a castle, containing sufficient accommodation to serve as the chief living-quarters permanently or in times of siege; also called a *donjon*.

Keldermans, Rombout (*c.* 1460–1531), *see* BELGIAN ARCHITECTURE.

Kent, William (1685–1748), painter, furniture designer, and landscape gardener as well as architect, was born in Bridlington of humble parents. He contrived to study painting in Rome for ten years and was brought back to London in 1719 by Lord BURLINGTON, whose friend and protégé he remained for the rest of his life. Whimsical, impulsive, unintellectual, in fact almost illiterate, he was the opposite of his patron – and as happy designing a Gothic as a classical building. Nevertheless, he allowed Burlington to guide his hand along the correct PALLADIAN lines in all his major commissions. His interior decoration is more personal, being, like his furniture, richly carved and gilt in a sumptuous manner deriving partly from Italian Baroque furniture and partly from Inigo JONES, whose designs he published in 1727 (though they are mostly by WEBB).

He did not turn architect until after 1730, by which time he was well into his forties. His masterpiece Holkham Hall (1734 onwards, executed by BRETTINGHAM) was designed partly by Burlington, whose hand is evident in the 'staccato' quality of the exterior and in such typical and self-isolating features as the VENETIAN WINDOW within a relieving arch. The marble apsidal entrance hall, based on a combination of a Roman basilica and the Egyptian Hall of VITRUVIUS, with its columns, coffered ceiling, and imposing staircase leading up to the *piano nobile*, is one of the most impressive rooms in England. His lavishly gilt and damask-hung state apartments, elaborately carved and pedimented doorframes, heavy cornices, and niches for antique marbles epitomize the English admiration for Roman magnificence. The Treasury (1733–7), 22 Arlington Street (1741), and 44 Berkeley Square (1742–4), all in London, are notable mainly for their interior decoration, especially the latter, which contains the most ingenious and spatially exciting staircase in London. Esher Place, Surrey, was the best of his neo-Gothic works (wings, now demolished, and other alterations, *c.* 1730). His last building, the Horse Guards, London (1750–59), is a repetition of Holkham, with the unfortunate addition of a clock-tower over the centre: it was executed after his death by John VARDY. Through Burlington's influence Kent was appointed Master Carpenter to the Board of Works in 1726, and Master Mason and Deputy Surveyor in 1735. He is perhaps more important historically as a designer of

gardens than as an architect. He created the English landscape garden, being the first to have 'leap'd the fence and seen that all nature is a garden'. This revolutionized the relation of house to landscape and led to less dramatic and forceful façades. From his time onwards the country house was designed to harmonize with the landscape, rather than to dominate and control it.

Colvin 1978; Summerson 1983; M. J. Wilson, *W.K. Architect, Designer, Painter, Gardener 1685–1748*, London 1984; J. Dixon Hunt, *W.K. Landscape Garden Designer*, London 1987.

Kentish rag. Hard unstratified limestone found in Kent and much used as an external building stone on account of its weather-resisting properties.

Key, Lieven de (*c.* 1560–1627), the first Dutch architect of note to work in the so-called 'Dutch Renaissance' style (similar to English Jacobean). He worked for some years in England before becoming municipal architect of Haarlem (1593), where he introduced the characteristic colourful use of brick with stone dressings (horizontal bands of stone, stone voussoirs set singly in brick above windows, etc.). His masterpieces are the façade of the Leiden Town Hall (1593–7), the Weigh House, Haarlem (1598), the Meat Market, Haarlem (1602–3), and the tower of the Nieuwekerk, Haarlem (1613).

Rosenberg 1977.

Key pattern, *see* FRET.

Keyser, Hendrick de (1565–1621), the leading architect of his day in Amsterdam, where he was appointed city mason and sculptor in 1595, worked in a style somewhat similar to English Jacobean. His plain utilitarian churches had great influence on Protestant church design in the Netherlands and Germany, especially his last, the Westerkerk in Amsterdam, built on a Greek cross plan (1620). His most important secular buidlings are the Amsterdam Exchange (1608) and Delft Town Hall (1618). In domestic architecture he simplified and classicized the traditional tall, gable-fronted Amsterdam house, introducing the ORDERS and reducing the number of steps in the gables. His works were engraved and published by Salomon de Bray as *Architectura moderna* (1631).

Rosenberg 1977.

Keystone. The central stone of an arch or a rib vault; sometimes carved. *See* Fig. 4.

Khmer architecture. The architectural style of the Khmer state which was founded in northern Cambodia with its capital at Angkor in the c9, expanded into present-day Vietnam, Laos and Thailand in the c11, but retracted in the c13. All the surviving buildings are religious (Hindu or Buddhist) and dedicated to a succession of god-kings, durable materials being reserved for this purpose, while all other buildings, including palaces, were of wood and have perished. Temples were built of stone, brick and LATERITE, without mortar but held together by iron clamps. As the only means of roofing was by corbelled vaults, interior spaces are of limited width. This is essentially an architecture of mass embellished with a jungly luxuriance of relief carving in a distinctive style often of the greatest refinement. Hinduism was introduced from India, but Indian prototypes had more influence on the ideas expressed than the means of expression. Angkor Wat, probably the largest temple in the world, covers an area of 20,000 sq. ft and was built for King Suryavarman II (1112–52), a self-styled avatar of Vishnu. It was conceived, like many Indian temples, as a symbolic representation of Mount Meru, on which the world rests; but it has a logical coherence never found in India – a plan of cosmic significance consisting of crosses in rectangles, a central stepped pyramid crowned by a spire repeated in diminishing scale at the corners of the platform and (originally) on those of the galleried wall surrounding the square enclosure within a moat. Indian tendencies towards multiplication of single elements were stretched as far as they would go. Another less vast temple at Angkor, the Bayon, was built on a more complex but similarly regular plan for a later king, Jayavarman VII (1181–1219), who was a Buddhist. His face, carved on a gigantic scale with the attributes of a Bodhisattva, stares out to the four points of the compass from each of its numerous spires. There are fine though relatively small Khmer-style temples elsewhere in Cambodia, notably Banteay Chmar (c11) and also in Thailand at Phanom Rung (c10–12) and Khao Phra Vjharn (c11), both on hill-top sites, and Muang Tam (late c10) and Phimai (late c11).

Kiesler, Frederick John (1890–1965). Austrian-born American architect, he built the Shrine of the Book, Jerusalem (1959–65, with A. Bartos), and published *Inside the Endless House* (New York 1966).

F.K., exh. cat., Bochum and Vienna 1975.

Kikutake, Kinonori (b. 1928). Leading member of the Japanese METABOLISM movement, e.g. his Marine Cities (eventually partly realized in the Aquapolis, Okinawa, 1975). His Sky House, Tokyo (1959), and the Miyakonoyo Civic Hall (1966) are notable. He wrote *Concepts and Planning* (Tokyo 1978).

King-post, *see* ROOF.

Kiosk. A light open pavilion or summerhouse, usually supported by pillars and common in Turkey and Persia. European adaptations are used mainly in gardens, as band-stands, for example, or for small shops selling newspapers.

Kleihues, Josef Paul (b. 1933), *see* GERMAN ARCHITECTURE; NEO-RATIONALISM.

Klenze, Leo von (1784–1864), a north German, was a pupil of GILLY in Berlin, and then of DURAND and PERCIER and FONTAINE in Paris. He was architect to King Jérome at Kassel in 1804–13, and to King Ludwig I in Munich from 1816. Klenze was at heart a Grecian, but he was called upon to work in other styles as well, and did so resourcefully. His chief Grecian buildings are the Glyptothek, or Sculpture Gallery (1816–34) – the earliest of all special public museum buildings – and the Propylaea, both in Munich. The Propylaea was begun in 1846, a late date for so purely Grecian a design. Grecian also, strangely enough, is that commemorative temple of German worthies, the Walhalla near Regensburg (designed 1816–21, built 1830–42), a Doric peripteral temple. Grecian,

too, is his addition to the Hermitage Museum, Leningrad (1839–49). But as early as 1816 Klenze did a neo-Renaissance palace (Palais Leuchtenberg), the earliest in Germany, even if anticipated in France. This was followed by the Königsbau of the Royal Palace, Munich (1826) – which has affinities with the Palazzo Pitti – and the freer, more dramatic Festsaalbau of the same palace (1832). In addition, Klenze's Allerheiligen church, again belonging to the palace (1827), is – at the king's request – neo-Byzantine. *See also* GÄRTNER.

Honour 1979; O. Hederer, *L. von K. Personlichkeit und Werk*, Munich (1964) 1981; Watkin and Mellinghoff 1987.

Klerk, Michel de (1884–1923). Leading member of the Amsterdam School who realized their EXPRESSIONIST aims on an urban scale – largely for working-class housing in Amsterdam, e.g. the eccentric Spaarndammerburt housing (1913–19) and the more sober Amstellan housing (1920–22).

S. S. Frank, *M. de K. 1884–1923. An Architect of the Amsterdam School*, Ann Arbor 1984.

Klint, Peder Vilhelm Jensen (1853–1930), is famous chiefly for his Grundtvig church at Copenhagen, won in competition in 1913 but, after further development of the design, built 1919–26. With its steeply gabled brick façade, all of a stepped organ-pipe design, and with its interior, Gothic in feeling, it stands mid-way between the HISTORICISM of the C19 and the EXPRESSIONISM of 1920, a parallel in certain ways to BERLAGE's earlier Exchange. The surrounding buildings, forming one composition with the church, are of 1924–6. Klint's son

Kaare (1888–1954) was one of the most distinguished of modern Danish furniture designers.

Hitchcock 1977.

Knapped flint. Flint split in two and laid so that the smooth black surfaces of the split sides form the facing of a wall; found especially in East Anglia. *See also* FLUSHWORK.

Kneeler. The block of stone set at the top of a brick or stone wall to finish the eaves of a parapet or coping; also called a pad-stone, kneestone, or skew.

Knight, Richard Payne (1750–1824), country gentleman and landscape gardening theorist, began in 1772 to build Downton Castle for himself: rough, irregular (the plan is anti-symmetrical rather than asymmetrical), and boldly medieval outside, smooth, elegant, and distinctly neo-classical within, it is the prototype of the picturesque country house 'castle' which was to remain popular for half a century. In 1794 he published *The Landscape – a Didactic Poem* attacking 'Capability' BROWN's smooth and artificial style of landscape gardening. It was dedicated to Uvedale PRICE, who published a lengthy reply differing on points of detail. Knight's much longer *Analytical Enquiry into the Principles of Taste* (1805) examines the PICTURESQUE philosophically.

Summerson 1983.

Knobelsdorff, Georg Wenzeslaus von (1699–1753). Court architect to Frederick the Great, with whom he was on terms of close friendship and whose sophisticated, eclectic tastes he faithfully mirrored although they quarrelled over the designs for Sanssouci. He was a Prussian aristocrat and began his career in the army, but in 1729 resigned his Captain's commission to train as a painter. By 1733 he was already on friendly terms with Frederick (then Crown Prince), for whom he built a little circular temple of Apollo in his garden in the garrison town of Neu-Ruppin. Frederick then enabled him to visit Italy and after his return commissioned him to enlarge the old border house of Rheinsberg (1737). Immediately after Frederick's accession to the throne in 1740 Knobelsdorff was sent off to Dresden and Paris to prepare himself for more ambitious projects. He added a wing to Monbijou for the Queen Mother (1740–42) and a wing to Charlottenburg for the king (1742–6) with a very grand, rich, colourful interior plastered with Rococo motifs (partly destroyed in the Second World War). In 1741 he began the Berlin opera house with a less exuberant interior and a severely Palladian exterior which owes much to English neo-Palladian models (burnt out 1843, renewed by K. F. Langhans; seriously damaged 1945 but now restored). While this was going forward he was appointed Surveyor General of Royal Palaces and Parks, Director in Chief of all buildings in the royal provinces, and a member of the Prussian Council of Ministers. In 1744 work began on the large Stadtschloss at Potsdam, colourful outside and in, and with one of the richest of all Rococo interiors (destroyed). He began Sanssouci, Potsdam, in 1745 in close collaboration with the king, who provided the general design. (Frederick's original sketch survives.) In 1746 he quarrelled with the king, who dismissed him and thus ended his architectural career, though he made posthumous amends by writing the 'Éloge de Knobelsdorff' which was read at the Berlin Academy in 1753. (His sketch design for a palace for Prince Heinrich in Unter den Linden, Berlin, was built by J. Boumann, 1748–66. It is now the Humboldt University.)

Hempel 1965; H. J. Kaddatz, *G.W. von K.*, Leipzig and Munich 1983.

Knöffel, Johann Christoph (1686–1752). He was a contemporary in Dresden of CHIAVERI and LONGUELUNE and was much influenced by the French classicism of the latter. His Wackerbarth Palais, Dresden (1723–8, destroyed 1945), and Kurlander Palais, Dresden (1728–9, destroyed 1945), were elegant examples of restrained pilastered town architecture. In 1734 he became Oberlandbaumeister in Dresden and in 1737 began his masterpiece, the Brihl Palais (destroyed 1899). He rebuilt the large hunting-lodge, Hubertusberg, between 1743 and 1751 and completed his rival Chiaveri's Hofkirche in Dresden after Chiaveri returned to Rome in 1748.

Hempel 1965; W. Hentschel and A. May, *J.C.K.*, Berlin 1973.

Knotted columns. A stone support carved in the form of two or four columns with their shafts tied into a knot, occasionally found in Romanesque architecture.

Koch, Gaetano (1849–1910), *see* ITALIAN ARCHITECTURE.

Kondo. The main hall of a Japanese Buddhist monastery.

Koolhaas, Rem (b. 1944), *see* DUTCH ARCHITECTURE.

Korb, Hermann (1656–1735). He began as a carpenter and was promoted architect by Duke Anton-Ulrich of Brunswick-Wolfenbüttel. He visited Italy in 1691, then supervised the construction of the Schloss at Salzdahlum designed by Johann Balthasar Lauterbach (1660–94) – a vast building with features anticipating DIENTZENHOFER's Pommersfelden and HILDEBRANDT's Upper Belvedere, but of mainly timber construction faced to simulate stone (demolished 1813). Also of wood was the interesting library he erected at Wolfenbüttel (1706–10). It was centrally planned (on the advice of Leibniz) with an oval interior lit by windows in the dome. His only surviving building of note is the church of the Holy Trinity, Wolfenbüttel (1705), with two tiers of galleries creating an octagonal central space.

Hempel 1965; G. Gerkens, *Das fürstliche Lustschloss Salzdahlum und sein Erbauer Herzog Anton Ulrich von Braunschweig-Wolfenbüttel*, Brunswick 1974.

Korsmo, Arne (1900–1986), *see* NORWEGIAN ARCHITECTURE.

Koteřa, Jan (1871–1923), *see* CZECHOSLOVAK ARCHITECTURE.

Krebs, Konrad (1491–1540), *see* GERMAN ARCHITECTURE.

Krejcar, Joromír (1895–1949), *see* CZECHOSLOVAK ARCHITECTURE.

Kremlin. A citadel or fortified enclosure within a Russian town, notably that in Moscow.

Krier, Leon (b.1946). Luxembourg architect, he worked for STIRLING 1968–70 and settled in London, where his anti-modern crusade to revitalize both vernacular and classicizing architecture was influential, but his only buildings to date have been small and somewhat 'folksy', of traditional wood construction at 'Seaside' in Florida, USA (1987). In 1989 he was chosen by the Prince of Wales to plan the Duchy of Cornwall's Poundbury development in Dorchester.

Krier, Rob (b. 1938). Luxembourg architect, trained in Germany and working since 1975 in Vienna. He is as anti-modern as his brother Leon, but a number of his projects have been realized, notably in Berlin (Rauchstrasse, 1982–4, and Ritterstrasse, begun 1982 and incorporating a reconstruction of SCHINKEL's Feilnerhaus of 1828–9). He has published *Rational Architecture* (London 1978) and *Architectural Composition* (London 1988).

Kroll, Lucien (b. 1927), *see* BELGIAN ARCHITECTURE.

Krubsacius, Friedrich August (1718–89). Architect and architectural theorist, author of *Betrachtungen über den wahren Geschmack der Alten in der Baukunst* (Dresden, 1747) attacking the Baroque style and reverting to the humanist idea that 'the noblest structure, man, the perfect proportions and graceful symmetry of his figure, were the first standards for architectural invention'. Though indebted to French theorists, he thought little of French architecture. He became royal architect and in 1764 professor of architecture at the new Academy of Arts in Dresden. But in his buildings he remained faithful to the Baroque. The most notable were the Neues Schloss at Neuwitz (1766–75; destroyed) and the Landhaus in Dresden (1770–76; burnt out 1944).

M. A. von Luttichau, *Die deutsche Ornamentkritik im 18 Jahrhundert*, Hildesheim 1983.

Krumpper, Hans (*c.* 1570–1635), *see* GERMAN ARCHITECTURE.

Kurokawa, Kisho Noriaki (b. 1934). Japanese architect, prominent in the METABOLISM movement of which his Takara Beautillion at the Osaka 1970 exhibition was exemplary. His Nagakin Capsule Tower, Tokyo (1972), and Sony Tower, Osaka (1979), are notable.

P. Drew, *The World of K.K.*, Tokyo 1975; F. Chaslin, *K.K.*, Tokyo 1988.

1

La Vallée, Simon de (d. 1642), son of an architect, settled in Sweden in 1637, becoming royal architect in 1639. He designed the Riddarhus in Stockholm (1641–2), derived from de BROSSE's Palais Luxembourg in Paris. He was succeeded as royal architect by his son Jean (1620–96), who travelled and studied in France, Italy, and Holland between 1646 and 1649. He completed his father's Riddarhus (with Justus VINGBOONS, who designed the façades), built the Oxenstjerna Palace, Stockholm (c. 1650–54), which introduced the Roman *palazzo* style, and designed the Katherinenkirka, Stockholm (1656), on a centralized plan probably derived from de KEYSER, as well as various palaces in Stockholm (e.g. for Field-Marshal Wrangel) and country houses (Castle Skokloster).

Paulsson 1958; T. O. Nordberg, *De la V. Ein Architektfamilij Frankrike Holland ech Sverige*, Stockholm 1970.

Label, *see* HOOD-MOULD.

Label-stop or **head stop.** An ornamental or figural BOSS at the beginning and end of a HOOD-MOULD.

Labrouste, Pierre-François-Henri (1801–75), won the Grand Prix in 1824, and was in Rome 1824–30. After his return he opened a teaching *atelier* which became the centre of rationalist teaching in France. His rationalism appears at its most courageous in the interior of his only famous work, the Library of Ste Geneviève by the Panthéon in Paris (1838–50). Here iron is shown frankly in columns and vault, and endowed with all the slenderness of which, in contrast to stone, it is capable. Labrouste's is the first monumental public building in which iron is thus accepted. The façade is in a nobly restrained Cinquecento style with large, even, round-arched windows, and there again, in comparison with the debased Italianate or the neo-Baroque of BEAUX ARTS type, which just then was becoming current, Labrouste is on the side of reason. The London architect James Bunstone Bunning (1802–63), in his Coal Exchange of 1846–9, since demolished, was as bold in his use of iron, but as an architect was lacking in the taste and discipline of Labrouste. Between 1854 and 1875 Labrouste also built the reading-room and the stack-rooms of the Bibliothèque Nationale, again proudly displaying his iron structure.

Hitchcock 1977; P. Saddy, *H.L. architecte 1801–75*, Paris 1978; Van Zanten 1987.

Laced windows. Windows pulled visually together vertically by strips, usually in brick of a different colour

FIG. 59. *Lancet window*

from that of the wall, which continue vertically the lines of the window surrounds. It was a popular motif *c.* 1720 in England.

Lacing course, *see* COURSE.

Lacunar. A panelled or coffered ceiling: also the sunken panels or COFFERING in such a ceiling.

Lady chapel. A chapel dedicated to the Virgin, usually built east of the CHANCEL and forming a projection from the main building; in England it is normally rectangular in plan.

Lafever, Minard (1798–1854), *see* UNITED STATES ARCHITECTURE.

Lajta, Béle (1875–1920), *see* HUNGARIAN ARCHITECTURE.

Lancet arch, *see* ARCH.

Lancet window. A slender pointed-arched window, much used in the early C13. *See* Fig. 59.

Langhans, Carl Gotthard (1732–1808). German neo-classical architect famous for the Brandenburg Gate in Berlin (1788–91), his one important work and the first of the Doric ceremonial gateways that were to be built all over Europe in the early C19. The Brandenburg Gate is still C18 in its elegant and rather un-Grecian proportions. His later buildings were more ponderous and cubic, e.g. the Potsdam Theatre (1795) and the theatre in Gdańsk (Danzig) (1798–1801). He also did the theatre at Charlottenburg Schloss in Berlin (1788–91). His son Carl Ferdinand Langhans (1782–1869) worked under SCHINKEL in the 1830s but continued his father's style in the palace of Kaiser Wilhelm I in Berlin (1836, burnt out 1945 but now restored externally), the old Russian Embassy in Berlin (1840–41) and the theatre at Wroclaw (Breslau) (1843).

T. W. Hinrichs, *C.G.L. ein schlesischer Baumeister 1732–1808*, Neudeln (1909) 1981; Watkin and Mellinghoff 1987.

Langley, Batty (1696–1751), the son of a Twickenham gardener, published some twenty architectural books, mostly manuals for the use of country builders and artisans, e.g. *A Sure Guide to Builders* (1729); *The Builder's Compleat Chest-Book* (1738). But his fame rests on his *Ancient Architecture Restored and Improved* (1741) in which he formalized KENT's neo-Gothic into 'orders'. He built little, and none of his works survives.

Colvin 1978; Harris 1990.

Lantern. A small circular or polygonal turret with windows all round, crowning a roof or dome. *See* Fig. 40.

Lantern cross. A churchyard cross with lantern-shaped top; usually with sculptured representations on the sides of the top.

Lantern tower. A tall lantern, often over the crossing of a church, e.g. Bell Harry Tower, Canterbury Cathedral.

Lasdun, Denys Louis (b. 1914). Leading English post-Second World War architect, began with Wells COATES 1935–7 and from 1938 to 1948 with TECTON. His principal buildings are the Royal College of Physicians, Regent's Park (1961–4), and the National Theatre (1967–76), both in London. He published *Architecture in the Age of Scepticism* (London 1984). He was knighted in 1977.

W. J. R. Curtis, *A Language and a Theme: the Work of D.L. and Partners*, London 1976.

Lassurance, Pierre Cailleteau, known as (1650–1724), *see* HARDOUIN-MANSART, Jules.

Lassus, Jean-Baptiste-Antoine (1807–57), *see* VIOLLET-LE-DUC, Eugène-Emanuel.

Laterite. A ferruginous substance found only in tropical regions which have heavy rainfall and great heat. When freshly excavated it may be cut with an axe, but it quickly becomes iron-hard when exposed to air. Blocks ground to fit against one another without need for mortar were extensively used as a building material in Cambodia and Thailand. As the surface cannot be carved in relief it was clad with sandstone (in KHMER ARCHITECTURE) or plastered with stucco.

R. L. Pendleton in the *Geographical Review* XXXI (1941), pp. 177–202.

Latin cross. A cross with three short arms and a long arm.

Latrobe, Benjamin Henry (1764–1820), the son of a Moravian minister in England, spent his boyhood and youth in England, in Germany, and again in England, where he worked under S. P. COCKERELL as an architect, and under Smeaton as an engineer. He must have been much impressed by SOANE's work. In 1795 he emigrated to America, where he was taken up by JEFFERSON and did the exterior of the Capitol at Richmond, Virginia. In 1798 he moved to Philadelphia, and there built the Bank of Pennsylvania (1799–1801) and in 1800 the Water Works (the latter largely an engineering job). The architecture of these two buildings was resolutely Grecian – the first examples of the GREEK REVIVAL in America – the former Greek Doric, and the latter Ionic. Of the same year 1799 is Sedgeley, the earliest GOTHIC-REVIVAL house in America. In 1803 Latrobe was called in at the Capitol in Washington, and there did some of his noblest interiors, with much vaulting in stone. The work dated from 1803–11, but the majority had to be redone after the fire of 1814, so what one now sees is mostly of Latrobe's maturity. But his most perfect work is probably Baltimore Cathedral (1804–18). Its interior in particular, on an elongated central plan, with the shallow central dome and the segmented tunnel vaults, is as fine as that of any church in the neo-classical style anywhere. Latrobe had at the beginning submitted designs in Gothic as well as classical forms, the Gothic being the earliest Gothic church design in America. Among his other buildings were the Baltimore Exchange (1816–20, destroyed 1904), the 'Old West' of Dickenson College, Carlisle, Pennsylvania (after 1811), and the Louisiana State Bank, New Orleans (begun 1819). Latrobe was the first fully trained architect in the United States. Yet his engineering training made it possible for him, throughout his career, to work as well on river navigation, docks, etc. – a combination which was to become typical of American C19 architects. His pupils included MILLS, STRICKLAND and William Small.

Hitchcock 1977; Whiffen and Koeper 1981.

Lattice window. A window with diamond-shaped LEADED LIGHTS or with glazing bars arranged like an open-work screen: also, loosely, any hinged window, as distinct from a SASH WINDOW.

Laugier, Marc-Antoine (1713–69), was a Jesuit priest and outstanding neo-classical theorist. His *Essai sur l'architecture* (1753) expounds a rationalist view of classical architecture as a truthful, economic expression of man's need for shelter, based on the hypothetical 'rustic cabin' of primitive man. His ideal building would have free-standing columns. He condemned pilasters and pedestals and all Renaissance and post-Renaissance elements. His book put NEO-CLASSICISM in a nutshell and had great influence, e.g. on SOUF-FLOT.

Herrmann 1962; Braham 1980; Rykwert 1980.

Laurana, Luciano (c. 1420–79), was born in Dalmatia, and appeared in Urbino c. 1466 at the humanist court of Federigo da Montefeltro, which included Piero della Francesca and, later on, FRANCESCO DI GIORGIO. He was appointed architect of the Palazzo Ducale, Urbino (1468–72), for which he designed numerous chimney-pieces, door-cases, etc., of extreme refinement and elegance, anticipating and surpassing the C18 in delicacy. His masterpiece is the Florentine-style *cortile* in the Palazzo Ducale, with a light springy arcade of Corinthian columns echoed by shallow pilasters between the windows on the upper storey.

Heydenreich and Lotz 1974.

Laves, Georg Ludwig Friedrich (1788–1864), was a nephew of H. C. JUSSOW, under whom he trained in Kassel. After travelling in Italy, France, and England he settled in Hanover in 1814. During the next fifty years Hanover was to be transformed by his romantic GREEK REVIVAL style almost as impressively as were Berlin and Munich by his great contemporaries SCHINKEL and KLENZE. The Leineschloss, later the Landtag (begun 1817), Wangenheim Palace (begun 1827) and the more Italianate Opera (1848–52) are his masterpieces, together with the layout of the Waterlooplatz (1855) and other new squares and streets. Laves was also an inventive and remarkably forward-looking engineer and submitted a startling design for the 1851 Exhibition Hall in London to be constructed largely of iron railway-track. It was an early attempt at prefabrication.

G. Hoeltje, *G.L.F.L.*, Hanover 1964; Watkin and Mellinghoff 1987.

Le Blond, Jean-Baptiste Alexandre (1679–1719), a minor Parisian architect credited with the introduction of the French Rococo style into Russia. Very little of his work survives. He began the vast Peterhof Palace, St Petersburg (1716, later enlarged by RASTRELLI).

Hamilton 1983.

Le Breton, Gilles (d. 1553). Master mason who carried out Francis I's enlargements at the Château de Fontainebleau and presumably designed them. His only surviving works are the Porte Dorée (1528–40), the north side of the

Le Corbusier

Cour du Cheval Blanc, and the now greatly mutilated portico and staircase in the Cour de l'Ovale (begun 1531). The buildings around the forecourt at Fleury-en-Bière, near Fontainebleau, have been attributed to him. Le Breton's simple and austere classicism, in his later works, derived from SERLIO and was to have some influence on the next generation of French architects, notably LESCOT.

Blunt 1982.

Le Corbusier, Charles-Édouard (Jeanneret) (1887–1966). Le Corbusier was born at La Chaux-de-Fonds in French Switzerland. He worked in PERRET's office in Paris in 1908–9, then for a short time in that of BEHRENS in Berlin. Le Corbusier was the most influential and most brilliant of C20 architects, of a fertility of formal invention to be compared only with Picasso's. But he was also restless and an embarrassingly superb salesman of his own ideas. It is no doubt relevant to an understanding of his mind and his work that he was an abstract or semi-abstract painter, comparable in some ways to Léger.

In Le Corbusier's early work three strains can be followed, continually interacting. One is the mass-production of housing (Dom-ino, 1914–15; Citrohan House, 1921; the abortive housing estate of Pessac, 1925). The second is town planning. Le Corbusier published and publicized a number of total plans for cities with a centre of identical skyscrapers, symmetrically arranged in a park setting, with lower building and complex traffic routes between. They are less realistic than GARNIER's Cité Industrielle of 1901, but far more dazzling (Ville Contemporaine, 1922; Plan Voisin, 1925; Ville Radieuse, 1935;

plan for Algiers, 1930). The third strain of Le Corbusier's early thought tends towards a new type of private house, white, cubist, wholly or partly on PILOTIS, with rooms flowing into each other. The earliest is the villa at Vaucresson (1922). Many followed, including the exhibition pavilion of the Esprit Nouveau at the Paris Exhibition of 1925, with a tree growing through the building. The most stimulating and influential villas were probably those at Garches (1927) and Poissy (1929–31). In the same years Le Corbusier did some designs for major buildings: for the League of Nations at Geneva (1927; not executed) and the Centrosojus in Moscow (1928). The designs had a great effect on progressive architects everywhere. Of the major buildings actually erected two must be referred to: the Salvation Army Hostel in Paris (begun 1929) with its long CURTAIN WALL; and the Swiss House in the Paris Cité Universitaire (1930–32), introducing a random-rubble baffle wall to contrast with the usual white-rendered concrete. In 1936 Le Corbusier was called to Rio de Janeiro to advise on the new building of the Ministry of Education which was subsequently executed by COSTA, NIEMEYER, Reidy (1909–64), and others. Their contribution has never been fully distinguished from his. In 1947 Le Corbusier was one of the group of architects to come to terms with the programme of the United Nations Headquarters in New York, and the Secretariat building, a sheer glass slab with solid, windowless end walls, is essentially his design.

At the same time, however, Le Corbusier began to abandon this rational smooth glass and metal style which until then he had been instrumental in propagating, and turned to a new anti-rational, violently sculptural, aggressive style which was soon to be just as influential. The first example is the Unité d'Habitation at Marseille (1947–52), with its heavy exposed concrete members and its fantastic roofscape. The proportions are worked out to a complicated system, called MODULOR, which Le Corbusier invented and pleaded for. The Unité was followed by another at Nantes (1953–5) and a third at Berlin (for the Interbau Exhibition, 1956–8). Le Corbusier's most revolutionary work in his anti-rational style is the pilgrimage chapel of Ronchamp not far from Belfort (1950–54), eminently expressive, with its silo-like white tower, its brown concrete roof like the top of a mushroom, and its wall pierced by small windows of arbitrary shapes in arbitrary positions. In his villas the new style is represented by the Jaoul Houses (1954–6), whose shallow concrete tunnel vaults soon became an international cliché. Of yet later buildings the Philips Pavilion at the Brussels Exhibition of 1958 had a HYPERBOLIC PARABOLOID ROOF, a form pioneered at Raleigh, North Carolina (1948–53). At Chandigarh Le Corbusier laid out the town and built the extremely powerful Law Courts and Secretariat (1951–6), the influence of which proved to be strongest in Japan. At the same time he did some houses at Ahmedabad (1954–6) which, like the buildings of Chandigarh, are of excessively heavy, chunky concrete members. In 1957 Le Corbusier designed the Museum of Modern Art for Tokyo and the Dominican Friary of La Tourette (1957–60), a ruthlessly hard block of immense force. His last important building was the Carpenter Art Centre at Harvard.

F. Chouay, *L.C.*, New York 1960; W. Boesiger (ed.), *L.C. Œuvres complètes*, Zurich (1935–65) 1970; C. Jencks, *L.C. and the Tragic View of Architecture*, London 1973; F. de Frandieu (ed.), *L.C. Sketchbooks*, London 1981–2; H. A. Brooks, *The L.C. Archive*, New York 1982.

Le Muet, Pierre (1591–1669), a *retardataire* MANNERIST, published *Manière de bien bastir pour toutes sortes de personnes* (1623), an up-to-date version of DU CERCEAU's first book of architecture, containing designs suitable for different income groups but going farther down the social scale. His best surviving buildings are the Hôtels Comans d'Astry (1647), de l'Aigle and Davaux in Paris. The Hôtel Duret de Chevry (1635, now part of the Bibliothèque Nationale) was for long attributed to him but is now known to be by Jean Thiriot. His later buildings, e.g. Hôtel Tubeuf, Paris (1650), are more classical but never entirely free of Mannerist traits.

Blunt 1982.

Le Nôtre, André (1613–1700), the greatest designer of formal gardens and parks, was the son of a royal gardener. He studied painting and architecture as well as garden design, and was appointed Contrôleur Général des Bâtiments du Roi in 1657. The enormous park at Versailles (1662–90), with its vast *parterres*, fountains, sheets of water, and radiating avenues, is his masterpiece. It extends the symmetry of LE VAU's architecture to the surrounding landscape and provides a perfect setting for the building. He began at Vaux-le-Vicomte (1656–61) and later worked at St Cloud, Fontainebleau, Clagny, Marly, and elsewhere, mostly for Louis XIV.

H. M. Fox, *A.L.N.*, London 1962; E. De Ganay, *A.L.N.*, Paris 1962; F. Hamilton Hazlehurst, *Gardens of Illusion. The Genius of A.L.N.*, Nashville 1980.

Le Pautre, Antoine (1621–81), designed the Hôtel de Beauvais in Paris (1652–5), the most ingenious of all Parisian *hôtel* plans considering the awkward site. But he is best known for the engraved designs in his *Œuvres* (first published 1652 as *Desseins de plusieurs palais*) of vast and fantastic town and country houses, which far exceed his contemporary LE VAU in Baroque extravagance. His influence is evident in the work of WREN and SCHLÜTER.

R. W. Berger, *A.L.P. – a French Architect of the Era of Louis XIV*, New York 1969; Blunt 1982.

Le Pautre, Pierre (*c.* 1643–1716), nephew of Antoine, was the leading decorator at Versailles under Jules HARDOUIN-MANSART and as influential as de COTTE in the evolution of the Rococo style, e.g. his Salon de L'Œil de Bœuf (1701) and chapel (1709–10), Versailles, and the choir of Notre Dame, Paris (1711–12).

Kalnein and Levey 1972.

Le Vau, Louis (1612–70), the leading Baroque architect in France, was less intellectual and refined than his great contemporary MANSART. He was also less difficult in character and headed a brilliant team of painters, sculptors, decorators, gardeners, with whom he created the Louis XIV style at Versailles. He was a great *metteur-en-scène* and could produce striking general effects with a typically Baroque combination of all the arts. Born in Paris, the son of a master mason by whom he was trained, he first revealed his outstanding gifts in the Hôtel Lambert, Paris (1642–4), where he made ingenious use of an awkward site and created the first of his highly coloured, grandiloquent interiors: the staircase and gallery are especially magnificent. In 1656 he began the Hôtel de Fontenay, Paris, and in 1657 he was commissioned by Fouquet, the millionaire finance minister, to design his country house at Vaux-le-Vicomte. This is his masterpiece and by far the most splendid of all French *châteaux*. Here grandeur and elegance are combined in a manner peculiarly French, and no expense was spared. The *château* was built in about a year and the luxurious interior, decorated by Lebrun, Guérin, and others, and the gardens laid out by LE NÔTRE were finished by 1661. In the same year Fouquet was arrested for embezzlement, whereupon his rival Colbert took over his architect and artists to work for the king. Le Vau was commissioned to rebuild the Galerie d'Apollon in the Louvre (1661–2), decorated by Lebrun (1663). In 1667 he was involved (with PERRAULT) in the design of the great east front of the Louvre in Paris. Work began on the remodelling of Versailles in 1669. Le Vau rose to the occasion, and his feeling for the grand scale found perfect expression in the new garden front. Unfortunately, this was ruined a few years later by HARDOUIN-MANSART's alterations and extensions, and nothing survives at all of the interiors he executed with Lebrun; these included the most spectacular of all, the Escalier des Ambassadeurs. In the Collège des Quatre Nations, Paris (now the Institut de France, begun 1661), which was built at the expense of Cardinal Mazarin, he came closer than any other Frenchman to the warmth and geniality of the great Italian Baroque architects. The main front facing the Seine is concave, with two arms curving forward from the domed centrepiece to end in pavilions. The sense of splendour both in planning and decoration is no less typical than the occasional lack of sensitivity in the handling of detail. Both here and at Versailles the chief member of his studio was François d'ORBAY, who carried out or completed several of his late works after his death.

Blunt 1982.

Leaded lights. Rectangular or diamond-shaped panes of glass set in lead CAMES to form a window. In general use in domestic architecture until the C18.

Leaf and dart. An OVOLO moulding decorated with a pattern of alternate leaf-like forms and darts, found especially on the ECHINUS of an Ionic capital.

Lean-to roof, see ROOF.

Lechner, Ödön (1845–1914). One of the most interesting of all representatives of ART NOUVEAU architecture. He started (like GAUDÍ) in a free Gothic ('Town Hall, Kecskemét, 1892, Museum of Decorative Art, Budapest, 1893–6) and developed towards a fantastic style with curvaceous gables and Moorish as well as folk-art connotations (Postal Savings Bank, Budapest, 1899–1902).

T. Bakonyi and M. Kubinsky, *O.L.*, Budapest 1981.

Ledoux, Claude-Nicolas (1736–1806), began as a fashionable Louis XVI architect, patronized by Mme du Barry, and developed into the most daring and extreme exponent of neo-

classicism in France. Only BOULLÉE among his contemporaries was his equal in imagination and originality, but most of Boullée's designs remained on paper. Neither was properly appreciated until recently. Despite its extreme geometrical simplicity their more advanced work is not abstract but expressive or *parlant*. Born at Dormans, Ledoux studied under J.-F. BLONDEL in Paris. He never went to Italy, though he was profoundly influenced by Italian architecture, especially by the cyclopean fantasies of PIRANESI. Though eccentric and quarrelsome, he was immediately and continuously successful and never lacked commissions. His first important buildings were the Hôtel d'Hallwyl, Paris (1766), the Château de Bénouville (1770–77), and the Hôtel de Montmorency, Paris (1770–72), the last displaying his originality in planning on a diagonal axis, with circular and oval rooms.

In 1771 he began working for Mme du Barry and the following year completed the Pavillon de Louveciennes, a landmark in the history of French taste. It was decorated and furnished throughout in the neo-classical style, the architectural treatment of the interior being confined to shallow pilasters, classical bas-reliefs, and delicate, honeycomb coffering. In 1776 he began the remarkable Hôtel Thélusson (demolished) in Paris, approached through an enormous triumphal arch leading into a garden laid out in the English landscape manner. This conception, in which the informality of the garden emphasized the stark simplicity and geometrical forms of the building, was repeated on a larger scale in the group of fifteen houses he built for the West Indian nabob Hosten in Paris

(1792, demolished). They, too, were informally disposed in a landscape garden.

Success and official recognition appear to have stimulated rather than dulled his powers of invention, for his most advanced and original work dates from after he became an Academician and Architecte du Roi in 1773. His masterpieces are the massive and rigidly cubic theatre at Besançon (1775–84, burnt out 1957), with its un-pedimented Ionic portico and, inside, a hemicycle with rising banks of seats surmounted by a Greek Doric colon-nade. Odder still is his saltworks at Arc-et-Senans (1775–9), some of which still survives in a dilapidated condition. It is the supreme expression of his feel-ing for the elemental and primeval. The glowering entrance portico is carved inside to emulate the natural rock out of which gushes water, pre-sumably saline though also carved in stone. Even more extreme were the buildings he envisaged for his 'ideal city' of Chaux, which were not, un-derstandably, executed: one was to have been a free-standing sphere and another an enormous cylinder set hori-zontally.

His Paris toll-houses of 1785–9 are less extreme, but they illustrate the wide range of his stylistic repertoire. Of those that survive the most exciting is the Barrière de La Villette in Place de Stalingrad, consisting of a Greek cross surmounted by a cylinder – a very successful essay in pure archi-tectural form. In 1783 he built a salt warehouse at Compiègne (only the massive arched façade survives) and in 1786 provided designs for a Palais de Justice and prison at Aix en Provence (not executed according to his designs). His career came to an end with the Rev-olution (he was imprisoned during the 1790s) and he spent his last years preparing his designs for publication: *L'architecture considérée sous le rapport de l'art, des mœurs et de la législation* (1804).

M. Gallet, *C.-N.L.*, Paris 1980; Braham 1980; A. Vidler, *C.-N.L.* Cambridge, Mass., 1988.

Lefuel, Hector-Martin (1810–80), won the Grand Prix in 1839 and in the same year went to Rome. In 1854, at the death of Louis Visconti (1791–1853), he became chief architect to the Louvre, which Napoleon III had in 1853 decided to complete by large and elaborate links connecting it with the Tuileries. The neo-Renaissance fashion originated here and soon became international (cf. HUNT). Lefuel also designed the palace for the International Exhibition of 1855.

Hitchcock 1977; Middleton and Watkin 1977.

Legrand, Jacques-Guillaume (1743–1808), *see* BÉLANGER, François-Joseph; GILLY, Friedrich.

Lemercier, Jacques (*c.* 1585–1654), was the son of a master mason who worked at St Eustache, Paris. He studied in Rome *c.* 1607–14, becoming Architecte du Roi soon afterwards. With Étienne Martellange (*c.* 1569–1641), who designed the Jesuit Nov-iciate, Paris (1630), he was the leading exponent of French classicism as ex-pounded by Fréart de Chambray (1606–76) in his *Parallèle de l'architec-ture* (1650) and ranks only just below MANSART and LE VAU. In 1624 he was commissioned by Louis XIII to plan extensions to the Louvre (the Pavil-lon de l'Horloge of 1641 is the most notable of his additions), in harmony with LESCOT's work of the previous century. But his principal patron was Cardinal Richelieu, for whom he designed the Palais Cardinal (Palais Royal), Paris (begun 1633); the Sorbonne, Paris (begun 1626); the *château* and church of Rueil and the *château* and town of Richelieu (begun 1631). Only a small domed pavilion of the office block survives from the enormous Château Richelieu, but the town still exists as laid out by Lemercier in a regular grid with houses of uniform design built of brick with stone quoins. As a designer of *hôtels* he was remarkably ingenious, and his solution at the Hôtel de Liancourt, Paris (1623), became a prototype which was followed by nearly all his successors. His church of the Sorbonne (begun 1635) is perhaps his finest work and is one of the first purely classical churches in France. His dome at the Val-de-Grâce, Paris, where he took over from Mansart in 1646, is also most dramatic and effective.

J. P. Babelon, *Demeures Parisiennes. Sous Henri IV et Louis XIII*, Paris 1965; Blunt 1982.

Lemyinge, Robert (d. 1628), *see* LIMINGE, Robert.

L'Enfant, Pierre Charles (1754–1825), a French architect and engineer who served as a volunteer major in the American army during the War of Independence, designed the old City Hall in New York and the Federal House in Philadelphia, but is remembered mainly for having surveyed the site and made the plan for the new federal capital in Washington, a grandiose conception based in some respects on Versailles. He would probably have been given the commission to design the Capitol and other buildings in Wash-

ington had he not become unmanageable. He was dismissed in 1792.

Whiffen and Koeper 1981.

Lennox, Edward (1854–1933), *see* CANADIAN ARCHITECTURE.

Leonardo da Vinci (1452–1519). The greatest artist and thinker of the Renaissance. His wide-ranging mind embraced architecture as well as many other fields of human activity. Although he built little or nothing, he provided a model for the dome of Milan Cathedral (1487; not executed), and during his last years in France produced a vast scheme for a new city and royal castle at Romorantin (not executed). But his influence was great, especially on BRAMANTE, who took over his interest in centralized churches. Leonardo was certainly involved in Bramante's work at S. Maria delle Grazie, Milan, though his role in Bramante's Tempietto in Rome is controversial. S. Maria della Consolazione at Todi (1508), begun by Cola da Caprarola (*fl.* 1499–1519), probably derived from one of his sketches by way of Bramante.

Heydenreich and Lotz 1974; C. Pedretti, *L. da V. Architect*, London 1981.

Leoni, Giacomo (*c.* 1686–1746), who was born in Venice, settled in England sometime before 1715, having previously worked in Düsseldorf. An apostle of PALLADIANISM, he published the first English edition of Palladio's *Architecture* (1715–20) and at Queensberry House (now Royal Bank of Scotland), London (1721, reconstructed 1792), provided that prototype English Palladian town house. In 1726 he published *The Architecture of L. B. Alberti*. His surviving buildings include Lyme

Park, Cheshire (1725–30); Argyll House, London (1723); and Clandon Park, Surrey (1731–5).

Colvin 1978; Summerson 1983; R. Hewlings in Brown 1985.

Leonidov, Ivan Ilich (1902–59). Leading exponent of CONSTRUCTIVISM in Moscow, where his most notable project (unrealized) was his Lenin Institute of 1927. His only notable work to be executed was the amphitheatre etc. at the Ordjohikedze Sanatorium, Kislovodsk (1932).

R. Koolhaus and G. Oorthuys, *I.L.*, New York 1981; A. Gozak and A. Leonidov, *I.L. The Complete Works*, London 1988.

Leper window, *see* LOWSIDE WINDOW.

Lequeu, Jean-Jacques (1757–after 1825). French neo-classical fantasist of neurotic power. He was born in Rouen, visited Italy in the early 1780s, and worked mainly as an architectural draughtsman until the Revolution and then as a cartographer. None of his few buildings survives. His fame rests on his drawings (Bibliothèque Nationale, Paris) in which the designs and ideas of BOULLÉE and LEDOUX appear to have gone to his head – monument to Priapus, vast and megalomaniac towers, a dairy to be built in the form of a cow, houses composed of both Gothic and antique motifs, etc., with much use of phallic and other symbols. In them he broke away from all conventions of symmetry, stylistic purity, proportion, and taste.

Braham 1980; P. Duboy, *J.-J.L. An Architectural Enigma*, London 1986.

Lesbian cymatium. A CYMA REVERSA moulding often decorated with LEAF AND DART.

Lescaze, William (1896–1964), *see* HOWE, George.

Lescot, Pierre (1500/15–1578). Son of a well-to-do lawyer, who gave him a good education. His only work to survive more or less intact is part of the square court of the Louvre (1546–51), which laid the foundations of French classicism. Essentially decorative, his style is very French and entirely lacks the monumentality of his Italian contemporaries. He had the great advantage of the sculptor Jean Goujon's collaboration, and his ornamental detail is therefore of the greatest refinement and delicacy. Though much altered, parts of his Hôtel Carnavalet, Paris (c. 1545–50), survive. The Fontaine des Innocents, Paris (1547–9), has been totally reconstructed.

Blunt 1982.

Lesene. A PILASTER without a base and capital often called a pilaster-strip and usually found on the exteriors of later Anglo-Saxon and early Romanesque churches. Although they were much used as decoration during the latter period, there is evidence in some Anglo-Saxon buildings to suggest that pilaster-strips as used by the Saxons were primarily functional. They served as bonding courses in thin rubble walls, and thus split up an unbroken expanse of wall, reducing cracking in the plaster and preventing longitudinal spread. The north nave wall at Breamore church shows long stones on end between flat stones, all clearly projecting some distance into the wall. This is a crude example of LONG AND SHORT WORK, but no claim can be made that the pilaster-strip and long and short work as used for QUOINS were evolved in any particular sequence. Other examples of the structural significance of the pilaster-strip are at Worth, where they are solid stone partitions, clearly of a piece with the long and short quoins, at Sompting and at Milborne.

Lethaby, William Richard (1857–1931), joined the office of Norman SHAW in 1877, became his trusted principal assistant, and set up on his own in 1889, helped on by Shaw. While he thus owed much to Shaw, as an artist and a thinker he owed more to MORRIS and Philip WEBB, and he played a significant part in the ARTS AND CRAFTS movement. He was as much an educator as a scholar and an architect, and indeed built very little. Foremost among his buildings are Avon Tyrrell in Hampshire (1891) and Melsetter on Orkney (1898), the church at Brockhampton in Herefordshire (1900–1902) – probably the most original church of its date in the world – and the Eagle Insurance Building in Colmore Row, Birmingham (1899), also of a startling originality, even if influenced by Webb. Lethaby was the chief promoter and the first principal of the London Central School of Arts and Crafts, which was established in 1894 on Morris's principles. It was the first school anywhere to include teaching workshops for crafts. Also in 1894, Lethaby (with Swainson) brought out a learned book on Hagia Sophia in Constantinople; in 1904 a general, very deeply felt book on medieval art; in 1906 and 1925 two learned volumes on Westminster Abbey; and in 1922 a collection of brilliant, convincingly forward-looking essays called *Form in Civilisation*.

Hitchcock 1977; G. Rubens, *W.L. His Life and Work 1857–1931*, London (1978) 1985; S. Backemeyer and T. Gronberg (eds.), *W.R.L. 1857–1931.*

Architecture, Design, Education, exh. cat., London 1984.

Levasseur, Noël (1680–1740), *see* CANADIAN ARCHITECTURE.

Levasseur, Pierre-Noël (1690–1770), *see* CANADIAN ARCHITECTURE.

Leverton, Thomas (1743–1824), the son of an Essex builder and not highly regarded in his own day, nevertheless designed some of the most elegant interiors in London, e.g. Nos. 1 and 13 Bedford Square (1775). His 'Etruscan' hall and other rooms at Woodhall Park (1778) are equally distinguished.

Summerson 1983.

Levi, Rino (1901–65), *see* BRAZILIAN ARCHITECTURE.

Lewerentz, Sigurd (1885–1975), *see* SWEDISH ARCHITECTURE.

Libera, Adalberto (1903–63), *see* RATIONALISM.

Libergier, Hugues (d. 1263). A French master mason whose funerary slab is now in Reims Cathedral. He is called Maistre on it and is represented holding the model of the major parish church of Reims, St Nicaise, which he designed and began in 1231. He also has a staff, an L-square, and compasses.

Branner 1965.

Liberty, stile, *see* ART NOUVEAU.

Libeskind, Daniel (b. 1946), *see* POLISH ARCHITECTURE.

Lierne, *see* VAULT.

Lights. Openings between the MULLIONS of a window.

Ligorio, Pirro (*c.* 1510–83). Painter and archaeologist as well as architect. He built the Villa d'Este, Tivoli (1565–

FIG. 60. *Linenfold*

72), and laid out its wonderful formal gardens with elaborate fountains and water-works. His masterpiece is the exquisite little Casino di Pio IV (1559–62) in the Vatican gardens, Rome, one of the most elegant of Mannerist buildings. Also in the Vatican, he transformed the exedra in BRAMANTE's Cortile del Belvedere into a gargantuan niche.

D. R. Coffin, *The Villa d'Este at Tivoli*, Princeton 1966; G. Smith, *The Casino of Pius IV*, Princeton 1976; Heydenreich and Lotz 1974.

Liminge, Lemyinge or **Lyming**, Robert (d. 1628). First recorded in 1607 as a carpenter, he was employed to design and supervise building at Hatfield House, Hertfordshire, in 1607–12. The loggia and frontispiece may be his, though Inigo JONES was consulted in 1609. At Blickling Hall, Norfolk (1616–17), he designed the last of the great Jacobean PRODIGY HOUSES in which Flemish ornament and planning were anglicized.

Colvin 1978; Summerson 1983.

Lindgren, Armas (1874–1929), *see* FINNISH ARCHITECTURE.

Linenfold. Panelling ornamented with a conventional representation of a piece of linen laid in vertical folds. One such piece fills one panel. First introduced in Flanders in the C15–16, it was much used in Tudor England for the decoration of both panelling and furniture. *See* Fig. 60.

Linstow, Hans Ditler Frants (1787–1851), *see* NORWEGIAN ARCHITECTURE.

Lintel. A horizontal beam or stone bridging an opening.

Lisboa, António Francisco (1730 or 1738–1814), *see* ALEIJADINHO.

Lissitsky, Eleazar Markevich, called El (1890–1941). Russian painter, typographer, designer and theorist as well as architect, Lissitsky became the apostle of CONSTRUCTIVISM in the West in the 1920s. He trained under Joseph OLBRICH at the College of Technology, Darmstadt (1909–14). In 1919 he became Professor of Architecture at Vitebsk, where he evolved his 'Proun' idea (Proun = 'For the New Art') which he described as an 'interchange station' between painting and architecture – an interplay between the pictorial and structural. His ideas owed something to both MALEVICH and TATLIN, then famous for his 1920 design for a spiral-shaped monument to the Third International. In 1920 Lissitsky designed his Lenin Tribune project which foreshadowed the prime Constructivist building, the Leningrad Pravda building projected by the VESNIN brothers in 1923. From 1922 until 1931 Lissitsky was in the West, where he knew and influenced the DE STIJL and other *avant-garde* architects. His 'Proun Cabinet' for the 1923 Berlin exhibition has been reconstructed at Eindhoven (Stedelijk van Abbe-museum), and his 'Abstract

Cabinet', created in 1926 for Dresden and in 1927 for Hanover and intended to 'allow abstract art to do justice to its dynamic properties', has been reconstructed in the Landesmuseum in Hanover. His most ambitious and forward-looking design – the 1924 *Wolkenbügel* project (with STAM) for office blocks in Moscow on upright or splayed legs straddling roads – never materialized. In 1939 he produced designs for the Soviet Pavilion restaurant at the New York World Fair.

S. Lissitsky-Kuppers, *E.L. Life, Letters, Texts,* London and New York 1968; *E.L.,* exh. cat., Cologne 1976.

Listel, *see* FILLET.

Liturgical orientation, *see* ORIENTATION.

Liwan, *see* IWAN.

Load-bearing or **load-carrying construction.** Construction in which walls, posts, columns or arcades support the weight of the ceilings, upper floors, etc., as distinct from FRAME CONSTRUCTION.

Lodge and Lodge books. Lodge was the medieval term for the masons' workshop or tracing house, with living-quarters, set up when a church, castle or house was to be built. In the case of cathedrals and great abbeys it was often permanent, under a resident master, to maintain the fabric of the building. Medieval masons' sketchbooks or notebooks are known as *lodge books; see* VILLARD DE HONNECOURT.

P. du Colombier, *Les Chantiers des cathédrales,* Paris, 1953; P. Booz, *Der Baumeister der Gotik,* Berlin 1956; Bucher 1979.

Lodoli, Carlo (1690–1761). A Venetian priest and architectural theorist.

His neo-classical and 'rationalist' ideas were published after his death by A. Memmo (*Elementi d'architettura lodoliana,* 1786) but they had been current for many years and were very influential, e.g. on Algarotti's *Saggio sopra l'architettura* (1753), Piranesi's *Della magnificenza ed architettura dei Romani* (1761) and on LAUGIER.

Herrmann 1962; L. Grassi, *Razionalismo architettonico dal L. a G. Pagano,* Milan 1966; Rykwert 1980; Wittkower 1982.

Log construction. Primitive form of timber construction still used in regions rich in timber. The walls are made of tree-trunks laid horizontally on top of one another, overlapping at the corners where they are slotted together. If round boles are used the joints are sealed with moss and mud, but the logs are usually adzed down to a plane surface. The only surviving log church in England is St Andrew, Greensted, of *c.* 1013 in which, however, the logs are set vertically in an oak sill. *See also* SCANDINAVIAN ARCHITECTURE.

H. J. Hansen, *Architecture in Wood: A History of Wood Building and its Techniques in Europe and N. America,* (Hamburg 1969) London 1971; T. Jordan, *American Log Building. An Old World Heritage,* Chapel Hill 1985.

Loggia. A gallery or room open on one or more sides, sometimes pillared; it may also be a separate structure.

Logorreta, Ricardo (b. 1930), *see* MEXICAN ARCHITECTURE.

Lombardo, Pietro (*c.* 1435–1515). A leading sculptor and architect in late C15 Venice. He was born at Carona in Lombardy, hence his name. He appears to have visited Florence before

1464, when he is first recorded working in Padua as a sculptor. Soon after 1467 he settled in Venice. Between 1471 and 1485 he designed and carved decorations for the chancel of S. Giobbe, Venice, a work of strongly Florentine character. His next and most important work was S. Maria dei Miracoli (1481–9), in which he successfully blended the Veneto-Byzantine and Renaissance styles – marble panelling inside and out and a Byzantine dome, combined with crisply carved Renaissance ornament. To give an illusion of greater size he resorted to various *trompe l'œil* devices which he repeated on a larger scale, but with less success, on the façade of the Scuola di S. Marco (1488–90, upper storeys completed by CODUSSI). He also introduced into Venice the large architectural sepulchral monument with a classical framework and abundance of classically inspired sculpture. Here he was much assisted by his sons Antonio (*c.* 1485–1516) and Tullio (*c.* 1455–1532). Various Venetian palaces have been attributed to Lombardo, notably Palazzo Dario (*c.* 1487).

Howard 1980; McAndrew 1980; R. Luciani, *P.L. Architetto*, Rome 1987.

Long and short work. Saxon QUOINS, consisting of long stones on end between flat ones, all bonded into the wall. The chancel arch JAMBS at Escomb (C7 or 8) may have a bearing on the origin of the technique; it may also have been evolved simultaneously and in association with pilaster-strip work (*see* LESENE). It is the insertion of the large flat stones which makes long and short work such a good bonding technique for corners, as in many cases they extend practically through the thickness of the walls; the upright

blocks alone are subject to diagonal thrust.

Superficially long and short work is of two kinds:

a. the 'upright and flat' type, where the full size of the horizontal stone is visible on both flanks;

b. the long and short strip quoin, where the horizontal stones have been cut back, making them flush with the upright blocks.

This was a refinement in the process of finding a solid cornering for stone buildings, but is not necessarily an indication of a later date (e.g. Deerhurst of the early C10 has the 'upright and flat' type). The method of construction is the same for both kinds.

Longhena, Baldassare (1597–1682), the only great Venetian Baroque architect, was born in Venice of a family of stone carvers and was trained under SCAMOZZI. In 1630 he won a competition for the design of the *ex voto* church of S. Maria della Salute, with which he was to be occupied off and on for the rest of his long life (it was not finally consecrated until 1687). Standing on an imposing site at the entrance to the Grand Canal, this church is a masterpiece of scenographic design, with a vast buoyant dome anchored by huge Baroque scrolls to an octagonal base, and a very complex façade which directs the eye through the main door to the high altar. The interior is conceived as a series of dramatic vistas radiating from the centre of the octagonal nave. Longhena realized a similarly theatrical concept in the design of his imposing double staircase for the monastery of S. Giorgio Maggiore (1643–5), which had considerable influence on later architects. In the domestic field he was less adventurous:

Palazzo Rezzonico (begun 1667) and Palazzo Pesaro (1649/52–82, façade begun 1676) on the Grand Canal – both completed after his death – with heavily rusticated basements, abundance of carving, and deep recesses which dissolve the surface of the exterior in patterns of light and shade, are merely Baroque variations on SAN-SOVINO's Palazzo Corner and the Mint. (G. Massari built the top floor of Palazzo Rezzonico in 1752–6.) A tendency towards wilful exaggeration of sculptural detail in these works reaches its fantastic peak in the little church of the Ospedaletto (1670–78), with a preposterously overwrought façade bursting with *telamones*, giant heads, and lion masks. He has been credited with numerous villas on the mainland, but none is of much interest.

Wittkower 1982; L. Puppi and G. Romanelli, *B.L. 1597–1682*, Venice 1982.

Longhi, Martino the younger (1602–60), the most important member of a family of architects working mainly in Rome, was the son of Onorio Longhi (1569–1619) and the grandson of Martino Longhi the elder (d. 1591). He continued his father's work on S. Carlo al Corso, Rome, and began S. Antonio de' Portoghesi, Rome (1638). His major achievement is the façade of SS. Vincenzo ed Anastasio, Rome (1646–50), a powerfully dramatic, many-columned composition in which Mannerist devices are used to obtain an overwhelming High Baroque effect of grandeur and mass.

Wittkower 1982; Varriano 1986.

Longuelune, Zacharias (1669–1748). French-born painter-architect who collaborated with Matthaeus PÖPPEL-MANN in Dresden from 1715 onwards on the designs for the vast new Saxon Palace. Very few of his own projects were executed but his grandiose designs, which embodied French classicist theory, exerted considerable influence both in Saxony and as far away as Poland and Denmark. He designed the formal park at Gross-Sedlitz (1726), additions to the Japanisches Palais in Dresden (1729 onwards) and the Blockhaus terminating the Hauptstrasse in Dresden Neustadt (1731) (burnt out 1945 but now reconstructed).

Colombier 1956.

Loop. A small, narrow and often unglazed light.

Loos, Adolf (1870–1933), was born at Brno in Moravia, studied at Dresden, spent three crucial years in the United States (1893–6), partly in Chicago, where he knew SULLIVAN and WRIGHT, and then worked in Vienna, strongly influenced by the doctrines just then expounded by Otto WAGNER. From the very first his designs (Goldmann shop interior, 1898) refused to allow any decorative features or any curves. His most important buildings are private houses of between 1904 (house, Lake Geneva) and 1910 (Steiner House, Vienna). They are characterized by unrelieved cubic shapes, a total absence of ornament, and a love of fine materials. In his theoretical writings, or rather his journalism, he was a rabid anti-ornamentalist, an enemy therefore of the Wiener Werkstätten and HOFFMANN, and a believer in the engineer and the plumber. His famous article called *Ornament and Crime* came out in 1908. As an architect, however, he wavered. His office building in the Michaelerplatz (1910) has Tuscan columns, his design for the Chicago

Tribune competition of 1923 is a huge closely windowed Doric column; but smaller domestic jobs, such as the house for the Dadaist Tristan Tzara in Paris (1926), remained faithful to the spirit of 1904–10. Loos was not a successful architect, but he was influential among some of the *avant-garde* in Europe. His collected essays have been published in English as *Spoken into the Void* (1982).

Hitchcock 1977; B. Gravagnuolo, *A.L. Theory and Works*, New York 1982; *The Architecture of A.L.*, exh. cat., London 1986.

Lorimer, Robert Stodart (1864–1929), *see* SCOTTISH ARCHITECTURE.

L'Orme, Philibert de (1500/15–1570) who was born in Lyon, the son of a master mason, went to Rome for three years, probably 1533–6, where he moved in high diplomatic-humanist circles but entirely misunderstood the point of Italian architecture. He was nothing if not original and as utterly French as his friend and admirer Rabelais. His buildings are notable for their ingenuity and sometimes outrageous experimentation. Almost everything he built has been destroyed, except for parts of Anet (Diane de Poitier's house) and the tomb of Francis I in St Denis (begun 1547). The frontispiece of Anet (begun before 1550, now in the École des Beaux Arts, Paris) is a good example of his style, correct in detail and rather more monumental than that of his contemporary LESCOT. The chapel (1549–52) and entrance front (*c.* 1552) are still *in situ*. He had a great influence on the development of French architecture, partly through his books, *Nouvelles Inventions* (1561) and *Architecture* (1567), the most practical architectural treatise of the Renaissance, containing a complete manual on the erection of a house. The decorative part of the screen in St Étienne-du-Mont, Paris, with its pierced balustrades and spiral staircase (*c.* 1545), is probably by de L'Orme.

A. Blunt, *P. de L'O.*, London 1958; L. Brion-Guerry, *P. de L'O.*, Milan 1965; Blunt 1982.

Loudon, John Claudius (1783–1843), was apprenticed to a landscape gardener in Scotland, and educated himself the hard way. He settled in London in 1803, and at once began writing on gardening and agriculture. He also took up farming, made money and lost it, travelled on the Continent (1814 as far as Moscow, 1819–20 in France and Italy). His *Encyclopaedia of Gardening* came out in 1822, an *Encyclopaedia of Agriculture* in 1825, an *Encyclopaedia of Plants* in 1829, and the architecturally important *Encyclopaedia of Cottage, Farm and Villa Architecture* in 1833. This is the standard book if one wants to see what ideals and what styles of the past English country houses followed, chiefly in the 1840s. Loudon also started and edited the *Gardener's Magazine* (from 1826) and the short-lived *Architectural Magazine* (1834). Garth, near Welshpool (1809, demolished), his own house of Tew End, Oxfordshire (1809), and possibly Hope End, near Ledbury (*c.* 1810, mostly demolished), were his main works as an architect.

E. B. MacDugall, *J.C.L. and the Early Nineteenth Century in Great Britain*, Washington, D.C., 1980; M. L. Simo, *L. and the Landscape: From Country Seat to Metropolitan 1783–1843*, London 1988.

Louis, Victor (1731–1800). French neo-classical architect working in a

FIG. 61. *Louvre*

somewhat florid style derived from ancient Rome and the city palaces (rather than the villas) of PALLADIO. Born in Paris, he was trained there and at the French Academy in Rome (1756–9). In 1765 he was called to Warsaw by Stanislas-Augustus but returned the next year without having built anything. His first work of importance is also his masterpiece, the theatre at Bordeaux (1772–80), a massive structure with a dodecastyle portico (without pediment) stretching the full length of the main façade. It contains a large stage, very grand auditorium and the most monumental staircase and foyer that had been realized up to that date. He did some other work in and around Bordeaux (e.g. Hôtel Saige, now the Préfecture, Château de Bouihl). He also had an extensive practice in Paris where his main work was the colonnades in the Palais Royal gardens (1780–85) and the adjoining Théâtre de la Comédie-Française (1786–90, rebuilt 1902). The original building had an iron and hollow-tile roof to reduce the danger of fires.

Kalnein and Levey 1972; Braham 1980: F.-G. Pariset, *V.L.*, Bordeaux 1980.

Louvre. 1. An opening, often with a LANTERN over, in the roof of a hall to let the smoke from a central hearth escape; either open-sided, or closed by slanting boards to keep out the rain. 2. One of a series of overlapping boards or slips of glass to admit air and exclude rain. *See* Fig. 61.

Lowside window. A window usually on the south side of the chancel, lower than the others, possibly intended for communication between persons outside the chancel and the priest within; perhaps also for the sanctus bell to be heard outside the church. It was formerly, and erroneously, called a *leper window.*

Lozenge. A diamond shape, i.e. a flat rectilinear figure with four equal sides but two angles sharper than the others.

Lubetkin, Berthold (1901–90), *see* TECTON.

Lucarne. 1. A small opening in an attic or a spire. 2. A DORMER WINDOW.

Ludovice, João Frederico (Johann Friedrich Ludwig, *c.* 1670–1752), the leading Late Baroque architect in Portugal, was born at Hall in Swabia, the son of a goldsmith whose craft he practised first in Rome (1697–1701) then in Lisbon. In about 1711 the king of Portugal commissioned him to build a small convent at Mafra. Gradually the size of the project was enlarged, and the building finally became one of the largest in Europe (built 1717–70). It includes a royal palace, a vast church, and conventual buildings for 300 monks. Mafra derives mainly from High Baroque Rome with a few south German and Portuguese overtones: the church, liberally decorated with Italian statues, is especially impressive. His only other works of importance are the library of Coimbra University (1717–23), with a very rich *mouvementé* façade, and the apse of Évora Cathedral (1716–46).

Kubler and Soria 1959; A. de Carvalho, *Don João V e arte do seu tempo*, Lisbon 1962.

Lundberg, Jon, *see* NORWEGIAN ARCHITECTURE

Lunette. A semicircular opening or TYMPANUM. The term can also be applied to any flat, semicircular surface.

Lurcat, André (1894–1970), *see* FRENCH ARCHITECTURE.

Lutyens, Sir Edwin Landseer (1869–1944). The leading 'Edwardian' architect and as expressive of his period as was Elgar in his music – sensitivity, imagination and impish humour being combined, not always happily, with the grandiose and majestic. After a short time with the country-house architects George & Peto, he set up on his own in 1889. His ambition was to emulate Norman SHAW but he was influenced by WEBB as well. In 1896 he designed Munstead Wood, Munstead, Surrey, for the gardener and garden designer Gertrude Jekyll, who revived the English cottage garden. A number of outstanding, small but usually quite opulent, houses followed, some of them masterpieces of ARTS AND CRAFTS architecture, notably Deanery Gardens, Sonning, Berkshire (1899–1902) for Edward Hudson, the founder of *Country Life* magazine. It is as skilful in its picturesque use of the vernacular as his reconstruction for the same client of Lindisfarne Castle, Northumberland, was to be two years later

in a romantic, dramatic vein. Other examples of his early, rambling, picturesque houses are Orchards, Munstead, Surrey (1897–9); Tigbourne Court, Witley, Surrey (1899–1901); Homewood, Knebworth, Hertfordshire (1901); Little Thakeham, Thakeham, Sussex (1902–3), and Folly Farm, Sulhamstead, Berkshire (1905). Their variety and ingenuity – especially in interior spatial play and in their imaginative interior–exterior relationships – make them comparable to Frank Lloyd WRIGHT's Prairie Houses of about the same date. They established Lutyens's reputation for originality and imaginative ability in coordinating vernacular forms. However, he was also attracted by classicism, at first of a William and Mary variety (Liberal Club, Farnham, Surrey, 1894–5); then in a wilfully eccentric and grandiose Vanbrughian way (Heathcote, Ilkley, Yorkshire, 1905–7); later more quietly neo-Georgian though on a grand scale (Nashdom, Taplow, Buckinghamshire, 1905–8, and Great Maytham, Rolvenden, Kent, 1907–9). Finally, in two late classical houses – The Salutation, Sandwich, Kent (1911), and Gledstone Hall, Yorkshire (1922–6) – his genius achieved solutions as convincing as any of his earlier picturesque houses. In the latter style his work culminated in Castle Drogo, Drewsteignton, Devon (1910–30), an enormous and imposing feudal fantasy which was never completed.

Lutyens shared to the full the imperial *folie de grandeur* of the Edwardian heyday and this made him the ideal architect for the layout and planning on a vast scale of New Delhi in India, where his Viceroy's House (1912–31, now Rashtrapati Bhavan) has a sense of solemnity and magnificence which BAKER in his buildings for New Delhi lacked. Though never on the scale of anything at New Delhi, some of his First World War memorials are even more impressive in their gravity and simplicity. The Cenotaph in Whitehall, London (1919–20), is the most famous, but the Memorial to the Missing of the Somme at Thiepval near Arras, France (1927–32), is overwhelming in its lonely, threnodic grandeur.

Of his later buildings – imposing in scale and as inventive and original as ever in detail – Britannic House, Finsbury Circus, London (1920–24), and the Midland Bank, Poultry, London (1924–37), should be mentioned, as also his two late, classicizing country houses: Halnaker House near Chichester, Sussex (1936), and Middleton Park, Middleton Stoney, Oxfordshire (1938). His great design for the Roman Catholic Cathedral of Liverpool (1929–44) was never to be realized – only the crypt was built (1933–41).

C. Hussey, *The Life of Sir E.L.*, London 1950; A. S. G. Butler, *The Architecture of Sir E.L.*, London 1950; C. Amery *et al.*, *L.*, exh. cat., London 1981.

Luzarches, Robert de (d. *c.* 1236), *see* ROBERT DE LUZARCHES.

Lych gate. A covered wooden gateway with open sides at the entrance to a churchyard, providing a resting-place for a coffin (the word *lych* is Saxon for corpse). Part of the burial service is sometimes read there.

Lyming, Robert (d. 1628), *see* LIMINGE, Robert.

m

Machicolation. A gallery or PARAPET projecting on brackets on the outside of castle towers and walls, with openings in the floor through which to drop molten lead, boiling oil, and missiles.

Machuca, Pedro (d. 1550), began as a painter, worked in Italy and returned to Spain in 1520. His masterpiece, the Palace of Charles V in the Alhambra at Granada (1527–68), is very Italian in the RAPHAEL–GIULIO ROMANO style; indeed, it is larger and more complete than any Bramantesque palace in Italy. But various Spanish or PLATER-ESQUE features crept into his design, e.g. the garlanded window frames.

E. E. Rosenthal, *The Palace of Charles V in Granada*, Princeton 1985.

Mackay, David John (b. 1933), *see* SPANISH ARCHITECTURE.

Mackintosh, Charles Rennie (1868–1928), studied at the Glasgow School of Art at the time when Glasgow painting had suddenly turned from a provincial past to new forms of considerable interest to people in England and even on the Continent. In 1893 and the following years he, his friend McNair, and the two Macdonald sisters, Margaret (later Mrs Mackintosh, 1865–1933) and Frances (later Mrs McNair), designed graphic work and repoussé metalwork in an ART NOUVEAU way,

inspired by *The Studio* (which started in London in 1893) and especially by Jan Toorop, the Dutchman. In 1896 Mackintosh won the competition for the new building of the Glasgow School of Art and erected a building inferior to none of its date anywhere in Europe or America – on a clear rational plan, with the basic external forms equally clear and rational (e.g. the studio windows), but with a centre-piece of complete originality and high fancifulness, influenced by VOYSEY, by the Scottish castle and manor-house tradition, and even a little by the current English 'Wrenaissance'. The metalwork of the façade and much of the interior achieve a unification of the crisply rectangular with the long, delicate, languid curves of Art Nouveau. It is in this unique harmony that Mackintosh's greatness lies, and it explains the deep impression his furniture and furnishings made on Austrian architects when they became familiar with him, first through *The Studio* and then through an exhibition at the Secession (*see* OLBRICH) in 1900. The Viennese were abandoning Art Nouveau for a clearer, saner style, and he both inspired and confirmed them.

Mackintosh had fully evolved his style in his interior work by 1899 – white lacquered chairs and cupboards, erect, elegant, clearly articulated, and with wistfully curved inlays in metal and pink, mauve, or mother-of-pearl enamel. There was no one else who could combine the rational and the expressive in so intriguing a way. His capital works at or near Glasgow are the tea-rooms for Mrs Cranston (Buchanan Street, 1897 onwards; Argyle Street, 1897 and 1905; Sauchiehall Street, 1904; Ingram Street, 1901, c. 1906, and c. 1911), now alas mostly destroyed or disused; two houses (Windyhill, Kilmacolm, 1899–1901, and Hill House, Helensburgh, 1902–3); a school (Scotland Street, 1906); and the library wing of the School of Art, Glasgow (1907–9), with its sheer, towering outer wall and its bewitchingly complex interior. In 1901 he had come second in a German publisher's competition for the house of an art-lover (Baillie Scott came first), and this consolidated his reputation abroad.

However, his erratic ways alienated clients. In 1913 he left the firm (Honeyman & Keppie) in which he had been a partner since 1904. He moved to Walberswick, then to London, then after the war to Port Vendres, and finally back to London, painting highly original, finely drawn landscapes and still-lifes, but never recovering an architectural practice.

T. Howarth, *C.R.M. and the Modern Movement*, London (1952) 1977; J. Cooper (ed.), *M. Architecture: The Complete Buildings and Selected Projects*, London and New York (1978) 1983; P. Nuttgens (ed.), *M. and his Contemporaries*, London 1988.

Mackmurdo, Arthur Heygate (1851–1942), came from a wealthy family and had plenty of leisure to evolve a style of his own. In 1874 he travelled to Italy with RUSKIN. About 1880 he seems to have built his first houses, of which 8 Private Road, Enfield (1887), is the most elegant. In 1882 he founded the Century Guild, a group of ARTS AND CRAFTS architects, artists and designers inspired by Ruskin and MORRIS. The group began in 1884 to publish a magazine, *The Hobby Horse*, which anticipated some of the features of book design recovered by Morris from the medieval past in his Kelmscott Press of 1890. As early as 1883, in the design for the cover of his book on Wren's City churches, Mackmurdo introduced those long flame-like or tendril-like curves which nearly ten years later were taken up, especially in Belgium, as a basis for ART NOUVEAU. But while in such two-dimensional designs, including a number for textiles (c. 1884) and in some early furniture (1882–3), Mackmurdo is the lone pioneer of Art Nouveau, the furniture he designed from 1886 onwards and a stand for an exhibition at Liverpool, also of 1886, established him as the forerunner of VOYSEY in clarity of structure, elegance, and originality in the sense of independence of the past. Specially characteristic, on the exhibition stand, are the long, tapering posts with a far-projecting flat cornice. In 1904 Mackmurdo gave up architecture; later he concentrated on economic thought and writing, his ideas being similar to those of Social Credit.

L. Lambourne, *Utopian Craftsmen: The Arts and Crafts Movement from the Cotswolds to Chicago*, London 1980; P. Stansky, *Redesigning the World: William Morris, the 1880s and the Arts and Crafts*, Princeton 1985.

Maclure, Samuel (1867–1929), *see* CANADIAN ARCHITECTURE.

Maderno, Carlo (c. 1556–1629), was

born at Capolago on Lake Lugano, and had settled in Rome by 1588, beginning as assistant to his uncle Domenico FONTANA. He was appointed architect of St Peter's in 1603, when he also completed the façade of S. Susanna, Rome, a revolutionary design with which he broke away from the current rather facile and academic MANNERISM and established his own lucid, forceful, and intensely dynamic style. S. Susanna and the majestic dome of S. Andrea della Valle, Rome, are his masterpieces, though he is best known for his work at St Peter's, where he had the unenviable job of altering MICHELANGELO's centralized plan by adding a nave and façade. Work began in 1607, and the façade was finished by 1612. Its excessive length is due to the later addition of towers, of which only the substructures were built and which now appear to form part of the façade. His Confessio before the high altar and his elegant fountain in the *piazza* are more successful. His secular buildings include Palazzo Mattei, Rome (1598–1618), Villa Aldobrandini, Frascati (1603–c. 1620), and Palazzo Barberini, Rome (1628, with BORROMINI), though the latter was almost entirely executed after his death by BERNINI, who made various alterations, notably to the main façade.

H. Hibbard, *C.M. and Roman Architecture 1580–1630*, London 1971.

Madrasa or **medrese**. An Islamic college for teaching theology and canon law. The form of the *madrasa* varies considerably throughout the Islamic world.

Maekawa, Kuneo (b. 1905), *see* MAYEKAWA, Kuneo.

Maher, George Washington (1864–1926), *see* ARTS AND CRAFTS.

Maiano, Benedetto da (1442–97), *see* BENEDETTO DA MAIANO.

Maiano, Giuliano da (1432–90), *see* GIULIANO DA MAIANO.

Maillart, Robert (1872–1940), a Swiss engineer, studied at the Zürich Polytechnic (1890–94), and set up on his own (1902). He worked on the unexplored possibilities of REINFORCED CONCRETE, and in the course of that work, arrived at a new aesthetic for concrete, using it to span by curves. His Tavenasa Bridge (1905) is the first in which arch and roadway are structurally one. He built many bridges afterwards, all of them of a thoroughbred elegance; the one across the Salzinatobel has a span of nearly 300 ft (1929–30). In 1908 he also began experimenting with concrete mushroom construction, at a time when this was being done independently in the United States; the technique involves a post and a mushroom top spreading from it that are one inseparable concrete unit. Maillart's first building of mushroom construction was a warehouse at Zürich (1910). *See also* SHELL.

M. Bill, *R.M.*, Zürich (1949) 1962; J. R. Abel *et al.* (eds.), *The M. Papers*, Princeton 1973; D. P. Billington, *R.M.'s Bridges. The Art of Engineering*, Princeton 1979.

Maillou, Jean (1668–1753), *see* CANADIAN ARCHITECTURE.

Maitani, Lorenzo (d. 1330). Sienese sculptor and architect. He was called in to advise on Orvieto Cathedral in 1310, being then described as 'universalis caputmagister', which testifies to his celebrity as an architect. From then until his death he was in complete control of all work on the façade of Orvieto Cathedral, including the sculpture some of which is probably by him. Two drawings for the façade survive, the second being probably by Maitani (Opera del Duomo, Orvieto). In 1317 he was mentioned as working on a fountain at Perugia and in 1322 he was on the commission for the new Baptistery of Siena Cathedral.

White 1987.

Majewski, Hilary (1837–97), *see* POLISH ARCHITECTURE.

Maki, Fumihiko (b. 1928), *see* JAPANESE ARCHITECTURE.

Makovecz, Imre (b. 1935), see HUNGARIAN ARCHITECTURE.

Malevich, Kasimir (1878–1935). Russian painter, pioneer of Suprematism (hard-edged abstractionism, developed *c.* 1915), who from *c.* 1920 – with his pupils at *Unovis* – turned his hand to ideal architectural models which he called *Arkhitektoniki* or *Planity.* Though his aesthetic was anti-utilitarian, hence strongly opposed to CONSTRUCTIVISM, he was a seminal influence on the modernist generations of, e.g., LISSITSKY and the BAUHAUS of the 1920s. [R. R. Milner-Gulland]

L. A. Zhadova, *M.: Suprematism and Revolution in Russian Art 1910–1930*, London 1982.

Mallet-Stevens, Robert (1886–1945), *see* ART DECO; FRENCH ARCHITECTURE.

Mandapa. A large open hall, especially one in a Hindu temple complex.

Mandorla, *see* VESICA.

Mannerism. In its primary sense, the acceptance of a manner rather than its meaning. Now Mannerism has also become a term to denote the style current in Italy from MICHELANGELO to the end of the C16. It is characterized by the use of motifs in deliberate opposition to their original significance or context, but it can also express itself in an equally deliberate cold and rigid classicism. The term applies to French and Spanish architecture of the C16 as well (de L'ORME; the Escorial), but how far it applies to the northern countries is controversial. Principal examples in Italy are Michelangelo's Medici Chapel and Laurentian Library, GIULIO ROMANO's works at Mantua, VASARI's Uffizi at Florence, and other works by these architects and LIGORIO, AMMANATI, BUONTALENTI, etc. PALLADIO belongs to Mannerism only in a certain limited aspects of his work.

J. Shearman, *M.*, Harmondsworth 1967; Heydenreich and Lotz 1974.

Manor house. A house in the country or a village, the centre of a manor. Architecturally the term is used to denote the unfortified, medium-sized house of the later Middle Ages.

M. Wood, *The Medieval English House*, London 1965.

Mansard roof, *see* ROOF.

Mansart, François (1598–1666), the first great protagonist of French classicism in architecture, holds a position parallel to Poussin in painting and Corneille in drama. He never went to Italy, and his style is extremely French in its elegance, clarity, and cool restraint. Though of scrupulous artistic conscience he was unfortunately both arrogant and slippery in his business relationships, and his inability to make and keep to a final plan not unnaturally enraged his clients. As a result, he lost many commissions. For the last ten years of his life he was virtually un-employed. He was seldom patronized by the Crown and never by the great nobility; his clients belonged mainly to the newly rich bourgeoisie, who had the intelligence to appreciate and the money to pay for his sophisticated and luxurious buildings.

Born in Paris, the son of a master carpenter, he probably began under de BROSSE at Coulommiers. By 1624 he had already established himself as a prominent architect in the capital. His early work derives from de Brosse, with Mannerist overtones in the style of DU CERCEAU, but his individual style began to emerge at the Château de Balleroy (1626), where the harmonious group-ing of massive blocks achieves an effect of sober monumentality. His first masterpiece, the Orléans wing of the *château* at Blois (1635–8), would have been a grander and more monumental Palais Luxembourg had it ever been completed. Only the central block and colonnades were built. But these dis-play to the full the ingenuity of plan-ning, clarity of disposition, and purity and refinement of detail which distin-guish his work. He also introduced here the continuous broken roof with a steep lower slope and flatter, shorter upper portion that is named after him. His style reached culmination at Maisons Lafitte (1642–51), the country house near Paris which he built for the im-mensely wealthy René de Longueil, who apparently allowed him a com-pletely free hand. (He pulled down part of it during construction in order to revise his designs!) It is his most com-plete work to survive and gives a better idea of his genius than any other. The oval rooms in the wings and the vesti-bule, executed entirely in stone without either gilding or colour, epitomize his

suave severity and civilized reticence in decoration. His design for the Val-de-Grâce in Paris (*c.* 1645) is con-temporary with Maisons Lafitte, but he was dismissed and replaced by LEMERCIER in 1646, when the build-ing had reached the entablature of the nave and the lower storey of the façade. The conception appears to derive from PALLADIO's Redentore.

His other important buildings are Ste Marie de la Visitation, Paris (1632–4); the Hôtel de la Vrillière, Paris (begun 1635, destroyed), wholly sym-metrical and the model for the classical type of Parisian *hôtel*; the Hôtel du Jars, Paris (begun 1648, now de-stroyed), in which he developed a freer, more plastic disposition of rooms which was to be very influential. His last surviving work is his remodelling of the Hôtel Carnavalet in Paris (1660–61). He was consulted by Colbert in the 1660s in connection with the Louvre and a royal chapel at St Denis, but his designs were not executed.

A. Braham and P. Smith, *F.M.*, London 1973; Blunt 1982.

Mansart, Jules Hardouin, *see* HARDOUIN-MANSART, Jules.

Mantelpiece. The wood, brick, stone or marble frame surrounding a fire-place, frequently including an over-mantel or mirror above; sometimes called *chimney-piece*.

Manueline style. An architectural style peculiar to Portugal and named after King Manuel the Fortunate (1495–1521). *See* PORTUGUESE AR-CHITECTURE.

Maqsura. A screen or grille of wood or metal in a mosque to protect the ruler from the other worshippers and forming a kind of royal box, usually near the MIHRAB and MIMBAR. Later the *maqsura* came to denote the detached part of the mosque set aside for communal prayers, taking the form of a domed square chamber. Mobile *maqsuras* of wood are also known.

Marchionni, Carlo (1702–86). Famous for his Villa Albani (now Torlonia), Rome (begun 1746), where the garden temples of *c.* 1760 reflect his friend Winckelmann's neo-classicism. He also designed SS. Annunziata, Messina (1763), and the Sacristy of St Peter's, Rome (1776–86).

E. Debenedetti (ed.), *C.M.*, Rome 1988.

Markelius, Sven Gottfrid (1889–1972). Swedish architect and town-planner. His concert hall at Hälsingbor (1925–32) is notable, but he is famous as city architect and planner to the city of Stockholm 1944–54, when he laid out the new suburb of Vällingby. Vällingby is not a SATELLITE TOWN, as it is not meant to have a completely independent existence, but is of an exemplary plan combining a truly urban-looking centre with peripheral housing of both high blocks of flats and small houses (1953–9).

S. Ray, *Il contributo svedese all'architettura contemporanea e l'opera di S.M.*, Rome 1969.

Marot, Daniel (*c.* 1660–1752), was the son of a minor French architect Jean Marot (*c.* 1619–79) who is chiefly remembered for his volumes of engravings *L'Architecture française* known as 'le grand Marot' and 'le petit Marot'. Born in Paris, Daniel emigrated to Holland after the Revocation of the Edict of Nantes (1685), becoming almost immediately architect to William of Orange. He developed an intricate style of ornamentation, similar to that of Jean Bérain (see his *Nouvelles cheminées à panneaux de la manière de France*), and was involved among other things with the design of the audience chamber or Trèveszaal in the Binnenhof, The Hague (1695–8), and the interior decoration and garden design at Het Loo. He followed William to England and designed the gardens (Grand Parterre) and perhaps some of the furnishings and interior decoration at Hampton Court, but though he later described himself as 'Architect to the King of England' no buildings can be ascribed to him (Schomberg House, London, *c.* 1698, appears to have been strongly influenced by him). He died at The Hague, where he designed part of the Royal Library (1734–8) and Stadthuis (1733–9). He published his *Œuvres* in Amsterdam in 1715 but his main buildings date from the following years and are all in The Hague – the German Embassy (1715), the Hôtel van Wassenaar and the façade of the Royal Library (1734, wings by Pieter de Swart, 1761).

Rosenberg 1977; Kuyper 1980.

Martellange, Étienne (d. 1641), see LEMERCIER, Jacques.

Martello tower. A round, low tower, with guns mounted on the flat roof, built for coastal defence in England from 1793 onwards, mainly during the Napoleonic wars but also later and on a wide scale. There are also examples in Jersey, Orkney, Ireland, Canada, South Africa and the USA (Key West, Florida). In form they derive from the traditional Mediterranean watch tower e.g. that on Cape Mortella, Corsica, hence the name.

S. Sutcliffe, *Martello Towers*, Cranberry, NJ, 1973.

Martienssen, Rex (1905–42), *see* SOUTH AFRICAN ARCHITECTURE.

Martin, Sir Leslie (b. 1908), was Architect to the London County Council from 1953 to 1956, in succession to Sir Robert MATTHEW, and later Professor of Architecture at Cambridge University. Under him the finest of all LCC housing estates was built, that at Roehampton for a population of about 10,000. Some of the brightest young architects in England were at that time working in the LCC office, and Martin gave them full scope. In the course of building the style of the scheme changed from one inspired by Sweden to that of LE CORBUSIER at Chandigarh, and Martin's own work in partnership with C.A. St J. Wilson has moved in the same direction – see, for example, the new building for Caius College, Cambridge (1960–62). Other later work includes College Hall, Leicester University (1958–61), the new Oxford libraries (1961–4) and Brunswick Centre, Bloomsbury, London (1962–8).

Martinelli, Domenico (1650–1718), quadratura painter and architect errant, who travelled widely and played an important part in the diffusion of the Italian Baroque style north of the Alps, was born in Lucca and ordained priest, but this did nothing to interfere with his wandering artistic career. His masterpiece is the Stadtpalais Liechtenstein in Vienna (1694–1705), which introduced the elaborate triumphal staircase which was to become an essential feature of Viennese palace architecture. Martinelli also designed the large but simpler Gartenpalais Liechtenstein, Vienna (1700–1711), and probably the Harrach Palais, Vienna (*c.* 1690), as well as a house for Graf von Kaunitz, Austerlitz. It is said that he also worked in Warsaw, Prague, and Holland.

He made designs for several palaces in Bohemia between 1692 and 1705 – Schloss Aussee and Schloss Landskron for Prince Liechtenstein, Schloss Austerlitz for Count Kaunitz, and for the Sternbeck Palace in Prague (1700 onwards).

H. Lorenz, *D.M.*, Vienna 1989.

Martorell, (Codina) Josep (Maria) (b. 1925), *see* SPANISH ARCHITECTURE.

Martyrium. A church or other building erected over a site which bears witness to the Christian faith, either by referring to an event in Christ's life or Passion, or by sheltering the grave of a martyr, a witness by virtue of having shed his or her blood. In Early Christian architecture martyria were usually circular whereas churches were rectangular (*see* BASILICA).

A. Grabar, *M. Recherches sur le culte des reliques et l'art chrétien antique*, Paris 1946.

Mascaron. A grotesque head viewed frontally. A decorative motif.

Mask stop, *see* STOPS.

Masonry. Work by a mason, for example brickwork, stonework. *See* ASHLAR, BRICKWORK, RUBBLE MASONRY, RUSTICATION.

Mason's lodge, *see* LODGE.

Mason's mark. A symbol, monogram or initial incised in stonework by the mason responsible for the execution of the building, frequently found on Romanesque and Gothic buildings.

Massari, Giorgio (1687–1766). Leading Venetian early C18 architect, a contemporary of Tiepolo with whom he often collaborated, e.g. Gesuati (1726–36), which is Palladian outside but with Rococo elements inside. His Santa Maria della Pietà (begun 1745) is more restrained, as is his Palazzo Grassi on the Grand Canal (begun 1748).

A. Massari, *G.M. architetto veneziano del settecento*, Vicenza 1971; Howard 1987.

Mastaba. Ancient Egyptian tomb, in form a massive brick or stone mound with battered walls on a rectangular base. The sarcophagal chamber was deep underground below.

Mathematical tiles. Small facing tiles usually the size of brick headers, applied to timber-framed walls to make them appear brick-built.

Mathey, Jean-Baptiste (c. 1630–95). He was probably born in Dijon and trained as a painter, but was taken to Prague in 1675 as architect to the archbishop and, despite local opposition, began to work in a classicizing French manner very different from that of F. CARATTI and others there. He built Schloss Troya (1679–96), and the quietly handsome Toscana Palace in Prague (1689–90) and, in a more exuberant style, two churches which influenced FISCHER VON ERLACH – that of the Crusader Knights (1679–88) and the abbey church of St Josef Malá Strana, both in Prague.

Hempel 1965.

Matthew, Sir Robert Hogg (1906–75). Architect to the London County Council 1946–53, i.e. the years of its notable housing and educational programmes, and of the Royal Festival Hall, London (1951, river-front remodelled 1962–4).

Of his and his firm's later work York University (1963) was remarkable – simple, un-monumental, and of rational construction yet pleasant to live in. The Hillingdon Civic Centre, Uxbridge (1973–8), marked a return to brick and traditional materials, the design being asymmetrical and picturesque, with pitched roofs.

Matthias of Arras (d. 1352), *see* CZECHOSLOVAK ARCHITECTURE.

Mausoleum. A magnificent and stately tomb. The term derives from the tomb of Mausolus at Halicarnassus *c.* 350 BC.

May, Hugh (1621–84), the son of a Sussex gentleman and prominent among the virtuosi of the Restoration, imported the placid spirit of Dutch PALLADIANISM into England and helped, with PRATT, to establish the type of house later known, erroneously, as the 'Wren' type. The east front of Cornbury House, Oxfordshire (1663–8), and Eltham Lodge, London (1663–4), are his only surviving works. He may also have designed Holme Lacy House, Hereford (begun 1673–4). His work at Windsor Castle (remodelling the Upper Ward including St George's Hall and the King's Chapel, 1675–83) was important but has been almost completely destroyed. It was the most fully developed example of a Baroque scheme of decoration in England – achieved with the aid of the painter Verrio and the sculptor Grinling Gibbons.

Colvin 78; Summerson 1983.

Mayan architecture, *see* MESOAMERICAN ARCHITECTURE.

Maybeck, Bernard Ralph (1862–1957). Active chiefly at Berkeley and

San Francisco. His is a curious, highly original STICK STYLE. Wood was his favourite material. Examples are the Faculty Club on the Berkeley campus (1899) and the first Church of Christ Scientist at Berkeley (1910–12). The mixture of vernacular, Gothic and Japanese in this building is irresistible. Many private houses show the same qualities, the interiors often being yet more stimulating than the exteriors. Maybeck's most spectacular house is Wynton on the McCloud River, built as a fancy castle for Mrs Hearst. The Lawson House at Berkeley is remarkable for being of reinforced concrete as early as 1907.

K. H. Cardwell, *B.M. Artisan, Architect, Artist*, Salt Lake City (1977) 1986; R. Longstreth, *On the Edge of the World. Four Architects in San Francisco at the Turn of the Century*, Cambridge, Mass., 1983.

Mayekawa, Kunio (b. 1905). Japanese architect; worked with LE COR-BUSIER 1928–30 and with RAYMOND 1930–35 and made his name as a pioneer of exposed concrete before the war. Later he refined its use in such buildings as the Harumi Apartments, Tokyo (1957), the Gakushuin University buildings, Tokyo (1960), and the Tokyo Metropolitan Festival Hall (1961). His later work is very restrained, e.g. the Miyagi Prefectural Art Museum, 1981. Kenzo TANGE worked in his office 1938–42.

A. Altherr, *Drei japanische Architekten, M., Tange, Sakakura*, Stuttgart 1968.

McIntire, Samuel (1757–1811), was a self-trained architect of great ability and the outstanding example of the early American craftsman-builder tradition, though most of his work dates from after the end of the Revolutionary War. He was a wood-carver by trade and lived in Salem, Mass. With the help of Batty LANGLEY's and WARE's books and perhaps an edition of Palladio (which he owned at his death), he taught himself the PALLADIAN style, which he adopted for his first houses, e.g. Pierce-Nichols House (1782) in Salem. His most ambitious effort was Salem Court House (1785, now demolished) with superimposed orders and a dome. In the 1790s he came under the influence of BULFINCH, who provided the general design for his most important private house, the Derby Mansion (1795–9, demolished 1815) and from whom he picked up the ADAM style which he used in his later and finest houses (mostly destroyed, but there are rooms from them in the Boston and Philadelphia museums).

Whiffen and Koeper 1981.

McKim, Charles Follen (1847–1909), studied first engineering at Harvard, then, in 1867–70, architecture in Paris at the École des Beaux Arts. On his return to the States he entered the office of H. H. RICHARDSON. When he set up his own practice, he went into partnership with William Rutherford Mead (1846–1928) and a little later with Stanford WHITE. In 1878 they were all interested in Colonial architecture, a highly unusual thing at the time. To this was added almost at once a liking for the Italian Renaissance which was first introduced, it seems, by Joseph Merrill Wells, who entered the office in 1879 and died early, in 1890. The Italian Renaissance meant to them the High Renaissance, not the Baroque exuberance of classical motifs then current. A first proof of this new taste was the impressive restrained group of the Villard Houses in Madison Avenue (1882), the second the Boston Public Library (1888–95) with its façade by McKim, inspired by LABROUSTE's Ste Geneviève Library. McKim believed in interior enrichment on a grand scale, and for the library was able to call in Sargent and Puvis de Chavannes. For the Chicago exhibition of 1893, McKim did the Agriculture Building.

Later jobs include the Germantown Cricket Club (1891), decidedly American Colonial; the lavish Madison Garden (1891), Spanish with a tall tower reminiscent of Seville; the Washington Triumphal Arch in New York in the style of the Étoile; Columbia University in New York with its library rotunda (1893) inspired by the Pantheon in Rome and JEFFERSON's Charlottesville (1817–26); the Morgan Library in New York (1903); and the Pennsylvania railway station also in New York (1906–10, demolished), a grandiose scheme echoing Imperial Roman *thermae*. Although Mead's retirement in 1919 left the firm without any of the original partners, it continued until 1961.

Hitchcock 1977; G. R. Wilson, *McK., Mead & White*, London 1983; L. M. Roth, *McK., Mead & White Architects*, London 1983.

Mead, William Rutherford (1846–1928), *see* MCKIM, Charles Fuller.

Meander, *see* FRET.

Medrese, *see* MADRASA.

Megalith. A large block of stone or boulder of irregular shape, only very roughly dressed or left as found. Prehistoric megalithic monuments, mostly in northern Europe, are now dated *c.* 4000–1000 BC and are of five main types: the menhir or single stone standing upright; the group or alignment of menhirs arranged in rows as at Carnac in Brittany where nearly 3,000 survive; circular settings as at Stonehenge (*c.* 1800 BC), which is architecturally unique (a circle of evenly spaced uprights with a continuous curving lintel, enclosing trilithons); chamber tombs walled and roofed with megaliths, known as dolmens or cromlechs though these terms are now obsolete in this sense in English (dolmen is still so used in French); and finally the apsidal megalithic temples of Malta, e.g. Mnajdra of *c.* 2800–1900 BC.

G. Daniel, *Megaliths in History*, London 1972; A Burl, *The Stone Circles of the British Isles*, New Haven and London 1976.

Megaron. A square or oblong room with a central hearth and usually four columns to support the roof, the lateral walls projecting forwards beyond the entrance wall to form the sides of a porch which is usually columned. Sometimes a second entrance wall, with a single opening like the first, is added to form an anteroom. It has been traditional in Greece since Mycenaean times and is sometimes thought to be the ancestor of the Doric temple. In Greek the word means simply 'large room'. Its technical use is modern.

Megastructure. A very large, multifunctional and wholly enclosed building complex. The megastructure replaces individual buildings when restructuring urban form, as in Paolo SOLERI's Arcologies. Scarborough College by ANDREWS was one of the first and most notable examples to be fully realized.

Banham 1976.

Meier, Richard (b. 1934). The most prolific and purist of the NEW YORK FIVE. His work was largely responsible for their being called the Whites, e.g. his Saltzman house, East Hampton, NY (1967–9), and the one-family house at Old Westbury, NY (1969–71). He has become one of the top American public architects, e.g. the Applied Art Museum, Frankfurt-am-Main (1979–80), the High Museum, Atlanta (1980–83), and the Getty Museum, Los Angeles (commissioned 1984).

J. Rykwert, *R.M. Architect 1964–84*, New York 1984; Klotz 1988.

Meissonnier, Juste-Aurèle (1695–1750). Leading Rococo designer and architect, born in Turin but settled in Paris *c.* 1714. Only one of his buildings survives (Chambre de Commerce, Bayonne) and his fame now rests on his engraved designs.

D. Nyberg (ed.), *Œuvres de J.-A.M.*, New York 1969.

Meldahl, Ferdinand (1827–1908), *see* DANISH ARCHITECTURE.

Melnikov, Konstantin Stepanovich (1890–1974). Russian architect who became prominent in the early 1920s for his 'Productivist' work, e.g. his wooden, demountable Sucharev Market, Moscow (1924–5), and his USSR Pavilion for the Paris 1925 exhibition which synthesized all the progressive elements in Soviet architecture. But he was out of public life from 1934 onwards until shortly before his death.

S. F. Starr, *M. Solo Architect in a Mass Society*, Princeton (1978) 1981; S. O. Khan-Magomedev, *Pioneers of Soviet Architecture: The Search for New Solutions in the 1920s and 1930s*, London 1987.

Mendelsohn, Erich or Eric (1887–1953). The boldness of Mendelsohn's vision of a sculptural architecture emerged early in his many small sketches for buildings that are not functionally determined but are highly expressive with their streamlined curves. In the years of German EXPRESSIONISM at and after the end of the First World War, he was just once enabled actually to build such a vision (the Einstein Tower at Potsdam, 1919–21); but vigorous curves carried round corners also characterize his remodelling of the Mosse Building in Berlin (1921), and appear much tempered by the more rational spirit of the INTERNATIONAL MODERN style of the later twenties and the thirties in his excellent Schocken stores for Stuttgart (1926) and Chemnitz (1928). As expressive as the Einstein Tower, but in terms of multi-angular roof shapes instead of curves, is another early work of Mendelsohn's, a factory at Luckenwalde (1923). Mendelsohn visited the United States in 1924 and was understandably impressed by the expressive qualities of the skyscrapers. Later Berlin buildings include the WOGA Bauten, Berlin (1924–6), the headquarters of the Metal Workers' Union (1929) and Columbushaus (1929–30). In 1933 Mendelsohn went to London and joined Serge CHERMAYEFF. Joint work are the de la Warr Pavilion at Bexhill (1935–6) and No. 64 Old Church Street, Chelsea (1936). But in 1934 he moved on to Israel, and in 1941 finally settled in the United States. In Israel he built, among other things, the Hadassah University Medical Centre on Mount Scopus, Jerusalem (1936–8), in America the Maimonides Hospital at San Francisco (1946–50).

Hitchcock 1977; B. Zevi, *E.M. Opera completa*, Milan 1970; S. Achenback, *E.M. (1887–1953). Ideen, Bauten, Projekte*, exh. cat., Berlin 1987.

Mengoni, Giuseppe (1829–77). Architect of the Galleria Vittorio Emanuele in Milan, won in competition in 1861. It was built in 1864–7 (though work on the decoration continued until 1877), and is the largest, highest, and most ambitious of all shopping arcades. It is cruciform, and the buildings through which it runs take part in the free Renaissance design of the *galleria*. Especially impressive is the façade towards the Piazza del Duomo.

J. F. Geist, *Arcades. The History of a Building Type*, Cambridge, Mass., 1983.

Menhir, *see* MEGALITH.

Merlini, Domenico (1730–97), *see* POLISH ARCHITECTURE.

Merlon, *see* BATTLEMENT.

Merovingian architecture, *see* FRENCH ARCHITECTURE.

Merrill, John O. (1896–1975), *see* SKIDMORE, OWINGS & MERRILL.

Meso-American architecture. The architecture of the civilizations that flourished from *c.* 1000 BC until the Spanish conquest in AD 1519–21 in Central America, i.e. the area south of the Pánuco river and north of Panama, comprising part of modern Mexico, Guatemala, Honduras, Belize, El Salvador and Nicaragua. Despite differences of language and ethnic type the peoples living in this region shared similar religious beliefs and rituals, as is evident in their architecture. Nearly

all surviving buildings were religious (others were of impermanent materials). The most notable are termed pyramids, though they differ from those of Egypt in both form and function – they are of varying plan (circular, oblong, square), flat-topped and conceived as artificial hills for the celebration of rites, like ZIGGURATS. Some were raised over the tombs of rulers. The earliest known *c.* C8 BC, of which only the core of layers of dried clay 100 ft high survives, was a truncated cone with ten ribs in a ceremonial centre of the Olmecs on the island of La Venta in the Tonolà river. At Cuicuilco (Valley of Mexico) a circular mound was raised by people of a different culture *c.* 200 BC, some 440 ft in diameter and 65 ft high of four stages faced with stone slabs laid in clay, the platform approached up ramps and steps from east and west. Slightly later and much better preserved are the buildings at Teotihuacán (near present-day Mexico City), a vast city – the earliest in the Americas of which substantial traces remain – covering some 8 sq. miles laid out AD C1–8 on an astronomically orientated grid plan. It has a central avenue 130 ft wide and $1\frac{1}{2}$ miles long, leading to a nearly 200-ft-high pyramid composed of layers of clay faced with rough stones and sited on axis with the point where the sun sets on the day of its zenith passage. Later and smaller pyramids at this site were more elaborately constructed with skeleton frameworks of piers and slabs of tufa, to stabilize earth and rubble fillings, and finely dressed masonry facing – notably that dedicated to Quetzalcoatl (*c.* AD 150–250) with relief carvings of plumed serpents and menacing heads.

Pyramids, often much higher in relation to the base, were built by the Maya, who lived in city states distributed over a wide area – Honduras, Guatemala, Belize, the whole Yucatan peninsula and the Mexican states of Tabasco and Chiapas. They were built in the ceremonial centres of cities among temples, sanctuaries, courts for the ball-game (a religious rite sometimes terminating with human sacrifice) and structures of more than one storey with many small ill-lit rooms which seem to have been intended less for habitation than for regal ceremonies and for storage. They were set on stone terraces and built of stone with a mortar composed of lime and sand. Openings have trabeated or triangular corbelled arches and interiors corbelled vaults, which appear for the first time in the Americas early in the C4 AD at Uaxactún. Much use was made of sculpture, often of very high quality – friezes, lintels, wall-panels, the treads of pyramid stairways and their borders – intricately carved in low relief with masks, serpents or representations of religious ceremonies, as at Cerros, Uxmal, Piedras Negras, Palenque, Yaxchilán and Chichen Itzá, though many were removed and are now in American and European museums. Maya buildings date from between the C2 BC and AD 900, when many of the cities were abandoned and the territory came under the rule of a different ethnic group usually identified as the Toltecs.

In southern Mexico, outside the Maya area, the distinct culture of the Zapotecs emerged at Monte Alban, where between the C4 and C10 a whole hill was covered with somewhat severe undecorated terraces, platforms and buildings linked by great staircases. A striking contrast is provided by the con-

temporary Tajín, the centre of the so-called Totonac culture where numerous buildings in a great variety of forms and with much sculptured decoration were constructed between the C5 or C6 and the C13, when the place was abandoned.

By the C10 when these early civilizations had begun to falter groups of invaders collectively known as the Chichimecs began to arrive from the north. The most important of them, the Toltecs, founded the city of Tula, where they built a grandiose pyramid dedicated to Tlahuizcalpantecuhtli, with savage sculptural decorations which include many references to human sacrifice. They appear to have taken over Chichen Itzá, where the latest buildings are sometimes said to have been erected by Toltecs, though they may be Mayan: the nine-storey pyramid called the Castillo, the Temple of the Jaguars, the Temple of the Warriors with a many-columned portico and the largest of all Meso-American ball courts.

The Toltec civilization was already in decline before the arrival of the Aztecs, who settled on the island of Texcoco in 1325 and soon dominated the entire Meso-American area. They took over the architecture of their predecessors, their only original contribution being the double pyramid. Their capital city Tenochtitlán and their holy city Cholula with many pyramids and temples were entirely destroyed by the Spaniards immediately after the conquest. Of surviving Aztec buildings the most important is the double pyramid at Tenayuca, with a monumental staircase up one side and a row of fiercely grimacing serpent heads projecting from the base on the other three sides. This pyramid appears to have been

rebuilt every fifty-two years for the ceremony of the New Fire, which initiated
each cycle of the Aztec calendar. The
present one dates from *c.* 1450-1500.
Other notable buildings include the
Pyramid at El Tepozteco (*c.* 1502-20),
constructed high on a rocky ridge, and
a complex of buildings hewn from the
living rock at Malinalco (1476-1520).
Although the bloodthirsty and warlike
Aztecs expanded their empire, in quest
of prisoners for human sacrifice as well
as land, one subject group maintained
cultural independence – the Mixtecs,
who occupied an area bordering the
Pacific and roughly corresponding to
the modern Mexican states of Oaxaca,
Puebla and Guerrero. The only important Mixtec site is Mitla, where there
are no pyramids, only palaces, notably
the Palace of the Columns decorated
with finely cut geometrical reliefs
which provide a striking contrast to the
terrifying grotesques on Aztec and
Toltec buildings. For post-conquest
architecture in the region, *see* MEXI-
CAN ARCHITECTURE.

Mesopotamian architecture, *see*
SUMERIAN AND AKKADIAN ARCHI-
TECTURE.

Metabolism. A Japanese movement
launched in 1960 in Tokyo, chiefly by
TANGE, who was joined by KIKUTAKE
and KUROKAWA and later by Fumihiko Maki (b. 1928). Kurokawa's work
typified the science-fiction-like image
of the group, which gradually dispersed after 1970.

K. Kurokawa, *The Concept of Metabolism,* Tokyo 1972; K. Kurokawa, *M.
in Architecture,* London 1977.

Metal structures. The use of metal
as a building material was discussed by
the Venetian theorist F. Venanzio in

Machinae Novae (1617) but only began
in practice in the late C18 with BRIDGES
and the first iron-framed buildings in
England (*see* INDUSTRIALIZED BUILD-
ING). The pioneer in the use of metal
for a complete structure (other than
bridges) was SCHINKEL, whose cast-
iron neo-Gothic Kreuzberg monument
in Berlin is of 1818. Other notable architects who were early in exploiting
metal include BÉLANGER, FONTAINE,
PAXTON, LABROUSTE, and BALTARD,
usually in conjunction with GLASS (*see
also* CONSERVATORIES). In 1843-4 a
prefabricated house of iron by John
Walker was erected on the Calaba river
in central Africa. As early as the 1840s
there were 'cast-iron districts' in American cities (*see* BOGARDUS), and though
there was nothing comparable in
Europe some remarkable exposed iron
façades went up in Britain between
1850 and 1880, the earliest in Glasgow
(36 Jamaica Street) by John Baird
(1798-1859) and in Liverpool by Peter
ELLIS. In 1854 Sir William Fairbairn
published in London *On the Application of Cast and Wrought Iron to Building Purposes* (reprinted 1970) and in
1865 D. B. Badger issued his *Illustrated
Catalogue of Cast-Iron Architecture* in
New York (reprinted 1981). Metal was,
of course, the essential element in the
development of the SKYSCRAPER and
the CURTAIN WALL, though it was not
always exposed. In Europe metal has
been largely replaced by REINFORCED
CONCRETE, which is cheaper, but it
continues to be used as an exposed element in the USA and Japan.

G. Roisecco, *L'architettura del ferro,*
Rome 1972-3; M. Gayle and E. V.
Gillo, *Cast Iron Architecture in New
York City,* New York 1974; Mainstone
1975; C. Behnisch and G. Hartung,
Eisenkonstruktion des 19 Jahrhunderts,

Munich 1982; B. Lemoine, *L'Architecture du fer. France XIX siècle*, Seyssel 1986.

Métezeau, Louis (1559/72–1615), was closely involved with the DU CERCEAUS in Henry IV's improvements to Paris, notably the Place des Vosges (1603 onwards) and at the Louvre, where he probably designed the south façade of the Grande Galerie. He also assisted in the interior decoration of the Petite Galerie, the Salle des Antiques and the Grande Galerie (1601–8). He collaborated with Dupérac on the interior decoration of the Hôtel de Jean de Fourcy, Paris (1601). His brother Clément or Jacques Clément Métezeau (1581–1652) may have been a more important architect. He was transitional between de BROSSE and LE VAU. He designed the Place Ducale at Charleville (1610), the portail of St Gervais, Paris (1616), the Orangerie du Louvre (1617), the Hôtel de Brienne (1630–32) and the Château de la Meilleraye (*c.* 1630). He worked with de Brosse at the Luxembourg in Paris *c.* 1615 and in 1611 was sent to Florence by Marie de' Medici to make drawings of Palazzo Pitti in connection with it, though they do not appear to have been used by de Brosse.

J. P. Babelon, *Demeures parisiennes. Sous Henri IV et Louis XIII*, Paris 1965.

Metope. The square space between two TRIGLYPHS in the FRIEZE of a Doric order; it may be carved or left plain. *See* Fig. 66.

Meurtrière. In military architecture, a small loophole, large enough for the barrel of a gun or musket and through which a soldier might fire under cover.

Mews. A row of stables with living accommodation above, built at the back of a town-house, especially in London. They are now nearly all converted into houses or 'mews flats'.

Mexican architecture. (For Pre-Columbian Mexican architecture, *see* MESO-AMERICAN ARCHITECTURE.) After the Spanish conquest Mexican architecture took on a Gothic (e.g. San Miguel de Actopan) or Spanish Renaissance character and then, from the late C16, Baroque (e.g. Mexico City Cathedral, 1563–1667, Puebla Cathedral, 1551–1664), sometimes of an extravagantly Churrigueresque kind (e.g. the Sanctuary at Ocotlán, *c.* 1745). Indeed Mexican Baroque architecture took Spanish Baroque to extremes, e.g. Governmental Palace, Guadalajara (1751–75). Mexican C20 architecture became known internationally in the 1930s with the Cardenas regime. José Villagrán García (b. 1901), Juan O'Gorman (1905–82) and Luis BARRAGÁN all began at this time, and in 1939 Hannes Meyer (1889–1954), who had for a short time succeeded GROPIUS as director of the BAUHAUS, settled in Mexico. However, it was not until after the Second World War that it won international acclaim with the new university city outside the capital, planned and largely built between 1950 and 1953. Notable are the School of Architecture and Museum of Art by Villagrán García, the School of Medicine by Pedro Ramírez Vásquez (b. 1919), the library with its vast exterior mosaics by O'Gorman and the Cosmic Ray building by CANDELA, who became, with Barragán, the best-known C20 Mexican architect. Ramírez Vásquez's programme for cheap mass-produced village schools was notable, as was also his Anthropological Museum in Mexico City of 1964. More recently the work of Richard Logorreta (b. 1931) has been acclaimed for his imaginative use of the vernacular, e.g. his Camino Real hotels of the 1970s.

Mey, Johann Melchior van der (1878-1949), *see* DUTCH ARCHITECTURE.

Meyer, Adolph (1881–1929), *see* GROPIUS, Walter.

Meyer, Hannes (1889–1954), *see* BAUHAUS; MEXICAN ARCHITECTURE.

Mezzanine. A low storey between two higher ones; also called an *entresol*.

Michael of Canterbury. A master mason working *c.* 1300, first at Canterbury for the cathedral, then in London, where he was the first master mason of St Stephen's Chapel (begun 1292) in the palace of Westminster and probably its designer. A Walter of Canterbury was in charge of work at the palace in 1322. A Thomas of Canterbury was working under him in 1324 and, in 1331, probably after Walter's death, was put in charge of work at St Stephen's Chapel. Thomas may have died in 1336.

Harvey 1984

Michaud, Joseph (1822–1902), *see* CANADIAN ARCHITECTURE.

Michelangelo Buonarroti (1475–1564). Sculptor, painter, poet, and one of the greatest of all architects, he was the archetype of the inspired 'genius' – unsociable, distrustful, untidy, obsessed by his work, and almost pathologically proud – in fact, the antithesis of the Early Renaissance ideal of the complete man so nobly exemplified in ALBERTI and LEONARDO. Deeply and mystically religious, he was consumed by the conflicts and doubts of the Counter-Reformation. As in his life, so in his art, he rejected the assumptions of the Renaissance and revolutionized everything he touched. Nowhere was his influence so profound or so enduring as in architecture. He invented a new vocabulary of ornament, new and dynamic principles of composition, and an entirely new attitude to space. His few dicta and his drawings reveal that he conceived a building as an organic growth and in relation to the movement of the spectator. He made clay models rather than perspective drawings, and appears to have eschewed the type of highly finished design which could be turned over to the builders ready for execution. He usually made considerable modifications as the building went up, and it is now impossible to tell exactly how his many incomplete works would have looked when finished or how he would have realized in stone those compositions which remained on paper – the façade of S. Lorenzo, Florence (1516), or the centrally planned S. Giovanni dei Fiorentini, Rome (1556 60).

His first work in architecture is the exterior of the chapel of Leo X in Castel Sant'Angelo, Rome (1514). In 1515 he received his first major commission, for the façade of BRUNELLESCHI's S. Lorenzo, Florence, which he conceived as an elaborate framework for more than life-size sculpture. In 1520, before his S. Lorenzo design was finally abandoned, he was commissioned to execute the Medici family mausoleum in the new sacristy of the same church, much of which was already built. He produced a revolutionary design in which, for the first time, the tyranny of the orders was completely rejected; windows taper sharply, capitals vanish from pilasters, tabernacles weigh down heavily on the voids of the doors beneath them. But the novelty of his design is less evident in this truculent misuse of the classical vocabulary than in the revolutionary conception of architecture which inspired it. He saw the wall not as an inert plane to be decorated with applied ornaments but as a vital, many-layered organism – hence the extraordinary form of the tabernacles with their strange elisions and recessions. The fact that he developed this new conception while the sacristy was in course of construction accounts for its many inconsistencies. The work was brought more or less to its present state by 1534 but never completed.

In 1524 he was commissioned to design a library for S. Lorenzo, Florence – the famous Biblioteca Laurenziana (reading-room designed 1525, vestibule 1526). The site determined its awkward shape and also limited the thickness of the walls. But he turned both these limitations to good effect, linking the structure to the decoration in a way never before achieved or imagined. Pilasters, which had hitherto been purely decorative elements applied to a structural wall, he used as the supports for the ceiling, while the cross-beams above the pilasters are echoed in mosaic on the floor so that the eye is drawn along the length of the room through a perspective of diminishing oblongs. He counteracted this longitudinal emphasis by stressing the verticality of the vestibule. Here the columns are set like statues in niches so that they appear to be merely decorative, though in fact they carry the roof. Other features are no less perverse – blind window-frames of aedicules with

pilasters which taper towards the base, consoles which support nothing, and a staircase which pours forbiddingly down from the library on to the entrance level (executed by AMMANATI). There is no figure sculpture, but the whole interior is treated plastically as if it were sculpture.

In 1528–9 Michelangelo was employed on the fortifications of Florence, which he designed, with characteristic perversity, for offence rather than defence. In 1534 he left Florence for Rome, where he spent the rest of his life. His first Roman commission was for the reorganization of the Capitol, to provide a suitable setting for the ancient statue of Marcus Aurelius and an imposing place for outdoor ceremonies (begun 1539). He laid out the central space as an oval – the first use of this shape in the Renaissance – and designed new fronts for Palazzo dei Conservatori and Palazzo del Senatore (neither finished before his death). His designs were strikingly original, e.g. in their use of a GIANT ORDER embracing two storeys, a device that was soon to become general. In 1546 he was commissioned to complete Antonio da SANGALLO's Palazzo Farnese. He converted the unfinished façade into one of the most imposing in Rome, redesigned the upper floors of the *cortile*, and planned a vast garden to link it with the Villa Farnesina on the far side of the Tiber (not executed). In the conception of this grandiose vista, as in his design for the Porta Pia (1561–5) at the end of a new street from the Quirinal, he anticipated the principles of Baroque town planning.

But his most important Roman commission was, of course, for the completion of St Peter's (1546–64). Here he was faced with the task of finishing a building begun by BRAMANTE and continued by Antonio da Sangallo. He reverted to the centralized plan of the former, but made it much bolder and stronger, and demolished part of the latter's additions. His work on the interior was entirely masked in the C17; on the exterior it is visible only on the north and south arms and the drum of the dome. (The dome itself is by della PORTA and differs substantially from Michelangelo's model.) But although his plans were much altered the church as it stands today owes more to him than to any other single architect. In his last years he designed the Cappella Sforza, S. Maria Maggiore, Rome (c. 1560), on an ingenious plan rather coarsely executed after his death. He also provided plans for the conversion of the central hall of the Baths of Diocletian into S. Maria degli Angeli (1561), but here his work was completely overlaid in the C18.

The story of his architectural career is one of constant frustration. Not one of his major designs was complete at the time of his death. Yet his influence was none the less great. The Mannerists took from him decorative details which were gradually absorbed into the European grammar of ornament. But it was not until the C17 that architects were able to appreciate and began to emulate his dynamic control of mass and space. Significantly, his true heir was to be another sculptor architect, BERNINI.

J. S. Ackerman, *The Architecture of M.*, London 1964–6; rev. edn with J Newman, Harmondsworth (1970) 1986; H. A. Millon and C. H. Smyth, *M. Architect*, Washington 1988.

Michelozzo di Bartolommeo (1396–1472), a sculptor and architect of extreme elegance and refinement, nevertheless lacked the genius of his great contemporaries Donatello and BRUNELLESCHI. Born in Florence, the son of Bartolommeo di Gherardo, who hailed from Burgundy, he worked as assistant to Ghiberti (1417–24), then shared a studio with Donatello (1425 33). In the mid-1430s he began to turn his attention to architecture and succeeded Brunelleschi as Capomaestro at the cathedral in 1446. His first important works were for the Medici family. In about 1433 he added the graceful courtyard and loggia to their castle-cum-villa at Careggi and eleven years later began the Palazzo Medici-Riccardi in Florence, the first Renaissance palace, with massive rusticated basement and slightly smoother rusticated upper floors capped by a prominent cornice. Behind this slightly forbidding fortress-like exterior there is an arcaded *cortile* derived from Brunelleschi's Ospedale degli Innocenti. His Medicean villa at Caffagiolo (1451) is again fortress-like, in contrast with his Villa Medici at Fiesole (1458–61: but considerably altered in C18), which is exquisitely light and elegant in style.

In 1437 he began work at S. Marco, Florence, where he designed the sacristy (1437–43), the cloisters and the light and harmonious library (1441). Between 1444 and 1455 he designed the tribune and sacristy of SS. Annunziata. The tribune (completed by ALBERTI) is centrally planned, inspired no doubt by Brunelleschi's S. Maria degli Angeli, but closer to an ancient Roman model, the temple of Minerva Medica. This was the first centralized building to be erected in the Renaissance, and it reflects both a desire to revive an antique form and a preoccupation with the circle as a symbol of the universe and eternity. At Pistoia he built the little church of S. Maria delle Grazie (1452), where he employed the Early Christian and Byzantine form of a square building with central dome and subsidiary domed chapels at the four corners. In about 1462 he was in Milan, probably working on the Medici Bank. He also built the Portinari Chapel in S. Eustorgio, Milan (c. 1462), which owes much to Brunelleschi's S. Lorenzo sacristy. With this chapel he introduced the Renaissance style to Lombardy. From 1462 to 1463 he was in Dubrovnik, where he designed the Palazzo dei Rettori.

W. Ferrara and F. Quintero, *M. di B.*, Florence 1984.

Michelucci, Giovanni (1891–1990). As one of the architects of Florence railway station (1933–6) he became a leading exponent of RATIONALISM. His later work was freer and more plasticly expressive, notably the Autostrada del Sole church at the Florence exit (1960–63).

F. Naldi, *G.M.*, Florence 1978; A. Bellucci and C. Conforti, *Lo spazio sacro di M.*, Florence 1987.

Mies van der Rohe, Ludwig (1886–1969), worked under Bruno Paul, and then from 1908 to 1911 in Peter BEHRENS's office in Berlin. His earliest independent designs are inspired by SCHINKEL and the Berlin Schinkel Revival of the early C20 (Kröller House, 1912). At the end of the First World War he was, like GROPIUS, caught up in the frenzy and enthusiasm of EXPRESSIONISM, and he designed then his revolutionary glass skyscrapers (1919–21). When Germany settled down to its rational responsible style of the later twenties and the early thirties,

Mies van der Rohe excelled in this as well (e.g. for DEUTSCHER WERKBUND, 1927). His true greatness as an architect was first revealed in the German Pavilion for the Barcelona Exhibition of 1929, with its open plan and masterly spatial composition, its precious materials – marble, travertine, onyx, polished steel, bottle-green glass – a sign of a striving after the highest quality and the most immaculate finishes. The planning principles of the Barcelona Pavilion were tested for domestic purposes in the Tugendhat House at Brno (1930), a private house.

From 1930 to 1933 Mies van der Rohe was director of the BAUHAUS, first at Dessau and then when it moved to Berlin for its last harassed phase of existence. In 1938 he was made Professor of Architecture at the Armour Institute (now Illinois Institute) of Technology in Chicago. In 1939 he designed a complete new campus for the Institute, whose plan has since developed and whose buildings have grown. They are characterized by cubic simplicity – envelopes which easily adapt to the various requirements of the Institute – and a perfect precision of details, where every member makes its own unequivocal statement. These qualities pervade all Mies van der Rohe's work. 'I don't want to be interesting, I want to be good,' he said in an interview. The volume of his work was remarkably small until after the Second World War, but then grew considerably. Among private houses the Farnsworth House at Plano, Illinois (1950), must be mentioned; among blocks of flats the Promontory Apartments (1947) with a concrete frame, and Lake Shore Drive (1951) with a steel frame, both at Chicago, and Lafayette Towers at Detroit (1963); among office buildings, the Seagram building in New York (1956–9), with a bronze and marble facing; and the new National Gallery in Berlin (1963–8). They are all a final triumphant vindication of the style created in the early C20 and assimilated gradually in the thirties, and they do not participate in the neo-sculptural tendencies of the last fifteen or twenty years.

F. Schulze, *M. van der R. A Critical Biography*, Chicago 1985; J. Zukowsky (ed.), *M. Reconsidered. His Career: Legacy and Disciples*, New York 1986; J. Zukowsky and H. P. Schwartz, *M. van der R.*, exh. cat., Frankfurt 1987.

Mihrab. The focus for prayer in a MOSQUE, usually a niche (sometimes a flat slab) in the centre of the QIBLA wall. It first appears in the late C7.

Milesian layout. A city plan of regular gridiron pattern with streets of uniform width and blocks of houses of approximately uniform dimensions. It probably originated in the Hittite, Assyrian and Babylonian empires and developed in Ionia in the C7 BC. It is named after the city of Miletus. Other notable examples in antiquity are Cyrene in Lydia (founded 630–24) and Paestum (built by Greek colonists in C6 BC). This type of plan was advocated by HIPPODAMOS, who is sometimes incorrectly said to have invented it.

Miller, Sanderson (1716–80), *see* GOTHIC REVIVAL.

Mills, Robert (1781–1855). Born in Charleston, South Carolina, he was discovered by JEFFERSON and articled to LATROBE, with whom he stayed from 1803 to 1808. His practice started in Philadelphia in 1808 (notably Washington Hall, perhaps influenced by

LEDOUX). He designed the former State House at Harrisburg in 1810 with a semicircular portico and a dome over the centre; a circular church at Charleston as early as 1804; an octagonal and a large circular one in Philadelphia in 1811–13 (the latter with 4,000 seats); and then the Washington Monument for Baltimore, an unfluted Doric column (1814–29). His principal later works are governmental buildings for Washington, all Grecian and competent (Treasury, 1836–9; Patent Office, 1836–40; Post Office, 1839 etc.), but his most famous work is the Washington Monument at Washington, won in competition in 1836 and completed only in 1884. It is an obelisk 555 ft high and was originally meant to have a Greek Doric rotunda at its foot. Mills also did engineering jobs and a number of hospitals. The Columbia Lunatic Asylum (1822) has none of the grimness of its predecessors. It is like a monumental hospital (Greek Doric portico), and has all wards to the south and a roof garden. It is of fireproof construction.

Hitchcock 1977; Whiffen and Koeper 1981; R. W. Liscombe, *The Church Architecture of R.M.*, Easly, S. Carolina, 1985.

Mimbar or **minbar**. The high pulpit in a MOSQUE. It stands to the right of the MIHRAB and is normally of wood (sometimes on wheels).

Minaret. A tall, usually slender tower or turret, connected with a MOSQUE. Minarets have one or more projecting balconies from which the muezzin calls the people to prayer. The first instance of a tower being utilized for this purpose was probably at Damascus in the early C8 (the Great Mosque). There are several regional variations, e.g. rec-

FIG. 62. *Minaret*

tangular in plan (North Africa), cylindrical (Iraq and Eastern Islamic world), slender, pencil-shaped and girdled with tiers of balconies (Turkey). *See* Fig. 62.

J. Bloom, *Minaret. Symbol of Islam*, Oxford 1990.

Minoan architecture, *see* CRETAN AND MYCENAEAN ARCHITECTURE.

Minster. Originally the name for any monastic establishment or its church, whether a monastery proper or a house of secular canons, it came to be applied to certain cathedral churches in England and abroad (e.g. York) and also other major churches.

Minute. In classical architecture a unit of measurement representing one sixtieth part of the diameter of a column at the base of its shaft. It may be either one sixtieth or one thirtieth part of a MODULE.

Mique, Richard (1728–94). Leading Louis XVI architect and the last of the royal architects at Versailles. He was trained under J.-F. BLONDEL in Paris, then employed by ex-King Stanislas at Nancy, who ennobled him (1761). On Stanislas's death in 1766 he returned to Paris. He built the Ursuline convent, now Lycée Hoche, at Versailles (1767–72) with quietly elegant conventual buildings and a church inspired by Palladio's Villa Rotonda, and in 1775 the Carmelite church at St Denis (now Justice de la Paix) with an Ionic portico and cupola. The same year he succeeded GABRIEL as first architect to Louis XVI and in this capacity was responsible for numerous minor works at Versailles – the decoration of the Petits Appartements of Marie Antoinette in the main palace, the theatre at the Petit Trianon, the exquisite circular Temple de l'Amour, the Belvédère, and, his best-known work, the picturesquely rustic Hameau with exposed beams and irregular roofs. He was finally guillotined.

Kalnein and Levey 1972; Braham 1980.

Misericord or **miserere.** Bracket on the underside of the seat of a hinged choir stall which, when turned up, served as a support for the occupant while standing during long services. The undersides were usually carved, often with figures.

M. D. Anderson, *Misericords. Medieval Life in English Woodcarving*, London 1954; G. L. Remnant, *A Catalogue of Misericords in Great Britain*, London 1969.

Mithraeum. A building, often semi-subterranean, for celebrating the cult of Mithras, originally a Persian demigod whose worship challenged early Christianity. A mithraeum contains a passage between broad shelves on which worshippers reclined during ceremonies, the end wall bearing a relief or fresco of Mithras. They are commonly found in the Roman provinces, e.g. Dura Europos, but also in Rome itself, e.g. below S. Clemente.

Mixtec architecture, *see* MESO-AMERICAN ARCHITECTURE.

Mnesicles. A prominent architect in Periclean Athens. He designed the grand entrance gateway to the Acropolis, Athens, 437–432 BC but never finished; also, probably, the earlier Erechtheum of *c.* 420 BC.

J. A. Bungaard, *M.*, Copenhagen 1957; C. Tiberi, *M. l'architetto dei propilei*, Rome 1964.

Modernism, *see* INTERNATIONAL MODERN.

Modernisme. Term given to a vigorous regional style which flourished in Catalonia *c.* 1880–1920 and which has influenced such recent architects as Bohigas and Martorell. *See* SPANISH ARCHITECTURE.

O. Bohigas, *Reseña y catálogo de la arquitectura modernista*, Barcelona 1971; J. L. Marfany, *Aspectes del Modernisme*, Barcelona 1975.

Modillion. A small bracket or CONSOLE of which a series is frequently used to support the upper member of a Corinthian or Composite CORNICE, arranged in pairs with a square depression between each pair. *See* Fig. 44.

Modular design. Design on the basis of fixed dimensions or MODULES, usually as a result of using prefabricated parts (*see* INDUSTRIALIZED BUILDING), but also reviving theoretical interest, e.g. MODULOR.

Module. A unit of measurement by which the proportions of a building or part of a building are regulated. 1. In classical architecture, either the diameter or half the diameter of a column at the base of its shaft, in either case divided into minutes so that the full diameter represents 60 minutes. 2. In modern architecture, any unit of measurement which facilitates prefabrication.

Modulor. The system of proportion advanced by LE CORBUSIER in his *Le Modulor* (1951). It is based upon the male figure and is used to determine the proportions of building units.

Moghul architecture, *see* INDIAN AND PAKISTANI ARCHITECTURE.

Molding, *see* MOULDING.

Molinos, Jacques (1743–1813), *see* BÉLANGER, François-Joseph; GILLY, Friedrich.

Moller, Georg (1784–1852), *see* GILLY, Friedrich.

Molnár, Farkas (1897–1945), *see* HUNGARIAN ARCHITECTURE.

Monastery. Monasticism originated in Egypt, where the first men to choose a monastic life were hermits. A more organized monastic existence was conceived by St Pachomius (346): monks now still lived on their own like hermits, but so close together that they had a joint chapel and a joint refectory. Such monks are known as coenobites. This form of monasticism reached Europe by way of the south of France and from there entered Ireland (Skellig Michael). But the monastic architecture of medieval England and the Continent is that created in the C6 as the expression of the rule of the order estab-

FIG. 63. *Plan of Fountains Abbey*

KEY:

1. Guest houses
2. Lay brothers' infirmary
3. Reredorter
4. Kitchen
5. Monks' refectory
6. Warming house
a = storerooms

7. Upstairs dormitory (shown by dotted lines)
8. Chapterhouse
9. Corridor
10. Infirmary hall
11. Infirmary chapel

lished by St Benedict at Montecassino. Its first surviving complete expression is the plan of *c.* 820 made by a cleric of Cologne for St Gall in Switzerland; here we have the axial arrangement of ranges – the coenobites' layouts were haphazard – the cloister with its arcaded walks, the chapterhouse and dormitory or dorter in the east range, the refectory, frater or dining hall in the range opposite the church, the stores in the west range. Abbots or priors usually lived near the west end as well, while the infirmary was beyond the claustral parts to the east. There were also a guest house, kitchens, brewhouse, bakehouse, smithy, corn-mills, stables, cowsheds, pigsties, etc., and workshops. In terms of architectural composition the monastery is infinitely superior to the medieval castle. *See* Fig. 63; CISTERCIAN ARCHITECTURE; CLUNY.

Braunfels 1973; W. Horn and E. Born, *The Plan of St Gall*, Berkeley and Los Angeles 1979.

Moneo, José Rafael (b. 1937), *see* SPANISH ARCHITECTURE.

Monolith. A single stone, usually in the form of a monument or column.

Monopteral. A term applied to a building with a single row of columns on all sides.

Monteiro, José Luis (1849–1942), *see* PORTUGUESE ARCHITECTURE.

Montereau, Pierre de (d. 1267), *see* PIERRE DE MONTREUIL.

Montferrand, August Ricard (1786–

1858). French Empire architect who emigrated to Russia and became, with ROSSI and STASOV, a leading post-Napoleonic architect in Leningrad. He was trained under PERCIER and worked at the Madeleine in Paris under VIGNON. His masterpiece is the vast and sumptuous St Isaac's Cathedral in Leningrad (1817–57). The dome (completed *c.* 1842) is framed in iron – an early example of the use of metal structure, preceding the dome of the Capitol in Washington by a decade. His enormous granite Alexander Column in Winter Palace Square (1829) is imposing though less original in conception than MILLS's almost contemporary Washington Monument in Washington.

G. Butikov, *St Isaac's Cathedral, Leningrad*, London 1980.

Montigny, A. J. V. Grandjean de (1776–1850), *see* BRAZILIAN ARCHITECTURE.

Montoyer, Louis Joseph (*c.* 1749–1811), *see* CZECHOSLOVAK ARCHITECTURE.

Montreuil, Pierre de (d. 1267), *see* PIERRE DE MONTREUIL.

Moore, Charles Willard (b. 1925). American POST-MODERN architect notable for his large-scale, eclectic, colourful and often extremely scenographic buildings and urban complexes, e.g. Kresge College, UC Santa Cruz (1973); Piazza d'Italia, New Orleans (1975–8); St Matthew's Episcopal Church, Pacific Palisades (1979–83), and Extensions Center and Alumni House, UC Irvine (1983–5).

D. Littlejohn, *Architect: The Life and Work of C.W.M.*, New York 1984; Klotz 1988.

Moosbrugger, Caspar, *see* MOOSBRUGGER, Caspar.

Morandi, Riccardo (b. 1902). Leading Italian concrete designer after NERVI. His Maracaibo bridge, Venezuela (1957), the underground automobile showroom, Turin (1959), and the autostrada bridge, Genoa (1960–67), made his name.

G. Boaga and B. Boni, *R.M.*, Milan 1962; L. V. Masini, *R.M.*, Rome 1974.

Morava school, *see* YUGOSLAV ARCHITECTURE.

Moretti, Luigi (1907–73), *see* ITALIAN ARCHITECTURE.

Morris, Robert (*c.* 1701/2–54), a relation of Roger MORRIS, was the theoretician of English Palladianism in his *An Essay in Defence of Ancient Architecture* (1728) and *Lectures on Architecture* (1734). *Rural Architecture* (1750), reissued as *Select Architecture* (1755), also had a wide influence, e.g. on JEFFERSON's Monticello.

Kaufmann 1955; Colvin 1978; Summerson 1983; Harris 1990.

Morris, Roger (1695–1749). One of the most gifted and original exponents of PALLADIANISM, though of the CAMPBELL rather than the BURLINGTON school. Most of his work was done in association with the 9th Earl of Pembroke, an amateur architect whose share in his designs is difficult to assess; works include Marble Hill, Twickenham (1724–9), White Lodge, Richmond (1727–8) and the Palladian Bridge at Wilton (1736). Later he turned neo-Gothic at Inveraray Castle, Argyllshire (1746 onwards).

Kaufmann 1955; Colvin 1978; Summerson 1983.

Morris, William (1834–96), was not

an architect, but holds an unchallenge-able place in a dictionary of architec-ture because of his great influence on architects. This influence acted in three ways. Morris had begun by studying divinity, then for a short time turned to architecture and worked in the Oxford office of STREET, and subse-quently in a desultory way learnt to paint under Rossetti. When he fur-nished his digs in London, and more so when, after his marriage, he wanted a house, he found that the architecture as well as the design of his day were not to his liking. So he got his friend Philip WEBB to design Red House for him, and this straightforward, red-brick, made-to-measure house had a great deal of influence (*see* ARTS AND CRAFTS). Secondly, as the result of the search for satisfactory furnishings, Morris and some friends created in 1861 the firm Morris, Marshall & Faulkner (later Morris & Co.), for which enterprise Morris himself designed wallpapers, the ornamental parts (and, rarely, the figure work) of stained glass, chintzes (i.e. printed textiles), and later also carpets, tap-estries and woven furnishing materials, and in the end (1890–96) even books and their type and decoration (Kelm-scott Press).

All his designs shared a stylized two-dimensional quality which con-trasted with the then prevailing natur-alism and its unbridled use of depth; but they also possessed a deep feeling for nature which itself contrasted with the ornamental work of a few slightly older English reformers (PUGIN; Owen Jones). These qualities im-pressed themselves deeply on younger architects of Norman SHAW's office and school, so much so that some of them took to design themselves. How-

ever, they might not have gone so far, if it had not been for Morris's third way of influencing architects, his lectures, which he began in 1877 and continued till his death frequently for the SPAB (Society for the Protection of Ancient Buildings), which he founded in 1877 and which enabled him to extol the simplicity and beauty of VERNACULAR buildings. They were impassioned pleas not only for better, more considered design, but for abolish-ing the ugliness of towns and buildings and of the things made to fill buildings, and for reforming the society re-sponsible for towns, buildings, and pro-ducts. Morris was a socialist, one of the founders of organized socialism in Eng-land. That he was also a poet would not be of relevance here, if it were not for the fact that his poetry and his prose romances developed from an avowed medievalism to a strongly implied social responsibility for the present. At the same time the medieva-lism, displayed, for example, by the self-conscious use of obsolete language, is a reminder of the medievalism – ad-mittedly adapted and even transmuted – of all his designs. There is, indeed, a medievalism even in Morris's theory, for his socialism is one of labour becoming once more enjoyable handi-craft. And although Morris fervently believed, harking back again to the Middle Ages, that all art ought to be 'by the people for the people', he could never resolve the dilemma that produc-tion by hand costs more than by machine, and that the products of his own firm therefore (and for other reasons) were bound to be costly and not 'for the people'. It needed a further reform and a revision of this one essen-tial tenet of Morris's to arrive at the C20 situation, where architects and artists design for industrial production and thereby serve the common man and not only the connoisseur. But Morris started the movement, and it was due to him that artists such as van de VELDE or BEHRENS turned designers, and that architects like VOYSEY did likewise. It was also due to him that the criteria of two-dimensional design rose from C19 to C20 standards. Webb's work for Morris had the same effect on furniture design.

P. Thompson, *The Work of W.M.*, London 1967; P. Henderson, *W.M., his Life, Work and Friends*, London 1967; Pevsner 1972; W. Stansky, *Redesigning the World. W.M., the 1880s and the Arts and Crafts*, Princeton 1984.

Mortar. A mixture of cement (or lime), sand and water, laid between courses of bricks or masonry to even out irregularities and gain greater adhesion; more loosely, any material for bedding and jointing brickwork or stonework.

Mortice and tenon joint. A joint formed by a projecting piece (or *tenon*) fitting into a socket (or *mortice*).

Mosaic. Surface decoration for walls or floors formed of small pieces or *tesserae* of glass, stone, or marble set in a mastic. The design may be either geometrical or representational. Mosaic reached its highest pitch of accomplishment in Roman and Byzantine buildings. *See also* TERRAZZO; TESSELLATED.

E. W. Anthony, *A History of Mosaics*, New York (1953) 1968; P. Portoghesi, *Mosaico e architettura*, Ravenna 1959.

Mosbrugger or **Moosbrugger**, Caspar (1656–1723), was born at Au in the Bregenzerwald – the headquarters of the Vorarlberg masons' guild – and was a founder of the Vorarlberg school of architects which included the BEER and THUMB families. He was apprenticed to a stone-cutter, then became a novice at the Benedictine monastery of Einsiedeln in 1682 and remained there as a lay-brother for the rest of his life. He became the greatest Swiss Baroque architect. Already in 1684 he was asked for advice at Weingarten Abbey, though building did not begin there until many years later. His masterpiece is the abbey church at Einsiedeln (begun 1719), a spatial composition of unusual complexity even for a Baroque architect. He did not live to see it completed. He also designed the parish church at Muri (1694–8). He probably played some part (even if only an advisory one) in the design of the vast Benedictine abbey church at Weingarten (1714–24), with a façade much like that at Einsiedeln, and he probably built the church at Disentis (1696–1712).

Hempel 1965; W. Oechslin (ed.), *Die Vorarlberger Barockbaumeister*, exh. cat., Einsiedeln and Bregenz 1973; N. Lieb and F. Dieth, *Die Vorarlberger Barockbaumeister*, Munich and Zürich (1960) 1983.

Moser, Karl (1860–1936), *see* SWISS ARCHITECTURE.

Mosque. An Islamic religious building for communal prayer. The earliest mosques mirror on a much larger scale Mohammed's own house, in which he worshipped, comprising a square, largely open enclosure, with a covered sanctuary on the QIBLA side and rooms along the east. From the c8 onwards most mosques had at least one MINARET (*see also* MIHRAB; MIMBAR; MAQSURA). A distinction should be drawn between a Friday mosque (or *jami*) large enough for the entire adult

FIG. 64. *Mouchette*

Muslim community to assemble for Friday prayers, and the simple oratory (or *masjid*) for daily prayers.

Mothe, Jean-Baptiste Michel Vallin de la (1729–1800), *see* VALLIN DE LA MOTHE, Jean-Baptiste Michel.

Motte. A steep mound, the main feature of many C11 and C12 castles. *See* MOTTE-AND-BAILEY.

Motte-and-bailey. A post-Roman and Norman defence system consisting of an earthen mound (the *motte*) topped with a wooden tower, placed within a BAILEY with enclosure ditch, palisade, and, rarely, an internal bank.

Mouchette. A curved DAGGER motif in curvilinear TRACERY, especially popular in England in the early C14. *See* Fig. 64.

Mouldings. The contours given to projecting members. *See* BEAD MOULDINGS; BEAKHEAD; BILLET; BOWTELL; CABLE MOULDING; CHEVRON; DOG-TOOTH; HOOD-MOULD; KEELMOULDING; NAILHEAD; NEBULE; OGEE MOULDING; OVOLO MOULDING; ROLL MOULDING; WAVE MOULDING.

Moya, John Hidalgo (b. 1920), *see* POWELL & MOYA.

Mozarabic. The style evolved by Christians under Moorish influence in Spain from the late C9 to the early C11, e.g. S. Miguel de Escalada near León (consecrated in 913) with its arcade of arches of horseshoe shape, Santiago de Peñalba (931–7) and Sta Maria de Lebeña (also C10). The style is Christ-

ian in inspiration but Islamic in conception and has many Islamic features such as the horseshoe arch. Mozarabic churches are usually small and stand in the open countryside. They form the largest and best preserved group of pre-Romanesque buildings in Europe.

J. F. Arenas, *Mozarabic Architecture*, Greenwich, Conn., 1973.

Mudéjar. Spanish Christian architecture in a purely Moslem style. (Literally, the term refers to Moslems who remained in Christian Spain after the reconquest.) The style was evolved by Moslems in Spain or by Christians working within the Spanish Moslem tradition. Notable examples are Alfonso VIII's early C13 chapel at the monastery of Las Huelgas, Burgos, and the C14 Alcázar, Seville, which has Kufic inscriptions extolling Christian rulers. Mudéjar motifs persisted in Spanish Gothic architecture and may also be found in PLATERESQUE buildings of the C16.

G. G. King, *Mudéjar*, Bryn Mawr 1927; Kubler and Soria 1959.

Mullion. A vertical post or other upright dividing a window or other opening into two or more LIGHTS.

Munday, Richard (d. 1740), *see* UNITED STATES ARCHITECTURE.

Munggenast, Josef (1680–1741). Nephew and pupil of PRANDTAUER, for whom he worked as foreman and whom he succeeded as architect at Melk. In collaboration with the Viennese sculptor, engineer and architect Matthias Steinl (1644–1727) he built the church for the Augustinian canons at Dürnstein, with a boldly *mouvementé* interior and outstandingly handsome tower (1721–7). His main independent work is the reconstruction of the monastery of Altenburg, where he provided a richly coloured, exuberantly Baroque casing for the Gothic church and created one of the best of all Baroque libraries (1730–33).

Hempel 1965; E. Munggenast, *J.M. der Stiftsbaumeister 1680–1741*, Vienna 1963; Brucker 1983.

Muntin. The vertical part in the framing of a door, screen, panelling, etc., butting into, or stopped by, the horizontal rails. *See* Fig. 41. In the USA a glazing bar or MULLION.

Muqarna, *see* STALACTITE WORK.

Murcutt, Glen (b. 1936), *see* AUSTRALIAN ARCHITECTURE.

Murphy/Jahn, *see* JAHN, Helmut.

Mushrabeyeh work. Elaborate wooden lattices used to enclose the upper windows in Islamic domestic architecture.

Muthesius, Hermann (1861–1927), *see* ARTS AND CRAFTS.

Mutule. The projecting square block above the TRIGLYPH and under the CORONA of a Doric CORNICE.

Mycenaean architecture, *see* CRETAN AND MYCENAEAN ARCHITECTURE.

Mylne, Robert (1733–1811), a contemporary and rival of Robert ADAM, descended from a long line of Scottish master masons. He was trained by his father in Edinburgh, then went to Paris (1754), and Rome (1755–9), where he had amazing success by winning First Prize at the Accademia di S. Luca in 1758. But he did not fulfil this early promise. His first work after settling in London (1759) was to be his most famous, Blackfriars Bridge (1760–69, demolished), in which he introduced elliptical arches. Thereafter he worked extensively both as architect and as engineer. His largest country house, Tusmore (1766–9, demolished), was neo-Palladian. More elegant and original is The Wick, Richmond (1775), a small suburban 'box', while his façade of the Stationers' Hall, London (1800), shows him at his most neoclassical.

Colvin 1978; Summerson 1983; Harris 1990.

n

FIG. 65. *Nailhead*

Nailhead. An Early English architectural enrichment consisting of small pyramids repeated as a band. *See* Fig. 65.

Naos. The sanctuary or principal chamber of a Greek temple, containing the statue of the god. In Byzantine architecture, the core and sanctuary of a centrally planned church, i.e. the parts reserved for the performance of the liturgy.

Narthex. 1. In a Byzantine church, the transverse vestibule either preceding nave and aisles as an inner narthex (esonarthex) or preceding the façade as an outer narthex (exonarthex). An esonarthex is separated from the nave and aisles by columns, rails or a wall. An exonarthex may also serve as the terminating transverse portico of a colonnaded ATRIUM or quadriporticus. 2. In a general medieval sense, an enclosed covered ANTECHURCH at the main entrance, especially if the direction is transverse and not east–west and several bays deep; sometimes called a GALILEE. *See* Fig. 10.

Nash, John (1752–1835), London's only inspired town-planner and the greatest architect of the PICTURESQUE movement. He was the exact opposite of his contemporary SOANE, being self-confident and adaptable, socially successful and artistically conservative, light-handed and slipshod in detail, but with an easy mastery of general effects on a large scale. Again, unlike Soane, he was an architect of exteriors rather than interiors. The son of a Lambeth millwright, he was trained under TAYLOR, but quickly struck out on his own and by 1780 was building stucco-fronted houses, then a novelty in London. In 1783 he went bankrupt, retired to Wales and recovered, and then joined the landscape gardener REPTON, with whom he developed a fashionable countryhouse practice. His output was enormous and in every conceivable style – classical (Rockingham, Ireland, 1810 (demolished)), Italian farmhouse (Cronkhill, *c.* 1802), castellated Gothic (Ravensworth Castle, 1808 (demolished)); Caerhays Castle, 1808), even Indian and Chinoiserie (Brighton Pavilion, 1802–21). He also built thatched cottages (Blaise Hamlet, 1811). With their fancy-dress parade of styles and irregular planning and silhouettes, these buildings epitomized the Picturesque in architecture. The same picturesque combination of freedom and formality marks his greatest work, the layout of Regent's Park and Regent Street in London (1811 onwards), a brilliantly imaginative conception foreshadowing the garden city of the future. He was already sixty, but still had the enthusiasm and organizing ability to carry the whole scheme through, and he lived to see it finished. The park is sprinkled with villas and surrounded by vast terraces and crescents of private houses built palatially with grandiose stucco façades. There are also cottage terraces and make-believe villages of barge-boarded and Italianate villas. Of his Regent Street frontages nothing now remains except the eye-catcher, All Souls, Langham Place (1822–5). During the 1820s he planned Trafalgar Square, Suffolk Street and Suffolk Place, built Clarence House and Carlton House Terrace, and began Buckingham Palace, all in London. But he shared in his royal patron's fall from public favour, was suspected of profiteering and sharp practice, and his career came to an abrupt end when George IV died in 1830. He was dismissed from Buckingham Palace (completed by Edward Blore) and from the Board of Works, of which he had been one of the Surveyors General since 1813. His reputation remained under a cloud for the next fifty years or more.

J. Summerson, *J.N.*, London (1935) 1980.

Nasoni or **Nazzoni**, Niccolò (d. 1773), who was born near Florence, settled in Portugal (1731), where he became one of the leading Baroque architects. His main work is São Pedro dos Clérigos, Oporto (1732–50), a large and impressive church on an oval plan with a very richly decorated façade, embraced by a bold pattern of ascending staircases.

Kubler and Soria 1959; R. C. Smith, *N.N. arqitecto de Porto*, Lisbon 1966.

Nave. The western limb of a church, that is, the part west of the CROSSING; more usually the middle vessel of the western limb, flanked by AISLES.

Nebule, nebulé or **nebuly moulding.** A moulding with wavy or serpentine lower edge.

Necking. A narrow, annular MOULDING round the bottom of a CAPITAL between it and the shaft of the column.

Necropolis. A burial-ground or cemetery, usually in or near a city.

Needle spire, *see* SPIRE.

Neo-classicism. The radical phase of late C18 CLASSICISM. It began with GABRIEL and others and ended, with BOULLÉE and LEDOUX, in an architecture of pure geometrical forms.

Neo-Gothic, *see* GOTHIC REVIVAL.

Neo-Palladian, *see* PALLADIANISM.

Neo-Rationalism. An Italian anti-Modernist movement of the 1960s, also known as the 'Tendenza', led by Aldo ROSSI. It rejected functionalism in favour of an autonomous architecture concerned with formal essences and not with technology. *Architettura della città* (1966) by Rossi and *La costruzione logica dell'architettura* (1967) by Giorgio Grassi (b. 1935) were seminal texts, as was also GREGOTTI's *Il territorio dell'architettura* (1966). Rossi's cemetery at Modena (1971–85) is the movement's chief monument. Oswald Mathis Ungers (b. 1926) and Josef Paul Kleihues (b. 1933) in Germany, Bruno Reichlin (b. 1941) and

Nepalese architecture

Fabio Reinhart (b. 1942) in Switzerland, as well as the KRIER brothers, have all been influenced by and loosely associated with the movement.

E. Bonfanti *et al.*, *Architettura razionale*, Milan 1973; Klotz 1986, 1988.

Nepalese architecture. The earliest surviving structures are STUPAS, probably C8–9 (though some may be enlargements of C3 BC originals) with later embellishments, e.g. the Svayambhu stupa near Kathmandu, a low semi-hemispherical brick mound surmounted by a square block with a huge pair of eyes inlaid on each side and a conical spire topped by a metal drum and umbrella. In Kathmandu the Kasthamandata, a pilgrims' hostel probably *c*. 1100 (though much restored), is in a style followed in the region for both secular and religious buildings until the present century – mainly of wood with wide-eaved roofs of truncated pyramidal form over each of its three storeys of diminishing size. Temples called *dega*, of two or three storeys, are somewhat similar in appearance to Chinese pagodas though more importance is given to their supporting brick walls, with much woodwork elaborately carved in relief, e.g. shrine of Pasupatinatha at Deo Patan (late C14). Stone-built Hindu temples dating from the C17 and later are in northern Indian styles, but usually with a stupa-like finial crowning the SIKHARA. The royal palace on the Durbar Square, Kathmandu, mainly C17–18, with buildings surrounding some fifty courts, is the most notable example of Nepalese domestic architecture, with much fine woodwork. The many C19–20 Rana palaces in the new town are in European styles.

Nering, Johann Arnold (1659–95). Prussian architect who, despite his early death, laid the foundations for architectural developments in C18 Berlin. He was trained as a military architect, sent to Italy and made Oberingenieur in 1680, later (1691) Oberbaudirektor. He was much employed on urban planning and built the Leipziger Tor (1683), the covered arcade with shops on the Muhlendamm in Berlin and the Friedrichstadt suburb with 300 two-storey houses, all in military order (1688 onwards). He enlarged the Burgkirche at Königsberg, on the model of the Nieuwekerk in The Hague (pre-1687), gave the Oranienburg Palace its present appearance (1689–95), began the Charlottenburg Palace, Berlin, the Arsenal, Berlin (1695, completed by SCHLÜTER and de BODT), and the Reformed Parish Church on an interesting quatrefoil plan. His style is severe and owed much to PALLADIO by way of the Dutch neo-Palladians.

Hempel 1965.

Nervi, Pier Luigi (1891–1979), took his degree in civil engineering in 1912, but had a long wait before he was allowed to establish himself as what he undoubtedly became, the most brilliant CONCRETE designer of the age. Nervi was as inventive and resourceful a technician as he was aesthetically sensitive an architect. He was moreover an entrepreneur and a university professor, a combination which would be impossible, because it is not permitted, in Britain.

The stadium in Florence was built in 1930–32; it seats 35,000, has a cantilever roof about 70 ft deep and an ingenious flying spiral staircase sweeping far out. In 1935, for a competition for airship hangars, he produced his idea of a vault of diagonally intersecting concrete beams with very massive flying-buttress-like angle supports. Such hangars were built at Orbetello from 1936 onwards (destroyed). A second type with trusses of precast concrete elements was carried out at Orbetello in 1940. 1948 is the date of Nervi's first great exhibition hall for Turin. The concrete elements this time are corrugated, an idea which went back to experiments of 1943–4. The second hall followed in 1950, again with a diagonal grid. The building of 1952 for the Italian spa of Chianciano is circular, and has a grid vault. By this time Nervi's fame was so firmly established that he was called in for the structure of the Unesco building in Paris (1953–6). His also is the splendid structure of the Pirelli skyscraper in Milan (1955–8; *see also* PONTI) – two strongly tapering concrete pillars from which the floors are cantilevered. With Jean PROUVÉ as the other consultant engineer, Nervi was responsible for the enormous new exhibition hall on the Rond-point de la Défense in Paris (1958): a triangle, each side 710 ft long, with three triangular sections of warped concrete roof, rising to a height of 150 ft.

Nervi's last buildings were the Palazzetto dello Sport in Rome (1959), circular with V-shaped supports for the dome all round; the Palazzo dello Sport, also in Rome (1960), with a 330-ft span and seating 16,000; yet another exhibition hall for Turin (1961), a square with sides 520 ft in length, supported on sixteen enormous cross-shaped piers; and the vast audience hall for the Pope in the Vatican (1970–71). He published *Arte o scienze del costruire?* (Rome 1954), *Structures* (New York 1956) and *Aesthetics and Technology in Building* (Cambridge, Mass., 1965).

Collins 1959; A. Pica, *P.L.N.*, Rome 1969; Mainstone 1975; P. Desideri *et al.*, *P.L.N. Pläne, Skizzen und Werkverzeichnis*, Zürich and Munich 1982.

Nesfield, William Eden (1835–88). He began in the ARTS AND CRAFTS manner (e.g. his Regent's Park Lodge of 1864) and until 1869 was in partnership with Norman SHAW, with whom he is credited with the Queen Anne revival. His Dutch C17 lodge at Kew Gardens (1866–7) probably inaugurated it, followed by his William and Mary–Louis XIII Kinmel Park, Denbighshire (begun 1867), and others. Some of his later buildings are in neo-Tudor and other styles, e.g. the remarkable Barclay's Bank, Saffron Walden, of 1875.

A. Saint, *Richard Norman Shaw*, New Haven and London 1976.

Neumann, Johann Balthasar (1687–1753), the greatest German Rococo architect, was master of elegant and ingenious spatial composition. He could be both wantonly sensuous and intellectually complex, frivolous and devout, ceremonious and playful. His churches and palaces epitomize the mid-C18 attitude to life and religion. But despite their air of spontaneity, few works of architecture have been more carefully thought out. His designs are as complex as the fugues of Bach; and for this reason he has been called an architect's architect.

The son of a clothier, he was born in Bohemia but worked mainly in Franconia, where he began in a cannon foundry and graduated to architecture by way of the Prince Bishop's artillery. He visited Vienna and Milan (1717–18) and soon after his return began the Bishop's new Residenz in Würzburg, consulting HILDEBRANDT and von

Welsch in Vienna and de COTTE and BOFFRAND in Paris about his designs. The influence of Hildebrandt is very evident in the finished palace, which was executed under a succession of five bishops over some sixty years, though it was structurally complete by about 1744. Outstanding here are the Hofkirche or Bishop's Chapel (1732–41, Hildebrandt collaborating on the decoration) and the magnificent ceremonial staircase leading up to the Kaisersaal (designed 1735, ceiling decoration by Tiepolo 1752–3). This staircase is one of his most original and ingenious conceptions, second only to his superb staircase at Bruchsal (1731–2, damaged in Second World War but restored). He later designed the imposing staircase at Schloss Brühl near Cologne (1743–8). These ceremonial staircases formed the most important single element in each palace and are at the same time masterpieces of engineering ingenuity and exhilarating spatial play. At Schloss Werneck (1734–45) he again collaborated with Hildebrandt, but this time impressed his own stamp on all parts of the building. His secular work was by no means limited to palace architecture; he was engaged in town planning and laid out whole streets of town houses, e.g. the Theaterstrasse at Würzburg. The house he built for himself in the Kapuzinergasse (No. 7) at Würzburg reveals his ability to work in a minor key.

He was much employed as a church architect, designing the parish church at Wiesentheid (1727), the pilgrimage church at Gössweinstein (1730–39), the church of St Paulinus, Trier (begun 1734), the church of Häusenstamm near Offenbach (1739–40), the Holy Cross Chapel at Etwashausen (1741) and additions to St Peter, Bruchsal

(1738) and the Dominican church at Würzburg (1741). In 1743 he began his great masterpiece, the pilgrimage church of Vierzehnheiligen (1742–53, completed 1772), where the foundations had already been built by a previous architect. His first task was to accommodate his own ideas to a somewhat inconvenient plan and this provided a spur to his genius. He worked out a remarkably complicated scheme based on the grouping of ovals, both in the vaulting and ground plan, which provides a breathtakingly exciting spatial effect, enhanced by the foaming and eddying Rococo decoration. Nowhere did the *mouvementé* quality of Rococo architecture find better expression; not only the statues but even the columns seem to be executing an elegant minuet. (The central altar, pulpit and much of the plasterwork were not completed until after Neumann's death.)

In the larger abbey church at Neresheim (begun 1747) he had a much freer hand and his plan is much simpler, though again based on ovals. By the use of very slender columns to support the large central dome he achieved an almost Gothic airiness. His last work of importance, the Marienkirche at Limbach (1747–52), is on a much smaller scale, but is unusual for him in being no less elaborately decorated on the exterior than inside.

Hitchcock 1968; C. F. Otto, *Space into Light: The Churches of B.N.*, Cambridge, Mass., 1979; T. Korth and J. Poeschke (eds.), *B.N.*, Munich 1987; E. Hubala, *B.N. – seine Kunst zu Bauen*, exh. cat., Wendlingen and Würzburg 1987–8.

Neutra, Richard Josef (1892–1970). He was Austrian by birth and studied in Vienna. In 1912–14 he worked under LOOS, and in 1921–3 he was with MENDELSOHN in Berlin. In 1923 he emigrated to Chicago, but finally settled down at Los Angeles in 1925. With his remarkable Lovell Health House, Los Angeles, of 1929, he became one of the chief propagators of the new European style in America. His work is predominantly domestic, and mostly of a wealthy and lavish kind. His forte is a brilliant sense for siting houses in landscape and linking building and nature: Desert House, Colorado, 1946; Kaufmann House, Palm Springs, 1947; and his own house at Silverlake, Los Angeles, 1933 and 1964. Neutra also designed some excellent schools and, towards the end of his life, some religious and commercial buildings. His style remained essentially that of his youth; it was unchanged in its direction by the anti-rational tendencies of the last ten or fifteen years. He published *Wie Baut Amerika?* (Stuttgart 1927) and *Survival Through Design* (New York 1954).

T. S. Hines, *R.N. and the Search for Modern Architecture*, New York 1982; A. Drexler, *The Architecture of R.N.*, New York 1982.

New Brutalism, *see* BRUTALISM.

New Towns. Those towns designed in the British Isles under the Act of 1946 – eight in the London region (Harlow, Crawley, Stevenage, etc.) and six in other parts of England, Scotland and Wales. More were added later. Although most of them have an existing town or village as a nucleus, they are entirely independent units, with populations of about 60,000 to 80,000. The development of these planned towns over the years has been of very great interest from sociological, architectural, and planning points of view. *See also* GARDEN CITIES and RADBURN PLANNING.

New York Five. A group of five American architects: EISENMAN, GRAVES, Charles Gwathmey (b. 1938), John Hejduk (b. 1929), and MEIER, also known as the 'Whites'. They exhibited together in New York in 1969 and later published *Five Architects* (New York 1972). They began a return to the INTERNATIONAL STYLE, notably to LE CORBUSIER, RIETVELD and Terragni. The group had dispersed by 1980.

Klotz 1988.

Newel, *see* STAIR.

Niccolini, Antonio (1772–1850), *see* ITALIAN ARCHITECTURE.

Niche. A vertical recess in a wall, pier, etc., usually arched and containing a statue, urn, or other decorative object.

Nicola Pisano, *see* PISANO, Nicola.

Niemeyer, Oscar (b. 1907), studied in his home town Rio de Janeiro, then worked in the office of Lucio COSTA and received his diploma in 1934. In 1936 he belonged to the team of Brazilian architects working with LE CORBUSIER on the new building for the Ministry of Education at Rio. He built the Brazilian Pavilion for the New York World Fair of 1939 with Costa, but only came fully into his own with the casino, club, and church of St Francis at Pampulha outside Belo Horizonte (1942–3). Here was a completely new approach to architecture, admittedly for non-utilitarian purposes: parabolic vaults, slanting walls, a porch canopy of a completely free double-curving form – a sculptural, frankly anti-rational, highly expressive style. The style suited BRAZIL, with its past of the extremest Baroque; it also became one of the elements in that general turn away from rationalism which is principally familiar in Le Corbusier's buildings after the Second World War.

Niemeyer was made architectural adviser to Nova Cap, the organization instituted to create Brasilia, the new capital, and in 1957 became its chief architect. He designed the hotel in 1958 and the exquisite president's palace in the same year. The palace has a screen of freely and extremely originally shaped supports in front of its glass façade, and Niemeyer has varied this theme in other buildings at Brasilia as well (Law Courts). The climax of the architectural composition of the capital is the Square of the Three Powers, with the Houses of Parliament – one with a dome, the other with a saucer-shaped roof – and the sheer, quite un-fanciful skyscraper of the offices be-tween. The slab blocks of the various ministries are also deliberately unfanci-ful. Niemeyer certainly varies his ap-proach according to the spiritual func-tion of buildings. Thus the cathedral of Brasilia, circular, with the excelsior of a bundle of curved concrete ribs rising to the centre, is highly ex-pressive; the block of flats for the Inter-bau Exhibition in Berlin (Hansa Quarter, 1957) is rational, without, however, lacking in resourcefulness; and Niemeyer's own house outside Rio (1953) is a ravishing interplay of nature and architecture. He published *Minha Experiencia en Brasilia* (Rio de Janeiro 1961; Paris 1963).

S. Papadaki, *The Work of O.N.*, New York 1950–60; R. Spade, *O.N.*, London 1971; N.W. Sodre, *O.N.*, Rio de Janeiro 1978; C. Hornig, *O.N. Bauten und Projekte*, Munich 1981; A. Fils, *O.N.*, Düsseldorf 1982.

Nobile, Pietro (1773–1854), a neo-classicist of a rather archaeologizing tendency, worked in Vienna (Thes-eustempel, a miniature of the Haiph-esteion, Athens, built to house a statue by Canova, 1820–23; the Burgtor, 1844) and in Trieste (S. Antonio, 1826–49).

Hitchcock 1977.

Nodding ogee arch, *see* ARCH.

Nogging, *see* BRICKWORK; TIMBER-FRAMING.

Noiers, Geoffrey de, *see* GEOFFREY DE NOIERS.

Nook-shaft. A shaft set in the angle of a PIER, a RESPOND, a wall, or the JAMB of a window or doorway.

Norman architecture, *see* ENGLISH ARCHITECTURE; ITALIAN ARCHITEC-TURE.

Norwegian architecture. (For medieval and earlier buildings in Norway *see* SCANDINAVIAN ARCHI-TECTURE.) Though Oslo was laid out regularly with a grid of streets and oblong blocks in 1824 – as was, even more regularly, Kristiansand in 1641 – Norway lagged behind Denmark and Sweden architecturally. Most Nor-wegian domestic architecture was still of wood, even in the C18. (The largest wooden building is Stiftsgården in Trondheim of 1774–8, nineteen windows wide with a pediment and some lacy Rococo ornament, though Danisgård at Bergen, also of the 1770s, is perhaps finer.) After 1814 Norway broke free of Denmark while remaining linked by a common monarch to Sweden, and the need for large official and public buildings led to the development in Oslo of some impressive Greek Revival monumental architecture. Apart from the Royal Palace by Hans Ditler Frants Linstow (1787–1851), the most notable buildings are by Christian Henrik Grosch (1801–65), who was appointed the city architect in 1828. By him are the Stock Exchange (1828), Bank of Norway (1830) and his Schinkelesque masterpiece, the University (1839–52). The castellated and turreted Oskarshall outside Oslo of 1848 (by Johann Henrik Nevelong, 1817–71) is a notable example of the c19 Gothic Revival. Thereafter Norway followed architectural developments elsewhere in Scandinavia, though seldom with great distinction, e.g. the brick-built City Hall in Oslo of 1917–50, heavy and very unromantic in comparison with ØSTBERG's City Hall in Stockholm. However, the work of Arne Korsmo (1900–1968) should be mentioned – Dammann House (1930–32) and

Hansen House (1936) in Oslo; also that of Jan Digerad (b. 1938) and Jon Lundberg (b. 1933), whose Akersverein 12–14 in Oslo is colourful.

Nosing, *see* STAIR.

Nouvel, Jean (b. 1945). French architect who made his name with the enormous Institut du Monde Arabe, Paris (1987). He was commissioned in 1987 to design the new National Theatre in Tokyo.

P. Goulet, *J.N.*, Paris 1987.

Nowicki, Matthew (1910–51), *see* HYPERBOLIC PARABOLOID ROOF.

Nüll, Eduard van der (1812–68), *see* AUSTRIAN ARCHITECTURE.

Nuraghi, *see* BEEHIVE HOUSE.

Nymphaeum. Literally a 'temple of the nymphs' but generally a Roman pleasure-house, especially one containing fountains and statues.

Nyrop, Martin (1849–1921), *see* DANISH ARCHITECTURE.

O

Obelisk. A tall tapering shaft of stone, usually granite, monolithic, of square or rectangular section, and ending pyramidally; prominently used in ancient Egypt, from whence several were brought to Europe under the Roman Empire (often re-erected later, e.g. in Piazza di S. Pietro, Rome) and again in the C19 (e.g. Cleopatra's needle, London).

L. Habachi, *Alles über Obelisk*, Mainz 1982.

Obrist, Hermann (1863–1927), *see* ART NOUVEAU.

Octagon. An eight equal-sided figure frequently used as a ground-plan from Roman (e.g. Nero's Golden House, atrium), Carolingian (e.g. Palatine Chapel, Aachen) and Medieval (Karlskirche, Prague; Chapterhouse, York Minster) to Renaissance and later buildings (e.g. the Octagon, Twickenham, by James GIBBS).

Octastyle. Of a portico with eight frontal columns.

Oculus. A circular opening in a wall or at the apex of a dome, e.g. Pantheon, Rome.

Odeon, odcion (Gr.) or **odeum** (Lat.). In Ancient Greek and Roman architecture a small roofed theatre, for concerts and lectures.

Odo of Metz, *see* CAROLINGIAN ARCHITECTURE.

O'Donnel, James (1774–1830), *see* CANADIAN ARCHITECTURE.

Œil-de-bœuf window. A small round or, more usually, oval window as in the Salon de l'Œil de Bœuf at Versailles. There are three ranges of them in the dome of St Peter's, Rome.

Œillet. In medieval architecture, a small opening in fortifications through which missiles could be discharged.

Off-set. The part of a wall exposed horizontally when the portion above it is reduced in thickness; often sloping, with a projecting drip mould on the lower edge to stop water running down the walls, e.g. in Gothic buttresses. Also called the *water-table*. *See* WEATHERING.

Ogee. A double-curved line made up of a convex and concave part (S or inverted S).

Ogee arch, *see* ARCH.

Ogee moulding, *see* CYMA RECTA *and* CYMA REVERSA.

Ogive. The French name for a pointed arch; hence *ogival*, a term applied to French Gothic architecture, but no longer used.

O'Gorman, Juan (1905–82), *see* MEXICAN ARCHITECTURE.

Olbrich, Joseph Maria (1867–1908), studied at the Vienna Academy, gained the Rome prize in 1893, returned to work under Otto WAGNER, and in 1897–8 built the Secession in Vienna, the premises of a newly founded society of the young progressive artists of Austria and the work which immediately established Olbrich's reputation. The little building, with its strongly cubic walls and its delightful hemispherical openwork metal dome, is both firm in its basic shapes and fanciful in its details. It is this unusual combination of qualities which attracted Ernst Ludwig Grand Duke of Hessen to Olbrich. So in 1899 Olbrich was called to Darmstadt and there, on the Mathildenhöhe, built the studio house (Ernst Ludwig Haus) and some private houses, including one for himself. The group of houses, some of them by other members of the group of artists assembled at Darmstadt (e.g. BEHRENS), was first built and furnished and then, in 1901, presented as an exhibition, the first of the kind ever held. Later Olbrich added another exhibition building and a tower, the Hochzeitsturm (1907). His last major building was the Tietz department store (now Kaufhof) at Düsseldorf (1906–9), the closely set uprights of whose façade, deriving from Messel's Wertheim store in Berlin, were very influential.

Olbrich's historical role is among those who succeeded in overcoming the vegetable weakness of ART NOUVEAU by providing it with a firmer system of rectangular coordinates. The other leading architects working in this direction were HOFFMANN and MACKINTOSH. Both Mackintosh and Olbrich succeeded in preserving the fancifulness of Art Nouveau sinuosity within this new, more exacting framework, whereas Hoffmann, and of course Behrens to a still greater extent, moved right away from Art Nouveau.

I. Latham, *O.*, London 1980; P. Haiko and B. Krimmel, *J.M.O. Architektur*, Berlin 1989.

Oliveira, Mateus Vicente de, *see* VICENTE DE OLIVEIRA, Mateus.

Olmec architecture, *see* MESO-AMERICAN ARCHITECTURE.

Olmsted, Frederick Law (1822–1903), the principal landscape architect of America after DOWNING's death and America's leading park designer, studied engineering and travelled widely in America, Europe, and even China, before being made superintendent for Central Park, New York (1857), which he designed with Calvert Vaux (1824–95). He visited European parks in 1859, then for a while supervised a mining estate in California (1863–5) and at that time suggested making the Yosemite area a reserve, and finally returned to the Central Park job in 1865. Olmsted also planned the parks system of Boston, the Niagara reserve, millionaires' estates, and the campus of the newly founded Leland Stanford University at Palo Alto. Among his pupils the most important was his nephew John Charles Olmsted (1853–1920).

L. W. Roper, *F.L.O.*, Baltimore and London (1973) 1983; C. C. McLaughlin (ed.), *The Papers of F.L.O.*, Baltimore 1983 onwards.

OMA (Office for Metropolitan Architecture), *see* DUTCH ARCHITECTURE.

Onion dome. A pointed bulbous dome common in Russia and Eastern Europe, especially on churches and church towers. Structurally it is not a true dome, i.e. it is not vaulted.

Opbergen, Antonius van (1543–1611), *see* DANISH ARCHITECTURE; POLISH ARCHITECTURE.

Opisthodomos. The enclosed section at the rear of a Greek temple, sometimes used as a treasury.

Optical refinements. Subtle modifications to profiles or surfaces to correct the illusion of sagging or disproportion in a building. *See* ENTASIS.

Opus Alexandrinum. Ornamental paving combining mosaic and OPUS SECTILE in guilloche design.

Opus incertum. Roman walling of concrete faced with irregularly shaped stones.

Opus listatum. Walling with alternating courses of brick and small blocks of stone.

Opus quadratum. Roman walling of squared stones.

Opus reticulatum. Roman walling of concrete faced with squared stones arranged diagonally like the meshes of a net.

Opus sectile. Ornamental paving or wall covering made from marble slabs cut in various, generally geometric, shapes.

Orangery. A garden building for growing oranges, with large windows on the south side, like a glazed LOGGIA. *See also* CONSERVATORY.

M. Woods and A. S. Warren, *A History of Greenhouses, Orangeries and Conservatories*, London 1988.

Oratory. A small private chapel, either in a church or in a house; or a church of the Oratorian order of S. Filippo Neri, e.g. the Brompton Oratory, London.

Orbay, François d' (1631–97). Chief assistant to LE VAU, several of whose late works he carried out, notably the Escalier des Ambassadeurs, Versailles, and the Collège des Quatre Nations (now the Institut de France), Paris. Of his independent works the Porte du Peyrou, Montpellier (*c.* 1689), is notable.

A. Laprade, *F. d'O. architecte de Louis XIV*, Paris 1960; Blunt 1982.

Orcagna (Andrea di Cione) (active 1343–68). He was primarily a painter – the most important in Florence after Giotto's death – but also a sculptor and architect. He was admitted to the Guild of Painters in 1343/4 and to the Guild of Stonemasons in 1352. By 1356 he was *capomaestro* at Orsanmichele, Florence, and by 1358 at Orvieto Cathedral, where he is frequently mentioned until 1362, though mainly in connection with the restoration of mosaics on the façade. In 1350 he became adviser on the construction of Florence Cathedral and until 1366 was active as a leading member of various commissions, including that which evolved the definitive design.

White 1987.

Orchaestra or **orchestra**. The circular 'dancing floor' of an ancient Greek theatre, whence the corresponding semicircular space in front of the stage or PROSCENIUM of an ancient Roman theatre.

Orchard, William (d. 1504), master mason, was probably designer of Bishop Waynflete's Magdalen College

FIG. 66. *Order (see also p. 318)*

KEY:

A. Entablature	D. Frieze	G. Shaft	1. Guttae	4. Abacus	7. Fluting
B. Column	E. Architrave	H. Base	2. Metope	5. Echinus	8. Dentils
C. Cornice	F. Capital	I. Plinth	3. Triglyph	6. Volute	9. Fascia

at Oxford (1468 onwards). The initials W.O. in the ingenious vault to the Divinity School, completed in the 1480s, allow it to be attributed to him, and if the attribution is correct, the similarity in design of the vaults of the Divinity School and the chancel of Oxford Cathedral make him a likely candidate for this even more ingenious vault. Both are characterized by the pendants which look like springers built on non-existing piers between a nave and aisles. It is a technically daring, highly original, and visually most puzzling solution.

Harvey 1984.

Order. 1. In classical architecture, a column with base (usually), shaft, capital, and entablature, decorated and proportioned according to one of

317

Tuscan   Roman Doric   Composite

the accepted modes – Doric, Tuscan, Ionic, Corinthian, or Composite. The simplest is the Tuscan, supposedly derived from the Etruscan-type temple, but the Doric is probably earlier in origin and is subdivided into Greek Doric and Roman Doric, the former having no base, as on the Parthenon and the temples at Paestum. The Ionic order originated in Asia Minor in the mid c6 BC. The Ionic capital probably developed out of the earlier Aeolic capital of uncertain origin. (The Aeolic capital has an oblong top supported by two large volutes with a PALMETTE filling the space between.) The Corinthian order was an Athenian invention of c5 BC, but was later developed by the Romans, who provided the prototype for the Renaissance form. The Composite order is a late Roman combination of elements from the Ionic and Corinthian orders. The Doric, Tuscan, Ionic, and Corinthian orders were described by VITRUVIUS, and in 1537 SERLIO published a book on the orders (coining the term Composite for what had previously been called Italic) which gave to each a range of expressive meanings as well as establishing the minutiae of proportions and embellishments for Renaissance and later architects. *See* Fig. 66; COLOSSAL ORDER.

2. Of a doorway or window, a series of concentric steps receding towards the opening.

J. Summerson, *The Classical Language of Architecture*, London (1963) 1980; R. Chilkam, *The Classical Orders of Architecture*, London 1985; Onians 1988.

Ordonnance. The disposition of the parts of a building. In French the term was used by C17–18 theorists in allusion to the choice of an appropriate order for a building and to its application.

Oriel, *see* BAY WINDOW.

Orientation. The planning of a building in relation to the rising sun, especially of West European churches which are usually orientated east–west with the altar at the east end. But there are many exceptions, e.g. St Peter's, Rome, which is orientated west–east.

Orthostat. A slab of stone set upright at the base of a wall or building to form the lower section of it, sometimes carved in relief, e.g. in ancient Hittite architecture in Turkey.

Østberg, Ragnar (1866–1945). His international fame derives entirely from his Stockholm City Hall (begun 1909, completed 1923), a building transitional – like BERLAGE's and KLINT's work – between C19 HISTORICISM and the C20. The City Hall makes extremely skilful use of elements of the Swedish past, Romanesque as well as Renaissance. Its exquisite position by the water suggested to Østberg certain borrowings from the Doge's Palace as well. But these motifs are converted

and combined in a highly original way, and the decorative details, rather mannered and attenuated, are typical of the ARTS AND CRAFTS of Germany, Austria, and central Europe in general about 1920. The City Hall was very influential in England in the twenties. Østberg had studied in Stockholm (1884–91) and travelled all over Europe as well as in America (1893–9). He also built the Patent Office (1921) and the Sea History Museum (1934–5), Stockholm, and was professor at the Stockholm Konsthögskola in 1922–32.

E. Cornell, *R. O. Svensk arkitekt*, Stockholm (1965) 1972.

Otaka, Masato (b. 1923), *see* JAPANESE ARCHITECTURE.

Otani, Sachio (b. 1924), *see* JAPANESE ARCHITECTURE.

Otto, Frei (b. 1925), pioneer of suspended roofs. Otto's thesis, presented in 1954, was about them. He built one a year later, for an exhibition at Kassel. Further exhibitions followed: Cologne 1957, Berlin (Interbau) 1957, Lausanne 1961, Hamburg 1963, Montreal 1967. The last named – German Pavilion, Expo '67 – made him world famous. The roofs are of steel-web or polyester-web freely suspended on cable nets stretched between heavier cables attached to masts and ground anchorages. He achieves much freer tent-like forms than did earlier pioneers, e.g. Nowicki and Severund's Raleigh Arena, N. Carolina (1952), Saarinen's Yale Hockey Rink (1953). He also designed the Conference Centre, Mecca, Saudi Arabia (1966–75), and imposing tensile structures for the Olympic Games at Munich in 1972, with Günter Behnisch (b. 1922). More recent buildings include the hotel and conference hall, Mecca (1974), and Government Offices, Riad, Saudi Arabia (1978–82). He has published *Tensile Structures* (1967) and *Schriften und Reden 1951–1983* (Wiesbaden 1984).

L. Glaeser, *The Work of F.O.*, exh. cat., New York 1972; P. Drew, *F.O. Form and Construction*, London 1983; L. Sachs, *Architekten heute, Porträt F.O.*, Berlin 1984; Klotz 1986.

Ottoman architecture, *see* TURKISH ARCHITECTURE.

Ottonian architecture. The style current in Germany *c.* 950–1050 under Otto the Great (reigned 936–73). The most notable surviving Ottonian buildings are Gernrode abbey church and Magdeburg Cathedral, both begun in 959, and the west choir of St Michael, Hildesheim (1010–33). *See also* CAROLINGIAN ARCHITECTURE; ROMANESQUE ARCHITECTURE.

Oubliette. In medieval architecture, a secret prison cell reached only through a trapdoor above, and into which a prisoner could be dropped and, presumably, forgotten.

Oud, Jacobus Johannes Pieter (1890–1963), worked for a short time under Theodor Fischer in Germany in 1911. In 1915 he met Theo van Doesburg and with him and RIETVELD he became a pillar of the group DE STIJL. Architecturally this group stood for an abstract cubism in opposition to the fanciful School of Amsterdam with its Expressionist compositions (de Klerk, Piet Kramer). There exist designs by Oud in a severely cubic manner which date from as early as 1917 and 1919. In 1918 he was made Housing Architect to the City of Rotterdam, a position he retained until 1927. His most important estates are one at Hoek van Holland (1924–7) and the Kiefhoek Estate (1925–30). Later Oud mellowed, abandoned the severity of his designing, and helped to create that curiously decorative, somewhat playful Dutch style which was nicknamed locally Beton-Rococo. The paramount example is the Shell Building at The Hague (1938–42).

G. Stamm, *J.J.P.O. Bauten und Projekte 1906–63*, Mainz and Berlin (1978) 1984.

Outram, John (b. 1934), *see* ENGLISH ARCHITECTURE.

Overdoor, *see* SOPRAPORTA.

Overhang. Projection of the upper storey of a house.

Oversailing courses. A series of stone or brick courses, each one projecting beyond the one below it.

Ovolo moulding. A convex moulding, usually a quarter of a circle and sometimes called a quarter round. It is often ornamented with EGG AND DART or other similar patterns.

Owings, Nathaniel A. (1903–84), *see* SKIDMORE, OWINGS & MERRILL.

P

Páckh, Janos (1796–1839), *see* HUN-
GARIAN ARCHITECTURE.

Padstone, *see* KNEELER; TEMPLATE.

Pagoda. European name (of Portuguese origin) for a Chinese or Japanese
Buddhist temple tower, usually a tiered
structure of several storeys. Its origin
is obscure, but it probably derived
from the superstructure of an Indian
Buddhist STUPA. It is called in Chinese
a *ta* (*t'a*), in Japanese a *shoro* if it served
as a bell-tower or a *tahoto* if it has a
single room with an elaborate superstructure. The term is also used,
loosely, for Buddhist temples in Nepal
and for *stupas* in Burma.

P'ai lou. A Chinese ornamental arch
or gateway, commemorative or triumphal in function, with one, three or five
openings. Usually built of stone but in
imitation of wooden prototypes, e.g.
stone beams are tenoned through the
columns.

Paine, James (1717–89), lived in
London but worked mainly as a
country-house architect in the Midlands
and north. Solid and conservative, he
began in the tradition of BURLINGTON
and KENT and he and Sir Robert
TAYLOR were said to have 'nearly
divided the practice of the profession
between them' in the mid-century. His
houses are practically planned and very
well built with dignified exteriors and
excellent Rococo plasterwork, e.g. the
Mansion House, Doncaster (1745–8).
Later he showed more originality and
preceded Robert ADAM in replacing
the C17 'house of parade' plan for
country houses with the compact, centrally planned 'villa with wings'. At
Kedleston (1759–60, later taken over
by Adam) he had the brilliant idea of
placing in sequence an antique basilica
hall and a Pantheon-like circular
saloon. At Worksop Manor (begun
1763 but only a third built, demolished
1843) he envisaged a gigantic Egyptian
Hall and at Wardour Castle (1770–76)
he designed a magnificent circular staircase rising towards a Pantheon-like
dome. But by this date he had been
superseded in the public eye by Robert
Adam, and his practice declined
rapidly. As a result of some domestic
trouble during his last years he retired
to France, where he died. Most of his
work is illustrated in his two volumes
of *Plans, Elevations and Sections of
Noblemen's and Gentlemen's Houses*
(1767 and 1783).

P. Leach, *J.P.*, London 1988; Harris
1990.

Pakistani architecture, *see* INDIAN
AND PAKISTANI ARCHITECTURE.

Palaestra. An exercise ground or
public building for athletes.

Paliotto. A canopy for an altar covering all four sides, as distinct from an ANTEPENDIUM, which covers the front only. The most famous is that of gold, silver partly gilt, enamel and semi-precious stones by Vuolvinius of the early C9 in S. Ambrogio, Milan.

Palladian window, *see* SERLIANA.

Palladianism. A style derived from the buildings and publications of PALLADIO. Its first exponent was Inigo JONES, who studied Roman ruins with Palladio's *Le antichità di Roma* and his buildings in and around Vicenza (1613–14), and introduced the style into England. Elsewhere in northern Europe, especially Holland (van CAMPEN) and Germany (HOLL), Palladian elements appear in buildings – temple fronts, the SERLIANA window, etc. – but here the leading influence was SCAMOZZI rather than Palladio. The great Palladian revival began in Italy and England in the early C18: in Italy it was confined to Venetia, but affected churches as well as secular buildings; in England it was purely domestic. The English revival, led by CAMPBELL and Lord BURLINGTON, was at the same time an Inigo Jones revival. Numerous books were published under Burlington's aegis and these provided a set of rules and exemplars which remained a dominant force in English architecture until late in the C18. From England and Venetia, Palladianism spread to Germany (KNOBELSDORFF) and Russia (CAMERON and QUARENGHI). At Potsdam accurate copies of Palladio's Palazzo Valmarana and Palazzo Thiene were built in the 1750s under the influence of Frederick the Great and his courtier, the Paduan Count Algarotti. From England the style also spread to the USA in the 1760s (JEFFERSON). Outside Italy the Palladian revival was concerned mainly with the use of decorative elements. Little attention was paid to Palladio's laws of HARMONIC PROPORTIONS except in Italy, where his ideas on this subject were examined by BERTOTTI-SCAMOZZI and elaborated by a minor architect, Francesco Maria Preti (1701–84).

R. Wittkower, *Palladio and Palladianism*, London 1974; W. M. Whitehall and F. D. Nicholls, *Palladianism in America*, Milan 1976; J. Harris, *The Palladians*, London 1981.

Palladio, Andrea (1508–80). The most influential and one of the greatest Italian architects (*see* PALLADIANISM). Smooth, elegant, and intellectual, he crystallized various Renaissance ideas, notably the revival of Roman symmetrical planning and HARMONIC PROPORTIONS. An erudite student of ancient Roman architecture, he aimed to recapture the splendour of antiquity. But he was also influenced by his immediate predecessors, especially BRAMANTE, MICHELANGELO, RAPHAEL, GIULIO ROMANO, SANMICHELI, and SANSOVINO, and to some extent by the Byzantine architecture of Venice. His style is tinged with MANNERISM, and it was understandably thought to be 'impure' by later neo-classical architects and theorists.

The son of Piero dalla Gondola he was born in Padua and began humbly as a stone-mason, enrolled in the Vicenza guild of bricklayers and stonemasons in 1524. Then, in about 1536, he was taken up by Giangiorgio Trissino, the poet, philosopher, mathematician, and amateur architect, who encouraged him to study mathematics, music, and Latin literature, especially

VITRUVIUS, and nicknamed him Palladio (an allusion to the goddess of wisdom and to a character in a long epic poem he was then writing). In 1545 Trissino took him to Rome, where he studied the remains of ancient architecture for two years. On returning to Vicenza he won a competition for the remodelling of the Early Renaissance Palazzo della Ragione or Basilica and work began in 1549. He surrounded it with a two-storey screen of arches employing a motive derived from SERLIO but henceforth called Palladian. This columned screen gives to the heavy mass of the old building a grandeur wholly Roman and an airy elegance no less distinctively Palladian. It established his reputation, and from 1550 onwards he was engaged in an ever-increasing series of overlapping commissions for palaces, villas, and churches.

The first of his palaces in Vicenza, Palazzo Thiene (begun 1542 perhaps on a design by Giulio Romano but never completed), gives an impression of massive power, emphasized by the rustication of the whole wall surface with rusticated Ionic columns on either side of the windows – barely emerging from chunky bosses – heavy quoins and voussoirs which contrast with smooth Corinthian pilasters. In plan it exploits a dynamic combination of rectangular rooms with a long aspidal-ended hall and small octagons similar to those of the Roman *thermae*. Palazzo Porto (begun *c.* 1548–52) is on a symmetrical plan derived from ancient Rome, with a façade inspired by Raphael and Bramante and much enriched with sculptured ornament. Soon afterwards he began the more original Palazzo Chiericati (completed in the late C17). This was built not in a narrow street but looking on to a large square; so he visualized it as one side of a Roman forum and designed the façade as a two-storey colonnade of a light airiness unprecedented in C16 architecture. For the convent of the Carità in Venice (planned 1561, but only partly executed) he produced what he and his contemporaries supposed to be a perfect reconstruction of an ancient Roman house; it also contains a flying spiral staircase, the first of its kind. But while his plans became ever more archaeological, his façades broke further away from classical tradition towards Mannerism, probably the result of a visit to Rome in 1554. Palazzo Valmarana (begun 1565) is a still more obviously Mannerist composition with a mass of overlapping pilasters and other elements which almost completely obscure the wall surface. The end bays are disquietingly weak, no doubt intentionally. The Loggia del Capitaniato (1571) is by far his richest building, with a mass of *horror vacui* relief decoration. His last building in Vicenza was the Teatro Olimpico (begun 1580 and finished by SCAMOZZI) – an elaborate reconstruction of a Roman theatre.

His villas show no similar process of development. In the 1550s he evolved a formula for the ideal villa – a central block of ruthlessly symmetrical plan, decorated externally with a portico and continued by long wings of farm buildings, either extended horizontally or curved forwards in quadrants, as at La Badoera (*c.* 1550–60), and linking the villa with the surrounding landscape. On this theme he composed numerous variations – from the stark severity of Poiana (1540s), with its undecorated shafts instead of columns, to the simplicity of La Malcontenta (1559–61) and the Villa Emo, Fanzolo (1560–65), where the windows are unmarked by surrounds and the decoration is limited to a portico on the main façade, to the elaboration of La Rotonda (1567), with its hexastyle porticos on each of its four sides. The use of temple-front porticos for houses was a novelty (Palladio incorrectly supposed that they were used on Roman houses). Sometimes they are free-standing but usually they are attached; and at Quinto (*c.* 1550) and Maser (later 1550s) he treated the whole central block as a temple front. The relation of the portico to the rest of the building and the sizes of the rooms inside were determined by harmonic proportions.

Temple fronts and harmonic proportions also play an important part in his churches, inspired by Alberti's S. Andrea in Mantua, all of which are in Venice: the façade of S. Francesco della Vigna (1562), and the churches of S. Giorgio Maggiore (begun 1566) and Il Redentore (begun 1576). The latter two appear inside to be simple basilicas, but as one approaches the high altar the curves of the transepts opening out on either hand and the circle of the dome overhead produce a unique effect of expansion and elation. Both churches terminate in arcades screening off the choirs and adding a touch of almost Byzantine mystery to the cool classical logic of the plan.

In 1554 Palladio published *Le antichità di Roma* and *Descrizione delle chiese . . . di Roma*, of which the former remained the standard guide-book for 200 years. He illustrated Barbaro's *Vitruvius* (1556) and in 1570 published his *Quattro libri dell'architettura*, at once a statement of his theory, a glorification of his achievements, and an advertisement for his practice. (His drawings of the Roman *thermae* were not published until 1730, by Lord BURLINGTON.)

He was the first great professional architect. Unlike his most notable contemporaries, Michelangelo and Raphael, he was trained to build and practised no other art. Though he was erudite in archaeology and fascinated by complex theories of proportions, his works are surprisingly unpompous and unpedantic. But the rules which he derived from a study of the ancients, and which he frequently broke in his own work, came to be accepted almost blindly as the classical canon, at any rate for domestic architecture.

Wittkower 1988; G. Zorzi (ed.), *Le opere di A.P.*, Venice 1959ff.; J. Ackerman, *P.*, Harmondsworth 1966; L. Puppi, *A.P.*, Milan (1973) 1977.

Palmer, John (*c.* 1738–1817), *see* CRESCENT.

Palmette. A fan-shaped decorative motif resembling a palmated leaf or a panicle of flowers. One type of ancient Greek palmette resembles honeysuckle flowers, another is more like a palm-leaf. Both were used in bands of ANTHEMION ornament, especially on Ionic buildings (e.g. Erechtheum, Athens), and the former type is sometimes incorrectly termed an anthemion. Ancient types of palmette were revived during the Renaissance and extensively used thereafter, especially in the late C18.

Palmstedt, Erik (1741–1803), *see* SWEDISH ARCHITECTURE.

Panel. Strictly any flat surface sunk or raised within a framework, e.g. Gothic stone panelling, but more usually a framed wooden surface as used in panelling to cover a wall. A *fielded panel* has a raised central flat surface often with bevelled edges, with a frame. Panelled walls developed in northern Europe from the C15 onwards when draught-proof rooms were demanded, LINENFOLD panelling being introduced first in Flanders, perhaps in imitation of curtaining. Painted, inlaid or carved panelling followed in the C16–17 and reached great sophistication in C18 France (*see* BOISERIE).

Pantheon dome. A dome similar to that of the Pantheon in Rome, though not necessarily open in the centre.

Pantile. A roofing tile of curved S-shaped section.

Papworth, John Buonarroti (1775–1847). Son of John, architect (1750–99), brother of Thomas, architect (1773–1814) and of George, architect, resident in Ireland (1781–1855); father of John Woody, architect (1820–70) and Wyatt Angelicus van Sandau, architect (1822–94). John B. Papworth's most important contribution to English architecture and planning is his work at Cheltenham mostly between 1825 and 1830. This comprises the Montpellier estate with the Rotunda (1825–6), the Lansdown estate with Lansdown Place and Lansdown Crescent (1825–9) and the church of St James (completion only, 1826–32). He also designed several country houses and a palace for the King of Württemberg at Cannstadt. The palace was not built, but Papworth received the title Royal Architect for it (1820). Papworth was interested in landscape gardening as well, and also in decoration and furnishings (notably shop windows). For one year (1836–7) he was director of the Government School of Design. Two much used picture books by Papworth were

Rural Residences (1818) and *Hints on Ornamental Gardening* (1823).

Colvin 1978; Summerson 1983.

Parabolic vault, see VAULT.

Paradise. 1. An open court or ATRIUM surrounded by porticos in front of a church (some medieval writers gave this name to the atrium of Old St Peter's). 2. The garden or cemetery of a monastery, in particular the main cloister cemetery (e.g. Chichester Cathedral, where the cloister-garth on the south side is called the 'paradise'). PARVIS seems to be a corruption of *paradisus*.

Parapet. A low wall, sometimes battlemented, placed to protect any spot where there is a sudden drop, for example, at the edge of a bridge, quay, or house-top.

Parclose. A screen enclosing a chapel or shrine and separating it from the main body of the church so as to exclude non-worshippers.

Parekklesion. In Byzantine architecture, a chapel, either free-standing or attached.

Pargeting. Exterior plastering of a TIMBER-FRAMED building, usually modelled in designs, e.g. vine pattern, foliage, figures; also, in modern architecture, the mortar lining of a chimney flue.

Parker, Barry (1867–1941), see UNWIN, Raymond.

Parler. The most famous family of German masons in the C14 and early C15. The name is confusing, as *Parlier* is German for the foreman, the second-in-command, in a masons' lodge and can thus occur in reference to masons not members of the family.

The family worked in south Germany, chiefly Swabia, and in Bohemia, chiefly Prague. More than a dozen members are recorded. The most important ones are Heinrich I and his son Peter. Heinrich I (b. *c.* 1300) was probably *Parlier* at Cologne, and then became master mason at Schwäbisch-Gmünd, one of the most important churches in Germany for the creation of the specifically German Late Gothic style (*Sondergotik*). It is likely that he designed the operative part, the chancel, a design on the HALL CHURCH principle which had great influence. A Heinrich of the same family, quite possibly he, also designed the chancel at Ulm (begun 1377).

Peter (1333–99) was called to Prague in 1352–3 to continue the cathedral begun in 1344 by Matthias of Arras (d. 1352). He completed the choir by 1385 and went on to the south transept, working first on a synthesis of the French cathedral plan with the hall principle of Gmünd and its consequences. In the chapels farther west he developed interesting and fanciful lierne vaults, curiously similar to English ones built a generation and more earlier. In 1357 he began the Charles Bridge in Prague. He probably designed and worked also at Kutná Hora (Kuttenberg) and the choir of St Barthelemy, Kolin (1378).

The Parlers, and especially Peter, also exercised great influence through the sculptural work of their lodges. Another member of the family, Johann, was master mason of the town of Freiburg from 1359 and perhaps designed the chancel of the minster there (1354–63). Yet another, again called Heinrich of Gmünd, was at Milan Cathedral in 1391–2 ('Enrico da Gamondia'), but left under a cloud, having been unable to win the authorities over to his ideas.

The Hans of Freiburg ('Annes de Firimburg') who, also in vain, made a report to the Milan authorities earlier in 1391 may be yet another Parler.

A. Legner (ed.), *Die P. und der schöne Stil 1350–1400. Europäische Kunst unter dem Luxemburger*, Cologne 1978–80; N. Nussbaum, *Deutsche Kirchenbaukunst der Gotik*, Cologne 1985; B. Schock-Werner in Recht 1989.

Parpen, parpent or **parpend**. A stone which passes through a wall with two smooth vertical faces. Also called a *through stone* or *bond stone*.

Parquet. Flooring of thin hardwood (about $\frac{1}{4}$ in. thick) laid in patterns on a wood sub-floor and highly polished. Inlaid or plated parquet consists of a veneer of decorative hardwood glued in patterns to squares of softwood backing and then laid on a wood sub-floor.

Parterre. In a garden, a level space, usually adjacent to the main house, laid out in low, formal beds of flowers as at the Grand Trianon, Versailles. In a theatre, that part of the auditorium on the ground floor lying behind the orchestra.

Parvis(e). 1. In France the term for the open space in front of and around cathedrals and churches; probably a corruption of *paradisus* (*see* PARADISE). 2. In England a term wrongly applied to a room over a church porch.

Pasqualini, Alessandro (d. before 1559), *see* DUTCH ARCHITECTURE.

Pastophory. A room in an Early Christian or Byzantine church serving as a DIACONICON or PROTHESIS; as a rule, flanking the apse of the church.

Patera. A small, flat, circular or oval ornament in classical architecture,

FIG. 67. *Patera and rosette*

often decorated with ACANTHUS leaves or rose petals. *See* Fig. 67.

Patio. In Spanish or Spanish American architecture, an inner courtyard open to the sky.

Paul, Bruno (1874–1968), *see* GERMAN ARCHITECTURE.

Pavilion. An ornamental building, lightly constructed, often used as a pleasure-house or summerhouse in a garden, or attached to a cricket or other sports ground; also a projecting subdivision of some larger building, usually square and often domed, forming an angle feature on the main façade or terminating the wings.

Pavilion roof, *see* ROOF.

Paxton, Sir Joseph (1803–65), the son of a small farmer, became a gardener and in 1823 worked at Chiswick in the gardens of the Duke of Devonshire. The Duke discovered his exceptional ability and in 1826 made him superintendent of the gardens at Chatsworth. He became a friend of the Duke, with him visited Switzerland, Italy, Greece, Asia Minor, Spain, etc., and in 1854 became Liberal MP for Coventry. He designed greenhouses for Chatsworth, the largest being 300 ft long (1836–40), tried out a new system

of glass and metal roof construction in them, laid out the estate village of Edensor (1839–41), and so, in 1850–51, moved into architecture proper by submitting, uninvited, his design for a glass and iron palace for the first international exhibition ever held. The Crystal Palace was truly epoch-making, not only because this was the most direct and rational solution to a particular problem but also because the detailing of this 1,800-ft-long building was designed in such a way that all its parts could be factory-made and assembled on the site – the first ever example of PREFABRICATION and large-scale INDUSTRIALIZED BUILDING. Paxton was also nominally responsible for a few large country houses (Mentmore, Ferrières, for members of the Rothschild dynasty), but they were partly or largely designed by his son-in-law. He was, further, one of the founders of the *Gardeners' Chronicle*, and was interested in public parks as well as private grounds (Birkenhead, 1843–7).

G. F. Chadwick, *The Works of Sir J.P. 1803–65*, London 1961; Hitchcock 1977.

Pearce, Sir Edward Lovett (*c.* 1699–1733). He was the leading exponent of PALLADIANISM in Ireland alongside CASTLE. His father was first cousin to VANBRUGH, like whom he began his career in the army. Nothing is known of his architectural training – if he had any – but he became one of the most interesting and original architects of the BURLINGTON school. His masterpiece is the Parliament House (now the Bank of Ireland) in Dublin (1728–39). The octagonal House of Commons was burnt in 1792 and later demolished. He also built the south front of Drumcondra House (1727) and Cashel Palace (*c.* 1731). He became Surveyor-General for Ireland in 1730.

Colvin 1978; Summerson 1983.

Pearson, John Loughborough (1817–97). A pupil of Ignatius BONOMI, SALVIN, and HARDWICK. Under Hardwick he worked on the Hall of Lincoln's Inn, where one may well discover his hand in the niceness of the detailing. In 1843 he set up practice, and almost at once was commissioned to design small churches. His first important church is St Peter, Kennington Lane, Lambeth, London (1863–5), French Gothic and vaulted throughout, the ribs of stone, the webs of brick. This building displays his faith in truth in building and in a nobility to fit the religious purpose. Pearson also designed country houses – e.g. Quar Wood, Stow-on-the-Wold, Gloucestershire (1857, mostly destroyed), which is Gothic, and Westwood, Sydenham, London (1881), which is French Renaissance – but essentially he is a church architect and a Gothicist. His best churches of the 1870s and 1880s are among the finest of their day not only in England but in Europe. Their style is C13 Franco-English, their decorative detail extremely sparing, and their spatial composition quite free and unimitative. Examples are St Augustine, Kilburn Park, London (1870–80); St Michael, Croydon (1871); St John, Red Lion Square, London (1874, demolished); Truro Cathedral (1879–1910); St John, Upper Norwood, London (1880–81); Cullercoats, Northumberland (1884), and St John's Cathedral, Brisbane, Australia (1887, unfinished). He was also surveyor to Westminster Abbey.

A. Quiney, *J.L.P. (1817–1897),* New Haven and London 1979.

Pebbledash, *see* ROUGHCAST.

Pedestal. In classical architecture, the base supporting a column or colonnade; also, more loosely, the base for a statue or any superstructure. *See* Fig. 68.

Pediment. Not a Greek or Roman term but signifying in classical architecture a low-pitched GABLE above a PORTICO, formed by running the top member of the ENTABLATURE along the sides of the gable; also a similar feature above doors, windows, etc. It may be straight-sided or curved segmentally. The terms *open pediment* and *broken pediment* are confused and have been employed to describe pediments open or broken either at the apex or base. For clarity, a pediment where the sloping sides are returned before reaching the apex should be called an *open-topped* or *broken-apex pediment*; and one with a gap in the base moulding an *open-bed* or *broken-bed pediment*.

Pei, Ieoh Ming (b. 1917). Chinese-born American architect, trained at MIT and Harvard. In 1948 he joined the urban developer William Zeckendorf in association with whom his first important buildings were designed, notably the Mile High Center, Denver, Colorado (1952–6) and the Place Ville-Marie complex in Montreal (1960). In 1955 he formed I. M. Pei & Partners, New York. Among their recent buildings are several for the new urban centre at Boston, including the John Hancock Tower; the John F. Kennedy Library, Harvard University; the National Airlines Terminal at Kennedy Airport, NY; the Collins Place development at Melbourne, Australia; the extension to the National Gallery, Washington, DC, completed 1978; the

FIG. 68. *Pedestal: Corinthian*

KEY: 1. Torus 3. Plinth
 2. Scotia 4. Die or dado

FIG. 69. *Pendant*

Xiang shan (Fragrant Hills) Hotel, Peking (1979–83); First Interstate Tower, Dallas (1986); the El Paso Tower, Houston (1981); and the glass 'Pyramide' or new entrance to the Louvre, Paris (1989).

B. Suner, *I.M.P.*, Paris 1988; C. Wiseman, *I.M.P*, New York 1990.

Peichl, Gustav (b. 1928), *see* AUSTRIAN ARCHITECTURE.

Pele-tower. A term peculiar to northern England and Scotland, signifying a small tower or house suitable for sudden defence.

Pellegrini, Pellegrino (1537–90), *see* TIBALDI, Pellegrino Pellegrini.

Pelli, Cesar (b. 1926), *see* UNITED STATES ARCHITECTURE.

Pendant. A BOSS elongated so that it hangs down; found in Late Gothic vaulting and, decoratively, in French and English C16 and early C17 vaults and also stucco ceilings. *See* Fig. 69.

Pendentive. A concave SPANDREL leading from the angle of two walls to the base of a circular DOME. It is one of the means by which a circular dome is supported over a square or polygonal compartment (*see* also SQUINCH), and is used in Byzantine (Hagia Sophia, Istanbul) and occasionally Romanesque architecture (Périgueux), and often in Renaissance, Baroque, and later architecture. *See* Fig. 40.

Penthouse. A subsidiary structure with a lean-to roof (*see* ROOF); also a separately roofed structure on the roof of a high block of flats.

Percier, Charles (1764–1838), studied in Paris under A.-F. Peyre and in Rome (1786–92) with his future partner P.-F.-L. FONTAINE. They worked together from 1794 until 1814, becoming the leading architects in Paris under Napoleon and creating the Empire style in decoration. For their joint works and publications, *see* FONTAINE.

Peressutti, Enrico (1908–73), *see* ROGERS, Ernesto Nathan.

Pergola. A covered walk in a garden usually formed by a double row of posts or pillars with BEAMS above and covered with climbing plants.

Peribolos. In ancient Greek architecture the wall or colonnade surrounding a temple or sacred enclosure, hence sometimes applied to the enclosure itself.

Peripteral. Of a building, surrounded by a single row of columns.

Peristyle. A range of columns surrounding a building or open court.

Perpendicular style or **Perp**. Historical division of English Gothic architecture from c. 1335–50 to c. 1530. *See* ENGLISH ARCHITECTURE.

Perrault, Claude (1613–88), a doctor by profession and amateur architect, was partly if not mainly responsible for the great east front of the Louvre in Paris (begun 1667), one of the supreme masterpieces of the Louis XIV style. LE VAU and the painter Lebrun were also members of the committee appointed to design this façade. It owes something to BERNINI's rejected project for the Louvre, and is notable for its great colonnade or screen of paired columns. He also designed the Observatoire, Paris (1667), and brought out an edition of VITRUVIUS (1674). In 1683 he published *Ordonnance des cinq espèces de Colonnes*. His brother Charles (1626–1703) was a theorist and Colbert's chief assistant in the Surintendance des Bâtiments.

M. Soriano, *Le Dossier C.P.*, Paris 1972; W. Herrmann, *The Theory of C.P.*, London 1973; Blunt 1982; A. Picon, *C.P. 1613–1688*, Paris 1988.

Perret, Auguste (1874–1954). The son of the owner of a building and contract-ing firm. After studies under Guadet he and two brothers joined the firm which was known from 1905 as Perret Frères. His first outstanding job was the house No. 25b rue Franklin near the Trocadéro in Paris, a block of flats on an interesting plan; it has a CONCRETE structure with the concrete members displayed and ART NOUVEAU faience infillings. Next came a garage in the rue Ponthieu (1905), even more demonstratively expressing its concrete frame. The Théâtre des Champs Élysées (1911–14) was originally designed by van de VELDE, but in its final form it is essentially Perret's, and its distinguishing feature is again the proud display of its concrete skeleton. Details, however, are decidedly classical, even if with a minimum of traditional motifs, and Perret was subsequently to develop in that direction. Nevertheless, until the mid-twenties bold concrete experiments still prevailed: the 65-ft arches across the vast workroom of the Esders tailoring establishment, Paris (1919), and the decorative concrete grilles of the windows and the concrete excelsior of the steeple of the churches of Notre Dame du Raincy (1922–3) and of Montmagny (1926). Examples of Perret at his most classical – basically the successor to the most restrained French c18 style – are the Museum of Public Works (1937, though with a brilliant curved flying concrete staircase inside) and the post-war work for Amiens (skyscraper 1947) and Le Havre (1945 onwards). The latter includes Perret's last work, the strange centrally planned church of St Joseph. He published *Une Contribution à une théorie de l'architecture*, Paris 1952.

B. Champigneulle, *P.*, Paris 1959; M. Zahar, *D'une doctrine d'architec-*

ture: A.P., Paris 1959; Collins 1959; E. Goldfinger, *A.P. Writings on Architecture*, London 1972.

Perron. An exterior platform ascended by steps and leading to the (usually first-floor) entrance to a house, church, etc. The door opens onto it. More loosely, the flight or flights of steps ascending to the platform.

Persian architecture. The nomadic peoples of Persia produced no architecture until after their conquest of Babylon in 539 BC. The only notable example of the succeeding Achaemenid period is the palace at Persepolis (518 – c. 460 BC), which reveals Assyrian influence in the extensive use of animal sculpture for the capitals of columns and in the use of large-scale relief decorations. Relief decorations in brightly coloured glazed brickwork (now in the Louvre, Paris) were also employed at Susa. The *apadana* or Hall of a Hundred Columns at Persepolis, so far as it can be reconstructed, shows that other elements were derived from Egypt though treated with greater lightness and elegance. Buildings erected under the Sassanian dynasty (226 BC–AD 642) were constructed of bricks and decorated with carved stucco; vaults and domes were much employed, as in the palace at Ctesiphon (AD 550). Other partially surviving Sassanian buildings of note are the palaces at Sarvistan (AD 350) and at Ferus-Abad (AD 223–41).

Persia made an important contribution to the development of ISLAMIC architecture, notably in the design of the cruciform mosque (in which an often very high vaulted niche is placed in each of the four walls of the court), e.g. the Friday Mosque in Isfahan (C12). The Persians made great use of internal and external revetments of glazed tiles of great beauty. Also they developed the domed tomb-chamber, the most notable being the mausoleum of Uljaitu, Sultaniyeh (c. 1309–13).

Some of the most impressive mosques were built under the Safavid dynasty (1502–1736), most notably in Isfahan, where the Masjid-i-Shah (1612–30) and Masjid-i-Shaykh Lutfullah (1602–4) stand on either side of a large square which is itself a fine example of urban planning. During this period many restorations of and additions to older buildings were carried out. Other achievements included bridges, notably the two-storey Pul-i-Khaj, Isfahan (1643–4), which serves also as a dam. Domestic architecture, especially pavilions in gardens, was developed with a refinement matching the decorative arts (notably carpets) of the period, e.g. Chihil Sutun, Isfahan.

After the fall of the Safavid dynasty there was little architectural activity until the rule of the Qajar (1794–1925), when conflicting tendencies – Islamic and Western – became evident, e.g. Gulistan Palace, Tehran. Tehran was developed as the capital and further Westernized under Riza Shah Pahlavi (1925–41).

Persius, Ludwig (1803–45), *see* SCHINKEL, Karl Friedrich.

Peruvian architecture. Remains of the earliest known buildings on the American continent are in Peru, notably at Chuquitanta in the centre of the coast – a c. 2000–1800 BC temple of stone-faced adobe walls on an artificial mound flanked by long wings. A ceremonial group at Chavin de Huantar in a valley of the central Andes built c. 900 BC is more impressive, with platforms surrounding a sunken court dominated by a square block about 240 ft wide and still standing 45 ft high, faced with well-cut stone, windowless but enclosing three stories of galleries connected by stairs and ramps and ingeniously ventilated by air shafts. The Mochica peoples in the north built *c.* 250 BC–AD 700 huge pyramids and also clustered dwellings of moulded adobes (e.g. at Moche). In the far south (modern Bolivia) at Tiahuanaco there is a large ceremonial centre begun AD *c.* 400 with the remains of buildings constructed from blocks of stone ingeniously dressed so that they could be bonded by grooves, slots or mortice and tenon joints but sometimes linked also by pouring molten copper into matching cavities. A new phase in the architectural history of Peru was initiated by the Incas, whose empire (founded in the C13) gradually expanded over most of the country and flourished until the Spanish conquest in 1532. At their capital Cuzco there are huge walls of polygonal masonry, tenoned together, of regular courses of rectangular blocks fixed by grinding the surface of one against those beneath and beside it. Both methods of construction were used *c.* 1500 at the fortified town of Machu Picchu, on a saddle of the Andes, which survives remarkably complete. Other notable Inca buildings are on the islands of Lake Titicaca, Pachacamac and Ollantayambo. Types of buildings were simple and standardized, rectangular and circular with windows and doors of trapezoid shape. Architectural decoration was sparse. Of colonial period buildings the cathedrals at Cuzco (1582–1654) and Lima (1582–1602), both largely by Francisco Becerra (*c.* 1545–1605), are in the austere Spanish style of the mid C16 apart from the façade of the former, which is in the rather heavy Baroque style that was developed in the church of the Compañía, Cuzco, and elsewhere. A more classical style was introduced by the amateur architect Manuel Amat, who was viceroy 1761–76 and designed the Nazarenas church at Lima. After the declaration of independence in 1821 the main influences were French for official buildings and a kind of South American vernacular for others, until the introduction of the INTERNATIONAL MODERN in the mid C20.

Peruzzi, Baldassare (1481–1536). One of the best High Renaissance architects in Rome. His works are much indebted to BRAMANTE and RAPHAEL, but have an almost feminine delicacy which contrasts with the monumentality of the former and the gravity of the latter. Born in Siena, he began as a painter under Pinturicchio. In 1503 he went to Rome, where he was employed by Bramante and assisted him with his designs for St Peter's. He probably built S. Sebastiano in Valle Piatta, Siena (*c.* 1507), a centralized Greek cross church derived from Bramante. His first important work was the Villa Farnesina, Rome (1508–11), one of the most exquisite of all Italian houses both for its architecture and for its interior decoration (frescoes by Peruzzi himself, Raphael, GIULIO ROMANO, Sodoma, and Ugo da Carpi), which combine to make it the outstanding secular monument of the High Renaissance. The plan is unusual: a square block with an open loggia in the centre of the garden front and projecting wings. The main rooms are on ground level. The façade decoration is rich with two superimposed orders of pilasters crowned with a boldly carved frieze of *putti* and swags in which the attic windows are set.

On Raphael's death (1520) Peruzzi completed his S. Eligio degli Orefici, Rome, and succeeded him as architect of St Peter's. In 1527 he fled from the Sack of Rome to Siena, where he was appointed city architect. In Siena he was mainly engaged on fortifications (near Porta Laterina and Porta S. Viene), but he also built Palazzo Polini and, outside Siena, the Villa Belcaro (now much altered). His last work, Palazzo Massimo alle Colonne, Rome (1532–6), is perhaps his most interesting, for its unorthodox design seems to echo the uneasy atmosphere of Rome in the years after the Sack. The façade is curved; there is a disturbing contrast between the ground floor with its deeply recessed loggia and the papery-thin upper part, with shallow window surrounds on the first floor and curious flat leathery frames round those on the floors above. In the *cortile* the sacrosanct orders are wilfully misused. The self-confidence of the High Renaissance has here given way to the sophisticated elegance and spiritual disquiet of MANNERISM.

Heydenreich and Lotz 1974; Lotz 1977; R. N. Adams, *B.P. Architect to the Republic of Siena 1527–1535*, Ann Arbor and London 1980; H. Wurm, *B.P. Architekturzeichnungen*, Berlin 1981.

Petersen, Carl (1874–1923), *see* DANISH ARCHITECTURE.

Petschnigg, Hubert (b. 1913), *see* HENTRICH, Helmut.

Pew. A fixed wooden seat in a church, in use at least by the C14. In medieval times pews were partially enclosed at the ends next to the aisles with *bench-ends*, which sometimes rise above the WAINSCOT and terminate in carved FINIALS (*see* POPPYHEAD). A *box-pew* is one with a high wooden enclosure all round and a small door; it is essentially a Georgian type.

Peyre, Marie-Joseph (1730–85), *see* WAILLY, Charles de.

Pharos. An ancient Roman lighthouse.

Piacentini, Marcello (1881–1960), *see* ITALIAN ARCHITECTURE; RATIONALISM.

Piano, Renzo (b. 1937). Italian HIGH TECH architect who made his name with the Centre Pompidou, Paris (1971–7), in partnership with Richard ROGERS. Of his later, independent work the Menil Collection gallery in Houston, Texas (1980–88), the travelling exhibition pavilion for IBM Europe (1984) and the Olympic Stadium, Bari (1989) are notable.

M. Dini, *R.P. Projects and Buildings 1964–83*, New York 1983; P. Goldberger, *R.P. Buildings and Projects 1971–89*, New York 1989.

Piano nobile. The main floor of a house, containing the reception rooms. It is usually higher than the other floors, with a basement or ground floor below and one or more shallower storeys above.

Piazza. 1. An open space, usually oblong, surrounded by buildings. 2. In C17 and C18 England, a long covered walk or LOGGIA with a roof supported by columns.

Picturesque. Originally a landscape

Pier

or building which looked as if it had come out of a picture in the style of Claude or Gaspar Poussin. In the late C18 it was defined in a long controversy between Payne KNIGHT and Uvedale PRICE as an aesthetic quality between the Sublime and the Beautiful, characterized in the landscape garden by wild ruggedness (chasms, dark impenetrable woods, rushing streams, etc.), and in architecture by interesting asymmetrical dispositions of forms and variety of texture – as in the COTTAGE ORNÉ and the Italianate or castellated Gothic country houses of John NASH and later in the work of DEVEY and the mid-C19 Domestic Revival in England. The notion of the 'picturesque' was the most important English aesthetic idea to have influenced architecture in Europe.

C. Hussey, *The Picturesque*, London 1927; Pevsner 1968; N. Pevsner (ed.), *The Picturesque Garden and its Influence*, Dumbarton Oaks, Washington, DC, 1974; D. Watkin, *The English Vision*, London 1982.

Pier. 1. A solid masonry support, as distinct from a COLUMN. 2. The solid mass between doors, windows, and other openings in buildings. 3. A name frequently given to Romanesque and Gothic pillars varying from a square to a composite section (*see* COMPOUND PIER).

Piermarini, Giuseppe (1734–1808). Leading neo-classical architect in Milan, he was trained in Rome under VANVITELLI and settled in Milan in 1769, then under Austrian rule. His most famous work is the façade of the Teatro alla Scala, Milan (1776–8). He also built several vast palaces, all rather severe with long façades, e.g. Palazzo Reale, Milan (1769–78), Palazzo Bel-

gioioso, Milan (1772–81) and Villa Reale, Monza (1777–80).

Meeks 1966; D. Cesarini, *G.P. Architetto neoclassico*, Milan 1983.

Pierre de Chelles, *see* JEAN DE CHELLES.

Pierre de Montreuil (or **Montereau**) (d. 1267). He may have been trained at Amiens. His early work for St Germain des Prés, Paris (1239–45), is destroyed. He is said to have been master mason at St Denis in the 1230s and 1240s, and the Sainte Chapelle in Paris has been attributed to him. But his sole surviving work is the upper part of the south arm terminal of the transept of Notre Dame, Paris (1258–67), where he took over from JEAN DE CHELLES. He succeeded Jean de Chelles as architect at Notre Dame in 1265. On his tombstone he is called *doctor lathomorum*.

D. Kimpel and R. Suckale, *Die gotische Architektur in Frankreich 1130–1270*, Munich 1985; R. Suckale in Recht 1989.

Pietilä, Reima (b. 1923), *see* FINNISH ARCHITECTURE.

Pietre dure. Italian term for semiprecious stones, such as agate, jasper and lapis lazuli, used from the C16 onwards for mosaics, sometimes covering complete interiors. The Cappella dei Principi, S. Lorenzo, Florence (begun 1604), is the most notable example. Such work was more usual on a small scale, to decorate altar frontals, furniture, etc. Sometimes called *commesso di pietre dure* or Florentine mosaic.

U. Baldini *et al.*, *La Cappella dei Principi e le pietre dure a Firenze*, Milan 1979.

Pigage, Nicolas de (1723–96), was born at Lunéville and trained in Paris, visited Italy and probably England, and in 1749 became architect to the Elector Palatine Carl Theodore in Mannheim, for whom his best work was done. His masterpiece is Schloss Benrath near Düsseldorf (1755–69), a large pavilion, apparently of one storey (but in fact of three), somewhat similar to Sanssouci at Potsdam, and decorated internally in the most exquisitely refined and restrained Rococo manner that hovers on the verge of Louis XVI classicism. At Schwetzingen he laid out the Elector's garden (1766), and built a miniature theatre and various follies, including a mosque, a romantic water castle, and a bath-house with a mirror ceiling.

Colombier 1956; W. Heber, *Die Arbeiten des N. de P. (1723–96) in der Residenzen Mannheim und Schwetzingen*, Worms 1986.

Pilaster. A shallow PIER or rectangular column projecting only slightly from a wall and, in classical architecture, conforming with one of the ORDERS.

Pilaster-strip, *see* LESENE.

Pilgram, Anton (d. *c.* 1515), was mason and sculptor first at Brno *c.* 1502 and Heilbronn (at Heilbronn he did the high-spired tabernacle for the Holy Sacrament), and later at St Stephan in Vienna, where the organ foot (1513) and the pulpit (1514–15) are his, both very intricate in their architectural forms and both including a self-portrait of the master.

K. Oettinger, *A.P. und die Bildhauer von St Stephan*, Vienna 1951; R. Feuchtmüller, *Die spätgotische Architektur und A.P.*, Vienna 1952.

Pilier cantonné. In medieval architecture, the combination of a simple monocylindrical support and engaged colonettes rising from floor to vault.

Pillar. A free-standing upright member which, unlike a COLUMN, need not be cylindrical or conform with any of the orders.

Pillar piscina, *see* PISCINA.

Pilotis. A French term for pillars or stilts that carry a building, thereby raising it to first-floor level and leaving the ground floor open.

Pinnacle. A small turret-like termination crowning spires, buttresses, the angles of parapets, etc.; usually of steep pyramidal or conical shape and ornamented, e.g. with CROCKETS. See Fig. 80.

Piper, Fredrik Magnus (1746–1824), *see* SWEDISH ARCHITECTURE.

Piranesi, Giovanni Battista (1720–78), who was mainly an engraver of views of Roman antiquities and an architectural theorist, exerted a profound influence on the development of the neo-classical and Romantic movements. Born in Venice, he was trained as an engineer and architect, and settled in Rome *c.* 1745. His highly dramatic views of Roman ruins and imaginative reconstructions of ancient Rome helped to inspire a new attitude to antiquity. In *Della magnificenza ed architettura dei Romani* (1761) he championed the supremacy of Roman over Greek architecture and in *Parere sull'architettura* (1765) advocated a free and imaginative use of Roman models for the creation of a new architectural style. He put his theories into practice only once, not very successfully, at S. Maria del Priorato, Rome (1764–6), which combines an antique flavour with allusions to the Knights of Malta, who owned the church; but it lacks the power and imagination of his engravings.

J. Wilton Ely, *The Mind and Art of P.*, London 1978; Rykwert 1980.

Pisano, Andrea (d. 1348/9). Not a relation of Giovanni PISANO but the finest Italian sculptor of the next generation and also an architect. As such he is traceable in records of Florence Cathedral as master mason, probably after GIOTTO's death in 1337 (the niche stage of the campanile is probably his). He was succeeded *c.* 1343 by TALENTI and from 1347 was master mason at Orvieto Cathedral, though by that time the most important sculptural and architectural work on its façade was over.

Trachtenberg 1971; White 1987.

Pisano, Nicola (d. *c.* 1280), and his son Giovanni (d. shortly after 1314), the greatest Italian sculptors of their generations, are also recorded as architects. In the case of Nicola we have no documents, but tradition (VASARI) and some stylistic arguments; in the case of Giovanni we are on firmer ground. He appears as master mason of Siena Cathedral in 1290 and at Siena some years earlier, during the time when the cathedral received its Gothic façade. About 1296 he moved to Pisa and was there probably also master mason.

White 1987.

Piscina. A stone basin in a niche near the altar for washing the Communion or Mass vessels; provided with a drain and usually set in or against the wall south of the altar. A free-standing piscina on a pillar can be called a *pillar piscina*.

Pisé or **terre pisé**. Clay or earth kneaded or mixed with gravel and used for building cottages, walls, etc. by being rammed between boards or formwork which is removed as it hardens. It was a building material common in the ancient Near East. *See also* COB.

Pitched roof, *see* ROOF.

Plaisance. A summerhouse or pleasure-house near a mansion.

Plan. The horizontal arrangement of the parts of a building or a drawing or diagram showing such arrangement as a horizontal section. *See also* AXIAL PLAN; CENTRALLY PLANNED.

Plaster, *see* STUCCO.

Plat band, *see* BAND.

Plate tracery, *see* TRACERY.

Plateresque. Literally 'silversmith-like', the name is given to an ornate architectural style popular in Spain during the C16. It is characterized by a lavish use of ornamental motifs – Gothic, Renaissance, and even Moorish – unrelated to the structure of the building to which it is applied. The main practitioners, many of whom were sculptors as well as architects, included Diego de SILOE, Alonso de COVARRUBIAS, Rodrigo GIL DE HONTAÑÓN.

Kubler and Soria 1959.

Playfair, William Henry (1790–1857), was the leading GREEK REVIVAL architect in Edinburgh alongside T. HAMILTON. He was the son of James Playfair (1755–94) who designed Melville Castle (1786) and Cairness House

(1791–7), the latter in an advanced neo-classical style with neo-Egyptian features inside. W. H. Playfair may have studied under SMIRKE in London but returned to Scotland in 1817 on being commissioned to complete R. ADAM's Edinburgh University. This established him professionally. He followed Adam's designs closely, but the interiors are his, notably the Library (c. 1827), which is among his finest works. In 1818 he also began the Academy at Dollar and the New Observatory on Calton Hill, Edinburgh, where he also built the National Monument (1824–9, unfinished), a Doric monument to his uncle John (1825) and another to Dugald Stewart (1831). His best-known works are the Royal Scottish Academy (1822, enlarged and modified 1831) and the National Gallery of Scotland (1850), Doric and Ionic respectively. The Surgeons' Hall (begun 1829), with its elegant and crisp Ionic portico, is perhaps his masterpiece. Though essentially a Greek Revival architect Playfair worked in other styles as well, e.g. neo-Gothic at New College, Edinburgh (1846–50) and neo-Elizabethan at Donaldson's Hospital, Edinburgh (1841–51).

A. J. Youngson, *The Making of Classical Edinburgh*, Edinburgh 1966; Crook 1972; Macaulay 1975.

Plečnik, Jošef (1872–1957). Trained in Vienna 1892–8 under Otto WAGNER, through whom he knew HOFFMANN, OLBRICH and KOTĚRA. He settled in Prague in 1911 and in 1920 began the reconstruction of Prague Castle and its gardens as the presidential palace for the new republic. But his most notable work is at Ljubljana (Yugoslavia), where pan-Slavic nationalism favoured his mixture of local Slovenian vernacular forms with modern, classical and Byzantine in a style expressive of his passionate 'regionalism'. Outstanding are the National University Library (1936–41), St Michael's church (1937–8), Zale cemetery (1938–40) and the bridges and river-bank promenades, all at Ljubljana.

F. Burckhardt, C. Eveno and B. Podrecca, *J.P. Architect 1872–1957*, Cambridge, Mass., 1989.

Plinth. The projecting base of a wall or column pedestal, generally CHAMFERED or moulded at the top. *See* Figs. 66, 68.

Plinth block. A block at the base of the architrave of a door, chimney-piece, etc., against which the skirting of the wall is stopped.

Pneumatic structures. Inflatable architecture, a special type of lightweight building, was developed by HAUS-RUCKER-CO and others.

T. Herzog, *Pneumatic Structures: A Handbook of Inflatable Architecture*, New York and Oxford 1976.

Poccianti, Pasquale (1774–1858), *see* ITALIAN ARCHITECTURE.

Podium. 1. A continuous base or plinth supporting columns. 2. The platform enclosing the arena in an ancient amphitheatre.

Poelaert, Joseph (1817–79), *see* BELGIAN ARCHITECTURE.

Poelzig, Hans (1869–1936), studied at the College of Technology in Berlin, and in 1899 was appointed to a job in the Prussian Ministry of Works. In the next year, however, he became Professor of Architecture in the School of Arts and Crafts at Breslau (Wrocław), and in 1903 its director. He stayed till 1916, then became City Architect of Dresden (till 1920), and after that Professor of Architecture in the College of Technology and the Academy of Arts in Berlin. In 1936 he accepted a chair at Ankara, but died before emigrating.

His first building of note was the water tower at Posen (Poznan), built in 1910 as an exhibition pavilion for the mining industry. It is of iron framing with brick infilling and details of exposed iron inside. Of 1911–12 are an office building at Breslau, with the motif of bands of horizontal windows curving round the corner – a motif much favoured in the 1920s and 1930s – and a factory at Luban, equally advanced in its architectural seriousness and its grouping of cubic elements. During and immediately after the First World War Poelzig was one of the most fertile inventors of Ex-PRESSIONIST forms, chiefly of a stalagmite or organ-pipe kind. These fantastic forms characterize his House of Friendship (1916), designed for Istanbul, his designs for a town hall for Dresden (1917), and those for a Festival Theatre for Salzburg (1919–20), none of which was executed. However, he did carry out the conversion of the Grosses Schauspielhaus in Berlin (1918–19), with its stalactitic vault and its highly Expressionist corridors and foyer. Later buildings were more conventionally modern (the enormous office building of 1928–31 for the Dye Trust, I. G. Farben, at Frankfurt (now the US Army headquarters) and the equally enormous building (1930–31) for the German Broadcasting Company in Berlin, now Radio Free Berlin).

T. Heus, *H.P. Bauten und Entwurfe. Das Lebensbild eines deutschen Baumeisters*, Stuttgart (1939) 1985; B. Miller-Lane, *Architecture and Politics in Germany 1918–1945*, Cambridge, Mass., 1968; J. Posener (ed.), *H.P. Gesammelte Schriften und Werke*, Berlin 1970.

Point-block housing. A point-block is a high block in which the centre is reserved for staircases, lifts, etc. and the flats fan out from that centre.

Pointed arch, *see* ARCH.

Pointing. The exposed mortar finishing to brick or masonry joints raked out to receive it. JOINTING is more durable. Old brickwork has to be 'repointed' by renewing decayed mortar. Pointing is usually flush at the edges ('flush pointing') or slightly recessed ('recessed pointing'). If flush but gently recessed in the middle, it is called 'bagrubbed pointing'. If deeply recessed to display the outline of each stone or brick, it is called 'hungry joint pointing'. If the joints are formed with a trowel, it is called 'ribbon pointing'.

Polish architecture. The oldest surviving building in Poland is the small quatrefoil Chapel of St Mary on the Wawel at Cracow. It is of the C10 and in this and all the rest the exact parallel to the oldest building of Bohemia, on the Prague Hradshin. The Romanesque style in Poland is part of that of Germany. Italian connections are largely explicable via Germany. The cathedral on the Wawel has its (German) crypt and parts of the west towers. At Gniezno splendid bronze doors of *c.* 1175 survive, at Strzelno some columns decorated with small figures under arches.

As in other countries the way was paved for the Gothic style by the CISTERCIANS. Their first abbey was at

Jedrzejow near Wroclaw in Silesia (1140 onwards), and there are a number of other abbeys. More determinedly Gothic are the buildings of the friars, starting with that of the Blackfriars at Sandomierz (1227 onwards). The east part of Wroclaw (Breslau) Cathedral, of 1244–72, has the straight ambulatory of Cistercian tradition. The nave followed in the C14, the century in which Cracow Cathedral on the Wawel was also rebuilt. Gniezno Cathedral of 1342–1415 has an ambulatory and a ring of straight-sided radiating chapels on the pattern of Cistercian architecture.

Late Gothic Polish churches have the high proportions and the ornate figured rib vaults of Germany. Wroclaw, Gdańsk (Danzig), Torun (Thorn), the Cistercian abbeys of Oliva and Pelplin, were of course all German. A characteristic Eastern feature however – though even this originated in Germany – is the so-called folded vaults, i.e. complicated space frames without ribs. Basilican sections are more frequent than halls. There are also a few two-naved halls. The church at Goslawice is an octagon with four cross-arms.

Of secular buildings by far the proudest is the Town Hall at Torun of about 1250, but mainly late C14, a bold oblong with blank giant arcading, an inner courtyard and one mighty tower. The surviving early buildings of Cracow University are also among the most interesting buildings of their kind anywhere in Europe.

The Renaissance reached Poland early, and probably by way of Hungary and Czechoslovakia. The Early Renaissance parts of the Wawel (castle) of Cracow were begun as early as 1502 and the domed chapel of King Sigismond attached to Cracow Cathedral in

1517–38; the architects in both cases were Italians. Yet closest to the windows of the Wawel palace is the Vladislav Hall at Prague, closest to the chapel that of 1507 at Esztergom. Specially characteristic of the indigenous later C16 and early C17 style are lively top crestings instead of battlements (Cracow, Cloth Hall, 1555) and courtyards or façades with arcading at two or three levels (Poznań, i.e. Posen, Town Hall, 1550–61, partially destroyed 1945, rebuilt). The former also occurs in the other East European countries, the latter in them and Germany. Castles in the country were often square or oblong with courtyards and with or without angle towers (Niepolomice, 1550 onwards; Baranow, 1579 onwards; Ujazdow, 1606 onwards). The Arsenal at Gdańsk (Danzig) of 1602–5 by the Flemish architect Antonius van Opbergen (1543–1611) is one of the great Netherlandish Renaissance buildings in this city. The remarkable new town of Zamosc, on the other hand, was built by a Venetian architect in 1587–1605.

Much interesting church work went on as well, with stuccoed tunnel vaults, their decoration being either Gothic Survival or simple geometrical patterns (Pultusk, 1556–63) or strapwork. Architects continued to be Italian and that remained so in the C17 as well. Poland has proportionately more churches of Italian inspiration in the C16 and early C17 than Germany.

The Italian church type of the Gesù in Rome was taken over before 1600 (Jesuit Church, Cracow, 1597 onwards, by J. M. Bernardone and J. Trevano); and Poland contributed much to the Italianate Baroque of the later C17 (Cracow University church, 1689). Besides longitudinal there are central churches. Klimontov, 1643 onwards, is oval, Gostyn, 1677 onwards, octagonal, and the church of the Holy Sacrament in Warsaw, 1688, round with four short arms. The latter is by the Dutch TYLMAN VAN GAMEREN, who became the leading Polish architect in the second half of the C17.

The plans of the C18, with their predilection for elongated central themes, show affinities with Bohemia and once more south Germany (Lwów, or Lvov, Dominicans, 1749–64, Berezwecz, with its curvaceous twin-tower façade, 1750 onwards). The principal country house of the first half of the C17 is Podhorce of 1635–40, still square with angle towers, and with the pedimented windows and superimposed orders of pilasters which one would find at the same time in Austria and Czechoslovakia. The full-blown Baroque came with Wilanow near Warsaw of 1681 etc. (by August Locci). In opposition to it was van Gameren's Franco-Dutch style (Warsaw, Krasiński Palace, 1682–94). This however did not apply to his ecclesiastical architecture throughout. St Anne at Cracow (1689 onwards) is thoroughly Italian and Baroque. The C18 saw a large activity both by the Saxon court and the native nobility. They culminated in PÖPPELMANN's designs for the Royal Palace. Style again varies from his exuberant Baroque to the classical French restraint of others.

Neo-classicism came early, and its earliest and finest phase corresponds with the reign of King Stanislaw Augustus Poniatowski (1764–85). Earlier still is the chapel belonging to the country palace of Podhorce. This is of 1752–66, by an architect signing himself C. Romanus. It is round, with a giant portico and a dome. Round and domed also, with a Roman Doric portico and

decidedly French, is the Protestant Church at Warsaw of 1777 by Simon Gottlieb Zug (1733–1807). The leading court architects of Stanislaw were Giacomo Fontana (1710–73) and Domenico Merlini (1730–97). Theirs is the Ujazdow Palace of 1768 onwards. By Merlini and the younger Jan Baptist Kamsetzer (1753–95) are the remodelling of the Lazienki Palace of Ujazdow (1788) and the excellent interiors of the Royal Palace (1780–85). Kamsetzer's church at Petrykosy of 1791 is wholly of the French Revolution type. At the same time the grounds of the country houses were converted in the English picturesque way (Arcadia, 1778 onwards, Natolin, Warsaw Belvedere). Between c. 1780 and c. 1825 Poland produced a number of spacious country houses in the classicist style and also the two Town Halls of Wilno and Grodno with detached giant porticos. But the most monumental of the giant porticos is that of Wilno Cathedral of 1777–1801, and that is by the Polish architect Wawrzyniec Gucewicz (1753–98). The leading early C19 architect in Warsaw was Antonio Corazzi (1792–1877). He designed the Polish Bank (1828–30), which is very French, and the Grecian Grand Theatre (1826–33). The later C19 went through the same historicist motions as all European countries, though the huge Poznanski textile factory and housing complex at Lodz, built from 1872 onwards by Hilary Majewski (1837–97), should be mentioned as a major 'historicizing' example of Industrial Architecture (it combines a BEAUX ARTS STYLE palace for the owner with the factory and blocks of workers' flats in earlier styles). In the early C20 Poland had a kind of national (in this case free neo-Romanesque) romanticism more characteristic of

Russia, Finland and Sweden than of the West. It is exemplified by the church of St James, Warsaw (1909–23), by the leading Polish architect of the inter-war period, Oscar Sosnowski (1880–1939). The *avant-garde* was less evident in Poland than in Czechoslovakia during these years despite contact with Russian Constructivism, e.g. the Warsaw Sanatorium of 1931. Since the Second World War several Polish architects have made their name internationally, e.g. Henryk Buszko (b. 1924) in partnership with Aleksander Franta (b. 1925) in Katowice, Wojciech Zablocki (b. 1930), whose Sports Centre, Warsaw (1974), may be mentioned, and Daniel Libeskind (b. 1946).

Polish parapet. A decorative device consisting of a large-scale cresting of blind arcades, pinnacles, pyramids, etc., used to crown the façades and mask the roofs of many Polish buildings, notably the Cloth Hall at Cracow (1555) and Town Halls of Poznán (*c.* 1550–61) and Culm (1567–97). It also occurs in Czechoslovakia.

Polk, Willis (1870–1924), *see* CURTAIN WALL.

Pollak, Leopoldo (1751–1806). He was born and trained in Vienna, settled in Milan in 1775 and became an assistant to PIERMARINI. His masterpiece is the Villa Belgioioso Reale (1793), now the Galleria d'Arte Moderna, a very large and grand but strangely frenchified version of PALLADIO, with a rusticated basement, giant Ionic order, and lavish use of sculpture. He built villas near Milan and laid out their gardens in the English style, e.g. Villa Pesenti Agliardi, Sombreno (*c.* 1800).

Meeks 1966; P. Mezzanotte, *Archi-tettura neoclassica in Lombardia*, Naples 1966.

Pollak, Mihály (1773–1855), the leading Hungarian classicist, was born in Vienna. His father was an architect, and his step-brother was Leopoldo POLLAK. He studied under his brother in Milan and settled in Budapest in 1798. His style is moderate, never *outré*, and not very personal. Occasionally he also used Gothic features (Pécs, or Fünfkirchen Cathedral, 1805 onwards). He built large private houses and country houses, but his *chefs-d'œuvre* are public buildings at Budapest, notably the Theatre and Assembly Room (completed 1832), the Military Academy (Ludoviceum, 1829–36), and the National Museum with its Corinthian portico and its splendid staircase (1836–45).

A. Zador, *M.P.*, Budapest 1960.

Pollini, Gino (b. 1903), *see* FIGINI, Luigi.

Polychromy. The ancient Greek use of many colours in architecture, especially on the exterior, was 'discovered' in 1830 by HITTORF, to the dismay of Greek purists. It was taken up in their own buildings by Hittorf and others, notably BINDESBØLL, DUBAN, LABROUSTE, KLENZE and SEMPER.

D. Van Zanten, *The Architectural Polychromy of the 1830s*, New York 1977.

Polygonal masonry. Masonry composed of blocks of stone dressed to fit one another with irregular polygonal exposed faces, rather than rectangular ones as in ASHLAR masonry. If some of the edges are curved it is called 'curvilinear'.

Pontelli, Baccio (1450–92/4). Florentine architect who worked at Urbino 1479–82, then in Rome until 1492. His most important work was the fortifications at Ostia. The Cancellaria, Rome (*c.* 1485), and S. Pietro in Montorio, Rome (*c.* 1490), have been attributed to him.

G. de Fiore, *B.P. architetto fiorentino*, Rome 1963; Heydenreich and Lotz 1974.

Ponti, Gio (1891–1979), Italian designer, architect, and also a painter and draughtsman in the twenties. His drawing reflects the style of the Vienna Secession (*see* OLBRICH), and his designs for porcelain of around 1925 may also be inspired by the Wiener Werkstätte. Ponti was a universal designer; his *œuvre* includes ships' interiors, theatrical work, light fittings, furniture and products of light industry. Much of his best work in these fields dates from after the war, e.g. the famous very delicately detailed rush-seated chair (1951). His fame as an architect rested for a long time on three buildings: the Faculty of Mathematics in the Rome University City, dated 1934 and one of the *incunabula* of INTERNATIONAL MODERN architecture in Italy (though preceded by TERRAGNI's few buildings); and then the two twin office buildings (1936 and 1951) designed for the Montecatini Company, both in Milan. The first, with its subdued modernity and its elegant detail, was a pioneer work and very personal. Ponti's finest building is the Pirelli skyscraper in Milan (1955–8, with NERVI); the building is 415 ft high, a slender slab of curtain walling with the long sides tapering to the slenderest ends. His Villa Planchart, Caracas, Venezuela (1955), is also remarkable,

as are his neo-Expressionist Taranto Cathedral and Denver Art Museum, Colorado. He published *In Praise of Architecture* (Milan 1957; New York 1960), and was for many years editor of the influential periodical *Domus*, which he founded.

L. L. Ponti, *G.P. The Complete Works*, London 1989.

Ponzio, Flaminio (1560–1613), official architect to Pope Paul V (Borghese), was able but rather unadventurous; he never developed far beyond the Late MANNERIST style in which he was trained. His most notable work is the Cappella Paolina in S. Maria Maggiore, Rome (1605–11), very richly decorated with sculpture and panels of coloured marbles and semi-precious stones. He also built the very long façade of Palazzo Borghese, Rome (1605–13), and the handsome Acqua Paola fountain on the Janiculum (1612). Early in the C17 he rebuilt, with a new dome, RAPHAEL and PERUZZI's S. Eligio degli Orefici, Rome.

H. Hibbard, *The Architecture of the Palazzo Borghese*, Rome 1962, and *C. Maderno and Roman Architecture 1580–1630*, London 1971.

Pope, John Russell (1874–1937), *see* UNITED STATES ARCHITECTURE.

Pöppelmann, Matthaeus Daniel (1662–1736). He was the architect of the Zwinger at Dresden, a Rococo masterpiece. He was born at Herford in Westphalia and settled in Dresden in 1686, being appointed Kondukteur in the Landbauamt in 1691, and eventually, in 1705, succeeding Marcus Conrad Dietze as Landbaumeister to the Elector of Saxony and King of Poland, Augustus the Strong. In 1705–15 he built the Taschenberg Palais in

Dresden for the Elector's mistress. For a state visit in 1709 he built a temporary wooden amphitheatre which the Elector then decided to replace with a stone construction (the Zwinger) which could be incorporated in the great new royal palace which Pöppelmann was commissioned to design. In 1710 he was appointed Geheim Cämmeriere and sent off to study and gather ideas in Vienna and Italy. His designs for the palace show some influence from both the Viennese Baroque of HILDE-BRANDT and the Roman Baroque of Carlo FONTANA. But the Zwinger itself could hardly be more original in general conception: a vast space surrounded by a single-storey gallery linking two-storey pavilions and entered through exuberant frothy gateways – the whole composition resembling a giant's Meissen table-centre. Only a section was ever built (1711–20; the Kronentor in 1713, the Wallpavillon in 1716. It was damaged in 1944 but is now rebuilt). The sculptural decoration was executed by Balthasar Permoser and the brilliance of the total effect is largely due to the successful collaboration between sculptor and architect. Pöppelmann's other buildings are far less exciting: the 'Indian' Wasserpalais at Schloss Pillnitz on the Elbe (1720–23) with CHINOISERIE roofs and painted figures of Chinamen under the eaves; the Bergpalais at Schloss Pillnitz (1724); Schloss Moritzburg, begun 1723, but executed under the direction of LONGUELUNE; and, from 1727 onwards, extensions to the Japanisches Palais in Dresden, executed under the direction of de BODT. His designs for the Dreikönigskirche in Dresden Neustadt (1732–9) were executed by Georg BÄHR. From 1728 onwards Pöppelmann collaborated with Longuelune in

Warsaw on the designs for a vast new Saxon Palace of which only the central section was built (c.1730). His son Carl Friedrich (d. 1750) succeeded him in Warsaw.

Hempel 1965; H. Heckmann, *M.D.P. (1662–1736) Leben und Werk*, Munich and Berlin 1972, and *M.D.P. und die Barockbaukunst in Dresden*, Berlin and Stuttgart 1986; H. Marx, *M.D.P. (1662–1736)*, Leipzig 1989.

Poppyhead. An ornamental termination to the top of a bench or stall-end, usually carved with foliage and fleur-de-lis type flowers, animals, or figures. A poppyhead is in fact a FINIAL.

Porch. The covered entrance to a building; called a PORTICO if columned and pedimented like a temple front.

Porta, Giacomo della (c. 1533–1602), a MANNERIST architect of Lombard origin working in Rome, is notable mainly as a follower of MICHEL-ANGELO, whom he succeeded as architect of the Capitol. Here he finished the Palazzo dei Conservatori to Michelangelo's design with slight alterations (1578) and also built the Palazzo del Senatore (1573–98) with rather more alterations. He followed VIGNOLA as architect of the Gesù, Rome, designing the façade (1571–84), which was destined to be copied for Jesuit churches throughout Europe. In 1573–4 he became chief architect at St Peter's, where he completed Michelangelo's exterior on the garden side and built the minor domes (1578 and 1585) and the major dome (1588–90) to his own design. The large dome is his masterpiece, though it is rather more ornate and much nearer in outline to the dome of Florence Cathedral than

Michelangelo's would have been. He also built the Palazzo della Sapienza (begun *c.* 1575); S. Maria ai Monti (begun 1580); the nave of S. Giovanni dei Fiorentini (1582–92); S. Andrea della Valle (1591, completed by MADERNO 1608–23); Palazzo Marescotti (*c.* 1590), and the very splendid Villa Aldobrandini, Frascati (1598–1603).

Heydenreich and Lotz 1974; V. Tiberia, *G. della P. Un architetto tra manierismo e barocco*, Rome 1974.

Portcullis. A gate of iron or iron-inforced wooden bars made to slide up and down in vertical grooves in the JAMBS of a doorway; used for defence in castle gateways.

Porte-cochère. A porch large enough for wheeled vehicles to pass through.

Portico. A roofed space, open or partly enclosed forming the entrance and centre-piece of the façade of a temple, house, or church, often with detached or attached columns and a PEDIMENT. It is called *prostyle* or *in antis* according to whether it projects from or recedes into a building; in the latter case the columns range with the front wall. According to the number of front columns it is called *tetrastyle* (4), *hexastyle* (6), *octastyle* (8), *decastyle* (10), or *dodecastyle* (12). If there are only two columns between pilasters or antae it is called *distyle in antis*.

Portoghesi, Paolo (b. 1931), *see* ITALIAN ARCHITECTURE.

Portuguese architecture. Until about 1500 Portugal participates in the development of Spanish architecture: there are Roman remains (temple at Évora); S. Frutuoso de Montélios is a C7 church on a Greek cross plan with horseshoe apses and domes, clearly inspired by Byzantium; Lourosa is MOZARABIC of 920; and the principal monuments of the Romanesque style also have their closest parallels in Spain. They are the cathedrals of Braga (begun *c.* 1100) and Coimbra (begun after 1150), inspired by Santiago de Compostela, in the style of the so-called pilgrimage churches of France: high tunnel-vaulted naves, arcades and galleries, and no clerestory lighting. On the other hand, they have no ambulatories. Individual buildings of special interest are the Templars' church of Tomar of the late C12, with a domed octagonal centre and a lower sixteen-sided ambulatory, and the Domus Municipalis of Braganza, a low irregular oblong with rows of short arched windows high up.

The Romanesque style died hard; the cathedral of Évora (begun 1186) is still pre-Gothic. The Gothic style was introduced by the Cistercians, and the outstanding Early Gothic building is the abbey of S. Maria Alcobaça (1178–1252) on the pattern of Clairvaux and Pontigny, i.e. with ambulatory and radiating chapels forming an unbroken semicircle. Its tall rib-vaulted interior is one of the noblest of the order in all Europe. The monastic quarters are well preserved and very beautiful too. But Alcobaça is an exception; for, generally speaking, the Gothic style does not begin in Portugal until the mid C13. Among the most important buildings are a number of friars' churches (S. Clara, Santarém) and a number of cathedral cloisters (Coimbra, Évora, Lisbon – all early C14).

But Portuguese architecture comes properly into its own only with the great enterprise of Batalha, a house of Blackfriars commemorating the battle of Aljubarrota. It was begun in 1388 with a vaulted nave of steep Spanish proportions and an east end of the type peculiar to the Italian friars. But after 1402 a new architect appeared, called Huguet or Ouguete, who continued the work until 1438. He introduced a full-blown Flamboyant, i.e. a Late Gothic style mixed with many reminiscences of the English PERPENDICULAR. The façade, the vaults of the cloister and chapterhouse, and the chapel of João I are his work. He also began a large octagon with seven radiating chapels east of the old east end, but this was never completed. Here, as in the link with the old east end, the vaults are of complex English types. The climax of the Late Gothic in Portugal is the MANUELINE STYLE, named after King Manuel I (1495–1521). It is the parallel to the Spanish style of the Reyes Católicos and, like it, springs from the sudden riches pouring in from overseas. But whereas the Spanish style is essentially one of lavish surface decoration, the most significant works of the Manueline style show a transformation of structural members as well, especially a passion for twisted piers. These appear at Belem, a house of the order of the Jerónimos (begun 1502) together with richly figured vaults and ample surface incrustation – and also at Setubal (1494–8). In addition there are the wildly over-decorated doorways and windows of Golegá and Tomar (1510 onwards). The portal to the unfinished east chapels of Batalha suggests East Indian inspiration. The leading masters were Diogo Boytac (*fl.* 1490–1525), a Frenchman, at Setúbal and Belem, Mateus Fernandes (*fl.* 1480–1515) in the portal of Batalha, and Diogo ARRUDA in the nave and windows of Tomar (1510–14).

But Tomar also contains the most important example in Portugal of the Italian Renaissance in its Roman Cinquecento forms. The building in question is the Great Cloister of the Cristo Monastery, Tomar (begun 1557), by Diogo de TORRALVA. But, as in Spain, the Renaissance had arrived earlier and in playful Quattrocento forms. Among cathedrals the Cinquecento style is represented by Leiria (begun 1551), the work of Afonso Álvares (*fl.* 1551–75). His nephew Baltasar (*fl.* 1570–1620) designed the Jesuit church of Oporto (*c.* 1590–1610) with its typically Mannerist, high and restless twin-tower façade. Also as in Spain, the Baroque was long in coming, but when it came it was less wild than in the neighbouring country; it influenced Brazil considerably (e.g. the Seminary at Santarém, 1676). The leading Baroque architects are João Turriano (1610–79) and João Antunes (1683–1734), and the most completely Baroque town is Aveiro. Octagonal and round plans are typical of Portuguese Baroque churches. The climax of the Baroque is well within the c18. It appears in the buildings of Niccolò NASONI (d. 1773), a native of Italy – such as the palace of Freixo and several churches at Oporto, notably S. Pedro dos Clérigos (1732–50) – and the buildings of J. F. LUDOVICE (*c.* 1670–1752), a native of Germany – such as the grand abbey of Mafra (1717–70) and the chancel of Évora Cathedral (1716–46). His pupil VICENTE DE OLIVEIRA designed the main block of the palace at Queluz (1747–52).

Opposition to the Baroque set in about the middle of the c18. There were two centres: Oporto, where the large hospital is by John CARR of York (design 1796) and the Terceiros church

345

has decoration inspired by Robert ADAM; and Lisbon, where rebuilding (to a plan) after the disastrous earthquake of 1755 was done on French principles. The most spectacular piece of the rebuilding is the Terreiro do Paço, the large square facing the Tejo. The whole area between the square and O Rocio was laid out by Eugenio dos Santos de Carvalho (1711–60) and is one of the most splendid surviving examples of C18 urbanism. Early C19 Portuguese architecture was dominated by several, not very distinguished, Italian architects; later C19 buildings are strongly Italian or French influenced, e.g. the Municipal Camera, Lisbon, of 1867–75, by Domingos Penente da Silva (1836–1901), and other public buildings in Lisbon by José Luis Monteiro (1849–1942), who had worked under BALLU on the rebuilding of the Hôtel de Ville, Paris. The metal structures by EIFFEL at Oporto and Lisbon – Ponte Maria Pia (1877) and Santa Justa Lift (1898–1901) – are exceptional.

In the conservative climate of pre-revolutionary C20 Portugal the tentative modernism of the Igreja do Sagrado Coração de Jesus in Lisbon (1962–7) by Nuno Porta and Castelo Branco, and the sensitive, AALTO-influenced buildings by Alvaro Siza (b. 1933) such as the Pinto e Sotto Mayor Bank in Oliveira de Azemeis (1971–4) were outstanding. Since 1974 Siza has designed some notable mass-housing at Bonça and at São Victor (both 1974–7).

Portzamparc, Christian de (b. 1944), *see* FRENCH ARCHITECTURE.

Post, George Browne (1837–1913), graduated in civil engineering and then worked in HUNT's office. He con-

ducted his own practice from 1860 and started again after the war in 1868. Post was an eclectic, without commitment to any one style in particular. He was interested in structure and planning, and late in life was partly responsible for evolving the standard American hotel plan with a bath to every room, a system which is complete in the Statler Hotel at Buffalo (1911–12). He did a number of millionaires' residences (Cornelius Vanderbilt, 1889 and 1895) and several prominent office buildings in New York, e.g. the Equitable building of 1869 (the first with lifts), the New York Produce Exchange (1881–5), the New York Times and Pulitzer buildings (both 1889), and the St Paul building (1897–9), which, with its twenty-two storeys, was the tallest in New York at that time.

Condit 1961; Whiffen and Koeper 1981.

Post, Pieter (1608–69), began as van CAMPEN's right-hand man at the Mauritshuis and Amsterdam Town Hall. He became a leading exponent of Dutch PALLADIANISM, an unpretentious, placid, and economic form of classicism, characterized by its use of brick with stone dressings and straightforward, almost diagrammatic use of pilasters. His masterpiece was the Huis-ten-Bosch near The Hague (1645–51; exterior ruined by C18 additions; interior decoration supervised by van Campen and C. Huygens), but the small Weigh-house at Leiden (1657), with its Tuscan pilasters on a rusticated base and supporting a simple pediment, is more typical. The Town Hall of Maastricht (begun 1659) is more ambitious. His style had great influence, and was later imported into England by Hugh MAY and others.

Kuyper 1980.

Post and lintel construction. An ancient and, structurally, the simplest type of construction: vertical members (columns, posts, piers or walls) support horizontal members (beams or lintels) as in ancient Egyptian or Greek temples. *See also* TRABEATED.

Postern. A small gateway, sometimes concealed at the back of a castle, town, or monastery.

Post-Modernism. A term coined in the 1940s but given currency by Charles Jencks in the 1970s for the reaction, primarily in architecture but also in the decorative arts, to Modernism and to Modernism's rational, functionalist ideals associated with the BAUHAUS. Pop Art led the way in America in the 1960s towards an anti-rationalist, pluralist aesthetic as did, in architecture, BRUTALISM. This encouraged eclecticism, especially one of a brash, uninhibited kind favouring 'elements which are hybrid rather than pure' and 'messy vitality over obvious unity' as the leading Post-Modernist architect Robert VENTURI wrote in his seminal book *Complexity and Contradiction in Architecture* in 1966. Post-Modern architecture emerged soon afterwards both in the USA and Europe with Michael GRAVES, Hans HOLLEIN, Philip JOHNSON, Charles MOORE, Robert STERN and others. The term has been adopted since then rather loosely by a variety of architects who have little in common apart from their opposition to Modernism and to such contemporary movements as HIGH TECH.

C. Jencks, *What is Post-Modernism?*, London 1986; Klotz 1988.

Posts. In TIMBER-FRAMED buildings the main vertical timbers of the walls. In ROOF construction vertical timbers which carry longitudinal ones.

Powell & Moya (A. J. Philip Powell and John Hidalgo Moya, b. 1921 and 1920) established themselves by winning the City of Westminster competition for the large housing estate in Pimlico, later named Churchill Gardens (1946). The clarity, precision, and directness of their style has been maintained in all their later work, such as the Mayfield School in Putney, London (1956), the Princess Margaret Hospital at Swindon (1957 onwards), the ingenious sets for Brasenose College, Oxford (1956 onwards), the Festival Theatre at Chichester (1962), large additions to St John's College, Cambridge (completed 1967), Christ Church, Oxford (completed 1968), Wolfson College, Oxford (1974) and the London Museum (1976).

Maxwell 1972.

Poyet, Bernard (1742–1824), *see* FRENCH ARCHITECTURE.

Pozzo, Andrea (1642–1709). Erroneously known as 'Padre Pozzo', he was a lay brother who entered the Jesuit order in 1665. Architect and painter, he was famous for illusionistic ceiling paintings, notably that in S. Ignazio, Rome (1691–4), and also those in the Chiesa della Missione, Mondoví (1676–7), and the Palais Liechtenstein, Vienna (1704–8). Born in Trento, he was trained in Milan and from 1681 worked in Rome (for a time in RAINALDI's studio) until 1702 when he settled in Vienna. He was extremely influential in the spread of the Baroque style from Italy to central Europe, through his engraved designs. His *Perspectivum pictorum et architectorum* (Rome 1693–1702) was frequently reprinted and had several foreign language editions as well. He designed the S. Ignazio altar in the Gesú, Rome (1697–8). His buildings are unexciting compared to his engraved designs. They include S. Ignazio, Dubrovnik (1699–1725), the Gesú and the interior of S. Maria dei Servi at Montepulciano (1702), the university church at Vienna (1705) and S. Francesco Saverio at Trento (begun 1708).

B. L. Kerber, *A.P.*, Berlin and New York 1971: Wittkower 1982; V. de Feo, *A.P. Architettura e illusione*, Rome 1988.

Prairie School. Architectural movement in American Midwest between *c.* 1900 and 1916, mainly in residential building. Inspired initially by SUL- LIVAN, it was given direction by Frank Lloyd WRIGHT. Horizontality, open plans and emphasis on the natural qualities of materials typified Prairie School buildings. After the first decade they became more varied and personal in expression and less local in scope, e.g. W. B. GRIFFIN.

H. A. Brooks, *The Prairie School*, Toronto 1972.

Prandtauer, Jakob (1660–1726), was the architect of Melk, Austria (1702– 14), perhaps the most impressive of all Baroque abbeys. The church, with its undulating façade, many-pinnacled towers, and bold dome, is clasped between two long ranges of monastic buildings which stretch forward to form a courtyard. Prandtauer took every advantage of the unusually dramatic site above the Danube to create a picturesque group of buildings which seems to rise out of the rock. The interior of the church (completed by other architects) is rich and *mouvementé*, with an almost Gothic sense of height. Prand-

tauer's other works are less exciting: the church at Sonntagberg (1706–17), a smaller version of Melk; completion of CARLONE's church at Christkindl; the magnificent stairway (1706–14), entrance portal (1712) and Marble Hall (1718–24) at St Florian near Vienna; the priory of Dürnstein (begun 1717); the little hunting-lodge of Hohenbrunn (1725–9); alterations to the Gothic cathedral at St Pölten (1722) and town houses in St Pölten. He belonged to an ancient tradition of master masons and (unlike HILDEBRANDT) supervised every stage of the works entrusted to him. Close sympathy with his religious patrons is suggested by his buildings no less than by his personal piety. He was a member of a lay confraternity and contributed handsomely to the expense of building his parish church at St Pölten (1722) and town houses in St Pölten. He was succeeded at Melk by his nephew Josef MUNGGENAST.

R. Feuchtmuller in *J.P. und sein Kunstkreis*, exh. cat., Vienna 1960; Brucker 1983.

Prang. Thai term for a type of spire with a rounded top. The form derives from structures symbolizing Mount Meru above the sanctuaries of Indian and Khmer temples. But in THAI AR- CHITECTURE the free-standing *prang* appears in Buddhist monasteries from the C13. The *prang* differs from a *chedi* (or STUPA) in that it has a small sanctuary for an image either at ground level or some way up and reached by external stairs. The most prominent example (mid-C19) is that of Wat Arun (Bangkok), encrusted with pieces of glazed pottery.

Pratt, Sir Roger (1620–85), a gentleman amateur, learned and widely travelled, was the most gifted of JONES's followers. His few buildings were very influential, but have all been destroyed or altered. At Coleshill (1650, now destroyed), Kingston Lacy (1663–5, altered by BARRY), and Horseheath (1663–5, destroyed) he invented the type of house later erroneously called the 'Wren' type. Clarendon House, London (1664–7, destroyed), was the first great classical house in London and was widely imitated and copied, e.g. at Belton House, Lincolnshire (1684–6).

Colvin 1978; Summerson 1983.

Precast concrete. Concrete components cast in a factory or on the site before being placed in position.

Pre-Columbian architecture, *see* MESO-AMERICAN ARCHITECTURE; PERUVIAN ARCHITECTURE.

Prefabrication. The manufacture of whole buildings or components in a factory or casting yard for transportation to the site. *See also* INDUSTRIALIZED BUILDING.

Presbytery. The part of the church which lies east of the choir and where the high altar is placed.

Prestressed concrete. A development of ordinary REINFORCED CONCRETE. The reinforcing steel is replaced by wire cables in ducts, so positioned that compression can be induced in the tension area of the concrete before it is loaded. This is done by stretching or tensioning the cables before or after casting the concrete. It results in more efficient use of materials and greater economy.

Preti, Francesco Maria (1701–84), *see* PALLADIANISM.

Price, Sir Uvedale (1747–1829),

landscape gardening theorist, was a friend of REPTON and R. P. KNIGHT, whom he joined in a revolt against the 'Capability' BROWN style. In reply to Knight's poem *The Landscape* he published a three-volume *Essay on the Picturesque* (1794), which defined the PICTURESQUE as an aesthetic category distinct from the Sublime and the Beautiful as defined by Burke. His approach was more practical than Knight's and laid great stress on the need for landscape gardeners to study the works of the great landscape painters.

Summerson 1983.

Primaticcio, Francesco (1504/5–70), was primarily a decorative painter and sculptor and, as such, head of the First School of Fontainebleau. His few buildings date from towards the end of his career, notably the Aile de la Belle Cheminée at Fontainebleau (1568) and the Chapelle des Valois at St Denis, largely built after his death by BULLANT and now destroyed.

Blunt 1982.

Principal, *see* ROOF.

Prior, Edward Schroeder (1852–1932), *see* ARTS AND CRAFTS.

Prix, Wolf D. (b. 1942), *see* COOP HIMMELBAU.

Prodigy houses. Recently coined term for a group of extravagant country houses built in England around 1600, e.g. Robert SMYTHSON's Wollaton Hall.

Summerson 1983.

Profile. The section of a MOULDING or, more generally, the contour or outline of a building or any part of it.

Projection, *see* AXONOMETRIC PROJECTION; ISOMETRIC PROJECTION.

Pronaos. The vestibule of a Greek or Roman temple, enclosed by side walls and a range of columns in front.

Proportion. A mathematical concept providing, in architecture and the visual arts, a set of norms comparable to metre in poetry and music. Canons of proportion based on the human figure and its members were established by the ancient Egyptians and ancient Greeks. VITRUVIUS is the only classical source on the various ancient theorists. Systems of proportion were developed by Renaissance architects, e.g. by LEONARDO, FRANCESCO DI GIORGIO and Luca Pacioli, whose *De divina proportione* was written in 1479 and published in 1509. (For ALBERTI and PALLADIO on proportion, *see* HARMONIC PROPORTIONS.) The *modulor* of LE CORBUSIER is the most notable modern instance of a canon of proportion.

P. H. Scholfield, *The Theory of Proportion in Architecture*, Cambridge 1958.

Propylaeum. The entrance gateway to an enclosure (usually temple precincts), as on the Acropolis at Athens.

Propylon. A free-standing classical gateway.

Proscenium. 1. In a Greek or Roman theatre, the stage on which the action took place. 2. In a modern theatre, the space between the curtain and orchestra, sometimes including the arch and frontispiece facing the auditorium.

Prostyle. Having free-standing columns in a row, as often in a PORTICO.

Prothesis. In Byzantine architecture, the room attached to or enclosed in the church and serving for the preparation and storage of the species of the Eucharist before Mass; generally used for the storage of the Eucharist after Mass.

Proto-Renaissance, *see* ITALIAN ARCHITECTURE.

Prouvé, Jean (1901–84). French architect and leading exponent of INDUSTRIALIZED BUILDING, he was trained as a metal craftsman in Nancy, where his father was a prominent Art Nouveau designer. A pioneer of the CURTAIN WALL, e.g. his Roland Garros Aereoclub, Buc (1937, dismantled 1940), he developed systems of metal cladding and replaceable wall components which were used by many architects, e.g. LE CORBUSIER and CANDILIS. His modifiable Maison du Peuple, Clichy (1937–9), and his housing estate of small units, made of aluminium, at Meudon (1949), were remarkable, as were his prefabricated 'Sahara' houses of 1958. His buildings could be very elegant, e.g. his Spa building at Évian of 1957.

B. Huber and J. C. Steinegger, *J.P. Prefabrication – Structural Elements*, Zürich and London 1971; D. D. Clayssen, *J.P. L'Idée constructive*, Paris 1983.

Pseudo-dipteral. In classical architecture, a temple planned to be DIPTERAL but lacking the inner range of columns.

Pseudo-peripteral. In classical architecture, a temple with porticos at either end and engaged columns or pilasters along the sides.

Pteroma. In a Greek temple, the space between the walls and colonnades.

Pteron. An external colonnade as in a Greek temple.

Pugin, Augustus Welby Northmore

(1812–52). His father, Augustus Charles (1769–1832), came from France to London in 1792, became a draughtsman in the office of NASH and later a draughtsman and editor of books on Gothic architecture (*Specimens*, 1821 onwards; *Gothic Ornaments*, 1828–31). The son helped on these, but soon received decorative and then architectural commissions. He designed furniture for Windsor Castle and stage sets for the theatre (*Kenilworth*, 1831) before he was twenty. He found himself shipwrecked off the Firth of Forth in 1830, got married in 1831, lost his wife one year later, got married again in 1833, lost his second wife in 1844, got married once more in 1849, and lost his mind in 1851.

He had a passion for the sea, and, after his conversion to Catholicism in 1834, a greater, more fervent passion for Catholic architecture, which had to be Gothic of the richest 'Second Pointed', i.e. late C13 to early C14 in style. He leaped to fame and notoriety with his book *Contrasts* (1836), a plea for Catholicism illustrated by brilliant comparisons between the meanness, cruelty, and vulgarity of buildings of his own day – classicist or minimum Gothic – and the glories of the Catholic past. Later he wrote more detailed and more closely considered books (*The True Principles of Pointed or Christian Architecture*, 1841 etc.), and in them showed a deeper understanding than anyone before of the connections between Gothic style and structure and of the function of each member. From these books he even appears a founder father of FUNCTIONALISM, though this is true only with qualifications.

His buildings mostly suffer from lack of means. He was rarely allowed to show in stone and wood the sparkling lavishness he could achieve on paper. He was as interested in furnishings, altars, screens, stained glass, metalwork, as in the building itself. This is how BARRY got him to work for the Houses of Parliament, where not only the Gothic details of the façades but even such fitments as inkstands and hatstands were designed by Pugin. He was a fast and ardent draughtsman. Perhaps his best churches are Cheadle in Staffordshire (1841–6), the cathedral of Nottingham (1842–4), and St Augustine, Ramsgate (1846–51), which he paid for himself and which stands next to his own house. As against earlier neo-Gothic churches, Pugin's are usually archaeologically correct, but often have their tower asymmetrically placed, and this started the calculated asymmetry of most of the best English C19 church design.

P. B. Stanton, *A.W.N.P.*, London (1967) 1971; Pevsner 1972; Hitchcock 1977; H. M. Port, *The Houses of Parliament*, London 1976.

Puig i Cadafalch, Josep (1869–1956), *see* SPANISH ARCHITECTURE.

Pulpit. An elevated stand of stone or wood for a preacher or reader, which first became general in the later Middle Ages (the AMBO was used in the early Middle Ages). Often elaborately carved, and sometimes with an acoustic canopy above the preacher called a *sounding board* or TESTER. Occasionally found against the outside wall of a church. The Anglican *three-decker pulpit* combines a reading desk and a clerk's stall with the preacher's stand, one on top of the other.

Pulpitum. A stone screen in a major

church erected to shut off the choir from the nave. It could also be used as a backing for the return choir stalls.

Pulvin. In Byzantine architecture, a DOSSERET above the capital supporting the arch above.

Pulvinated. Convex in profile; a term usually applied to a FRIEZE.

Purbeck marble. A dark fossiliferous limestone quarried on the Dorset coast of England, called after the Isle of Purbeck. Not a marble but used as one on account of its capacity to take a high polish. In fashion in England from the later C12 onwards and favoured particularly in the C13. Used for COMPOUND PIERS in churches. Purbeck shafts in conjunction with shafts of normal limestone give a striking effect of light and dark. Also used for effigies all over England.

Purlin, see ROOF.

Putlock holes, putlog holes or **putholes.** Holes in a wall to support scaffolding during construction. They are frequently left after construction is finished. Putlocks or putlogs are the short horizontal timbers which bear the scaffolding boards.

Pycnostyle. With an arrangement of columns set 1½ times their diameter apart. *See also* ARAEOSTYLE; DIASTYLE; EUSTYLE; SYSTYLE.

Pylon. In ancient Egyptian architecture, the rectangular, truncated, pyramidal towers flanking the gateway of a temple; also, more loosely, any high isolated structure used decoratively or to mark a boundary.

Pyramid. In ancient Egyptian architecture, a sepulchral monument in the form of a huge stone structure with a square base and sloping sides meeting at an apex: also, more loosely, any structure of this form.

I. E. S. Edwards, *The Pyramids of Egypt*, New York 1972.

Pythius (*fl.* 353–334 BC). Architect and theorist working in Asia Minor. With Satyros he designed and wrote an account of the most famous and elaborate sepulchral monument of antiquity, the richly sculptured Mausoleum built for the Carian satrap Mausolos at Halicarnassus and numbered among the seven wonders of the world (begun before 353 BC and finished after 350; sculptured fragments now in the British Museum). He was also the architect of the large temple of Athena Polias at Priene (dedicated 334; fragments now in Berlin and in the British Museum) in which the Ionic order was thought to have achieved its canonical form. In a treatise on this building (known to Vitruvius but now lost) he extolled the perfection of its proportions, criticized the Doric order and, apparently for the first time, recommended a wide training for the architect who, he said, 'should be able to do more in all the arts and sciences than those who, by their industry and exertions, bring single disciplines to the highest renown'.

Lawrence 1983.

q

Qibla. The direction in which every Muslim must turn when praying. Originally Jerusalem, but in 624 Mohammed changed it to Mecca. In mosques it is indicated by the *qibla* wall. *See also* MIHRAB.

Quadrangle. A rectangular courtyard enclosed by buildings on all sides and sometimes within a large building complex. The arrangement is often found in colleges and schools.

Quadratura. *Trompe l'œil* architectural painting of walls and ceilings. In the C17 and C18 it was frequently executed by travelling painters who specialized in it and were known as *quadraturisti*.

Quadrifrons. A four-arched structure, often placed by the ancient Romans at an intersection of right-angled thoroughfares. It was usually on a square plan.

Quadriga. A sculptured group of a chariot drawn by four horses, often used to crown a monument or façade.

Quadripartite vault, *see* VAULT.

Quarenghi, Giacomo (1744–1817), a very prolific architect, was much admired and patronized by Catherine II of Russia. Born near Bergamo, he went to Rome in 1763 to study painting, but soon turned to architecture.

He designed the interior of S. Scolastica, Subiaco (1770–76), in a light, elegant vein of neo-classicism. In 1779 he accepted an invitation to St Petersburg, where he spent the rest of his life. His first important building is the English Palace, Peterhof (1781–9, destroyed), a sternly aloof Palladian house with no decoration apart from a vast projecting portico on one side and a recessed loggia on the other. He employed a similar formula for the State Bank (1783–90) and the Academy of Sciences (1783–9), both in Leningrad. The Hermitage Theatre, Leningrad (1783–7), is smaller and richer. His later work is more accomplished and excellent in its precision and clarity of mass, e.g. Imperial Pharmacy, Leningrad (1789–96), Jusopov Palace, Leningrad (begun 1790), Alexander Palace, Tsarskoe Selo (1792–6), the Riding School (1805–7) and Smolny Institute (1806–8), both in Leningrad.

Hamilton 1983; V. Zanella, *G.Q. Architetto a Pietroburgo. Lettere e altri scritti*, Venice 1988.

Quarry or **quarrel**. A small, usually diamond-shaped pane, or a square one placed diagonally, with which medieval leaded windows were glazed. The term can also apply to any small quadrangular opening in the TRACERY of a window. The word probably derives

Quarry faced

FIG. 70. *Quoins*

from the French *carré*. Various devices and patterns were painted on quarries, particularly during the Perpendicular period. The lead supports are called *canes*.

Quarry faced. Ashlar left as it comes from the quarry, squared off only for the joints. *See also* RUSTICATION.

Quatrefoil, *see* FOIL.

Queen Anne style, *see* SHAW, Richard Norman.

Queen-post, *see* ROOF.

Quincunx. An arrangement of five verticals, with four at the angles of a rectangle and the fifth in the centre. The term is also applied to a Christian (usually Byzantine) church on a CROSS-IN-SQUARE plan with a central dome, four rectangular bays covered by barrel vaults and four smaller bays covered by domes at the angles of the cross.

Quirk. A sharp V-shaped incision in a moulding and between mouldings.

Quoins. The dressed stones at the corners of buildings, usually laid so that their faces are alternately large and small. From the French *coin* (corner). *See* Fig. 70.

r

Rabbet or **rebate**. A rectangular recess made along an edge or any channel or groove cut along the face of a piece of stone, wood, etc., so as to receive a tongue or edge of another piece.

Rabirius (*fl.* AD 81–96). Roman architect who, according to Martial, was employed by Domitian to build the palace on the Palatine in Rome which became the permanent residence of Roman emperors (the word palace is derived from it) and was still in use in the late c6. Enough survives to reveal the grandeur of this vast building or complex of buildings, erected on two levels of the hill and incorporating a hippodrome, libraries and courtyard gardens as well as innumerable state and private apartments. It was both a symbol of the Emperor's power and a perfect setting for the ceremony of his court (poets were quick to associate the several domes above the official rooms with the arc of the heavens). With its rich decorations and many fountains splashing in marble-lined courtyards it was the epitome of luxurious opulence. He has been credited with many other buildings, without evidence, but was probably responsible for Domitian's villa near Albano, of which little survives.

MacDonald 1965; Ward-Perkins 1981.

Radburn planning. A planning idea conceived in the United States after the First World War by a group including Lewis Mumford, Clarence Stein, Henry Wright, and others. It was first tried out at Radburn, New Jersey, in 1929, which was intended to be a self-contained new town (not a commuter suburb as it became). The main object of the plan is the complete segregation of traffic and pedestrians. Areas known as superblocks are ringed by roads from which cul-de-sac service roads lead to the interior. All paths and walks linking the blocks with each other and the town centre pass over or under the roads. Examples of towns planned under some such system are Vällingby, near Stockholm, and Cumbernauld, one of the NEW TOWNS in Scotland.

D. Schaffer, *Garden Cities of America: The Radburn Experience*, Philadelphia 1982.

Radiating chapels. Chapels projecting radially from an AMBULATORY or APSE. *See also* CHEVET.

Rafters, *see* ROOF.

Raggle. A groove cut in masonry, e.g. to receive the edge of a roof.

Ragstones, *see* RUBBLE MASONRY.

Raguzzini, Filippo (*c.* 1680–1771). The most original and spirited Rococo architect in Rome, where he built the hospital and church of S. Gallicano (1725–6) and Piazza di S. Ignazio (1727–8). The latter is a masterpiece of scenic town planning.

D. T. Metzger, *Piazza S. Ignazio, Rome, in the Seventeenth and Eighteenth Centuries*, London 1981; M. Rotili, *F.R. nel terzo centenario della nascità*, Naples 1982.

Rail. A horizontal member in the frame of a door, window, panel, etc.

Rainaldi, Carlo (1611–91), was born and lived in Rome. Son of a minor architect, Girolamo Rainaldi (1570–1655), he came into his own only after his father's death. He evolved a typically Roman grand manner notable for its lively scenic qualities and for its very personal mixture of MANNERIST and north Italian features with the High Baroque style of his great contemporaries, especially BERNINI. With his father he began S. Agnese in Piazza Navona, Rome, on a conservative Greek cross plan in 1652, but was dismissed in the following year when BORROMINI took over the work. His principal buildings are all in Rome – S. Maria in Campitelli (1663–7); the façade of S. Andrea della Valle (1661–5); the exterior apse of S. Maria Maggiore (1673); and the artfully symmetrical pair of churches in Piazza del Popolo, S. Maria in Monte Santo and S. Maria de' Miracoli (1662–79), which punctuate the beginning of the three main streets radiating into the centre of the city (Bernini replaced him as architect of the former in 1673).

Wittkower 1982.

Rainwater head. A box-shaped structure of metal, usually cast iron or lead, and sometimes elaborately decorated, in which water from a gutter or parapet is collected and discharged into a down-pipe.

Ramírez Vásquez, Pedro (b. 1919), see MEXICAN ARCHITECTURE.

Ramp. 1. A slope joining two different levels. 2. Part of a staircase handrail which rises at a steeper angle than normal, usually where winders (*see* STAIR) are used.

Rampart. A stone or earth wall surrounding a castle, fortress, or fortified city for defence purposes.

Ramping arches. Arches which are made asymmetrical to follow the ramp of a staircase.

Ramsey, *see* WILLIAM OF RAMSEY.

Random ashlar. Masonry composed of rectangular stones set without continuous joints.

Raphael (Raffaello Sanzio, 1483–1520). The greatest exponent of High Renaissance classicism in architecture as well as in painting. His buildings are few, but they quickly took their place beside ancient Roman buildings and the late works of BRAMANTE as architectural models. Though he owed much to Bramante, his style is sweeter, softer, and simpler. Born in Urbino, he was trained as a painter under Pietro Perugino at Perugia. An early painting of *The Betrothal of the Virgin* (1504, Brera Gallery, Milan) is dominated by a domed building, which reveals an exquisite sensitivity to architecture and a particular interest in centrally planned structures. In 1508 he settled in Rome, where he was almost immediately employed by Pope Julius II to paint the Stanza della Segnatura in the Vatican, including *The School of*

Athens with its wonderful architectural perspective of coffered vaults. His first building was S. Eligio degli Orefici, Rome (designed *c.* 1511–12, construction begun 1514. The dome was begun, probably under PERUZZI, in 1526 and completed in 1542: but the whole church was rebuilt, with a new dome, by Flaminio PONZIO in the early C17). He designed the Palazzo Bresciano-Costa, Rome (*c.* 1515, now demolished), the Palazzo Pandolfini, Florence (*c.* 1517, but executed by Giovanni Francesco Sangallo and, after 1530, by Aristotile Sangallo) and Palazzo Branconio dell'Aquila (Rome 1518–20, demolished). These derive from Bramante's Palazzo Caprini with notable variations, e.g. unbroken horizontal lines of rustication on the basement, and at Palazzo Costa alternate triangular and segmental pediments above the windows on the first floor, between clusters of three pilasters. (Palazzo Vidoni-Caffarelli, Rome, of *c.* 1525 has often been attributed to Raphael but is not by him.)

In 1515 he was appointed Superintendent of Roman Antiquities and probably proposed a scheme (also attributed to Bramante) for measuring and drawing all the Roman remains and restoring a large number of them. The most notable result of his archaeological interests was the design for Villa Madama, Rome (begun 1517, but never completed), with a circular courtyard and numerous apsed and niched rooms inspired by the Roman *thermae* and Pliny's description of his villa at Laurentium. It greatly impressed PALLADIO. The only part completed was decorated with exquisitely subtle stucco reliefs and GROTESQUE paintings by Giovanni da Udine and GIULIO ROMANO, who worked in his studio and may have assisted in some of his architectural designs also. Raphael here re-created the elegance of Roman interior decoration as effectively as Bramante had reproduced the solemnity and monumental grandeur of Roman architecture. He was appointed architect of St Peter's (1514) with Fra GIOCONDO and A. da SANGALLO, and drew up a basilican variant to Bramante's plan. His centrally planned Chigi Chapel in S. Maria del Popolo, Rome, of *c.* 1513 onwards, represents his reply to Bramante's more restricted view of ancient architecture. The chapel was completed, with some modifications, by BERNINI.

Heydenreich and Lotz 1974; M. Tafuri and C. L. Frommel, *R. architetto*, Rome 1984; C. L. Frommel *et al.*, *R. Das architektonisch Werk*, Stuttgart 1987.

Rastrelli, Bartolomeo Francesco (Varfolomey Varfolomeevich, 1700–1771), the leading architect of the 'Petersburg Baroque' period. He came to Russia from France at fifteen with his father, Bartolomeo Carlo (*c.* 1675–1744), a sculptor and occasional architect, and both settled there. Rastrelli probably studied in Paris but dates and details are unclear. His first independent buildings date from the 1720s; the earliest to have survived (1730s) were for Biron (Bühren) at Mitau (Yelgava, Latvia). Thereafter follow twenty years of uninterrupted work on a series of major commissions, mostly for the Empress Elizabeth, during which Rastrelli as chief court architect headed a large atelier of architects and designers, and the characteristic features of 'Rastrellian Baroque' – which had repercussions far beyond St Petersburg – were established. The chief surviving works are

St Andrew's church, Kiev (1747–67, realized by I. Michurin); extensions and remodelling of Peterhof (1745 onwards); the Vorontsov and Stroganov palaces, St Petersburg (1750s); the *ensemble* of the Smolny Cathedral (1748–57) and Convent, St Petersburg (not realized as originally planned – a belfry was intended); the Great Palace of Tsarskoe Selo, now Pushkin (1749–52), incorporating CHEVAKINSKY'S palace; and finally the Winter Palace, St Petersburg (1754–62).

Most of his interiors, Rococo in spirit, have been lost or altered. His exteriors, exuberant as they are with their colour-washed stucco, rhythmically massed columns and delicate fenestration, nevertheless have the solid monumentality of the High Baroque rather than the curvilinear lightness of true Rococo. The origins of his style, variously attributed to France, Italy, south Germany, and Russia, are still obscure: his lesser works have affinities with FISCHER VON ERLACH'S domestic buildings. His grander commissions achieve a uniquely Russian synthesis: gigantic as they are, they are cheerful rather than overwhelming. The modest three storeys of the Winter Palace set a ceiling on subsequent Petersburg building that has helped to preserve the city's remarkable visual wholeness.

With the rejection of his plans for the Market Building (Gostiny Dvor) in St Petersburg in 1761 (*see* VALLIN DE LA MOTHE), Rastrelli's dominance in Russian architecture was abruptly terminated and a new generation of neo-classically orientated architects associated with the Academy of Arts (founded 1759) swept his influence away in the subsequent reign of Catherine. His last years were embittered by an unsuccessful search for commissions. [R. R. Milner-Gulland]

Hamilton 1983; M. Onsjannilior, *F. B. R.*, Leningrad 1982.

Rationalism. Italian movement led by the 'Gruppo 7' founded in 1926 by FIGINI, POLLINI, TERRAGNI and a few others, notably Marcello Piacentini (1881–1960), and expanded in 1928 by Adalberto Libera (1903–63) and others to form MIAR (Movimento Italiano per l'Architettura Razionale). Its ostensibly 'modern' programme derived partly from SANT'ELIA's Futurist projects. Terragni was its outstanding exponent, but the movement foundered in its alliance with Fascism, which led to the eclecticism of Piacentini's buildings for Rome University (1932) and eventually to the nationalistic and reactionary monumentality of the buildings for the 1942 Universal Exhibition, now EUR, Rome.

E. Mantero (ed.), *Il razionalismo italiano*, Bologna 1984; R. A. Etlin, *Modernism in Italian Architecture 1890–1940*, Cambridge, Mass., 1989; T. Schumacher, *Surface and Symbol. G. Terragni and the Italian Rationalist Movement*, Princeton 1990.

Rauch, John (b. 1930), *see* VENTURI, Robert.

Ravelin. In military architecture, an outwork formed of two faces of a salient angle and constructed beyond the main ditch and in front of the CURTAIN WALL.

Raymond, Antonin (1889–1976), *see* JAPANESE ARCHITECTURE.

Raymond du Temple (active *c.* 1360–1405). Master mason to Charles V and Charles VI (Maître des Œuvres de Maçonnerie du Roi). He was held in high esteem. The king made presents to him and was godfather to a son of his. In 1363 he became master mason at Notre Dame. In 1367–70 he built the Chapel of the Célestins, of which some outstanding sculpture is now in the Louvre. In the seventies the Vis du Louvre, the famous external spiral staircase, was added by him to the Louvre. In 1387 he contracted to build the Collège de Beauvais, a university college in Paris. He was also active in the country.

Ph. Henwood in *Bulletin de la Société de l'histoire* 105, 1978/9.

Rayonnant. The Gothic style prevailing in France from *c.* 1230 to *c.* 1350, named after the radiating arrangement of lights in rose windows. Ste Chapelle, Paris (1241–8), epitomizes the style.

Branner 1965.

Rear arch. The arch on the inside of a wall spanning a doorway or window opening.

Rear vault. The small vaulted space between the glass of a window and the inner face of the wall, when the wall is thick and there is a deep SPLAY.

Rebate, *see* RABBET.

Redan. A small RAVELIN.

Redman, Henry (d. 1528), was the son of the master mason of Westminster Abbey, and is first found working there in 1496. He succeeded his father at the Abbey in 1516 and also worked for the king, holding the post of King's Master Mason from 1519, jointly with William VERTUE, and in the end alone. He was called in with Vertue for an opinion at King's College Chapel, Cambridge, in 1509, and again appears with him at Eton for the design of Lupton's Tower in 1516. He was also Cardinal Wolsey's architect, and may have designed Hampton Court. At Christ

Church, Oxford (Cardinal College), he was, jointly with John Lebons or Lovyns, in charge from the beginning (1525).

Harvey 1984.

Reeding. Decoration consisting of parallel convex mouldings touching one another.

Re-entrant corners. Corners with angles pointing inwards.

Refectory, *see* MONASTERY.

Reginald of Ely (d. 1471). First master mason, and so probably the designer, of King's College Chapel, Cambridge (begun 1446). However, his design did not include the present fan vaulting; it seems that he intended a lierne vault (*see* VAULT) instead. Reginald in all probability designed Queens' College too (1446 onwards), and perhaps the archway of the Old Schools (begun 1470), now at Madingley Hall.

Harvey 1984.

Regulus. The short band between the TENIA and GUTTAE on a Doric ENTABLATURE.

Reichlin, Bruno (b. 1941), *see* SWISS ARCHITECTURE, NEO-RATIONALISM.

Reidy, Affonso Eduardo (1909–64), *see* BRAZILIAN ARCHITECTURE.

Reinforced concrete. Since concrete is strong in compression and weak in tension, steel mesh or rods are inserted to take the tensile stresses which, in a simple beam, occur in the lower part; the concrete is thus reinforced. Also called *ferro-concrete*. *See* CONCRETE.

J. Faber and D. Alsop, *Reinforced Concrete Simply Explained*, London 1979; A. Allen, *Reinforced Concrete Design to BS 8110*, London 1988.

Reinhardt, Fabio (b. 1942), *see* SWISS ARCHITECTURE; NEO-RATIONALISM.

Relieving arch, *see* ARCH.

Renaissance. The Italian word *rinascimento* (rebirth) was already used by Renaissance writers themselves to indicate the restoration of ancient Roman standards and motifs. Today the term means Italian art and architecture from *c.* 1420 (BRUNELLESCHI) to the mid C16. It was followed by MANNERISM and BAROQUE, though the old mistaken custom is still occasionally found of extending Renaissance to include the Baroque. In countries other than Italy the Renaissance started with the adoption of Italian Renaissance motifs, but the resulting styles – French Renaissance, German Renaissance, etc. – have little in common with the qualities of the Italian Renaissance, which are details of ancient Roman derivation and a sense of stability and poise. For Proto-Renaissance, *see* ITALIAN ARCHITECTURE. *See also* CLASSICISM; and BELGIAN, CZECHOSLOVAK, DUTCH, FRENCH, GERMAN, HUNGARIAN, ITALIAN, POLISH, RUSSIAN, SPANISH and SWISS ARCHITECTURE.

Rendering. The plastering of an outer wall.

Rennie, John (1761–1821), son of a farmer, was trained by an inventive millwright and then at Edinburgh University. In 1784 he was put in charge of installing the new Boulton & Watt steam engine at the Albion Works in London. In 1791 he set up in business on his own. He was first interested in canals (Kennet and Avon), later also in fen drainage, harbours and docks, lighthouses, and also bridges. He designed Kelso Bridge (1800–1803), Waterloo Bridge (1811–17, demolished), Southwark Bridge (1815–19, demolished) and London Bridge (1824–31), built by his sons George (1791–1866) and Sir John (1794–1874), which was demolished in 1967 and re-erected at Lake Harasu City, Arizona, USA.

C. T. G. Boucher, *J.R. 1761–1821. The Life and Work of a Great Engineer*, Manchester 1963; Summerson 1983.

Renwick, James (1818–95), the son of an English engineer who emigrated to America and became the most prominent man in his field in the United States, graduated at Columbia College, New York, and became famous as an architect of churches (Grace Church, Broadway, 1843 onwards, St Patrick's Cathedral, 1853–87). His other best-known buildings are the sweetly picturesque neo-Norman Smithsonian Institution in Washington (1846), and Vassar College, an essay in a free Renaissance mixture (1865).

S. Rattner, *R.'s Design for Grace Church. Religious Doctrine and the Gothic Revival*, New York 1969; Hitchcock 1977; Whiffen and Koeper 1981.

Repton, Humphry (1752–1818), the leading English landscape gardener of the generation after BROWN, was a contemporary of PRICE and KNIGHT, with whose defence of wildness and ruggedness, however, he did not agree. The innovation of his layouts, an innovation which pointed forward into the C19, is the treatment of the garden close to the house not naturally and picturesquely, but formally with parterres and terraces, to which in his late work he added such 'Victorian' motifs as rose-arbours, aviaries etc. He also was responsible for a certain amount of architectural work though this was mostly left to his sons John Adey (1775–1860) and George (1786–1858).

Repton had lived as a country gentleman until a financial setback forced him to make a living out of his passion for gardening. He was at once successful, and the total of parks and gardens treated by him is in the neighbourhood of two hundred. He wrote *Sketches and Hints on Landscape Gardening* in 1795, *Observations on the Theory and Practice of Landscape Gardening* in 1803, *An Inquiry into the Changes of Taste in Landscape Gardening* in 1806, and *Fragments on the Theory and Practice of Landscape Gardening* in 1816. The term 'landscape gardening' is his.

D. Stroud, *H.R.*, London 1962.

Reredos. A wall or screen, usually of wood or stone, rising behind an altar, and as a rule decorated.

Respond. A half-PIER bonded into a wall and carrying one end of an arch; often at the end of an ARCADE.

Retable. A superstructure found since C11, either painted or carved, on the rear of the altar or on its own pedestal behind the altar, especially one with carved figures in the *corpus* or central part, flanked by carved and/or painted wings.

Retaining wall. A wall, usually battered, which supports or retains a weight of earth or water; also called a *revetment*.

Reticulated, *see* TRACERY.

Retro-choir. The space behind the high altar in a major church.

Return. The side or part which falls away, usually at right angles, from the front or direct line of a structure. Two particular uses of the term are: (a) that part of a dripstone or HOOD-MOULD which, after running downwards, turns off horizontally; (b) the western row of choir stalls which runs north–south, set against the screen at the west end of the choir.

Reveal. That part of a JAMB which lies between the glass or door and the outer wall surface. If cut diagonally, it is called a SPLAY.

Revell, Viljo (1910–64), *see* CANADIAN ARCHITECTURE; FINNISH ARCHITECTURE.

Revetment. 1. *See* RETAINING WALL. 2. The facing (e.g. of marble) applied to a wall built of some other material.

Revett, Nicholas (1720–1804), *see* STUART, James 'Athenian'.

Reyns, *see* HENRY OF REYNS.

Rib. A projecting band on a ceiling or vault, usually structural but sometimes purely decorative, separating the CELLS of a groined VAULT.

Ribbon development. The construction of continuous strings of houses along main roads. This was responsible for much spoliation of the English countryside during the first quarter of this century, but was largely halted by the passing of the Ribbon Development Act of 1935.

Ribera, Pedro de (*c.* 1683–1742), the leading Late Baroque architect in Madrid, carried the CHURRIGUERESQUE style to its ultimate point of elaboration. In the neo-classical period he was held up for derision by one authority, who published a complete list of his buildings as an object lesson to students, with the result that his *œuvre* is unusually well documented. Of Castilian origin, he began working for the city council of Madrid in 1719, and became its official architect in 1726. With the exception of the tower of Salamanca Cathedral (*c.* 1738) and a chapel attached to S. Antonio, Ávila (1731), all his buildings are in Madrid. His most celebrated work is the doorway to the Hospicio S. Fernando (*c.* 1722), an overpowering extravaganza of boldly and somewhat coarsely carved draperies, festoons, top-heavy ESTÍPITES, urns, and flames rising in staccato leaps above the roofline. In 1718 he built the little church of the Virgen del Puerto, which has an exterior like a garden pavilion, with a picturesque bell-shaped spire, and an octagonal interior with a CAMARÍN behind the altar. Other works include the Toledo Bridge (designed 1719, built 1723–4), with elaborately carved tabernacles perched above the arches; the Montserrat church (1720, incomplete); and S. Cayetano (1722–32, incomplete).

Kubler and Soria 1959.

Ricardo, Halsey (1854–1928), *see* ARTS AND CRAFTS.

Ricchino, Francesco Maria (1583–1658). The most important Lombard architect of the Early Baroque. His S. Giuseppe in Milan (1607–30) broke away from the prevailing academic MANNERISM as decisively as did MADERNO'S S. Susanna in Rome (1603). Both in its plan (a fusion of two centralized units) and in its aedicule façade S. Giuseppe is entirely forward-looking. Nearly all his later churches have been destroyed. Of his surviving works the best are the concave façades of the Collegio Elvetico, Milan (1627), and the Palazzo di Brera, Milan (1651–86), with its noble courtyard. His vast central cortile of the Ospedale Maggiore, Milan, was designed with G.-B. Pessina (1625–49, restored 1950s).

Wittkower 1982.

Richardson, Henry Hobson (1838–86), studied at Harvard, and then studied architecture at the École des Beaux Arts in Paris (1859–62), where, after the Civil War, he returned to work under LABROUSTE and then HITTORF. Back at Boston in 1865 he started a practice, and in 1870 won the competition for the Brattle Square church, in 1872 that for Trinity church (1873–7). These established him as an original, and at the same time a learned, architect. His favourite style was a very massive, masculine Romanesque, inspired by architects such as VAUDREMER. But the tower of the Brattle Square church, with its frieze of figures right below the machicolated top, is Romanesque only in so far as it is round-arched. In 1882 he travelled in Europe, and only then saw French and north-Spanish Romanesque buildings at first hand. The Romanesque suited him as a style: it was direct and powerful, thus capable of fulfilling American requirements. Rockfaced rustication was also a favourite with him. In fact, he was always attracted by utilitarian jobs. The most monumental of these was the Marshall Field Wholesale Warehouse in Chicago (1885–7, demolished *c.* 1935). He also designed small railway stations in the eighties. Before then he had done some small libraries (North Easton, 1877; Quincy, 1880), two buildings for Harvard (Sever Hall, 1878, which is remarkably independent of any stylistic imitation; Austin Hall, 1881, which is Romanesque), and also some private houses (the SHINGLE-faced, very original and forward-pointing Stoughton House at Cambridge, Massachusetts, 1882–3; the Glessner House at Chicago, 1855) which illustrate his ARTS AND CRAFTS affiliations. Richardson was a *bon vivant*, a designer of zest and conviction. His Romanesque was soon widely imitated – to its detriment – but helped greatly in liberating America from the indiscriminate imitation of European revivals. Among his pupils were McKIM and WHITE, and he also influenced ROOT and SULLIVAN decisively.

Hitchcock 1977; J. K. Ochsner, *H.H.R. (1838–1886). Complete Architectural Works*, Cambridge, Mass., 1984; J. F. O'Gorman, *H.H.R. Architectural Forms for an American Society*, Chicago 1987.

Rickman, Thomas (1776–1841), moved late from medicine and business into architecture. From sketching and writing about old churches he went on to open a practice as an architect. This was in 1817, the year in which he also published some lectures under the title *An Attempt to Discriminate the Styles of Architecture in England.* This little book established our terms Early English, Decorated, and Perpendicular. As a church architect Rickman could be remarkably conscientious in trying to create credible Gothic interiors. Such churches as those at Hampton Lucy (1822–6) and Oulton (1827–9) must have struck his contemporaries as archaeologically convincing. They were done in partnership with Henry Hutchinson (1800–1831), his former pupil, who was also largely responsible for Rickman's most familiar building: New Court, St John's College, Cambridge (1826–31), with the attached so-called Bridge of Sighs. Rickman was a Quaker, but late in life turned Irvingite.

Hitchcock 1977.

Ridge, *see* ROOF.

Ridge-rib, *see* VAULT.

Ridinger or **Riedinger,** Georg (1568–after 1616). Leading German Renaissance architect, a contemporary of Elias HOLL, Heinrich SCHICKHARDT and Jacob WOLFF. His masterpiece was Schloss Aschaffenburg (1605–14, destroyed but rebuilt) built for the Archbishop of Mainz, Ulrich von Gemmingen (the patron of Matthias Grünewald), and his successor Johann Schickard von Kronberg. The square ground-plan of four wings and corner towers round a central courtyard was probably derived from French *château* design through DU CERCEAU'S engravings. Though still rather medieval and fortress-like, the elevations were articulated with strong horizontal mouldings and occasional Netherlandish ornamentation. Ridinger thought it 'heroic'. It had great and long-lasting influence in Germany, e.g. on Petrini's (1624–1701) Marquardsburg of almost a hundred years later.

Hitchcock 1981; B. von Rode, *Schloss Aschaffenburg und Pompejanum,* Munich 1982.

Ried von Piesting, Benedikt, *see* RIETH VON PIESTING, Benedikt.

Riemerschmid, Richard (1868–1957). He was more important as a designer than as an architect, being one of the earliest to work for industrialized mass production. But in 1907 he planned the first German GARDEN CITY at Hellerau near Dresden (begun 1909) for which he also designed several buildings (1910–13). His small theatre in the Munich Schauspielhaus (1901 with Max Littmann) is a notable late ART NOUVEAU work. His Reckendorf pavilion for the Cologne

Werkbund in 1928 was also remarkable.

W. Nerdinger (ed.), *R. R. Vom Jugendstil zum Werkbund*, Munich and Nuremberg 1982.

Rieth von Piesting, Benedikt (*c.* 1454–1534). German mason, Master of the King's Works in Bohemia. His *chef-d'œuvre* at Prague is the Vladislav Hall in the castle with its intricate lierne vault, including curved ribs, and its curious italianizing details of windows and doorways, Quattrocento in style, but including strange Gothic twists. This work belongs to the years 1493–1502. By Rieth also may be the Organ Gallery in Prague Cathedral, fancifully Late Gothic (*c.* 1490–93). It has ribs in the form of naturalistically imitated branches. At St Barbara, Kutná Hora, Rieth altered the existing plans for the nave and aisles, and designed the vault, a vault whose ribs form a net of lozenges (executed after his death, 1540–48). Equally intricate is the vault of Laun city church, his last work.

G. Fehr, *B.R.*, Munich 1961; Hitchcock 1981; F. Seibt (ed.), *Renaissance in Böhmen*, Munich 1985.

Rietveld, Gerrit Thomas (1888–1964). Dutch designer, famous for his Red-Blue chair (1918), he became the leading DE STIJL architect. His paradigmatic masterpiece is the Schroeder House, Utrecht (1924), which foreshadowed all the features of the INTERNATIONAL STYLE – asymmetrical composition, unrelieved cubic shapes, slab roof cantilevered out at the corners, white rendering and large windows in horizontal strips with flexible continuous interior spaces made possible by steel skeleton construction. His later buildings include terrace houses and the Vreeburg Cinema, Utrecht (1930 and 1934). He enjoyed a revival in his old age, designing the sculpture pavilion for Sonsbeck Park, Arnhem (1954, re-erected at Otterlo 1964), and the Rijksmuseum Vincent van Gogh, Amsterdam, built posthumously with modifications (1963–72).

T. M. Brown, *The Work of G.R. Architect*, Cambridge and Utrecht 1958; A. Buffinga, *G.T.R.*, Amsterdam 1971; P. Overy *et al.*, *Das Rietveld-Schröder Haus*, Brunswick and Wiesbaden 1988.

Rinaldi, Antonio (*c.* 1709–94). One of the leading Late Rococo architects in Russia. His main works are the Peter III Palace and the Chinese Palace (1758–62 and 1762–8), Oranienbaum, now Lomonossow, with a pretty CHINOISERIE interior, and the Marble Palace, Leningrad (1768–72), derived from JUVARRA'S Palazzo d'Ormea, but rather more austere and classical, faced with red granite and grey Siberian marble. It is of interest also as the first ever example of the use of iron beams in architecture. The castle at Gattschina (1766–81) is tentatively classicizing.

Hamilton 1983.

Rinceau. An ornamental motif of scrolls of foliage, usually vine.

Rise. Of an arch or vault, the vertical distance between the SOFFIT at the crown and the level of the SPRINGING LINE.

Riser, *see* STAIR.

Robert de Luzarches (d. *c.* 1236). The master mason who began the nave of Amiens Cathedral in 1220. He was succeeded by Thomas de Cormont, who built the choir and aisles *c.* 1236–40.

Branner 1965.

Roberto, Marcelo (1908–64) and Milton (1914–53), *see* BRAZILIAN ARCHITECTURE.

Roberts, Henry (1803–76). Designed the Fishmongers' Hall, London (1832–5), in a Greek Revival style in the manner of SMIRKE, but is notable as a pioneer in improving working-class housing. He built model working-class houses in London from the 1840s onwards and published extensively on the subject.

J. S. Curl, *The Life and Works of H. R. 1803–76*, London 1983.

Rocaille. The amorphous, rock-like material used in grottoes, and on fountains, hence suggestive of water and mutability, which together with shells was perhaps the main inspiration and origin of ROCOCO ornament. The name is used especially for this type of Rococo ornament.

H. Bauer, *R., zur Herkunft und zum Wesen eines Ornament-Motivs*, Berlin 1962.

Roche, Eamonn Kevin (b. 1922). Born in Dublin, he went to the USA in 1948, worked with Eero SAARINEN 1951 61 and then in partnership with John Dinkeloo (1918 81). The Ford Foundation headquarters in New York (1963–8) made his name. A year later came the headquarters of the Knights of Columbus, New Haven, Connecticut (1965–9), then the Creative Arts Center, Wesleyan University (1971), at Middletown, Connecticut. Recent work includes the United Nation Plaza Hotel (1969–79), Metropolitan Museum extension (1967–78), both in New York, General Foods Corp. headquarters, Rye (1977–83), and the Morgan Bank headquarters, New York (1983–7).

F. Dallo, *K.R.*, London 1986.

Rococo architecture. The Rococo is not a style in its own right, like the BAROQUE, but the last phase of the Baroque. The great breaks in European art and thought take place at the beginning of the Baroque and again at the beginning of NEO-CLASSICISM. The Rococo is chiefly represented by a type of decoration initiated in France (*see* BOFFRAND; MEISSONNIER), by lightness in colour and weight, where the Baroque had been dark and ponderous, and, in south Germany and Austria, by a great spatial complexity (notably NEUMANN), which, however, is the direct continuation of the Baroque complexity of BORROMINI and GUARINI. The new decoration is often asymmetrical and abstract – the term for this is ROCAILLE – with shell-like, coral-like forms and many C- and S-curves. Naturalistic flowers, branches, trees, whole rustic scenes, and also Chinese motifs are sometimes playfully introduced into *rocaille*. In French external architecture the Rococo is only noticeable by a greater elegance and delicacy. England has no Rococo, apart from occasional interiors. But the playful use of Chinese, Indian, and also Gothic forms in garden furnishings can well be ascribed to Rococo influence.

Rodríguez Tizon, Ventura (1717–85), the leading Spanish Late Baroque architect, began under SACCHETTI at the Royal Palace, Madrid, and was employed by the Crown until 1759. His first important work was the Church of S. Marcos, Madrid (1749–53), built on an oval plan derived from BERNINI'S S. Andrea al Quirinale, Rome. In 1753 he built the Transparente in Cuenca Cathedral. In 1760 he became professor at the Madrid academy and his work began to assume a more dogmatic appearance under French neo-classical influence. The Royal College of Surgery, Barcelona (1761), is almost gaunt in its severe renunciation of ornament. His noblest work is the façade of Pamplona Cathedral (1783), with a great Corinthian portico flanked by square towers, archaeologically correct in detail yet still reminiscent of early C18 Rome.

T. F. Reese, *The Architecture of V.R. (1717–1785)*, New York 1976.

Roebling, John A. (1806–69), *see* BRIDGE.

Rogers, Ernesto Nathan (1909–69). Founded BBPR in Milan in 1932 with Enrico Peressutti (1908–73). The Torre Velasca, Milan (1957–60), made his name, but he was also influential as editor of *Domus* and *Casabella*.

Rogers, Isaiah (1800–1869). Born in Massachusetts and a pupil of WILLARD in Boston. His first important job was a hotel, the Tremont House, Boston (built 1828–9), which was immediately followed by the Astor House, New York (1832–6). Other major hotels by Rogers were the Exchange, Richmond, Virginia (1841), the Charleston, Charleston, South Carolina (opened 1839), with a memorable Corinthian colonnade, the St Charles, New Orleans (*c.* 1851), Maxwell House, Nashville (1859–69), and Burnet House, Cincinnati (1854–6). He also designed the Romanesque St John Episcopal Church, Cincinnati, with its diagonally placed towers, the Bank of America, New York (1835), whose façade became the entrance feature of Pine Lodge Park, Methuen Hall and the Mercantile Exchange, New York (1836–42), with its central rotunda

and long colonnade, now part of the National City Bank.

Hitchcock 1977.

Rogers, Richard (b. 1933). Leading English HIGH TECH architect, cousin of Ernesto N. ROGERS, was in partnership with Norman FOSTER in 'Team 4' until 1967 and became known internationally in the 1970s with the Centre Pompidou, Paris (1971–7), designed with Renzo PIANO. His later independent works include the Inmos Factory, Newport (1982); Coin Street development plans for South Bank, London (1983, unrealized); laboratories etc. for PA Technology, Princeton, NJ (1984), and the new Lloyd's of London building (completed 1986).

B. Appleyard, *R.R. A Biography*, London and Boston 1986; P. Cook *et al.*, *R.R. and Architects*, London and New York 1986.

Rohault de Fleury, Charles (1801–75), *see* HITTORF, Jakob Ignaz.

Roll moulding. Moulding of semicircular or more than semicircular section.

Roman, Jacob (1640–*c.* 1716). Dutch sculptor and architect who designed the Town Halls at Deventer (1693) and de Voorst (1695–1700) and succeeded MAROT at Het Loo.

Kuyper 1980.

Roman architecture. Whereas GREEK ARCHITECTURE is tectonic, built up from a logical series of horizontals and verticals (the Doric temple has been called 'sublimated carpentry'), Roman architecture is plastic with much use of rounded forms (arch, vault, and dome), so that buildings tend to look as if they had been made of concrete poured into a mould. In

Greek and HELLENISTIC ARCHITEC-TURE the column was the most import-ant member; in Rome the column was frequently degraded to merely de-corative uses, while the wall became the essential element. Hence the Roman predilection for the PSEUDO-PERIPTERAL (Temple of Fortuna Virilis, Rome, late C2 to mid C1 BC; Maison Carrée, Nîmes, begun *c.* 19 BC), for the Corinthian order, and for elaborately carved ENTABLATURES and other ornamentation. It was the de-velopment of CONCRETE used in con-junction with brick that made possible the construction of the great Roman domes and vaults. Concrete proved as economical of materials as of labour, since the masons' rubble could be used for filling. Surfaces were either stuccoed or clad in marble. The earliest concrete dome is C2 BC (Stabian Baths, Pompeii), while the earliest large-scale concrete vault is that of the Tabularium in Rome of 78 BC, where the half columns are used ornamentally – the first important instance of the divorce of decoration and function. The con-crete barrel vault on a large scale appears in Nero's Golden House, Rome, by the architect SEVERUS (mid C1 AD) and in the palace buildings by RABIRIUS for Domitian on the Pala-tine in Rome (late C1 AD). Later vaulted buildings of importance in-clude the Baths of Caracalla (*c.* AD 215), Baths of Diocletian (AD 306), and the Basilica Nova of Maxentius (AD 310–13), all in Rome.

Roman architecture reaches its apogee in the Pantheon, Rome (*c.* AD 100–125, with a dome 141 ft in diam-eter), which is both a feat of engineer-ing and a masterpiece of simple yet highly satisfying proportions – it is based on a sphere, the heights of the walls being equal to the radius of the dome. Comparison of the Pantheon with the Parthenon reveals the contrast between the tectonic and extrovert nature of Greek and the plastic, in-trovert nature of Roman architecture. This is equally evident in the most typically Roman of all buildings, the BASILICA, which, with its interior colonnades, is like a Greek temple turned outside in. Other typically Roman buildings are: THERMAE, with their rich decoration and complicated spatial play; AMPHITHEATRES, of which the Colosseum, Rome (AD 69–79), is the largest; and TRIUMPHAL ARCHES, a purely decorative type of building of which the earliest recorded examples were temporary structures of the C2 BC. Always of the Corinthian or Composite ORDER, these arches vary from the relative severity of that at Susa near Turin to the elaboration of that at Orange in the south of France (*c.* 30 BC). City gateways were hardly less profusely decorated, e.g. Porta Nigra at Trier (late C3 or early C4 AD).

In domestic architecture three types were developed; the *domus* or town-house; the *insula* or multi-storey apart-ment house or tenement block; and the *villa* or suburban or country house. The *domus* derived from the Greek and Hellenistic house and was usually of one storey only and inward-looking, the rooms being grouped axially and symmetrically around an atrium and one or more peristyle courts. The street façade was plain and without windows, or was let off as shops, as can still be seen at Pompeii. The *insula* had several identical but separate floors and was often vaulted throughout with concrete construction. A decree of Augustus limited their height in Rome to 75 ft. During the Neronian rebuilding of

Rome after the fire of AD 64 new quarters of *insulae* were laid out symmetrically along arcaded streets and round public squares. The *villa* derived from the traditional farm-house and was more casual and straggling in plan than the *domus*. It was also more outward-looking, and great variety in planning and room shapes was attained in the more luxurious examples. The exteriors were enlivened with porticos and colonnades, rooms were designed to catch the view, or the sun in winter or the shade in summer, as at Pliny's villa at Laurentum.

Hadrian's fantastic sprawling villa at Tivoli (*c.* AD 123) illustrates almost the whole range of Imperial Roman architecture at its sophisticated best. Indeed it is perhaps over-sophisticated already. The last great architectural monument of the Roman Empire is Diocletian's Palace at Split in Yugoslavia (*c.* AD 300), built after the Pax Romana had begun to disintegrate. Yet even here the Roman genius for experimentation was still at work. Certain decorative elements, e.g. engaged columns standing on isolated corbels, anticipate the language of BYZANTINE ARCHITECTURE.

Romanesque architecture. The style current until the advent of GOTHIC. Some experts place its origins in the C7, others in the C10: the former view includes CAROLINGIAN in Romanesque architecture, the latter places the beginning of Romanesque at the time of the rising of the Cluniac order in France and the Ottonian Empire in Germany. The first view also includes Anglo-Saxon architecture, the second identifies the Romanesque in Britain with the Norman.

The Romanesque in the northern countries is the style of the round arch. It is also characterized by clear, easily comprehended schemes of planning and elevation, the plan with staggered apses (*en échelon*) at the east end of churches, the plan with an ambulatory and radiating chapels, plans (mainly in Germany) with square bays in nave, transepts, and chancel, and square bays in the aisles one quarter the area. The compositions of the walls also stress clearly marked compartments, e.g. in the shafts which in Norman churches run from the ground right up to the ceiling beams.

The Early Romanesque had not yet the skill to vault major spans. Experiments began about 1000, but remained rare till after 1050. Then various systems were developed which differentiate regional groups: tunnel vaults in France, often pointed (Burgundy, Provence), and also in Spain; groin vaults in Germany; domes in the south-west of France; rib vaults at Durham and in Italy. The spread of the rib vault and the pointed vault, however, is usually a sign of the approaching Gothic style. In the exteriors the two-tower façade plus a tower over the crossing is most typical of England and Normandy, whereas screen façades with no towers are characteristic of the south of France, and a multitude of towers over the west as well as the east parts is typical of Germany. *See also* ENGLISH ARCHITECTURE; GERMAN ARCHITECTURE; ITALIAN ARCHITECTURE; SPANISH ARCHITECTURE.

Romanian architecture, *see* BYZANTINE ARCHITECTURE.

Romano, *see* GIULIO ROMANO.

Rood. Originally the Saxon word for a cross or crucifix. In churches this was set at the east end of the nave, flanked by figures of the Virgin and St John. It was usually wooden, and fixed to a special beam stretching from RESPOND to respond of the CHANCEL ARCH, above the ROOD LOFT. Sometimes the rood is painted on the wall above the chancel arch.

Rood loft. A gallery built above the ROOD SCREEN, often to carry the ROOD or other images and candles; approached by stairs either of wood or built in the wall. Rood lofts were introduced in the C15, and many were destroyed in the Reformation.

Rood screen. A screen below the ROOD, set across the east end of the nave and shutting off the chancel.

Roof
Construction

Roofs are generally called after the principal structural component, e.g. *crown-post*, *hammerbeam*, *king-post*, etc. *See below* under *Elements*.

A *single-framed* roof is constructed with no main trusses. The rafters may be fixed to a wall-plate or ridge, or longitudinal timbers may be absent altogether. A *common rafter* roof is one in which pairs of rafters are not connected by a collar-beam. A *coupled rafter* roof is one in which the rafters are connected by collar beams.

A *double-framed* roof is constructed with longitudinal members such as purlins. Generally there are principals or principal rafters supporting the longitudinal members and dividing the length of the roof into bays.

A *slab roof* is a flat roof composed either of single slabs stretching from one side of an enclosed space to another, or one of concrete which has the appearance of a thick slab.

Elements
Ashlar piece. A short vertical timber connecting an inner wall-plate or timber pad to a rafter above.

Blades, *see* CRUCKS.

Braces. Subsidiary timbers set diagonally to strengthen the frame. *Arch braces:* a pair of curved braces forming an arch, usually connecting the wall or post below with the tie- or collar-beam above. *Passing braces:* straight braces of considerable length, passing across other members of the truss. *Scissor braces:* a pair of braces which cross diagonally between pairs of rafters or principals. *Wind-braces:* short, usually curved braces connecting side purlins with principals. They are sometimes decorated with cusping.

Collar-beam. A horizontal transverse timber connecting a pair of rafters or principals at a height between the apex and the wall-plate.

Crown-post. A vertical timber standing centrally on a tie-beam and supporting a collar purlin. Longitudinal braces usually rise from the crown-post to the collar purlin. When the truss is open lateral braces generally rise to the collar-beam, and when the truss is closed they go down to the tie-beam.

Crucks, *see* CRUCK CONSTRUCTION and CRUCKS.

Hammerbeam. Horizontal brackets projecting at wall-plate level on opposite sides of the wall like a tie-beam with the centre cut away. The inner ends carry vertical timbers called hammer-posts and braces to a collar-beam. The famous hammerbeam roof in Westminster Hall, London, of 1394–1406 was devised by the king's carpenter, Hugh Harland.

Hammer-post. A vertical timber set on the inner end of a hammerbeam to support a purlin; it is braced to a collar-beam above.

King-post. A vertical timber standing centrally on a tie- or collar-beam and rising to the apex of the roof where it supports a ridge.

Principals. The pair of inclined lateral timbers of a truss which carry common rafters. Usually they support side purlins and their position corresponds to the main bay division of the space below.

Purlin. A horizontal longitudinal timber. *Collar purlin:* a single central timber which carries collar-beams and is itself supported by crown-posts. *Side purlins:* pairs of timbers occurring some way up the slope of the roof, they carry the common rafters and are supported in a number of ways: *butt purlins* are tenoned into either side of the principals; *clasped purlins* rest on queen-posts or are carried in the angles between the principals and the collar; *laid-on purlins* lie on the backs of the principals; *trenched purlins* are trenched into the backs of the princpals.

Queen-posts. A pair of vertical, or near vertical, timbers placed symmetrically on a tie-beam and supporting side purlins.

Rafters. Inclined lateral timbers sloping from wall-top to apex and supporting the roof covering. *Common rafters:* rafters of equal scantling found along the length of a roof or sometimes interrupted by main trusses containing principal rafters. *Principal rafters:* rafters which act as principals but also serve as common rafters.

Ridge, ridge-piece. A horizontal, longitudinal timber at the apex of a roof supporting the ends of the rafters.

Sprocket. A short timber placed on the back, and at the foot of a rafter to form projecting eaves.

Strut. A vertical or oblique timber which runs between two members of a roof truss but does not directly support longitudinal timbers.

Tie-beam. The main horizontal, transverse timber which carries the feet of the principals at wall-plate level. A *baulk-tie* joins the wall posts of a timber roof and prevents the walls from spreading.

Truss. A rigid framework of timbers which is placed laterally across the building to carry the longitudinal roof timbers which support the common rafters.

Wall-plate. A timber laid longitudinally on the top of a wall to receive the ends of the rafters. In a timber-framed building the posts and studs of the wall below are tenoned into it.

See Fig. 71.

Shape

The following terms are used to describe the shape rather than the construction of roofs. In principle most of these shapes can be formed by more than one type of construction.

A *Belfast* or *bowstring roof* is constructed with curved timber trusses and horizontal tie-beams, connected by light diagonal lattices of wood.

A *coupled* roof is constructed without ties or collars, the rafters being fixed to the wall-plates and ridge pieces.

A roof is *double-framed* if longitudinal members (such as ridge beam and purlins) are used. Generally the rafters are divided into stronger ones called principals and weaker subsidiary rafters.

A *gable roof* is a *pitched roof* (*see below*).

A *gambrel* roof terminates in a gablet at the ridge; in the USA a *gambrel* roof is simply a *mansard* roof.

A *helm roof* has four inclined faces joined at the top, with a gable at the foot of each.

King-post roof

Arched brace roof

Crown-post roof

Hammerbeam roof

FIG. 71. *Roofs*

KEY:

1. Ridge	8. Post	14. Trenched purlin	20. Hammer-post
2. Common rafter	9. Wall-plate	15. Windbrace	21. Ashlar piece
3. Principal	10. Scissor brace	16. Arched brace	22. Pad
4. Brace	11. Collar purlin	17. Arched brace	23. Hammerbeam
5. Butt purlin	12. Crown-post	18. Sprocket	24. Bracket
6. Tie-beam	13. King post	19. Cornice	25. Principal rafter
7. Collar-beam			

A *hipped roof* has sloped instead of vertical ends.

A *lean-to roof* has one slope only and is built against a vertical wall.

A *mansard roof* has a double slope, the lower being longer and steeper than the upper; named after François MANSART.

A *pavilion roof* slopes, or is hipped, equally on all four sides.

A *pitched roof* is the commonest type of roof with gables at both ends. Also called a *gable roof*.

A *saddleback roof* is the name given to a normal pitched roof, when used over a tower.

Suspended roof, see OTTO, Frei.

In a *wagon roof*, by closely set rafters

Root

FIG. 72. *Roof; types*

with arched braces, the appearance of the inside of a canvas over a wagon is achieved. Wagon roofs can be panelled or plastered (ceiled), or left uncovered. Also called a *cradle roof*.

See HYPERBOLIC PARABOLOID ROOF; Fig. 72.

Root, John Wellborn (1850–91), was born in Georgia, USA, went to school near Liverpool and studied at Oxford. He then took an engineering degree at the University of New York. In 1871 he went to live in Chicago. There he met BURNHAM and went into partnership with him, a suitable partnership to which Burnham contributed his organizational acumen and interest in planning, Root his resourcefulness and his aesthetic accomplishments, which included not only drawing but also music. On the work of the partnership *see* BURNHAM.

D. Hoffmann (ed.), *The Meaning of Architecture: Buildings and Writings by*

J.W.R., New York 1967; D. Hoffmann, *The Architecture of J.W.R.*, Baltimore 1973.

Roriczer or **Roritzer**. A family of C15 German masons, master masons of Regensburg Cathedral for three generations. Wenzel died in 1419. His style was so clearly influenced by Prague and the PARLERS that he must have been trained in their lodge. The surviving drawing of the west front of the cathedral may be his. Konrad, his son (d. 1477), is mentioned as master mason to the cathedral in 1456 and 1474. Concurrently, he had the same job at St Lorenz in Nuremberg (*see* HEINZELMANN) from 1439 onwards. At Regensburg he probably designed the triangular porch. He was consulted for St Stephan in Vienna in 1462, and for the Frauenkirche in Munich in 1475. His son Matthäus or Mathes (1430–*c.* 1495) worked under his father at S. Lorenz, Nuremberg, becoming master mason there 1463–6. Between 1466 and 1473 he was a member of the Brotherhood of Masons at Regensburg and worked with Hans BÖBLINGER at Esslingen. He was in Munich in 1473 and in 1476 became a citizen of Regensburg, where in 1477 he followed his father as master mason at the cathedral, of which the west façade, the Eichel turret (1487–8) and the tabernacle (1493) are his. He published an important booklet on how to set out Gothic finials, *Büchlein vor des fialen Gerechtigkeit* (Regensburg, 1486); also *Winpergbüchlein* and *Geometria deutsch*, Regensburg (1486–90). His brother Wolfgang was appointed his successor. Wolfgang was executed for political reasons in 1514.

L. R. Shelby, *Gothic Design Techniques: The Fifteenth Century Design*

Booklets of M.R. and Hans Schutter-mayer, Carbondale 1977; A. Hubel in Recht 1989.

Rose window or **wheel window**. A circular window with FOILS of patterned TRACERY arranged like the spokes of a wheel.

Rosette. A rose-shaped PATERA. *See* Fig. 67.

Rossellino, Bernardo di Matteo Gamberelli called (1409–64), was primarily a sculptor. Precocious, he was still only in his twenties when he completed the Misericordia at Arezzo (1433) and the Chiostro degli Aranci in the Badia, Florence (1436–7). In the 1440s he was concerned mainly with sculpture, but in the 1450s in Rome he became *ingegnere di palazzo* to Pope Nicholas V and also knew ALBERTI. Later, back in Florence, he superintended the building of Alberti's Palazzo Rucellai and completed the lantern on BRUNELLESCHI's *duomo*. His chief works in architecture are the *piazza* and surrounding buildings at Pienza (1460–62), commissioned by Pope Pius II (Piccolomini), notably the cathedral and Palazzo Piccolomini. It was the first ideal city of the Renaissance to be realized.

Heydenreich and Lotz 1974; C. R. Meek, *Studies in the Architectural Career of B. di M.G. called R.*, Ann Arbor and London 1980; C. R. Mack, *Pienza. The Creation of a Renaissance City*, London 1987.

Rossetti, Biagio (*c.* 1447–1516). Architect and town-planner, he was responsible for the expansion of Ferrara under Duke Ercole I by a planned extension to the north on a site enclosed by a wall – the Addizione Erculea. It is the most important piece of systematic Renaissance town planning in Italy, and contains four churches and eight palaces by Rossetti. He is first recorded working at Palazzo Schifanoia, Ferrara, under Pietro Benvenuti (d. 1483), whom he succeeded as ducal architect. In 1492 he began work on the Addizione Erculea. His most important building is the Palazzo dei Diamanti (after 1498), but the Casa Rossetti and the Palazzi Bevilacqua and Rondinelli in Piazza Nuova (1490s) are very accomplished too. His Palazzo di Lodovico Moro is *c.* 1500. S. Francesco and S. Cristoforo are the best preserved of his four churches, S. Maria in Vado and S. Benedetto being much altered or damaged.

B. Zevi, *B.R. architetto ferrarese*, Turin 1960; Heydenreich and Lotz 1974.

Rossi, Aldo (b. 1931). Controversial and stimulating theorist, the leading proponent of the Italian anti-Modernist NEO-RATIONALISM movement or 'Tendenza' of which his book *L'architettura della città* (1966) was the seminal text. His cemetery at Modena (designed 1971–6, built 1980–85) is his and the movement's masterpiece so far, though his residential block for AYMONINO's Gallaratese 2 complex, Milan (1970–73), should be mentioned along with his school at Falagnano Olana (1972) and the floating, demountable theatre for Venice (1980). Recent works include his renovation and addition to the Carlo Felice theatre, Genoa (1982–9), the Palazzo Hotel, Fuknoto (1987), the Historisches Museum, Berlin, and New School of Architecture, Miami, Florida. He published *A Scientific Autobiography* (Cambridge, Mass.) in 1981.

V. Scully and R. Moneo, *A.R. Build-*

ings and Projects, Cambridge, Mass., 1985; Klotz 1988; A. Ferlin, *A.R. Architecture 1959–1987*, Cambridge, Mass., 1989.

Rossi, Giovanni Antonio de' (1616–95). A prolific Roman High Baroque architect. His most important work is in the domestic field, e.g. the grandiose Palazzo Altieri, Rome (1650–54 and 1670–76), and the smaller, more elegant Palazzo Asti-Bonaparte, Rome (*c.* 1665), which set a pattern for c18 architects in Rome. In his ecclesiastical work he showed a preference for oval plans and lavish sculptural decoration. His Cappella Lancellotti in S. Giovanni in Laterano, Rome (*c.* 1680), and S. Maria in Campo Marzo, Rome (1676–86), are minor masterpieces of Roman High Baroque.

Wittkower 1982.

Rossi, Karl Ivanovich (1775–1849). The leading architect in post-1815 St Petersburg, where he was responsible for replacing the Greek Revival style of THOMON, VORONIKHIN and ZAKHAROV with a much juicier Rome-inspired brand of classicism. The son of an Italian ballerina, he was trained in Russia and visited Italy only in 1802. Until 1816 he worked mainly in Moscow, but his principal buildings are in Leningrad: the New Michael Palace (now the Russian Museum, 1819–28) together with the square and surrounding buildings, the huge and richly Roman General Staff Arch and the vast hemicycle of office buildings on either side; the Alexander, now Pushkin, Theatre (1827–32); and the Senate and Synod (1829–34). But he is perhaps less important for these than for the town planning around them.

M. Z. Taranovskaya, *K.R.*, Leningrad 1980; Hamilton 1983.

Rostral column. *See* COLUMNA ROSTRATA.

Rotunda. A building (often surrounded by a colonnade) or room circular in plan and usually domed, e.g. the Pantheon.

Roughcast. An external rendering of rough material, usually applied in two coats of cement and sand on to which gravel, crushed stone, or pebbles are thrown before the second coat is dry; also called *pebbledash*.

Rousseau, Pierre (1751–1810), *see* FRENCH ARCHITECTURE.

Rubble masonry. Rough unhewn building stones or flints, generally not laid in regular courses. *Coursed rubble* is walling with the stones or flints roughly dressed and laid in deep courses. *Snecked* or *speckled rubble* is walling with stones of varying sizes with small rectangular fillings or snecks between them.

Rudnyev, Ljew Wladimirowitsch (1885–1956), *see* RUSSIAN ARCHITECTURE.

Rudolph, Paul (b. 1918), was a pupil of GROPIUS at Harvard. In 1958 he became head of the school of architecture at Yale University, New Haven, for which he designed the new building (1961–4), but shortly after left Yale. The building for the school unmistakably belongs to the trend often termed BRUTALISM, but Rudolph – like SAARINEN and Philip JOHNSON – is one of those who do not feel compelled to adhere to one style in all their designs, even those of the same years, though this in no way impairs his sincerity. Rudolph's other principal buildings are the Sarasota High School (1958–9), Cocoon House, Siesta Key,

FIG. 73. *Running dog*

Florida (1960–61), the fortress-like Endo Laboratories at Garden City, New York (1961–4), and the State Service Center in the Government Center, Boston (1962, 1967–72).

S. Moholy-Nagy, *Introduction to the Architecture of P.R.*, New York 1970; R. Spade, *P.R.*, London and New York 1971.

Rundbogenstil. German C19 'round-arched style' deriving in various degrees from Early Christian, Byzantine, German and Italian Romanesque and even Italian Early Renaissance styles. It corresponds to the neo-Romanesque of C19 France and the USA and to the neo-Norman of C19 England but is much more prominent, having been used by GÄRTNER, KLENZE, SCHINKEL and many other architects. The term seems to have been coined by H. Hübsch in 1828. *See also* HISTORICISM.

Running dog. A classical ornament often used in a frieze, similar to the wave ornament. It is sometimes called a *Vitruvian scroll. See* Fig. 73.

Ruskin, John (1819–1900), was not an architect, but the source of an influence as strong on architecture as it was on the appreciation of art. This influence made itself felt in two ways: by the principles which Ruskin tried to establish, and by the styles whose adoption he pleaded for.

As for the former, they are chiefly the principles of the *Seven Lamps of Architecture*, which came out in 1849: Sacrifice (architecture, as against mere building, takes into account the venerable and beautiful, however 'unnecessary'); Truth (no disguised supports, no sham materials, no machine work for handwork); Power (simple grand massing); Beauty (only possible by imitation of, or inspiration from, nature); Life (architecture must express a fullness of life, embrace boldness and irregularity, scorn refinement, and also be the work of men as men, i.e. handwork); Memory (the greatest glory of a building is its age, and we must therefore build for perpetuity); Obedience (a style must be universally accepted: 'We want no new style', 'the forms of architecture already known are good enough for us'). From this last point, Ruskin proceeded to list the styles of the past which are perfect enough to be chosen for universal obedience. They are the Pisan Romanesque, the Early Gothic of west Italy, the Venetian Gothic, and the earliest English Decorated. This last, the style of the late C13 to early C14, had in fact been the choice of PUGIN, of the Cambridge Camden Movement (*see* BUTTERFIELD), and of SCOTT. But Ruskin's next book on architecture was *The Stones of Venice* (1851–3), which, being in praise of the Venetian Gothic, led admirers of Ruskin to imitate that style – G. F. BODLEY, J. P. SEDDON, J. Prichard, early STREET, early GODWIN and the Irish architects Benjamin Woodward (1815–61) and Thomas Deane (1792–1871), whose University Museum, Oxford (1854–60), was a notable essay in Ruskinian Gothic. But *The Stones of Venice* also contains the celebrated chapter *On the Nature of Gothic*, which for the first time equated the beauties of medieval architecture and decoration with the pleasure taken by the workman in producing them. This was the mainspring that released the work of MORRIS as creator of workshops and as social reformer.

Hitchcock 1954; Pevsner 1972; E. Blau, *Ruskinian Gothic: The Architecture of Deane and Woodward 1845–61*, Princeton 1982; M. Swenarton, *Artisans and Architects. The R. Tradition in Architectural Thought*, London 1989; M. W. Brooks, *J. R. and Victorian Architecture*, London 1990.

Russian architecture. The architectural history of Russia is conditioned by Orthodox Eastern Europe: unlike the West, yet similarly, if tenuously, linked with the traditions of classical antiquity (through Byzantium), and experiencing from time to time westernizing movements that culminated in the comprehensive reforms of Peter the Great (*c*. 1700). Uniquely among Orthodox lands, Russia has preserved buildings of aesthetic significance from all periods in nearly 1,000 years of architectural development. Since Russia did not experience the Renaissance, the first seven centuries of its architectural history after the official conversion to Christianity (AD 988) may broadly be termed medieval. Thereafter the same standard categories of periodization (Baroque, neo-classic, etc.) are applied as in the rest of Europe.

From prehistoric times the material of vernacular Russian architecture was wood, used until this century not only for domestic buildings but in quite elaborate structures (fortresses, churches, palaces). The early development of such architecture is hard to establish, since no surviving building appears to be older than the church of the Muromsky monastery on Lake Onega (standing in 1391), and few antedate the C17. Indirect evidence suggests an elaborate wooden architecture as early as the C10 (any links with Viking Scandinavia are so far unelucidated).

With the transplanting of Byzantine Orthodox culture into Kievan Russia at the Conversion, ambitious brick and stone buildings begin to be commissioned (masonry may indeed have appeared earlier, in the Grand Prince's palace). Excavations of the so-called Tithe church in Kiev (late C10) revealed a cross-domed BYZANTINE cathedral with rich decoration. The earliest standing churches, of the C11, are located on or near the great trade route 'from the Vikings to the Greeks', axis of the Old Russian state. The Transfiguration Cathedral at Chernigov (*c*. 1036) is unique in showing the longitudinal tendencies of a domed basilica. All other Old Russian churches are based on the classic middle-Byzantine CROSS-IN-SQUARE plan, generally a cross-vaulted and centrally domed quincunx with apses to east and narthex to west. Santa Sophia ('Holy Wisdom') – the 'Great Church' of Kiev, begun in 1037 – is uniquely elaborate with its seven naves, staircase-towers, thirteen domes on elongated drums grouped pyramidally, and mixed fresco and mosaic decoration. Santa Sophia of Novgorod (1045) is starker and the vertical tendency more emphatic.

Russian C11–12 architecture (particularly in Novgorod) is characterized by simple forms and a craggy monumentality; exterior decorative effect is often achieved through mixed brick-and-stonework set in prominent bands of pink (brick-dust) mortar – later concealed by whitewash and (in the south) stuccoed Baroque accretions. Around

the mid C12 new strivings towards refinement and decorative complexity
appear, and considerable variegation in
architectural patterns is seen within the
fragmented Russian principalities. The
shift of the Grand Prince's capital from
Kiev to Vladimir in the north-eastern
forest zone is marked by the construction of a splendid group of churches in
fine white local limestone, some of
which (notably St Demetrius, Vladimir, 1199, and Yuryev-Polsky, 1230)
are covered externally with low-relief
figurative sculpture, of complex iconography and uncertain provenance.
(Scholars have attempted to demon-
strate variously Romanesque, Transcaucasian, Serbian, Byzantine and
native Russian elements in these remarkable structures, without definitive
conclusions.) A portion of the royal
palace at Bogolyubovo near Vladimir
(1158) is the earliest surviving Russian
domestic building. Meanwhile architectural innovation proceeded in a different direction in the west Russian
lands, and subsequently Novgorod; the
Yefrosinyev monastery cathedral at
Polotsk (mid-C12) and the church of
St Michael at Smolensk (1191) add a
central element with curved gable-ends
(*bochka*, 'barrel') beneath the central
drum, thus creating the outline of a
stepped pyramid – a development that
was crucially to affect the history of the
cross-domed church in Russia in the
later Middle Ages. The brick-built
Pyatnitsky church in Chernigov
(*c.* 1200) takes the process further;
superposed gable-ends (pointed,
though Gothic influence is unlikely)
rise in a dramatic series of steps that
clearly foreshadow the later Muscovite
kokoshniki (small tiered decorative
arches). Ogees are seen at Yuryev-
Polsky and Suzdal (1222), their form

reminiscent of the characteristic Russian 'onion dome' (whose early history
is obscure, though it had evolved out
of the 'helmet' dome by the C13,
probably in Novgorod).

The Tatar invasion (sack of Kiev,
1240) and 240 years of occupation
checked but did not completely arrest
building activity. Novgorod recovered
its prosperity before the turn of the
century, and numerous small churches
– inventively varying the trefoil-gabled
roof-line – testify to its merchants'
patronage. The C14 rise of Moscow as
successor to Vladimir leads to a series
of 'white stone' churches (Zveni-
gorod, *c.* 1399; Trinity Cathedral, Zag-
orsk, 1422; Andronikov Monastery,
Moscow, before 1427), carrying the use
of *kokoshniki* to daring heights. From
c. 1480, with the sack of Novgorod and
liberation from the Tatars, Moscow's
dominance in Russia is complete, and
architectural patronage is concentrated
there. Ivan III embarked on a grand
programme of construction in his
capital: from 1475 to 1505 there
successively appear the Dormition
Cathedral, the 'Faceted Chamber', the
Kremlin walls, the Annunciation
Cathedral, the Ordination church, the
first stages of the great belfry and the
Cathedral of the Archangel Michael.
Mistrustful of Moscow masons, Ivan
employed a team of builders from
Pskov (in several smaller churches)
and a succession of Italian engineers (notably Aristotele Fioravanti
(*c.* 1415–86), who arrived via Hungary
in 1474) to oversee the main Moscow
works, e.g. the Dormition Cathedral.
Nevertheless the basic forms of the
cross-domed church are re-affirmed,
and Italianisms are noticeable only in
certain applied features: faceted stonework on the Chamber; Renaissance

cornices, scallops and stucco decoration on the Archangel Cathedral; swallowtail battlements on the walls.

Official church architecture of the centralized Muscovite state (c16–17) is grandiose, styleless and perfunctory: whitewashed brick replaces white stone, flat metal roofs vulgarize the subtly curved façades of earlier times, proportions become dumpy, decorative features coarsened and huddled. But an astonishing architectural development from (probably) the 1520s gives rise to a small number of bizarrely impressive 'spire' or 'tent' churches that at last move away from the tenacious cross-in-square ground-plan; techniques of popular wooden architecture are demonstrably influential. The most *outré* of these structures, the amalgam of nine churches on Red Square known as St Basil's (1555), weirdly combines elements used earlier at Kolomenskoe (1532) and Dyakovo (1547); it had no successors, though variations on the 'tent' principle (declared uncanonical in the 1650s) continue. Particularly on smaller churches decorative features (window surrounds, porches, polychrome masonry and ceramic inlays) multiply wildly; the treatment is manneristic, calculatedly picturesque and unstructural. From the c15 secular masonry architecture slowly evolves: palaces (Moscow, Novgorod, Uglich); fine monastic complexes; domestic buildings (not numerous from before 1700, but good surviving examples in Moscow, Pskov, Gorokhovets); above all great brick fortresses patterned on the Moscow Kremlin (Smolensk, Tula, Novgorod). But wood continues to be the dominant material for all building purposes: a culmination of this architecture is reached in the multi-domed c18 churches of Kizhi.

The complex westernization of Russian architecture begins before Peter's reforms, with the adoption of isolated RENAISSANCE and BAROQUE decorative motifs (e.g. pediments over window surrounds) from the mid c17 (Residential Palace, Moscow Kremlin, 1635). The moment of transition comes with the 'Moscow Baroque' of the 1680s–90s – sometimes called Naryshkin Baroque – an original and impressive style, already showing some understanding of the orders and classical symmetry, but still medieval in fundamental respects. Among notable surviving buildings are Dubrovitsy Palace (1690–1704), with freestanding sculpture, Fili Palace (1693) and the *ensemble* of the Novodevichy Convent, Moscow. The re-incorporation of the west Russian lands (under Poland since the Tatar period) provided a pool of culturally Westernized personnel; Ukrainian Baroque has its own characteristics, however, and stylistically the interaction with Muscovy is less significant than was once thought. In the 1700s rule-of-thumb methods of design are superseded and Western textbooks become better known; with the foundation of St Petersburg (1703) enormous architectural opportunities are opened, though till 1714 Moscow continues to be the chief 'laboratory' for new trends.

'Petrine Baroque' is generally stylistically rather restrained. Prototypes seem to be largely north-European, but there are some idiosyncratic developments (e.g. towers of several diminishing storeys, often topped with a flèche). Peter imported Western architects (LE BLOND, SCHÄDEL, SCHLÜTER, Mattarnovi, Konrad, D. TREZZINI, etc., of whom the last had the greatest impact), but certain native architects show individual personality: O. Startsev and Y. Bukhvostov in the 1690s, D. Aksamitov (Lefortovo Palace, 1697) and above all I. Zarudny (d. 1727), whose work is poised remarkably between the old and the new. Peter's death (1725) heralds a decline in the fortunes of St Petersburg and building activity generally; it picks up again with the reign of Elizabeth (1741–62) and the last, grandest stage of the Baroque in Russia, associated above all with the name of RASTRELLI (though CHEVAKINSKY, Michurin, D. Ukhtomsky, A. Kvasov, and F. Argunov have their own importance). Save for interior work and some house-plans of Argunov and K. I. Blank it is not really appropriate to designate this architecture Rococo. It was an age of immense palaces (Winter Palace, etc. in Leningrad; Tsarskoe Selo; Peterhof; Apraksin House in Moscow), but also of revived church architecture: monastic *ensembles* with tall belfries and cross-domed churches recall Old Russia.

'Petersburg Baroque' terminated with startling abruptness in the last year of Elizabeth's reign; even in the provinces it scarcely lingered beyond the 1760s. Neo-classicism found an early exponent in J.-B. M. VALLIN DE LA MOTHE. Catherine II (1762–96), consciously emulating Peter, commissioned large scale urban building schemes in the capital and provinces, tempting leading progressive European architects (CAMERON and QUARENGHI) to settle in Russia. The last-named was an influential proponent of PALLADIANISM, yet already before his arrival native-born architects (KAZAKOV, STAROV, Jeger Velten, 1730–1801) had evolved a neo-classical manner of exceptional purity and unforced grace. BAZHENOV, one of the most original figures of the period, stands slightly apart. He and Kazakov also reflected the antiquarian tastes of the age in a number of inventive mock-Gothic buildings (with Old Russian features) from as early as the 1760s.

By the end of the century the stark primitivism associated with LEDOUX and BOULLÉE had a foothold in Russia (cf. THOMON, ZAKHAROV, STASOV), and the reign of Alexander I saw the next great age of Russian neo-classicism – more vigorous and cheerful perhaps than most in Western Europe. From Kazakov to Zhilyardi (Domenico Gigliardi, 1788–1845) several major architects concentrated on work in Moscow, particularly after the fire of 1812; in the provinces this was the classic age of the Russian country house with its park and outbuildings. Meanwhile Petersburg was taking on its final shape (with the vast schemes of ROSSI) as one of the most consistently neo-classical cities of Europe, its stuccoed and colour-washed façades, with details picked out in white, giving a theatrical yet delicate effect.

Eclecticism, visible in church architecture (VORONIKHIN, MONTFERRAND) before vernacular neo-classicism had lost its hold on the townscape, led to the characteristic mid-c19 mixing of motifs and loss of sense of scale (prominently seen in the work of Konstantin Andrejewitsch Thon (1794–1881), e.g. Great Kremlin Palace, Moscow, 1838) Medieval revivalism during the rest of the century seldom led to convincing results, perhaps through sheer lack of knowledge of the character of Old Russian building (cf. the misapprehensions of VIOLLET-LE-DUC, one of its keenest proponents, in his *L'Art russe*, 1877), until the church at Abramtsevo by A. Vasnetsov and others (1882) and the Yaroslavl railway terminus in Moscow (1903) by Fedor Osipovich Shekhtel (1859–1926).

There is some interesting ART NOUVEAU work in Moscow and Leningrad (Ryabushinsky House, Moscow, by Shekhtel), associated with the pioneers of the Modern Movement in art, often featuring external ceramic work (e.g. by Vrubel on Metropole Hotel, Moscow, 1899). More characteristic of turn-of-the-century building, however, was an 'Edwardian' mannered eclecticism giving rise to occasionally quite successful pastiche buildings in various classical (sometimes *style russe*) idioms. Architects such as V. A. Shchuko, Ljew Wladimirowitsch Rudnyev (1885–1956), I. Fomin and I. V. Zholtovsky, characteristically adaptable, not only made their mark at this period but were on hand much later, when Stalin's Russia rejected modernism in the 1930s, to re-establish the heavy classical motifs that dominated building of *c.* 1934–55.

War and revolution disrupted architectural activity; when it resumed a new generation of radically modern theorists was ready. Ambitions towards the total remodelling of townscape in the spirit of an exalted proletarian consciousness (Mayakovsky: 'Streets are our brushes, squares our palettes') found expression first in street décor for huge popular pageants, then in TATLIN's and LISSITSKY's visionary schemes; the notion of architectural design as a sort of aesthetic 'laboratory for the future' (MALEVICH) was eventually to clash with functionalist principles and practical needs. Meanwhile revolutionary Russia gave the world the name (coined by A. Gan, 1919) and early theory of CONSTRUCTIVISM, a utilitarian modernism of great

subsequent importance (e.g. at the BAUHAUS). Resources for large-scale building became available only in the mid-1920s, and some of the most forward-looking Constructivist designs (e.g. by LEONIDOV) remained on paper. Nevertheless the achievements of a decade or so of modernist architecture were considerable: in public buildings (e.g. *Izvestiya* offices, Moscow, by G. Barkhin, 1927), workers' clubs (e.g. the Rusakov Club, Moscow, by MELNIKOV and the Zuyev Club, Moscow, 1926–8, by Ilyal A. Golosov, 1883–1945, and others by the VESNIN brothers), monuments (Lenin's Mausoleum in Red Square (1930) by Alexie V. Shchusev, 1873–1949), houses (e.g. Melnikov's in Moscow of 1929), exhibition design (Lissitsky) and, most interestingly, in large integrated schemes incorporating factories, housing, theatres, etc., notably the Likhachev Car Works in Moscow of 1934 by the Vesnins, also, for example, in Kharkov and Leningrad.

The anti-modernist reaction of the 1930s may partially correspond to an international shift in taste, but the rhetorical architecture of the late 1940s and early 1950s is like nothing anywhere else: notably, the half-dozen skyscrapers facetiously dubbed 'Stalinist Gothic' that encircle the centre of Moscow, culminating in the Lamonossow University (1949–53) by Rudnyev. Unfortunately this period also witnessed unimaginative reconstruction in the major Soviet cities (many war-damaged). From the later 1950s simplicity and modern methods of construction have been dominant, sometimes with successful results (Palace of Congresses, Moscow Kremlin, 1961), and mass prefabricated housing schemes, e.g. the Kalinin Pro-

FIG. 74. *Rusticated column*

smooth   cyclopean

diamond-pointed   vermiculated

FIG. 75. *Rustication*

spekt development, Moscow (1969), have led to a more sensitive approach to town planning. An interesting locale in which to assess changes of Soviet style over forty years is the Moscow Underground railway, whose stations evolve from Constructivist reminiscences through unimaginable ornateness to contemporary functionalism. [R. R. Milner-Gulland]

Rusticated column. A BLOCKED column whose SHAFT is interrupted by rusticated square blocks. *See* Fig. 74.

Rustication. Masonry cut in massive blocks (sometimes in its crude, quarry-dressed state) separated from each other by deep joints, employed to give a rich and bold texture to an exterior wall and normally reserved for the lower part of it. Various types have been used: *banded*, with only the horizontal joints emphasized; *chamfered*, with smooth stones separated by V joints, as in *smooth* rustication described below; *cyclopean* (or *rock-faced*), with very large rough-hewn blocks straight from the quarry (or artfully carved to look as if they were); *diamond-pointed*, with each stone cut in the form of a low pyramid; *frosted*, with the surface of the stones carved to simulate icicles; *smooth*, with blocks, neatly finished to present a flat face, and chamfered edges to emphasize the joints; *vermiculated*, with the blocks carved with shallow curly channels like worm tracks. Sometimes it is simulated in stucco or other compositions, e.g. by PALLADIO. *See* Fig. 75.

Ry, Paul du, *see* DU RY, Paul.

S

Saarinen, Eero (1910–61), the son of Eliel SAARINEN, went with his father to the United States, but spent part of his study years in Paris (1929–30). In 1931–4 he was at Yale, in 1935–6 back in Finland and from 1936 onwards he taught at his father's Cranbrook Academy of Art together with Charles EAMES. They were to pioneer a new approach to architecture and furniture design. As an architect his important works are all of the post-war years, and taken together they are admirable for their variety and sense of visual and structural experiment. The General Motors' Technical Centre at Warren, Michigan (1948–56), has severely rectangular buildings in the style of MIES VAN DER ROHE, plus a circular auditorium with a shallow aluminium-roofed dome, and a highly original water-tower 132 ft high as a vertical accent. The Kresge Auditorium of the Massachusetts Institute of Technology at Cambridge (1953–5) has a warped roof on three supports, and the chapel there has undulating inner brick walls and a central opening in a dome whose top is of an abstract sculptural form. The chapel of Concordia Senior College (1953–8) has a steeply pointed, decidedly Expressionist roof, while the Yale University Hockey Rink (1953–9) has a central arch of double curve spanning the length, not the width of the building. The Trans-World Airline's Kennedy Terminal, New York (1956–62), with its two dramatically outward-swinging arches, is consciously symbolic of flight and has elements inside of almost GAUDÍ-like heavy curving. After that the T. J. Watson Research Centre at Yorktown, New York (1957–61), is, with its 1,000-ft curved shape, perfectly crisp and unemotional; but the Ezra Stiles and Morse Colleges at Yale (1958–62), a unified composition, have the stepping-forward-backward-and-upward movements so characteristic of Louis KAHN's Medical Research Building in Philadelphia, begun one year earlier. Saarinen's last fling was the Dulles Airport for Washington (1958–63), with a long down-curving roof ridge on lines of closely set, heavy and outward-leaning concrete supports. Saarinen also designed the United States Embassies in London (1955–61) and Oslo (1959 onwards).

A. Temko, *E.S.*, New York and London 1962; R. Spade, *E.S.*, London and New York 1971; R. A. Kuhner, *E.S. His Life and Work*, Monticello 1975.

Saarinen, Eliel (1873–1950). His most famous building is the railway station at Helsinki, which was built in 1905–14 after a competition he won in 1904.

The style is inspired by the Vienna Secession (*see* OLBRICH), but in a highly original version, and the building takes its place in the series of outstanding central European railway stations characteristic of the years from the end of the C19 to the First World War (Hamburg, begun 1903; Leipzig, 1905; Karlsruhe, 1908; Stuttgart, 1911). Saarinen took part in the Chicago Tribune competition of 1922, and his design, though placed second, was much admired. As a result he left Finland and emigrated to the United States, where his great achievement was the Cranbrook Academy. He designed the buildings for it at Bloomfield Hills, Michigan (1926–43), and became president of the academy of art in 1932, attracting there Charles EAMES and his son Eero as teachers. It had great influence on design in the USA. He published *The Cranbrook Development* (1931), *Search for Form* (1939) and *The City: Its Growth, Its Decay, Its Future* (1943). In 1949 he designed Christ Church, Minneapolis.

A. Christ-Janer, *E.S. (1873–1950). Finnish-American Architect and Educator*, Chicago and London 1979.

Sacchetti, Giovanni Battista (1700–1764). A pupil of JUVARRA, whom he followed to Spain and whose designs he executed for the garden façade of the palace La Granja at S. Ildefonso (1736–42). His main work is the Royal Palace, Madrid (begun 1738), where he greatly enlarged Juvarra's scheme by reference to BERNINI's Louvre project: the result is imposing, almost overpowering and rather top-heavy. He also laid out the area of the city surrounding the palace.

Kubler and Soria 1959; Pommer 1967.

Sacconi, Count Giuseppe (1853–1905). His *magnum opus* is the National Monument to Victor Emmanuel II in the centre of Rome, won in competition in 1884 (completed 1911). Among other works the Assicurazioni Generali in Piazza Venezia, Rome (1902–7), might be mentioned.

Meeks 1966; P. Portoghesi, *L'eclettismo a Roma 1870–1922*, Rome 1968.

Sacristy. A room in a church for sacred vessels and vestments.

Saddle bars. In CASEMENT glazing, the small iron bars to which the leaded panels are tied.

Saddle stone, *see* APEX STONE.

Saddleback roof, *see* ROOF.

Saénz de Oíza, Francisco (b. 1918), *see* SPANISH ARCHITECTURE.

Safdie, Moshe (b. 1938). Israeli architect, trained under KAHN, he settled in 1964 in Montreal, Canada, where his 'Habitat' at the 1967 Expo made his name. Its dramatic approach to 'assembly' raised prefabricated building to a new architectural level. His later work is no less remarkable in its emotive use of vernacular forms, e.g. Yeshivat Porat Yosef Rabbinical College (1971–9) and the Mamilah project (1972), both in Jerusalem. In 1988 he was commissioned to build the new National Gallery of Canada at Ottawa. He has published *Beyond Habitat* (1970), *For Everyone a Garden* (1974) and *Form and Purpose* (1982).

P. Drew, *The Third Generation: The Changing Meaning of Architecture*, New York 1972.

Sail vault, *see* DOME.

Sakakura, Junzo (1904–69), *see* JAPANESE ARCHITECTURE.

Sala terrena. A ground-floor room opening directly onto the garden, a feature especially of C17–18 palaces. They were often decorated with *trompe l'œil* painted vegetation or like a grotto to suggest their intermediary function between the built and the natural world.

Sally-port. A POSTERN gate or passage underground from the inner to the outer works of a fortification.

Salomónica. Spanish term for SOLOMONIC COLUMN, much used in Spanish Baroque architecture.

Salvi, Nicola (1697–1751), designed the Trevi Fountain in Rome (1732–62), a Late Baroque masterpiece. It consists of a classical palace-façade, based on a Roman TRIUMPHAL ARCH; this is set on an enormous artificial outcrop of rock out of which fountains gush into a lake-size basin at the bottom. Marble tritons and Neptune in a shell preside over the whole fantastic composition.

J. A. Pinto, *The Trevi Fountain*, New Haven and London 1986.

Salvin, Anthony (1799–1881), came of an old North Country family and was the son of a general. A pupil of NASH, he became an authority on the restoration and improvement of castles, and his work in that field includes the Tower of London, Windsor, Caernarvon, Durham, Warwick, Alnwick, and Rockingham. But he by no means devoted himself exclusively to castles, though he was emphatically a domestic rather than an ecclesiastical architect. The range of styles used by him includes the sober Tudor of Mamhead in Devon (1826–38, a remarkably early use of the Tudor style), the ecclesiological of Kilndown church, Kent (1839–40), the C13 fortress of Peckforton Castle, Cheshire (1846–50), the lush Italian Renaissance interiors of Alnwick (1854 etc., not designed but approved by him), and the elaborate Jacobean of Thoresby, Nottinghamshire (1864–75). But his most stunning building is quite an early one: Harlaxton in Lincolnshire (1835–43), which is in an elaborate, indeed grossly exuberant, Elizabethan. The building was carried on by W. Burn.

J. Allibone, *A.S. Pioneer of Gothic Revival Architecture*, Cambridge 1988.

Sambin, Hugues (1515/20–1601/2). French Mannerist architect, sculptor and furniture designer. He worked in Burgundy, where he led a school of gifted provincial architects who indulged in rich surface effects with elaborately cut rustication (e.g. Petit Château at Tanlay, *c.* 1568) or with high-relief sculpture (e.g. Maison Milsand, Dijon, *c.* 1561). Sambin also built the Palais de Justice at Besançon and his style had considerable influence, even in Paris, e.g. Hôtel de Sully. He published *Œuvre de la diversité des termes* (1572).

A. Castan, *L'Architecteur H.S.*, Besançon and Dijon 1891; Blunt 1982.

Sanctuary. Area around the main altar of a church (*see* PRESBYTERY).

Sanfelice, Ferdinando (1675–1748), a leading Neapolitan architect of his day, was spirited, light-hearted, and unorthodox. He is notable especially for his ingenious scenographic staircases, e.g. Palazzo Sanfelice, Palazzo Serra di Cassano (1720–38).

G. A. Ward, *The Architecture of F.S.*, New York and London 1988.

Sangallo, Antonio da (Antonio Giamberti), the elder (1455–1534), was born in Florence. His only notable building is one of the great master-pieces of Renaissance architecture, S. Biagio, Montepulciano (1518–34). It was inspired by BRAMANTE's plan for St Peter's, i.e. a Greek cross with central dome and four towers (only one of which was built) between the arms.

Heydenreich and Lotz 1974; Lotz 1977.

Sangallo, Antonio da (Antonio Cordiani), the younger (1483–1546), who was born in Florence, was the most notable member of the Sangallo family: nephew of Antonio the elder and Giuliano. He became the leading High Renaissance architect in Rome for two decades after RAPHAEL's death. He began as an architectural draughtsman, employed first by BRAMANTE then by PERUZZI. In 1516 he became Raphael's assistant as architect at St Peter's, and was employed there to strengthen Bramante's work. He designed Palazzo Palma-Baldassini, Rome, 1515?–46. His masterpiece is Palazzo Farnese, Rome (begun c. 1519, completed after 1546 by MICHELANGELO), the most monumental of Renaissance palaces. The façade is astylar and the walls are smooth except for string courses dividing the storeys and bold quoins, which combine to give a horizontal emphasis stressing the gravity of the composition. It is at once sober, elegant, and restful. Several other palaces have been attributed to him, notably Palazzo Sacchetti, Rome (begun 1542), which was his own palace. In 1539 he became chief architect of St Peter's, and supplied designs for the alteration of Bramante's plan (not executed). He designed the interior of the Cappella Paolina in the Vatican (1540–46). For many years he was employed as a military engineer on the fortifications around Rome. On his death he was succeeded as architect of St Peter's by Michelangelo, whose dynamic style makes a striking contrast to Sangallo's suave, self-confident classicism.

G. Giovannoni, *A. da S. il Giovane*, Rome 1959; Frommel 1973; Heydenreich and Lotz 1974; Lotz 1977.

Sangallo, Giuliano da (Giuliano Giamberti, 1445–1516), military engineer and sculptor as well as architect, was born in Florence. The brother of Antonio da Sangallo the elder, he was one of the best followers of BRUNELLESCHI, and maintained the Early Renaissance style into the age of BRAMANTE and RAPHAEL. Most of his buildings are in and around Florence. Villa del Poggio a Caiano (1480–97?, later altered internally); S. Maria delle Carceri, Prato (1484–91), the first Renaissance church on a Greek cross plan, with marble-clad exterior, Brunelleschian interior; the atrium of S. Maria Maddalena de' Pazzi, Florence (c. 1490–95); the sacristy of S. Spirito, Florence (in collaboration with CRONACA, 1492–4); probably Palazzo Corsi, Florence (now the Museo Horne); and Palazzo Gondi, Florence (1490–94), with a rusticated façade deriving from Palazzo Medici-Riccardi and a monumental staircase rising from the interior courtyard. Between 1489 and 1490 he made a model for Palazzo Strozzi, Florence, in which the Florentine city palace found its perfect expression. It was later executed by BENEDETTO DA MAIANO and Cronaca, but its conception was probably his. He left Florence after the death of Lorenzo the Magnificent. His Palazzo Rovere at Sarona (now much altered) dates from these years. He also worked in Rome, where he built S. Maria dell'Anima (1514) and provided a project for St Peter's (c. 1514).

Heydenreich and Lotz 1974; Lotz 1977; S. Bardazzi and E. Castellani, *La villa medicea a Poggio a Caiano*, Prato 1981; P. Morselli and G. Corti, *La chiesa di S. Maria delle Carceri in Prato*, Florence 1982.

Sanmicheli, Michele (c. 1484–1559), the leading MANNERIST architect in Verona, was famous as a military engineer; most of his works have a rather fortress-like appearance, and the façade he designed for S. Maria in Organo, Verona (1547–59), might almost be mistaken for one of the fortified gateways to the city. He is often compared with PALLADIO, who was indebted to him and succeeded him as the leading architect in the Veneto, but there is a striking contrast between the massive muscularity of Sanmicheli's works and the far more intellectual and polished buildings of Palladio.

Born in Verona, the son of an architect, he went to Rome c. 1500. He supervised work on the Gothic façade of Orvieto Cathedral (1510–24), where he also designed the altar of the Magi (1515). In 1526 he was employed by the Pope on the fortifications of Parma and Piacenza, and in the following year he settled in Verona. He was much in demand as a military architect, fortifying Legnago (1529), in charge of the fortifications at Verona (from 1530) and Venice (from 1535), and also in Corfu and Crete. The buildings he designed in this capacity are among his best – boldly rusticated gateways and whole fortresses with robust Doric columns and a few strongly effective ornaments such as coats of arms and giant heads frowning out of keystones, e.g. Porta Nuova, Verona (1539–50), Forte di S. Andrea a

Lido, Venice (1535–49), Porta S. Zeno, Verona (1547–50), and most forceful of all, the Porta Palio, Verona (1548–59).

His palaces begin in the tradition of BRAMANTE and RAPHAEL with Palazzo Pompei, Verona (c. 1527–57), but he soon developed a more individual style, making much play with strong contrasts of light and shade. Palazzo Canossa, Verona (c. 1530), has a very high rusticated base and simplified SERLIAN windows on the first floor; Palazzo Bevilacqua, Verona (c. 1530), is richer, with an elaborate pattern of windows, spiral columns, and a rather oppressive use of sculpture. Here he adopted a device which later became very popular, projecting the triglyphs of the order to form consoles for a balcony. In his later palaces he strove towards the elimination of the wall surface, and at Palazzo Grimani, Venice (begun 1557, later altered), he almost entirely filled the spaces between the pilasters and the columns with windows. He was little employed for churches, but the Capella Pellegrini which he added to S. Bernardino, Verona (c. 1528), and Madonna di Campagna, Verona (1559), are of interest for their domes, rather squat, on high drums decorated with alternating groups of two blank arches and three windows.

Heydenreich and Lotz 1974; Lotz 1977; L. Puppi, *M.S. architetto. Opera completa*, Rome 1986.

Sansovino, Jacopo d'Antonio Tatti, called (1486–1570) who was primarily a sculptor, introduced the High Renaissance style of architecture to Venice. Born in Florence, the son of Antonio Tatti, he was trained under Andrea Sansovino, whose name he took. From 1505 he worked mainly in Rome as a sculptor and restorer of antique statues. In 1517 he quarrelled with MICHEL-ANGELO, and at the Sack of Rome (1527) he fled to Venice, intending to go to France, but he was commissioned to repair the main dome of S. Marco, appointed Protomagister of S. Marco in 1529, and then stayed on in Venice for the rest of his life. Friendship with Titian and Aretino introduced him into the Venetian 'establishment', and he soon became the leading architect, a position he maintained until the arrival of PALLADIO, who owed much to him.

Apart from Palazzo Gaddi, Rome (1518), his main buildings are all in Venice: the Library and Mint (1537–45) facing the Doge's Palace, and the near-by Loggetta (1537–40) at the foot of the Campanile. They show a happier fusion of architecture and figure sculpture than had previously been achieved in Venice and together make a remarkable urbanistic contribution to the city. Probably influenced by SERLIO's theories, he used the orders expressively to indicate the functions of the buildings – rusticated Doric for the Mint, Composite for the Loggetta (a meeting place for patricians) and so on. Palladio called the Library the richest building erected since classical times. Sansovino built several churches, notably S. Francesco della Vigna (1534, completed by Palladio) and the façade of S. Giuliano (1553–5). In Palazzo Corner on the Grand Canal he adapted a Roman-type palace to Venetian requirements (before 1561). On the mainland he built Villa Garzoni, Pontecasale (c. 1530), a somewhat severe structure surrounding a wide courtyard, where he came nearer to the feeling of an antique villa than any other C16 architect.

D. Howard, *J.S.*, London (1975) 1988.

Sant'Elia, Antonio (1888–1916), the architect of Italian Futurism. He was killed in the war, too early to have had a chance to do any actual building. However, his drawings, chiefly of 1913–14, and those of Mario Chiattone (1891–1957) create a remarkable vision of the industrial and commercial metropolis of the future, with stepped-back skyscrapers, traffic lanes at different levels, factories with boldly curved fronts. The forms are influenced by the Vienna Secession (*see* OLBRICH), but are also curiously similar to those of MENDELSOHN's sketches of the same years. The metropolitan content, however, is Futurist.

L. Caramel, *A. S.'E. Complete Works*, New York 1988.

Santini-Aichel, Jan Blazej (1667–1723). A Bohemian architect of Italian extraction born in Prague but trained in Italy. He also made visits to England and Holland. He worked sometimes in a Baroque (derived from BORROMINI and GUARINI) and sometimes in a neo-Gothic or rather a Baroque–Gothic style of his own devising. His secular work was in the former style, e.g. town palaces in Prague and Schloss Karlskrone (1721–2), his ecclesiastical work in the latter style – gay, naïve and very personal, with a predilection for star-shaped forms in his elegant and airy vaulting. His Baroque–Gothic churches include those at Sedlec (1702–6), at Kladruby (1712–26) and the pilgrimage church on Zelena Hora (Green Hill), Žd'ár (1720–22), all in Czechoslovakia. But he was a freak and had no influence at all.

Hempel 1965; B. Queysanne, *J.B.S.-A. Un architecte baroque-gothique en Bohème (1667–1723)*, Paris 1986.

Saracenic architecture, *see* ISLAMIC ARCHITECTURE.

Sash window. A window formed with sashes, i.e. sliding glazed frames running in vertical grooves; imported from Holland into England in the late C17. *See* WINDOW.

Sassanian architecture, *see* PERSIAN ARCHITECTURE.

Satellite town. A self-contained town which is nevertheless dependent upon a larger centre for certain facilities, such as higher education. Though distinct from they were greatly influenced by GARDEN CITIES such as Letchworth (*see* Sir Ebenezer HOWARD).

Saucer dome, *see* DOME.

Sauvage, Henri-Frédéric (1873–1932), *see* FRENCH ARCHITECTURE.

Scagliola. A material used since ancient Roman times to imitate marble and especially popular in the C17 and C18 for columns, pilasters and other interior architectural features. It is composed of pulverized selenite, applied to a wet gesso ground, fixed under heat and highly polished, hence sometimes called *stucco lustro*. It was also developed from the C16 onwards in Italy, especially for table-tops etc., in imitation of Florentine mosaic work.

Scallop. An ornament carved or moulded in the form of a shell.

Scalloped capital, *see* CAPITAL.

Scamozzi, Ottavio Bertotti (1719–90), *see* BERTOTTI-SCAMOZZI, Ottavio.

Scamozzi, Vincenzo (1552–1616), the most important of PALLADIO's immediate followers, was a conservative and rather pedantic formalist who maintained the principles of the C16

into the age of the Baroque. But he designed a handful of buildings of outstanding merit. Born in Vicenza, he was the son of a carpenter-cum-architect, from whom he received his training. In 1575–8 he built his masterpiece, the Rocca Pisana at Lonigo, a villa perched on a hilltop and commanding spectacular views which the windows were designed to frame in an unprecedented manner. The villa is an 'improved' version of Palladio's Rotonda (which Scamozzi had completed), with an inset portico on the main façade and Venetian windows on the others. (Lord BURLINGTON took elements from both villas for Chiswick House.) His masterpiece as a town palace is Palazzo Trissino, now the Palazzo del Comune, Vicenza (1592), where he was indebted to PERUZZI as well as Palladio. His later houses, e.g. Villa Molin alla Mandria near Padua (1597), tended to be enlargements and elaborations of Palladian themes. From 1578 to 1580 he travelled in south Italy, visiting Naples and Rome, where he gathered material for his *Discorsi sopra le antichità di Roma* (1582). After Palladio's death he took over several of his unfinished works, notably S. Giorgio Maggiore, Venice. At the Teatro Olimpico, Vicenza, he added the elaborate permanent stage set (1585). In 1588 he designed a similar theatre at Sabbioneta, predecessor of the Teatro Farnese, Parma (1618–28), by Giovanni Battista Aleotti (1546–1636). In 1582 he began the somewhat overweighted church of S. Gaetano, Padua. The same year he won the competition for the Procuratie Nuove in Piazza S. Marco, Venice, with a design based on Sansovino's Library – later much elongated and heightened by a third storey. Also in Venice, in 1595, he began S. Nicolo dei Tolentini, a derivation from Palladio's Redentore. In 1599 he went to Prague, then across Germany to Paris, returning to Venice in 1600; four years later he visited Salzburg, where he made designs for the cathedral (not executed), a cross between the Redentore and S. Giorgio Maggiore. In Venice his late buildings include San Lazzaro dei Mendicanti (1601–34) and Palazzo Contarini (1609–16). The fruits of his travels were incorporated in his *L'idea dell'architettura universale* (1615), the last and most academic of the theoretical works of the Renaissance and the first to mention medieval as well as classical and Renaissance buildings. It also provided the final codification of the ORDERS and thus exercised a wide and lasting influence especially in northern Europe.

F. Barbieri, *V.S.*, Vicenza 1952; Howard 1987; M. Muraro, *Venetian Villas*, Milan 1986.

Scandinavian architecture. The beginnings are auspicious: the ship-shaped houses of *c.* 1000 near Trelleborg in Denmark, sixteen of them, each nearly a hundred feet long, and with an outer veranda all round, arranged in four squares of four, all in one round enclosure, and the superb and frightening decoration of the Oseberg ship, cart and sledges, all superb Viking work of *c.* 800. The Vikings were heathens and intrepid explorers. They conquered parts of England, settled down in Normandy, and reached Iceland, Greenland and America. At the same time the Swedes conquered Russia and reached the Dnieper. The christianization of Denmark and Sweden took place from north Germany in the C9 and C10, of Norway only at the end of the C10. The style of the intricate

Viking ornamentation continued in the next outstanding contribution of Norway, the STAVE CHURCHES of the C12 (Urnes, Borglund, Lom) with their timber arcading structurally as ingenious as it is visually fascinating. Apart from stave churches there were also straightforward log churches of the type of Greensted in Essex. The best examples are Hedared and St Mary Minor at Lund in Sweden of *c.* 1020. But the most impressive Swedish contribution to timber architecture is her detached bell-towers of unboarded skeletal construction. Where stone was used, the northern countries looked primarily to Germany for guidance (cf. for an early example the C11 WESTWORK of Husaby). Another source, though less pronounced, is Anglo-Saxon England (e.g. Sigtuna, St Peter). The principal C12 cathedrals were Lund (in Sweden) which became an archbishop's see in 1104, Viborg and Ribe (in Denmark). Their twin west towers, their projecting transepts, their hall crypts and their details all derive from Germany. Lund is the most interesting. Its origin is Speier in Germany and via Speier, Lombardy. A master Donatus working at Lund may well have been Italian himself. At Ribe the dome over the crossing seems southwest French in origin, but the mid-C13 *eexpartite* rib vaults of the nave are Early French Gothic. Brick may have reached Denmark from Lombardy and was at once adopted (Ringsted, 1160 onwards, the Cistercian Sorø, 1161 onwards). The most interesting Danish building of the Middle Ages is of brick: the church of Kalundborg, a centrally planned late C12 building with a centre on the Byzantine (Russian?) inscribed-cross plan, but with four arms of equal length, projecting and crowned by four towers, which with the broader and higher central tower creates a splendid skyline.

Of brick also is Roskilde Cathedral, much changed by picturesque later additions. Its ambulatory is French Romanesque, but other elements mark the transition to the Gothic style. The two most important Norwegian cathedrals point unmistakably to England. Stavanger has a nave of *c.* 1130 onwards with typically English short round piers and a Gothic chancel of 1272 onwards, equally English. Trondheim has a singular east end in which the straight-ended chancel is continued by an octagon to house the shrine of St Olav. The corona of St Thomas at Canterbury, evidently the source for the centrally planned east shrine, had been completed in 1185. Trondheim must have been begun just about then. The details of octagon and choir are derived from Lincoln, begun in 1192. The screen between chancel and octagon is of *c.* 1330 and has its parallels also in England. The west front, left incomplete, is entirely English too, of the screen type with late C13 sculpture and two west towers set outside the aisle fronts. The finest secular building of the Middle Ages in Scandinavia is King Haakon's Hall at Bergen, completed in 1261. The largest Scandinavian cathedral is that of Uppsala, begun *c.* 1270 and with a French Gothic ambulatory and radiating chapels and continued from 1287 by Étienne de Bonneuil. Linkøping Cathedral, also C13, has a nave of hall type more probably derived from English hall choirs such as those of Salisbury and the Temple Church than from Germany. But German HALL CHURCHES, more and more the favourite church type in that country, also had an impact

on the north, and an increasing impact (Malmö St Peter, Aarhus Cathedral). The friars, settling from the 1230s onwards, preferred halls. One of the earliest friars' churches is that of the Dominicans at Sigtuna (*c.* 1240), one of the finest is that of the Carmelites at Elsinore (Helsingborg) of the late C15. Both have brickwork in the decoratively enriched patterns so dear to the north German builders. Altogether the churches of the Late Gothic period depend on north Germany and especially Westphalia. Examples are the cathedrals of Strängnäs and Västerås in Sweden with their figured rib vaults. Swedish parish churches are notable for the survival of a large number of Late Gothic wall paintings. For later Scandinavian architecture, *see* DANISH, NORWEGIAN, and SWEDISH ARCHITECTURE.

Scarp, *see* ESCARP.

Scarpa, Carlo (1906–78). Venetian architect known for his exhibition and museum designs, more sensitive than those by ALBINI, e.g. Museo Castelvecchio, Verona (1964). His Olivetti building, Venice (1957–68), and Brion cemetery complex, San Vito d'Altivole, Treviso (1970–72), are also notable.

F. Dal and G. Mazzariol, *C.S. The Complete Works*, Venice 1985; M. A. Crippa, *C.S. Theory, Design, Projects*, Cambridge 1987.

Scarpagnino, Antonio Abbondi, called, *see* BON or BONO, Bartolomeo.

Schädel, Gottfried (d. 1752), went to St Petersburg with SCHLÜTER in 1713 and built the vast, exuberantly Baroque palace for Prince Menshikov at Oranienbaum (1713–25), the first large Western-style palace in Russia. In 1735 he settled in Kiev, where he built the Sophia Cathedral and Andreas Cathedral (1747–52).

Hamilton 1983.

Scharoun, Hans (1893–1972), presents us with the curious case of an architect who, because of his style, stood in the forefront when he was thirty, who through a shift in style among others fell into oblivion, and who, with a return to something approaching the style which had been his in his youth and which he had never felt compelled to change, found himself in the forefront once again at the age of sixty-five to seventy. Scharoun belongs among the EXPRESSIONISTS and fantasts of post-1918 Germany; like them he freely penned his dreams. In the later twenties he built some houses and flats, but major jobs were offered him only in the post-Second World War years when sympathy with the twenties played such an important part; then the *Wirtschaftswunder* made it possible to build what had remained on paper forty years earlier. Among his last jobs were an estate at Charlottenburg-North, Berlin (1955–61); Romeo and Juliet, a twin scheme of flats at Stuttgart (1955–9); the Berlin Philharmonie (1956–63); the German Embassy, Brasilia (1970); the Maritime Museum, Bremen (1970); and the spacious new National Library, Berlin (finished 1978), opposite the new National Gallery by MIES.

P. Blundell Jones, *H.S. A Monograph*, London 1978; E. Janofske, *Die Architekturauffassung H.S.*, Darmstadt 1982, and *Architektur-Räume: Idee und Gestalt bei H.S.*, Brunswick 1984.

Schickhardt, Heinrich (1558–1635). One of the first German Renaissance architects, less well known than Elias HOLL because none of his buildings survives, but of great historical importance. He was trained by Georg Beer (d. 1600), whom he helped to design the Neues Lusthaus at Stuttgart (1584–93, demolished). In 1590 he became official architect to the Duke of Württemberg, with whom he visited Italy (1598–1600). His newly acquired knowledge of Italian Renaissance architecture was manifested in the new wing he added to the Schloss at Stuttgart on his return (1600–1609, destroyed 1777) – a symmetrical building with some sixty Tuscan columns in the ground-floor stables. He also designed and laid out the small town of Freudenstadt around a large central arcaded square with church, town hall, market hall and hospital at the corners (destroyed in the Second World War but rebuilt) – an unusually progressive example of north European town planning. The church (1601–9) is L-shaped, with altar and pulpit in the corner.

Hitchcock 1981; *Der Württembergische Baumeister H.S. 1558–1635*, exh. cat., Herrenberg and Freudenstadt 1982.

Schindler, Rudolph M. (1887–1953). Born and trained in Vienna. In 1913 he emigrated to America, where in 1918 he began to work under Frank Lloyd WRIGHT. In 1921 he started practising on his own in Los Angeles. About 1925 he had developed his personal style inspired by Wright and the INTERNATIONAL MODERN, especially of OUD. Cubism also must have inspired him. From 1925 onwards, for a few years, he worked in partnership with NEUTRA. Like Neutra, Schindler specialized in expensive private houses. His *magnum opus* is Beach House

Schinkel

(Lovell House) at Newport Beach (1925–6). Of his later buildings Buck House (1934) and the Falk Apartments (1939), Los Angeles, should be mentioned.

D. Gebhard, *S.*, New York 1972; A. Sarnitz, *R.M.S. Architect 1887–1953*, New York 1989.

Schinkel, Karl Friedrich (1781–1841), the greatest German architect of the C19, was Prussian and worked almost exclusively in Prussia. He was the son of an archdeacon, went to school in Berlin, and received his architectural training there too, under GILLY, in whose father's house he boarded, and at the newly founded Academy. He was powerfully influenced by the original and francophile style of Gilly. He stayed in Italy and in Paris in 1803–5, then worked as a painter of panoramas and dioramas, and a little later (chiefly *c.* 1810–15) did independent paintings too, in an elevated Romantic style (landscapes and Gothic cathedrals). This led on to theatrical work, and Schinkel designed for the stage from 1816 right into the thirties (forty-two plays, including *The Magic Flute*, *Undine*, *Käthchen von Heilbronn*). Meanwhile, however, he had begun to submit architectural designs, hoping to attract attention to himself. The first was for a mausoleum for the much beloved Prussian Queen Luise. This was eminently romantic in the Gothic style, with coloured glass in the windows and life-size white angels by the head of the sarcophagus. It was followed by church designs, e.g. a cathedral in the trees, centrally planned with a steep Gothic dome. In 1810 Schinkel had secured a job in the administration of Prussian buildings, with the help of Wilhelm von Humboldt. In 1815 he was made Geheimer Oberbaurat in the newly created Public Works Department, a high title for so young a man, and in 1830 he became the head of the department.

All his principal buildings were designed between 1816 and 1830. The earliest are pure Grecian, yet always serviceable, functionally planned, and with the motifs of the façade, in the spirit of Gilly, modified with originality to ensure that the stylistic apparatus does not interfere with the use of the building. The Neue Wache or New Guard House in Unter den Linden, Berlin, came first (1816; Greek Doric portico, transformed internally 1966), then the Theatre (1818–21), large, with a raised Ionic portico and excellent interiors (badly damaged 1945 but restored), and after that the Old Museum (1823–30, interior partly destroyed 1945), with its unbroken row of slender Ionic columns along the façade, its Pantheon-like centre rotunda, taken obviously from DURAND, and its staircase open to the portico and picturesquely introducing a degree of interpenetration of spaces not to be expected from outside. This is the first sign of hidden resources in Schinkel, making it impossible to label him a Grecian and leave it at that. Side by side with these major buildings, Schinkel designed the War Memorial on the Kreuzberg (1818), Gothic and of cast iron, Tegel, Humboldt's country house (1822–4), in a characteristic domestic Grecian, and the Werdersche Kirche (1821–31). The design for this last was submitted in a classical and a Gothic version, both vaulted; the Gothic version won, evidently inspired by the English type of Late Gothic Royal Chapels with their four angle turrets.

Schinkel was, indeed, keenly interested in England and in 1826 travelled through the country, after staying for a while in Paris. It was not his first major journey since Italy: in 1816 he had been to the Rhine, where he developed an interest in the preservation of monuments, and in 1824 he went again to Italy. In England he was more interested in industrial developments than in architecture proper, the promotion of crafts and industry being part of his official responsibilities.

His principal late works show a remarkable change of style and widening of possibilities. They include unexecuted designs for an exchange or merchants' hall with warehouse (1827?) and for a library (1830s), both utilitarian without any period trimmings. Among executed works, the Nikolaikirche at Potsdam (1830–37, badly damaged 1945 but restored) is classical, whereas the building for the Academy of Architecture is only vestigially period (north Italian Quattrocento), but essentially also unenriched functional (1831–6). A widening in another direction led to projects for centrally and longitudinally planned churches in arcuated styles, vaguely Early Christian or Italian Romanesque (the so-called RUNDBOGENSTIL of Lombardy; see GÄRTNER), while a broadening of yet another kind is represented by two small buildings in the park of Potsdam – Charlottenhof and the Roman Bath (1826 and 1833) – and the costly projects for a palace on the Acropolis (1834) and in the Crimea (1838), in all of which Grecian motifs are applied to picturesquely irregular compositions where architecture and nature collaborate. Of his immediate followers Ludwig Persius (1803–45) was outstanding, e.g. Friedenskirche, Potsdam

(1845–87), built from his designs after his death.

E. Forssmann, *K.F.S. Bauwerk und Baugedanken*, Munich 1981; A. Haus, *K.F.S. Bauten, Gemälde, Industriedesign, Bühnenbilder*, Munich 1987; Watkin and Mellinghoff 1987.

Schlaun, Johann Conrad (1695–1773). A Westphalian Baroque architect who began with small and simple churches for Capuchin friars, e.g. Brakel (1715–18). He then studied under NEUMANN at Würzburg (1720–21), travelled to Rome and returned to Münster by way of France and Munich (1724). In 1725 he was appointed architect to Clemens August, Elector of Cologne, for whom he began Schloss Brühl (later altered by CUVILLIÉS) and the very elegant little cruciform hunting-lodge Clemenswerth, near Sögel (c. 1736–50). For the Elector's minister, Graf von Plettenberg, he erected various buildings in the park at Nordkirchen, notably the Oranienburg (from 1725). Still clinging to the Baroque style, by then rather *démodé*, he built the Clemenskirche, cleverly inserted into a corner of the House of the Brethren of Mercy at Münster (1745–53), the Borrominesque church of St Johann Nepomuk at Rietberg (1744–8), the Erbdrostenhof in Münster (1754–7) and the Schloss at Münster (1767–73). The two houses he built for himself are remarkably original: the Rüschhaus outside Münster (1745–8) in the Westphalian rustic tradition with a few sophisticated Baroque flourishes, and a town house in Münster (1753–5) stylistically similar.

Hempel 1965; *J.C.S.*, exh. cat., Münster 1973.

Schlüter, Andreas (c. 1659–1714). He was equally distinguished as sculptor and architect. As an architect he ranks slightly below his great contemporaries HILDEBRANDT and FISCHER VON ERLACH. He was trained in Danzig (and was probably born there) but is first heard of in Warsaw in 1689–93 as the sculptor of pediments on the Krasiński Palace. He does not seem to have worked as an architect in Poland. In 1694 he was called to Berlin by the Elector Friedrich III, who sent him to France and Italy to study. On his return in 1696 he was commissioned to carve the very elaborate sculptural keystones for windows and doors on the Berlin Arsenal designed by NERING. He succeeded Nering as architect at the Arsenal in 1698. In the same year he was put in charge of the building of the Royal Palace in Berlin, and in 1698 became its Surveyor General. The Royal Palace (1698–1706, completed by Eosander; bombed 1945, demolished 1950) was his masterpiece. Some of his sculptural decoration on the Lustgarten façade, on the great staircase and Baronial Hall, was fortunately removed before demolition in 1950. The influence of BERNINI and LE PAUTRE is evident in the design, as well as that of Fischer von Erlach and Nicodemus TESSIN, both of whom were in Berlin while it was being built. In 1701–4 he also built the Old Post Office in Berlin (demolished 1889), but he fell into disgrace shortly afterwards as a result of the collapse of the Munzturm water-tower at the north-west corner of the Royal Palace. He was dismissed from his appointments in 1707. In 1711–12 he built the Villa Kamecke in Dorotheenstadt, Berlin (destroyed 1945, but fragments preserved in the Bode Museum, East Berlin). After the king's death he left Berlin and settled in St Petersburg in 1713, where he died.

Hempel 1965; G. Peschken and W. Klunner, *Das Berliner Schloss*, Berlin 1982.

Schmidt, Friedrich von (1825–91), *see* AUSTRIAN ARCHITECTURE.

Schmuzer, Joseph (1683–1752). The best known of a dynasty of Bavarian stuccadors and architects in Wessobrunn. His Rococo interiors of the parish church at Oberammergau (1736–42), the abbey church of Rottenbuch (1737–42) and at Ettal (1744–52) are notable.

Hitchcock 1968.

Schoch, Johannes or Hans (*c.* 1550–1631). His masterpiece is the Friedrichsbau in Heidelberg Castle (1601–7) in which the architectural elements are closely knit and vigorously moulded though still somewhat heavy-handed as compared with later and more accomplished German Renaissance buildings, e.g. Jacob WOLFF's Pellerhaus in Nuremberg of the same years. Schoch may have worked with Speckle (1536–89) on the Neuer Bau at Strassburg (1582–5) and perhaps also on the Grosse Metzig in Strassburg (1586). The Fleischhalle at Heilbronn (*c.*1600) and the south wing of the Arsenal at Amberg (1604) may derive from designs by Schoch.

Hitchcock 1981.

Schuricht, Christian Friedrich (1753–1832), *see* CZECHOSLOVAK ARCHITECTURE.

Schutze, Philip Trammell (1890–1982), *see* CLASSICISM.

Sconce. In military architecture, a small fort or earthwork, usually built as a counter-fort or to defend a pass, castle gate, etc.

FIG. 76. *Scotia*

Scotia. A concave moulding which casts a strong shadow, as on the base of a column between the two TORUS mouldings. *See* Figs. 68, 76.

Scott, Sir George Gilbert (1811–78), the son of a clergyman and himself an evangelical, regarded himself as an architect of the multitude, not of the chosen few, and his sturdy stand on the *juste milieu* secured him an unparalleled multitude of buildings. He started with workhouses – a speciality of Sampson Kempthorne, the architect under whom he had worked – and he did them in partnership with W. B. Moffatt. The Royal Wanstead School at Wanstead, Essex, formerly an Orphan Asylum, is their first important work; it is Jacobean in style. But one year later they built St Giles, Camberwell, London (1841–3), and here Scott found his feet. This is a Gothic church which was substantial, no longer papery as the earlier neo-Gothic churches had been, and which was, moreover, both knowledgeable and, with its properly developed chancel, ritualistically acceptable to the Cambridge Camden group. In the same year Scott began to restore Chesterfield church, and so started on his career as a busy, undaunted restorer. In the next year, 1844, he won the competition for St Nicholas at Hamburg with a competent German Gothic design which established him internationally. He restored more cathedrals and parish churches than can be remembered, was made surveyor of Westminster Abbey in 1849, and built – to name but a few – the grand Doncaster parish church (1854 onwards), the chapels of Exeter College, Oxford (1856), and St John's College, Cambridge (1863–9), and the parish church of Kensington, London (1869–72). His style is Anglo-French High Gothic (late C13 to early C14).

He was also active as a secular architect. Examples are Kelham Hall, Nottinghamshire (1857 onwards), the St Pancras Station Hotel in London (1868–74), the Albert Memorial (1863–72), the group of houses in Broad Sanctuary, just west of Westminster Abbey (1854), and Glasgow University buildings (begun 1868). Scott even wrote a persuasive book to prove that the Gothic style was as suited to secular as to clerical C19 tasks (*Remarks on Secular and Domestic Architecture*, 1858), and was deeply hurt when he found himself forced by Lord Palmerston to do the new Government offices, now the Foreign Office, in Whitehall in the Renaissance style (1862–73). Scott was ambitious and fully convinced he was as good an architect as any; this comes out clearly in his *Personal and Professional Recollections* (1879). He was, in fact, a highly competent architect, but he lacked genius. As a restorer he believed in careful preservation, but was ruthless in action. In spite of this he was quite a medieval scholar, as is demonstrated by his *Gleanings from Westminster Abbey* (1862).

His sons George Gilbert (1839–97) and John Oldrid (1842–1913) were both Gothicists too, competent and careful like their father, but they had in addition a sensitivity which belongs to the Late as against the High Victorian milieu. George Gilbert's *chef d'œuvre* was St Agnes, Kennington, London

(1877), remarkably bare and grand; John Oldrid, following his brother, did the grand Catholic church of Norwich (1844–1910).

Pevsner 1972; D. Cole, *The Work of Sir G.S. (1811–78)*, London 1980; G. Fisher, G. Stamp *et al.*, *Catalogue of the Drawings Collection of the R.I.B.A. The Scott Drawings*, London 1981; I. Toplis, *The Foreign Office. An Architectural History*, London and New York 1987.

Scott, Sir Giles Gilbert (1880–1960), the son of George Gilbert and grandson of Sir George Gilbert, rose to sudden and very early fame with his design for Liverpool Cathedral, won in competition in 1904 and very evidently inspired by BODLEY. This means that it is still Gothicist in the C19 manner. However, it has an originality of plan and a verve of verticals which promised much. Scott's early ecclesiastical buildings, such as St Joseph, Lower Sheringham, Norfolk (1909–35), and the Charterhouse School Chapel (1922–7), are indeed both original and bold, and in addition much less dependent on a style from the past. Scott exploited a surprising variety of possibilities. The results included Battersea Power Station in London (1932–4), which became the pattern for post-war brick-built power stations all over England, and the new Waterloo Bridge (1939–45), with the fine sweep of its shallow arches. However, his official representational architecture lost the early tensions and turned commonplace: Cambridge University Library (1931–4), the new building for the Bodleian Library, Oxford (1936–46), Guildhall Building, London (1954–8).

V. L. Cotton, *The Book of Liverpool Cathedral*, London 1964.

Scott, Mackay Hugh Baillie (1865–1945), see ARTS AND CRAFTS.

Scott, Michael (b. 1905), see IRISH ARCHITECTURE.

Scott-Brown, Denise (b. 1931), see VENTURI, Robert.

Scottish architecture. Prehistory is characteristically represented by Neolithic chamber-tombs (Maes Howe, Orkney), a Bronze Age stone circle (Callanish), hut circles and round houses, and Iron Age *brochs* – round stone houses built without mortar. Roman occupation lasted from AD 58 to 100 and from 140 to 200 and was superficial. Several forts were built, but the most familiar monument is the Antonine Wall of 143. The Dark Ages produced beehive huts and high crosses. The Ruthwell Cross of *c.* 700 is the most accomplished in Britain. The figure sculpture surpasses anything of the same date in all Europe. Round church towers, an Irish feature, begin in Scotland as in Ireland in the C10 (Brechin, Egilsay). The Romanesque style starts in the C11, but the major Norman works belong to the C12: Dunfermline (*c.* 1150) under Durham influence, Jedburgh Abbey of the same date with the so-called giant arcading of Romsey and Oxford, and Kelso of the late C12 with the west transept of Ely and Bury St Edmunds. Castles of stone appeared in the late C12; but Scotland did not go in for keeps. To the Transitional from Norman to Gothic belong the Cistercian Dundrennan Abbey and the elegant nave of Jedburgh. Fully Gothic are the choir of Glasgow Cathedral with its vaulted undercroft, the beautiful west end of Elgin and the nave of Dunblane. The paramount example of the c14 and c15 is Melrose, which has some French features. We shall find such direct inspiration from France again later. As for the c15 and early c16 the climax in ecclesiastic architecture is Rosslyn Chapel (c. 1450), in its abundance of decoration reminiscent of Spain, and in secular architecture Borthwick (c. 1430) with its majestic Great Hall covered by a pointed tunnel vault. In the c15 and c16 secular architecture is on the whole more eventful than church architecture. As for the latter, it is enough here to mention St Giles at Edinburgh, with a fine tierceron vault and a so-called crown on its tower and a few other town parish churches (Linlithgow, Stirling, Dundee). Concerning castles, Inverlochy of the c13 has a nearly square *enceinte* with four round corner towers, Caerlaverock has a big c13 to c15 gatehouse, and there are the many TOWER-HOUSES. They are high and forbidding. Characteristic of them are the many TOURELLES, a French not an English feature. Elphinstone, the oldest part of Glamis and Affleck represent the type. The Great Hall of Edinburgh Castle dates from c. 1505 and has a wooden roof. Of about the same date is the impressive gatehouse of Stirling Castle.

As in England the Renaissance comes in the first half of the c16 as a mode of decoration applied to indigenous buildings or elements. Such is the case of the Great Halls of Edinburgh Castle and Stirling Castle and later of Falkland Palace (c. 1540). In all these cases the source is not the Renaissance of Italy but of France and her Loire *châteaux*. Equally French is, for example, Huntly Castle (1602), whereas Crichton Castle (1581–91) derived its façade of diamond-cut ashlar blocks

from Ferrara or Spain. The castles and tower houses of the Elizabethan and Jacobean decades are Scotland's most memorable contribution to pre-Victorian architecture. Half-a-dozen names are all that can be given here: Kellie of 1573, Balmanno of about the same time, Dundarave of 1596, Cawdor of about the same time, Crathes of 1595 and Fyvie also mostly late c16. Jacobean and after are the north quarter of Linlithgow Palace (1618–21) and the east quarter of Caerlaverock (c. 1620–35). Inside such buildings is often good plasterwork and far more often than in England ceiling painting (mostly of folk quality). The most monumental Scottish building of the mid c17 is Heriot's Hospital in Edinburgh of 1628–59. This has a large courtyard and four sturdy angle towers.

A Scottish c17 speciality is reformed churches of more monumental intentions than they are in England. Burntisland is square with a square tower above the middle (1592); Lauder is a Greek cross (1673); Dairsie (1621) and several others are Gothic Survival.

The Inigo Jones–Christopher Wren style took some time to get entry into Scotland. The interpreter was William BRUCE. An early example is Holyrood House (1671 onwards). It has superimposed pilasters and a pediment, once again more French than English. A pedimented centre was also introduced by Bruce at Hopetoun House in 1703. This part of the mansion and also a house like Kinross belong to the English group round Coleshill. After Scotland had thus submitted to the London taste, Scottish Georgian is on the whole the same as English Georgian. The ADAMS worked in the north as they did in the south – see the major parts of Hopetoun and Robert Adam's

Mellerstain (1778) and his Edinburgh University (1789–94). His Culzean (1777–92) is the most dramatically sited of the several remarkable, almost astylar, castles which he designed towards the end of his life for Scottish clients, e.g. Seton Castle near Edinburgh. (They are very different from his earlier neo-Gothic work in England.) The most important architectural event in C18 Scotland however is the laying-out of Edinburgh's New Town. The design is of 1767, by James Craig (1744–95). But Charlotte Square was built to designs by Robert Adam (1791).

So to the C19. Scotland was stronger in the Grecian than in the Gothic mode. Of Gothic buildings reference might be made to the gorgeous Taymouth of 1806–10 by Archibald and James Elliot (1760–1823 and 1770–1810) and St John at Edinburgh of 1816–18 by William Burn (1789–1870), who initiated the 'Scottish Baronial' style for country houses c. 1830, though it was his pupil David Bryce (1803–76) who became its most celebrated exponent. As for Grecian, the Edinburgh High School of 1825 (by T. HAMILTON) is one of the most serious Doric compositions in Britain. Also at Edinburgh are PLAYFAIR's Royal Scottish Academy (Doric, 1822–36) and National Gallery (1850). The Perth Waterworks of 1832 (by W. Anderson) deserve to be better known. But the most interesting neo-Greek phenomenon in Scotland is the work of Greek THOMSON, who expressed himself in that style at a time when it was thoroughly unpopular all over Europe (but cf. the Vienna Parliament of 1873–83 by HANSEN). His churches handle the Greek amazingly freely, with a dash of Egyptian, whereas his terraces of well-to-do houses such as Moray Place, Glasgow, of 1859 are clearly derived from SCHINKEL. Thomson also did commercial premises, though in that field the most interesting building is the house at the corner of Argyll Street and Jamaica Street, Glasgow, which is of 1855–6 by John Baird (1798–1859) and has an arcuated cast-iron front. Other styles used in the mid C19 are the Gothic (Glasgow Stock Exchange of 1877 by John Burnet, 1814–1901) and the Elizabethan (Donaldson's Hospital, Edinburgh, of 1841–51, by Playfair).

Nothing in such buildings would have led anybody to expect that by the 1890s Scotland would possess the most brilliant architect in Europe, Charles Rennie MACKINTOSH. His synthesis of sinuous Art Nouveau decoration with precisely rectangular panels, his synthesis (in the Glasgow School of Art of 1907–9) of functional considerations with freely playing ornament, his synthesis of sympathy for the Scottish past and daring innovation, his sense of spatial interpenetrations – all this was nowhere else to be seen combined in one man. His almost exact contemporary, Robert Stodart Lorimer (1864–1929), began as an ARTS AND CRAFTS architect and went on, like Lutyens, to work in various styles from the classical, e.g. his distinguished and elegant New Library, St Andrews University, St Andrews (1907–9), to the Gothic, e.g. Thistle Chapel, St Giles's Cathedral, Edinburgh (1910), to the Scottish Baronial, often with a touch of the vernacular sensitively used. His Scottish National War Memorial in Edinburgh Castle was his last and best-known work. Among recent buildings the controversial megastructure town centre at Cumbernauld New Town near Glasgow (1963), St Bride

FIG. 77. *Scroll*

at East Kilbride (1958) by Jack Coia (1898–1981) and the student accommodation (1964–9) and Arts Centre (1974–5) at St Andrews University, St Andrews, by STIRLING were notable.

Screen. A partition wall of wood or stone, with one or more doors, as at the kitchen end of a medieval hall where it usually supports a gallery. *See also* PARCLOSE; ROOD SCREEN.

Screens passage. The space at the service end of a medieval hall between the screen and the buttery, kitchen and pantry entrances.

Scroll. 1. An ornament in the form of a scroll of paper partly rolled. 2. In classical architecture, the VOLUTE of an Ionic or Corinthian CAPITAL. 3. In Early English and Decorated Gothic architecture, a moulding in such a form *See* Fig. 77.

Secession or **Sezession.** A group of architects and artists who seceded from the conservative academy in Vienna and established the Wiener Sezession in 1897. Notable among them were the painter Klimt and the architects HOFFMANN and OLBRICH. Olbrich designed their exhibition building in Vienna in 1898. They were later joined by Otto WAGNER and became very influential, German ART NOUVEAU (or *Jugendstil*) being sometimes called *Sezessionstil*.
  R. Weissenberger, *Die Wiener Sezession*, Vienna 1972.

Section. A diagrammatic drawing of a vertical plane cut through a building.

Sedding, John Dando (1838–91), *see* ARTS AND CRAFTS.

Seddon, John Pollard (1827–1906), in partnership with John Pritchard 1852–62. His most spectacular work is the former hotel (now university) at Aberystwyth (1867 – after 1872). This displays a rather wild Gothic. Gothic and rather capricious too is the church of Ayot St Peter (1875). Much quieter is Chigwell Row (1867). The Powell Almshouses, Fulham, London (1869), are small and engaging. Finally, and unexpectedly, the beautiful church of Hoarwithy (1880s), in the Italian Romanesque style with detached campanile. Seddon was on friendly terms with the Pre-Raphaelites and MORRIS.
  M. Darby, *J.P.S. (1827–1906)*, London 1984.

Sedilia. Seats for the clergy, generally three (for priest, deacon and sub-deacon), and of masonry, in the wall on the south side of the CHANCEL.

Segal, Walter (1907–85), *see* COMMUNITY ARCHITECTURE.

Segment. Part of a circle smaller than a semicircle.

Segmental. Of an arch or other curved member, having the profile of a circular arc substantially less than a full circle.

Segmental arch, *see* ARCH.

Seidler, Harry (b. 1923), *see* AUSTRALIAN ARCHITECTURE.

Selva, Giovanni Antonio (1753–1819), a leading neo-classical architect in Venice, trained under TEMANZA, then visited Rome, Paris, and London (1779–83). His early works are in a sim-

plified neo-Palladian style, e.g. Teatro
La Fenice, Venice (1788–92, burnt
down but rebuilt to his design). But he
developed a much stronger neo-classical manner later on, e.g. Duomo,
Cologna Veneta (1806–17), with its
vastly imposing octastyle Corinthian
portico.

E. Bassi, *G.S. architetto veneziano*,
Padua 1936; Howard 1987.

Semper, Gottfried (1803–79), the
most important German architect of
the Early and High Victorian decades,
was born at Hamburg and studied at
Göttingen, and then in Munich (under
GÄRTNER). In 1826, after fighting a
duel, he fled to Paris, where he worked
under GAU and HITTORF. The years
1830–33 were spent in Italy and Greece,
and after that journey Semper published a pamphlet on polychromy in
Greek architecture, immediately influenced by Hittorf. In 1834 he was appointed to a chair at the Dresden Academy and there built his finest buildings.
The Opera came first (1838–41). It
was, in its original form, neo-Cinquecento, with subdued ornamentation
and an exterior that expressed clearly
its interior spaces. The semicircular
front was inspired by Moller's theatre
at Mainz (*see* GILLY). After that
followed the synagogue, a mixture of
Lombard, Byzantine, Moorish, and
Romanesque elements (1839–40); the
Quattrocento Villa Rose (1839); and
the Cinquecento Oppenheim Palace
(1845). Then came the Picture Gallery,
closing with its large arcuated façade
the Baroque Zwinger at the time left
open to the north (1847–54), and the
Albrechtsburg, a grand terraced
Cinquecento villa above the river
Elbe (1850–55), symmetrical, yet the
German equivalent of, say, Osborne.

After the revolution of 1848 Semper
fled Germany and went first to Paris
(1849–51)–an unsuccessful time, which
made him contemplate emigration to
America – and then to London (1851–
5), where he did certain sections of the
1851 Exhibition and advised Prince
Albert on the tasks for the museum
which is now the Victoria and Albert.

Semper was, in fact, keenly interested in art applied to industry, and his
Der Stil (1861–3, only two volumes
published) is the most interesting application of materialist principles to
craft and design, an attempt at proving
the origin of ornament in certain techniques peculiar to the various materials
used. In architecture Semper believed
in the expression of the function of a
building in its plan and exterior, including any decorative elements.

In 1855 Semper went to the Zürich
Polytechnic and taught there till 1871.
During that time he made designs for
the Wagner National Theatre (1864–6)
which considerably influenced the
building as it was erected at Bayreuth
(by O. Brückwald, 1841–1904; opened
1876). Semper's last years were spent
in Vienna. His style then, as is clearly
seen in the Dresden Opera (redesigned
1871 after a fire), was more Baroque,
less disciplined, and looser. This is also
evident in the two large identical
museum buildings for Vienna, forming
a forum with the Neue Hofburg (1872
and 1881 onwards), and in the Burgtheater (1873). These last buildings
were executed by Karl von Hasenauer
(1833–94), but the well-thought-out,
clearly articulated plans are Semper's.
His writings on architecture have
been translated as *The Four Elements of
Architecture and Other Writings. G.S.*,
ed. H. F. Mallgrave (Cambridge
1989).

FIG. 78. *Serliana*

Pevsner 1972; W. Herrmann, *G.S. (1803–1879). In Search of Architecture*, Cambridge, Mass., and London 1984.

Senmut (*fl. c.* 1520 BC), *see* EGYPTIAN ARCHITECTURE.

Sens, *see* WILLIAM OF SENS.

Sepulchre, *see* EASTER SEPULCHRE and HOLY SEPULCHRE.

Serbian architecture, *see* BYZANTINE ARCHITECTURE.

Serliana or **Serlian motif.** An archway or window with three openings, the central one arched and wider than the others: so called because it was first illustrated in SERLIO's *Architettura* (1537), though it probably derived from BRAMANTE. It was much used by PALLADIO, and it became one of the hallmarks of PALLADIANISM, especially in C17–18 England. It is more commonly known as a Venetian or Palladian window. *See* Fig. 78.

Serlio, Sebastiano (1475–1554),

painter and architect, was more important as the author of *L'Architettura*, published posthumously in 1584, which had appeared in six parts between 1537 and 1551 (augmented from his drawings 1575). This was the first book on architecture whose aim was practical as well as theoretical, and the first to codify the five ORDERS: it diffused the style of BRAMANTE and RAPHAEL throughout Europe, and provided builders with a vast repertory of motifs. (The first English translation appeared in 1611 as *The Five Books of Architecture*.) His approach to classical architecture was more critical than that of earlier theorists, he paid great attention to the meanings that different styles could convey and virtually created a vocabulary to describe aesthetic responses to buildings. Born and trained in Bologna, he went to Rome *c.* 1514, and remained there until the sack of 1527 as a pupil of PERUZZI, who bequeathed him plans and drawings used extensively in his book. He then went to Venice until 1540, when he was called to France, and advised on building operations at Fontainebleau. Here he built a house for the Cardinal of Ferrara, known as the Grand Ferrare (1544–6, destroyed except for the entrance door) and the *château* at Ancy-le-Franc, near Tonnerre (begun 1546), which survives. The Grand Ferrare established the standard form for the HÔTEL or town house in France for more than a century. The fantastic designs, especially for rusticated portals, in the later parts of his books, published in France, were much imitated by French MANNERIST architects.

Heydenreich and Lotz 1974; M. N. Rosenfeld, *S.S. On Domestic Architecture*, Cambridge and New York 1978; Onians 1988; Harris 1990.

Sert, José Luis (1902–83). He came from Barcelona, worked from 1929 to 1932 for LE CORBUSIER, returned to Barcelona, where he built the Dispensari Antitubercolosi (1934–6), emigrated to America in 1939 and succeeded GROPIUS at Harvard in 1953–69. He designed the Students' Hall of Residence for Harvard in 1962 – a restless design. Other works are the US Embassy, Baghdad (1959–60), the Fondation Maeght, St Paul de Vence, near Nice (1959–64), and the Fundación Miró, Barcelona (1972–5).

M. L. Borràs (ed.), *S: Mediterranean Architecture*, Boston 1975; J. Freixa (ed.), *J.L.S.*, Zürich 1980.

Servandoni, Giovanni Niccolò (1695–1766), born in Florence and trained as a painter under Pannini, began as a stage designer in France in 1726, but soon turned to architecture. In 1732 he won the competition for the west façade of St Sulpice, Paris. Though not executed until 1737, and revised meanwhile, this is among the earliest manifestations of a reaction against the Rococo. He later worked in England, designing the gallery of Roger MORRIS's Brandenburg House, Hammersmith (1750, demolished 1822).

Colvin 1978; Rykwert 1980.

Severus (*fl.* AD 64). Roman architect employed by Nero to build the Domus Aurea on the Esquiline after the disastrous fire of AD 64. Tacitus and Suetonius testify to the grandeur of the whole concept, the spacious gardens with which the buildings were integrated, the size, number and richness of the rooms decorated with gold, gems, mother of pearl and ivory, the baths of sea water and sulphur water, the dining-rooms fitted with devices for sprinkling the guests with scent from the ceiling. Nero is reported to have remarked that he was 'beginning to be housed like a human being'. The parts which survive reveal the architect's genius in designing a large series of rooms of contrasting forms and creating ingenious systems of indirect lighting. He was assisted by the engineer Celer in this work and also in a project to build a canal from Lake Avernus to the Tiber. It is probable that he was also in charge of the rebuilding of Rome after the fire and the author of the new city building code.

MacDonald 1965.

Severy. A compartment or bay of a vault.

Sexpartite vault, *see* VAULT.

Sgraffito. Decoration on plaster of incised patterns, the top coat being cut through to show a differently coloured coat beneath.

Shaft. The trunk of a column between the base and CAPITAL. *See* Fig. 66. Also, in medieval architecture, one of several slender columns attached (in a cluster) to a pillar or pier, door jamb or window surround. *See* COMPOUND PIER; Fig. 30.

Shaft-ring or **annulet** or **corbel-ring.** A motif of the C12 and C13 consisting of a ring round a SHAFT.

Sharawadgi. Artful irregularity in garden design and, more recently, in town planning. The word, probably derived from the Japanese, was first used in 1685 to describe the irregularity of Chinese gardens; it was taken up again and popularized in mid-C18 England and, in connection with town planning, some forty or fifty years ago.

Shaw, Richard Norman (1831–1912), was a pupil of William Burn (1789–1870), a very successful, competent, and resourceful architect of country houses, and won the Academy Gold Medal in 1854, after having travelled in Italy, France, and Germany. He published a hundred of the travel sketches in 1858 as *Architectural Sketches from the Continent* and in the same year went as chief draughtsman to STREET, following WEBB in this job. He started in practice with a friend from Burn's office, W. Eden NESFIELD, but they mostly worked separately. Shaw began in Gothic style, and did a number of churches, some of them remarkably powerful (Bingley, Yorkshire, 1864–8; Batchcott, Shropshire, 1891–2), and one at least partaking of his happily mixed, mature style (Bedford Park, London, 1877). But this style was not reached by Shaw and Nesfield at once. A few years intervened of highly picturesque, still somewhat boisterous country mansions, timber-framed as well as of stone (Leys Wood, Sussex, 1868; Cragside, Northumberland, 1870). At the same time, however, a change took place to a more intimate style, simpler details, and local materials (Glen Andred, Sussex, 1868; Grim's Dyke, Harrow, now a hotel, 1870–72). This was called their 'Old English Style' and influenced the ARTS AND CRAFTS movement. This both architects have entirely in common. Shaw published *Sketches of Cottages and Other Buildings* (London 1878).

Shaw and Nesfield's mature style is much more subdued, and its period sources are mid-C17 brick houses under Dutch influence and the William and Mary style, rather than Gothic and Tudor. It was popularly known as the 'Queen Anne style'. Decoration is more refined than was usual, and interior decoration was here and there left to MORRIS's firm. Which of the two architects really started this style is not certain. Nesfield is the more likely – see his Dutch C17 lodge at Kew Gardens (1866) and his William-and-Mary-cum-Louis-XIII Kinmel Park, Denbighshire (begun 1867) – but Shaw made an international success of it. That some inspiration from Webb stands at the beginning is indubitable. The key buildings were New Zealand Chambers in the City of London (1871–3, now demolished), Lowther Lodge, Kensington (1873, now Royal Geographical Society), Shaw's own house, 6 Ellerdale Road, Hampstead (1875), and the exquisite Swan House, Chelsea Embankment (1876). At the same time Shaw was associated with Bedford Park, Turnham Green, London, as the earliest garden suburb ever. It was not until the 1880s that he received his first public commission, New Scotland Yard, London (1887–90), a vigorous and impressive redbrick and stone building with TOURELLES and a lively skyline. A second block was added in 1890, which Shaw is said to have regretted. About 1890 (e.g. Bryanston, Dorset, 1889–94) Shaw turned away from the dainty elegance of his earlier domestic style towards a grand classicism with giant columns and Baroque details (Chesters, Northumberland, 1891; Piccadilly Hotel, 1905); this also was very influential.

A. Saint, *R.N.S.*, New Haven and London 1976.

Shchusev, Alexie V. (1873–1949), *see* RUSSIAN ARCHITECTURE.

Shekhtel, Fedor Osipovich (1859–1926), *see* RUSSIAN ARCHITECTURE.

Shell. A thin, self-supporting membrane on the eggshell principle (*see* STRESSED-SKIN CONSTRUCTION), developed in the early C20 by FREYSSINET and other CONCRETE designers, notably TORROJA and MAILLART, whose Cement Industry Pavilion at Zürich (1938–9) is a paradigmatic shell structure, and above all, NERVI, SAARINEN and CANDELA, who pioneered HYPERBOLIC PARABOLOID vaulting in Mexico in the early 1950s.

J. Joedicke, *Shell Architecture*, New York 1963.

Shepheard, Edward (d. 1747), *see* WOOD, John.

Sheppard, Richard (b. 1910). The most interesting buildings by R. Sheppard, Robson & Partners to date are Churchill College, Cambridge (1959 onwards), with a number of small and medium-sized courts grouped loosely round the towering concrete-vaulted hall; hostels for Imperial College, London (1961–3); the School of Navigation of Southampton University (1959–61); Digby Hall, Leicester University (1958–62); the West Midland Training College at Walsall (1960–63); and the City University, St John Street, London (1976).

Shingle style. The American term for the Domestic Revival of the 1870s and 1880s, influenced initially by Norman SHAW, but replacing his tile-hanging by SHINGLE-hanging. The pioneer building is the Sherman House at Newport, Rhode Island, by RICHARDSON (1874). McKIM, Mead & WHITE also participated. The masterpiece is Richardson's Stoughton House at Cambridge, Massachusetts (1882–3). The shingle style is almost exclusively a style of the medium-sized private house, and its most interesting and most American feature, not implied in the name, is open internal planning.

V. Scully, *The Shingle Style and the Stick Style*, New Haven 1971, and *The Architecture of the American Summer. The Flowering of the Shingle Style*, New York (1971) 1988.

Shingles. Wooden tiles for covering roofs, walls and spires. They were sometimes of other materials (e.g. asbestos, cement) but were always cut to standard shapes and sizes.

Shinohara, Kazuo (b. 1925), *see* JAPANESE ARCHITECTURE.

Shopping centre, *see* GRUEN, Victor (1903–80).

Shouldered arch, *see* ARCH.

Shute, John (d. 1563), the author of the first English architectural book, *The First and Chief Groundes of Architecture* (1563), described himself as a painter and architect, and was a member of the household of the Duke of Northumberland, who sent him to Italy about 1550. His book included illustrations of the five orders, derived mainly from SERLIO. It went into four editions before 1587 and must have been widely used.

Summerson 1983; Harris 1990.

Shuttering, *see* FORMWORK.

Siccard von Siccardsburg, August (1813–68), *see* AUSTRIAN ARCHITECTURE.

Sikhara. The spire or tower of a Hindu temple, over the sanctuary.

Sill or **cill.** The horizontal member at the base of a timber-framed wall into which the posts and studs are normally tenoned. Also the horizontal member at the bottom of a window-opening or door-frame.

Siloe, Diego de (*c.* 1495–1563), was a sculptor as well as an architect, and one of the main practitioners of the PLATERESQUE style. Born in Burgos, he studied in Italy (Florence and possibly Rome), where he acquired a Michelangelesque style of sculpture and picked up the vocabulary of Renaissance architecture. His finest work as both sculptor and architect is the Escalera Dorada in Burgos Cathedral (1519–23) – a very imposing interior staircase rising in five flights and derived from that designed by BRAMANTE to link the terraces of the Belvedere Court. To decorate it *putti*, portraits in roundels, winged angel heads and other Renaissance motifs are used with a still Gothic profusion. In 1528 Siloe began his masterpiece, Granada Cathedral, where his main innovation was a vast domed chancel very skilfully attached to the wide nave. Here he adopted a purer and more severe manner which was to have wide influence in Spain. His other buildings include the tower of S. María del Campo, near Burgos (1527); Colegio Fonseca courtyard, Salamanca (1529–34); the Salvador church, Ubeda (1536); Guadix Cathedral (1549); and S. Gabriel, Loja (1552–68), with its unusual trefoil *chevet*.

Kubler and Soria 1959; E. E. Rosenthal, *The Cathedral of Granada*, Princeton 1961.

Silva, Domingos Penente da (1836–1901), *see* PORTUGUESE ARCHITECTURE.

Sima recta, *see* CYMA RECTA.

Sima reversa, *see* CYMA REVERSA.

Simatium, *see* CYMATIUM.

Simón de Colonia (d. *c.* 1511). Son of Juan de Colonia (d. 1481), and father of Francisco de Colonia (d. 1542). Juan no doubt came from Cologne, and, indeed, the spires of Burgos Cathedral (1442–58) look German Late Gothic. Juan was also the designer of the Charterhouse of Miraflores outside Burgos (1441 onwards). Simón, sculptor as well as architect, followed his father at Burgos Cathedral and Miraflores and designed, in a typically Spanish wild Late Gothic, the Chapel of the Constable of the cathedral (1486 onwards) and the façade of S. Pablo at Valladolid (1486–99). He became master mason of Seville Cathedral in 1497. Francisco, who probably completed the façade of S. Pablo, is responsible (with Juan de Vallejo) for the crossing tower of Burgos Cathedral (1540 onwards), still essentially Gothic, though Francisco had done the Puerta de la Pellejería of the cathedral in the new Early Renaissance in 1516. Francisco was made joint master mason with JUAN DE ÁLAVA at Plasencia Cathedral in 1513, but they quarrelled over the job and also over Álava's work at Salamanca Cathedral. Álava commented on Francisco's *'poco saber'*.

Kubler and Soria 1959; M. Dezzi Bardeschi, *La cattedrale di Burgos*, Florence 1965.

Sinan (1489–1578 or 1588), the greatest Turkish architect. He worked for Suleiman I 'The Magnificent' throughout the Ottoman Empire, from Budapest to Damascus, and, according to himself, built no less than 334 mosques, schools and hospitals, public baths, bridges, palaces, and so on. His mosques developed from Hagia Sophia, the most famous being the enormous Suleymaniye in Istanbul (1551–8), though the Shezade mosque (1544–8) and the small Sokollu Mehmet Pasha mosque (1570–74), both in Istanbul, are perhaps finer. He considered his masterpiece to be the Selimiye at Edirne (Adrianople, 1569–74).

A. Stratton, *S.*, New York 1972; E. Egli, *S.*, Zürich 1976; A. Kuran, *S: The Grand Old Master of Ottoman Architecture*, Washington and Istanbul 1987.

Singhalese or **Sinhalese architecture,** *see* SRI LANKAN ARCHITECTURE.

Site, *see* UNITED STATES ARCHITECTURE.

Sitte, Camillo (1843–1903), Austrian town-planner and architect, was director of the Trades' School of Salzburg (1875–93), and then of Vienna (1893 onwards). His fame rests entirely on his book *Der Städtebau* (1889), which is a brilliant essay in visual urban planning. Sitte, with the help of a large number of diagrammatic plans, analyses open spaces in towns and the many ways in which irregularities of plan can cause attractive effects. His subject is really 'townscape'.

G. R. Collins, *C.S. and the Birth of Modern City Planning*, New York 1965.

Six-light window, *see* WINDOW.

Siza, Alvaro (b. 1933), *see* PORTUGUESE ARCHITECTURE.

Skeleton construction. A method of construction consisting of a framework (*see* FRAMED BUILDING) and an outer covering which takes no load (*see* CLADDING). The skeleton may be visible from the outside.

W. Blaser, *Filigrane Architecture.*

Metall- und Glaskonstruktion Skin und Skeleton in Europa und den USA, Basel and New York 1980.

Skew, *see* KNEELER.

Skewback. That portion of the ABUTMENT which supports an arch.

Skidmore, Owings & Merrill (known as SOM). One of the largest and at the same time best architectural firms in the USA, named after the founding partners Louis Skidmore (1897–1962), Nathaniel A. Owings (1903–84) and John O. Merrill (1896–1975). SOM has branches in New York, Chicago and other centres, each with its own head of design. Gordon Bunshaft (b. 1909), a partner in 1945, is an especially distinguished designer. Outstanding among the works of the firm, which in the 1950s and 1960s became synonymous with what is now known as 'Corporate Modernism', were the following: Lever House, New York (completed 1952), which started the international vogue for curtain-walled SKYSCRAPERS rising on a podium of only a few storeys, and which has, moreover, a garden-court in the middle of the podium; the Hilton Hotel at Istanbul (begun 1952); the United States Air Force Academy at Colorado Springs (begun 1955). Other important buildings are the Manufacturers' Trust Bank in New York (1952–4), memorably low in a city of high buildings and (although a bank and in need of security) largely glazed to the outside; the Connecticut General Life Insurance at Hartford (1953–7), beautifully landscaped and detailed; the Pepsi-Cola Company Building, New York (1960); and the Chase Manhattan Bank, New York (1961). SOM's style is developed from that of MIES VAN DER ROHE and, until recently, rarely departed from its crispness and precision. For some years now the firm has gone in for concrete used in pre-cast members. In this field their Banque Lambert in Brussels of 1959 has proved as influential as Lever House less than a decade before. In some others of their recent buildings a playfulness – even though a structural playfulness – has appeared which is less convincing. Among their more notable recent buildings are the John Hancock Tower, Chicago (1970), the Hirschorn Museum, Washington, DC (1973), 33 West Monroe Building, Chicago (1980), the National Commercial Bank Building and International Airport buildings at Jeddah, Saudi Arabia (1982), and the Canary Wharf Scheme, Isle of Dogs, and Broadgate development, Liverpool Street, both in London, of the 1990s. Owings published *The Spaces in Between, an Architect's Journey* (Boston 1973).

E. Danz, *Architecture of SOM 1950–1962*, New York 1962; A. Drexler and A. Menges, *Architecture of SOM 1963–1973*, New York 1974; A. Bush-Brown, *Architecture of SOM 1973–1983*, New York 1984; C. H. Krinsky, *Gordon Bunshaft of SOM*, Cambridge, Mass., 1988.

Skirting. The edging, usually of wood, fixed to the base of an internal wall

Skylight. A window set into a roof or ceiling to provide top-lighting.

Skyscraper. A multi-storey building constructed on a steel skeleton, provided with high-speed electric elevators and combining extraordinary height with ordinary room-spaces such as would be used in low buildings. The term originated in the United States in the late 1880s, about ten or twelve years after office buildings in New York had reached the height of ten or twelve storeys or *c.* 250 ft. To go much beyond this was impossible with traditional building materials, and further development was based on the introduction of metal framing. This took place at Chicago in 1883 (*see* JENNEY). Steel skeleton construction for skyscrapers was first established by HOLABIRD & ROCHE's Tacoma Building in Chicago (1887-8), which had twenty-two storeys and a complete steel skeleton. The highest skyscraper before the First World War was C. Gilbert's Woolworth building in New York (792 ft). The Empire State Building, New York (1930–32), is 1,250 ft high; the twin towers of the World Trade Center, New York (1970–74, by YAMASAKI), are 1,350 ft. The Sears Tower, Chicago (completed 1974 by SKIDMORE, OWINGS & MERRILL), is 1,454 ft. The Eiffel Tower is 985 ft.

Condit 1964; P. Goldberger, *The Skyscraper*, New York 1981; Hart 1985; Zukowsky 1988; T. A. P. van Leeuwen, *The Skyward Trend of Thought*, Cambridge, Mass., 1988.

Slab roof, *see* ROOF.

Slate-hanging. A wall covering of overlapping rows of slates on a timber substructure.

Sleeper wall. An underground wall either supporting SLEEPERS, or built between two PIERS, two walls, or a pier and a wall, to prevent them from shifting. The foundation walls of an ARCADE between nave and aisle would thus be sleeper walls.

Sleepers, *see* BEAM.

Slype. A covered way or passage, especially in a cathedral or monastic church, leading east from the cloisters between transept and chapterhouse.

Smeaton, John (1724–92). Civil engineer notable as an architect for his arched bridges (Perth, Banff and Coldstream) and for the third Eddystone lighthouse (1756–9).

A. W. Skempton (ed.), *J.S., F.R.S.*, London 1981.

Smirke, Sir Robert (1780–1867), the leading GREEK REVIVAL architect in England, nevertheless lacked the genius of his almost exact contemporary in Germany, SCHINKEL, by whom he may have been influenced. The son of a painter and Academician, he was articled to SOANE, but quarrelled after a few months. From 1801 to 1805 he travelled in Italy, Sicily, and Greece, sketched most of the ancient buildings in the Morea, and on his return to London published the first and only volume of his projected *Specimens of Continental Architecture* (1806). His first buildings were medieval in style – Lowther Castle (1806–11) and Eastnor Castle (*c.* 1810–15). He made his name with Covent Garden Theatre (1808, destroyed), the first Greek Doric building in London and as such very influential. It showed with what simple means gravity and grandeur might be achieved. His cool businesslike efficiency quickly brought him fame and fortune, and in 1813 he reached the head of his profession when he joined Soane and NASH as Architect to the Board of Works. His masterpieces came in the next decade, first the British Museum (1823–47), then the General Post Office (1824–9, demolished), both large in scale and massively Grecian in style. Though less uncompromising and less impressive than Schinkel's Altes Museum in Berlin (1823–30) the British Museum with its tremendous Ionic colonnade has a noble dignity and illustrates his admirable directness and scholarly detailing at their best. Knighted in 1832, he retired in 1845.

J. M. Crook, *The British Museum*, London 1972; Crook 1972; Colvin 1978.

Smithson, Peter and Alison (b. 1923 and 1928). Their school at Hunstanton in Norfolk (1954) was one of the most controversial buildings of the time; it is not informal but a symmetrical group, and in its details is inspired by MIES VAN DER ROHE. The Smithsons then turned in the direction of BRUTALISM, but their biggest and most mature building, for the *Economist* in London (1962–4), has none of the quirks of that trend. It is a convincingly grouped scheme of various heights, with a façade to St James's Street that succeeds in establishing a *modus vivendi* with the C18 clubs around, and with two high blocks of different heights behind. Their more recent Robin Hood Gardens, London (1968–72), is less successful. They have published *Urban Structuring* (London 1967) *Without Rhetoric; an Architectural Aesthetic 1955–1972* (London 1973) and *The Shift* (London 1981).

5 Architekten Zeichnen für Berlin, exh. cat., Berlin 1976.

Smythson, Robert (*c.* 1535–1614), the only Elizabethan architect of note, perfected the spectacular if rather outlandish country-house style developed by the courtiers and magnates of the period. First heard of at Longleat, where he worked as principal freemason (1568–75), he built his masterpiece, Wollaton Hall, during the next decade (1580–88). This was a revolutionary building – a single pile with corner towers and a central hall, planned symmetrically on both axes. The plan probably derives from SERLIO and the whimsical Flemish carved ornamentation of banded shafts, strapwork, etc., from de VRIES, but the fantastic and romantic sham-castle silhouette is his own invention and wholly English. He settled near Wollaton, acquiring property there and the style of a 'gentleman'. But he almost certainly had a hand in the design of three later houses of note, Worksop Manor (c. 1585, now destroyed), Hardwick Hall (1590–97) and Burton Agnes (1601–10). His son John (d. 1634) designed Bolsover Castle (c. 1612–34), perhaps the most romantic of all the sham castles.

M. Girouard, *R.S. and the Elizabethan Country House*, London 1983.

Soane, Sir John (1753–1837). The most original English architect after VANBRUGH. His extremely personal style is superficially neo-classical but, in fact, romantic or 'picturesque' in its complicated and unexpected spatial interplay. Intense, severe, and sometimes rather affectedly odd, his buildings reflect his tricky character. He was always slightly unsure of himself and, despite his genius, never achieved complete confidence and authority even in his own style. The son of a Berkshire builder, he trained under DANCE and HOLLAND, then studied for three years in Italy, where he probably knew PIRANESI; but French influence, especially that of PEYRE and LEDOUX, was more profound. He returned to London in 1780, but his career only really began with his appointment as Surveyor

to the Bank of England in 1788. His work at the Bank, now destroyed, was among the most advanced in Europe. The Stock Office (begun 1792) and the Rotunda (begun 1796) must have seemed shockingly austere, with their shallow domes and general emphasis on utility and structural simplicity, not to mention his reduction of classical ornamentation to rudimentary grooved strips and diagrammatic mouldings. The romantic or picturesque element in his work is felt increasingly after 1800, notably in Pitzhanger Manor (Ealing Public Library, 1800–1803) and in the Dulwich College Art Gallery (1811–14, restored 1953), a 'primitivist' construction in brick with each element curiously detached by some slight break or recession, and, above all, in his own house, No. 13 Lincoln's Inn Fields, London (1812–13), now Sir John Soane's Museum. This is highly eccentric and personal to the point of perversity, especially inside, with congested, claustrophobic planning, complicated floor-levels, ingenious toplighting, hundreds of mirrors to suggest receding planes and blur divisions, and hanging, Gothic-inspired arches to detach ceilings from walls. The exterior perfectly illustrates his linear stylization and emphasis on planes rather than masses. His last buildings of note are the astylar utilitarian stables of Chelsea Hospital, London (1814–17), St Peter's, Walworth (1822), and Pell Wall House, Staffordshire (1822–8) with curious features reminiscent of VANBRUGH. He was made Professor of Architecture at the Royal Academy in 1806 and knighted in 1831. He published *Designs in Architecture* (London, 1778, re-issued 1790).

P. de la Ruffinière du Prey, *J.S. The Making of an Architect*, London 1982;

Socle

J. Summerson *et al.*, *J.S.*, London 1983; D. Stroud, *Sir J.S.*, London 1984; E. Schumann-Bacia, *Die Bank von England und ihr Architekt J.S.*, Munich 1989.

Socle. A base or pedestal.

Soffit. The underside of any architectural element, e.g. an INTRADOS.

Soffit cusps. Cusps springing from the flat soffit or INTRADOS of an arched head, and not from its chamfered sides or edges.

Solar. A private chamber on an upper floor of a medieval house, usually a bedroom or living-room on the first floor adjoining the hall at the high-table end.

Solari, Guiniforte (1429–81), a Milanese 'last-ditch' Gothic conservative, completed FILARETE's Renaissance Ospedale Maggiore in the Gothic style, built the simplified Gothic nave of S. Maria delle Grazie, Milan (1465–90, completed by BRAMANTE), and worked on the Gothic Milan Cathedral.

Heydenreich and Lotz 1974.

Solari, Santino (1576–1646), one of the first Italian architects to work extensively in Germany and Austria, came of a large family of artists from Como. His main work is Salzburg Cathedral (1614–28), an entirely Italian basilican church with dome and with twin towers flanking the west façade. For the Bishop of Salzburg he built the Italianate *Lustschloss* at Hellbrunn, outside Salzburg (1613–19). He also designed (*c.* 1620) the solemn little shrine of the black-faced Virgin at Einsiedeln, Switzerland, later surrounded by MOOSBRUGGER's fantastic Baroque abbey church.

Hempel 1965.

Solarium. A sun terrace or LOGGIA.

Solea. In an Early Christian or Byzantine church, a raised pathway projecting from the BEMA to the AMBO.

Soleri, Paolo (b. 1919). Italian architect trained in Turin, worked with Frank Lloyd WRIGHT 1947–8, returned to Italy and built the Solimene ceramic factory, Vietri, near Salerno, 1951–4, then returned to the USA and started the Cosanti Foundation, Scottsdale, Arizona, in 1955 to pursue alternative urban planning. In 1966 he published *Arcology: The City in the Image of Man* (Cambridge, Mass., and London) and by 1970 had designed thirty Arcologies – a series of high-density MEGASTRUCTURES of which one, Arcosanti, has been under construction since 1970.

D. Wall, *Visionary Cities: The Arcology of P.S.*, London 1971; Banham 1976; *P.S. Architectural Drawings*, exh. cat., New York 1981.

Solomonic column. A spirally fluted or shaped column commonly called a 'barley-sugar column'. Such columns in St Peter's, Rome, were traditionally believed to have come from Solomon's Temple, hence the name.

SOM, *see* SKIDMORE, OWINGS & MERRILL.

Sommaruga, Giuseppe (1867–1917). Milanese architect, studied under the historicizing, late Romantic architects Luca Beltrami (1854–1933) and Camillo Boito (1836–1914) but turned to ART NOUVEAU and became, side by side with Ernesto Basile (1857–1932; Casa Basile, Palermo, 1904) and Raimondo d'Aronco (1857–1932; buildings for the Turin exhibition 1902), its most important representative in Italy. His principal works are the Palazzo Castiglioni, Milan (1901), the Clinica Colombo, Milan (1909), and the Hotel Tre Croci, Campo dei Fiori, near Varese (1909–12).

Pevsner and Richards 1973; Nicoletti 1978.

Sonck, Lars (1870–1956), *see* FINNISH ARCHITECTURE.

Sondergotik, *see* GERMAN ARCHITECTURE.

Sopraporta. A painting above the door of a room, usually framed in harmony with the door-case to form a decorative unit.

Sosnowski, Oscar (1880–1939), *see* POLISH ARCHITECTURE.

Soufflot, Jacques Germain (1713–80), the greatest French neo-classical architect, was the son of a provincial lawyer against whose wishes he went off to Rome to study architecture in 1731. He stayed seven years, settling on his return in Lyon, where he was commissioned to build the enormous Hôtel Dieu (1741 onwards). This made his reputation, and in 1749 he was chosen by Mme de Pompadour to accompany her brother, M. de Marigny, to Italy, where he was to spend two years preparing himself for his appointment as Surintendant des Bâtiments. The tour was very successful and may be regarded as marking the beginning of NEO-CLASSICISM in France, of which the great masterpiece was to be Soufflot's Ste Geneviève (called the Panthéon since the Revolution) in Paris (begun 1757). This was a revolutionary building for France and was hailed by the leading neo-classical critic and theorist, LAUGIER, as 'the first example of perfect architecture'. It perfectly expresses a new, more serious, not to say solemn attitude towards antiquity, and combines Roman regularity and monumentality with a structural lightness derived from Gothic architecture. Soufflot himself said (1762) that one should combine the Greek orders with the lightness one admired in Gothic buildings. He continued working on his masterpiece to the end of his life, but did not live to see it finished. His other buildings are of less interest, e.g. École de Droit, Paris (designed 1763, built 1771 onwards) and various follies in the Château de Menars park (1767 onwards) including a rotunda, nymphaeum, and orangery, all in an elegant but rather dry neo-classical style.

Braham 1980; Rykwert 1980; M. Gallet *et al.*, *S. et son temps*, Paris 1980; D. Ternois and F. Perez, *L'Œuvre de S. à Lyon*, Lyon 1982.

Sounding board, *see* PULPIT.

South African architecture. There is no unified, consistent representative of South African architecture any more than there is a unified South African culture; the reasons are of course the same. In typical colonial fashion, indigenous traditions were neglected and models from the countries of origin (Holland and Britain) were copied, imperfectly but sometimes with happy results. Although South Africa is no longer colonial, cultural integration is actively opposed and consequently foreign influences, now American rather than European, continue to prevail.

The first of these influences, following on the occupation of the Cape by the Dutch East India Company in 1652, was Dutch–Flemish, resulting in a regional style of mainly domestic architecture known as Cape Dutch. This style was based on short-span, symmetrical, rectangular-plan forms, usually with E, H, T or U configurations. The houses were single-storeyed, with thick lime-washed walls and relatively narrow, economically disposed door- and window-openings, thatched with reeds and adorned with local versions of Baroque and then Rococo gables, e.g. Groot Constantia (altered *c.* 1792) in Constantia; Stellenberg House, 1790, in Kenilworth; and Morgenster House, 1786, in Somerset West.

More sophisticated influences were brought to the Cape by particular individuals, notably Anton Anreith (1754–1822), a skilled sculptor and woodcarver from Germany who arrived in 1776, and Louis Michel Thibault (1750–1815), who had studied under GABRIEL *c.* 1775 and came as a military engineer with the French occupying forces in 1783. In their work they maintained the continuity of the Cape Dutch tradition, but added new ideas and elements, and a great deal of refinement, e.g. Lutheran church, Cape Town, which Anreith refaced 1787–92.

After the Napoleonic wars, the British found themselves the reluctant masters of a strategically important but otherwise unprofitable colony. Expenditure on development was small, but a style based on English Georgian architecture gradually established itself in Cape Town, while a modified English vernacular tradition was planted in the Eastern Cape, where about 4,000 British immigrants were settled in 1820 in an effort to stabilize the troubled frontier.

British imperialism with its concomitant colonial technology developed rapidly in the C19 and when, in the 1870s, first diamonds and then gold were discovered in South Africa, there was available a 'ready-made' political and administrative apparatus accompanied by a literally ready-made architecture. Victorian patterns, executed in Victorian corrugated- and cast-iron, proliferated throughout the country. At the same time, the new prosperity attracted original talents and Cecil Rhodes's architect, Herbert BAKER (strongly influenced by LUTYENS), was the central figure in a new wave of external influence on South African architecture.

Baker was appreciative of the Cape Dutch tradition and sought, in his early work in Cape Town (e.g. Groot Schuur, 1890), to incorporate its elements into his already eclectic but sensitive and skilful architecture. His major works, after the Second Anglo-Boer War, included the Rhodes Memorial in Cape Town (1905–8), the Pretoria railway station (1908), the Supreme Court Buildings, Johannesburg (1911) and the Union Buildings, Pretoria (1910–13). His former associates and other architects influenced by him, notably J. M. Solomon, who designed the University of Cape Town campus (1915), and Gordon Leith, who practised in the Transvaal and Orange Free State, exerted a powerful influence on all South African architecture until the beginnings of the Modern Movement in the 1920s.

From about 1925 the influence of contemporary movements abroad became evident, mainly through the architectural schools and the *South African Architectural Record*. A. Stanley Furner, editor of the *SAAR* from 1926–9, introduced most contemporary movements to the profession. His students, under the leadership of Rex Martienssen (1905–42) and recent immigrants from Europe, responded to these influences, mainly from the heroic period of the INTERNATIONAL MODERN style. House Munro, Pretoria (1932 by McIntosh) was followed by others of which House Harris, Johannesburg (1933 by Hanson, Tomkin and Finkelstein) is a good example, a two-storey white cube showing formal and spatial characteristics derived from GROPIUS and MIES VAN DER ROHE. A rapid development of domestic architecture followed, culminating in Casa Bedo, Johannesburg (1936 by Cowin and Ellis), a free-plan form and Miesian spatial organization adapted to local conditions by wide eaves and a hipped roof reminiscent of Sir Herbert Baker and Frank Lloyd WRIGHT. This adaptation is typical and produced a model for many houses of the next two decades.

A similar pattern of development occurred in other building types. Early International Style buildings gave the lead for buildings in Johannesburg such as Hotpoint House (1934), Reading Court (1936) and Denstone Court (1937 by Hanson, Tomkin and Finkelstein), Aiton Court (1938 by W. R. Stewart, A. Stewart and Bernard Cooke), Peterhouse (1936 by Fassler, Martienssen, and Cooke) and in Cape Town the Cavalla Factory (1938 by Policansky).

Local conditions, technology, and inventiveness led to adaptations towards a contemporary vernacular: examples in Johannesburg include the 20th Century Fox Cinema and offices (1936 by Hanson, Tomkin and Finkelstein) and the innovative work of W. B. Pabst; in Cape Town the work of P. E. Pahl, M. Policansky, Prof. L. Thornton Whyte and others; in Durban such buildings as the Technical College Clubhouse (1943 by Jackson and Park Ross).

By the 1950s a fairly widespread contemporary vernacular had emerged albeit with regional differences and notwithstanding attempts by Fassler, Hanson, and others to establish a neo-classical style based on the work of PERRET. The country was growing rapidly, commercialism was the order of the day, and in general architecture and the cities were eroded by pragmatic immediacy. There were notable exceptions. Norman Eaton (1902–55) developed a fine regional architecture, e.g. Greenwood House and Village, Pretoria (1951), Wachthuis, Pretoria (1960), and the Netherlands Bank, Durban (1965). Other examples of regionally sensitive and appropriate architecture are the Club Building, Pretoria (1963 by John Templar), houses in Durban by Biermann and Hallen, and the houses of Revel Fox in the Cape.

The next discernible wave of influence occurred in the early 60s with the return of young architects who had done graduate study under Louis KAHN, Romualdo Giurgola, Paul RUDOLPH, Robert VENTURI and others in America. Examples of this influence are, in Cape Town, the Truworths Factory (1968 by R. S. Uytenbogaardt), in Johannesburg, House Robinson (1966 by Meyer and Gallagher) and House Britz (1972 by Britz) and in Durban, the work of Hallen and Theron.

With continued prosperity foreign architects were commissioned to design major buildings, mainly in Johannesburg, e.g. Carlton Centre (1966–72 by SKIDMORE, OWINGS & MERRILL),

Space-frame

FIG. 79. *Space-frame*

Standard Bank (1971 by HENTRICH) and the IBM building (1975 by Philip Dowson). These years have also seen the emergence of diverse local talents attempting a revalidation of architectural language, e.g. in the Cape, the Naude House (1968 by A. and A. de Sousa Santos) and Werdmuller Centre (1976 by R. S. Uytenbogaardt) and in Johannesburg, the RAU University (Meyer *et al.*) and the Miller House (1974 by Stan Field). Outstanding is the Portuguese-born Amancio d'Alpoim Miranda Guedes (b. 1925), who has developed a highly individual and exhilarating style combining Gaudí and Kahn with the local vernacular. Though long resident in South Africa and since 1975 professor and head of the department of architecture at Witwatersrand University, Johannesburg, most of his work has been in Mozambique, e.g. the Smiling Lion Hotel, Lourenço Marques (1956–8), with Ndebele-inspired external murals, and the Governor's Palace, Vila Pery (1973). [I. Prinsloo and J. Moyle]

Space-frame. A three-dimensional framework for enclosing spaces, in which all members are interconnected and act as a single entity, resisting loads applied in any direction. Systems can be designed to cover very large spaces, uninterrupted by support from the ground, and the surface covering can be integrated to play its part in the structural whole. Some types have the appearance of egg-boxes (pyramidal in their elements), others are based on hexagonal or other geometric figures. The chief exponents to date are Zygmunt S. Makowski (*space-grid*), Bruno TAUT, Konrad WACHSMANN, Jean PROUVÉ, and Buckminster FULLER, whose dome, designed for the Union Tank Car Co., Baton Rouge, USA (1958), has a diameter of 384 ft. *See* Fig. 79.

Z. S. Mackowski, *Steel Space Structures*, London 1965.

Span. The distance between the supports of an arch, beam or roof.

Spandrel. The triangular space between the side of an arch, the horizontal drawn from the level of its apex, and the vertical of its springing; also applied to the surface between two arches in an arcade, and the surface of a vault between adjacent ribs.

Spanish architecture. After the Roman aqueducts, etc., the first noteworthy monuments in Spain are a few relics of the Visigothic age, notably S. Juan de Baños (661), originally with a very odd plan with a square chancel and square chapels of the same size attached to the long narrow transepts. The plan of S. Miguel at Tarrasa (C9 or earlier) – Tarrasa being one of the rare surviving examples of a 'church family' – is of the Early Christian and Byzantine inscribed-cross plan, that of S. Pedro de Nave (C7) a composition of square or oblong compartments like the English *porticus*. This latter scheme became that of the eminently interesting Asturian churches of the C9 such as S. Julián de los Prados, Oviedo (*c*. 830), with its astonishing Pompeian interior decoration, Sta Cristina de Lena and S. Miguel de Linio. One of them, now a church, was originally a royal hall (Sta Maria de Naranco, 843–50).

Meanwhile the Muslims had captured most of Spain (711), and the Mosque of Cordoba had been begun in 786. It grew to be in the end a vast rectangle of *c*. 550 × 420 ft, filled with a forest of columns so as to form nineteen parallel naves. The most ornate parts date from *c*. 970. The vaults of these parts with their intersected ribs must have inspired certain Gothic and certain Baroque vaults. However, Islam's architecture also immediately inspired Spanish Christian architecture. The term MOZARABIC means such mixtures of Islamic and Christian elements as are exemplified by S. Miguel de Escalada (consecrated in 913), with its arcade arches of horseshoe shape, Santiago de Penalba (931–7) and Santa Maria de Lebeña (also C10). The term MUDÉJAR refers to Christian architecture in a purely Moslem style, and this remained characteristic of secular architecture in Spain nearly to the end of the Middle Ages. No wonder, considering the glories and luxurious comforts of the Alhambra of Granada, which – in the one remaining Moslem part of the peninsula – was built as late as the C14. Among the Christians such Mudéjar towers of the C13 as those of Teruel look back at the splendour of the Giralda at Seville of *c*. 1172–90, and palaces of Christian rulers established Islamic forms of decoration, of plan and of life. The palace of Tor-

desillas is of the 1340s, the Alcázar at Seville of the years of Pedro the Cruel (1349–68), and at Seville the so-called House of Pilate carried Mudéjar right into the C16, even if the last-built parts of the house (which was not completed in 1553) take full note of Gothic as well as developed Renaissance motifs.

But this anticipates the story by several centuries. The Romanesque style had started in the early C11 in Catalonia in a version similar to that of Lombardy (Ripoll, 1010–32, desperately restored; Cardona, consecrated 1040). The C11 in Spain is particularly important for decorative sculpture. It seems that ever since S. Pedro de Nave in the C10 the Spanish were ahead of the French in this field. There is certainly nothing in France to compare with the capitals of Jaca. The French Romanesque of the great pilgrimage churches has an outstanding representative in the far north-west corner of Spain in the celebrated church of Santiago de Compostela (begun *c*. 1075 and completed with the splendidly sculptured Pórtico de la Gloria in 1188). Other Romanesque churches are S. Martin de Frómista of *c*. 1060, S. Isidoro at León with its antechurch known as the Panteón de los Reyes also of *c*. 1060, and Lugo Cathedral, a direct descendant of Santiago, and S. Vicente at Ávila, both of the C12. The Late Romanesque of Spain is best represented by the Old Cathedral of Salamanca and the Cathedral of Zamora, both with curious domes of west and south-west French affinities, but essentially original.

To determine the date when the Gothic style arrived is as difficult for Spain as for England. The Old Cathedral of Salamanca for instance has pointed arches almost entirely. But pointed arches are not necessarily Gothic. The CISTERCIANS who came directly or indirectly from Burgundy brought the pointed arch as a Burgundian Romanesque motif. The Cistercians arrived in Spain in 1131, and soon large buildings were erected by them in many places: Moreruela, Meira, La Oliva, Huerta, Veruela, Poblet, Santas Creus have the standard French plan with chancel and transeptal east chapels. But while these are mostly straight-ended it is also usual in Spain to have the chancel apsed (Oliva, Huerta, Meira) or even an ambulatory and apsed radiating chapels (Moreruela, Poblet, Veruela). Whereas in many of these churches one can be in doubt as to what to regard as Romanesque, what as Gothic, La Oliva must clearly be considered Gothic, and the date of the beginning is 1164.

With the C13 the north French cathedral style entered Spain. The most French cathedrals of the C13 are those of Burgos (1221 onwards), Toledo (1226 onwards), and León, but the most original version of the Spanish Gothic is Catalan (Barcelona Cathedral, 1298 onwards; Sta María del Mar, Barcelona, 1329 onwards; Palma Cathedral, Majorca), with very wide and high naves and very high aisles or with aisles replaced by chapels between internal buttresses (Sta Catalina, Barcelona, 1223 onwards; Sta María del Pino, Barcelona, c. 1320; and Gerona Cathedral, whose nave with a span of 74 ft is the widest in Europe). The Late Gothic style was much influenced by Germany and the Netherlands, as is shown by such works as the towers of Burgos Cathedral by Juan de Colonia (*see* SIMÓN DE COLONIA) (begun 1442). Late Gothic vaults with their lierne rib patterns also have

German origins. Spatially, however, Spain was entirely Spanish: the vast rectangles of her cathedrals hark back to the mosques of Islam, but their height and the height of the aisles are her own. Seville Cathedral was begun in 1402 and is 430 ft long and 250 ft wide, with a nave 130 ft high and aisles 85 ft high. Spain continued to embark on new cathedrals on this scale right up to the time of the Reformation. Salamanca was started in 1512, Segovia in 1525. In Spain those were the years of greatest wealth, resulting in the many funerary monuments and the excessively lavish decoration of such buildings as the Constable's Chapel at Burgos Cathedral (1482 onwards) and S. Juan de los Reyes, Toledo (1476 onwards), or of such façades as those of S. Pablo (1486 onwards) and S. Gregorio (*c.* 1492), both at Valladolid. No square inch must lack its complicated and lacy carving. The spirit of Islam re-asserted itself in this, and the desire to over-decorate surfaces was carried on with Renaissance details in the C16 (PLATERESQUE style) and with Baroque details in the C18 (CHURRIGUERESQUE style).

Spain is the country of the most spectacular castles. For the C12 the most magnificent display is the walls of Ávila, for the C13 the castle of Alcalá de Guadaira, for the C14 Bellver on Majorca (1309–14), which is round and has a round courtyard, for the C15 Coca, vast and all of brick.

The Italian Renaissance had actually reached Spain early, and such monuments as the courtyard of the castle of La Calahorra (1509–12) or the staircase of the Hospital of Toledo (1504 onwards) are pure and perfectly at ease. But almost at once the crowding of motifs started again, and the façade of the University of Salamanca (*c.* 1515 onwards) is no more than a furnishing of the Late Gothic façade with new motifs. Soon, however, the pure Italian High Renaissance also entered Spain. The first and for a while the only example is Charles V's unfinished palace on the Alhambra (1527–86 by MACHUCA), with its circular courtyard and its motifs reminiscent of RAPHAEL and GIULIO ROMANO. The severest and vastest palace in the Italian style is Philip II's Escorial (1563 onwards by Juan Bautista de TOLEDO and HERRERA). Ecclesiastical architecture in the C16 reached its climax in the east end of Granada Cathedral by SILOE (1528 onwards), and the parts of Valladolid Cathedral by Herrera of 1585 onwards. But such austerity remained rare, and Spain came once again into her own when, in the late C17, she developed that style of excessive Baroque surface decoration which culminated in such buildings as the façade of Santiago de Compostela (1738 onwards), the sacristy of the Charterhouse of Granada (1727 onwards), the Transparente by TOMÉ in Toledo Cathedral (1721–32), the portal of the Hospital of S. Ferdinand in Madrid (1722) and that of the Dos Aguas Palace at Valencia (1740–44). Greater sobriety in an Italian and French sense characterizes the circular Sanctuary of St Ignatius of Loyola, begun in 1689 and designed by Carlo FONTANA, the Royal Palace in Madrid by G. B. SACCHETTI begun in 1738, the Royal Palace of La Granja, partly by Filippo JUVARRA (1719 onwards), and the Royal Palace at Aranjuez, rebuilt in 1748–68 after Herrera's designs by Santiago Bonavia (d. 1759). Among the Spanish academics Ventura RODRÍGUEZ TIZON was the most conspicuous figure; his giant portico for Pamplona Cathedral was built in 1783. Of 1787 is the even more neo-classical design for the Prado in Madrid by Juan de VILLANUEVA.

C19 conservatism was broken only towards the end of the century by the lively Catalonian version of Art Nouveau known in Spain as 'Modernisme'. GAUDÍ was the great genius of the movement, but Lluis Doménech i Montaner (1850–1923) and Josep Puig i Cadafalch (1869–1956) were hardly less eccentrically individual, e.g. Doménech's Palau de la Musica (1904–8) and Puig i Cadafalch's Casaramona factory (1912), both in Barcelona. The 1929 Barcelona International Exhibition introduced the INTERNATIONAL MODERN style with one of its masterpieces, MIES VAN DER ROHE's Barcelona Pavilion (now restored), and in the 1930s TORROJA and SERT designed several notable buildings. Barcelona has remained the centre of innovative architecture, with José Antonio Coderch (1913–84), whose Casa Ugalde (1952), Cocheras flats (1968) and Trade Office Building (1965) in Barcelona are notable; followed by the partnership Martorell–Bohigas–Mackay formed in Barcelona in 1962 by Josep Martorell (b. 1925), Oriol Bohigas (b. 1925) and David Mackay (b. 1933), whose free-ranging experimentation extends from the vernacular to the 'machine-age' (Santa Aguada Housing, Benicassim, of 1966 and Thau School, Barcelona, of 1972–4). In 1962, also, Ricardo BOFILL founded his Taller de Arquitectura and has since become famous internationally – indeed most of his recent work has been outside Spain. In 1962, again, Francisco Saénz de Oìza (b. 1918) built his remarkable Wrightian Torres

Blancas apartment tower in Madrid. More recently José Rafael Moneo (b. 1937) has made his name with a series of notable buildings: the Diestre factory, Saragossa (1963–7); Bankinter Building, Madrid (1975); Town Hall, Logroño (1978); and the National Museum of Roman Art, Merida (1985).

Speer, Albert (1905–81). Hitler's architect and, after 1942, armaments minister. Imprisoned 1945–66. He made his name with his spectacular settings for Nazi Party rallies in the 1930s, notably by his dramatic use of massed flags and searchlights creating 'bowls of light'. His buildings were on an increasingly grand and eventually megalomaniac scale – Zeppelin Field, Nuremberg (1934–7, partly demolished), the New Reich Chancellery, Berlin (1938–9, demolished) and many unrealized projects for Berlin. In comparison TROOST almost seems refined. His reputation has been re-assessed by certain POST-MODERN architects, and the Japanese Embassy, Berlin, has been rebuilt to his designs. He published *Inside the Third Reich* (New York–London 1970) and *Spandau: The Secret Diaries* (New York–London 1976).

B. Miller-Lane, *Architecture and Politics in Germany 1918–1945*, Cambridge, Mass., 1968; L. Krier (ed.), *A.S.*, Brussels 1985.

Spence, Sir Basil Urwin (1907–76), *see* ENGLISH ARCHITECTURE.

Spere. A fixed structure which serves as a screen at the lower end of an open (medieval) hall between the hall proper and the SCREENS PASSAGE. It has a wide central opening between posts and short screen walls, and there is often a movable screen in the opening. The top member is often the tie-beam of the roof truss above; screen and truss are then called a *spere-truss*.

Spezza, Andrea (d. 1628), *see* CZECHOSLOVAK ARCHITECTURE.

Spiral stairs, *see* STAIR.

Spire. A tall pyramidal, polygonal, or conical structure rising from a tower, turret, or roof (usually of a church) and terminating in a point. It can be of stone, or of timber covered with SHINGLES, or lead. A *broach spire* is usually octagonal in plan, placed on a square tower and rising without an intermediate parapet. Each of the four angles of the tower not covered by the base of the spire is filled with an inclined mass of masonry or broach built into the oblique sides of the spire, carried up to a point, and covering a SQUINCH. A broach spire is thus the interpenetration of a lower-pitch pyramid with a much steeper octagon. A *needle spire* is a thin spire rising from the centre of a tower roof, well inside a parapet protecting a pathway upon which scaffolding could be erected for repairs. *See* Fig. 80.

Spirelet, *see* FLÈCHE.

Splay. A sloping, chamfered surface cut into the walls. The term usually refers to the widening of doorways, windows, or other wall-openings by slanting the sides. *See also* REVEAL.

Spoerry, François (b. 1912), *see* FRENCH ARCHITECTURE.

Springing line. The level at which an arch springs from its supports. The bottom stone of the arch resting on the IMPOST each side can thus be called a *springer*. *See also* SKEWBACK; Fig. 4.

1. Octagonal spire over tower with pinnacles

2. Spire and octagon over tower with flying buttresses

3. Broach spire

4. Needle spire

FIG. 80. *Spire*

Sprocket, *see* ROOF.

Spur. An ornament, usually of foliage, on the corner of a square plinth surmounted by a circular PIER; also called a *griffe*.

Spur stone. A stone projecting from the angle of a corner or arch to prevent damage by passing traffic: it is usually circular in section.

Squinch. An arch or system of concentrically wider and gradually projecting arches, placed diagonally at the internal angles of towers to fit a polygonal or round superstructure on to a square plan. *See* Fig. 40.

Squint. An obliquely cut opening in a wall or through a PIER to allow a view of the main altar of a church from places whence it could not otherwise be seen; also called a *hagioscope*.

Sri Lankan architecture. The earliest surviving buildings in Sri Lanka (formerly Ceylon) are Buddhist

419

STUPAS, locally called dagobas. Buddhism was introduced from India in the mid C3 BC and the Thuparama dagoba in the ancient capital city of Anuradhapura dates back to this time, though the original hemisphere was subsequently enlarged. The building of dagobas has continued to the present day, the Sinhalese majority being Buddhist: there are slight variations in form, bell-shaped, bulbous or spreading (likened to a heap of rice), each with a spire rising from a rectangular block. They are set on terraced bases and some were originally surrounded by colonnades. Remains of early monastic buildings and, perhaps, palaces are limited to stone supports which give no indication of the form of their wooden superstructures. But steps to the platforms of the more important ascend from semicircular slabs called moonstones, often very delicately carved, and also have carvings on their risers and balustrades. At Polonnaruwa, the capital c. 1055–1270, there are more substantial remains of monastic and palatial buildings. Here much use was made of brick for piers, walls and also tunnel vaults. The most impressive structure is the Tivanka image house (c. 1160–1200), with much relief sculpture, similar to south Indian work, on the exterior but quite unlike any Indian temple in form. Another type of monument indigenous to the island, called a vatadage, consists of a raised stepped circular platform with a small dagoba or statue of the Buddha in the centre, surrounded by at least one ring of monolithic columns and sometimes a wall, usually said to have been roofed, though its structure is uncertain. Notable examples are at Tiriyai on the east coast (founded C8), Polonnaruwa and nearby Medirigiriya (both

C11). At Yapahuwa there is an impressive stone-built gatehouse, all that remains of a royal palace of 1273–84, perched on a mountain side and approached up a very long and steep flight of steps. Later buildings are mainly of wood – the temple of the Holy Tooth at Kandy (the royal capital 1592–1815) and others nearby – apart from those constructed by the Dutch from 1658 (fortifications and churches at Jaffna, Galle and Colombo) and throughout the island during the British occupation of 1815–1948. Of recent buildings those by Geoffrey BAWA are outstanding.

Staddle stones. Mushroom-shaped stones used as bases to support timber-built granaries or hay barns, especially in Sussex.

Stadium. In ancient Greece a running-track; now a large, usually unroofed, sports ground for athletic events.

Stair, staircase. There are special names for the various parts of a stair: the *tread* is the horizontal surface of a step; the *nosing* is the overhanging edge of a tread, usually a half-round; the *riser* is the vertical surface; a *winder* is a tread wider at one end than the other. A *newel, spiral, vice, winding,* or *turnpike* (Scot.) *staircase* is a circular or winding staircase with a solid central post in which the narrow ends of the steps are supported. The *newel* is also the principal post at the end of a flight of stairs; it carries the *handrails* and the *strings* which support the steps. A *dogleg staircase* consists of two flights at right angles, with a half landing. *See* Fig. 81. A *flying stair* is cantilevered from the stairwell without a newel. A *geometric* stair is a flying stair whose

1. Straight-stair
2. Quarter-turn with landing
3. Quarter-turn with winders
4. Dog-leg stair
5. Half-turn with landings
6. Spiral stair
a. Riser
b. Tread
c. String
d. Newel
e. Handrail
f. Baluster

FIG. 81. *Stair*

inner edge describes a curve; it can be built on either a circular or elliptical plan. A *well stair* is a stair within an open well, especially a *half-turn stair* which climbs up three sides of the well with corner landings.

Staircases seem to have existed as long as monumental architecture: a staircase of *c*. 6000 BC has been discovered in the excavations of Jericho. Monumental staircases also existed at Knossos in Crete and Persepolis in Iran. The Greeks and the Romans were not apparently much interested in making an architectural feature of the staircase, and medieval staircases were also utilitarian as a rule. In the Middle Ages the accepted form was the newel staircase, which could assume a monumental scale (Vis du Louvre, Paris, late C14), but only did so to any extent after 1500 (Blois). The standard form of the Italian Renaissance is two flights, the upper at an angle of 180° to the lower, and both running up between solid walls. However, a few architects, notably FRANCESCO DI GIORGIO and LEONARDO DA VINCI, worked out on paper a number of other, more interesting types, and these seem to have been translated into reality in the C16, mostly in Spain. There is the staircase which starts in one flight and returns in two, the whole rising in one well, called *double-return* stairs; the staircase which starts in one and turns at right angles into two (BRAMANTE'S Belvedere Court in the Vatican; Escalera Dorada, Burgos); and, the most frequent type, the staircase which runs up in three flights at right angles round an open well, i.e. a squared spiral stair with intermediate landings. But Bramante in the Vatican still built a normal spiral stair, though also with an open well, and BERNINI (Palazzo Barberini) made this oval, a characteristically Baroque turn. PALLADIO invented the geometrical or flying staircase (Academy, Venice), a spiral staircase without any support other than the bonding of the steps into the outer wall.

The Baroque is the great age of monumental and inventive staircases. The finest of all are in Germany (Würzburg, Brühl, and especially Bruchsal, all by NEUMANN), but there are excellent ones also in France (MANSART at Blois) and in Italy (Naples).

In C20 architecture the staircase has assumed a new significance as the element in a building which is most expressive of spatial flow. The earliest staircase in a glass cage is GROPIUS's at the Cologne Werkbund exhibition (1914). Since then much has been made of flying staircases, staircases without risers, and similar effects.

A. Chastel and J. Guillaume, *L'Escalier dans l'architecture de la Renaissance*, Paris 1988; C. Baldon and I. Melchior, *Steps and Stairways*, New York 1989.

Stalactite work or **muqarna**. Ceiling ornament in ISLAMIC ARCHITECTURE formed by corbelled SQUINCHES made of several layers of brick scalloped out to resemble natural stalactites.

Stall. A carved seat of wood or stone in a row of similar seats; if hinged, often carved on the underside (*see* MISERICORD).

Stam, Mart or Martinus Adrianus (1899–1986). Dutch architect closely associated with the Russian CONSTRUCTIVISTS and the BAUHAUS. An uncompromising socialist, he worked in Russia with LISSITSKY and Ernst May and, after 1948, in East Germany. He is famous as the inventor of the tubular steel chair (1924).

R. Blijstra, *M.S. Documentation of his Work 1920–1965*, London 1970; G. Dorthuys, *M.S.*, London 1970.

Stanchion. A vertical supporting member, nowadays mainly of steel.

Starling. A pointed projection on the PIER of a bridge to break the force of the water. *See* CUTWATER.

Starov, Ivan Yegorovich (1744–1808). Russian neo-classical architect. Unlike the older BAZHENOV and KAZAKOV, with their predominantly urban commissions, he frequently worked in the provinces and may be considered the initiator of the classic age of Russian country-house architecture. Born in Moscow, he trained at the Academy in Petersburg and in Paris under de WAILLY (1762–8). Outstanding among his early works are the *ensemble* of Nikolskoye-Gagarino (Moscow Province, 1773 – its notable columned rotunda belfry destroyed 1941) and Taitsy (1774) near Leningrad; in each the main house has an un-Palladian dynamism reminiscent of Bazhenov. Later came grander, more sober buildings: the somewhat heavy cathedral of the Alexander Nevsky Monastery in Petersburg (1778); the hugest of all Russian country houses at Pella on the Neva (1785, soon afterwards dismantled); and his masterpiece, the Tauride Palace in Petersburg (1783), very extensive but (with its single-storeyed galleries) not overwhelming. From 1771 to the 1790s he was extremely influential in the planning of new and reconstructed towns throughout the Russian Empire. [R. R. Milner-Gulland]

Hamilton 1983.

Stasov, Vasily Petrovich (1769–1848). With ROSSI the leading architect of the later neo-classical period in St Petersburg, but more experimental. Some of his work has the stark geometricity of LEDOUX. Public commissions included vast military and cavalry complexes (incorporating five domed churches) in Petersburg; the laconic Victualling Store in Moscow (1832, designed 1821) and his last Petersburg masterpiece, the triumphal Moscow Gate (1834), a Greek Doric propylaea in cast iron. He rebuilt much of the interior of the Winter Palace after a fire (1837). Outside the capitals his best-known work is at Arakcheev's estate of Gruzine, with beacon-towers and a belfry (destroyed in the last war) that looked like an even more aggressively geometric variant of the Leningrad Admiralty spire (*see* ZAKHAROV). [R. R. Milner-Gulland]

Hamilton 1983.

Stave church. A timber-framed and timber-walled church; the walls are of upright planks with corner-post columns. The term is applied exclusively to Scandinavian churches built from the early or mid CII onwards. Later stave churches usually have inner rows of posts or piers, sometimes an external covered arcade, and roofs arranged in tiers. A third system was also used from *c.* 1200, incorporating a central column from the floor to the roof.

Steenwinckel, Hans the elder (*c.* 1545–1601), Hans the younger (1587–1639), and Lourens van (*c.* 1585–1619), *see* DANISH ARCHITECTURE.

Steeple. The tower and spire of a church taken together.

Steindl, Imre (1839–1902), *see* HUNGARIAN ARCHITECTURE.

Steiner, Rudolf (1861–1925), *see* SWISS ARCHITECTURE.

Stella, Paolo della (d. 1552), *see* CZECHOSLOVAK ARCHITECTURE.

Stereobate. A solid mass of masonry serving as a base, usually for a wall or a row of columns.

Stereotomy. The art and science of cutting, or making sections of, solids, e.g. pre-cutting stones to fit in their allocated place, especially in an arch or vault, where the geometry of their planes is complex.

Stern, Robert A. M. (b. 1939). American POST-MODERN architect and polemicist. His early buildings shared VENTURI's sophisticated populism, e.g. Ehrman House, Armonk, NY (1975), but his later work has developed a wide historical–associational range, e.g. Observatory Hill Dining Hall, University of Virginia, Charlottesville (1982–4); Point West Place, Framingham, Massachusetts (1983–5), and his almost Schinkelesque villa in New Jersey (1983–8). He published *Modern Classicism* in 1988.

V. Scully, *R.A.M.S. Buildings and Projects 1981–85*, New York 1985.

Stethaimer or **Stettheimer,** Hans (d. 1432), worked at Landshut in Bavaria. He came from Burghausen, is usually called Hans von Burghausen and may not have been called Stethaimer. He began St Martin's, the chief parish church of Landshut, in 1387. On his funerary monument other works of his are mentioned: they include the chancel of the Franciscan church at Salzburg (begun 1408). He was one of the best of the German Late Gothic architects, believed in the HALL CHURCH, in brick as a material, where he could use it, and in a minimum of decoration. At Salzburg the most fascinating motif is that of the long slender piers of the chancel with one of them placed axially, due east, so that the eye faces not an interstice but a pier with the light from the east playing round it. Stethaimer's monument may indicate that he was also concerned with sculpture. His source is the style of the PARLER family.

Frankl 1972; T. Herzog, *Meister Hans von Burghausen, gen. S. Sein Leben und sein Werk*, Landshut 1958.

Stick style. Popular late C19 type of

timber-built house in the USA, picturesque and rustic, deriving partly from the balloon-frame buildings but also from other vernacular styles, e.g. the Swiss chalet and with wide surrounding verandas. It reached its height with HUNT's houses in Newport, Rhode Island, of the 1870s.

Stiff-leaf. A late C12 and early C13 type of sculptured foliage, found chiefly on CAPITALS and BOSSES, a development from the CROCKETS of crocket capitals; almost entirely confined to Britain. *See* Fig. 24.

Stijl, De, *see* DE STIJL.

Stile. The vertical member to which the RAILS of a door, window or other frame are joined.

Stile floreale. Italian term for ART NOUVEAU, especially that of the early, flamboyant buildings by D'ARONCO and SOMMARUGA.

Stile liberty. The Italian term for ART NOUVEAU.

Stilted arch, *see* ARCH.

Stirling, James (b. 1926). His early buildings, designed in partnership with James Gowan (b. 1923), moved from a mild BRUTALISM (Ham housing estate, 1958) to a highly original and imposing proto-HIGH TECH style (Engineering Department, Leicester University, 1959–63). The latter established his reputation. His later independent buildings were less impressive, e.g. History Faculty, Cambridge (1965–8). In 1977 he won the competition for the Neuestaatsgalerie at Stuttgart with designs which combined his sense of grandeur with a new sophistication and historical allusiveness which perhaps owed something to POST-MODERN-ISM. Completed in 1984, it is his masterpiece to date, more imaginative and accomplished than his Clore Gallery, London (1980–87). His controversial designs for No. 1 Poultry, Mansion House Square, London, followed in 1985.

P. Arnell and T. Bickford, *J.S. Buildings and Projects*, London 1984.

Stoa. In Greek architecture, a covered colonnade, sometimes detached. In Byzantine architecture, a covered hall, its roof supported by one or more rows of columns parallel to the rear wall; in Latin, porticus.

J. J. Coulton, *The Architectural Development of the Greek Stoa*, Oxford 1976.

Stoep. The Dutch term for veranda.

Stone, Edward Durell (1902–78). Successful American architect who liked to clothe his façades with an ornamental veil, usually including arched elements, e.g. the US Embassy, New Delhi (1954–8); the Huntington Hartford Museum, New York (1958–9); the Kennedy Center for the Performing Arts, Washington, DC (1971).

Stop-chamfer. An ornamental termination to a CHAMFER, common in the Early English period and very much favoured by Victorian architects bringing the edge of the pared-off stone or beam back to a right angle; also called a *broach-stop*. See Fig. 82.

Stops. Projecting stones at the ends of HOOD-MOULDS, STRING COURSES, etc., against which the mouldings finish: often carved, e.g. *a mask stop*. *See also* LABEL-STOP.

Storey or **story.** The space between any two floors or between the floor and roof of a building. In England the

FIG. 82. *Stop-chamfer*

FIG. 83. *Strapwork*

ground-level storey is usually called the ground floor, in America the first floor, in France the *rez-de-chaussée*.

Storey posts. The principal posts of a timber-framed wall.

Stoup. A vessel to contain holy water, placed near the entrance of a church; usually in the form of a shallow dish set against a wall or pier or in a niche.

Strainer arch, *see* ARCH.

Strapwork or **rollwork.** Ornament consisting of interlaced bands, reminiscent of leather thongs or carved fretwork. Its origin is uncertain (*see* ARABESQUE) but it appears in the Galerie de François I at Fontainebleau (1533–5). It became popular in northern Europe, especially the Netherlands, where fantastic, typically MANNERIST, variations of it were published by DIETTERLIN, FLORIS and de VRIES. It was generally used on ceilings, screens and panelling and was popular in Elizabethan England. *See* Fig. 83.

P. Ward-Jackson, in *Victoria & Albert Museum Bulletin*, April 1967.

Street, George Edmund (1824–81), a pupil of George Gilbert SCOTT, was in practice in 1849, after having already designed some churches in Cornwall. In 1850–51 he travelled in France and Germany, in 1853 in north Italy (resulting in a book on the marble and brick buildings of north Italy which came out in 1855), in 1854 in Germany again, in 1861–3 three times in Spain (his important book on Spanish Gothic architecture was published in 1865). In 1852 Street started a practice at Oxford and among his first assistants were WEBB and MORRIS. The first important building is the Cuddesdon Theological College. Street was a High Church man much appreciated by the Cambridge Camden group (*see* BUTTERFIELD), a tremendous worker and a fertile draughtsman who liked to design all details himself. His first large church was St Peter, Bournemouth (1853 onwards).

The practice was moved to London in 1855, and there Street's most characteristic early church is St James the Less, off Vauxhall Bridge Road (1860–61), a very strong design encouraged no doubt by Butterfield but not imitating him, and inspired by RUSKIN. The Gothic is continental rather than English. Among Street's most notable churches are Oakengates, Shropshire (1855); Boyne Hill, Berkshire (1859); St Philip and St James, Oxford (1860–62); All Saints, Clifton, Bristol (1863–8); St John, Torquay (1861–71); St Mary Magdalen, Paddington, London (1868–78); St Paul's, Rome (1872–6); and Holmbury St Mary built at his own expense (1879). Street is always unconventional and inventive, yet hardly ever as aggressive as Butterfield. His principal secular work is the Law Courts, won in competition in 1866. It is a high-minded essay in C13 Gothic, yet picturesque in grouping. The Great Hall inside is particularly impressive.

Meeks 1966; Hitchcock 1977; D. Brownlee, *The Law Courts. The Architecture of G.E.S. (1824–1881)*, Cambridge, Mass., and London 1984.

Street furniture. Benches, bollards, railings, lamp-posts, pillar-boxes, telephone kiosks, etc., usually of cast-iron or other metal and sometimes notable in design, e.g. the Dutch 'telefoon' booths by BRINKMAN and the British telephone kiosks designed by Sir G. G. SCOTT (model 2 of 1926 and model 6 of 1936).

Street Furniture, Design Council catalogue, London 1979; G. Stamp, *Telephone Boxes*, London 1989.

Stressed-skin construction. A form of construction in which the outer skin or SHELL acts with the frame members to contribute to the flexural strength of the unit as a whole.

Stretcher, *see* BRICKWORK.

Strickland, William (1788–1854), a pupil of LATROBE in Philadelphia, rose to fame with the Bank of the United States, Philadelphia, now the Custom House. This had first been designed by Latrobe, but was then built to a modified design by Strickland (1818–24). It is Grecian in style, whereas Strickland's earlier Masonic Temple (1810) had been Gothic. His finest buildings are the Philadelphia Merchants' Exchange (1832–4), with its elegant corner motif crowned by a copy of the Lysicrates Monument, and the Tennessee State Capitol at Nashville (1845–59). He also built the United States Mint, Washington (1829–33), in

a style similar to MILLS's, and the United States Naval Asylum (1827) with an Ionic portico and tiers of long balconies left and right. Strickland was a very versatile man: in his early days he painted and did stage design, and he was also throughout his later life engaged in major engineering enterprises (canals, railways, the Delaware Breakwater).

A. A. Gilchrist, *W.S. Architect and Engineer*, Philadelphia 1950; Hitchcock 1977.

String course. A continuous horizontal band set in the surface of an exterior wall or projecting from it and usually moulded.

Strings. The two sloping members which carry the ends of the treads and risers of a STAIRCASE. *See* Fig. 81.

Strut, *see* ROOF.

Stuart, James 'Athenian' (1713–88), a minor architect, is nevertheless important in the history of GREEK REVIVAL architecture for his temple at Hagley (1758), the earliest Doric Revival building in Europe. He and Nicholas Revett (1720–1804) went to Greece in 1751–5 and in 1762 published the *Antiquities of Athens* (2nd vol. 1789), which had little immediate influence except on interior decoration. Indolence and unreliability lost him many commissions, and he built very little. He designed several first-floor rooms at Spencer House, London (1760 onwards). His No. 15 St James's Square, London (1763–6), was later altered internally by James WYATT (c. 1791). The Triumphal Arch, Tower of the Winds, and Lysicrates Monument in the park at Shugborough are his best surviving works (1764–70). His chapel at Greenwich Hospital (1779–88) seems to have been designed largely by his assistant William Newton.

D. Watkin, *Athenian S. Pioneer of the Greek Revival*, London 1982; Harris 1990.

Stuart architecture, see ENGLISH ARCHITECTURE.

Stucco. A slow-setting plaster composed basically of gypsum, sand and slaked lime with other substances to facilitate modelling and ensure durability. The term is used in English for a type introduced from Italy in the C18, with marble dust as a binder and strengthener; also, more loosely, for various types of fine plaster used both as a medium for internal decorative work and externally as a rendering or protective coating and for architectural features, in lieu of stone.

Of ancient but unknown origin, stucco was developed by the ancient Romans for ceiling decorations etc. and later by Islamic architects for both external and internal decorative work, e.g. STALACTITE (*muqarna*) domes as at the Alhambra, Granada. In Renaissance and Baroque Europe it was used on a large scale for interior decorative schemes, e.g. at the Château de Fontainebleau, reaching great refinement in C17–18 Germany, where it was often combined with BOISERIES, e.g. by Dominikus ZIMMERMANN in the Residenz, Munich, and, more typically of German Rococo, at his country church at die Wies, with the addition only of occasional paint and gilding. In England such craftsmen as Joseph Rose (1745–99) carried out decorative schemes in stucco, especially ceilings, to designs by the ADAM brothers. The use of stucco for large-scale decorative schemes was revived briefly by ART NOUVEAU architects, notably August

ENDELL's Elvira Studio, Munich (1897–8).

Laing 1978; G. Beard, *Stucco and Decorative Plasterwork in Europe*, London 1983; D. Garsting, *Giacomo Serpotta and the Stuccatori of Palermo 1560–1790*, London 1984; W. Jahn, *Stukkatoren des Rokoko. Bayreuther Hofkünstler in markgräflichen Schlössern und in Würzburg*, Sigmaringen 1988; H. Schnell and U. Schedler, *Lexikon der Wessobrunner Künstler und Handwerker*, Munich and Zürich 1988.

Stucco lustro, see SCAGLIOLA.

Studs. In TIMBER-FRAMED buildings secondary vertical timbers of the walls. *See* Fig. 85.

Stupa. The earliest Indian Buddhist (and Jain) religious monument, in origin a hemispherical funerary mound. The first were built to enshrine the cremated remains of Buddha and his disciples; later they commemorated the teaching of Buddha (or of Mahavira, the founder of Jainism) though enshrining the relics of other teachers. Early stupas, such as those at Sanchi of C3–1BC, consist of hemispheres of earth and rubble raised on low cylindrical bases and faced with bricks or stone. Miniature stone railings mark the square platform at the summit, with a central stone mast supporting a finial with one or more umbrella-like tiers, called a *chattra*. A relic casket is embedded below. A paved pathway for worshippers to perform the rite of *pradakshina* by circumambulation surrounded the stupa, usually with a stone railing and four gateways, often bearing elaborate sculptural decorations. The stupa itself is undecorated, but it is imbued with complex cosmological and/or Buddhist symbolism.

The stupa is called a *chorten* in Bhutan, Nepal and Tibet and a *dagoba* in Sri Lanka, where it became bell-shaped. The bell-shape form evolved several variants in Burma, Thailand, Cambodia and Indonesia

A. Snodgrass, *The Symbolism of the Stupa*, Ithaca 1985.

Stylobate. The substructure on which a colonnade stands; more correctly, the top step of the structure forming the CREPIDOMA.

Suardi, Bartolomeo, called Bramantino (*fl.* 1503–36). He was primarily a painter but was responsible for one outstanding building in his native Milan, the octagonal Trivulzio chapel, S. Nazaro Maggiore. It is a masterpiece of classical restraint and geometrical purity. It was begun in 1512.

W. Suida, *Bramante e il Bramantino*, Milan 1955.

Suger, Abbot (1081–1151), was not an architect; neither does he seem to have been responsible, even as an amateur, for any architectural work. But as he was abbot of St Denis, outside Paris, when the abbey church was partly rebuilt (*c.* 1135–44) and as this was the building where the Gothic style was to all intents and purposes invented, or where it finally evolved out of the scattered elements already existing in many places, his name must be recorded here. He wrote two books on the abbey in which the new building is commented on, but nowhere refers to the designer or indeed explicitly to the innovations incorporated in the building.

E. Panofsky, *S. Abbot of Saint-Denis 1081–1151*, Princeton 1979; S. McK. Crosby, *The Royal Abbey of Saint Denis from its Beginnings to the Death of S. 475–1151*, New Haven 1987.

Sullivan, Louis Henry (1856–1924), was of mixed Irish, Swiss, and German descent. He was born in Boston, studied architecture briefly at the Massachusetts Institute of Technology, and moved to Chicago in 1873. He worked there under JENNEY, then, after a year in Paris in VAUDREMER's *atelier*, returned to Chicago. In 1879 he joined the office of Dankmar Adler (1844–1900), who had emigrated from Germany in 1854 and was established as an architect in Chicago by 1869. The firm became Adler & Sullivan in 1881. Their first major building, and no doubt the most spectacular in Chicago up to that time, was the Auditorium (1886–90), which was strongly influenced by RICHARDSON. The auditorium itself is capable of seating more than 4,000. Sullivan's interior decoration is exceedingly interesting, of a feathery vegetable character, derived perhaps partly from the Renaissance in an ARTS AND CRAFTS spirit but at the same time pointing forward to the licence of ART NOUVEAU. His two most familiar skyscrapers, the Wainwright building, St Louis (1890), and the Guaranty building, Buffalo (1894), have not the exclusively functional directness of HOLABIRD & ROCHE's Marquette building of 1894, but they do express externally the SKELETON structure and the cellular interior arrangements. However, Sullivan, though pleading in his *Kindergarten Chats* (1901) for a temporary embargo on all decoration, was himself as fascinated by ornament as by functional expression, and this appears even in the entrance motifs of his major building, the Carson, Pirie & Scott Store (1899–1904), which is most characteristic of the CHICAGO SCHOOL. For the Chicago Exhibition of 1893 Sullivan designed the Transportation building, with its impressively sheer giant entrance arch. He recognized the setback which the classicism otherwise prevailing at the exhibition would mean to the immediate future of American architecture.

Adler died in 1900, and after that time Sullivan's work grew less until it dried up almost entirely, though his National Farmer's Bank, Owatonna, Minnesota (1907–8), should be mentioned. He was a difficult man, uncompromising and erratic, but his brilliance is undeniable – see the passages which his pupil WRIGHT has devoted to his *Lieber Meister*.

Condit 1964; R. Twombly, *L.S. His Life and Work*, New York 1987; Zukowsky 1988.

Sumerian and Akkadian (Babylonian, Assyrian) architecture. As early as the fourth millennium the Sumerians in the Euphrates delta had evolved a complex architecture. The main material was brick; techniques included the arch, the dome, and the vault (though the latter appears to have been used only for underground burial chambers). Having solved these basic problems of construction, architects, applied themselves to decoration. An astonishing proof of their ability is provided by the great ZIGGURAT temple of the Uruk period (late fourth millennium) at Warka (Biblical Erech): the surface was decorated with a mosaic of red-, black- and buff-coloured terracotta cones arranged in geometrical patterns. The façades were further articulated by a succession of decorative buttresses – a device that was to distinguish sacred buildings in Mesopotamia until Hellenistic times. The temple at Al 'Ubaid near Ur, built by King A-

annipadda, *c.* 2600 BC, shows that by this date painted and relief decorations were used not merely as ornaments but to emphasize the structure. But perhaps the most remarkable of these early constructions is the vast ziggurat at Ur, built in the C22 BC – an extremely sophisticated building with dramatic staircases ascending to the shrine on top and with every line subtly curved to correct optical illusions. The principles of this architecture were taken over by the Assyrians of northern Mesopotamia towards the end of the second millennium. So far as may be judged from the excavated sites (unfortunately their great cities at Nineveh and Nimrud yield little for the student of architecture), the Assyrians could not make any technical advances of importance on the Sumerians, but they demanded effects of greater grandeur with lavish use of brilliant colour and much sculpture in the round as well as in relief. The Palace of Sargon at Khorsabad reveals that they achieved their effects of splendour by the multiplication of units rather than by bold over-all designing.

Superimposed orders. The ORDERS used one above the other in an arcaded or colonnaded building, using Doric, Ionic, and Corinthian in that order upwards.

Superstudio, *see* ITALIAN ARCHITECTURE.

Suspended roofs, *see* HENTRICH, Helmut; OTTO, Frei.

Sustris, Friedrich (1524–99 or 91?). Netherlandish MANNERIST painter and architect working in Munich at the same time as Peter CANDID and the Mannerist sculptor Hubert Gerhard. He studied in Italy, where he acquired a sophisticated Mannerist style derived from VASARI. His main work in architecture is the chancel and transept of St Michael's church in Munich (1592, built after the collapse of a tower in that year). He probably designed the Grotto Court (*c.*1581) in the Residenz, very Florentine Mannerist in style. In 1584 he remodelled the parish church of Dachau. The court and interior decoration of Schloss Landshut survive (1573–8); the Akademie der Wissenschaften (1585–97, formerly the Jesuit College) in Munich is attributed to him.

Hitchcock 1981

Swag. A FESTOON in the form of a piece of cloth draped over two supports.

Swan-neck. An OGEE-shaped member, e.g. the curve in a staircase handrail where it rises to join the newel post.

Swedish architecture. (For medieval and earlier architecture in Sweden, *see* SCANDINAVIAN ARCHITECTURE.) Though the present-day centre of Stockholm was laid out on a grid shortly after 1625 (as were also Kalmar, after 1647, and Karlskrona after 1679), the Renaissance made itself felt slowly and reached Sweden mainly from the Netherlands. Justus VINGBOONS visited Sweden in 1653–7, but already before then the style of van CAMPEN and POST had been developed. The de Geer House in Stockholm of 1646 is a perfect example of it. The initiator may have been Simon de LA VALLÉE, who had arrived in 1637 and died in 1642, or his son Jean. The Riddarhus in Stockholm of *c.* 1641–71 was begun by Simon de la Vallée and completed by Vingboons and Jean de la Vallée. At the same time Jean provided in the Oxenstjerna Palace of *c.* 1650–54 an example of the Roman *palazzo* façade.

Churches are of course all Protestant and hence all variations on Dutch types. There are a remarkable number of them, starting with St Katherine in Stockholm by the younger LA VALLÉE begun in 1656. It is a Greek cross with a dome and four corner turrets. Kalmar Cathedral by Nicodemus TESSIN the Elder of 1660 onwards is also basically a Greek cross with corner turrets, but the west and east arms are lengthened and apsed. To the churches must be added the Kagg Mausoleum at Floda of 1661, again a Greek cross, and the grand Carolean Mausoleum attached to the Riddarholm church at Stockholm by the elder Tessin with its splendid columnar exterior. This was designed in 1671.

Openness to influences from several countries remained characteristic of Scandinavia in the C18, or rather of Denmark and Sweden; for Norway had been left behind ever since the Middle Ages. The most monumental building of Scandinavia, the Royal Palace in Stockholm by the younger TESSIN, begun in 1697, reflects more powerfully than any other palace in Europe the impact made by BERNINI's plans for the Louvre in Paris. In 1693 Tessin had made a similar design for the King of Denmark. Tessin knew both Rome and Paris. His country house Steninge of 1694–8 has an entirely French plan, derived from Vaux-le-Vicomte. His father's Drottningholm of the 1660s and Eriksberg had been French throughout, as was also Svartsjö – a completely French *maison de plaisance* – of 1735–9 by Carl Hårleman (1700–1753), the architect of the great East

India Company Warehouse at Göteborg of *c.* 1740 – an outstanding example of early industrial architecture, nineteen windows wide and four storeys high. About the middle of the C18 the PICTURESQUE movement made its mark in Sweden, inspired by England, which had been visited by Fredrik Magnus Piper (1746–1824) before he designed the landscape park at Haga and followed an English *jardinier* in dealing with the landscape park at Drottningholm, both near Stockholm.

The outstanding neo-classical buildings in Sweden are the theatre of Gripsholm Castle (1782) by Erik Palmstedt (1741–1803) and the Uppsala Botanicum (1788) and other buildings by Jean-Louis Desprez (1743–1804), who had belonged to the most advanced Parisian artistic circles before settling in Sweden in 1784. Between that year and the death of Gustavus III in 1792 he was the fount of the strictest Scandinavian classicism. However, such was the mood of the later C18 that he also designed in the Chinese style for the park at Haga, near Stockholm. The work of Carl August Ehrensvard (1745–1800) was much more severe – indeed his are among the most radical neo-classical designs anywhere. For C19 HISTORICISM the best examples in Sweden are late, e.g. the grandiose Renaissance-style university buildings at Uppsala of 1879–87 by Herman Theodor Holmgren (b. 1842) and the Nordisk Museum, Stockholm, of 1890–1907 by Isak Gustaf Clason (1856–1930) in what might be called a northern Renaissance style. But already from the 1890s onwards Swedish architects had begun to join the vanguard of those who tried to get away from Historicism by some 'modern'

fusion of styles, both historical and vernacular. ØSTBERG's City Hall in Stockholm of 1909–23 is the best-known exemplar of this trend, though the earlier Engelbrekst church, Stockholm, of 1906–14 by Lars Israel Wahlman (1870–1952) is an even more strikingly romantic fantasy. Sweden was to reach its own distinctive and distinguished C20 style through a conjunction of national sources: the large-scale and carefully designed industrial (usually hydro-electric) installations, such as those at Trollhättan of 1906–16, followed by ALMQUIST's power-stations near Hammerfors and Krangfors of 1925–8 combined with the so-called 'Nordic Classicism' of Ivar Tengbom (1878–1968), the most prolific Swedish architect of his day, whose Stockholm concert-hall of 1920–26 is typical of the style which culminated in ASPLUND's Stockholm City Library of 1920–28. Asplund collaborated with Sigurd Lewerentz (1885–1975) at the Woodlands Cemetery, Stockholm, where Lewerentz's Resurrection Chapel of 1927 was followed in 1935–40 by Asplund's famous crematorium. By that date Asplund had achieved his unique brand of the INTERNATIONAL MODERN, delicate, refined, with thin steel and much glass, and eminently tactful, as in his law-courts addition to the Göteborg Town Hall of 1934–7. Later Lewerentz was to break away from its restraints towards a more personal and uncompromising, almost Brutalist, idiom in his two late churches of St Mark, Stockholm (1956–60), and St Peter's, Klippan (1963–6).

The new town of Vällingby, an outer suburb of Stockholm, not a satellite town, was planned by MARKELIUS in 1949 and began to be built in 1953. It has something of the informality and freshness of a carnival. Among the more recent buildings of note in Sweden those by ERSKINE should be mentioned – his Ski Resort hotel at Borgafjäll of 1948–54 and his Stockholm University library, students' centre and sports hall of 1973–83.

Swiss architecture. Switzerland has all the architectural advantages and disadvantages of a position between three larger countries (Germany, France and Italy): the advantage of variety of styles, the disadvantage of little visual identity.

The country is uncommonly rich (given its small size) in early buildings. At Romainmôtier a small, aisleless C5 church with two transeptal porticos (in the English sense of the word) has been excavated, and a larger church consecrated in 753 and still of the same archaic plan. Chur has the C8 east end of St Lucius with a ring-crypt and above it three parallel apses on Italian Early Christian precedent. The same east end is at St Martin at Chur, Müstair and Disentis. The famous ideal plan for the monastery of St Gall is of *c.* 820 (the surviving church and library are C18).

The earliest Romanesque churches are inspired by Burgundy and especially the second church of Cluny. They are the third building of Romainmôtier with a typically Burgundian antechurch, and Payerne. Both are C11. Schaffhausen on the other hand of the late C11 and early C12 looks to Germany and the chief German Cluniac centre Hirsau. The Romanesque style culminates in the cathedral of Basel, connected closely with Alsace. It contains a little of the early C11, but dates mostly from *c.* 1180 and later.

At that same time the cathedral of Lausanne had already been begun, and this as well as Geneva Cathedral are again orientated towards France and now a Gothic France. Lausanne Cathedral in particular actually belongs to the Burgundian school of the C13. The principal Late Gothic churches on the other hand are an outlier of south Germany: Berne Minster (1421 onwards), St Oswald at Zug (1478 onwards) and St Leonard at Basel (1489 onwards).

It is understandable that the Renaissance appears first in the cantons bordering on Italy. The portal of St Salvator at Lugano of 1517 is close to Como in style. Of later C16 buildings it is enough to refer to the three-storeyed courtyard arcades of the Ritter House at Lucerne (1556–61) and to the Geltenzunft (1578) and Spiesshof (late C16) at Basel, both more classical than such buildings usually are in Germany. The Spiesshof in particular with its SERLIANA windows is indeed closely dependent on SERLIO.

The C17 gives a mixed impression. There is the fascinating Gothicism of the church of the Visitandes at Fribourg, a quatrefoil in plan but with the most intricate rib vaults (1653–6), there is the Zürich Town Hall, still Renaissance rather than Baroque, though as late as 1694–8, and there are the beginnings of a German Baroque in such a church as that of Muri, designed by MOSBRUGGER and begun in 1694. Its centre is a spacious octagon. Mosbrugger then designed the spatially complex Einsiedeln abbey church (1719–23).

The C18 in Switzerland stands under the sign of the contrast between the dazzling and melodramatic south German Baroque (abbey church of St Gallen of 1748–60 by Peter THUMB and others) and the cool restrained

French Dix-huitième (private houses, Geneva). There is in this of course also a contrast between Catholic and Protestant. Typically Protestant churches of unusual interior are the entirely French Temple at Geneva (1707–10 by Vennes), and Holy Ghost, Berne (1726–9 by Schildknecht). The church at Berne is oblong and has four entries in the middle of the four sides and as its only asymmetrical accents a (German) west tower and the pulpit inside close to the east end. The cathedral of Solothurn of 1762 onwards (by G. M. Pisoni) is mildly classicist, the noble west portico of Geneva Cathedral of 1752–6 (by Count ALFIERI) much more radically so. But the most exactingly neo-classicist building of the late C18 in Switzerland is the town hall of Neufchâtel of 1782–90, by Pierre-Adrien Pâris (1745–1819).

For the C19 the most interesting series of buildings are the *hôtels*, but they have not yet been sufficiently studied. For the C20 Switzerland contributed good architecture in the pre-first-war years (Badischer Bahnhof, Basel, by Curjel & Moser, 1912–13), outstanding EXPRESSIONISM of the same and the immediate post-first-war years, e.g. Goetheanum Dornach, 1913 and again after a disastrous fire 1923–8, by Rudolf Steiner (1861 1925), and much good and early work in the INTERNATIONAL MODERN of the twenties and thirties. Some of the churches were highly influential abroad, e.g. St Anthony, Basel (1925–31), by Karl Moser (1860–1936). LE CORBUSIER, who was born at La Chaux-de-Fonds, contributed one block of flats at Geneva (1931–2) and the Centre Le Corbusier at Zürich (1964–6). Max BILL's domestic work in wood of the 1940s was remarkable, but

his most distinguished building is in Germany (Hochschule für Gestaltung, Ulm, 1953–5). Two late Expressionist buildings are of note: the pilgrimage church at Neviges (1963–8) by Gottfried BÖIIM and the church centre at Hérémence (1963–71) by Walter-Maria Förderer (b. 1928). More recently the so-called Ticino School made its name internationally with such distinguished small buildings as the Casa Tonino, Torricella, of 1972–4, by Bruno Reichlin (b. 1941) and Fabio Reinhart (b. 1942), and especially work by Mario BOTTA.

Synagogue. A Jewish place of worship, in origin a meeting-house, not a temple. The earliest of which traces survive seem to have developed from the ancient Roman BASILICA, like EARLY CHRISTIAN churches. The Ark of the Covenant (*Aron Hakodesh*), for the Scrolls of the Law, originally had no fixed position but a niche (as at Dura Europos) or an apse (as at Beth Alpha) became usual, generally in front of the end wall. Later the Ark and the reading desk were raised on steps (*see* TEBAM). Architecturally, synagogues have adopted the styles current wherever they were built – Romanesque, Gothic, Renaissance, Baroque, Rococo, etc. The C14 Gothic synagogue in Prague, the Altneuschule, is one of the oldest to survive intact. Erich MENDELSOHN's domed synagogue in Cleveland, Ohio, 1945, is one of the most recent notable examples.

J. S. M. Chiat, *Handbook of Synagogue Architecture*, Chicago 1982; C. H. Krinsky, *Synagogues of Europe. Architecture, History, Meaning*, Cambridge, Mass., London (1985) 1987.

Synclastic. Of a surface, having curvatures in the same sense (concave or convex) in all directions through any point, as in a simple DOME and in contrast to an ANTICLASTIC surface.

Synthronon. In Early Christian and Byzantine churches, the bench or benches reserved for the clergy in the semicircle of the apse or in rows on either side of the BEMA.

Systyle. With an arrangement of columns spaced two diameters apart. *See also* ARAEOSTYLE; DIASTYLE; EUSTYLE; PYCNOSTYLE.

t

T'a, *see* PAGODA.

Tabernacle. A canopied recess to contain an image; an ornamental receptacle for the consecrated host, usually in the form of a miniature building placed on an altar in a Catholic church; the portable shrine in which the Jewish Ark of the Covenant was housed.

Tablinum. In ancient Roman architecture, a room with one side open to the ATRIUM or central courtyard.

TAC (The Architects' Collaborative), *see* GROPIUS, Walter.

Taenia, *see* TENIA.

Tahoto, *see* PAGODA.

Takeyama, Minoru (b. 1934), *see* JAPANESE ARCHITECTURE.

Talenti, Francesco (*fl.* 1340–69). Florentine architect who completed the windowed upper stories of the campanile after he succeeded Andrea PISANO there in *c.* 1343. From 1350 he was *capomastro* at the Duomo (*see* ARNOLFO DI CAMBIO), of which little was built until after 1357, to an enlarged and modified plan by Talenti; his final design of 1366–7 included the octagon (*see* BRUNELLESCHI). Francesco Talenti's son Simone (1340/45–81) was the principal architect of the Loggia dei Lanzi, Florence (1376–82).

Trachtenberg 1971; White 1987.

Tall building, *see* SKYSCRAPER.

Taller de Arquitectura, *see* BOFILL, Ricardo.

Talman, William (1650–1719), WREN's most distinguished contemporary, was the leading country-house architect until eclipsed by VANBRUGH. Little is known about him personally, though he seems to have been difficult and quarrelsome. His country houses are by far the largest and most lavish of their period in England, and display a mixed French and Italian Baroque character. They were very influential, e.g. in the use of giant pilasters with architrave and frieze to frame a façade, the cornice alone continuing across. Thoresby (1683–5, destroyed), the south and east front of Chatsworth (1687–96), Dyrham Park (1698–1704), Dorchester House, Surrey (*c.* 1700), and the new front at Drayton (*c.* 1701) were his main works, all country houses. He probably designed the state apartments at Burghley House, Northants (1688, destroyed). He succeeded Hugh MAY as Comptroller of the Office of Works in 1689, serving under Wren, whose design for Hampton Court he probably revised and altered in execution.

J. Harris, *W.T. Maverick Architect*, London 1982.

Tambour. 1. The core of a Corinthian or Composite CAPITAL. 2. The circular wall carrying a DOME or CUPOLA (*see* DRUM).

Tange, Kenzo (b. 1913), studied at Tokyo University 1935–8, then joined the office of Kunio MAYEKAWA, but returned to Tokyo University 1942–5 as a graduate. His mature buildings are all dramatically plastic: the Kagawa prefectural offices at Takamatsu (1958), with a ruthlessly expressed post-and-beam structure; the waterfront Dentsu offices at Osaka (1960); the Atami Gardens Hotel at Atami (1961), meticulously furnished by Isamu Kenmochi; the challenging Kurashiki (1960), standing four-square and quakeproof; St Mary's Roman Catholic Cathedral, Tokyo (1965), a cruciform arrangement of paraboloids; and the joyful Golf Club at Totsuka (1962), in which an upswept traditional roof is typically contrasted with aluminium curtain walls. With Yoshokatsu Tsuboi as engineer, Tange designed the magnificent tensile catenary roof spanning the 15,000-seat National Gymnasium for the Tokyo Olympic Games in 1964. Tange's leadership of the younger generation principally results from his research work into town planning at Tokyo University, the absence of which has reduced Japan's expanding industrial cities to a critical state of congestion. Tange's plan for Tokyo (1960) shows a logical hierarchy of rapid transit roads within connecting ring roads, enclosing environmental areas of high-density housing; his idea was to extend the city in this way on piles over Tokyo Bay. He won the international competition for replanning Skopje in Yugoslavia (1965), with a system of multi-purpose blocks. He has designed prototypes of these for the Dentsu building and Tsukiji area, Tokyo (1965), with flying bridges clad in criss-cross concrete grilles, and for the Yamanashi broadcasting centre, Kofu (built 1966–7), which is held together by sixteen cylindrical towers of lifts and services. Tsuboi was engineer for Dentsu, and Fugaku Yokoyama for the astonishing Yamanashi project. In 1967 Tange was also appointed (with Uzo Nikiyama) master planner of the international exhibition of 1970 at Osaka. Thereafter he changed course, and in his recent buildings, e.g. Akasaka Prince Hotel, Tokyo (1983), visual delicacy and metallic precision replace his former plastic exuberance.

Banham 1976; H. R. von der Möll *et al.*, *K.T.*, Zürich 1978.

Tarsia. A form of mosaic or inlay made up of different coloured woods popular in C15–C16 Italy especially for the decoration of studies and small rooms in palaces and for the choirs of churches.

Tas-de-charge. The lowest courses of a vault or arch, laid horizontally and bonded into the wall.

Tatlin, Vladimir (1885–1953). Tatlin began and ended his career as a painter, but became famous as pioneer of abstract sculpture, theatre designer and creator of a single major architectural model, one of the most visionary, perhaps notorious of modern times; his activity provided much of the inspiration for CONSTRUCTIVISM. Acquaintance with Picasso's early collages (1913) inspired his 'counter-reliefs', utilizing *objets trouvés*, that take on architectonic significance in his décor (with G. Yakulov) for the Moscow Café Pittoresque (1917). He was closely associated with the literary Futurists, for whom artistic and political revolution were complementary. In 1919 he embarked on his project for a monument to the Third International: a gigantic building, spanning the River Neva, in the form of a double skew spiral of open-work girders, with revolving halls suspended at various levels. Unrealized and probably unrealizable, this great symbol of revolutionary modernism – an 'answer' to the Eiffel Tower – was endlessly discussed, and several scale models have been constructed. Tatlin's organic theories of art and society led after 1930 to many years' work on *Letatlin*, a glider with movable wings, and to various utilitarian projects and educational activities. But his 'culture of materials' smacked of aestheticism to extreme Constructivists and of formalism to traditionalists, and he became a lonely figure; from the mid-1930s his only public activity was in theatre design, and from *c.* 1944 until 1962 his heritage was virtually ignored in Russia. [R. R. Milner-Gulland]

J. Milner, *V.T. and the Russian Avant-Garde*, New Haven and London 1983; L. A. Zsadova (ed.), *T.*, London 1988.

Taut, Bruno (1880–1938). A pupil of Theodor Fischer, he settled in Berlin in 1908 and was first noticed for his highly original glass pavilion at the 1914 WERKBUND exhibition in Cologne, a polygonal building with walls of thick glass panels and a glass dome, the elements set in lozenge framing (a SPACE-FRAME). In the years of the wildest Expressionism he wrote his *Alpine Architektur* (1917–18, English edn 1972) and *Die Stadtkrone* (1919) and designed fantastic buildings for imprecisely formulated purposes. Later he developed functional theories for mass-housing, e.g. his Britz housing, Hufeisen, Berlin, 1925–31, with Martin Wagner (1885–1957). After 1933 he emigrated to Japan (1933–6) and then to Turkey (1936–8).

R. H. Bletter, *B.T. and Paul Schubart's Vision. Utopian Aspects of German Expressionist Architecture*, New York 1979; I. Boyd-White, *B.T. and the Architecture of Activism*, Cambridge, Mass., 1983.

Taut, Max (1884–1967). He worked with MIES VAN DER ROHE 1906–11 and then with his brother Bruno, 1914–31. His most notable buildings were concrete-frame office blocks in Berlin, e.g. Verband der Deutschen Buchdrucker (1922–5) with Mart STAM. Some of his post-1945 housing is notable, e.g. Reuther Siedlung, Bonn (1949–52), and August-Thyssen Siedlung, Duisberg (1955–64).

M.T., exh. cat., Berlin 1964.

Taylor, Sir Robert (1714–88), son of a mason-contractor, trained as a sculptor under Cheere and visited Rome *c.* 1743. Though sufficiently successful to be commissioned by Parliament to design and carve the monument to Captain Cornwall in Westminster Abbey (1744), he soon abandoned sculpture for architecture and by assiduity and businesslike methods quickly built up a large practice. He and PAINE were said to have 'nearly divided the practice of the profession between them' during the mid-century. He was highly competent and worthily carried on the neo-Palladian tradition of BURLINGTON and KENT; indeed he went some way beyond it in his late work. Most of his work has been destroyed, notably that in the Bank of England, which included his last and by far his most original work, the Reduced Annuities Office, a top-lit hall with circular clerestory carried on shallow segmental arches which anticipate his pupil SOANE. (The Court Room of 1767–70 has been reconstructed.) Asgill House, Richmond (1758–67), and Stone Building, Lincoln's Inn, London (begun 1775), are the best of his surviving buildings. He was knighted when sheriff of London, 1782–3, and left the bulk of his large fortune to found the Taylorian Institute in Oxford.

M. Binney, *Sir R.T.: From Rococo to Neo-Classicism*, London 1984.

Tebam. A dais or rostrum for the reader in a synagogue. Adjoining it to the east is the Chief Rabbi's seat.

Tecton. A team established in London in 1932 by Berthold Lubetkin (1901–90) to which among others LASDUN belonged. They did the Highpoint Flats I and II at Highgate, London, in 1936 and 1938, the Finsbury Health Centre in 1938–9, and the blocks of flats in Rosebery Avenue in 1946–9. Their most popular work was for the London Zoo (1934–8). The details here of freely moulded concrete are prophetic of the 1950s. The group disbanded in 1948.

P. Coe and M. Reading, *Lubetkin and T. Architecture and Social Commitment*, London and Bristol 1981.

Telamones, *see* ATLANTES.

Telford, Thomas (1757–1834), son of a Scottish shepherd, trained as a mason, worked in Edinburgh, then in London, and by 1784 had been made supervisor of works on Portsmouth Dockyard. In 1788 he became surveyor to the county of Shropshire. He built several churches in the county, notably

Bridgnorth (1792), and several bridges, notably Buildwas Bridge (1795–8, demolished), which was of iron (the Coalbrookdale Bridge had been built in iron in 1777) and had a 130 ft span. In 1793 work started on the Ellesmere Canal, and Telford was put in charge. He built the Chirk Aqueduct at Ceiriog, 700 ft long and 70 ft high (1796–1801), and the Pont Cysylltau Aqueduct, 1,000 ft long and 120 ft high (1795–1805). In 1800 he suggested the rebuilding of London Bridge with a single span of 600 ft. Telford was responsible for other canals (Caledonian, 1804; Göta, 1808), for the St Katherine's Docks (1827; *see* HARDWICK), for fen drainage, for roads, and for further bridges, including the beautiful Dean Bridge, Edinburgh, of stone (1829), the Menai Straits Suspension Bridge, of iron, with a 530 ft span (1819–26), and the Conway Suspension Bridge, also of iron (1821–6).

L. T. C. Rolt, *T.T.*, London 1958; Colvin 1978; A Penfold (ed.), *T.T. Engineer*, London 1980.

Temanza, Tommaso (1705–89). The most sensitive of Venetian neo-Palladians. His masterpiece is the little church of the Maddalena, Venice (begun 1763), with its interior freely derived from PALLADIO's chapel at Maser. He wrote *Le vite dei più celebri architetti e scultori veneziani* (1778).

Meeks 1966; Howard 1987; Wittkower 1982.

Template. The block of stone set at the top of a brick or rubble wall to carry the weight of the JOISTS or roof-trusses; also called a *pad stone*.

Temple, Raymond du (active *c.* 1360–1405), *see* RAYMOND DU TEMPLE.

Tengbom, Ivar (1878–1968), *see* SWEDISH ARCHITECTURE.

FIG. 84. *Term*

Tenia. The small moulding or fillet along the top of the ARCHITRAVE in the Doric ORDER.

Tenon, *see* MORTICE AND TENON JOINT.

Term. A pedestal tapering towards the base and usually supporting a bust; also a pedestal merging at the top into a sculptured human, animal, or mythical figure; also called *terminal figures* or *termini* (*see also* CARYATID). *See* Fig. 84.

Terrace. 1. A level promenade in front of a building. 2. A row of attached houses designed as a unit, flat-faced and flush with those on either side, a feature of Victorian England, though their kinship with Georgian Bath and London is apparent, e.g. Bedford Square, London.

S. Muthesius, *The English Terrace House*, New Haven and London 1982.

Terracotta. Fired but unglazed clay, used mainly for wall covering and ornamentation as it can be fired in moulds.

Terragni, Giuseppe (1904–43). Leading exponent of Italian RATIONALISM, he began with a five-storey concrete block of flats in Como, 'Novocomun', in 1927–8. His masterpiece, the Casa del Fascio, Como, followed in 1932–6. The Asilo Sant'Elia, Como (1936–7), the Casa Bianca, Seveso (1936–7), the Casa del Fascio, Lissone (1938–9), and the Casa Giuliani, Como (1939–40), are only slightly less distinguished. His Danteum library and museum project for Rome (1937) was never built.

B. Zevi (ed.), *G.T.*, Bologna 1980; A. F. Marcianò, *G.T. L'opera completa 1925–1943*, Rome 1987; S. Germer and A. Preis, *G.T. 1904–43, Moderne und Faschismus in Italien*, Munich 1990; T. Schumacher, *Surface and Symbol, G.T. and the Italian Rationalist Movement*, Princeton 1990.

Terrazzo. A flooring finish of marble chips mixed with cement mortar and laid *in situ*; the surface is then ground and polished.

Terry, Quinlan (b. 1937), *see* ENGLISH ARCHITECTURE.

Tessellated. Of a cement floor or wall covering, having TESSERAE embedded in it.

Tessenow, Heinrich (1876–1950), *see* GERMAN ARCHITECTURE.

Tesserae. The small cubes of glass, stone, or marble used in MOSAIC.

Tessin, Nicodemus, the elder (1615–81), a leading Baroque architect in Sweden, was born at Stralsund and

439

began by working under Simon LA VALLÉE. In 1651–2 he made a tour of Europe and in 1661 was appointed city architect of Stockholm. His main work is Drottningholm Palace (begun 1662), built in an individual Baroque style, derived from Holland, France, and Italy. His other works include Kalmar Cathedral (1660), Göteborg Town Hall (1670), the Carolean Mausoleum attached to the Riddarholm church, Stockholm (designed 1671), and numerous small houses in Stockholm. His son Nicodemus the younger (1654–1728) succeeded him as the leading Swedish architect. Trained under his father, he travelled in England, France, and Italy (1673–80), and completed his father's work at Drottningholm. His main building is the vast royal palace in Stockholm (begun 1697), where he adopted a Baroque style reminiscent of, and probably influenced by, BERNINI's Louvre project.

Paulsson 1958; B. R. Kommer, *N.T. der Jüngere und das Stockholmer Schloss*, Heidelberg 1974.

Tester. A canopy suspended from the ceiling or supported from the wall above a bed, throne, pulpit, etc.

Tetrastyle. Of a PORTICO with four frontal columns.

Teulon, Samuel Sanders (1812–73). Goodhart-Rendel called Teulon a rogue-architect, together with Edward Buckton Lamb (1806–69) and Bassett Keeling (1836–86). Teulon was a Gothicist, but the motifs he used – motifs of the late C13 and early C14 – are treated freely and with a heaviness not to be found *c.* 1300. His churches are domineering, his details coarse. These qualities are already fully exhibited in so early a mansion as Tortworth Court

(1849–52), Avon. Teulon's most overpowering country house is Shadwell Park, Norfolk (1856–60), an addition to an older building. Of the churches designed by Teulon the most characteristic are St Mary, Ealing (1866–73), St Stephen, Hampstead (1869–76), and Silvertown (1859), all in London, though St John, Huntley, Gloucestershire (1861–3), is more enterprising.

M. Saunders in Brown 1985.

Thai architecture. The earliest surviving buildings are KHMER, dating from C9–13 in north-east and central Thailand. A distinctive architecture with some Khmer elements but more inspiration from SRI LANKA, whence Theravada Buddhism had been introduced as the state religion, was developed in the kingdom founded in the mid C13 at Sukhothai. Domestic buildings were of wood and have perished, but there are imposing remains of STUPAS (called *chedis* in Thai), PRANGS and monastic halls, notably at Sukhothai, Sisatchanalai and Kaemphaeng Phet. They are built of LATERITE and/or brick and were originally covered with stucco modelled in relief and painted. In an independent northern kingdom with its capital at Chiang Mai (founded 1297) a similar style was evolved from the same roots, although the most notable monument is quite different – Wat Chet Yot, Chiang Mai, a free interpretation of the great Buddhist shrine at Bodh Gaya in India, a cube decorated with stucco reliefs and supporting five spires (begun 1455). From the mid C16 this area was occupied by the Burmese, who influenced its later architecture. The rest of Thailand was gradually united in the kingdom founded in 1350 at Ayutthaya and extending at times into Burma and Cambodia as well as down the Malay peninsula. Numerous *chedis* survive, also some monastic halls – for daily prayers, ordinations and display of images – with timber-framed tiled roofs. After the sack of Ayutthaya by the Burmese in 1767 a new capital was founded some 50 kms to the south at Bangkok where, from the early C19, the royal palace and monastic complexes were built in a richer and more grandiose style, later adopted throughout the kingdom. The most notable buildings are monastic halls with very steeply pitched tiled roofs constructed in such a way that the uppermost, with the longest ridge-pole, seems to float above the others that extend the building at either end. Prominent upward-curving *naga*, or snake-head finials, terminating the ridge-poles are often elaborately carved and add notably to the buildings' distinctive character. Such halls are still being built on the same model, though ferro-concrete for supports and iron girders for beams are now used instead of stuccoed brick and wood. Western techniques and (for secular buildings) historical styles were introduced in the late C19 as part of a royally instigated campaign of modernization. But nearly all houses continued to be built of wood in traditional vernacular styles, varying from region to region (many examples are preserved in the open-air museum, 'Ancient City', near Bangkok). The INTERNATIONAL MODERN style was introduced in the 1950s for office buildings, shops, hotels, etc. A version taking local conditions into account has been developed by the Western-trained Sumet Jumsai (b. 1939). Other Thai architects have adopted POST-MODERNISM with sometimes astonishing results – in

Bangkok a high-rise block of flats crowned by a Palladian villa.

Thatch. A roof covering of straw, reeds or other vegetable material, held in place by stones, ropes or poles, or interspersed with layers of mud. Thatch of even the best materials lasts no more than eighty years. Very little is known about ancient methods of thatching.

Davey 1961; R. West, *Thatch. A Manual for Owners, Surveyors, Architects and Builders*, London 1987.

Theatre. A place for viewing dramas or other spectacles, open-air in ancient Greece and Rome, usually covered in Europe since the C16.

Thermae. In Roman architecture public baths, usually of great size and splendour and containing libraries and other amenities as well as every provision for bathing. Their remains in Rome were closely studied by architects from PALLADIO onwards and had great influence on planning.

Thermal window. A semicircular window divided into three lights by two vertical mullions, also known as a Diocletian window because of its use in the Thermae of Diocletian, Rome. Its use was revived in the C16 especially by PALLADIO and is a feature of PALLADIANISM.

Tholos. A beehive-shaped chamber of stone and roofed by CORBELLING, e.g. 'Treasury of Atreus' at Mycenae.

Thomas, William (1799–1860), *see* CANADIAN ARCHITECTURE.

Thomas of Canterbury (*fl.*1324–31), *see* MICHAEL OF CANTERBURY.

Thomon, Thomas de (1754–1813). Leading neo-classical architect in

Russia. He was born in Berne, probably studied under LEDOUX in Paris and completed his training in Rome *c.* 1785. In 1789 he followed the Comte d'Artois into exile to Vienna, where he found a patron in Prince Esterhazy. From there he went to Russia. His designs for the Kazan Cathedral were rejected (1799) but in 1802 he became architect to the Court of Alexander I in St Petersburg and immediately obtained important commissions – the Grand Theatre (1802–5, demolished) and the Bourse (designed 1801–4, built 1805–16), a Tuscan Doric temple with blank pediments, great segmental lunettes and flanking *columna rostrata*. The Bourse is his masterpiece and a major neo-classical building of the most severe and radical kind, more advanced than anything in Paris at that date. In 1806–10 he built a Doric mausoleum to Paul I in the park at Pavlovsk. He published *Recueil de plans et façades des principaux monuments construits à St Petersburg* (1808, republished in Paris 1819 with an amended title).

Hamilton 1983.

Thomson, Alexander (1817–75), lived and worked in Glasgow, and was in practice from about 1847. He was known as 'Greek' Thomson, and rightly so, for to be a convinced Grecian was a very remarkable thing for a man belonging to the generation of PUGIN, SCOTT, and RUSKIN. The formative influence on his style was SCHINKEL rather than English Grecians. This comes out most clearly in such monumental terraces as Moray Place (1859), where the purity of proportion and the scarcity of enrichment suggests a date some thirty years earlier. His churches, on the other hand, though essentially Grecian, are far from pure: they exhibit an admixture of the Egyptian, even the Hindu, as well as a boldness in the use of iron, which combine to produce results of a fearsome originality. The three churches – all United Presbyterian – are the Caledonian Road church (1856), the St Vincent Street church (1859), and the Queen's Park church (1869, burnt 1942). They are among the most forceful churches of their date anywhere in Europe. Equally interesting are Thomson's warehouses, especially the Egyptian Halls.

A. Gomme and D. Walker, *The Architecture of Glasgow*, London 1969; Crook 1972; Pevsner 1972; R. McFadzean, *The Life and Works of A.T.*, London 1979.

Thon, Konstantin Andrejewitsch (1794–1881), *see* RUSSIAN ARCHITECTURE.

Thornton, William (1759–1828), was an English physician who emigrated from the West Indies to the USA and became an American citizen in 1788. He designed the Philadelphia Library Company building in 1789 and in 1793 won the competition for the Capitol, Washington, though his runner-up, Stephen Hallet, was put in charge of the execution of his designs. The foundation stone was laid by George Washington in the same year. Hallet modified Thornton's designs and was replaced in 1795 by James HOBAN who proposed further alterations and was dismissed in 1798. But by 1800 the north wing containing the Senate had been completed substantially to Thornton's designs. In 1803 LATROBE took charge and completed the south wing by 1807. He also supervised the rebuilding after the Capitol had been sacked and burnt by British troops in 1814.

Thumb

Latrobe followed Thornton's designs for the exterior though not for the interior. In 1827 BULFINCH connected the two wings, again following the original design. (The dome and further extensions were added by T. U. WALTER, 1857–63.) Thornton also designed the Octagon House, Washington (1800), and Tudor Place, Washington (1815).

E. Stearns and D. N. Yerkes, *W.T. A Renaissance Man in the Federal City*, Washington, DC, 1976.

Thorpe, John (*c.* 1565–1655), an unimportant clerk in the Office of Works and later a successful land surveyor, was not, as is sometimes thought, the architect of Longleat, Kirby, Wollaton, Audley End, and other great Elizabethan and Jacobean houses. Plans and a few elevations of these and many other Elizabethan buildings are in a volume of drawings by him in the Sir John Soane Museum, London.

Colvin 1978; Summerson 1983.

Through stone, *see* PARPEN.

Thrust. The outward force of an ARCH or VAULT counterbalanced if necessary by BUTTRESSES.

Thumb, Michael (d. 1690). He was born at Bezau in the Bregenzerwald and was a founder of the Vorarlberger school of architects which included, beside the Thumb family, the MOSBRUGGER family and the BEER family. The latter intermarried with the Thumb family. The long series of buildings of this school, mostly for Benedictine monasteries in south-west Germany and Switzerland, was eventually to mark the triumph of German over Italian elements in south German Baroque architecture (i.e. over the domination of such Italians as

ZUCCALLI and VISCARDI from the Grisons). Michael Thumb's pilgrimage church of Schönenberg near Ellwangen (begun 1682) is a prototype of the Vorarlberger Münsterschema – a pillared HALL CHURCH, the internal buttresses being faced with pilasters and projecting so deep as to form chapels, usually connected above by a gallery. He continued the type at the Premonstratensian abbey church of Obermarchtal (1686–92). Both churches are notable for their plainspoken dignity. His son Peter (1681–1766) worked as a foreman for Franz BEER from 1704 and married his daughter. He later occupied an influential position at Constance. As an architect he developed a much more sophisticated manner than his father and achieved a wonderfully light and sparkling Rococo unity of effect in his best interiors. In 1738 he built the library of the monastery of St Peter in the Black Forest, successfully adapting the Vorarlberger Münsterschema of internal buttresses with columns and a balcony swirling round them. His masterpiece is the pilgrimage church of Birnau on Lake Constance (1746–58), where he had the collaboration of Feuchtmayer on the decoration. At the great Benedictine abbey of St Gallen he worked for eleven years (1748–58) but the extent of his contribution to the abbey church is uncertain. He was probably mainly responsible for the great central rotunda and he probably influenced the design of the two-towered east façade, built by Johann Michael BEER in 1760–69. For the library in the monastery at St Gallen (1758–67) he employed the same system as at St Peter in the Black Forest.,

Christian Thumb (1683–1726) worked with Michael Thumb at

443

Schönenberg and at Obermarchtal, where he continued after Michael's death in 1690. His masterpiece is the Schlosskirche at Friedrichshafen (1695–1701). He probably collaborated with Andreas Schreck at the abbey church at Weingarten (1716–24).

Hitchcock 1968; H. M. Gubler, *Der Barockmeister P.T. 1681–1766*, Sigmaringen 1972; N. Lieb and F. Dieth, *Die Vorarlberger Barock Baumeister*, Munich and Zürich (1960) 1983.

Thura, Laurids de (1706–59), *see* DANISH ARCHITECTURE.

Tibaldi, Pellegrino Pellegrini (1527–96). He began as a painter in Bologna but became the protégé of St Carlo Borromeo, who established him in Milan where he worked mainly as an architect from 1564 onwards, succeeding ALESSI as the leading architect. His more notable works include the Collegio Borromeo at Pavia, begun 1564; the austere Canonica cortile in the Archiepiscopal Palace in Milan, commissioned 1565 and begun *c.* 1572; S. Fedele in Milan, begun 1569 (the year after the Gesù in Rome) and S. Sebastiano, Milan, begun 1576. He was made chief architect of Milan Cathedral in 1567 and built the crypt under the choir and the high barriers between the choir and the ambulatory. From 1586 to 1594 or 1595 he was in Spain, working as a painter at the Escorial.

Heydenreich and Lotz 1974; A. Mazzocca and G. Panizza, *P.P. L'architettura*, Milan 1990.

Tibetan architecture. The earliest permanent buildings were c8 Buddhist temples and STUPAS (e.g. Samye near Lhasa). In the C11 Buddhism was revived or reintroduced and many monastic complexes date back to this period, notably at Toling and Mangnang. Indian and, after the C13, Chinese influences are evident (the latter in the form of roofs), but a highly distinctive Tibetan style was developed in connection with tantric Buddhism. No architecture is more obsessively symbolic, in orientation, planning (based on mandalas), proportions and the number of columns, openings, storeys, etc., as well as ornament. Tibetan stupas, called *chorten*, have interior spaces and vary in form: that begun 1425 in the Palkhor monastery, Gyantse, is unique – octagonal in plan, four storeys high with 73 interior shrines. The famous Potala dominating Lhasa was built mainly in the C17 (on the site of earlier structures) as the palace of the Dalai Lama and a monastery with a very severe exterior rising to nine storeys and with innumerable richly decorated – though often very small – rooms inside.

Tie-beam, *see* ROOF.

Tierceron, *see* VAULT.

Tigerman, Stanley (b. 1930). Chicago architect who has exploited the metaphorical possibilities of architecture, e.g. Daisy House, Porter, Indiana (1977), for the owner of a striptease club. He published *The Architecture of Exile* (New York 1988).

R. Miller and D. M. Habel, *Versus. An American Architect's Alternatives. S.T.*, New York 1982.

Tile-hanging. A wall covering of overlapping rows of tiles on a timber structure, like SLATE-HANGING.

Tiles. The use of glazed pottery tiles for pavement or wall decoration is of ancient Near Eastern origin, like that of GLAZED BRICKS. Glazed tiles survive

FIG. 85. Timber-framing

KEY:

1. Wall-plate	5. Window sill
2. Post	6. Cross-rail
3. Brace	7. Sill
4. Stud	8. Plinth

from C9 BC Ashur (East Berlin) and C7 BC Susa (Louvre, Paris). They were not used by the ancient Greeks or Romans but were revived on a large scale with the rise of Islam, and both the interior and exterior walls of mosques were frequently clad with them, as were also domes. In the C15, tilework was transplanted from Islamic North Africa to Spain, where it is called ALICATADOS, and also Portugal (*see* AZULEJOS). The export to Italy of Spanish tiles led to their production there and in Holland and France in the C15–17. After a decline in the early C19 tiles returned to favour in both Europe and the USA in the late C19, notable use being made of them for exterior wall cladding by ART NOUVEAU architects, e.g. Otto WAGNER.

A. Barendsen, *Tiles*, London 1967; A. Vallet, *La Céramique architecturale*, Paris 1982.

Timber-framing. A method of construction (called colloquially *half-timbering*) in which walls are built of interlocking vertical and horizontal timbers. The spaces are filled with non-structural walling of wattle and daub, lath and plaster (known as nogging), etc. Sometimes the timber-frame is covered by plaster, boarding laid horizontally (*see* WEATHERBOARDING) or MATHEMATICAL TILES to make it seem brick-built. *See also* BEAM; BRACE; BRESSUMER; CROSS-RAIL; CRUCKS; JETTY; JOISTS; POSTS; SILL; STUDS; WEALDEN HOUSE. *See* Fig. 85.

R. W. Brunskill, *Timber Building in Britain*, London 1985; R. J. Brown, *Timber-Frame Buildings of England*, London 1986.

Tithe barn, *see* BARN.

Todt, Fritz (1891–1942), *see* GERMAN ARCHITECTURE.

Toko-no-ma. The alcove in which a painting or print is hung and a flower vase placed in a Japanese house.

Toledo, Juan Bautista de (d. 1567), philosopher and mathematician as well as architect, spent many years in Italy and for some time before 1559 was architect to the Spanish Viceroy in Naples. In 1562 he was appointed architect of the Escorial, drew up the entire ground plan, but built only the two-storeyed Court of the Evangelists, modelled on SANGALLO's Palazzo Farnese, Rome, and the vast severe south façade.

Kubler and Soria 1959; G. Kubler, *Building the Escorial*, Princeton 1982.

Toltec architecture, *see* MESO-AMERICAN ARCHITECTURE.

Tomb-chest. A chest-shaped stone coffin, the most usual medieval form of funerary monument. *See also* ALTAR-TOMB.

Tomé, Narciso (active 1715–42), began as a sculptor with his father and brothers on the façade of Valladolid University (1715). His famous Transparente in Toledo Cathedral (1721–32) is the most stupefying of all Baroque extravaganzas in spatial illusionism. It goes farther than anything invented by Italian Baroque architects and is exceptional even for Spain.

Kubler and Soria 1959.

Torana. Indian gateway, especially one on the enclosure of a Buddhist STUPA.

Torralva, Diogo de (1500–1566), the leading Portuguese Renaissance architect, was the son-in-law of ARRUDA but abandoned his rich MANUELINE style for one much simpler, sterner, and more Italianate. His main work is the cloister of the Cristo Monastery, Tomar (1557), with the SERLIAN MOTIF used as an open arcade on the upper floor. He designed the apse for the Jeronimite Church at Belem (1540–51). Several other buildings have been attributed to him, notably the octagonal church of the Dominican Nuns at Elvas (1543–57).

Kubler and Soria 1959; Smith 1968.

Torroja (y Miret), Eduardo (1899–1961). Spanish concrete engineer and architect and a pioneer of SHELL construction. The Algeciras Market Hall (1933) made his name internationally, followed by his Zarzuela racecourse grandstand and the SHELL roof of the Fronton Recoletos (destroyed), both of 1935. The sinuous roof of the Las Cortes football stadium, Barcelona, of 1943 is also remarkable. He published *Philosophy of Structure* (Berkeley, California, 1958) and *The Structures of E.T.* (New York 1958).

J. Joedicke, *Shell Architecture*, New York 1963.

Torus. A large convex moulding of semicircular profile, e.g. at the base of a column. *See also* ASTRAGAL; Fig. 68.

Touch. A soft black marble quarried near Tournai, used chiefly for monuments.

Tourelle. A turret CORBELLED out from the wall.

Tower house. A medieval Scots type of fortified house with the main hall raised above the ground and with one or more storeys above. It continued into the C17 with modifications and elaborations, e.g. Glamis Castle. *See also* SCOTTISH ARCHITECTURE.

Town, Ithiel (1784–1844), *see* DAVIS, Alexander Jackson.

Townsend, Charles Harrison (1851–1928). English Late Victorian 'rogue' architect whose small-scale public buildings challenge those of his more successful, pompous contemporaries such as Aston WEBB. Outstanding are the Bishopsgate Institute (1892–4), Whitechapel Art Gallery (1895–9) and, most original of all, the Horniman Museum (1898–1901), all in London.

Service 1977.

Trabeated. Constructed on the POST AND LINTEL principle, as Greek buildings were, in contrast to ARCUATED.

Tracery. The ornamental intersecting work in the upper part of a window, screen, or panel, or used decoratively in blank arches and vaults. The earliest use of the term so far traced is in Sir Christopher WREN, the medieval word being *form-pieces* or *forms*.

In windows of more than one light in Early Gothic churches the SPAN-

DREL above the lights is often pierced by a circle, a quatrefoil, or some such simple form. This is known as *plate tracery*. Later, and first at Reims (1211), the circle is no longer pierced through a solid spandrel; instead the two lights are separated by a moulded MULLION and the mouldings of this are continued at the head forming bars of circular, quatrefoil, etc., forms and leaving the rest of the spandrels open. This is called *bar tracery*, and throughout the later Middle Ages it was one of the principal decorative elements of churches. The patterns made by the bars were first the simple geometrical forms already indicated (*geometrical tracery*), later fantastical forms including double curves (*flowing tracery*), and later still – at least in England – plain, vertical, arched panels repeated more or less exactly (*panel tracery*). In Germany, France, and Spain forms similar to the English flowing tracery became the rule in the late Middle Ages. With the end of the Middle Ages tracery generally disappeared.

Bar tracery, introduced at Reims and brought to England *c.* 1240, consists of intersecting ribwork made up of slender shafts continuing the lines of the mullions up to a decorative mesh in the window-head.

Flowing tracery is made up of compound or OGEE curves, with an uninterrupted flow from curve to curve; also called *curvilinear* or *undulating tracery*. It was used from the beginning of the C14 in England, and throughout the C15 in France, where it rapidly became fully developed and FLAMBOYANT, with no survival of the geometrical elements of the early flowing tracery of England.

Geometrical tracery is characteristic of *c.* 1250–1300 and consists chiefly of circles or foiled circles.

Plate tracery (C13)

Geometrical (bar) tracery (C13)

Intersecting tracery (C13–14)

Reticulated tracery (C13–14)

Curvilinear or flowing tracery (C14)

Late C14 tracery

Panel tracery (C14)

FIG. 86. *Tracery*

447

In *intersecting tracery* each mullion of a window branches into curved bars continuous with the mullions. The outer arch of the window being of two equal curves (*see* ARCH), all subdivisions of the window-head produced by these tracery bars following the curves of the outer arch must of necessity be equilateral also. The bars and the arch are all drawn from the same centre with a different radius. Such a window can be of two, or usually more, lights, with the result that every two, three, or four lights together form a pointed arch. Additional enrichment, e.g. circles, CUSPING, is always of a secondary character. The form is typical of *c.* 1300.

Kentish tracery is FOILED tracery in a circle with barbs between the foils.

Panel tracery is Perpendicular tracery formed of upright, straight-sided panels above the lights of a window, also called *rectilinear*.

Plate tracery is a late C12 and early C13 form where decoratively shaped openings are cut through the solid stone infilling in a window-head.

Reticulated tracery, a form used much in the early to mid C14, is made up entirely of circles drawn at top and bottom into OGEE shapes resulting in a net-like appearance.

In *Y-tracery* a mullion branches into two forming a Y shape; typical of *c.* 1300.

See Fig. 86.

Trachelion. The neck of a Greek Doric column, between the SHAFT-RING and HYPOTRACHELIUM.

Tracing house. The house or room in which the medieval mason drew or scratched details of mouldings and other details as instructions to those working under him (*super moldas in trasura*). The tracing could also be done on sand on the floor of the room. *See also* LODGE AND LODGE BOOKS.

Tramello, Alessio (*c.* 1470/5–*c.* 1529). He worked for most of his life in and around Piacenza in a style which owes much to the Milanese buildings of BRAMANTE. His more notable buildings include S. Sisto (1499) and the centrally planned Madonna di Campagna (1522), both at Piacenza. In 1525 he was consulted about the Steccata at Parma which had been begun in 1521 by Giovanfranceso Zaccagni, who resigned in 1525.

Heydenreich and Lotz 1974.

Transenna. An openwork screen or lattice, usually of marble, in an Early Christian church.

Transept. The transverse arms of a cross-shaped church, usually between NAVE and CHANCEL, but also occasionally at the west end of the nave as well, and also doubled, with the eastern arms farther east than the junction of nave and chancel. The latter form is usual in English Gothic cathedrals.

Transitional architecture. A term usually referring to the period of transition from the ROMANESQUE to the GOTHIC, or in Britain from the NORMAN to the EARLY ENGLISH style. Sometimes details of the later styles are used on the general forms of the earlier.

Transom. A horizontal bar of stone or wood across the opening of a window or across a panel.

Transparente, *see* TOMÉ, Narciso.

Transverse arch, *see* VAULT.

Tread, *see* STAIR.

Trefoil, *see* FOIL.

Trezzini or **Tressini** (spelt in Russian Trezini), Domenico (1670–1734), a Swiss, was one of the first foreign architects to come to Russia at the invitation of Peter the Great; he was engaged (by the Russian ambassador in Copenhagen, where he had been working on Frederick IV's palace) just before St Petersburg was founded (1703), and with his characteristic adaptability and compliance to Peter's wishes he was extremely active in the city's early construction. Of the numerous buildings his atelier designed, there survive: Peter's modest Summer Palace (1711); the Cathedral of SS. Peter and Paul (1714), replacing a wooden predecessor and likewise sporting a dramatic flèche, gilded and topped with an angel, designedly higher than the Moscow belfry 'Big John' – the cathedral as a whole a somewhat awkwardly articulated domed basilica with prominent volutes on the west front, though it is now hard to envisage it with its original Baroque detail (note the magnificent carved-wood ICONOSTASIS by Zarudny); and Trezzini's masterpiece, the 'Twelve Colleges' – i.e. Government ministries, subsequently housing the University – strung end-to-end across the tip of Vasilyev Island, each with a colossal order of pilasters under a high hipped roof, linked originally by a continuous open gallery and a 600-metre long corridor. His younger relative (once thought to be his son) Pietro Antonio (in Russia 1726–51) was also a busy architect, notable for pioneering the reintroduction of the Old Russian five-domed centralized church-plans to Petersburg Baroque. [R. R. Milner-Gulland]

Hamilton 1983.

Triangulation. The achievement of rigidity, or at least the prevention of completely free relative movement, in an assembly of struts and ties, by arranging them in a continuous series of triangles in one or more planes.

Tribune. 1. The APSE of a BASILICA or basilican church. 2. A raised platform or rostrum. 3. The GALLERY in a church.

Triclinium. The dining-room in an ancient Roman house.

Triconch. Clover-leaf or trefoil in plan, e.g. a church ending in three apsidally ended arms at right-angles to one another.

Triforium. An arcaded wall-passage facing on to the NAVE, at a level above the arcade and below the CLERESTORY windows (if there are any). The term is often wrongly applied to a TRIBUNE or GALLERY.

Triglyphs. Blocks separating the METOPES in a Doric FRIEZE. Each one has two vertical grooves or glyphs in the centre and half grooves at the edges. If the half grooves are omitted (as occasionally in post-Renaissance architecture) the block is called a diglyph. See Fig. 66.

Trilithon. A prehistoric monument consisting of a horizontal MEGALITH resting on two upright ones, as at Stonehenge.

Trim. The framing or edging of openings and other features on a façade or indoors. It is usually of a colour and material (wood, stucco, or stone) different from that of the adjacent wall surface.

Triumphal arch. A free-standing monumental gateway of a type which originated in Rome in the C2 BC in richly decorated temporary structures erected by Roman magistrates for such festive occasions as the triumphs decreed to victorious generals. From the late C1 BC similar structures were erected in stone, and often richly decorated with sculpture, as city gates or as entrances to *fora* but also frequently as urban decorations with no more than a commemorative purpose: some twenty survive from the reign of Augustus, mostly in Italy and Gaul. They were built throughout the Roman Empire and numerous AD C2 and C3 examples survive in North Africa. There are two main types – those with a single archway (Arch of Augustus at Susa, Piedmont, 9–8 BC, Arch of Titus in Rome, *c*. AD 82) and those with a large archway flanked by two small archways (Arch of Septimius Severus in Rome, AD 203, and Arch of Constantine in Rome, AD 315). Sometimes they seem to have been designed primarily as richly ornamented bases for gilt bronze statues. The form was revived in the Italian Renaissance, once again as a type of temporary festival architecture, which remained popular until the late C18. Many were built in stone during the C18 and C19 often in direct imitation of Roman prototypes, e.g. Arco di S. Gallo, Florence, by J.-N. JADOT DE VILLE ISSY (1739), Arc du Carrousel, Paris, by PERCIER and FONTAINE (1806–7), Arc de Triomphe, Paris, by CHALGRIN (1806–35), the Marble Arch, London, by J. NASH (1828), etc. By extension the term 'triumphal arch' is sometimes applied to structures with one large and two small doorways, e.g. the choir screen in a medieval church. A Chinese type of triumphal or commemorative arch is called a P'AI LOU.

M. P. Nilsson, *The Origin of the Triumphal Arch*, Lund 1932; U. West-fehling, *Triumphbogen in 19 und 20 Jahrhunderts*, Munich 1975; G. A. Mansuelli *et al.*, *Studi sull'arco onorario romano*, Rome 1979.

Triumphal column. A massive column erected as a public monument. The first were set up in Republican Rome but these appear to have been relatively small and simple in comparison with Trajan's column completed AD 113 and 125 ft high. It is adorned with a continuous spiral of low relief carving illustrating Trajan's two Dacian wars. This and the similar Antonine Column (or Column of Marcus Aurelius), probably completed in AD 193, set a pattern for such monuments. Their progeny included the columns of Theodosius the Great of 386 and of Arcadius of 403, both in Constantinople (and both destroyed), and in much later times the pair of columns flanking the Karlskirche in Vienna by FISCHER VON ERLACH (begun 1716) and the Vendôme Column in Paris with bronze reliefs (1806–10, thrown down 1871 and re-erected 1874). The majority of commemorative columns, though often on bases imitated from the Roman prototypes, have plain shafts, e.g. the Monument, London (1671–7) by WREN, the Washington Monument in Baltimore (1814–29) by Robert MILLS, and Nelson's Column, Trafalgar Square, London, designed by William Railton (1839–42).

G. Becatti, *La colonna coclide istoriata*, Rome 1960.

Troost, Paul Ludwig (1878–1934), *see* GERMAN ARCHITECTURE.

Trophy. A sculptured group of arms or armour used as a memorial to victory, sometimes with floreated motifs intermingled to form a FESTOON.

Trulli, *see* BEEHIVE HOUSE.

Trumeau. The stone MULLION supporting the middle of a TYMPANUM of a doorway.

Truss. A number of timbers framed together to bridge a space or form a BRACKET, to be self-supporting, and to carry other timbers. The trusses of a roof are usually named after the particular feature in their construction, e.g. king-post, queen-post, etc. *See* ROOF.

Tschumi, Bernard (b. 1944), *see* FRENCH ARCHITECTURE.

Tudor arch, *see* ARCH.

Tudor flower. An upright ornamental motif, rather like a formalized ivy leaf, often used in English Late Gothic and Tudor architecture, especially for BRATTISHING.

Tufa. The commonest Roman building stone, formed from volcanic dust; it is porous and grey.

Tumulus. A mound covering an ancient burial or tomb, usually of earth but sometimes of stones. The latter is called a *cairn*. Earth mounds, round or elongated, are called *barrows* or *long barrows*, and in England belong to the Early and Middle Neolithic period, though burial under a round mound continued occasionally until Roman and Anglo-Saxon times.

Tunnel vault, *see* VAULT.

Turkish architecture. The *c.* 7000 BC Neolithic settlements at Catal Hüyük and Hacilar are among the earliest known, consisting of rectangular mud-brick buildings juxtaposed. Access is through the roofs only. Impressive remains of Hittite buildings survive at Bogazkoy (*c.* 1360 BC), notably monumental gateways with figurative reliefs. C7 BC Urartian temples and fortresses at Altintepe and Kofkalesi are impressive. (For later pre-Islamic architecture in Turkey, *see* HELLENISTIC ARCHITECTURE; BYZANTINE ARCHITECTURE.)

The battle of Manzikert in 1071 opened Anatolia to Islam, but not until the turn of the C13 were the Seljuks sufficiently established to begin sponsoring monumental architecture. Notable among Seljuk buildings in Anatolia are the mosque of Khuand Khatun, Kayseri (1237–8), the mosque and hospital, Divrik (1228–9), the Cifte Minareli MADRASA, Erzerum (1253), and the Karatay *madrasa* (1252) and Ince Minareli *madrasa* (1258) at Konya. With the advent of the Ottomans a distinctive style developed typified by lead-covered domes, pencil-thin minarets and lavish tilework and marble relief decorations on limestone. The Yeshil mosque, Iznik (1378–92), the Ulu mosque (1395–9) and Yeshil mosque (1421), Bursa, and especially the Uch Sherefeli mosque, Edirne (1438–47), are outstanding early Ottoman buildings. After the conquest of Constantinople in 1453 Hagia Sophia and other Christian churches were converted into mosques and Byzantine influence is felt in later Ottoman architecture, notably in that of the greatest Ottoman architect, SINAN, of whose numerous buildings the Shezade mosque (1544–8), Suleymaniye mosque (1551–8) and Sokollu Mehmet mosque (1570–74) in Istanbul and his great Selimiye mosque (1569–74) in Edirne may be mentioned. Of later Ottoman mosques that of Sultan Ahmed in Istanbul (1610–16) is outstanding. Of secular Ottoman buildings the kiosk is typical, though the famous Chinli Kiosk, Istanbul (1472), is unique. Most domestic architecture was of wood and little survives. Of c19 buildings the Dolmabahçe Palace, Istanbul (1852), is an unusually lavish example of an orientalized Louis XVI and French Empire style.

In the early c20 the Italian *stile Liberty* architect Raimondo d'ARONCO (1857–1932) and the German functionalist Bruno TAUT both worked in Turkey, but the most notable contemporary buildings are by the Turkish architect Sedad Hakki Eldem (b. 1908), whose work ranges from his rather stern but imposing university buildings in Istanbul (1942) and Ankara (1943) to the notable Social Security Agency Complex at Zehreh, Istanbul (1962–4), and the genial Koç Foundation, Ataturk Library, Istanbul (1973). His luxurious waterside country houses or *yalis* along the Bosphorus – e.g. the Rahmi Koç villa at Tarabya (1975–80) – and his embassy buildings at Ankara (1964–77) are also notable. The distinctly Turkish–Ottoman character which marks his work is all the more effective for being so unforced.

Turnpike stair, *see* STAIR.

Turret. A very small and slender tower.

Tuscan order, *see* ORDER.

Tusking. Stones left projecting from a wall for subsequent bonding into another wall.

Tylman van Gameren (before 1630–1706). Dutch architect chiefly responsible for introducing the Baroque style into Poland, where he settled in 1665. His three centralized churches in Warsaw – Holy Sacrament (1688), St Casimir (1688–9) and St Boniface (1690–92) – reveal him as a somewhat stolid, classicizing master of the Baroque. St Anne, Cracow (1689–1705), is livelier, but this may be due to collaboration with Baldassare Fontana. He rebuilt the palace of Prince Sanguszko, Warsaw (enlarged c18), designed Castle Nieborów (1680–83) and completed the Krasinski Palace, Warsaw (1682–94).

Hempel 1965; S. Mossakowski, *T.G.*, Breslau, Warsaw and Cracow 1973.

Tympanum. The area between the LINTEL of a doorway and the arch above it; also the triangular or segmental space enclosed by the mouldings of a PEDIMENT.

U

Undercroft. A vaulted room, sometimes underground, below an upper room such as a church or chapel.

Ungers, Oswald Mathias (b. 1926), *see* GERMAN ARCHITECTURE; NEO-RATIONALISM.

United States architecture. The earliest buildings were those erected by Spanish settlers in what is now New Mexico, e.g. Governor's Palace, Santa Fe (1610–14), and San Estaran, Acoma (c. 1630). In C17 New England architecture was modest, first Dutch in inspiration, then English, e.g. St Luke's, Isle of Wight County, Virginia (1632), Bacon's Castle, Surrey County, Virginia (c. 1655, rebuilt), Capen House, Topsfield, Massachusetts (1683). Original and unique to New England were the meeting houses, square halls serving both secular and religious functions. The Old Ship Meeting House, Hingham, Massachusetts (1681 with C18 additions), survives. The most complete surviving example of Colonial architecture is Williamsburg, Virginia, though it is much restored – the Capitol (1701–5, rebuilt 1928–34), the College of William and Mary (1716–1859) and the Palace of the Governors (1749–51, rebuilt 1928–34). In Philadelphia the Independence Hall of 1731–91 was rebuilt by STRICKLAND in 1832. C18 churches are entirely Georgian, often influenced in their spires by GIBBS. Houses are equally Georgian, in the country as well as the towns, e.g. Colony House, Newport, Rhode Island (1739), by Richard Munday (d. 1740) (*see also* Peter HARRISON and Samuel McINTIRE). But in both houses and churches timber plays a prominent part alongside, or instead of, brick. Among the best churches are Christ Church, Philadelphia (1727 and 1754); Christ Church, Cambridge (1759–61); St Michael, Charleston (1753); and the Baptist Church at Providence (1775). The finest Early Georgian house is Westover, Virginia (1726–30). From the mid C18 notable examples are Mount Airey, Virginia (perhaps by John ARISS), Mount Pleasant, Philadelphia, and Whitehall, Maryland, with giant Corinthian portico. Later porticos tend to have attenuated columns (Homewood, Baltimore). As town *ensembles* Salem and Nantucket (Massachusetts) and Charleston (South Carolina) may be singled out. The United States has still quite a few C18 public buildings: Old State House, Boston (1710); Faneuil Hall, Boston (1742); and so to the Capitol in its original form (1792) and the Boston State House by BULFINCH (1795–8). The earliest university buildings are also Georgian: at Yale (1750–52); and then Thomas JEFFERSON's University

453

of Virginia at Charlottesville (1817–26), the first American CAMPUS, i.e. with buildings composed round a spacious lawn. Jefferson's own house, Monticello, was built 1770–79, remodelled 1796–1808. In the wide diffusion of this Georgian style in the late C18 and early C19 such books as *The Country Builder's Assistant* (1797), *The American Builder's Companion* (1806) and others by Asher Benjamin (1773–1845) played a significant part. His works are illustrated with contemporary American buildings and he assumed that his readers would probably build in wood.

The Greek Revival starts with LA-TROBE's Doric Bank of Pennsylvania of 1799–1801. From 1803 he did much in a Grecian taste inside the Capitol in Washington (begun by William THORNTON and finished by T. U. WALTER). His finest work, comparable with that of SOANE in elegance and originality, is Baltimore Cathedral (begun 1804). But for this building he also submitted a Gothic design; a country house of his (Sedgeley, Philadelphia) was Gothic too. His near contemporary Maximilien GODEFROY was similarly ambidextrous. However, except in church design, Gothic made slow progress, and the most thoroughly Grecian years are the 1820s and 1830s, with HAVILAND and STRICKLAND in Philadelphia, WILLARD in Boston, the big government buildings in Washington by HADFIELD, HOBAN and, above all, MILLS and several state capitols by Town & DAVIS (North Carolina, Connecticut, Illinois, Indiana, Ohio) and Strickland (Tennessee). Davis experimented in many styles, including the Egyptian and the Old-English cottage. The most prominent Gothic churches are RENWICK's

Grace Church, New York (1846), UPJOHN's Church of the Holy Trinity, Brooklyn (1841–6), and others in New York by Minard Lafever (1798–1854). (*See also* WARE & VAN BRUNT; CRAM; GOODHUE.) Henry Austin (1804–91) deserves a special mention; if ever there was a rogue architecture, his New Haven railway station (1848–9) is it. Its style cannot be derived from any clear direction. The USA has been rich in such highly gifted eccentrics and loners, e.g. Frank FURNESS, Bernard MAYBECK and Bruce GOFF.

Already in the second quarter of the century certain American specialities began to appear. One is hotels, especially of the size and type that became standard in Europe later (*see* Isaiah ROGERS and George Browne POST); another is such technical equipment as bathrooms and lifts.

The United States moved from a marginal to a central position with the work of H. H. RICHARDSON, both in the field of the massive uncompromising commercial building for which his style was a French-inspired Romanesque (Marshall Field Wholesale Warehouse, Chicago, 1885–7) and in the field of the informal, comfortable, moderately dimensioned private house (Sherman House, Newport, 1874–6 – *see* SHINGLE STYLE). Even more independent are some of the houses designed in their early years by McKIM, Mead & WHITE, notably one at Bristol, Rhode Island (1887, demolished). Otherwise that firm is principally remembered for their Italian Renaissance Revival (Villard Houses, New York, 1885; Boston Public Library, 1888–95), Colonial Revival, and also Palladian Revival, the latter on a grand scale (Pennsylvania Station,

New York, 1906–10, demolished). Their assistant Henry Bacon (1861–1924) and disciple John Russell Pope (1874–1937) carried on the tradition into the C20 with, respectively, the Lincoln Memorial (1917) and Jefferson Memorial (1934–43) in Washington, where Paul CRET worked in a freer BEAUX ARTS style during the same years.

Meanwhile, however, Chicago had established a style of commercial architecture all her own and vigorously pointing forward into the C20 (CHICAGO SCHOOL). It started from the introduction of the principle of steel framing (*see* SKYSCRAPER) in 1883 with JENNEY's Home Insurance building (demolished) and reached its climax in such buildings as the Tacoma (1887–8) by HOLABIRD & ROCHE, the Marquette (1894) by the same firm, the Masonic Temple (1892, demolished) by BURNHAM and ROOT and, most personal, the Wainwright building at St Louis (1890) by SULLIVAN. With Sullivan's Carson, Pirie & Scott Store, Chicago (1899–1904), a totally unhistoricist style of unrelieved verticals and horizontals was reached, though Sullivan was perhaps at his most original in his feathery, decidedly ART NOUVEAU ornament.

Sullivan's principal pupil was Frank Lloyd WRIGHT, the greatest American architect to date, who bridges the whole period from *c.* 1890 to nearly 1960. His early PRAIRIE houses culminated in his first, brilliantly original, style of sweeping horizontals and of intercommunication between spaces inside a house and between inside and outside spaces. Almost contemporaneously in California another pupil of Sullivan, Irving GILL, developed a new domestic style which was taken

further, again partly under Wright's inspiration, by GREENE & GREENE and others, including Rudolph SCHINDLER. In the East the influence of Europe still predominated with the so-called INTERNATIONAL MODERN style, introduced by such prominent buildings as the Philadelphia Savings Fund building by HOWE & Lescaze (1929–32 – relatively late in European terms) and the McGraw-Hill building, New York, by Raymond HOOD (1931); but the spectacular development of C20 architecture in the United States belongs to the years after the Second World War. The flowering was fostered by such distinguished immigrants as GROPIUS, MIES VAN DER ROHE, NEUTRA, and BREUER. The first stage belongs to the rational, cubic, crisp so-called International Modern and culminates in Mies van der Rohe's houses and blocks of flats of *c.* 1950 onwards and most of the work of SKIDMORE, OWINGS & MERRILL, whose so-called 'Corporate Modernism' marked the 1950s and 1960s in the north-east and mid-West. In California some remarkable and internationally influential experiments were made in INDUSTRIALIZED BUILDING, most notably by Charles EAMES in 1949 for John Entenza's Case Study programme. Case Study House No. 18, Beverly Hills (1955–8), by Craig Ellwood (b. 1922), and the work of SCBSD (State of California Building Systems Development) under Ezra Ehrenkrantz (b. 1933) are also notable.

The second stage was that of the neo-sculptural, anti-rational, highly expressive style current in many countries in the 1960s. The United States is richer than any other part of the world in such buildings, from a love of novelty as well as from a prosperity that encourages display. Trends within this trend cannot here be separated: they run from the powerful concrete curves of Eero SAARINEN to the smooth professionalism of Ieoh Ming PEI. They include such mercurial and controversial figures as Philip JOHN-SON, Paul RUDOLPH, Louis KAHN, Minoru YAMASAKI, Kevin ROCHE and Robert VENTURI. The intellectual sophistication of the latter has earned him the (perhaps unwanted) position of high priest to POST-MODERNISM, whose chief exponents in the USA are Michael GRAVES, Charles MOORE, Robert A. M. STERN and Stanley TIGERMAN. Partly in reaction to this trend the NEW YORK FIVE emerged in 1969, of whom Peter EISENMAN and Richard MEIER are notable. Outside these two currents flourish several architects of note: Frank O. Gehry (b. 1929), Cesar Pelli (b. 1926) and James Wines (b. 1932), who launched the disruptive group SITE in 1969.

A postscript on American technical achievements: first FULLER's geodesic domes, of which the largest has a diameter of 384 ft; second the even higher SKYSCRAPERS of New York: Woolworth by GILBERT, 1913, 792 ft; Empire State by Shreve, Lamb & Harmon, 1930–32, 1,250 ft; World Trade Center by Yamasaki, 1970–74, 1,350 ft; and the Sears Tower, Chicago, by Skidmore, Owings & Merrill, 1974, 1,454 ft; thirdly and finally roadworks. The American freeways, parkways, trunk roads, turnpikes have no competitors. Their boldness and their intricacies of junction are stupendous. But they place the motor vehicle above man. They led to the invention by Victor GRUEN of the out-of-town shopping centre or supermarket marooned in an enormous car-park.

Unwin, Sir Raymond (1863–1940). The leading English town-planner of his day and the man who – in partnership from 1896 to 1914 with Barry Parker (1867–1941) – translated into reality the GARDEN CITY scheme conceived by Ebenezer HOWARD. The 'First Garden City', as the company for its realization was actually called, was Letchworth in Hertfordshire (begun 1903). Unwin published *The Garden City* (London 1905). However, while the growth of Letchworth did not progress as rapidly or as smoothly as had been anticipated, two garden suburbs did extremely well, the Hampstead Garden Suburb outside London (begun 1907), and Wythenshawe outside Manchester (begun 1927). The Hampstead Garden Suburb in particular must be regarded as the *beau idéal* of the garden city principles of domestic and public planning, with its formal centre – the two churches and the institute designed by LUTYENS – its pattern of straight main and curving minor vehicular roads and its occasional pedestrian paths, its trees carefully preserved and its architectural style controlled in no more than the most general terms of a free neo-Tudor. Unwin also showed his sense of subtle visual planning effects in his *Town Planning in Practice*, first published in 1909, and a textbook to this day.

Mumford 1961; W. L. Creese, *The Search for Environment. The Garden City: Before and After*, New Haven and London (1960) 1966, and *The Legacy of R.U. A Human Pattern for Planning*, Cambridge, Mass., and London 1967; F. Jackson, *Sir R.U. (1863–1940)*, London 1985.

Upjohn, Richard (1802–78), was born

at Shaftesbury, where he was later in business as a cabinet-maker. He emigrated to America in 1829 and opened a practice as an architect at Boston in 1834. His speciality was Gothic churches: the first came in 1837, and the principal ones are Trinity Church, New York (1841–6), an effort in a rich Anglo-Gothic, and Trinity Chapel, West 25th Street (1853), also Anglo-Gothic. He built in other styles (Trinity Building, New York, 1852, is Italianate). Upjohn was first president of the American Institute of Architects.

E. Upjohn, *R.U. Architect and Churchman*, New York 1939; P. B. Stanton, *The Gothic Revival and American Church Architecture. An Episode in Taste 1840–56*, New York 1968.

Urban renewal. The replanning of existing towns or centres to bring them up to date and to improve amenities and traffic circulation.

Utzon, Jørn (b. 1918), *see* AUSTRALIAN ARCHITECTURE; DANISH ARCHITECTURE.

V

Vaccarini, Giovan Battista (1702–68), was born in Palermo. He studied under Carlo FONTANA in Rome and settled in Catania (1730), where his exuberant Sicilian Rococo style is seen in the façade of the cathedral (begun 1730), Palazzo Municipale (1732), Collegio Cutelli (1754), and S. Agata (begun 1735).

G. Alajmo Alessandro, *G.B.V. e le sconosciute vicende della sua vita,* Palermo 1950; A. Blunt, *Sicilian Baroque,* London 1968.

Vaccaro, Domenico Antonio (1681–1750). With SANFELICE, a leading Neapolitan architect of his day. His small ingeniously planned churches are notable, e.g. S. Maria delle Grazie, Calvizzano, near Naples, of *c.* 1743. But he is known mainly for his maiolica cloister at S. Chiara, Naples (1739–42).

Blunt 1975.

Valadier, Giuseppe (1762–1839), archaeologist, town-planner, and a prolific though rather reactionary architect. His main buildings are neo-Palladian rather than neo-classical, e.g. interior of Spoleto Cathedral (1784), interior of Urbino Cathedral (1789), and façade of S. Rocco, Rome (1833), though the boldly simple S. Pantaleo, Rome (1806), is more in tune with his times. His masterpiece is the reorganization of Piazza del Popolo, Rome, for which

he published a design in 1794 and which he began in 1813 (executed 1816–20).

P. Marconi, *G.V.,* Rome 1964.

Valle, Gino (b. 1923), *see* ITALIAN ARCHITECTURE.

Vallin de la Mothe, Jean-Baptiste Michel (1729–1801), came to Russia in 1759 at the invitation of Count I. I. Shuvalov to teach architecture at the newly founded St Petersburg Academy of Arts. The Academy itself (1765), very French and rather cold in contrast with the near-contemporary Russian Palladian buildings in its neighbourhood, was apparently designed by de la Mothe in collaboration with A. F. Kokorinov (1726–72), Director of the Academy, and himself a considerable architect whose work was already adumbrating the turn away from the Baroque. For the Academy building – the first prominent neo-classical structure of Petersburg – they seem to have reworked a plan previously commissioned from J.-F. BLONDEL, de la Mothe's uncle. But de la Mothe had earlier (1761) produced a more humdrum but historically significant contribution to the overthrow of RASTRELLI's Baroque in his Market Building on Nevsky Prospekt. Continuing his role of neo-classical pioneer, de la Mothe built the 'small' Hermitage next to the Winter Palace for Catherine (1764), and undertook the construction of the great classical archway to the port area of 'New Holland' begun by CHEVAKINSKY. He left Russia in 1776. [R. R. Milner-Gulland]

Hamilton 1983.

Van Alen, William (1882–1954), *see* ART DECO.

Van Brunt, Henry (1832–1903), *see* WARE & VAN BRUNDT.

Van Campen, Jacob (1595–1657), *see* CAMPEN, Jacob van.

Van de Velde, Henry (1863–1957), *see* VELDE, Henry van de.

Van den Broek, Johannes Hendrik (1898–1978), *see* DUTCH ARCHITECTURE.

Van Eyck, Aldo (b. 1918), *see* DUTCH ARCHITECTURE.

Vanbrugh, Sir John (1664–1726), soldier, adventurer, playwright, and herald, was also the outstanding English Baroque architect. His father was a Flemish refugee who became a rich sugar-baker and married the daughter of Sir Dudley Carleton. He was brought up as a gentleman and commissioned in the Earl of Huntingdon's regiment in 1686. In 1690 he was arrested in Calais for spying and imprisoned for two years, part of the time in the Bastille. After his release he took London by storm with his witty and improper comedies *The Relapse* and *The Provok'd Wife*. Then he switched his talents to architecture – 'without thought or lecture', said Swift – having been invited by the Earl of Carlisle to try his hand at designing Castle Howard (1699). Lord Carlisle also had him appointed Comptroller at the

Office of Works (1702), and thus he became, without any training or qualifications, WREN's principal colleague. But he turned out to be an architect of genius. The Tories later deprived him of his Comptrollership, but he was reinstated after the death of Queen Anne and knighted (1714). Witty and convivial, a friend of Tonson and Congreve and a member of the Kit Cat Club, he lived on familiar terms with the great men who became his clients.

His style derives from Wren at his grandest – e.g. Greenwich Hospital – and probably owes much to HAWKSMOOR, his assistant from 1699 onwards. But every building that he designed is stamped with his own unique personality – expansive, virile, and ostentatious, more Flemish than English and often rather coarse and theatrical. Castle Howard (1699–1726) is an amazing trial of strength by a young undisciplined genius. His great opportunity came in 1705 at Blenheim Palace, the nation's gift to Marlborough in honour of his victories. Here he had almost unlimited funds at his disposal and the whole megalomaniac conception suited his temperament perfectly. He was always at his best on the largest possible scale, and his genius for the dramatic and heroic, for bold groupings of masses and for picturesque recessions and projections and varied skylines had full play.

His style reached sudden maturity at Blenheim – indeed, English Baroque architecture culminates there – and it changed little afterwards. The best of his surviving houses are Kimbolton (1707–9), King's Weston (1711–14), Seaton Delaval (1720–28), Lumley Castle (entrance front and interior alterations, 1722), and Grimsthorpe (north range only, c. 1722–6). He said he wanted his architecture to be 'masculine' and to have 'something of the Castle Air', and nowhere does his peculiar version of the Baroque come closer to the massiveness of a medieval fortress than at Seaton Delaval. Sombre and cyclopean, this extraordinary house is unlike any other building in England or anywhere else. His strong sense of the picturesque led him to further and more explicit medievalisms elsewhere, notably at his own house at Greenwich (after 1718), which is castellated and has a fortified-looking round tower. He seems here to have foreshadowed the romantic spirit of later Gothic revivals.

Colvin 1978; Summerson 1983; G. Beard, *The Work of J.V.*, London 1986; K. Downes, *Sir J.V. A Biography*, London 1987; C. Saumarez Smith, *The Building of Castle Howard*, London 1990.

Vanvitelli, Luigi (1700–1773), was born in Naples, the son of the painter Gasper van Wittel, studied painting as an architect only in the 1730s. He under his father in Rome, and emerged worked at Pesaro, Macerata, Perugia, Loreto, Siena, Ancona, and Rome (monastery of S. Agostino and remodelling of S. Maria degli Angeli) before he was summoned to Naples by Carlo III in 1751 to build the enormous 1,200-room palace at Caserta. This is the last great Italian Baroque building. Its immense internal vistas, ceremonial staircase and central octagonal vestibule rival the most extravagant stage-set in scenographic fantasy, though the exterior already veers towards neo-classical restraint. Almost equally impressive are his Chiesa dell'Annunziata (1761–82), Piazza Dante (1757–63), and twenty-five-mile-long Acquedotto Carolino (1752–64).

Blunt 1975; F. Strazzullo (ed.), *Le lettere di L.V.*, Galatina 1976–7; Wittkower 1982.

Vardy, John (1718–65). Friend and close associate of KENT, whose designs for the Horse Guards, London, he carried out (with W. Robinson, 1748 onwards). His most important surviving work is Spencer House, London (1756–65), an excellent example of PALLADIANISM freely interpreted.

Colvin 1978; Summerson 1983; R. White in Brown 1985.

Vasari, Giorgio (1511–74). A painter and author of the famous *Vite de' più eccellenti architetti, pittori e scultori italiani* (1550, revised 1568), which by its eulogistic account of MICHELANGELO exerted an important influence on architectural taste. As an architect he had a hand, with VIGNOLA and AMMANATI, in designing the Villa Giulia, Rome (1551–5). His most important independent work is the Uffizi, Florence (begun 1560), with a long narrow courtyard stretching down towards the river and closed by a range with two superimposed Serlian arcades – an adaptation of Michelangelo's Laurentian Library to external architecture – completed by BUONTALENTI, who designed the famous *tribuna* (1584). In his native town, Arezzo, he designed the abbey church of SS. Fiora e Lucilla (begun 1566), and the imposing Logge Vasariane (1573). In Florence his renovations of the interiors of S. Maria Novella in 1565–72 and S. Croce in 1566–84 were important. Following the ideas of the Council of Trent, he 'purified' them to create open, clarified interior spaces, removing the medieval screens, choir stalls, etc.

Heydenreich and Lotz 1974; L. Satkowski, *Studies on V.'s Architecture*, New York 1977.

Vásquez (Vázquez), Lorenzo (*fl.* 1489–1512), to whom the earliest works of the Renaissance in Spain are now attributed, was master mason to Cardinal Mendoza and for the Cardinal the Colegio de Santa Cruz at Valladolid, begun in 1486, was transformed in 1491 by Vásquez, with its Quattrocento frontispiece medallion. The next buildings in order of date were also commissioned by the Mendoza family: the palace at Cogolludo (probably 1492–5), with windows still floridly Late Gothic; the palace at Guadalajara (before 1507); and the castle of La Calahorra (1509–12). In the latter case, however, it is known that Michele Carlone of Genoa was called in to take charge. For other early major Renaissance designs in Spain *see* EGAS.

Kubler and Soria 1959.

Vásquez, Pedro Ramírez (b. 1919), *see* MEXICAN ARCHITECTURE.

Vauban, Sébastien le Prestre de (1633–1707). Architect, town-planner and the most famous of all military engineers. According to Voltaire he constructed or repaired the fortifications of 150 'places de guerre' and he was said to have directed some 53 sieges. A close friend of Louvois (minister of war 1666–91) and of Colbert, he became Commissaire Général des Fortifications in 1677. In 1703 he was made a Maréchal de France. His genius as a military engineer lay in the resourcefulness with which he used and adapted traditional means rather than in the invention of new ones. His ingenuity is well displayed at difficult sites, e.g. Mont-Louis in the Pyrenees and Mont-Dauphin and Château

Queyras on the Savoy frontier. But his most famous fortifications are those of Lille (1668–74), Maubeuge (1683–5) and Neuf-Brisach (1697–1708). Some of his fortresses were in effective military use up to the 1914–18 war, notably Langwy (built 1678). He laid out the new towns he brought into being, such as Neuf-Brisach, and occasionally designed individual buildings, e.g. the governor's house, church and arsenal at Lille and churches at Givet and Briançon. He restored the *châteaux* of Auney and Ussé. But his merit as an architect is best appreciated in the massive simplicity of such ramparts as those of Oléron, Gravelines and Bayonne and in his monumental gateways which range from the Baroque splendour of the Porte de Paris at Lille, enriched with columns, entablatures, trophies and sculptured panels, to the simple grandeur of the Mons Gate at Maubeuge. In these Vauban approached the noble severity and grandeur achieved by his contemporaries Libéral BRUANT and François BLONDEL. His memoirs, *Plusieurs maximes bonnes à observer pour tous ceux qui font bâtir*, contain a complete treatise on building. He also published *Véritable manière de bien fortifier. De Mr de Vauban* (Amsterdam 1702)

M. Parent and J. Verroust, *V.*, Paris 1971

Vaudoyer, Léon (1803–72). French architect. His *chef d'œuvre* is Marseilles Cathedral (begun in 1852), which combines convincingly a Romanesque plan with a Byzantine elevation and the polychrome horizontal striping of, e.g., Siena Cathedral.

Hitchcock 1977; Van Zanten 1987.

Vaudremer, Joseph-Auguste-Émile (1829–1914), after a training under the

Vault

FIG. 87. *Vault*

KEY:
a. Tunnel vault   c. Rib vault
b. Groin vault   d. Fan vault

1. Transverse rib   5. Tiercerons
2. Diagonal rib   6. Liernes
3. Transverse ridge-rib 7. Boss
4. Longitudinal ridge-rib

sober utilitarian architects Blouet and Gilbert, started with the large Santé Prison, Paris (1862 onwards), in the same spirit. However, in 1864 he was commissioned to build the church of St Pierre de Montrouge in Paris (1864–70), and here his very sobriety and directness made him choose the Romanesque rather than the Gothic style. The building must have impressed H. H. RICHARDSON. Romanesque also, but internally with much grander stone vaults, is Notre Dame, rue d'Auteuil, Paris (1876 onwards). The much larger and more famous Sacré Cœur on Montmartre is by Paul Abadie (1812–84) and was started in 1876. It is inspired by St Front at Périgueux, which Abadie disastrously restored.

Hitchcock 1977; *Entre archéologie et modernité. Paul Abadie architecte*, exh. cat., Paris 1988/9.

Vault. An arched ceiling or roof of stone, brick or concrete, sometimes imitated in wood or plaster.

Barrel vault, see tunnel vault.

Cloister vault, see domical vault.

Cross-vault, see groin vault.

Domical vault. A dome rising direct on a square or polygonal base, the curved surfaces separated by GROINS. *See* DOME. In America called a *cloister vault*. *See* Fig. 40.

A *fan vault* consists of solid concave-sided semi-cones, meeting or nearly meeting at the apex of the vault. The areas between are flat and, if the cones meet, form concave-sided lozenges. The cones and centres are decorated with panelling so as to give the appearance of a highly decorated rib vault. *See* Fig. 87.

A *groin vault* is produced by the intersection at right angles of two tunnel vaults of identical shape. *See* Fig. 87.

Handkerchief vault, see DOME.

Hyperbolic paraboloid vault, see HYPERBOLIC PARABOLOID ROOF.

Lierne. A tertiary rib, that is, one which does not spring either from one of the main springers or from the central BOSS. *See* Fig. 87. A *lierne vault* is a ribbed vault with liernes.

For *net vault* see definition under RIETH.

Parabolic vault. A thin shell covering, usually of reinforced concrete, of parabolic section, i.e. in form a cone cut parallel to one edge. Such vaults are light and little subject to tensional stresses. *See also* HYPERBOLIC PARABOLOID ROOF; SHELL.

A *ploughshare vault* or *stilted vault* has the wall ribs sprung from a higher level than the diagonal ribs, in order to increase the light from a clerestory window.

In a *quadripartite vault* one bay is divided into four quarters or CELLS.

A *rampart vault* is a wagon vault with abutments at different heights.

A *rib vault* is a framework of diagonal arched ribs carrying the cells which cover in the spaces between them. *See* Fig. 87.

Ridge-rib. The rib along the longitudinal or transverse ridge of a vault, at an angle of approximately 45° to the main diagonal ribs. *See* Fig. 87.

Sail vault, see DOME.

In a *sexpartite vault* one bay of quadripartite vaulting is divided transversely into two parts so that each bay has six compartments.

Shell vault, see SHELL.

A *stellar vault* is one with the ribs, liernes and tiercerons arranged in a star-shaped pattern.

Tierceron. A secondary rib, which springs from one of the main springers, or the central boss, and leads to a place on the ridge-rib. *See* Fig. 87.

A *transverse arch* separates one bay of a vault from the next. It can be either plain in section or moulded.

Tunnel vault (also called *barrel vault* and *wagon vault*). The simplest form of vault, consisting of a continuous vault of semicircular or pointed sections, unbroken in its length by cross vaults. BUTTRESSING is needed to ground the thrust, which is dispersed all along the wall beneath. Tunnel vaults can be subdivided into bays by transverse arches. *See* Fig. 87.

Wagon vault, see tunnel vault.

Vaulting shaft. The vertical member leading to the springer of a vault.

Vauthier, Louis (*c.* 1810–77), *see* BRAZILIAN ARCHITECTURE.

Vaux, Calvert (1824–95), *see* DOWNING, Andrew Jackson; OLMSTED, Frederick Law.

Vázquez, Lorenzo (*fl.* 1489–1512), *see* VÁSQUEZ, Lorenzo.

Velarium. An awning hung over a courtyard or, in ancient Rome, over an amphitheatre.

Velde, Henry van de (1863–1957). He was born at Antwerp of a well-to-do family and was first a painter influenced aesthetically by the Neo-Impressionists (Pointillists), socially by the ideals which at the time also inspired van Gogh. About 1890, under the impact of RUSKIN and MORRIS, he turned from painting to design and in 1892 produced the first works that are entirely his own and at the same time are entirely representative of ART NOUVEAU, the anti-historical movement just then emerging. They are works of typography and book decoration, with long flexible curves, and an appliqué panel called *The Angels Watch*. Their stylistic source seems to be the Gauguin of Pont Aven and his circle, especially Émile Bernard.

In 1895 van de Velde designed a house and furnishings at Uccle near Brussels for his own young family. It was his first achievement in architecture and interior design, and both now became his principal concerns. He was commissioned to design interiors for Bing's newly established shop L'Art Nouveau in Paris (1895) and then showed most of this work at an exhibition in Dresden (1897). In both centres its impact was great, but whereas reactions were largely hostile in France, they were enthusiastic in Germany, and so van de Velde decided to leave Brussels and settle in Berlin. In the next years he did much furnishing work for the wealthy and the refined, including the shop of the imperial barber (Haby, 1901). In 1901 he was called to Weimar as consultant on the coordination of crafts, trades, and good design. He furnished the Nietzsche-Archive there (1903), and rebuilt the Art School and the School of Arts and Crafts (1904, 1907), of which latter he became director. He also did the interior of the Folkwang Museum at Hagen (1901–2) and the Abbe Monument at Jena (1908).

His style is characterized by the long daring curves of Art Nouveau, which he endowed with a peculiar resilience, and in architecture also by the use of the curve rather than the angle – e.g. for roofs. For the Werkbund Exhibition at Cologne in 1914 (*see* GROPIUS; TAUT) he did the theatre, also with curved corners and a curved roof.

Being Belgian he left his job in Germany during the war, lived through restless years of émigré life and only in 1925 settled down again, now back in Brussels. However, the years of his great successes and his European significance were over. His late style is less personal, close to that of the Amsterdam School, notably his University Library, Ghent (1936), and the Kröller-Müller Museum at Otterlo in Holland, beautifully coordinated with the heath scenery around (1937–54).

He published *Déblaisement d'art* (Brussels 1894); *Aperçus en vue d'une synthèse d'art* (Brussels 1895); *Vom neuen Stil* (Leipzig 1907); and, posthumously, his autobiography, *Geschichte meines Lebens* (Munich 1962).

A. M. Hammacher, *Le Monde de H. van de V.*, Antwerp and Paris 1967; K. J. Sembach, *H. van de V.*, London 1989.

Velten, Jeger (1730–1801), *see* RUSSIAN ARCHITECTURE.

Venetian door. An adaptation of the SERLIANA to a doorway, i.e. with the central opening arched and flanked by tall narrow square-topped windows.

Venetian window, *see* SERLIANA.

Vennecool, Steven Jacobs (1657–1719), *see* DUTCH ARCHITECTURE.

Venturi, Robert (b. 1925). Leading American POST-MODERN architect in partnership since 1964 with John Rauch (b. 1930) and since 1967 with his wife Denise Scott-Brown (b. 1931) and later with Steven Izenour (b. 1930). His early buildings were small and built at low cost, notably his mother's house at Chestnut Hill, Pennsylvania (1961–5). In 1966 he published *Complexity and Contradiction in Architecture* in which he argued for complexity, contradiction, ambiguity and paradox in place of the purity, clarity and simplicity of the INTERNATIONAL STYLE. To MIES VAN DER ROHE's *dictum* 'less is more' Venturi replied 'less is a bore'. In 1972 he published, with Denise Scott-Brown and Steven Izenour, *Learning from Las Vegas*. These books provided a theoretical basis for Post-Modernism and made Venturi famous internationally. His later buildings have the provocativeness and scholarly refinement of his writings, notably the Dixwell Fire Station, New Haven (1970–74), extension to the Allen Memorial Art Gallery, Oberlin, Ohio (1976), the Brant Johnson House, Vail, Colorado (1976), the Busco Showroom, Philadelphia (1979), and his 1986 extension to the National Gallery, London.

R. Maxwell and R. A. M. Stern, *V. and Rauch*, London 1978; D. Dunster, *V. and Rauch*, London 1978; Klotz.

Veranda. An open gallery or balcony with a roof supported by light, usually metal, supports.

Verge, John (1782–1861), *see* AUSTRALIAN ARCHITECTURE.

Vergeboard, see BARGEBOARD.

Vermiculation. Decoration of masonry blocks with irregular shallow channels like worm tracks. *See* Fig. 75.

Vernacular architecture. A term of recent usage indicating, by analogy with language (native or local dialects), buildings in indigenous styles constructed from locally available materials following traditional building practice and patterns and not architect-designed – e.g. North American farm houses, often of CLAPBOARD, without any or with only a few superficial classical features; or in England medieval BARNS or timber-framed houses of which the WEALDEN HOUSE was a notable type. The C16–17 Kelmscott Manor, owned by William MORRIS, is a prime example of English, specifically Oxfordshire, vernacular architecture. Although a taste for such buildings formed a part of the PICTURESQUE from the late C18

(e.g. the COTTAGE ORNÉ), they were generally scorned until the mid to late C19, when professional architects associated with Morris and the ARTS AND CRAFTS movement (notably DEVEY, Philip WEBB, Norman SHAW and VOYSEY) drew inspiration from them in their search for a way out of HISTORICISM while preserving contact with national or local history and traditions. More recently, vernacular architecture has been emulated and its materials – brick, rubble-masonry, knapped flint, wood, etc. – favoured in contrast to the impersonal concrete and glass of the INTERNATIONAL MODERN style. The vernacular has also been studied more closely than before in reaction against an elitist approach to history. There are, nevertheless, underlying connections between buildings in vernacular and 'polite' styles, the latter usually preceding the former, and since, until the C20, both were conditioned by local aesthetic preferences, the difference between them is often no more than one of degree. When used in a global context the term 'vernacular architecture' indicates what has been called, more appropriately, 'architecture without architects'.

R. W. Brunskill, *Illustrated Handbook of Vernacular Architecture*, London 1987; A. Clifton Taylor, *The Pattern of English Building*, London 1987; J. Kemp, *American Vernacular*, New York 1988.

Vertue, Robert (d. 1506) and William (d. 1527), were brothers and both masons. Robert, the elder, appears at Westminster Abbey from 1475. About 1501 both brothers were master masons for Bath Abbey, begun at that time by Bishop King. This grandly

Perpendicular building has a fan VAULT which, so they told the bishop, would be such that 'there shall be none so goodly neither in England nor in France'; and as at that moment neither the vault of King's College Chapel, Cambridge, nor that of Henry VII Chapel in Westminster Abbey, nor that of St George's Chapel, Windsor, existed (though the latter was building), the claim was just. The Vertues' precise connection with these three works cannot be proved, but as they were jointly the King's Master Masons, with Robert Janyns and John Lebons (*see* REDMAN), it is likely that a connection existed. William, in any case, signed a contract with another (John Aylmer) to vault the chancel at Windsor, and visited King's College Chapel once in 1507, once (with Redman) in 1509, and once (with WAS-TELL) in 1512, if not more often.

In 1516 William appeared at Eton (with Redman), where he made a design (the design?) for Lupton's Tower. From 1515 he was joint King's Mason with Redman. In 1526 he probably designed the fan-vaulted cloister chapel in the Palace of Westminster.

Harvey 1984.

Vesica. An upright almond shape; found chiefly in medieval art to enclose a figure of Christ enthroned. Also called a *mandorla*.

Vesnin, Aleksandr (1883–1959), almost always worked with one or both of his brothers – Leonid (1880–1933) and Viktor (1882–1950) – as the most successful architectural partnership (in terms of buildings actually erected) of the era of Russian CONSTRUCTIVISM; Aleksandr was their theoretician and editor of the influential journal *Contemporary Architecture*. Already in-

itiators of modernistic simplicity of design by 1914, the Vesnins' major opportunities came in the 1920s and early 1930s: as well as various monumental projects and stage-designs, they particularly specialized in workers' clubs and theatres. Their largest commissions included the great Dnieper dam and ancillary works at Zaporozhye, and the replanning of the whole region around the Simonov Monastery and Likhachyov Car Works in Moscow (1930–37). [R. R. Milner-Gulland]

S. O. Khan-Magomedov, *A.V. and Russian Constructivism*, London 1987.

Vestibule. An anteroom or entrance hall.

Viaduct. A long series of arches carrying a road or railway.

Vice. *See* STAIR.

Vicente de Oliveira, Mateus (1710–86), the leading Portuguese ROCOCO architect, began under LUDOVICE but forsook his grandiose manner for one more delicate and intimate. His masterpiece is the palace of Queluz (1747–52, interior destroyed), where a large building is disguised behind an exquisitely frivolous façade swagged with garlands of carved flowers. He also designed the very large Estrêla church in Lisbon (1778).

Kubler and Soria 1959; Smith 1968.

Victorian architecture, *see* ENGLISH ARCHITECTURE.

Vignola, Giacomo (or Jacopo) Barozzi da (1507–73), the leading architect in Rome after the death of MICHEL-ANGELO, was born at Vignola, near Modena, and studied painting and architecture at Bologna. In 1530 he settled in Rome. He seems to have played the leading part in designing the Villa Giulia, Rome (1551–5), in collaboration with AMMANATI and VASARI. It is a masterpiece of Mannerist architecture and garden design, with much play with vistas from one courtyard to another, hemicycles echoing each other, a curious rhythmical use of the orders, and very shallow relief decorations applied to the surfaces.

In 1559 he began work on the Palazzo Farnese at Caprarola, which had already been started on a pentagonal plan. He designed the rather stern façades, the elegant circular interior courtyard and the ingenious arrangement of rooms. The famous circular staircase is also his, and he probably designed the gardens as well. In about 1550 he built the little Tempietto di S. Andrea, Rome, for Pope Julius III, using for the first time in church architecture an oval plan which he was to repeat on a larger scale in his design for S. Anna dei Palafrenieri, Rome (begun 1573), and which was to be used extensively by Baroque architects. His most influential building was the Gesù, Rome (begun 1568); it has probably had a wider influence than any church built in the last 400 years. The plan, which owes something to ALBERTI'S S. Andrea, Mantua, combines the central scheme of the Renaissance with the longitudinal scheme of the Middle Ages. The aisles are replaced by a series of chapels opening off the nave, and various devices – e.g. lighting and the placing of the nave pilasters – direct attention to the high altar. (The interior was redecorated in High Baroque style in 1668–73.) In 1558 he designed the plan for the Palazzo Farnese in Piacenza, on which work stopped soon after 1560 so that barely a third was built. He may also have designed the Portico dei Banchi at Bologna.

Vignola was architect to St Peter's (1567–73) and continued Michelangelo's work there faithfully. In 1562 he published *Regole delle cinque ordini*, a simple MODULAR interpretation of the architectural ORDERS which, on account of its straightforward approach, enjoyed immense popularity. It became one of the most important textbooks ever written (translated into English in 1655).

Heydenreich and Lotz 1974; J. Coolidge, W. Lotz *et al.*, *La vita e le opere di J.B. da V.*, Vignola 1974; Harris 1990.

Vignon, Pierre-Alexandre (1762–1828). French Empire architect famous for the Madeleine in Paris (1806–45), his one important building. He was trained under J.-D. Leroy and LEDOUX and in 1793 became Inspecteur Général des Bâtiments de la République. His Madeleine is an enormous peripteral Corinthian temple on a high podium, as imposingly and imperially Roman in scale as in its slightly vulgar ostentation. It superseded a building designed by Pierre Contant d'Ivry (1698–1777) in 1764, revised c. 1777 by G. M. Couture (1732–99). This had hardly begun to be built when Napoleon called in Vignon in 1806, having decided that it should be a *Temple de la Gloire* and not a church. But he reversed this decision in 1813 after the Battle of Leipzig and the loss of Spain. Vignon did not live to see his masterpiece completed and it was finished by J.-J.-M. Huvé (1783–1852).

M. L. Biver, *Le Paris de Napoléon*, Paris 1963.

Vihara. A residential building for monks and other ascetic groups in an Indian Buddhist monastery. Viharas followed a standard pattern, small cells opening off a square or rectangular court. In the middle of one side is the entrance. The cell opposite usually accommodates a votive STUPA or Buddha image. Like CHAITYA HALLS, the earliest were rock-cut, but brick remains of structural monasteries have survived. Indian Buddhist monasteries are essentially groups of viharas, as at Ajanta and Nalanda.

Villa. In Roman architecture, the landowner's residence or farmstead on his country estate; in Renaissance architecture, a country house; in C19 England, a detached house 'for opulent persons', usually on the outskirts of a town; in modern architecture, a small detached house. The basic type developed with the growth of urbanization: it is of five bays, on a simple corridor plan with rooms opening off a central passage. The next stage is the addition of wings. The courtyard villa fills a square plan with subsidiary buildings and an enclosure wall with a gate facing the main corridor block. As a building-type the Palladian villa was to have enormous influence (*see* PALLADIANISM).

G. A. Mansuelli, *Le ville del mondo romano*, Milan 1958; J. Ackerman, *The Villa. Form and Ideology of Country Houses*, London 1990.

Villagrán García, José (b. 1901), *see* MEXICAN ARCHITECTURE.

Villanueva, Carlos Raúl (1900–1975). Notable Venezuelan architect working in Caracas, to whose rapid growth he contributed several remarkable housing projects on a very large scale, e.g. the Dos de Diciembre estate (1943–5) for over 12,000 people and the El Paraiso complex (1954). But he is best known for his stadium, auditorium and other buildings for Caracas University (1950–57).

S. Moholy-Nagy, *C.R.V.*, New York 1964.

Villanueva, Juan de (1739–1811), the leading Spanish neo-classical architect, was the son of a sculptor under whom he trained. He began in the CHURRIGUERESQUE tradition, then became a draughtsman to SACCHETTI in Madrid and adopted an Italianate Baroque style. He was sent by the Royal Academy to Rome (1759–65), and on his return his brother Diego (1715–74) published his *Colección de papeles críticos sobre la arquitectura* (1766), the first neo-classical attack on the Churrigueresque and Rococo to appear in Spain. Rather tentatively he began to put these ideas into practice in the Palafox Chapel in Burgo de Osma Cathedral (1770), Casita de Arriba at the Escorial (1773), and Casita del Príncipe at El Pardo (1784). His outstanding work is the Prado Museum, Madrid, designed (1787) as a museum of natural history but later adapted to house the royal collection of pictures. With its sturdy Tuscan portico in the centre and its boldly articulated wings with Ionic colonnades at first-floor level, it is an effective and undoctrinaire essay in neo-classicism.

Kubler and Soria 1959.

Villard de Honnecourt, a French architect who was active around 1225–35 in the north-west of France and probably worked at Cambrai Cathedral, which no longer exists, and perhaps at Reims *c.* 1228–33. Villard is known to us by the book of drawings with short texts compiled for learners in his lodge, the masons' workshop and office. The most famous of LODGE BOOKS, it is in the Bibliothèque Nationale in Paris and contains plans of buildings (both copied and invented), elevational details, figure sculpture, figures drawn *au vif*, foliage ornament, a lectern, a stall end, a *perpetuum mobile*, and in addition many small technical drawings, more of an engineering kind, which were added to the book by two successors of Villard. From the text and the examples illustrated it is certain that Villard knew Reims, Laon, Chartres, Lausanne, and that he travelled as far as Hungary. The sculptural style of his figures connects him with work of about 1230 at Reims. Villard's book gives us the clearest insight we can obtain into the work of a distinguished master mason and the atmosphere of a lodge. It has been suggested that he was an artist, not an architect or mason, but this seems improbable.

H. R. Hahnloser, *V. de H.*, Vienna (1937) 1972; T. Bowie (ed.), *The Sketchbook of V. de H.*, Bloomington and London 1968; Bucher 1979; C. F. Barnes, *V. de H. the Artist and his Drawings*, Boston, Mass., 1982, and in Recht 1989.

Vimana. In Hindu temples the shrine proper and its superstructure, but also, more loosely, a Hindu temple comprising sanctuary and attached porches.

Vincidor, Tommaso (*c.* 1495–1560), *see* DUTCH ARCHITECTURE.

Vingboons or **Vinckeboons**, Philip (1607/8–78), was the leading exponent of van CAMPEN's Dutch classicism for middle-class domestic architecture in Amsterdam. He worked for the prosperous merchants while Pieter POST was patronized by the upper class. Being Roman Catholic he obtained no commissions for public buildings or churches. He created a new type of town house, sober, unpretentious and eminently practical, with strictly sym-

metrical planning and severely simple elevations. His designs, published as *Œuvres d'architecture* in two volumes (1648 and 1674), were very influential especially in England. His brother Justus (*fl.* 1650–70) designed the façades of LA VALLÉE's Riddarhus in Stockholm (1653–6) and built the imposing Trippenhuis in Amsterdam (1662).

Kuyper 1980; K. Ottenheym, *P.V. (1607–1678)*, Zutphen 1989.

Viollet-le-Duc, Eugène-Emanuel (1814–79), was born into a wealthy, cultured, and progressive family. His opposition to the 'establishment' began early: he helped to build barricades in 1830 and refused to go to the École des Beaux Arts for his training. In 1836–7 he was in Italy studying buildings with industry and intelligence. His future was determined by his meeting with Prosper Mérimée (1803–70), author of *Carmen* and Inspector in the newly founded Commission des Monuments Historiques. Viollet-le-Duc, inspired by Victor Hugo's enthusiasm on the one hand and by Arcisse de Caumont's scholarship on the other, now turned resolutely to the French Middle Ages and soon established himself both as a scholar and as a restorer. His first job was Vézelay (1840). He then did the Sainte Chapelle in Paris with Félix-Jacques Duban (1797–1870), and Notre Dame with Jean-Baptiste-Antoine Lassus (1807–57). The number of his later restorations is legion, e.g. the whole town of Carcassonne (1844 onwards). Some of his restorations have recently been removed in the course of further 'restoration', notably at St Sernin, Toulouse.

As a scholar he developed new and highly influential ideas on the Gothic style, which to him is socially the outcome of a lay civilization succeeding the sinister religious domination of the earlier Middle Ages. The Gothic style to Viollet-le-Duc is also a style of rational construction based on the system of rib vault, flying buttress, and buttress. The ribs are a skeleton, like a C19 iron skeleton; the webs or cells are no more than light infilling. All thrusts are conducted from the ribs to the flying buttresses and buttresses, and thin walls can be replaced by large openings. These ideas were laid down and made universal property by Viollet-le-Duc's *Dictionnaire raisonné de l'architecture française* (published 1854–68). A comparison between Gothic skeleton and C19 iron skeleton building was drawn, or rather implied, in Viollet-le-Duc's *Entretiens* (2 vols., published 1863 and 1872), and especially in the second volume. Here Viollet-le-Duc appears as a passionate defender of his own age, of engineering, and of new materials and techniques, especially iron for supports, for framework, and for ribs. The plates to the *Entretiens* are extremely original, but aesthetically they are none too attractive. As an architect Viollet-le-Duc had in fact little merit. Time and again one is struck by the discrepancy between the consistency and daring of his thought and the looseness and commonplace detailing of his original buildings, e.g. St Denys-de-l'Estrée, St Denis (1864–7).

Pevsner 1972; Van Zanten 1987; F. Bercé *et al.*, *V.-le-D. Architect*, Washington, DC, 1988.

Viscardi, Giovanni Antonio (1647–1713). He was born in the Grisons and went, like his compatriot and bitter rival ZUCCALLI, to work in Munich, where he became master mason to the Court in 1678 and chief architect in 1685. Zuccalli helped to oust him from this post in 1689 but he was in charge of enlarging Nymphenburg palace from 1702 onwards (he began the saloon and added pavilions etc.) and he was reinstated as chief architect 1706–13. His most important building is the Mariahilfkirche at Freystadt (1700–1708), with a very high central dome, on a plan that was to have widespread influence even beyond Bavaria (BÄHR used it as a model for the Frauenkirche in Dresden). He also designed the Cistercian church of Fürstenfeld (1701–47). His last works were the Jesuit assembly hall or Bürgersaal, Munich (1709–10), and the church of the Holy Trinity in Munich (1711–14).

Hempel 1965; K.-L. Lippert, *G.A.V.*, Munich 1969.

Visconti, Louis-Tullius-Joachim (1791–1853), *see* LEFUEL, Hector-Martin.

Vitozzi, Ascanio (*c.* 1539–1615). He began as an officer and military engineer, serving at Lepanto in 1571 and later in Tunis and in Spain and Portugal. In 1584 he was called by Duke Carlo Emanuele I of Savoy to Turin, where he built S. Maria del Monte or dei Cappuccini (begun 1585) and the Trinità (begun 1598), but his masterpiece is the enormous centrally planned pilgrimage church at Vicoforte di Mondovì, in Piedmont (begun 1596).

Wittkower 1982.

Vitruvian opening. A doorway or window of which the sides incline slightly inwards towards the top, giving it a heavy, Egyptian look. It was described by Vitruvius.

Vitruvian scroll, see RUNNING DOG.

Vitruvius Pollio, Marcus (active 46–30 BC), a Roman architect and theorist of slight importance in his own time but of enormous influence from the Early Renaissance onwards, served under Julius Caesar in the African War (46 BC), built the basilica at Fano (destroyed), and in old age composed a treatise on architecture in ten books *De architectura*, written in a somewhat obscure style and dedicated to Augustus. This is the only complete treatise on architecture to survive from antiquity. Several manuscript copies were known and used in the Middle Ages. In 1414 Poggio Bracciolini drew attention to a copy at St Gall, and the treatise soon came to be regarded as a vade-mecum for all progressive architects. Both AL-BERTI and FRANCESCO DI GIORGIO derived much from it for their writings and buildings. The first printed text was published in Rome *c.* 1486 and the first illustrated edition by Fra GIO-CONDO in 1511; an Italian translation was prepared under RAPHAEL's direction *c.* 1520, and another translation was printed in 1521 with an extensive commentary by Cesare Cesariano and numerous illustrations. A vast number of subsequent editions and translations in nearly all European languages appeared (into English in 1692). The obscurity of the text, which made a strong appeal to the Renaissance intellect, enabled architects to interpret its gnomic statements in a variety of ways.

MacDonald 1965; Ward-Perkins 1981; H. Knell (ed.), *V. – Kolloquien des Deutschen Archäologen-Verbandes*, Darmstadt 1984; Harris 1990.

Vittone, Bernardo (1702–70), a little-known architect of real if rather freakish genius, worked exclusively in Piedmont, where he was born. He studied in Rome and edited GUARINI's posthumous *Architettura civile* (1737). His secular buildings are dull; not so his numerous churches, mostly small and scattered in remote villages, in which the unlikely fusion of Guarini and JUVARRA had surprising and original results in a gay Rococo vein. Of his structural inventions the pendentive-squinch (e.g. S. Maria di Piazza, Turin, 1751–4) and fantastic three-vaulted dome are the most successful. His churches at Vallinotto (1738–9), Brà (1742), and Chieri (1740–44) show his structural ingenuity at its prettiest. Later churches – Borgo d'Ale, Rivarolo Canavese, Grignasco – are larger, less frivolous, but suavely calm and sinuous. He had several followers and disciples in Piedmont, but no influence whatever farther afield.

Pommer 1967; Wittkower 1982; Varriano 1986.

Volute. A spiral scroll on an Ionic CAPITAL; smaller versions appear on Composite and Corinthian capitals. *See* Fig. 66.

Voronikhin, Andrei Nikiforovich (1760–1814), one of the leading figures in the neo-classical transformation of St Petersburg, was born a serf on the estates of Count Stroganov, who sent him to study in Moscow, then on a European tour (1786–90), and finally employed him to design the state apartments in his palace. His main works are in Leningrad, e.g. Cathedral of the Virgin of Kazan (1801–11), the most Catholic and Roman church in Russia, and the Academy of Mines (1806–11), with a dodecastyle Paestum portico.

Hamilton 1983.

Voussoir. A brick or wedge-shaped

stone forming one of the units of an arch. *See* Fig. 4.

Voysey, Charles Francis Annesley (1857–1941). He worked first under SEDDON and from 1880 with DEVEY, on whose vernacular manner his own early work was based. He set up in practice in 1882. He was as interested in design as in architecture, under the general influence of MORRIS and of MACKMURDO in particular, and became a leading member of the ARTS AND CRAFTS movement. His earliest designs for wallpapers and textiles are of 1883 and are indeed very reminiscent of Mackmurdo. His first commissions for houses date from 1888–9, and from then until the First World War he built a large number of country houses and hardly anything else. They are never extremely large, never grand, never representational; instead they are placed in intimate relation to nature – perhaps an old tree preserved in the courtyard – and developed informally. They spread with ease and, having lowish comfortable rooms, are often on the cosy side. The exteriors are usually rendered with pebbledash and have horizontal windows. They are no longer period imitations at all – in fact, more independent of the past than most architects ventured to be before 1900 – but they never lack the admission of a sympathy for the rural Tudor and Stuart traditions. Voysey designed the furniture and all the details, such as fireplaces, metalwork, etc., himself, and the furniture is again inspired by Mackmurdo's (and in its turn inspired MACKINTOSH's). It is reasonable, friendly, and in the decoration not without a sweet sentimentality; the same is true of textiles and wallpapers.

Among his houses which had a tremendous influence at home (right down to the caricatures produced between the wars by speculative builders) and abroad, the following may be listed: Cottage, Bishops Itchington, 1888; Perrycroft, Colwall, 1893; Annesley Lodge, Hampstead, London, 1896; Merlshanger (Grey Friars), Hog's Back, Guildford, 1896; Norney, Shackleford, 1897; Broadleys and Moor Crag, both Gill Head, Windermere, 1898; The Orchard, Chorley Wood, 1900–1901, designed for himself. After the war Voysey was rarely called upon to do any architectural work.

D. Gebhard, *C.F.A.V. Architect*, Los Angeles 1975; J. Brandon-Jones, *C.F.A.V. Architect and Designer 1857–1941*, exh. cat., Brighton 1978; D. Simpson, *C.F.A.V. (1857–1941). An Architect of Individuality*, London 1979.

Vries, Hans Vredeman de (1527–1606), began as a painter, settled in Antwerp, and published fantastic ornamental pattern-books – *Architectura* (1565), *Compertimenta* (1566), *Variae Architecturae Formae* (1601) – which had enormous influence on architecture all over northern Europe including England (e.g. SMYTHSON's Wollaton). His style lacks FLORIS's grace and wit but well represents the Flemish and Dutch contribution to MANNERISM and expresses the northern feeling for flat pattern in STRAPWORK or carved decoration of interlaced bands and forms similar to fretwork or cut leather.

Gerson and ter Kuile 1960.

Vyse. A spiral staircase or a staircase winding round a central column.

W

Wachsmann, Konrad (1901–80). A pioneer of INDUSTRIALIZED BUILD-ING, he was experimenting with standardized elements for pre-fabricated buildings by 1925 and after emigrating to the USA he developed his General Panel System with GROPIUS in the 1940s. In 1946 he launched his Mobilar Structures and in 1961 published *The Turning Point in Building. Structures and Design* (New York).

Klotz 1986; T. Herzog *et al., Vom Sinn des Detail. Zum Gesamtwerk von K.W.*, Cologne 1988.

Wagner, Martin (1885–1957), *see* TAUT, Bruno.

Wagner, Otto (1841–1918), became professor at the Academy in Vienna in 1894, and delivered an inaugural address pleading for a new approach to architecture, for independence of the past, and for rationalism ('Nothing that is not practical can be beautiful'). Before that time he had himself designed in the neo-Renaissance style. His most familiar achievement is some stations for the Vienna Stadtbahn (1894–1901), ART NOUVEAU with much exposed iron, though more restrained than Hector GUIMARD's contemporary ones for the Paris Métro. But his most amazingly modern and C20-looking job is the Post Office Savings Bank, Vienna (1904–6), the exterior faced with marble slabs held in place by aluminium bolts and the interior featuring a glass barrel vault realized with a clarity and economy hardly matched by anyone else at so early a date. Wagner had a decisive influence on the best younger architects of Vienna (*see* HOFFMANN, LOOS, OLBRICH) and outside Austria through his pupil Jan Kotěra (1871–1923) in Czechoslovakia and through his assistant Jože PLEČNIK in Prague and Ljubljana in the 1930s. Wagner's most monumental building, closer to the style of the Secession, is the Steinhof Asylum chapel, Vienna (1906). He published *Moderne Architektur* (Vienna 1896; English translation by H. F. Mallgrave, Chicago 1988).

H. Geretsegger and M. Peifner, *O.W. 1841–1918*, London (1964) 1979; O. A. Graf, *O.W.*, Vienna 1985; P. Haiko (ed.), *Sketches, Projects and Executed Buildings by O.W.*, London 1987.

Wagon roof, *see* ROOF.

Wagon vault, *see* VAULT.

Wahlman, Lars Israel (1870–1952), *see* SWEDISH ARCHITECTURE.

Wailly, Charles de (1730–98). Notable Louis XVI architect trained under BLONDEL, SERVANDONI and at the French Academy in Rome (1754–6).

His talent ranged from interiors of a somewhat theatrical opulence (salone of Palazzo Spinola, Genoa, 1772–3) to the austerity of his most celebrated building, the Odéon, Paris (1779–82), designed in collaboration with Marie-Joseph Peyre (1730–85). It was twice burnt but little altered in rebuilding (1807 and 1818). De Wailly's other works are no less remarkable, e.g. the Château de Montmusard near Dijon (1764–72, unfinished), the first *château* in France in which the influence of antiquity is preponderant, and various *hôtels* in Paris.

Gallet 1964; M. Mosser and D. Rabreau, *C. de W. 1730–1798: Peintre architecte dans l'Europe des lumières*, exh. cat., Paris 1979; Braham 1980.

Wainscot. The timber lining to walls. The term is also applied to the wooden panelling of PEWS.

Wall arcade. A blind arcade.

Wall-plate, *see* ROOF.

Wall rib, *see* FORMERET.

Wallot, Paul (1841–1912), *see* GERMAN ARCHITECTURE.

Walsingham, Alan of, *see* ALAN OF WALSINGHAM.

Walter, Thomas Ustick (1804–87), was of German descent, and was born in Philadelphia, where his father was a mason. He studied under STRICKLAND and started on his own in 1830. As early as 1833 he was commissioned to design Girard College, an ambitious, wholly peripteral (and thus functionally dubious) white marble building. In 1851 he began the completion of the Capitol in Washington: he added the wings, and the dominant dome on a cast-iron framing is his. He also com-

pleted MILLS's Treasury. Like nearly all the leading American architects, Walter was also capable of major engineering works – e.g. a breakwater he built in Venezuela (1843–5).

Hitchcock 1977; Whiffen and Koeper 1981.

Walter of Canterbury (*fl.c.* 1322), *see* MICHAEL OF CANTERBURY.

Warchavchik, Gregori (1896–1972), *see* BRAZILIAN ARCHITECTURE.

Ward. The courtyard of a castle; also called a *bailey*.

Wardell, William (1823–99), *see* AUSTRALIAN ARCHITECTURE.

Ware, Isaac (*c.* 1717–66). A protégé of Lord BURLINGTON and a strict Palladian. His buildings are competent but uninspired, e.g. Chesterfield House, London (1749, destroyed), and Wrotham Park (*c.* 1754). However, his *Complete Body of Architecture* (1756) was very influential and became a standard textbook.

Colvin 1978; Summerson 1983; Harris 1990.

Ware & van Brunt. William Robert Ware (1832–1915) took a Harvard BS degree and was then a pupil of HUNT. Henry van Brunt (1832–1903) also took a Harvard degree and was also a pupil of Hunt. The two were in partnership from 1863 to 1881. Ware created the first American school of architecture (1865) at the MIT and the second (1881) at Columbia. The educational system was influenced by the École des Beaux Arts in Paris. Both Ware and van Brunt started as Gothicists, inspired by RUSKIN. Their best Gothic churches are First Church, Boston (1865–7), St John, Cambridge, Massachusetts (1869–70), and – more original – Third Universalist, Cambridge (1875), and St Stephen Lynn, Massachusetts (1881). Ware often judged competitions and took a great interest in the affairs of the American Institute of Architects, whereas van Brunt was a brilliant architectural writer. He translated VIOLLET-LE-DUC's *Entretiens* in 1875, and when Ware was commissioned to do internal alterations to the Harvard Library, he took his inspiration from LABROUSTE. Van Brunt moved to Kansas City in 1884. In his last phase he designed many railway stations. His Electricity Building at the Chicago Exhibition of 1893 is classical. His partner on this was Frank Howe.

Hitchcock 1977; Whiffen and Koeper 1981.

Wastell, John (d. *c* 1515), lived at Bury St Edmunds and, though evidently highly appreciated, was not in the King's Works. He had probably started under and with Simon CLERK, and followed him both at the abbey of Bury and at King's College Chapel, Cambridge, where he appears from 1486 and was master mason throughout the years when the glorious fan VAULT was built and the chapel completed. The vault can therefore with some probability be considered his design, though the King's Masons, William VERTUE and Henry REDMAN, visited the building in 1507, 1509, and 1512. Wastell was also Cardinal Morton's mason and then the master mason of Canterbury Cathedral, where he was presumably the designer for Bell Harry, the crossing tower of the cathedral (built 1494–7). Other buildings have been attributed to him on stylistic grounds.

Harvey 1984.

Watanabe, Hitoshi (b. 1905), *see* JAPANESE ARCHITECTURE.

Waterhouse, Alfred (1830–1905), started in practice at Manchester in 1856 and moved to London in 1865. In Manchester he won the competitions for the Assize Courts (1859) and Town Hall (1869–77), both excellently planned and externally in a free, picturesque Gothic which yet does not depart too far from symmetry. Soon after, his style hardened and assumed that odd character of sharp forms and harsh imperishable materials (terracotta, best red brick) which one connects with him. He remained a planner of great clarity and resourcefulness and used ironwork freely for structural purposes. But he was a historicist all the same, happiest in a rigid matter-of-fact Gothic, but also going in for a kind of Romanesque (Natural History Museum, London 1873–81) and for French Renaissance (Caius College, Cambridge, 1868 onwards). Of his many buildings the following may be mentioned: some very interestingly planned Congregational churches (Lyndhurst Road, Hampstead, 1883; King's Weigh House Chapel, 1889–91); the headquarters of the Prudential Assurance in Holborn (1876 onwards); The City and Guilds Institute in Kensington (1881); St Paul's School (1881–4, demolished); the National Liberal Club (1884); and a number of country mansions (Hutton Hall, Yorkshire, 1865; enlargement of Eaton Hall, Cheshire, 1870–83, demolished 1961).

Hitchcock 1977; M. Girouard, *A.W. and the Natural History Museum*, New Haven and London 1980; C. Cunningham *et al.*, *A.W. 1830–1905*, exh. cat., London 1983.

Water-leaf. A leaf shape used in later

CI2 CAPITALS. The water-leaf is broad, unribbed, and tapering, curving out towards the angle of the ABACUS and turned in at the top. *See* Fig. 24.

Water-table, *see* OFF-SET.

Wattle and daub. A method of wall construction consisting of branches or thin laths (wattles) roughly plastered over with mud or clay (daub), sometimes used as a filling between the vertical members of TIMBER-FRAMED houses.

Wave moulding. A compound moulding formed by a convex curve between two concave curves; typical of the Decorated style.

Wealden house. A medieval TIMBER-FRAMED house of distinctive form. It is peculiar to England and found mainly in the south-east. It has a central open hall flanked by bays of two storeys. The end bays are JETTIED to the front but a single roof covers the whole building, thus producing an exceptionally wide overhang to the eaves in front of the hall. They are supported by diagonal, usually curved, braces starting from the short inner sides of the overhanging wings and rising parallel with the front wall of the hall towards the centre of the eaves.

Weatherboarding. Overlapping horizontal boards covering a TIMBER-FRAMED wall; the boards are wedge-shaped in section, the upper edge being the thinner.

Weathering. A sloping horizontal surface on sills, tops of buttresses, etc., to throw off water. *See* OFF-SET.

Web. A compartment or bay of a VAULT, between the ribs, also called a cell or *severy*.

Webb, Sir Aston (1849–1930). Perhaps the most successful of the providers of large public buildings in suitable styles around 1900, together with his partner Edward Ingress Bell (1837–1914). His favourite style, especially earlier in his career, was a free François I. Later there are also buildings in the Imperial-Palladian of the years of Edward VII. Chief buildings: Law Courts, Birmingham (with Ingress Bell, 1886–91); Metropolitan Life Assurance, Moorgate (with Bell, 1890–93), one of his best; Victoria and Albert Museum (1891–1909); Royal Services Institute, Whitehall (with Bell, 1893–5); Christ's Hospital, Horsham (with Bell, 1894–1904); Royal Naval College, Dartmouth (1899–1904); Royal College of Science (1900–1906); University, Birmingham (1900–1909), Byzantino-Italian; Imperial College, Kensington (1900–1906); Admiralty Arch (1908–9); façade of Buckingham Palace (1912–13).

Service 1977.

Webb, John (1611–72). Pupil and nephew by marriage of Inigo JONES, whose right-hand man he appears to have been from the 1630s onwards. He was responsible for the reconstruction of the staterooms at Wilton in 1649 after a fire, including the famous double-cube room which was for long thought to be one of Jones's masterpieces. However, Webb's independent work mostly dates from after his master's death and much of it has been destroyed, e.g. Gunnersbury House (*c.* 1658–63, demolished) and Amesbury House (*c.* 1660, rebuilt). The portico of The Vine (1654–6) and the King Charles block at Greenwich Palace (1664–9) survive. His reputation has been overshadowed, unjustly, by that of Jones.

Colvin 1978; Summerson 1983; J. Bold, *J.W.: Architectural Theory and Practice in the Seventeenth Century*, Oxford 1989.

Webb, Philip Speakman (1831–1915), hardly ever designed anything but houses, all outstanding examples of the ARTS AND CRAFTS movement, of which he became the main theorist. Among the architects of the great English Domestic Revival, he and Norman SHAW stand supreme: Shaw much more favoured, more inventive, more voluble, more widely influential; Webb harder, more of a thinker, totally deficient in any architectural bedside manner, and perhaps more deeply influential, even on Shaw himself. Webb chose his clients and never agreed to having a stable of assistants. His style is strangely ruthless: from the first he mixed elements from the Gothic and the C18, not for the fun or devilry of it, but because one should use the most suitable motifs regardless of their original contexts. He also liked to expose materials and show the workings of parts of a building. For Webb, LETHABY wrote, architecture was first of all a common tradition of honest building. Though he did not publish or exhibit he was very influential largely through his work for the SPAB (*see* MORRIS). His buildings showed how traditional building crafts could be used inventively.

His first job was Red House (1859) for William Morris, whose closest friend he remained throughout. For Morris's firm he designed furniture of a rustic Stuart kind, and also table glass and metalwork. He also joined in the stained glass work. His principal town houses are No. 1 Palace Green (1868) and No. 19 Lincoln's Inn Fields

(1868–9). Of his country houses Joldwyns, Surrey (1873), Smeaton Manor, Yorkshire (1878), and Conyhurst, Surrey (1885), come nearest to Shaw in character – gabled, cheerful, with weatherboarding, tilehanging, and white window trim. Standen, East Grinstead, Sussex (1891–4), is best preserved. Clouds, Wiltshire (1876–91), is the largest and least easy to take, strong no doubt, but very astringent indeed, designed, as it were, in a take-it-or-leave-it mood. Webb's interiors from the later seventies onwards often have white panelling and exhibit a marked sympathy with the C18 vernacular. In 1901 he retired to a country cottage and ceased practising.

H. Lethaby, *P.W. and His Work*, Oxford 1935; S. Kirk, *P.W. (1831–1915). Domestic Architecture*, London 1985.

Weinbrenner, Friedrich (1766–1826), was born at Karlsruhe and visited Berlin (1790) and Rome (1792). His major achievement is the transformation of Karlsruhe into a neo-classical city, rather like a miniature version of Leningrad. The Marktplatz (1804–24), with balancing but not identical buildings and a pyramid in the centre, and the circular Rondellplatz (1805–13), with the Markgräfliches Palais are masterpieces of neo-classical town planning. He also built a handsome circular Catholic church (1808–17).

D. B. Brownlee (ed.), *F.W. (1766–1826) Architect of Karlsruhe*, exh. cat., Philadelphia, Karlsruhe, Cambridge, Mass., 1986/7.

Wells, Joseph Merrill (d. 1890), *see* MCKIM.

Wells Coates (1895–1958), *see* COATES, Wells.

Werkbund, see DEUTSCHER WERK-BUND.

Westwork. The west end of a Carolingian or Romanesque church, consisting of a low entrance hall and above it a room open to the nave and usually flanked or surrounded by aisles and upper galleries. The whole is crowned by one broad tower, and there are occasionally stair turrets as well. In the main upper room stood an altar as a rule.

Wheel window, see ROSE WINDOW.

White, Stanford (1853–1906), was of old New England stock and was brought up in a cultured house. He was a pupil of RICHARDSON and from 1879 a partner of McKIM and Mead. White was a rich *bon vivant*, a man who entertained sumptuously, and exuberant in other ways as well. He was a brilliant and effortless designer, his range stretching from magazine covers to a railway carriage, including Gordon Bennett's yacht, and houses more original than any by anyone anywhere at the time. The temerity of the Low House at Bristol, Rhode Island (1887, demolished), with its enormous spreading pitched roof, is almost beyond belief. For other buildings *see* McKIM. White was shot dead during a theatre rehearsal in 1906.

L. M. Roth, *McKim, Mead & W. Architects*, London 1978; L. Wodehouse, *W. of McKim Mead & W.*, London and New York 1988.

Wilkins, William (1778–1839), son of a Norwich architect, was educated at Caius College, Cambridge, where he was elected Fellow in 1802. He travelled in Greece, Asia Minor, and Italy (1801–4) and published *Antiquities of Magna Graecia* (1807) on his return.

He pioneered the GREEK REVIVAL in England with his designs for Downing College, Cambridge (begun 1806), Haileybury College (1806–9), and the temple-style country house Grange Park (1809), with its Theseum peristyle and other rather pedantically Athenian references. In fact, he was rather priggish and doctrinaire, and his rival SMIRKE had little difficulty in overtaking his lead in the movement. But Downing College is important historically as the first of all university CAMPUSES – separate buildings round a park-like expanse of lawn – preceding JEFFERSON's Charlottesville. His other university buildings in Cambridge were neo-Gothic, e.g. New Court, Trinity (1821–3), and the screen and hall-range at King's (1824–8). He had greater opportunities in London to develop his neo-Greek style but muffed them – University College (1827–8), St George's Hospital (1828–9), and finally the National Gallery (1834–8), which ruined his reputation. Only the main block of University College is his, and though the portico itself is very imposing he seems to have been unable to unite it satisfactorily with the rest of the composition. This inability to subordinate the parts to the whole resulted at the National Gallery in a patchy façade unworthy of its important site.

Colvin 1978; R. W. Liscombe, *W.W. 1778–1839*, Cambridge 1980.

Willard, Salomon (1783–1861). Massachusetts architect. First a carpenter and as such in 1808 built the ingenious spiral staircase in the Exchange Coffee House in Boston. He was also busy as a carver in wood (e.g. ships' figureheads) and stone. However, he moved into architecture – e.g. the Bunker Hill Monument, mostly by him (1825–42), the Doric United States Bank in Boston (1824-6), two County Court Houses at Boston (Suffolk County) and Dedham (Norfolk County) and the Town Hall at Quincy (1844).

Whiffen and Koeper 1981.

William of Ramsey (d. 1349). A member of a family of masons who worked in Norwich and London from about 1300 onwards, William appears first in 1325 as a mason working on St Stephen's Chapel in the Palace of Westminster (*see* MICHAEL OF CANTERBURY). In 1332 he became master mason of the new work at St Paul's Cathedral, which meant the chapterhouse and its cloister. In 1336 he was appointed Master Mason to the King's Castles south of Trent, which included the Palace of Westminster and St Stephen's Chapel. William was also commissioned in 1337 to give his *sanum consilium* on Lichfield Cathedral. In the early thirties he may have been master mason to Norwich Cathedral also: the cloister there was taken over by one William of Ramsey from John of Ramsey, probably his father, who was already master mason to the cathedral in 1304. William was evidently an important man, and what we know from an old illustration and surviving fragments of the chapterhouse of St Paul's indicates that the creation of the Perpendicular style was due to him, or at least that he made a style out of elements evolved in London and especially at St Stephen's Chapel in the decade preceding 1330.

Harvey 1984.

William of Sens (d. *c.* 1180). Designer and master mason of the chancel of Canterbury Cathedral, rebuilt after a fire had destroyed it in 1174. He was a Frenchman (or else his successor would not have been known as William the Englishman) and came from Sens Cathedral, which was begun *c.* 1140 and which contained features repeated at Canterbury (also in the Englishman's work, no doubt on the strength of drawings left in the lodge by William of Sens). He was, however, also familiar with more recent French work, notably Notre Dame in Paris (begun 1163), St Rémi at Reims, Soissons, and buildings in the north-west such as Valenciennes. William, as the true master mason of the Gothic Age (*see also* VILLARD DE HONNECOURT), was familiar with wood as well as stone and with devices to load stone on to ships. He had been chosen at Canterbury from a number of English and French masons assembled for consultation on action to be taken after the fire.

Webb 1965.

William of Wynford (d. *c.* 1405-10), was made master mason of Wells Cathedral in 1365, after having worked at Windsor Castle, where William of Wykeham was then clerk of the works. Wynford remained in the royal service and in 1372 received a pension for life. He also remained William of Wykeham's protégé, and worked for him at Winchester College and from 1394 at Winchester Cathedral, where he probably designed the new nave and west front. New College, Oxford, has also been attributed to him. He was obviously a much appreciated man; he dined with William of Wykeham, at the high table of Winchester College, and at the prior's table at the cathedral, and received a furred robe once a year from the cathedral. On several occasions he appeared, no doubt for consultations, together with YEVELE.

Wind-brace

Harvey 1984.

Wind-brace, *see* ROOF.

Winde, William (d. 1722), was born in Holland, the son of a Royalist exile. He followed GERBIER as architect of Hampstead Marshall (1662–88), of which only the gate piers survive, and became, with PRATT and MAY, a leader of the Anglo-Dutch school. His Buckingham House, London (1705, destroyed), with its unpedimented attic storey, forebuildings, and quadrant colonnades, was very influential. None of his buildings survives unless Belton House, Lincolnshire (1685–8), is his.

Colvin 1978; Summerson 1983.

Winder, *see* STAIR.

Winding stair, *see* STAIR.

Window. 1. An opening made in a wall to light or ventilate an enclosed space. Early windows, from considerations of security and architectural stability, were little more than incisions in the wall. Their SILLS and the REVEAL of the JAMBS might be SPLAYED to increase the flow of light. They became much larger in Roman times, when glazing was introduced (by AD 65 according to Seneca). The spread of glazing and developments in skeletal vaulting in the Middle Ages both made larger windows possible. These would be divided into LIGHTS by MULLIONS (and later horizontally divided by TRANSOMS), whose heads in Gothic architecture were elaborated into steadily more complex TRACERY. Gothic windows are usually protected externally by a HOOD-MOULD, and the reveals may be enriched by colonnettes and MOULDINGS. In classical architecture a window may be framed externally by a simple ARCHITRAVE, with or without a crowning ENTABLATURE or PEDIMENT, or it may be more richly set in an AEDICULE.

2. *Window* is also used to refer to the glass held in wood or metal frames within the opening. Such frames, with QUARRIES of glass held in lead CAMES braced by SADDLE BARS, were originally hinged when required to open inwards or outwards – the CASEMENT WINDOW. When larger panes of *crown glass* became available in the C17, these were incorporated in wooden SASH WINDOWS sliding up and down one in front of the other. These were at first held in place by pegs, and then (the *'double-hung' sash*) by cords with counter-balancing weights inside the jambs. These were invented in Holland in the 1680s, and on their introduction to England (first recorded as replacements in the Banqueting House, Whitehall, in 1685) they rapidly replaced casements in all but the smallest houses. In the course of the C18 the *glazing bars* became slenderer and the panes of glass larger, but only in the C19 did the ready availability of large panes of *sheet glass* allow the abandonment of glazing bars, and thus a delicate relationship between the proportions of the glazing and those of the building as a whole.

The need for light in the factories and ever more mammoth office blocks of the C19 and C20 has made windows steadily more prominent in relation to the wall. (Repeal of the excise duty on glass in England was in 1845, and of the window tax in 1851.) The development of SKELETON CONSTRUCTION, together with more efficient heating systems and the invention of air-conditioning, have removed the traditional constraints upon this process; and much of modern architecture can be seen as the acceptance, followed by the aesthetic exploitation, of the new relationship of the window to the *skeleton frame*. Modern buildings employ metal-frame windows which, where they open at all, are usually sliding, or of the side and vertical *pivot-hung* type. *Double-glazing* is becoming common.

Special types of window include: *bay*, *bow*, and *oriel windows*, which are all forms of projection from a house front containing fenestration. *Oriel windows* generally project from an upper storey (though not necessarily, viz. college halls), supported on some form of CORBELLING or BRACKET. *Bay windows* are canted projections rising from the ground; *bow windows* are rounded projections, often only of the window frame itself. *Biforate windows*, common in Italian medieval architecture and called *bifore*, are divided vertically by a column to form two separate arched openings. *French windows* are, as the French name (*croisée*) for them suggests, casement windows carried down to the floor so as to open like doors. They made their appearance at Versailles in the 1680s. *Dormer windows* are windows placed vertically in a sloping roof with a roof of their own. The name derives from the fact that they usually lighted sleeping quarters. For the *Palladian* or *Venetian window*, see SERLIANA. The *Diocletian* or *thermal window*, whose use was revived by PALLADIO himself and became another feature of PALLADIANISM, is a semicircular window divided into three lights by two vertical mullions. It derives its name from its use in the THERMAE of Diocletian at Rome. *Picture window* is a name often used to describe a large window in a house, containing a single un-interrupted pane of glass. A *Wyatt window* has three lights recessed under a segmental relieving arch. *See also* CHICAGO WINDOW; FANLIGHT; GLASS; LANCET; LATTICE; LOW-SIDE; ŒIL-DE-BŒUF; SKYLIGHT. [A. Laing]

Wines, James (b 1932), *see* UNITED STATES ARCHITECTURE.

Wit or **Witte,** Peter de, *see* CANDID.

Wohlmut (Wolmuet), Bonifaz (d. 1579), *see* CZECHOSLOVAK ARCHITECTURE.

Wolff, Jacob the elder (*c.* 1546–1612). Master mason to the city of Nuremberg. His most notable work was the *überherrliche* (super-magnificent) house which he and Peter Carl built for Martin Peller in Nuremberg (1602–7, destroyed in the Second World War but partially rebuilt). Martin Peller had been a consul in Venice and the Pellerhaus is a curious compromise between Venetian and German taste, its three heavily rusticated storeys being crowned with a rich three-storey German gable. On the Marienberg, above Würzburg, he connected the wings of the existing castle to make a vast elongated rectangular court (1600–1607) very sparingly decorated. His son Jacob Wolff the younger (1571–1620) travelled and studied in Italy and brought back a more highly developed Italian Renaissance style which he used in a striking manner in his additions to the Nuremberg Town Hall (1616–22, destroyed in the Second World War but rebuilt).

Hempel 1965; Hitchcock 1981.

Wood, John, the elder (1704–54), a competent exponent of PALLADIANISM (e.g. Prior Park near Bath,

1735–48), and the author of the eccentric *The Origin of Building* (1741), revolutionized town planning with his scheme for Bath (1727), unfortunately only partly executed. He began with Queen Square (1729–36), treating the north side as a palace front with a rusticated ground floor and attached central pediment. (This had recently been attempted in Grosvenor Square, London, *c*. 1730, by Edward Shepheard (d. 1747) but only partially realized.) Entirely original was the Circus (1754), a circular space with three streets radiating out of it; the elevations have superimposed orders so that it looks like the Colosseum turned outside in. He intended to follow the Circus with a Forum, of which North and South Parades are fragments, and an enormous Gymnasium (unexecuted), and thus make Bath once more into a Roman city. He died soon after placing the first stone of the Circus, but his work was carried on by his son John Wood the younger (1728–81), who took it a step further towards open planning with his Royal Crescent (1767–75), the first of its kind and an artistic conception of great originality and magnificence. It has been widely copied ever since (*see* CRESCENT). His other buildings – e.g. the Assembly Rooms (1769–71) and Hot Baths (1773–8) – are excellent late examples of Palladianism.

Colvin 1978; Summerson 1983; T. Mowl and B. Earnshaw, *J.W. Architect of Obsession*, Bath 1988; Harris 1990.

Woods, Shadrach (1923–73), *see* CANDILIS, Georges.

Woodward, Benjamin (1816–61), *see* RUSKIN, John.

Wren, Sir Christopher (1632–1723).

The greatest English architect. His father was Dean of Windsor and his uncle Bishop of Ely, both pillars of the High Church. He was educated at Westminster School and at fifteen became a demonstrator in anatomy at the College of Surgeons; then he went up to Oxford. Experimental science was just then coming to the fore, and he found himself in company with a group of brilliant young men who were later to found the Royal Society. He was entirely engrossed in scientific studies. Evelyn called him 'that miracle of a youth' and Newton thought him one of the best geometricians of the day. In 1657 he was made Professor of Astronomy in London, in 1661 in Oxford; but two years later his career took a different turn with his appointment to the commission for the restoration of St Paul's. After the Great Fire of London he was appointed one of the Surveyors under the Rebuilding Act (1667) and in 1669 became Surveyor General of the King's Works. Then he resigned his Oxford professorship and was knighted (1673). He was twice MP (1685–7 and 1701–2) and, despite his Tory connections, survived the Whig revolution of 1688, but on the accession of George I in 1714 he lost his office. He was twice married, first to a daughter of Sir John Coghill, and secondly to a daughter of Lord Fitzwilliam of Lifford. He died aged ninety-one having, as he wrote, 'worn out (by God's Mercy) a long life in the Royal Service and having made some figure in the world'.

If Wren had died at thirty he would have been remembered only as a figure in the history of English science. His first buildings, the Sheldonian Theatre, Oxford (1664–9), and Pembroke College Chapel, Cambridge

(1663–5), are the work of a brilliant amateur though the trussed roof of the Sheldonian already displays his structural ingenuity. In 1665–6 he spent eight or nine months studying French architecture, mainly in Paris, and may well have visited Flanders and Holland as well. He met BERNINI in Paris, but learnt more from MANSART and LE VAU, whom he probably knew and whose works he certainly studied. French and Dutch architecture were to provide the main influences on his own style. The Fire of London in 1666 gave him his great opportunity. Though his utopian city plan was rejected, every facet of his empirical genius found scope for expression in the rebuilding of St Paul's and the fifty-one city churches. The latter especially revealed his freshness of mind, his bounding invention, and his adventurous empiricism. There were, of course, no precedents in England for classical churches except in the work of Inigo JONES. Wren's city churches were built between 1670 and 1686, nearly thirty being under construction in the peak year of 1677. Plans are extremely varied and often daringly original, e.g. St Stephen, Walbrook (1672–9), which foreshadows St Paul's, and St Peter's, Cornhill (1675–81), in which his two-storeyed gallery church with vaulted nave and aisles was first adumbrated. This type was later perfected at St Clement Danes (begun 1680) and St James's, Piccadilly (1676–84). But his originality and fertility of invention are best seen in the steeples, which range from the neo-Gothic of St Dunstan in the East to the Borrominesque fantasy of St Vedast and St Bride.

More scholarly and refined in detail than his sometimes rather hastily conceived and crudely executed city churches is his masterpiece, St Paul's Cathedral. Nothing like it had ever before been seen in England. It was a triumph of intellectual self-reliance, and the dome is one of the most majestic and reposeful in the world, purely classical in style. Baroque influences are evident elsewhere in the building, notably in the towers, the main façade, and such illusionist features as the sharm-perspective window niches and the false upper storey in the side elevations to conceal the nave buttresses. The interior is ostensibly classical, but contains many Baroque gestures. It was begun in 1675, and Wren lived to see it finished in 1709.

His secular buildings range from the austere Doric barracks at Chelsea Hospital (1682–92) to the grandest and most Baroque of all his works, Greenwich Hospital (1696 onwards), where the Painted Hall (1698) is the finest room of its kind in England. Of his vast and elaborate additions and alterations to Whitehall Palace, Winchester Palace, and Hampton Court only a fragment of the latter survives (and this was probably revised and altered by his assistant William TALMAN). Like nearly all his work, these great schemes were carried out for the Office of Works. (The question of his delegation of designs to assistants and associates, notably to Robert HOOKE, is controversial.) Of his few independent commissions the best are Trinity College Library, Cambridge (1676–84), and Tom Tower, Christ Church, Oxford (1681–2). Apart from Marlborough House, London (1709–10, now much altered), no town or country house can be certainly attributed to him, though his name has been optimistically given to many e.g. Winslow Hall, Buckinghamshire. HAWKSMOOR was his only pupil of note, but he had a wide and profound influence through his long reign at the Office of Works.

E. F. Sekler, *W. and His Place in European Architecture*, London 1956; Colvin 1978; Summerson 1983; K. Downes, *The Architecture of W.*, London 1982.

Wright, Frank Lloyd (1869–1959). The greatest American architect to date. His *œuvre* ranges over more than sixty years and is never repetitive, routine, or derivative. He first worked with J. L. Silsbee, a SHINGLE STYLE architect, then with SULLIVAN, whom he never ceased to admire, and was responsible for much of his master's domestic work until 1893. In 1894 he helped found the Chicago ARTS AND CRAFTS Society. The first type of building he developed as an independent architect is what he called the PRAIRIE house – low, spreading, with rooms running into each other, terraces merging with the gardens, and roofs far projecting. Houses of this type are located in the outer suburbs of Chicago (Oak Park, Riverside, etc.). The development was extremely consistent, ending up with designs more daringly novel than any other architect's in the same field. The series was heralded by houses before 1900 and was complete by about 1905; its climax is the Robie House, Chicago (1908). Concurrently he had done one church, Unity Temple, Oak Park (1905–6), and one office building, Larkin Building, Buffalo (1904, demolished 1950) – both with the same stylistic elements and the same freshness of approach as the private houses. The Larkin Building might well be called the most original office building of its date anywhere.

Some bigger jobs came along about the time of the First World War: Midway Gardens, Chicago (1913, demolished), a lavish and short-lived entertainment establishment, and the no longer surviving Imperial Hotel at Tokyo (1916–20). His assistant here, Antonin Raymond (1889–1976), then settled in Japan. Both these buildings were very heavily decorated, and the elements of this decoration, polygonal and sharp-angled forms, are entirely Wright's, favoured by him from the very beginning, but less in evidence in the prairie houses, at least externally. The houses of the twenties introduced a new technique which allowed Wright to use surface decoration on the outside as well: precast concrete blocks.

In fact, from then onwards, Wright went more and more his own way, and it is very rare for his work to run parallel to international developments and conventions. One exception is Falling Water, Bear Run, Pennsylvania (1937–9), which is closer to the so-called INTERNATIONAL MODERN of Europe (and by then of America) than anything else Wright designed. His own work which, about 1914–17, influenced GROPIUS as well as the Dutch DE STIJL group is not represented in Europe at all, as his harmless little Memorial Hostel for Venice was prevented from being executed. In his autobiography Wright tells of many such calamities, but as a writer he was biased and monotonously convinced that he was always right and blameless. This attitude seems to have distinguished his Taliesin Community in Wisconsin from the fraternity ideals of RUSKIN: it was more of a master-and-disciples than a guild relationship. Wright built at Taliesin three times (1911, 1914, and 1925 onwards), and then added a Taliesin Winter Camp in

Arizona (1927 onwards), eminently fantastical and very exciting.

World-wide recognition came late to Wright, and only in his last twenty years or so, that is from the time when he was nearly seventy, did large commissions come his way fairly evenly. The first was the Johnson Wax Factory at Racine, Wisconsin (1936–9). Here he built an office block with walls of brick and glass tubes, and an interior with reinforced concrete mushroom columns (*see* MAILLART). The laboratory tower was added in 1949. The chapel of Florida Southern College dates from 1940, the Unitarian Church at Madison from 1947, the design for the Guggenheim Museum in New York from 1942 (completed 1960), and the office skyscraper at Bartlesville, Oklahoma, was completed in 1955. The museum, designed as a spiral ramp on a circular plan, is functionally indefensible but formally certainly startling. The skyscraper and the two ecclesiastical buildings display Wright's inborn passion for sharp angles more radically than any of his earlier buildings, and it is interesting to observe that the recent turn of architecture towards aggressive sharp angles (*see* BREUER; SAARINEN) has given this pre-1900 passion of Wright's new topicality. He lived through three phases of free decorative play in international architecture: the Arts and Crafts, Expressionism, and the most recent antirationalism.

Wright's writings on architecture have been collected and edited by F. Gutheim as *F.L.W. on Architecture: Selected Writings 1894–1940* (New York 1941) and as *In the Cause of Architecture: Essays by F.L.W. for the Architectural Review 1908–1952* (New York 1975).

R. L. Sweeney, *F.L.W. An Annotated Bibliography*, Los Angeles 1978; R. C. Twombly, *F.L.W. His Life and Architecture*, New York 1979; W. A. Storrer, *The Architecture of F.L.W. A Complete Catalogue*, Cambridge, Mass., and London (1974) 1982; B. Gill, *Many Masks. A Life of F.L.W.*, New York 1988.

Wyatt, Benjamin Dean (1775–*c.* 1855). The son of James WYATT, he was notable for his lavish Louis XV interiors at Lancaster House, London (1825, begun by SMIRKE 1820) and Apsley House, London (1828). He also designed Drury Lane Theatre (1811, present portico later) and the Duke of York's Column (1831–4), both in London.

Colvin 1978; J. M. Robinson, *The W.s. An Architectural Dynasty*, London 1979.

Wyatt, James (1746–1813), the most successful architect of his day, rivalled the ADAM brothers and even overshadowed CHAMBERS, whom he succeeded as Surveyor-General in 1796. But his brilliance was superficial, and his reputation now rests mainly on his neo-Gothic extravaganzas, though the best of these have been destroyed. The son of a Staffordshire timber-merchant and builder, he went to Italy in 1762. He was in Venice for two years studying under the painter-architect Visentini, then in Rome. He leapt to fame on his return to London in about 1768 with the Pantheon in Regent Street (1772, now destroyed), an astonishing neo-classical version of Hagia Sophia in Constantinople. He was inundated with commissions from then onwards, despite his outrageously bad manners to clients and his general unreliability. His classical houses, very smooth and elegant, include Heaton House (1772), Heveningham (interior *c*. 1780–84), Castle Coole in Northern Ireland (1790–97), and Dodington, Gloucestershire (1798–1813), the latter very solemn and severe, owing much to the Greek Revival. His neo-Gothic work ranges from the exquisite miniature Lee Priory (1785–90, destroyed, but one room survives in the Victoria and Albert Museum) to the fabulous Fonthill Abbey (1796–1812, destroyed) for William Beckford and the almost equally extravagant Ashridge (1808–13). His numerous and ruthless restorations and 'improvements' to Gothic buildings include work at Salisbury, Durham, and Hereford Cathedrals, and earned him the name of 'Wyatt the Destroyer'.

Colvin 1978; J. M. Robinson, *The W.s. An Architectural Dynasty*, London 1979; Summerson 1983.

Wyatt, Sir Matthew Digby (1820–77), *see* WYATT, Thomas Henry.

Wyatt, Samuel (1737–1807). The elder brother of James WYATT, he began under Robert ADAM at Kedleston in 1759 and later worked with his brother on the Pantheon in London. His country houses are austere versions of his brother's – e.g. Doddington Hall, Cheshire (1777–98). He is notable for his structural innovations. His Albion Mills, London (1783–6), was founded on a structural raft and he was experimenting with cast-iron construction in the 1780s, taking out a patent in 1800 for building cast-iron bridges, warehouses, etc.

Colvin 1978; J. M. Robinson, *The W.s. An Architectural Dynasty*, London 1979.

Wyatt, Thomas Henry (1807–80), and his brother Sir Matthew Digby (1820–77), are not related to James WYATT. Thomas Henry's *chef-d'œuvre* is Wilton Church, Wiltshire (1842–3), in an Early-Christian-Italian-Romanesque manner; it is perhaps the finest example of that style of the 1840s, rarer in England than in Germany. He also designed many Gothic churches (for a time in partnership with David Brandon). Sir Matthew Digby Wyatt belonged to the circle of Henry Cole and Owen Jones, who were responsible for much of the work on the Exhibition of 1851; Wyatt himself was Secretary of the Executive Committee. He was a poor architect (*see* the architectural parts of Paddington Station, 1854–5), but an extremely intelligent and far-seeing architectural journalist, a believer in the new materials of his century and the possibilities of machine production.

Hitchcock 1954; Pevsner 1972.

Wyatt window, *see* WINDOW.

Wyatville, Sir Jeffry (1766–1840). He was the nephew of James WYATT, under whom he trained and whose work at Ashridge he completed in 1817 (adding the north entrance, east wing and stables). Although a competent classical architect (e.g. his entrance hall and stable court at Longleat, 1806–13), he specialized in neo-Gothic and 'Tudor collegiate' mansions. His masterpiece is Windsor Castle, which he remodelled for George IV between 1824 and 1837, giving it a picturesque silhouette by raising the Round Tower 33 ft to make it a dominant feature around which to group his newly battlemented and machicolated towers. He added the George IV Gateway and Lancaster Tower and rebuilt the Chester and Brunswick Towers. His

Waterloo Gallery and new royal apartments are still in use. He changed his name to Wyatville when he began work at the Castle and was knighted in 1828.

D. Linstrum, *Sir J.W.*, Oxford 1972; Colvin 1978; J. M. Robinson, *The W.s. An Architectural Dynasty*, London 1979.

Wynford (d. *c.* 1405–10), *see* WILLIAM OF WYNFORD.

X

Xystus. In a church, an AMBULATORY. In Greek architecture, a long portico used for athletic contests; in Roman architecture, a long covered or open walk bordered by colonnades or trees.

y

Yamasaki, Minoru (b. 1912). Born in Seattle, he trained there and in New York. The St Louis Airport (1953–5), designed with Hellmut and Leinweber, made him famous. Its crossing concrete vaults are eminently impressive. Later buildings tended to be playful and weak: American Concrete Institute, Detroit, 1958; the Pruitt-Igoe public housing, St Louis (1958, demolished 1972); Reynolds Metals Building, Detroit, 1959; Conference Center and Education Building, Wayne State University, Detroit, 1958 and 1961; Michigan Consolidated Gas Company, Detroit, 1962; School of Music, Oberlin College, 1964. But his twin-towered World Trade Center, New York, 1970–74, is a landmark. He published *A Life in Architecture* (New York 1979).

Ybl, Miklos Nikolaus (1814–91), *see* HUNGARIAN ARCHITECTURE.

Yevele, Henry (d. 1400), was admitted a citizen of London in 1353, became mason to the Black Prince about 1357, to the king (for Westminster, the Tower, and other palaces and castles) from 1360, and to Westminster Abbey from 1388 at the latest. It is probable that he had designed the nave of the abbey (as begun *c.* 1375), and that of Canterbury Cathedral, built *c.* 1379–1405, has also been attributed to him. He designed Westminster Hall in 1394. He was a wealthy man with property in many places, and he engaged in business both in connection with and apart from his duties as the king's Master Mason.

Harvey 1984.

Yorke, Francis Reginald Stevens (1906–62), *see* ENGLISH ARCHITECTURE.

Yorkshire lights. In a mullioned window, a pair of lights, one fixed and the other sliding horizontally.

Yoshisaka, Takamasa (1917–80), *see* JAPANESE ARCHITECTURE.

Yugoslav architecture, see BYZANTINE ARCHITECTURE.

Z

Zablocki, Wojciech (b. 1930), *see* POLISH ARCHITECTURE.

Zakharov, Andreyan Dmitrievich (1761–1811), the leading Russian neo-classicist and perhaps the greatest Russian architect, was trained at the St Petersburg Academy of Arts, then in Paris under CHALGRIN (1782–6), and travelled in Italy. His masterpiece is the Admiralty, Leningrad (1806–20), vast, bold, and solid, with a façade a quarter of a mile long, a huge columned tower supporting a needle-like spire over the central gate, and dodecastyle Tuscan porticos at the ends. To give expression to such an immense front-tage without breaking its unity was a major achievement. But the end blocks are still more successful, the nearest approach to BOULLÉE's architecture of geometrical shapes on a grand scale: each is in the form of a cubic pavilion capped by a low cylindrical drum, pierced by a vast semicircular portal, and flanked by colonnades. Another of his notable works is the cathedral of St Andrew in Kronstadt. He and VORONIKHIN were the leading architects in the committee that planned the Petersburg Bourse and adjacent townscape (*see* THOMON).
Hamilton 1983.

Zapotec architecture, *see* MESO-AMERICAN ARCHITECTURE.

Zehrfuss, Bernard-Louis (b. 1911), *see* BREUER, Marcel.

Zhilyardi (or Gigliardi), Domenico (1788–1845), *see* RUSSIAN ARCHITECTURE.

Ziggurat or zikkurat. A rectangular temple-tower in the form of a truncated pyramid built in diminishing stages, each stage being reached by ramps, erected by the Sumerians and their successors. The best-known examples are those of Ur and Babylon, the fabled Tower of Babel. The largest and best preserved is that at Choga Zanbil (Iran) of 1250 BC. *See* Fig. 88.

Zimbalo, Giuseppe (active 1659–86). The chief exponent of the wildly exuberant and rather coarse Baroque style developed at Lecce, e.g. Prefettura (1659–95), Cathedral (1659–82), S. Agostino (1663), and Chiesa del Rosario (1691). His pupil Giuseppe Cino (1645–1722) carried his style on into the c18.
M. Calvesi and M. Manieri-Elia, *Architettura barocca a Lecce e in terra di Puglia*, Rome 1971.

Zimmermann, Dominikus (1685–1766), one of the greatest south German Rococo architects, but a craftsman before he was an architect, retained to the last his peasant vitality,

FIG. 88. *Ziggurat*

spontaneity, and unquestioning piety. Perhaps it is significant that his master-piece, die Wies, was built neither for a great prince nor for the abbot of a rich monastery but for a simple rustic com-munity. Born at Wessobrunn, he began there as a stucco worker, then settled at Füssen (1698), and finally at Lands-berg (1716), where he eventually became mayor. He continued to work as a stuccoist after becoming an ar-chitect and frequently collaborated with his brother Johann Baptist (1680–1758), who was a painter. His earliest building is the convent church at Mödi-gen (1716–18), but his mature style first becomes apparent in the pilgrim-age church of Steinhausen (1728–31), which is the first wholly Rococo church in Bavaria. It broke away decisively from its Baroque predecessors, the mystical indirect lighting and rich velvety colour of ASAM giving place to flat even lighting and a predominantly white colour scheme – bright, brittle, and porcellaneous. The colours used are all symbolical, as are the motifs in both painted and carved decoration. At the Frauenkirche, Günzburg (1736–41), he adopted an oblong plan, and at die Wies (1745–54) he combined an oval with an oblong, using the former for the nave with its wide ambulatory (necessary for a pilgrimage church), and the latter for the rather long chancel, which is treated with an in-tensified, predominantly pink colour scheme. Here stucco work, white-painted wooden statues, and frescoes combine with architecture to delight and instruct the pilgrim, be he never so humble or so sophisticated. In more ways than one it is the meeting-place of the courtly Rococo style and an anci-ent tradition of craftsmanship which stretches back to the Middle Ages.

H.-R. Hitchcock, *German Rococo. The Z. Brothers*, London 1968; H. and A. Bauer, *J.B. and D.Z.*, Regensburg 1985.

Zítek, Josef (1832–1909), *see* CZECH-OSLOVAK ARCHITECTURE.

Zoomorph. A boulder carved by the Maya with animal and other forms, as distinct from a megalith cut and carved into the form of a STELE.

Zoophorus. A frieze with animal reliefs, as on the Theseum in Athens.

Zuccalli, Enrico (1642–1724). Bar-oque architect, born in the Grisons, who settled in Munich where he and his rival VISCARDI dominated the ar-chitectural scene for several years. He succeeded BARELLI as architect to the Elector in 1672. In Munich he com-pleted Barelli's Theatine church of St Cajetan, reducing the size of the dome. He supervised the decoration of the Residenz (Imperial suite 1680–1701; Alexander and Summer Suite 1680–85) and built the Portia Palace (1694).

Outside Munich, at Schleissheim, he built the Lustheim or Banqueting House (1684–9) and began the main palace (1701, completed by EFFNER). In 1695 he began rebuilding the palace at Bonn (completed after 1702 by de COTTE). He rebuilt the abbey church of Ettal (1709–26, partly burnt and rebuilt 1742). His kinsman Giovanni Gaspare (active 1685) built two Italianate churches at Salzburg: St Erhard (1685–9) and St Cajetan (1685–1700).

S. Heym, *H.Z. (1642–1724). Der kurbayerische Hofbaumeister,* Munich 1984; Brucker 1983.

Zug, Gottlieb Simon (1733–1807), *see* POLISH ARCHITECTURE.

Bibliographical Abbreviations

Banham 1960	R. Banham, *Theory and Design in the First Machine Age*, London 1960
Banham 1976	R. Banham, *Megastructures*, London 1976
Baum 1956	J. Baum, *German Cathedrals*, London 1956
Benevolo 1971	L. Benevolo, *History of Modern Architecture*, London (1960) 1971
Blunt 1975	A. Blunt, *Neapolitan Baroque and Rococo Architecture*, London 1975
Blunt 1982	A. Blunt, *Art and Architecture in France: 1500–1700*, Harmondsworth (1953) 1982
Boethius 1978	A. Boethius, *Etruscan and Early Roman Architecture*, Harmondsworth (1970) 1978
Bognar 1985	B. Bognar, *Contemporary Japanese Architecture*, London 1985
Bony 1979	J. Bony, *The English Decorated Style*, Oxford 1979
Bony 1983	J. Bony, *French Gothic Architecture Twelfth to Thirteenth Century*, Berkeley and London 1983
Braham 1980	A. Braham, *The Architecture of the French Enlightenment*, London 1980
Branner 1965	R. Branner, *St Louis and the Court Style in Gothic Architecture*, London 1965
Braunfels 1973	W. Braunfels, *Monasteries of Western Europe*, Princeton 1973
Brown 1985	R. Brown (ed.), *The Architectural Outsiders*, London 1985
Brucker 1983	G. Brucker, *Barockarchitektur in Österreich*, Cologne 1983
Bucher 1979	F. Bucher, *Architector. The Lodge Books and Sketchbooks of Medieval Architects*, New York 1979
Clarke 1969	B. F. L. Clarke, *Church Builders of the Nineteenth Century*, Newton Abbot (1938) 1969
Collins 1959	P. Collins, *Concrete. The Vision of a New Architecture. A Study of Auguste Perret and his Precursors*, New York and London 1959

Biographical Abbreviations

Collins 1965   P. Collins, *Changing Ideals in Modern Architecture (1750–1950)*, London 1965

Colombier 1956   P. du Colombier, *L'Architecture française en Allemagne au XVIIIe siècle*, Paris 1956

Colvin 1978   H. Colvin, *Biographical Dictionary of British Architects 1600–1840*, London (1954) 1978

Conant 1979   K. J. Conant, *Carolingian and Romanesque Architecture: 800–1200*, Harmondsworth (1959) 1979

Condit 1961   C. Condit, *American Building Art – The Twentieth Century*, New York 1961

Condit 1964   C. Condit, *The Chicago School of Architecture*, Chicago 1964

Condit 1968   C. Condit, *American Building Materials*, Chicago 1968

Crook 1972   J. M. Crook, *The Greek Revival*, London 1972

Crook 1987   J. M. Crook, *The Dilemma of Style*, London and Chicago 1987

Davey 1961   N. Davey, *A History of Building Materials*, London 1961

Davies 1988   C. Davies, *High Tech Architecture*, London 1988

DBI   *Dizionario biografico degli italiani*, Rome 1960 onwards

Dixon and Muthesius 1978   R. Dixon and S. Muthesius, *Victorian Architecture*, London 1978

Downes 1966   K. Downes, *English Baroque Architecture*, London 1966

Ettinghausen and Grabar 1988   R. Ettinghausen and O. Grabar, *The Art and Architecture of Islam 650–1250*, Harmondsworth 1988

Frankfort 1970   H. Frankfort, *The Art and Architecture of the Ancient Orient*, Harmondsworth 1970

Frankl 1962   P. Frankl, *Gothic Architecture*, Harmondsworth 1962

Frankl 1977   P. J. Frankl, *The Gothic*, Princeton (1960) 1977

Frommel 1973   C. L. Frommel, *Der Römischen Palastbau des Cinquecento*, Tübingen 1973

Gallet 1964   M. Gallet, *Demeures Parisiennes à la époque de Louis XVI*, Paris 1964

Gerson and ter Kuile 1960   H. Gerson and E. H. ter Kuile, *Art and Architecture in Belgium 1600–1800*, Harmondsworth 1960

Giedion 1967   S. Giedion, *Space, Time and Architecture: The Growth of a New Tradition*, Cambridge, Mass., and Oxford (1941) 1967

Goldthwaite 1980   R. A. L. Goldthwaite, *The Building of Renaissance Florence*, Baltimore and London 1980

Goodwin 1971   G. Goodwin, *A History of Ottoman Architecture*, London 1971

Hamilton 1983   G. H. Hamilton, *The Art and Architecture of Russia*, Harmondsworth (1954) 1983

Harris 1990   E. Harris and N. Savage, *British Architectural Books and Writers 1556–1785*, Cambridge 1990

Hart 1985   F. Hart, W. Henn and H. Sontag, *Multi-Storey Buildings in Steel*, London 1985

Harvey 1984   J. Harvey, *English Medieval Architects. A Biographical Dictionary down to 1580*, London (1954) 1984

Hempel 1965   E. Hempel, *Baroque Art and Architecture in Central Europe*, Harmondsworth 1965

Herrmann 1962   W. Herrmann, *Laugier and Eighteenth Century French Theory*, London 1962

Heydenreich and   L. H. Heydenreich and W. Lotz, *Architecture in Italy*
Lotz 1974   *1400–1600*, Harmondsworth 1974

Hitchcock 1954   H.-R. Hitchcock, *Early Victorian Architecture in Britain*, New Haven and London 1954

Hitchcock 1968   H.-R. Hitchcock, *Rococo Architecture in Southern Germany*, London 1968

Hitchcock 1977   H.-R. Hitchcock, *Architecture: Nineteenth and Twentieth Centuries*, Harmondsworth (1958) 1977

Hitchcock 1981   H.-R. Hitchcock, *German Renaissance Architecture*, Princeton 1981

Honour 1977   H. Honour, *Neo-Classicism*, Harmondsworth (1968) 1977

Honour 1979   H. Honour, *Romanticism*, Harmondsworth 1979

Howard 1987   D. Howard, *Architectural History of Venice*, London (1980) 1987

Jencks 1988   C. Jencks, *Architecture Today*, London 1988

Kalnein and   W. Kalnein and M. Levey, *Art and Architecture of the*
Levey 1972   *Eighteenth Century in France*, Harmondsworth 1972

Kaufmann 1955   F. Kaufmann, *Architecture in the Age of Reason*, Cambridge, Mass., 1955

Klotz 1986   H. Klotz (ed.), *Vision der Moderne*, Munich 1986

Klotz 1988   H. Klotz, *The History of Postmodern Architecture*, Cambridge, Mass., 1988

Krautheimer 1986   R. Krautheimer, *Early Christian and Byzantine Architecture*, Harmondsworth (1965) 1986

Kubler 1984   G. Kubler, *Art and Architecture of Ancient America*, Harmondsworth (1962) 1984

Kubler and   G. Kubler and M. Soria, *Art and Architecture in Spain and*
Soria 1959   *Portugal and their American Dominions 1500–1800*, Harmondsworth 1959

Biographical Abbreviations

Kuyper 1980   W. Kuyper, *Dutch Classicist Architecture*, Delft 1980

Laing 1978   A. Laing in A. Blunt (ed.), *Baroque and Rococo Architecture and Decoration*, London 1978

Lawrence 1983   A. W. Lawrence, *Greek Architecture*, Harmondsworth (1957) 1983

Lieberman 1982   R. Lieberman, *Renaissance Architecture in Venice*, New York 1982

Lotz 1977   W. Lotz, *Studies in Renaissance Architecture*, Cambridge, Mass., 1977

Loyer 1979   F. Loyer, *Art Nouveau Architecture*, London 1979

Loyer 1982   F. Loyer, *Architecture of the Industrial Age 1789–1914*, New York 1982

Loyer 1987   F. Loyer, *Paris XIX siècle. L'immeuble et la rue*, Paris 1987

McAndrew 1980   J. McAndrew, *Venetian Architecture of the Early Renaissance*, Cambridge, Mass., 1980

Macaulay 1975   J. Macaulay, *The Gothic Revival 1745–1845*, Glasgow 1975

MacDonald 1965   W. L. MacDonald, *The Architecture of the Roman Empire*, Vol. 1, New Haven and London 1965

MacDonald 1986   W. L. MacDonald, *The Architecture of the Roman Empire*, Vol. 2, New Haven and London 1986

Mainstone 1975   R. Mainstone, *Developments in Structural Form*, London 1975

Maxwell 1972   R. Maxwell, *New British Architecture*, London 1972

Meeks 1966   C. L. V. Meeks, *Italian Architecture 1750–1914*, New Haven and London 1966

Middleton and Watkin 1977   R. D. Middleton and D. Watkin, *Neo-Classical and Nineteenth Century Architecture*, London 1977

Middleton 1982   R. D. Middleton, *The Beaux-Arts and Nineteenth Century French Architecture*, London 1982

Miller Lane 1968   B. Miller Lane, *Architecture and Politics in Germany 1918–1945*, Cambridge, Mass., 1968

Mumford 1961   L. Mumford, *The City in History. Its Origins, its Transformations and its Prospects*, London 1961

Nicoletti 1978   G. M. Nicoletti, *L'architettura liberty in Italia*, Bari and Rome 1978

Onians 1988   J. Onians, *Bearers of Meaning. The Classic Orders in Antiquity, the Middle Ages and the Renaissance*, London 1988

Paulsson 1958   T. Paulsson, *Scandinavian Architecture*, London 1958

Pevsner 1968   N. Pevsner, *Studies in Art, Architecture and Design*, London 1968

Pevsner 1972 — N. Pevsner, *Some Architectural Writers of the Nineteenth Century*, Oxford 1972

Pevsner and Richards 1973 — N. Pevsner and J. M. Richards (eds.), *The Anti-Rationalists*, Wisbech 1973

Pierson and Jordy 1970 — W. H. Pierson and W. Jordy, *American Builders and their Architects. The Colonial and Neo-Classical Styles*, New York 1970

Pommer 1967 — R. Pommer, *Eighteenth Century Architecture in Piedmont: The Open Structures of Juvara, Alfieri and Vittone*, New York and London 1967

Recht 1989 — R. Recht (ed.), *Les Bâtisseurs des cathédrales gothiques*, Strasbourg 1989

Robertson 1969 — D. S. Robertson, *A Handbook of Greek and Roman Architecture*, Cambridge (1943) 1969

Rosenberg 1977 — J. Rosenberg, S. Slive and E. H. ter Kuile, *Dutch Art and Architecture 1600–1800*, Harmondsworth (1966) 1977

Roth 1979 — L. M. Roth, *A Concise History of American Architecture*, New York 1979

Rykwert 1980 — J. Rykwert, *The First Moderns*, London 1980

Service 1977 — A. Service, *Edwardian Architecture*, London 1977

Smith 1968 — R. C. Smith, *The Art of Portugal 1500–1800*, London 1968

Smith and Simpson 1981 — W. S. Smith and W. K. Simpson, *The Art and Architecture of Ancient Egypt*, Harmondsworth 1981

Summerson 1983 — J. Summerson, *Architecture in Britain 1530–1830*, Harmondsworth (1953) 1983

Tafuri 1966 — M. Tafuri, *L'architettura del Manierismo nel cinquecento europeo*, Rome 1966

Trachtenberg 1971 — M. Trachtenberg, *The Campanile of Florence Cathedral. 'Giotto's Tower'*, New York 1971

Van Zanten 1987 — D. Van Zanten, *Designing Paris. The Architecture of Duban, Labrouste, Duc and Vaudoyer*, Cambridge, Mass., 1987

Varriano 1986 — J. Varriano, *Italian Baroque and Rococo Architecture*, New York and Oxford 1986

Ward-Perkins 1981 — J. B. Ward-Perkins, *Roman Imperial Architecture*, Harmondsworth 1981

Watkin and Mellinghoff 1987 — D. Watkin and T. Mellinghoff, *German Architects and the Classical Ideal 1740–1840*, London 1987

Webb 1965 — G. Webb, *Art and Architecture in Britain: The Middle Ages*, Harmondsworth 1965

Whiffen and Koeper 1981 — M. Whiffen and F. Koeper, *American Architecture 1607–1976*, London 1981

Biographical Abbreviations

White 1987   J. White, *Art and Architecture in Italy 1250–1400*, Harmondsworth (1966) 1987

Wittkower 1974   R. Wittkower, *Palladio and Palladianism*, London 1974

Wittkower 1982   R. Wittkower, *Art and Architecture in Italy 1600–1750*, Harmondsworth (1965) 1982

Wittkower 1988   R. Wittkower, *Architectural Principles in the Age of Humanism*, London (1949) 1988

Zukowsky 1988   J. Zukowsky, *Chicago Architecture 1872–1922. The Building of a Metropolis*, Chicago 1988

Discover more about our forthcoming books through Penguin's FREE newspaper...

Penguin **Quarterly**

It's packed with:

- exciting features

- author interviews

- previews & reviews

- books from your favourite films & TV series

- exclusive competitions & much, much more...

Write off for your free copy today to:
Dept JC
Penguin Books Ltd
FREEPOST
West Drayton
Middlesex
UB7 0BR
NO STAMP REQUIRED

READ MORE IN PENGUIN

In every corner of the world, on every subject under the sun, Penguin represents quality and variety – the very best in publishing today.

For complete information about books available from Penguin – including Puffins, Penguin Classics and Arkana – and how to order them, write to us at the appropriate address below. Please note that for copyright reasons the selection of books varies from country to country.

In the United Kingdom: Please write to *Dept. JC, Penguin Books Ltd, FREEPOST, West Drayton, Middlesex UB7 OBR*

If you have any difficulty in obtaining a title, please send your order with the correct money, plus ten per cent for postage and packaging, to *PO Box No. 11, West Drayton, Middlesex UB7 OBR*

In the United States: Please write to *Penguin USA Inc., 375 Hudson Street, New York, NY 10014*

In Canada: Please write to *Penguin Books Canada Ltd, 10 Alcorn Avenue, Suite 300, Toronto, Ontario M4V 3B2*

In Australia: Please write to *Penguin Books Australia Ltd, 487 Maroondah Highway, Ringwood, Victoria 3134*

In New Zealand: Please write to *Penguin Books (NZ) Ltd, 182–190 Wairau Road, Private Bag, Takapuna, Auckland 9*

In India: Please write to *Penguin Books India Pvt Ltd, 706 Eros Apartments, 56 Nehru Place, New Delhi 110 019*

In the Netherlands: Please write to *Penguin Books Netherlands B.V., Keizersgracht 231 NL–1016 DV Amsterdam*

In Germany: Please write to *Penguin Books Deutschland GmbH, Friedrichstrasse 10–12, W–6000 Frankfurt/Main 1*

In Spain: Please write to *Penguin Books S. A., C. San Bernardo 117–6° E–28015 Madrid*

In Italy: Please write to *Penguin Italia s.r.l., Via Felice Casati 20, I–20124 Milano*

In France: Please write to *Penguin France S. A., 17 rue Lejeune, F–31000 Toulouse*

In Japan: Please write to *Penguin Books Japan, Ishikiribashi Building, 2–5–4, Suido, Tokyo 112*

In Greece: Please write to *Penguin Hellas Ltd, Dimocritou 3, GR–106 71 Athens*

In South Africa: Please write to *Longman Penguin Southern Africa (Pty) Ltd, Private Bag X08, Bertsham 2013*